Vital Records of Uxbridge, Massachusetts, to the Year 1850

Uxbridge

Nabu Public Domain Reprints:

You are holding a reproduction of an original work published before 1923 that is in the public domain in the United States of America, and possibly other countries. You may freely copy and distribute this work as no entity (individual or corporate) has a copyright on the body of the work. This book may contain prior copyright references, and library stamps (as most of these works were scanned from library copies). These have been scanned and retained as part of the historical artifact.

This book may have occasional imperfections such as missing or blurred pages, poor pictures, errant marks, etc. that were either part of the original artifact, or were introduced by the scanning process. We believe this work is culturally important, and despite the imperfections, have elected to bring it back into print as part of our continuing commitment to the preservation of printed works worldwide. We appreciate your understanding of the imperfections in the preservation process, and hope you enjoy this valuable book.

VITAL RECORDS

OF

UXBRIDGE

MASSACHUSETTS,

TO THE YEAR 1850.

COMPILED BY THOMAS W. BALDWIN, A.B., S.B., MEMBER
OF THE NEW ENGLAND HISTORIC
GENEALOGICAL SOCIETY.

BOSTON, MASS.
1916.

Number of births printed 6,354
Number of marriages printed . 2,091 × 2 = 4,182 names
Number of deaths printed 1,981

Total 12,517

BOSTON
WRIGHT & POTTER PRINTING COMPANY,
32 DERNE STREET.

UXBRIDGE.

Established June 27, 1727, from part of Mendon.

Part included in the new town of Upton June 14, 1735.

Certain lands granted to Uxbridge June 5, 1736.

Certain lands annexed April 16, 1742.

Part of the district of New Sherborn annexed June 4, 1746.

Bounds between Uxbridge and Mendon established April 10, 1754.

Bounds between Uxbridge and Sutton established June 29, 1769.

Part annexed to Mendon April 24, 1770.

Part established as the District of Northbridge July 14, 1772.

Boundary line between Uxbridge and Northbridge established and part of each town annexed to the other April 30, 1856.

Boundary between Uxbridge and Douglas established April 25, 1864.

Bounds between Uxbridge and Northbridge established April 17, 1908.

Population by Census: —

1765 (Prov.), 1,213;	1865 (State), 2,838;
1776 (Prov.), 1,110;	1870 (U. S.), 3,058;
1790 (U. S.), 1,308;	1875 (State), 3,029;
1800 (U. S.), 1,404;	1880 (U. S.), 3,111;
1810 (U. S.), 1,404;	1885 (State), 2,948;
1820 (U. S.), 1,551;	1890 (U. S.), 3,408;
1830 (U. S.), 2,086;	1895 (State), 3,546;
1840 (U. S.), 2,004;	1900 (U. S.), 3,599;
1850 (U. S.), 2,457;	1905 (State), 3,881;
1855 (State), 3,068;	1910 (U. S.), 4,671;
1860 (U. S.), 3,133;	1915 (State), 4,921.

EXPLANATIONS.

1. When places other than Uxbridge or Massachusetts are named in the original records they are given in the printed copy.

2. In all items from the records the original spelling of the names is given and any additions made to the spelling of the record are enclosed in brackets.

3. The various spellings of a name should be examined as items about the same family or individual may be found under different spellings.

4. The birth of a married woman is recorded under her maiden name when it is known, but if the maiden name is unknown the entry appears under the husband's name with a dash enclosed in brackets, i.e., [———] to signify that the maiden name is not known.

5. In taking records from gravestones it is often the case that the family name of a woman as given on the stone is not that under which she was born, so, therefore, many births may appear under a married name instead of the original, which is not shown on the stone. In many cases names are evidently those of wives though not so specified.

6. Marriages and intentions are printed under the name of both parties. When both the marriage and intention are recorded, only the marriage record is printed and the date of the intention is not given, except when needed to make more clear the date of the marriage. When the marriage appears without the intention recorded it is designated with an asterisk.

7. Additional information, which does not appear in the original town record, i.e., any difference shown in other records of the same person is enclosed in parenthesis with the source of the information indicated.

8. The births and deaths from the records of the Uxbridge Monthly Meeting are mostly of families living outside of Uxbridge, but who were members of the societies represented in the Monthly Meeting. Where in the record the name of a place is given the same is given in the printed text.

ABBREVIATIONS.

a. — age; aged
abt. — about
b. — born
bp. — baptized
bur. — buried
ch. — child
c.r.1. — church record, First Congregational Society (Unitarian)
c.r.2. — church record, First Evangelical Congregational Society
c.r.3. — from records of Smithfield, R. I., Monthly Meeting
c.r.4. — from records of Uxbridge Monthly Meeting
d. — daughter; died; day
Dea. — deacon
dec. — deceased
dup. — duplicate entry
g.r.1. — grave record, Prospect Hill Cemetery
g.r.2. — grave record, St. Mary's Catholic Cemetery
g.r.3. — grave record, Daniels Cemetery, South Mendon road
g.r.4. — grave record, Bassett Cemetery, South Mendon road
g.r.5. — grave record, Darling Cemetery, east side of town
g.r.6. — grave record, Norton or Swedish Cemetery
g.r.7. — grave record, Cook Cemetery
g.r.8. — grave record, Tucker Cemetery, Scadeen
g.r.9. — grave record, Tiffany Cemetery, Scadeen
g.r.10. — grave record, Aldrich Cemetery, Scadeen
g.r.11. — grave record, Shove Cemetery near Schockalog
g.r.12. — grave record, Royal Taft Cemetery, near Schockalog
g.r.13. — grave record, White Cemetery, southwest corner of town
g.r.14. — grave record, Joseph Richardson Cemetery, southwest part of Uxbridge

ABBREVIATIONS.

G.R.15. — grave record, Mowry Cemetery, South Uxbridge
G.R.16. — grave record, Aldrich Cemetery, South Uxbridge
G.R.17. — grave record, Morse Cemetery, South Uxbridge
G.R.18. — grave record, De Wolfe Cemetery, near Ironstone
G.R.19. — grave record, Richardson Cemetery, near Ironstone
G.R.20. — grave record, Southwick Cemetery, South Uxbridge
G.R.21. — grave record, Cemetery at Quaker meeting-house
G.R.22. — grave record, Gifford Cemetery, near Ironstone
G.R.23. — grave record, Quaker City Cemetery
G.R.24. — grave record, Albee Cemetery, east side of town
G.R.25. — grave record, Buffum Cemetery on Douglas line
h. — husband; hours
inf. — infant
int. — publishment of intention of marriage
Jr. — Junior
md. — married
min. — minutes
mo. — month
prob. — probably
rep. — reputed
s. — son
Sr. — Senior
T.R. — town record
unm. — unmarried
w. — wife, weeks
wid. — widow
widr. — widower

UXBRIDGE BIRTHS.

To the Year 1850.

ADAMS, Aaron, s. of John and Mary, Sept. 28, 1752.
Abigail, d. of Samuel and Susannah, Nov. 15, 1794.
Abner, s. of John and Mary, Nov. 4, 1757.
Abraham, s. of William and Mary, Mar. 19, 1731–2.
Andrew, s. of John and Mary, Nov. 7, 1759.
Angeline Day, ——, 1824. G.R.1.
Anna, d. of James and Elisabeth, Apr. 8, 1753. Twin.
Betsey, d. of Samuel and Susannah, Jan. 30, 1792.
Betsey, d. of Benjamin and Betsey, May 20, 1804.
Catharine C. (Catherine Capron, C.R.2), d. of Lyman and Cynthia S., Aug. 25, 1846.
Christien Isabella, d. of Fleming and Rebecca, June 9, 1844.
Cynthia S., Oct. 13, 1806. G.R.1.
David, s. of Joseph and Elisabeth, Oct. 13, 1766.
Dolly, d. of Joseph and Dolley, Mar. 26, 1808.
Dorothy [——], w. of Joseph, ——, 1770. G.R.1.
Elias, s. of Samuel and Susannah, Apr. 18, 1802.
Elisabeth, d. of James and Elisabeth, May 6, 1749.
Elizabeth Smith, d. of Lyman and Cynthia, Jan. 27, 1841.
Elsezabeth, d. of Joseph and Elisabeth, Jan. 21, 1773.
Fannie C. [——], w. of John, Mar. 9, 1801. G.R.1.
Fanny, d. of Benjamin and Betsey, Nov. 12, 1794.
Francis, s. of James and Elisabeth, Feb. 3, preceding the year 1747.
George, s. of Benjamin and Betsey, Feb. 25, 1802.
George, ——, 1819. G.R.1.
George A., s. of George and Clarissa, Aug. 12, 1847.
Harriet, Dec. 15, 1804. G.R.1.
Israil, s. of James and Elisabeth, Apr. 8, 1753. Twin.
James, s. of James and Elisabeth, Dec. 22, 1742.
James, s. of James and Elisabeth, Aug. 14, 1764.
Jerusha A. Keith [——], w. of William W., ——, 1834. G.R.1.

ADAMS, John, s. of John and Mary, Nov. 26 or 28, 1746.
John, s. of Benjamin and Betsey, Mar. 31, 1798.
John, s. of Joseph and Dolley, Nov. 16, 1800.
Jonathan, s. of John and Mary, Feb. 26, 1747-8.
Joseph, s. of Joseph and Elisabeth, Aug. 25, 1763.
Josiah, s. of Benjamin and Betsey, Jan. 15, 1796.
Josiah Augustus, s. of wid. Harriot, bp. Sept. 18, 1831. c.r.1.
Lydia, d. of James and Elisabeth, Aug. 3, 1756.
Lyman, Feb. 4, 1808. g.r.1.
Mary, d. of John and Mary, Aug. 1, 1749.
Mary, d. of Joseph and Dolley, Dec. 1, 1803.
Moses, s. of James and Elisabeth, Jan. 10, 1760.
Moses, s. of Joseph and Elisabeth, Dec. 10, 1769.
Moses, s. of Samuel and Susannah, Oct. 19, 1796.
Moses, s. of Joseph and Dolley, Aug. 11, 1806.
Nathan, s. of John and Mary, July 17, 1754.
Nehemiah, s. of John and Mary, May 21, 1751.
Nethaniel, s. of James and Elisabeth, Jan. 3, preceding the year 1745.
Rebekah, d. of William and Mary, Apr. 30, 1733.
Ruth, d. of Joseph and Elisabeth, May 11, 1757. (Ruth, d. of Joseph and Susanna, bp. Sept. 4, 1757. c.r.1.)
Sally, d. of Samuel and Susannah, Jan. 20, 1800.
Sally, d. of Benjamin and Betsey, Jan. 12, 1806.
Samuel, s. of James and Elisabeth, May 11, 1751.
Samuel, s. of Joseph and Elisabeth, Oct. 25, 1760.
Samuel Craggin, s. of Benjamin and Betsey, June 3, 1800.
Sarah, d. of John and Mary, May 3, 1756.
Suky, d. of Joseph and Dolley, Sept. 5, 1798.
William W., ——, 1832. g.r.1.

ALBEE, Abial, d. of James and Prudnance, Apr. 28, 1756.
Abigail, d. of James and Prudnance, May 25, 1751.
Alpheus, s. of James and Prudnance, Feb. 15, 1761.
Alpheus, s. of James and Ruth, Oct. 25, 1801.
Benjamin, s. of Eleazer and Ruhamah, Aug. 20, 1781.
Betsey, d. of James and Ruth, Sept. 8, 1786.
Bulah, rep. d. of Eleazer and real d. of Bethiah Woodward, Sept. 15, 1749.
Cyntha, d. of James and Ruth, July —, 1796.
Eliza, d. of Ellis and Lavinia, May 14, 1827.
Ellis, s. of James and Ruth, Apr. 25, 1784.
Ellis, s. of Ellis and Lavinia, May 2, 1830.
Eunice, d. of James and Prudnance, Apr. 28, 1763.

ALBEE, Hepzibah, d. of James and Prudnance, May 17, 1772.
Hopestill, d. of James and Prudnance, Jan. 17, 1768.
James, s. of James and Prudnance, Mar. 11, 1753.
James, s. of James and Ruth, Oct. 30, 1798.
Jesse, s. of James and Ruth, Mar. 27, 1782.
Laura Southwick, d. of Ellis and Lavinia, May 16, 1829.
Lois, d. of James and Prudnance, Feb. 15, 1759.
Nella, d. of James and Ruth, May 4, 1788.
Phila, d. of James and Ruth, Nov. 17, 1779.
Prudance, d. of James and Prudnance, Jan. 3, preceding the year 1747-8.
Prudance, d. of James and Prudnance, Nov. 18, 1770.
Rachel, d. of James and Prudnance, June 26, 1749.
Silvea, d. of James and Ruth, Mar. 22, 1790.

ALDRICH, ——— [———], 2d w. of Ephraim, 24th day, 4th mo. 1773. c.r.4.
———, s. of William and Dinah, Feb. 19, 1798. Twin.
———, s. of Daniel H. and Phebe M., Dec. 25, 1843 (Dec. 5, 1843 dup.).
———, s. of Thomas J. and Lydia, Jan. 5, 1847.
Aaron, s. of Jacob and Joanna, July 18, 1742.
Abby Elizabeth, d. of Valentine M. and Abigail, Mar. 18, 1848.
Abby Emma, d. of Welcome and Maria, b. in Northbridge, Jan. 29, 1849.
Abel, s. of Abel and Doras Cartwrite, Nov. 14, 1741.
Abel, s. of Joseph and Elisabeth, Nov. 16, 1749.
Abel, s. of Abel and Elizabeth, Feb. 28, 1792.
Abigail, d. of Jacob and Joanna, Oct. 28, 1740.
Abigail, d. of Enoch and Deborah, June 22, 1793.
Abigal, d. of Solomon and Elisabeth, July 24, 1757.
Able, s. of Seth and Amey, Apr. 30, 1780.
Abraham, s. of Noah and Sarah, Dec. 25, 1743.
Abraham, s. of Asa and Susanna, 3d day, 12th mo. 1774. c.r.4.
Abraham, s. of Seth and Amey, July 18, 1782.
Adaline, d. of Asahel and ———, Oct. 1, 1806.
Aderline, d. of Jesse and Susannah, Nov. 17, 1811.
Adin, s. of Noah and Elisabeth, 22d day, 7th mo. 1795. c.r.4.
Ahaz, s. of Alexander and Abigail, Jan. 17, 1767.
Ahaz, s. of Seth and Amey, Nov. 22, 1767.
Ahaz, s. of Enoch Jr. and ———, July 15, 1798.
Alexander, s. of Jeremiah and Hannah, Nov. 10, 1736.
Alexander, s. of Alexander and Abigail, May 2, 1768.
Allen Dan Scott, s. of Sarah Scott, bp. Jan. 1, 1837. c.r.2.

ALDRICH, Allen P., s. of Jacob and Mahitabel (Mary in pencil), Oct. 24, 1830.
Almy [――――], w. of Paul Jr., 2d day, 2d mo. 1785. c.r.4.
Alzada Ellen, d. of Asahel and Skerherezade, Jan. 31, 1837.
Amanda Malvina, d. of Justus and Pamela, in Bellingham, Jan. 27, 1834.
Amanda Maria, d. of Seth Jr. and Audary, 22d day, 1st mo. 1824. c.r.4.
Amariah, s. of Jacob and Mehetabel, 22d day, 4th mo. 1772. c.r.4.
Amasa, s. of Noah and Elisabeth, 11th day, 12th mo. 1791. c.r.4.
Amasa, s. of Asahel and ――――, May 3, 1808.
Amety, d. of John and Elisabeth, 7th day, 4th mo. 1791. c.r.4.
Amey, d. of Seth and Amey, May 8, 1785.
Amey, d. of David and Mary, 2d day, 6th mo. 1786. c.r.4.
Amos, 12th day, 11th mo. 1768. c.r.4.
Amy Maria, d. of Savel and Wait, Sept. 16, 1807. (Alma Meria, 16th day, 3d mo. 1807. c.r.4.)
Ananias, s. of Jacob and Mehetabel, 4th day, 4th mo. 1770. c.r.4.
Anna [――――], w. of Nehemiah, 9th day, 4th mo. 1749. c.r.4.
Anna [――――], 2d w. of John, 30th day, 11th mo. 1765. c.r.4.
Anna, d. of Arnold and ――――, Mar. 10, 1809.
Anna Cog, d. of Seth 3d and Audary, Dec. 10, 1802.
Anna Elisabeth, d. of Elisabeth, 18th day, 5th mo. 1819. c.r.4.
Anne, d. of Nehemiah and Anna, Oct. 11, 1788.
Apeme, ch. of Daniel and Mary, 1st day, 1st mo. 1783. c.r.4.
Arnold, s. of Abel and Olive, Sept. 11, 1785.
Arnold, s. of Arnold and ――――, May 30, 1811.
Asa, s. of Samuel and Huldah, Apr. 12, 1753. (2d day, 2d mo. 1752 o. s. c.r.3.) (2d day, 4th mo. 1752. c.r.4.)
Asahel, s. of Jacob and Joanna, Mar. 16, 1751–2.
Asahel, s. of Nathaniel and Rachel, May 4, 1780.
Asahel, s. of Asa and Susanna, 3d day, 4th mo, 1782. c.r.4.
Asahel, s. of Enoch and Deborah, July 6, 1782.
Asahel Ferdinand, s. of Asahel and Skerherezade, Dec. 17, 1832 (Dec. 7 dup.).
Ashel, s. of Jesse and Susannah, Sept. 9, 1796.
Audary [――――], w. of Seth Jr., 18th day, 12th mo. 17――. c.r.4.
Azuba [――――], w. of Willard, 2d day, 5th mo. 1783. c.r.4.
Barnabus, s. of Jeremiah and Hannah, Oct. 17, 1745.
Bathsheba, d. of John and Mary, July 29, 1768.
Bathsheba, d. of Justus and Pamela, in Bellingham, Jan. 1, 1832.

ALDRICH, Baylies W., s. of Valentine M. and Abigail, Dec. 5, 1849.
Benajah, s. of Stephen and Mary, 10th day, 11th mo. 1761. c.r.3.
Benjamin, s. of Abel and Elisabeth, May 1, 1733.
Benjamin, s. of Solomon and Elisabeth, Feb. 12, 1759.
Benjamin, s. of Seth 3d and Audary, Apr. 18, 1804.
Benjamin D., s. of Seth Jr. and Audary, 9th day, 9th mo. 1809. c.r.4.
Betsey, d. of Joseph and Harriet, Oct. 2, 1812.
Betsey Wheelock, d. of Sarah Scott, bp. Jan. 1, 1837. c.r.2.
Brice, s. of Peter and Issabel, 8th day, 1st mo. 1772. c.r.4.
Brown, s. of David and Mary, 9th day, 1st mo. 1785. c.r.4.
Brown W., s. of John and Anna, 18th day, 3d mo. 1809. c.r.4.
Bulah, d. of Peter and Esther, June 14, 1758.
Caleb, s. of Benjamin and Lydia, Sept. 19, 1768.
Cata, d. of Nathaniel and Rachel, Mar. 3, 1791.
Catharina, d. of John and Mary, Aug. 24, 1750.
Chad, s. of Stephen and Mary, 12th day, 2d mo. 1773. c.r.4.
Chalkley, s. of Noah and Elisabeth, 23d day, 3d mo. 1800. c.r.4.
Chancey, s. of Willard and Azubah, 27th day, 2d mo. 1814. c.r.4.
Charles Luther, s. of Lamond and Scynthia, June 28, 1834. "The above Charles L. was the son of Mathias Rice by his wife Hannah." [See Rice.]
Cheney, s. of Joseph and Harriet, Dec. 8, 1819.
Chloa, d. of Solomon and Elisabeth, Jan. 3, 1766.
Chloa, d. of Peter and Esther, Apr. 27, 1766.
Chloe [———], 2d w. of Joel, 14th day, 12th mo. 1779. c.r.4.
Chloe M., d. of Hosea and Mary Ann, Jan. 17, 1838.
Chloe Matildah, d. of Peleg and Huldah, 20th day, 3d mo. 1817. c.r.4.
Christopher Cog, s. of Seth 3d and Audary, Apr. 4, 1806.
Cynthia M., Nov. 28, 1818. g.r.23.
Daniel, s. of Daniel and Mary [no date]. c.r.4.
Daniel, s. of Jacob and Joanna, Sept. 3, 1733.
Daniel, s. of Benjamin and Lydia, Aug. 5, 1766.
Daniel H., s. of Ephraim and Dorcas, July 14, 1806.
Daniel H., s. of Samuel Jr. and Sarah, 23d day, 12th mo. 1813. c.r.4.
David, s. of John and Mary, July 21, 1757.
David, s. of Nehemiah and Anna, Feb. 17, 1784.
David, s. of David and Martha, 10th day, 1st mo. 1794. c.r.4.
David, s. of Nathan and Eunice G. 2d, Sept. 15, 1848.

ALDRICH, David Edwin, s. of Amos and Betsey, May 3, 1838.
Davis, s. of Justus and Pamela, May 25, 1841.
Deborah, d. of Jacob and Joanna, Apr. 26, 1745.
Deborah, d. of Peter and Issabel, 8th day, 2d mo. 1775. C.R.4.
Delphia, d. of Willard and Azubah, 22d day, 7th mo. 1817. C.R.4.
Dexter, s. of George and Rozilla of Adams, in Adams, Dec. 26, 1788.
Deziah, d. of John and Penellepy, Dec. 2, 1739.
Dinah, d. of Jeremiah and Hannah, Feb. 6, 1733-4.
Dinah, d. of Edward and Dinah, May 3, 1734.
Dinah [―――], w. of William, 10th day, 6th mo. 1761. C.R.4.
Dorcas, d. of Stephen and Mary, 30th day, 7th mo. 1767. C.R.4.
Dorcas [―――], w. of Ephraim, 22d day, 10th mo. 1771. C.R.4.
Dorcas, d. of Noah and Elisabeth, 21st day, 9th mo. 1811. C.R.4.
Dorcas, d. of Peleg and Huldah, 1st day, 1st mo. 1827. C.R.4.
Dorcas H. (Dorcas Hall, C.R.4), d. of Daniel H. and Phebe M., Sept. 17, 1841.
Duty, s. of Jesse and Susannah, Oct. 3, 1802.
Ebenezer, s. of Jacob and Mehetabel, 1st day, 2d mo. 1774. C.R.4.
Eber, s. of Enoch and Deborah, Apr. 24, 1785.
Edmund Horace, s. of Asahel and Skerherezade, Oct. 9, 1840.
Edward, s. of Edward and Dinah, Aug. 29, 1738.
Edwin O., s. of Jacob and Mahitabel (Mary in pencil), Dec. 6, 1823.
Eleanor W. (Eleanor Williams, C.R.2), d. of Valentine M. and Abigail, July 27, 1845.
Elijah, s. of John and Mary, Mar. 30, 1762.
Elisa, d. of Ebenezer and Isebel, 31st day, 7th mo. 1802. C.R.4.
Elisabeth, d. of Abel and Orana, Aug. 25, 1742.
Elisabeth [―――], w. of John, 4th day, 3d mo. 1765. C.R.4.
Elisabeth [―――], w. of Noah, 25th day, 5th mo. 1767. C.R.4.
Elisabeth, d. of John and Elisabeth, 22d day, 1st mo. 1795. C.R.4.
Eliza Brown, d. of Samuel Jr. and Sarah, 20th day, 11th mo. 1808. C.R.4.
Eliza Elvira, d. of Ahaz and Mary, May 17, 1823.
Elizabeth [―――], w. of A[bel], Jan. —, 1764. G.R.1.
Elizabeth, d. of Seth and Mary, July 12, 1775.
Elizabeth, d. of Abel and Olive, Dec. 4, 1789.
Ellis, s. of Abel and Olive, July 25, 1781.
Enoch, s. of Abel and Orana, Jan. 19, 1752-3.
Enoch, s. of Seth and Amey, Nov. 14, 1773.

ALDRICH, Ephraim, s. of Seth and Mary, Oct. 11, 1769.
Ephraim, s. of Ephraim and Dorcas, Feb. 17, 1805.
Esek, s. of Stephen and Mary, 29th day, 8th mo. 1779. c.r.4.
Esther, d. of Jacob and Joanna, Oct. 26, 1750.
Esther, d. of Peter and Esther, Jan. 30, 1756.
Esther, d. of Paul and Susanna, 21st day, 8th mo. 1782. c.r.4.
Esther [———], w. of Joel, 21st day, 8th mo. 1782. c.r.4.
Eunice, d. of Joseph and Elisabeth, Mar. 1, 1756.
Eunice, d. of Abel and Olive, Oct. 2, 1775.
Ezekiel, s. of Solomon and Elisabeth, Sept. 30, 1763.
Gardner, s. of Samuel and Huldah, 3d day, 6th mo. 1766. c.r.3.
George, s. of Benjamin and Lydia, Oct. 26, 1770.
George Anthony, s. of Abel Jr. and Phebe, Oct. 2, 1821.
George C., s. of Paul and Mary, 10th day, 9th mo. 1807. c.r.4.
Gideon Mowry, s. of Daniel H. and Phebe M., June 29, 1834.
Gilbert, s. of Jacob and Mahitabel (Mary in pencil), Apr. 20, 1821.
Gilbert F., s. of Lamond and Scynthia, July 26, 1834.
Hannah, d. of Edward and Dinah, Apr. 16, 1736.
Hannah, d. of Jonathan and Mary, Apr. 5, 1756.
Hannah, d. of Peter and Esther, Apr. 7, 1764.
Hannah, d. of Nehemiah and Anna, Mar. 7, 1778.
Hannah, d. of Ebenezer and Isebel, 1st day, 6th mo. 1798. c.r.4.
Hannah D. [———], w. of Peleg Brown, 6th day, 8th mo. 1833. c.r.4.
Harriet Marinda, d. of Thomas J. and Lydia, July 29, 1844.
Harris, s. of Asa and Susanna, 1st day, 6th mo. 1777. c.r.4.
Henry Clay, s. of Nathan 2d and Maria, Aug. 5, 1833.
Hetta [———], w. of Jacob, 9th day, 4th mo. 1797. c.r.4.
Hopestil, d. of Samuel and Huldah, Apr. 18, 1746. (13th day, 2d mo. 1746 o. s. c.r.3.)
Hosea, s. of Seth and Amey, Feb. 24, 1776.
Hosea, s. of Enoch Jr. and ———, Mar. 14, 1803.
Huldah [———], w. of Samuel, 15th day, 8th mo. 1728. c.r.4.
Huldah, d. of Samuel and Huldah, 30th day, 3d mo. 1774. c.r.4.
Huldah [———], w. of Peleg, 14th day, 1st mo. 1797. c.r.4.
Huldy, d. of Samuel Jr. and Sarah, 27th day, 1st mo. 1805. c.r.4.
Ira, s. of David and Mary, 15th day, 9th mo. 1788. c.r.4.
Ira, s. of Abel and Elizabeth, May 5, 1796.
Ira A., s. of Welcome and Maria, Feb. 3, 1845.
Isabel, d. of John and Mary, Oct. 29, 1752.

ALDRICH, Isabel, d. of Ephraim and Dorcas, 31st day, 8th mo. 1797. c.r.4.
Isabel, d. of John A. and Emeline W., b. in Maine, Nov. 30, 1848.
Israel, 2d day, 3d mo. 1765. c.r.4.
Israel, s. of Seth Jr. and Audary, 8th day, 7th mo., 1815. c.r.4.
Jacob, s. of Jacob and Joanna, Dec. 15, 1736.
Jacob, s. of Jacob and Joanna, Oct. 16, 1746.
Jacob, s. of Jacob and Mehetabel, 13th day, 4th mo. 1776. c.r.4.
Jacob, s. of Seth and Mary, Aug. 24, 1792.
James, s. of Solomon and Elisabeth, Sept. 26, 1768.
James, s. of Solomon and Elisabeth, Mar. 24, 1771.
James, s. of Paul and Susanna, 17th day, 10th mo. 1791. c.r.4.
James K. P., s. of Thomas and Louisa, Feb. 10, 1846.
Jane Mariah, d. of Welcome and Maria, Feb. 7, 1832.
Jemima, d. of Enoch and Deborah, Nov. 16, 1779.
Jesse, s. of Noah and Sarah, July 26, 1746.
Jesse, s. of Asahel, 13th day, 5th mo. 1773. c.r.4.
Jesse, s. of Stephen and Mary, 23d day, 9th mo. 1777. c.r.4.
Jesse, s. of David and Mary, 4th day, 3d mo. 1797. c.r.4.
Jestus, s. of Enoch Jr. and ———, June 6, 1807.
Joanna, d. of Jacob and Joanna, Feb. 16, 1743–4.
Joanna, d. of Aaron, 24th day, 10th mo. 1770. c.r.4.
Joanna, d. of Seth and Amey, Oct. 14, 1771.
Joanna, d. of Jacob and Mehetabel, 22d day, 6th mo. 1778. c.r.4.
Joanna, d. of Nathaniel and Rachel, Sept. 30, 1785. (30th day, 8th mo. 1785. c.r.4.)
Joel, s. of Seth and Mary, July 14, 1772.
John, s. of John and Mary, Sept. 21, 1759.
John, s. of John and Elisabeth, 16th day, 8th mo. 1798. c.r.4.
John M., s. of Thomas J. and Lydia, b. in Rochester, N. H., July 17, 1849.
John Seagrave, s. of Joseph and Harriet, Dec. 13, 1814.
John W., s. of Asahel and Skerherezade, Dec. 10, 1838.
Jonathan, s. of Jonathan and Mary, Sept. 16, 1749.
Jonathan R. (Jonathan Richard, c.r.4), s. of Daniel H. and Phebe M., Oct. 31, 1838.
Joseph, 29th day, 9th mo. 1718. c.r.4.
Joseph, s. of Seth and Mary, Aug. 2, 1764.
Joseph, s. of Seth and Mary, May 13, 1784.
Joseph, s. of Abel and Olive, Jan. 8, 1788.
Joseph, s. of David and Martha, 10th day, 11th mo. 1801. c.r.4.

ALDRICH, Joseph, Feb. 16, 1834. G.R.1.
Joshua, s. of Joseph and Elisabeth, Feb. 6, 1752-3. (12th day, 2d mo. 1752. C.R.4.)
Joshua, s. of John and Elisabeth, 24th day, 9th mo. 1788. C.R.4.
Joshua, s. of William and Dinah, Apr. 27, 1790.
Josiah C., s. of Nathan and Sarah S., b. in Douglas, July 9, 1848.
Josiah Wilcox, s. of Daniel H. and Phebe M., Feb. 12, 1831.
Justus, s. of Ahaz and Mary, May 14, 1834.
Lamond, s. of Willard and Azubah, 12th day, 9th mo. 1805. C.R.4.
Leander H., s. of Jacob and Mahitabel (Mary in pencil), July 1, 1828.
Lennard, s. of Solomon and Elisabeth, July 18, 1773.
Lepha, d. of Abel and Olive, Sept. 21, 1779.
Lois, d. of Daniel and Mary, Feb. 26, 1791.
Lot, s. of John and Mary, Oct. 30, 1754.
Lovel, s. of Abel and Olive, Sept. 3, 1783.
Lucina S., d. of Savel and Wait, Nov. 9, 1804. (Lorina, 3d day, 11th mo. 1804. C.R.4.)
Lucy G., d. of Savel and Wait, Feb. 24, 1806. (21st day, 2d mo. 1806. C.R.4.)
Lydia [———], w. of Benjamin, 17th day, 5th mo. 1740. C.R.4.
Lydia, d. of Jeremiah and Hannah, May 16, 1743.
Lydia, d. of Peter and Esther, June 5, 1769.
Lydia, d. of Daniel and Mary, 9th mo. 1775. C.R.4.
Lydia, d. of Benjamin and Lydia, Aug. 6, 1783.
Lydia, d. of Jesse and Susannah, May 2, 1794.
Lymon, s. of Samuel and Huldah, 6th day, 12th mo. 1768. C.R.3.
Manson Ahaz, s. of Ahaz and Mary, Dec. 16, 1824.
Marcy, d. of Samuel and Huldah, 18th day, 1st mo. 1761. C.R.3.
Margrey, d. of Noah and Sarah, June 10, 1749.
Maria F., d. of Nathan and Eunice G., May 9, 1847.
Marinda, d. of Abel and Elizabeth, June 10, 1794.
Martha, d. of Peter and Esther, July 25, 1749.
Martha, d. of Stephen and Mary, 7th day, 8th mo. 1763. C.R.4.
Martha, d. of Samuel Jr. and Sarah, 20th day, 4th mo. 1788. C.R.4.
Martha A., d. of Nathan and Sarah, Apr. 20, 1847.
Martin, s. of Jesse and Susannah, Jan. 3, 1806.
Mary, d. of Jacob and Joanna, Feb. 17, 1735-6.
Mary [———], w. of Stephen, 12th day, 12th mo. 1740. C.R.4.
Mary, d. of Jonathan and Mary, May 8, 1741.
Mary, d. of Abel and Orana, June 5, 1747.

ALDRICH, Mary, d. of Joseph and Elisabeth, July 1, 1747.
Mary, d. of Samuel and Huldah, July 24, 1748. (26th day, 5th mo. 1748. c.r.3.)
Mary [———], w. of David, 13th day, 6th mo. 1763. c.r.4.
Mary, d. of Seth and Amey, Sept. 1, 1769.
Mary [———], 2d w. of Paul, 23d day, 2d mo. 1781. c.r.4.
Mary, d. of Seth and Mary, Feb. 23, 1781.
Mary, d. of Samuel Jr. and Sarah, in Northbridge, 28th day, 7th mo. 1794. c.r.4.
Mary, d. of William and Dinah, Nov. 11, 1802.
Mary Brayton, d. of Daniel H. and Phebe M., Feb. 20, 1832.
Mary Brown, d. of David and Mary, 1st day, 12th mo. 1803. c.r.4.
Mary Cordelia, d. of Justus and Pamela, in Bellingham, Jan. 5, 1838.
Mary Jane, d. of Jacob and Mahitabel (Mary in pencil), Feb. 12, 1826.
Mary Jerusha, d. of Ahaz and Mary, June 10, 1826.
Mehetabel, d. of George and Meriam, Aug. 31, 1796.
Mercy, d. of Samuel Jr. and Sarah, 11th day, 8th mo. 1802. c.r.4.
Meriathanina, d. of Jonathan and Mary, May 1, 1753.
Milley, d. of Samuel and Huldah, 22d day, 3d mo. 1758. c.r.3.
Molley, d. of Solomon and Elisabeth, June 11, 1754.
Molley, d. of John and Mary, Apr. 30, 1765.
Molly, d. of Abel and Olive, Oct. 2, 1773.
Narcissa, d. of Paul Jr. and Almy, 2d day, 4th mo. 1809. c.r.4.
Nathan, s. of Peter and Esther, Aug. 13, 1762.
Nathan, s. of Seth and Amey, Mar. 28, 1788.
Nathan, s. of Paul and Susanna, 23d day, 3d mo. 1797. c.r.4.
Nathan, s. of Nathan and Martha, his 2d wife, May 16, 1843.
Nathan[ie]l, s. of Joseph and Elisabeth, Jan. 3, 1753.
Nathaniel, 1st day, 2d mo. 1754. c.r. 4.
Nathaniel, s. of Asahel and ———, Feb. 13, 1810.
Nehemiah, s. of Jacob and Joanna, May 20, 1749.
Nehemiah, s. of Nehemiah and Anna, Dec. 7, 1785.
Nella, d. of Nathaniel and Rachel, Nov. 8, 1784. (8th day, 3d mo. 1784. c.r.4.)
Noah, s. of Noah and Sarah, Sept. 16, 1741.
Noah, s. of Noah and Rachel, June 7, 1759.
Noah, s. of Seth and Mary, Oct. 4, 1766.
Olive, d. of Abel and Olive, Sept. 1, 1777.
Olney, s. of Nehemiah and Anna, Mar. 27, 1782.
Omar, s. of Paul and Mary, 19th day, 6th mo. 1805. c.r.4.

ALDRICH, Orinda Barber, d. of Ahaz and Mary, Oct. 3, 1831.
Oscar De Wilton, s. of Daniel H. and Phebe, 25th day, 12th mo. 1843. C.R.4.
Otis, s. of Peter and Elizabeth, Mar. 14, 1774.
Otis, s. of Enoch and Deborah, Mar. 4, 1788.
Patience A. [———], w. of Gideon M., Jan. 4, 1835. G.R.1.
Paul, s. of Peter and Esther, July 8, 1751. (Paul, 19th day, 7th mo. 1751. C.R.4.)
Paul, s. of Paul and Susanna, 19th day, 12th mo. 1784. C.R.4.
Peleg, s. of Samuel Jr. and Sarah, in Northbridge, 30th day, 6th mo. 1790. C.R.4.
Peleg Brown, s. of Peleg and Huldah, 19th day, 12th mo. 1824. C.R.4.
Penellepy, d. of John and Mary, Nov. 26, 1748.
Penllepy, d. of Joseph and Elisabeth, Jan. 30, 1742–3.
Peter, 19th day, 9th mo. 1722. C.R.4.
Peter, s. of Peter and Esther, Nov. 11, 1754.
Phebe, d. of Daniel and Mary [no date]. C.R.4.
Phebe, d. of Paul and Susanna, 15th day, 10th mo. 1799. C.R.4.
Phebe, d. of Noah and Elisabeth, 5th day, 9th mo. 1802. C.R.4.
Phebe [———], w. of Daniel H., 19th day, 9th mo. 1808. C.R.4.
Phebe Ann, d. of Sarah Scott, bp. Jan. 1, 1837. C.R.2.
Phebe Saben, d. of Paul Jr. and Almy, 27th day, 9th mo. 1815. C.R.4.
Phila, d. of Paul and Susanna, 23d day, 4th mo. 1787. C.R.4.
Phile, d. of Peter and Esther, May 26, 1760.
Phillip, s. of Ebenezer and Isebel, 10th day, 4th mo. 1800. C.R.4.
Pliny, s. of Noah and Elisabeth, 25th day, 8th mo. 1797. C.R.4.
Polly Adaline, d. of Wheeler and Polly, Mar. 12, 1844.
Prise, d. of Paul and Susanna, 3d day, 4th mo. 1794. C.R.4.
Pruda, d. of Jacob and Mehetabel, 20th day, 10th mo. 1782. C.R.4.
Prudence, d. of Aaron, 7th day, 7th mo. 1769. C.R.4.
Rachel, d. of Jeremiah and Hannah, May 29, 1735.
Rachel, d. of Jacob and Joanna, Mar. 19, 1754. Twin. (Rachel, w. of Nathaniel, Mar. 19, 1753 dup.)
Rachel, d. of Joseph and Elizabeth, May 18, 1761.
Rachel, d. of Seth and Mary, Sept. 28, 1788.
Rachel, d. of Asahel and ———, Oct. 15, 1804.
Rachel, d. of Paul and Mary, 3d day, 3d mo. 1813. C.R.4.
Rhoda, d. of Samuel and Huldah, Jan. 20, 1751–2. (20th day, 12th mo. 1750. C.R.3.)
Rhoda, [———], w. of Amos, 11th day, 12th mo. 1769. C.R.4.

ALDRICH, Rhoda, d. of Samuel Jr. and Sarah, in Northbridge, 17th day, 2d mo. 1786. c.r.4.
Rhoda, d. of George and Meriam, Aug. 7, 1799.
Rhoday, d. of Enoch and Deborah, Mar. 3, 1775.
Richard, s. of Enoch and Deborah, Apr. 7, 1777.
Richard, s. of Paul Jr. and Almy, 20th day, 3d mo. 1807. c.r.4.
Robert Bruce, s. of Peleg and Huldah, 15th day, 5th mo. 1819. c.r.4.
Robert H., s. of Seth Jr. and Audary, 14th day, 9th mo. 1811. c.r.4.
Robert Hall, s. of Ephraim and Dorcas, Aug. 19, 1801.
Royal, s. of Stephen and Mary, 20th day, 6th mo. 1769. c.r.4.
Royal, s. of George and Rozilla of Adams, in Adams, June 16, 1787.
Rufus, s. of Benjamin and Lydia, June 13, 1773.
Rufus T., s. of Seth Jr. and Audary, 3d day, 6th mo. 1813. c.r.4.
Ruth, d. of Joseph and Elisabeth, June 29, 1741.
Ruth, d. of Jacob and Joanna, Mar. 19, 1754. Twin.
Ruth, d. of Stephen and Mary, 1st day, 5th mo. 1771. c.r.4.
Ruth [———], 2d. w. of Ephraim, 24th day, 4th mo. 1773. c.r.4.
Ruth, d. of Nathaniel and Rachel, Sept. 12, 1776. (1st day, 9th mo. 1776. c.r.4.)
Ruth, d. of Nehemiah and Anna, Oct. 3, 1791.
Ruth, d. of Willard and Azubah, 20th day, 3d mo. 1803. c.r.4.
Ruth, d. of Jesse and Susannah, Aug. 25, 1808.
Ruth Mowry, d. of Paul Jr. and Almy, 14th day, 2d mo. 1818. c.r.4.
Sabra Salinda, d. of Ahaz and Mary, Mar. 4, 1830.
Salley, d. of Daniel and Mary, May 29, 1789.
Sally, d. of Hosea and Rachel, Feb. 14, 1799.
Samuel, 2d day, 2d mo. 1726. c.r.4.
Samuel Jr. (s. of Samuel and Huldah, c.r.3), in Northbridge, 1st day, 9th mo. 1763. c.r.4.
Samuel, s. of Samuel Jr. and Sarah, 4th day, 7th mo. 1792. c.r.4.
Samuel, s. of George and Meriam, Aug. 3, 1794.
Samuel, s. of Seth Jr. and Audary, 25th day, 3d mo. 1821. c.r.1.
Samuel, ———, 1823. g.r.21.
Samuel B., s. of Peleg and Huldah, 18th day, 2d mo. 1821. c.r.4.
Samuel Clarke, s. of Samuel and Melisia, Apr. 12, 1845.
Samuel Willod, s. of Samuel Jr. and Sarah, in Northbridge, 15th day, 5th mo. 1800. c.r.4.

ALDRICH, Sands, ch. of Daniel and Mary, 11th mo. 1779. c.r.4.
Sarah, d. of Edward and Dinah, Dec. 20, 1740.
Sarah, d. of Joseph and Elisabeth, Apr. 1, 1745.
Sarah, d. of Jonathan and Mary, Nov. 29, 1746.
Sarah, d. of Abel and Orana, May 22, 1750.
Sarah, d. of Samuel and Huldah, 29th day, 8th mo. 1755. c.r.3.
Sarah [———], w. of Samuel Jr., in Providence, 13th day, 9th mo. 1766. c.r.4.
Sarah, d. of Aaron, 4th day, 4th mo. 1773. c.r.4.
Sarah, d. of Seth and Amey, Mar. 6, 1778.
Sarah, d. of Benjamin and Lydia, Sept. 18, 1778.
Sarah, d. of David and Sarah, 18th day, 8th mo. 1791. c.r.4.
Sarah, d. of Enoch and Deborah, Nov. 4, 1795.
Sarah, d. of Samuel Jr. and Sarah, in Northbridge, 15th day, 9th mo. 1797. c.r.4.
Sarah, d. of Joseph and Harriet, Aug. 15, 1817.
Sarah, d. of Peleg and Huldah, 24th day, 1st mo. 1823. c.r.4.
Sarah Ann, d. of Willard and Azubah, 16th day, 2d mo. 1811. c.r.4.
Sarah D., d. of Jacob and Mahitabel (Mary in pencil), Nov. 8, 1819.
Sarah Jane, d. of Nathan and Martha, Feb. 26, 1845.
Savel, s. of Nathaniel and Rachel, July 12, 1781. (20th day, 7th mo. 1781. c.r.4.)
Seth, s. of Abel and Elisabeth, Apr. 26, 1736.
Seth, s. of Jacob and Joanna, Dec. 6, 1738. (Seth, b. 8th day, 12th mo. 1738. c.r.4.)
Seth, s. of Abel and Orana, June 22, 1744.
Seth, s. of Benjamin and Lydia, Nov. 16, 1775.
Seth, s. of Daniel and Mary, 10th mo. 1777. c.r.4.
Seth, s. of Noah and Elisabeth, 22d day, 2d mo. 1790. c.r.4.
Seth, s. of Ebenezer and Isebel, 2d day, 11th mo. 1804. c.r.4.
Seth, s. of Ahaz and Mary, June 29, 1828.
Seth R., s. of Arnold and ———, July 12, 1815.
Silas, s. of Experiance Thayer, Sept. 29, 1774.
Silvia, d. of Joseph and Harriet, Mar. 19, 1822.
Simon, s. of Jonathan and Mary, May —, 1760.
Solomon, s. of John and Penellepy, Mar. 28, 1730.
Solomon, s. of Solomon and Elisabeth, Jan. 26, 1761.
Solomon C., s. of Asahel and Skerherezade, May 25, 1835.
Stephen, 28th day, 11th mo. 1726. c.r.4.
Stephen, s. of Stephen and Mary, 15th day, 5th mo. 1765. c.r.4.
Stephen, s. of William and Dinah, Apr. 14, 1795.

ALDRICH, Susan Ann, d. of John and Betsey, July 2, 1843.
Susanna [―――], w. of Asa, 21st day, 5th mo. 1751. C.R.4.
Susanna [―――], w. of Paul, 30th day, 11th mo. 1756. C.R.4.
Susanna, d. of Paul and Susanna, 27th day, 4th mo. 1789. C.R.4.
Susanna, d. of Joel and Esther, Dec. 11, 1804.
Susannah, d. of Jonathan and Mary, Nov. 29, 1743.
Susannah, d. of Abel and Orana, Nov. 15, 1753.
Sylama, d. of Nathaniel and Rachel, Aug. 13, 1778.
Sylvanus Scott, s. of Sarah Scott, bp. Jan. 1, 1837. C.R.2.
Sylvester Welcome, s. of Welcome and Maria, Nov. 12, 1830.
Sylvia Ann, d. of Hosea and Mary Ann, July 20, 1844.
Thankful, d. of William and Dinah, Feb. 19, 1798. Twin.
Thomas, s. of Willard and Azubah, 30th day, 10th mo. 1808. C.R.4.
Thomas Paul, s. of Paul Jr. and Almy, 6th day, 11th mo. 1820. C.R.4.
Timothy, s. of Jeremiah and Hannah, Oct. 7, 1739.
Turnner, s. of Peter and Esther, Jan. 8, 1768.
Tyler D., s. of Asahel and ―――, Sept. 15, 1813.
Valentine M., s. of Jacob and Mahitabel (Mary in pencil), Apr. 2, 1815.
Wait [―――], w. of Savel, 10th day, 1st mo. 1782. C.R.4.
Wanton, s. of Asa and Susanna, 4th day, 4th mo. 1780. C.R.4.
Watee E., d. of Hosea and Mary Ann, Sept. 1, 1840.
Welcome, s. of Abel and Elizabeth, June 18, 1798.
Wheeler, s. of William and Dinah, July 26, 1792.
Willard, s. of Nathaniel and Rachel, Apr. 23, 1775 (1774, C.R.4).
Willard Ansel, s. of Lamond and Scynthia, Mar. 20, 1836.
William, s. of Jacob and Joanna, Jan. 13, 1731-2.
William, s. of Joseph and Elisabeth, Apr. 14, 1758.
William, s. of Enoch and Deborah, Mar. 6, 1791. Twin.
William H., s. of Seth Jr. and Audary, 30th day, 4th mo. 1819. C.R.4.
Willis, s. of Stephen and Mary, 17th day, 1st mo. 1776. C.R.4.
Willis, s. of Nehemiah and Anna, Mar. 4, 1780.
Willis, s. of Enoch and Deborah, Mar. 6, 1791. Twin.
Wily, s. of Jesse and Susannah, Apr. 25, 1799.
Zacheus, s. of Stephen and Mary, 10th day, 8th mo. 1781. C.R.4.

ALEXANDER, Alanson, s. of Whitney and Hannah, Dec. 23, 1840.
Charlotte [―――], w. of George E., June 21, 1822. G.R.1.

ALEXANDER, George E., Nov. 4, 1828. G.R.1.
Gidean, s. of Elijah and Elisabeth, Aug. 13, 1767.
Jane E. Taft [――――], w. of Mason, Apr. 4, 1836. G.R.1.
Mason, Nov. 10, 1830. G.R.1.
Matilda, d. of Whitney and Hannah, Oct. 26, 1838.
Sarah E., d. of Isaac, b. in Mendon, and Mary Jane, b. in Bolton, Nov. 9, 1849.

ALGER, Benajah, s. of John and Elisabeth, June 3, 1782. Twin.
Elisabeth, d. of John and Elisabeth, Oct. 25, 1775.
John, s. of John and Elisabeth, Oct. 2, 1778.
Josiah, s. of John and Elisabeth, June 3, 1782. Twin.
Martha, d. of John and Elisabeth, Aug. 11, 1774.
Samuel, s. of John and Elisabeth, Feb. 14, 1786.

ALLEN, Abagail, d. of Moses and Comfort, 5th day, 12th mo. 1778. C.R.4.
Abigail, d. of Micah and Mary, bp. July 26, 1752. C.R.1.
Abraham, s. of Moses and Comfort, 25th day, 9th mo. 1768. C.R.4.
Arnold S., ――――, 1846. G.R.1.
Comfort [――――], w. of Moses, 11th day, 12th mo. 1745. C.R.4.
Comfort, d. of Moses and Comfort, 12th day, 7th mo. 1774. C.R.4.
Ebenezer, s. of Samuel and Bethany, July 5, 1795.
Ezra, 18th day, 10th mo. 1747. C.R.4.
Ezra, s. of Ezra and Lucy, 3d day, 8th mo. 1781. C.R.4.
Hannah, d. of Moses and Comfort, 24th day, 9th mo. 1776. C.R.4.
Henry Clay, s. of Whipple and Amanda N., Nov. 11, 1844.
Jerathmeel, s. of Moses and Comfort, 11th day, 5th mo. 1770. C.R.4.
John Clark, s. of Diarca and Joanna, bp. May 5, 1824. C.R.1.
Joseph, s. of Joseph and ――――, of Providence, bp. at Providence, June 26, 1751. C.R.1.
Joseph, s. of Micah and Mary, bp. Sept. 1, 1754. C.R.1.
Lucy [――――], w. of Ezra, 15th day, 11th mo. 1749. C.R.4.
Lydia, d. of Ezra and Lucy, 3d day, 12th mo. 1772. C.R.4.
Margaret, d. of Moses and Comfort, 18th day, 8th mo. 1783. C.R.4.
Martha, d. of Moses and Comfort, 3d day, 6th mo. 1781. C.R.4.
Mary, d. of Samuel and Mary, July 11, 1746.
Moses, 30th day, 11th mo. 1745. C.R.4.
Moses, s. of Moses and Comfort, 25th day, 5th mo. 1772. C.R.4.

ALLEN, Polly, d. of Samuel and Bethany, Dec. 18, 1788.
Ruth, d. of Ezra and Lucy, 27th day, 4th mo. 1770. C.R.4.
Samuel, s. of Samuel and Bethany, July 19, 1791.
Sarah F., ———, 1824. G.R.1.
Seth, s. of Samuel and Bethany, May 31, 1786.
Silence, d. of Micah and Mary, bp. Nov. 5, 1758. C.R.1.
Sophia R. Seagrave [———], w. of Arnold S., ———, 1847. G.R.1.
Tamar, d. of Ezra and Lucy, 23d day, 7th mo. 1774. C.R.4.
Willis Arnold, s. of John and Azuba, Apr. 21, 1832.

AMIDOWN (see Ammadown), Mary, d. of Phillip and Submit, May 5, 1732.
Mehitable, d. of Phillip and Submit, Mar. 27, 1738–9.

AMMADOWN (see Amidown), Caleb, s. of Philip and Submit, bp. Oct. 17, 1736. C.R.1.
Joseph, s. of Philip and Submit, bp. Nov. 25, 1733. C.R.1.

ANDREWS, Emeline Paine, d. of Hawkins and Lucinda, Nov. 15, 1843.
Matilda [———], w. of Geo[rge], Apr. 4, 1838. G.R.1.

ANSON, Else Ann, d. of Manning and Susan, Aug. 29, 1829.
Ezekiel, s. of Manning and Susan, Nov. 7, 1836.
Henry, s. of Manning and Susan, Jan. 30, 1828.
Manning Walter, s. of John and Esther, Oct. 31, 1799.
Mary Thwing, d. of Manning and Susan, Dec. 2, 1834.
Minerva Adelaide, d. of Manning W. and Susan, July 7, 1844.
Sarah Allen, d. of Manning and Susan, Aug. 18, 1833.

ANTHONY, Elisha Leander, s. of Elisha and Roxcellana, May 14, 1845.

ARCHER, Abner, s. of Job and Bethany, Sept. 16, 1764.
Bethemydier, d. of Job and Bethany, May 9, 1771.
David, s. of Benjamin and Elisabeth, Feb. 8, 1743–4.
Elisabeth, d. of Benjamin and Elisabeth, Mar. 9, 1745–6.
Job, s. of Benjamin and Elisabeth, Dec. 5, 1741.
Lucy, d. of Job and Bethany, Mar. 24, 1763.
Mary, d. of Benjamin and Mary, Sept. 11, 1760. (Mary, d. of Benjamin and Mary dec., bp. July 12, 1761. C.R.1.)

ARCULESS, ———, d. of Isaac and Mary, Apr. 28, 1846.

ARMSTRONG, David Newell, s. of Seth W. and Maria C., July 20, 1843.

ARNOLD, Alice A., d. of Alfred, b. in Mendon, and Sarah S., b. in Leicester, Oct. 21, 1849.
Alise, d. of Elisha and Theodate, 19th day, 4th mo. 1788. c.r.4.
Benedict, 27th day, 4th mo. 1752. c.r.4.
Benedict, s. of William and Hannah, 2d day, 1st mo. 1803. c.r.4.
Daniel, s. of Oliver and Abigail, 28th day, 8th mo. 1815. c.r.4.
Dorcas, d. of Benedict and Sarah, 14th day, 10th mo. 1775. c.r.4.
Dorcas, d. of William and (Hannah, c.r.4), July 21, 1809. (31st day, 7th mo. 1809. c.r.4.)
Edmond, s. of Alfred and Sarah, Sept. 17, 1839.
Elisha, 24th day, 4th mo. 1756. c.r.4.
Elisha, s. of Oliver and Abigail, 6th day, 5th mo. 1820. c.r.4.
George Washington, s. of Welcome and Rebecca, May 20, 1844.
George Willard, s. of George and ———, July 24, 1809.
Hannah [———], w. of William, Dec. 11, 1779. g.r.21.
Huldah, d. of Elisha and Theodate, 7th day, 8th mo. 1791. c.r.4.
Israel, s. of Elisha and Theodate, 20th day, 2d mo. 1784. c.r.4.
Israel, s. of Oliver and Abigail, 2d day, 1st mo. 1812. c.r.4.
James G., 22d day, 9th mo. 1824. c.r.4.
Lucy, d. of William and (Hannah, g.r.21), July 10, 1807.
Lucy, d. of Oliver and Abigail, 27th day, 4th mo. 1818. c.r.4.
Maria, d. of William and Hannah, 30th day, 1st mo. 1801. c.r.4.
Mary, d. of Benedict and Sarah, 1st day, 12th mo. 1781. c.r.4.
Mary, d. of Oliver and Abigail, 2d day, 3d mo. 1814. c.r.4.
Mary Smith, d. of William and Hannah, 10th day, 11th mo. 1811. c.r.4.
Minerva Eveline, d. of Alfred and Sarah, Aug. 22, 1837.
Oliver, s. of Elisha and Theodate, 10th day, 12th mo. 1777. c.r.4.
Patience, d. of Elisha and Theodate, 24th day, 8th mo. 1799. c.r.4.
Ruth, d. of Elisha and Theodate, 20th day, 2d. mo. 1775. c.r.4.
Sam[ue]l A., 4th day, 1st mo. 1827. c.r.4.
Sarah [———], w. of Benedict, 27th day, 4th mo. 1754. c.r.4.
Sarah, d. of William and (Hannah, c.r.4), Sept. 27, 1805.
Theodate [———], w. of Elisha, 5th day, 11th mo. 1752. c.r.4.
Thomas L., s. of Welcome J. and Charlotte B., Oct. 26, 1846. Removed to Millbury.
Waity, d. of Elisha and Theodate, 12th day, 11th mo. 1780. c.r.4.
William, s. of Benedict and Sarah, 31st day, 1st mo. 1777. c.r.4. (Jan. 30, 1777. g.r.21.)

ATTWOOD, Frances, 23d day, 5th mo. 1728. c.r.4.

BACHELDER, ———, s. of Bridgham and Mary, May 4, 1847.
Lydia, d. of William and Lydia, Dec. 23, 1767.

BACON, Amos, s. of Jonathan and Ruth, bp. Apr. 15, 1739. c.r.1.
Betsy Snow, d. of ——— and Ester, bp. Sept. 5, 1802. c.r.1.
Bulah, d. of Jonathan and Martha, May 19, 1764.
Damerus, d. of Jonathan and Martha, Feb. 26, 1757.
Diadame, d. of Jonathan and Martha, Mar. 12, 1772.
Dorothy, d. of William and Mary, bp. May 4, 1755. c.r.1.
Dorothy, d. of William and Mary, bp. June 15, 1760. c.r.1.
E. O., ———, 1832. g.r.1.
Eunice, d. of William and Mary, bp. Aug. 30, 1767. c.r.1.
George Hall, s. of George and Esther, Feb. 15, 1802.
Hannah Sophia, d. of George H. and Lucy, June 27, 1827.
Jane E. [———], w. of E. O., ———, 1835. g.r.1.
Jepthah, s. of Jonathan and Martha, Mar. 31, 1770.
Joel, s. of William and Mary, bp. Nov. 10, 1771. c.r.1.
Jonathan, s. of Jonathan and Martha, Oct. 27, 1754.
Jonathan, s. of Jonathan and Martha, Apr. 30, 1759.
Nathan, s. of Jonathan and Ruth, bp. May 8, 1737. c.r.1.
Nathan, s. of William and Mary, bp. Sept. 23, 1764. c.r.1.
Ruth, d. of Jonathan and Ruth, May 20, 1736.
Ruth, d. of William and Mary, bp. Sept. 23, 1764. c.r.1.
Solomon, s. of Jonathan and Martha, July 3, 1763.
Sophia, d. of ——— and Ester, bp. Sept. 5, 1802. c.r.1.
Timothy, s. of Jonathan and Ruth, Feb. 23, 1734-5.
William, s. of William and Mary, bp. Apr. 10, 1757. c.r.1.
Zilpha, d. of Jonathan and Martha, Feb. 6, 1767.
Zipporah, d. of Jonathan and Martha, Jan. 19, beginning the year 1750.

BAKER, Amey, d. of Amos and Rachel, 1st day, 8th mo. 1785. c.r.4.
Amos, 9th day, 6th mo. 1756. c.r.4.
Anna [———], w. of Obediah, 20th day, 8th mo. 1774. c.r.4.
Bezaleel Sawyer, s. of Manasseh and Lois, Sept. 13, 1802.
Caleb Strong, s. of Manasseh and Lois, July 30, 1816. Twin.
Catey, 23d day, 12th mo. 1765. c.r.4.
Chloe Taft, d. of Manasseh and Lois, Dec. 17, 1807.
Daniel, s. of Obediah and Anna, 3d day, 1st mo. 1795. c.r.4.
Dinah [———], w. of ———, 17th day, 9th mo. 1741. c.r.4.
Elisabeth, 25th day, 5th mo. 1767. c.r.4.

BAKER, Elisabeth, d. of Obediah and Anna, 30th day, 11th mo. 1796. c.r.4.
Esther [———], w. of ———, 16th day, 7th mo. 1714. c.r.4.
Esther, d. of ——— and Dinah, 22d day, 10th mo. 1775. c.r.4.
Hannah, d. of ——— and Dinah, 21st day, 1st mo. 1772. c.r.4.
Hannah, d. of Joseph and Molley, ———, 1775.
Hannah Dike, d. of Manasseh and Lois, Nov. 8, 1813.
Huldah, d. of ——— and Dinah, 10th day, 2d mo. 1771. c.r.4.
John Brooks, s. of Manasseh and Lois, July 30, 1816. Twin.
John Williams, s. of Manasseh and Lois, Sept. 29, 1810.
Mary, d. of Obediah and Anna, 20th day, 10th mo. 1798. c.r.4.
Mary Sawyer, d. of Manasseh and Lois, Apr. 1, 1800.
Rachel [———], w. of Amos, 5th day, 10th mo. 1760. c.r.4.
Rachel, d. of Amos and Rachel, 11th day, 6th mo. 1787. c.r.4.
Randal, 25th day, 1st mo. 1770. c.r.4.
Samuel, s. of Joseph and Molley, Sept. 2, 1773.
Sarah Williams, d. of Manasseh and Lois, Feb. 8, 1796.
Sawyer, s. of Manasseh and Lois, Nov. 5, 1797.
Stephen, 23d day, 8th mo. 1764. c.r.4.
Stephen, s. of ——— and Dinah, 23d day, 6th mo. 1768. c.r.4.
Thankful, d. of Amos and Rachel, 7th day, 12th mo. 1783. c.r.4.
William Henry, s. of Manasseh and Lois, June 8, 1805.

BALCOM (see Balcum), Aaron Benson, s. of Ebenezer and Polly, bp. Sept. 18, 1831. c.r.1.
Elijah, s. of Joseph and Pheeby of New Sherborn, July 26, 1729.
Joel Chapin, s. of Ebenezer and Polly, bp. Sept. 18, 1831. c.r.1.
Mary, d. of Joseph and Pheeby of New Sherborn, Dec. 12, 1725.
Mary, d. of Ebenezer and Polly, bp. Sept. 18, 1831. c.r.1.
Samuel, s. of Joseph and Pheeby of New Sherborn, Mar. 10, 1726–7.

BALCUM (see Balcom), Elijah, s. of Elijah and Ruth, Apr. 5, 1755.

BALDWIN, Ephraim, s. of Jonas and ———, bp. Oct. 6, 1771. c.r.1.
Jonas Cutler, s. of Samuel and Millicent, Jan. 3, 1769.
Samuel, s. of Samuel and Millicent, Oct. 13, 1766.

BALLOU, Mary Emma, d. of Welcome, b. in Burrillville, and Sarah, Nov. 23, 1849.

BAMFORTH, Bentley, Aug. 28, 1840. g.r.1.

BANCROFT, Anna, d. of William and Mary, May 3, 1764.
Sarah, d. of William and Mary, Dec. 7, 1767.

BARBER, James Henry, inf. s. of James and Betsey Ann, bp. Jan. 1, 1846. C.R.2.

BARDEEN (see Bardens), Ferdinand, s. of Ferdinand and Amy, Aug. —, 1846. G.R.18.

BARDENS (see Bardeen), Eunice, d. of James and Jerusha, Sept. 27, 1749.
Lucy, d. of James and Tryfeney, Mar. 24, 1764.
Moses, s. of James and Mary, July 15, 1756.
Stephen, s. of James and Mary, Mar. 18, 1754.
Thomas, s. of James and Jerusha, Aug. 8, 1747.

BARNES, Carrie J., ——, 1841. G.R.1.
Elizabeth J. [———], w. of William G., ——, 1807. G.R.1.
William G., ——, 1805. G.R.1.

BARRETT, Abigail, d. of Jaazanaih and Rhoda, 10th day, 3d mo. 1791. C.R.4.
Hannah, d. of Jaazanaih and Rhoda, 19th day, 5th mo. 1783. C.R.4.
Jaazanaih, 21st day, 1st mo. 1752. C.R.4.
Jaazaniah, s. of Jaazanaih and Rhoda, 6th day, 12th mo. 1788. Richmond, C.R.4.
John, s. of Jaazanaih and Rhoda, 13th day, 7th mo. 1781. C.R.4.
Jonathan, s. of Jaazanaih and Rhoda, 18th day, 1st mo. 1786. C.R.4.
Rhoda [———], w. of Jaazanaih, 24th day, 5th mo. 1760. C.R.4.

BARRY, Margaret Maher [———], w. of Thomas, Mar. 25, 1829. G.R.2.
Thomas, Nov. 15, 1824. G.R.2.

BARTEE, Elijah Balcom, s. of Phebe, bp. June 14, 1741. C.R.1.
Samuel, s. of Phebe, bp. June 14, 1741. C.R.1.

BARTLETT, Elizabeth, youngest d. of Walter Price and Elizabeth of Salem, Feb. 11, 1783. G.R.1.
Mary E., d. of Eber and Deborah, 1st day, 12th mo. 1833. C.R.4.
Tho[ma]s Edward, s. of Eber and Deborah, 17th day, 4th mo. 1838. C.R.4.

BARTON, Henry H., s. of Theron, b. in Charlton, and Betsey, July 3, 1849.

BASSET (see Bassett), Artimus, s. of William and Margery, 19th day, 6th mo. 1782. c.r.4.
Cyrus, s. of William and Margery, 31st day, 3d mo. 1779. c.r.4.
Daniel, s. of William and Margery, 19th day, 12th mo. 1784. c.r.4.
Ellis, s. of William and Margery, 2d day, 7th mo. 1787. c.r.4.
Isaac, s. of Joseph and Hannah, 1st day, 7th mo. 1781. c.r.3.
Lydia, d. of William and Margery, 31st day, 8th mo. 1780. c.r.4.
Margery [———], w. of William, 16th day, 10th mo. 1754. c.r.4.
Martha, d. of William and Margery, 6th day, 7th mo. 1789. c.r.4.
William, 29th day, 10th mo. 1747. c.r.4.
William, s. of William and Margery, 13th day, 8th mo. 1791. c.r.4.

BASSETT (see Basset), Amey, d. of Joseph and Rachel, Apr. 11, 1793.
Anna, d. of Joseph and ———, 23d day, 11th mo. 1784. c.r.4.
Ephraim, 7th day, 9th mo. 1789. c.r.4.
Hannah, d. of Joseph and Rachel, May 23, 1791.
Hannah Smith, d. of Ephraim and Mary, his 2d w., 4th day, 4th mo. 1832. c.r.4.
Isaac, s. of Ephraim and Mary (Mercy, c.r.4), Apr. 17, 1812.
James C. (James Cumstock dup.), s. of Ephraim and Mary (Mercy, c.r.4), July 18, 1815 (June 18, 1815 dup.).
Joseph, 25th day, 3d mo. 1752. c.r.4.
Mary Smith [———], w. of Ephraim, ——— 1804. g.r.4.
Mercy [———], w. of Ephraim, 14th day, 4th mo. 1791. c.r.4.
Rachal [———], w. of Joseph, 18th day, 5th mo. 1761. c.r.4.
Rachel, d. of Joseph and Rachel, July 6, 1799.
Rowland G. (Rowland Green dup.), s. of Ephraim and Mary (Mercy, c.r.4), Dec. 17, 1817.
Ruth, d. of Joseph and Rachel, May 19, 1795.
Samuel Smith, s. of Ephraim and Mary, his 2d w., 4th day, 9th mo. 1828. c.r.4.

BATES, Abbie M. Whittemore [———], w. of Ira D., Sept. 3, 1841. g.r.1.
Ira Delaven, s. of Stephen and Mary, Dec. 25, 1843.

BATTEY (see Battie), Amos, s. of Nicholas and Thankful, Feb. 21, 1800.
Benjamin, 7th day, 9th mo. 1737. c.r.4.
Benjamin, s. of Nicholas and Thankful, Apr. 20, 1794.
David, s. of Jesse and Nancy, 30th day, 3d mo. 1790. c.r.4.
Elisabeth W., d. of Richard and Rachel A., 30th day, 9th mo. 1840. c.r.1.
Ezra, s. of Nicholas and Thankful, Mar. 24, 1789.
Jesse, s. of Benjamin and Mercy, 29th day, 11th mo. 1763. c.r.4.
Joanna, d. of Nicholas and Thankful, Dec. 7, 1791.
Joel, s. of Nicholas and Thankful, Feb. 4, 1787.
Joseph, s. of Benjamin and Mercy, 26th day, 5th mo. 1768. c.r.4.
Joseph, s. of Nicholas and Thankful, June 8, 1797.
Lydia, d. of Nicholas and Thankful, Feb. 1, 1785.
Mary, d. of Nicholas and ———, 2d day, 6th mo. 1781. Gloucester. c.r.4.
Mercy [———], w. of Benjamin, 3d day, 10th mo. 1737. c.r.4.
Nancy [———], w. of Jesse, 21st day, 9th mo. 1770. Gloucester. c.r.4.
Nicholas, 29th day, 10th mo. 1758. Gloucester. c.r.4.
Ruth S., d. of Richard and Rachel A., 17th day, 9th mo. 1835. c.r.4.
Sarah, d. of Benjamin and Mercy, 1st day, 8th mo. 1761. c.r.4.
Sarah Jane, d. of Richard and Rachel A., 27th day, 1st mo. 1832. c.r.4.
Thankful [———], 2d w. of Nicholas, 24th day, 9th mo. 1758. Coventry. c.r.4.

BATTIE (see Battey), Anne, d. of Richard and Rachel A., Aug. 30, 1830.

BATTLES, Alpeous, s. of Edward and Ruth, Apr. 5, 1773.
Deland, s. of Edward and Ruth, Jan. 21, 1771.
Joanna, d. of Edward and Ruth, Feb. 26, 1778.
Perla, d. of Edward and Ruth, Sept. 21, 1767.
Ruth, d. of Edward and Ruth, Aug. 12, 1775.

BAXTER (see Baxtor), Joseph, s. of Joseph and ———, bp. Apr. 2, 1749. c.r.1.

BAXTOR (see Baxter), Mary, d. of Joseph and Jemima, Dec. 24, 1740.

BAYLIES, Abigail, d. of Nicholes and Abigail, Sunday, June 21, 1772.
Adolphas, s. of Alpheus and Sarah, Jan. 22, 1800.
Adolphus, s. of Nicholas and Elisabeth, Monday, Mar. 24, 1745-6.
Adolphus, s. of Nicholes and Abigail, May 6, 1780.
Alpheus, s. of Nicholes and Abigail, Friday, June 29, 1770.
Alpheus Wood, s. of Adolphus and Mary, Mar. 15, 1832.
Eleanor, d. of Nicholes and Abigail, Mar. 21, 1785.
Elizabeth, d. of Nicholes and Abigail, Sunday, Nov. 24, 1765.
Ellen Augusta, d. of Adolphus and Mary, Oct. 15, 1840.
Ephraim, s. of Alpheus and Sarah, June 6, 1795.
Fraedrick, s. of Nicholas and Elisabeth, Saturday, July 18, 1741.
George, s. of (Dea., c.r.1) Nicholes and Hannah, May 29, 1791.
George Nicholas, s. of Ephraim and Henrietta, July 10, 1832.
Gustaves, s. of Nicholas and Elisabeth, Saturday, June 20, 1752.
Gustavus, s. of Nicholes and Abigail, Monday, July 6, 1761.
Henrietta Whitney [———], w. of Dea. Ephraim, ———, 1797. g.r.1.
Hodijah, s. of Nicholas and Elizabeth, bp. Sept. 19, 1756. c.r.1.
Josiah, s. of Alpheus and Sarah, Feb. 28, 1806.
Mary, d. of Nicholes and Abigail, Thursday, Aug. 4, 1774.
Mary Elizabeth (Maria Elizabeth, c.r.1), d. of Ephraim and Henrietta, Sept. 3, 1825.
Mary Elizabeth, d. of Adolphus and Mary, Mar. 24, 1834.
Nancy, d. of Nicholes and Abigail, Apr. 20, 1782.
Nicholas, s. of Nicholas and Elisabeth, Thursday, Nov. 15, 1739.
Nicholas, s. of Nicholes and Abigail, Saturday, Apr. 9, 1768.
Sarah, d. of Alpheus and Sarah, bp. July 22, 1810. c.r.1.
Submit, d. of Nicholes and Abigail, Jan. 7, 1788. (Submit, d. of Nicholas and Abigail dec., bp. Jan. 18, 1788. c.r.1.)
Susan Maria (Susanna Maria, c.r.1), d. of Ephraim and Henrietta, Jan. 21, 1824.
Susannah, d. of Nicholes and Abigail, Monday, Aug. 10, 1778.
Thomas Sargent, s. of Nicholas and Elisabeth, Tuesday, Oct. 18, 1748.
Timothy, s. of Nicholes and Abigail, Tuesday, Oct. 5, 1763.
William, s. of Nicholas and Elisabeth, Thursday, Nov. 24, 1743.

BEALS, Samuel George Bamfield, s. of Samuel R. and Hannah B., Mar. 24, 1830.

BEATH, Elizabeth, d. of Jeremiah and Elizabeth, bp. May 26, 1751. c.r.1.
Margaret, d. of Jeremiah and Margaret, bp. May 8, 1748. c.r.1.

BENNET, Asahel, s. of John and Mary, 16th day, 7th mo. 1766. c.r.4.
David, s. of John and Mary, 3d day, 7th mo. 1764. Twin. c.r.4.
Deborah, d. of John and Mary, 3d day, 7th mo. 1764. Twin. c.r.4.
Joanna, d. of John and Mary, 12th day, 2d mo. 1778. c.r.4.
Mary, d. of John and Mary, 15th day, 12th mo. 1768. c.r.4.
Nehemiah, s. of John and Mary, 28th day, 8th mo. 1770. c.r.4.

BENSON, Amasa, s. of Benjamin and Martha, Mar. 15, 1770.
Charles Augustus, s. of Ezra T. and Pamela, Sept. 26, 1832.
Eunice S. [———], w. of Amasa B., ———, 1821. g.r.1.
Sarah W., d. of Amasa B. and Eunice S., ———, 1848. g.r.1.
Timothy, s. of Benjamin and Martha, Aug. 19, 1771.

BERRIGEN, Bedilia, d. of John and Mary, Aug. 14, 1843.

BERRY, Mary, d. of Richard and Catharine, both b. in Ireland, in Blackstone, Oct. 19, 1848.

BILLINGS, Etta Parker [———], w. of Linn L., May 18, 1838. g.r.1.
Linn L., ———, 1844. g.r.1.

BILLS, Cordelia Ellen, d. of Davis and Julia E., June 29, 1846.
Davis, s. of Samuel and ———, Sept. 10, 1804.

BISHOP, James, s. of Sarah, bp. Dec. 25, 1771. c.r.1.
Seth, s. of Josep[h] and Niomi, Mar. 11, 1775.

BLAIR, Joseph H., ———, 1844. g.r.1.

BLAKE, Asa, s. of Joseph and Mary, May 1, 1755.
Banis (Bernice, c.r.1), d. of Joseph and Mary, Mar. 18, 1759.
Barness, d. of Asa and Joanna, bp. Oct. 29, 1786. c.r.1.
Benjamin, s. of Joseph and Mary, Dec. 6, 1739.
Elizabeth, d. of Joseph and Mary, bp. Nov. 9, 1756. c.r.1.
Hannah, d. of Joseph and Mary, July 14, 1751.
Hannah, d. of Asa and Joanna, bp. Sept. 4, 1796. c.r.1.
James, s. of Joseph and Mary, Aug. 15, 1744.
Joseph, s. of Asa and Joanna, bp. June 9, 1793. c.r.1.
Lucy, d. of Simeon and Sarah, Oct. 19, 1780.
Molley, d. of Simeon and Sarah, Oct. 11, 1782.
Molly, d. of Joseph and Mary, July 25, 1746.
Reuben, s. of Asa and Joanna, bp. Feb. 13, 1786. c.r.1.

BLAKE, Samuel, s. of Joseph and Mary, Dec. 12, 1740.
Simeon, s. of Joseph and Mary, bp. Nov. 9, 1756. C.R.1.
Simeon, s. of Asa and Joanna, bp. Aug. 24, 1794. C.R.1.
Susan, d. of Joseph and Mary, June 16, 1756.
Susanna, d. of Asa and Joanna, bp. Feb. 13, 1786. C.R.1.

BLANCHARD, ———, s. of Joseph and Nancy, Feb. 13, 1846.
D. F., ———, 1813. G.R.1.
Lydia [———], w. of D. F., ———, 1819. G.R.1.
Phebe [———], w. of D. F., ———, 1807. G.R.1.
Phebe Ann, d. of Joseph and Nancy, May 25, 1844.

BLOOD, Augustus, rep. s. of Isaac and real s. of Sally Thayer, June 15, 1817.

BLY, Ebenezer, s. of Oliver and Mercy, bp. Oct. 26, 1740. C.R.1.

BOLSTER, Abigail, d. of John and Abigail, bp. Nov. 26, 1769.
Anna, d. of Richard and Anna, Feb. 27, 1757.
Asael, s. of Isaac and Sarah, Oct. 1, 1777.
Asahel, s. of Richard and Anne [no date].
Barak, s. of John and Abigail, bp. Oct. 31, 1763. C.R.1.
Betty, d. of Isaac and Hepzebah, Dec. —, 1740.
David, s. of John and Abigail, bp. May 7, 1759. C.R.1.
David, s. of John and Abigail, Mar. 6, 1760.
George W., Capt., Apr. 20, 1832. G.R.1.
Hipsebath, d. of John and Abigail, bp. June 12, 1771. C.R.1.
Isaac, s. of Isaac and Hepzebah, Apr. 28, 1737.
James, s. of John and Abigail, bp. Oct. 4, 1767. C.R.1.
Jemima, d. of John and Abigail, May 19, 1754.
Joel, s. of John and Abigail, June 17, 1761.
Kezia, d. of John and Abigail, June 16, 1752.
Mary, d. of Isaac and Abigail, Oct. 10, 1732.
Nathan, s. of John and Abigail, Apr. 28, 1756.
Phebe A. [———], w. of Washington, Oct. 1, 1812. G.R.1.
Washington, Sept. 26, 1806. G.R.1.
William, s. of Isaac and Hepzebah, Mar. 10, 1735–6.

BOND, Henry, ———, 1809. G.R.1.
John Adams, s. of Henry, b. in England, and Dolly, Aug. 27, 1848.

BOON, Samuel Willard, s. of Francis and Mary, Feb. 11, 1787.

BOSWORTH, Ichabod, s. of Jonathan and ———, bp. June 4, 1745. C.R.1.

BOVIEN, Joseph, s. of Elar, ———, 1847.

BOWEN, Anne, d. of David and Hopstill, Sept. 30, 1765.
Anne, d. of John and Phebe, 6th day, 4th mo. 1788. c.r.4.
Benjamin, s. of John and Phebe, 14th day, 4th mo. 1786. c.r.4.
Charles, s. of Thomas and Elisabeth, 16th day, 9th mo. 1800. c.r.4.
Dorcas, d. of John and Phebe, 17th day, 4th mo. 1790. c.r.4.
Eddy, s. of Lemuel and Hannah, 30th day, 1st mo. 1788. c.r.4.
Elisabeth [———], w. of Thomas, 30th day, 12th mo. 1765. c.r.4.
Eliza Ann, d. of Thomas and Elisabeth, 24th day, 2d mo. 1808. c.r.4.
Ephraim, s. of Lemuel and Huldah, 11th day, 8th mo. 1784. c.r.4.
Ephraim, s. of John and Phebe, 19th day, 5th mo. 1796. c.r.4.
Gideon, s. of Lemuel and Huldah, 19th day, 10th mo. 1783. c.r.4.
Gustavus Vaugn, s. of John A. and Mary M., Jan. 22, 1845.
Hannah, d. of Lemuel and Huldah, 25th day, 5th mo. 1786. c.r.4.
Huldah [———], w. of Lemuel, 27th day, 5th mo. 1756. c.r.4.
Isaac, s. of Thomas and Elisabeth, 24th day, 7th mo. 1796. c.r.4.
John, 16th day, 5th mo. 1737. c.r.4.
Jonathan, s. of John and Phebe, 18th day, 7th mo. 1782. c.r.4.
Lemuel, 16th day, 3d mo. 1755. c.r.4.
Martha, d. of Lemuel and Martha, 20th day, 3d mo. 1791. c.r.4.
Mercy Ann, d. of Thomas and Elisabeth, 16th day, 11th mo. 1791. c.r.4.
Molle, d. of David and Hopstill, Nov. 18, 1767.
Pardon, s. of John and Phebe, 3d day, 6th mo. 1794. c.r.4.
Phebe [———], w. of John, 14th day, 8th mo. 1738. c.r.4.
Phebe, d. of John and Phebe, 24th day, 6th mo. 1792. c.r.4.
Sarah, 27th day, 4th mo. 1770. c.r.4.
Sarah, d. of Thomas and Elisabeth, 9th day, 11th mo. 1789. c.r.4.
Sarah, d. of Lemuel and Huldah, 20th day, 2d mo. 1793. c.r.4.
Smith, s. of Thomas and Elisabeth, 24th day, 4th mo. 1803. c.r.4.
Smith A., Oct. 23, 1836. g.r.19.
Susan Richardson, Jan. 13, 1828. g.r.19.
Susana, d. of John and Phebe, 15th day, 4th mo. 1784. c.r.4.
Thomas, 16th day, 4th mo. 1763. c.r.4.

BRADY, John, s. of John and Margarett, Oct. 10, 1845.
Mary A. [———], w. of Patrick, ———, 1838. G.R.2.
Mary E., d. of John and Margaret, both b. in Ireland, Dec. 9, 1849.
Patrick, ———, 1834. G.R.2.

BRAMAN, Ann Louisa W. (Ann Louisa Whitin, C.R.2), d. of William T. and Sylvia K., Aug. 3, 1843.
B. Whitman, ———, 1821. G.R.1.
Cornelia Pittman, d. of Sylvia, bp. Nov. 22, 1846. C.R.2.
Elizabeth J. [———], w. of B. Whitman, ———, 1824. G.R.1.
Ella Gertrude, d. of Leonard, b. in Stafford, Conn., and Rosetta, b. in Douglas, May 18, 1849.
Herbert D., s. of Leonard and Rosetta, May 25, 1847.
Ida Livonia, adopted d. of Whitman P. and Elisabeth J., and real d. of William Bowen, b. in Monson, and Betsey, b. in Brattleboro, Vt., in Northbridge, Jan. 11, 1849.
Leonard, May 15, 1823. G.R.1.
Rosetta C. Marsh [———], w. of Leonard, Jan. 12, 1826. G.R.1.

BRANCH, Augustus Hamlet, s. of Nath[anie]ll, Sept. 8, 1816.
Caroline Elisabeth, d. of Nath[anie]ll, Jan. 15, 1820.
George Curien, s. of Nathaniel and Rachel, Dec. 8, 1799.
Hamlet, s. of Nathaniel and Rachel, June 17, 1813.
Henrietta Maria Ann Jeannette, d. of Nathaniel and Rachel, Dec. 7, 1807.
Lafayette, s. of Nathaniel and Rachel, June 10, 1810.
Ophelia, d. of Nathaniel and Rachel, Apr. 25, 1805.
Silas Wheelock, s. of Nathaniel and Rachel, Apr. 9, 1802.

BRASTOW, Betsy, d. of David and Abigail, May 15, 1780.
Nabby, d. of David and Abigail, Feb. 29, 1784.
Salley, d. of David and Abigail, Feb. 3, 1782.

BRAYTON, David, 6th day, 6th mo. 1737. C.R.4.
Hannah [———], w. of ———, 7th day, 7th mo. 1764. C.R.4.
Hannah, d. of ——— and Hannah, 27th day, 8th mo. 1800. C.R.4.
Mary [———], w. of David, 3d day, 4th mo. 1757. C.R.4.
Seril, ch. of David and Mary, 2d day, 12th mo. 1802. C.R.4.

BREWER, Eunice [———], w. of Simeon, ———, 1785. C.R.4.

BRICK, Nora, ———, 1839. G.R.2.
Patrick, ———, 1822. G.R.2.

BROODWICK, ——, d. of Demus and Margaret, Oct. —, 1847.

BROOKING, Olney, s. of Thomas and Susan, Apr. 17, 1846.

BROWN, ——, ch. of Salmon, May 19, 1840.
Aaron, s. of Josiah and Mary, Feb. 12, 1747–8.
Abba Eliza, d. of Lieut. Pemberton and Abba Eliza, June 30, 1833.
Abba Frances, d. of Clark and Frances, Apr. 28, 1845.
Adin Ballou, s. of Lieut. Pemberton and Abba Eliza, Nov. 14, 1831.
Alpheus, s. of Aaron and Jemima, Oct. 7, 1781.
Amity, 7th day, 9th mo. 1769. Providence, c.r.4.
Andrus, s. of Elihu and Marcy, Nov. 13, 1794.
Chloa, d. of Josiah and Mary, Feb. 16, 1758.
Chloe, d. of Aaron and Jemima, Jan. 29, 1784.
Clara Ida, d. of Martin S., b. in Burrillville, R. I., and Clarissa L., b. in Grafton, Sept. 1, 1849.
Deborah, d. of Aaron and Jemima, Jan. 16, 1778.
Elisabeth, ——, 1775. c.r.4.
Elizabeth, d. of William and Rebecca, bp. Apr. 11, 1736. c.r.1.
Elizabeth W. [——], w. of Seth G., ——, 1840. g.r.1.
Ephraim, ——, 1827. g.r.1.
Hannah, d. of Elihu and Marcy, Sept. 29, 1792.
Hannah Jacobs [——], w. of Andrus, Sept. 17, 1800. g.r.1.
Henry Harrison, s. of Lieut. Pemberton and Abba Eliza, June 26, 1840.
Hepzibah, d. of Aaron and Jemima, Feb. 22, 1776.
Huldah, 26th day, 9th mo. 1762. c.r.4.
Jennett, d. of Alpheus and ——, Dec. 28, 1807.
John, ——, 1831. g.r.2.
John Davis, s. of Lieut. Pemberton and Abba Eliza, Oct. 14, 1842.
Josephine, d. of Lieut. Pemberton and Abba Eliza, Jan. 29, 1830.
Josiah, s. of Aaron and Jemima, Jan. 25, 1790.
Lydia, d. of Josiah and Mary, July 4, 1745.
Marcy, d. of Elihu and Marcy, Dec. 17, 1796.
Marianna [——], w. of James A., ——, 1832. g.r.1.
Mary, d. of John and Sarah, bp. Nov. 25, 1744. c.r.1.
Mary Buckman, d. of Elihu and Marcy, July 16, 1798.
Merrick D. F., s. of Martin S. and Clarissa L., Dec. 12, 1847.
Olive, d. of Aaron and Jemima, Oct. 14, 1779.
Paulina Whitmore, in Sutton, ——, 1807. g.r.1.

BROWN, Pemberton Whitmore, s. of Lieut. Pemberton and Abba Eliza (s. of Pemberton and Paulina dup.), Jan. 18, 1845.
Pemela, d. of Elihu and Marcy, Oct. 4, 1790.
Pemperton, s. of Elihu and Marcy, Oct. 11, 1801.
Phila Plina, d. of Clark and Frances, Nov. 27, 1843.
Ruth, d. of Josiah and Mary, Feb. 25, 1753.
Seth G., ——, 1833. G.R.1.
Susan E. Alverson [——], w. of Ephraim, ——, 1822. G.R.1.
Terrissa Gregory, d. of Lieut. Pemberton and Abba Eliza, Oct. 3, 1828.
Welcome C., s. of Clark and Frances, Apr. 5, 1847.
William, s. of William and Mary, in Douglas, Jan. 24, 1768.
Willis, s. of Alpheus and ——, July 22, 1809.

BROWNING, W[illia]m A., ——, 1842. G.R.1.

BUFFUM, Benjamin, 15th day, 2d mo. 1725. C.R.4.
Candis, d. of Jedediah and Sarah, 29th day, 1st mo. 1776. C.R.4.
Charles Eustis, s. of Benjamin Jr. and Rosamond, Apr. 22, 1847.
Elisabeth [——], w. of Benjamin, 29th day, 5th mo. 1725. C.R.4.
Emeline S., d. of Benjamin and Hannah, Sept. 26, 1827.
Eseck, s. of Jedediah and Sarah, 6th day, 4th mo. 1763. C.R.4.
Farnum, Dec. 4, 1822. G.R.25.
Hannah, d. of Benjamin and Elisabeth, 30th day, 8th mo. 1769. C.R.4.
Harriet A., d. of Benjamin and Hannah, June 8, 1832.
Jedediah, 17th day, 8th mo. 1737. C.R.4.
Jedediah, s. of Jedediah and Sarah, 8th day, 4th mo. 1767. C.R.4.
Joshua, s. of Benjamin and Elisabeth, 13th day, 8th mo. 1766. C.R.4.
Louisa M., d. of Benjamin and Hannah, Sept. 18, 1825.
Phebe, 8th day, 8th mo. 1754. C.R.4.
Phebe, d. of Benjamin and Hannah, Feb. 26, 1823.
Robert, s. of Jedediah and Sarah, 10th day, 3d mo. 1765. C.R.4.
Sally W., d. of Benjamin and Hannah, July 1, 1818.
Sarah [——], w. of Jedediah, 5th day, 9th mo. 1736. C.R.4.
Sarah, d. of Jedediah and Sarah, 22d day, 10th mo. 1769. C.R.4.
Sarah, 5th day, 4th mo. 1782. C.R.4.
Stephen, s. of Benjamin and Elisabeth, 27th day, 12th mo. 1762. C.R.4.
Susan, d. of Benjamin and Ellen H., 4th day, 3d mo. 1848. C.R.4.
William, s. of Jedediah and Sarah, 4th day, 6th mo. 1772. C.R.4.

BULLARD, Beveth, s. of David and Hopestel, May 30, 1767.
Catharine Messinger, d. of Luther and Hannah, Feb. 20, 1822.
Charles Henry, s. of Luther and Hannah, Feb. 13, 1820.
Elias Dudley, s. of Luther and Hannah, Nov. 12, 1828.
Fisher, s. of Baruch and Julia, Oct. 9, 1794.
George Austin, s. of Luther and Hannah, Dec. 26, 1824.
Henry Messenger, s. of Baruch and Julia, May 30, 1790.
John Dudley, s. of Luther and Hannah, Mar. 8, 1817.
Julia Ann, d. of Luther and Hannah, Oct. 5, 1815.
Luther, s. of Baruch and Julia, in Northbridge, Dec. 5, 1788.
Otis, s. of Baruch and Julia, in Northbridge, Sept. 23, 1786.
Samuel Willard, s. of Baruch and Julia, Jan. 27, 1799.
Sarah [――――], w. of George A., Mar. 24, 1829. G.R.1.

BULLER, Almon, ――, 1807. G.R.1.
Rebecca E. [――――], w. of Almon, ――, 1821. G.R.1.

BURBECK, Mary G., Dec. 25, 1803. G.R.1.

BURKE, Sarah, mother of Andrew Burns, ――, 1810. G.R.2.

BURNS, Andrew, ――, 1841. G.R.2.
Margaret J. Geary [――――], w. of Andrew, ――, 1835. G.R.2.

BURRILL, Abram F., s. of Amos C. and Elethear, in Smithfield, R. I., June 30, 1840.
Edgar F., s. of Amos C., b. in Burrillville, R. I., and Elethear, b. in Providence, R. I., in Woonsocket, R. I., Dec. 15, 1848.
George Willson, s. of Narcisus E. and Harriet N., Aug. 10, 1835.
Henry Ruthven, s. of Narcisus E. and Harriet N., Sept. 21, 1837.

BUSHEE, Ellen A., d. of John I. and Mary, Apr. 8, 1846.

BUXTON, Anna, d. of Henry and ――――, in Smithfield, Apr. 19, 1798.
Benson Hanson, s. of Leonard and Sarah, Feb. 18, 1825.
Chloe, d. of Peleg and Chloe, Dec. 11, 1811.
Deborah, d. of Henry and ――――, in Smithfield, Apr. 5, 1782.
Eliza, d. of Peleg and Chloe, Apr. 25, 1808.
Eliza, d. of Leonard and Sarah, Feb. 6, 1827.
Esther [――――], w. of James, 5th day, 4th mo. 1755. C.R.4.
Henry Martin, s. of Henry and ――――, Apr. 4, 1794.

BUXTON, Job, s. of Peleg and Chloe, July 6, 1806.
John, s. of Peleg and Chloe, Nov. 26, 1803.
Leonard, s. of Peleg and Chloe, June 10, 1801.
Lydia, d. of Henry and ———, in Smithfield, Apr. 2, 1800.
Sabra, d. of Henry and ———, Apr. 2, 1796.

CADWELL, Josephine B., Jan. 29, 1830. G.R.1.

CALLAM (see Callum), Albert, s. of George and Olive, 24th day, 9th mo. 1813. C.R.4.
Elma Maria, d. of George and Olive, 15th day, 9th mo. 1817. C.R.4.
George, 11th day, 7th mo. 1777. C.R.4.
Jeremiah B., s. of George and Olive, 23d day, 10th mo. 1810. C.R.4.
Lydia, d. of George and Olive, 10th day, 4th mo. 1807. C.R.4.
Olive [———], w. of George, 14th day, 4th mo. 1785. C.R.4.
Olive, d. of George and Olive, 24th day, 8th mo. 1821. C.R.4.

CALLUM (see Callam), Henry Clay, s. of Lyman and Cynthia, June 3, 1830.

CAPEN (see Capin), Abigail, d. of Samuel and Anna, bp. Aug. 5, 1739. C.R.1.

CAPIN (see Capen), Samuel, s. of Solomon and Joanna, bp. Aug. 6, 1758. C.R.1.

CAPRON, Abigail [———], w. of John, in Mendon, Mar. 2, 1759. G.R.1.
Abigail Read, d. of John W. and Catharine, Apr. 12, 1833.
Ardinette, d. of Luther and Henrietta M. A., Dec. 18, 1828.
Asenath [———], w. of John, in Pomfret, Conn., Nov. 28, 1764. G.R.1.
Asenath Cargill, d. of John and Asenath, Nov. 5, 1792 (Oct. 5, 1792 dup.).
Caleb Congdon, s. of Effingham L. and Phebe C., July 10, 1825.
Catharine Adelaide, d. of John W. and Catharine (Catharine B. dup.), Dec. 11, 1846.
Catharine Messenger, d. of John W. and Catharine (Catharine B. dup.), June 27, 1844.
Charles Cargill, s. of John W. and Abigail, Aug. 7, 1841.
Chloe D. [———], w. of William C., ———, 1800. G.R.1.
David I., s. of Charles and Jehoshabe, July 29, 1799.

CAPRON, Effingham Lawrence, s. of John and Asenath, in Pomfret, Conn., Mar. 29, 1791.
Elizabeth Congdon, d. of Effingham L. and Phebe C., Oct. 3, 1821.
Elizabeth Read, d. of John W. and Abigail, Dec. 3, 1820. (w. of Dr. Truman Rickard. G.R.1.)
Gilbert Everingham, s. of Effingham L. and Phebe C., Apr. 1, 1820.
Helen Maria (Hiller Maria dup.), d. of William C. and Chloe D., Jan. 26, 1826.
J. A. [————], w. of Henry, ———, 1822. G.R.1.
John, in Cumberland, R. I., July 28, 1757. G.R.1.
John, s. of John W. and Abigail, May 26, 1838.
John Henry, s. of William C. and Chloe D., Nov. 25, 1828.
John Willard, s. of John and Asenath, Feb. 14, 1797.
Laura Ann Washburn, d. of (Dea., c.r.2) William C. and Chloe D., May 13, 1837.
Laura Southwick, d. of Effingham L. and Phebe C., July 8, 1823.
Laura Waldo, d. of John and Asenath, Oct. 22, 1794.
Lucy Waldo, d. of John and Asenath, Aug. 11, 1799. Twin.
Lydia B. [————], w. of Effingham L., 23d day, 3d mo. 1805. G.R.1.
M. J. [————], w. of Henry, ———, 1839. G.R.1.
Maranda, d. of John and Asenath, in Pomfret, Conn., Nov. 20, 1789.
Maria, d. of Charles and Jehoshabe, July 27, 1801.
Mary Ann, d. of John W. and Abigail, Sept. 9, 1827.
Olivia, d. of Effingham L. and Phebe C., July 21, 1827.
Phebe, d. of John and Asenath, in Pomfret, Conn., Mar. 26, 1786.
Phebe C. [————], w. of Effingham L., 8th day, 8th mo. 1791. G.R.1.
Polly, d. of John and Asenath, in Pomfret, Conn., Feb. 17, 1784.
Samuel John Mills, s. of William C. and Chloe D., May 15, 1832.
W[illia]m Banfield, s. of John and Asenath, in Pomfret, Conn., Jan. 11, 1788.
William Banfield, s. of William C. and Chloe D. (the son of John, the son of Charles, the son of Banfield, 2d, the son of Banfield who was the first Capron who came to America), Apr. 14, 1824.
W[illia]m Cargill, s. of John and Asenath, Aug. 11, 1799. Twin.
Willet Southwick, s. of Effingham L. and Phebe C., Sept. 23, 1818.

CARLY, Rebeckah, d. of Ichabod and Mary, Apr. 18, 1763.
William Sergant, s. of Ichabod and Mary, in Bolton, Conn., Aug. 27, 1765.

CARPENTER, ———, s. of Joseph, b. in Smithfield, R. I., and Sabra, b. in Scituate, R. I., July 14, 1849.
Bernice, d. of Joseph and Sabra, Jan. 30, 1847.
Charles Valentine, s. of Daniel and Eunice, Oct. 28, 1803. Twin.
Clara Caroline, d. of Daniel and Eunice, Oct. 28, 1803. Twin.
Daniel, s. of Joseph and Percis, Oct. 28, 1773.
David George, s. of Daniel and Eunice, Apr. 27, 1801.
Edwin Ruthven, s. of John and Anna, Apr. 16, 1817.
Ellen Lucretia, d. of Edwin R. and Delphia F., Dec. 2, 1845.
Emily, d. of George and Charlotte, Dec. 16, 1823.
Eunice, d. of Daniel and Eunice, Aug. 24, 1805.
Florentia (Florentia D., G.R.1), d. of John and Anna, Mar. 14, 1830.
George, s. of Joseph and Percis, Mar. 29, 1786.
Hannah, d. of Joseph and Percis, Sept. 30, 1793.
Hellen Louisa, d. of Daniel George and Waity, Sept. 28, 1823.
Henry, s. of Joseph and Percis, Sept. 10, 1791.
John, s. of Joseph and Percis, Aug. 28, 1788.
John Henry, s. of Edwin R. and Delphia, July 13, 1841.
Joseph, s. of Daniel and Eunice, Mar. 10, 1814.
Josephus, s. of Joseph and Percis, Dec. 5, 1775.
Julius Angelo, s. of Charles V. and Esther, Aug. 19, 1827.
Maria, d. of George and Charlotte, Oct. 7, 1826.
Maria Eugenia, d. of Charles V. and Esther, in New York City, July 3, 1833.
Maria Theresa, d. of Daniel and Eunice, June 14, 1797.
Maria Theresa 2d, d. of Daniel and Eunice, Mar. 25, 1799.
Marianne, d. of Daniel George and Waity, May 16, 1821.
Martha Ann, d. of Daniel and Eunice, Mar. 6, 1808.
Mary Green, d. of John and Anna, Apr. 18, 1820.
Nancy, d. of Joseph and Percis, June 5, 1783.
Parmelia, d. of William and Abiel, Feb. 5, 1796.
Sally Bartlet, d. of William and Abiel, Apr. 17, 1799.
Sally Bartlet, d. of William and Abiel, May 8, 1801.
Sarah, d. of Joseph and Percis, Feb. 5, 1781.
Sarah Ann, d. of John and Anna, Aug. 10, 1822.
Sarah Ann, d. of John and Anna, Aug. 10, 1824.
Stephen, s. of Joseph and Percis, Aug. 13, 1778.
William, s. of Joseph and Percis, in Providence, Oct. 3, 1771.

CARROLL, Ann, ——, 1818. G.R.2.
Catherine, ——, 1847. G.R.2.
John, ——, 1837. G.R.2.

CARTER, Lucy E. Spaulding [——], w. of Edwin, Apr. 23, 1837. G.R.1.
Richard, ——, 1833. G.R.1.

CASS, Daniel, 29th day, 11th mo. 1724. C.R.4.
Daniel Jr., 24th day, 10th mo. 1733. C.R.4.
Daniel, s. of Daniel Jr. and Lydia, 30th day, 7th mo. 1783. C.R.4.
Deborah [——], w. of Josiah, 19th day, 1st mo. 1736. C.R.4.
Jonathan, s. of Daniel Jr. and Lydia, 7th day, 3d mo. 1782. C.R.4.
Lydia [——], w. of Daniel Jr., 20th day, 11th mo. 1758. C.R.4.
Lydia, d. of Daniel Jr. and Lydia, 28th day, 3d mo. 1785. C.R.4.
Mordecai, s. of Daniel, 23d day, 12th mo. 1765. C.R.4.
Nathan, s. of Josiah and Deborah, 19th day, 2d mo. 1777. C.R.4.

CHACE (see Chacse, Chase), Polly, d. of Ebenezer and Mary, Feb. 23, 1779.

CHACSE (see Chace, Chase), Lemual, s. of Thomas and Hannah, Feb. 17, 1766.

CHANDLER, Samuel, s. of Samuel, June 7, 1793.

CHAPEN (see Chapin), Amariah, s. of Joseph and Ruth, Apr. 20, 1762.
Daniel, s. of Samuel and Bulah, Sept. 24, 1765.
Josiah, s. of Samuel and Bulah, Nov. 4, 1779.
Marcy, d. of Joseph and Ruth, Nov. 21, 1760.
Mary, d. of Garshom and Deborah, Mar. 1, 1774.
Moses, s. of Joseph and Ruth, May 24, 1776.
Phila, d. of Joseph and Ruth, June 5, 1765.
Samuel, s. of Samuel and Bulah, Feb. 17, 1776.
Zadock, s. of Samuel and Bulah, Jan. 4, 1764.

CHAPIN (see Chapen), ——, s. of Phineas and Eunice, Oct. 15, 1815.
——, s. of Royal and Maria Theresa, July 20, 1827.
Abigail (Nabby dup.); d. of Phinehas and Eunice, Feb. 1, 1796.
Abigail Adams, d. of Moses and Betsey, Sept. 4, 1809.
Adaline, d. of Moses and Betsy, bp. May 14, 1820. C.R.1.

CHAPIN, Adela, d. of John S. and Polly, Sept. 24, 1808.
Adolphus, Nov. 12, 1796. G.R.1.
Amory, s. of Amiriah and Olive, May 7, 1802.
Annah, d. of Samuel and Anna, May 12, 1731.
Annette M., d. of Samuel A. and Maria, Dec. 9, 1845.
Asenath Cargill, d. of John S. and Polly, Sept. 22, 1818.
Bartlet Judson, s. of Royal and Maria Theresa, Sept. 27, 1825.
Betsey Taft, d. of Moses and Betsey, Oct. 14, 1807.
Bezaleel Taft, s. of Phineas and Eunice, Oct. 21, 1810.
Caleb Taft, s. of Phinehas and Eunice, Feb. 6, 1806.
Caroline, d. of Joseph and Louisa, bp. Aug. 14, 1828. C.R.1.
Charles Cargill, s. of John S. and Polly, Aug. 27, 1807.
Chloe, d. of Phinehas and Eunice, Apr. 8, 1802.
Deborah, d. of Samuel and Anna, Jan. 17, 1737.
Derias, s. of Solomon and Joanna, Dec. 11, 1756.
Diana Maria, d. of Moses and Betsey, Mar. 29, 1812.
Edwin F., s. of Caleb T. and Clarrissa, June 7, 1836. Twin.
Ephraim, s. of Samuel and Anna, May 24, 1735.
Eunice, d. of Joshua and Mary, bp. Feb. 4, 1770. C.R.1.
Eunice M., d. of Caleb T. and Clarrissa W., May 1, 1832.
Eunice Taft [———], w. of Dea. Phineas, ———, 1774. G.R.1.
Ezra W., s. of Caleb T. and Clarrissa, June 7, 1836. Twin.
Gardner Spring, s. of Phinehas and Eunice, Oct. 2, 1817.
Gardner Spring, s. of Bezaleel T. and Martha, in Solon, Me., Feb. 14, 1833.
George Hoyt, s. of Bezaleel T. and Martha, Jan. 26, 1841.
Hannah, d. of Garshom and Betty, July 17, 1759.
Jacob, s. of Amiriah and Olive, June 5, 1793.
John, s. of Solomon and Joanna, Sept. 23, 1755.
John Capron, s. of John S. and Polly, Apr. 30, 1825.
John Shearman, s. of Gershom and Mary, Aug. 2, 1779.
Joseph, s. of Moses and Betsey, July 15, 1797 (July 26 dup.).
Josiah, s. of Amiriah and Olive, July 27, 1788.
Josiah Godard, s. of John S. and Polly, Nov. 23, 1810.
Josiah Spring, s. of (Dea., C.R.1) Phinehas and Eunice, Aug. 24, 1820.
Laura Ann Fletcher, d. of Bezaleel T. and Martha, June 17, 1835.
Laurinda, d. of Phinehas and Eunice, Feb. 6, 1798.
Lelia Maria, d. of Samuel A. and ———, Jan. 1, 1844.
Margaret Ann, d. of Phinehas and Eunice, June 16, 1808.
Maria Kellogg [———], w. of Samuel Austin, in Sheffield, Jan. 19, 1816. G.R.1.

CHAPIN, Mary Judson, d. of Samuel A. and Maria, Jan. 1, 1844.
Mary Warren, d. of Phinehas and Eunice, Feb. 27, 1804.
Moses Smedley, s. of Moses and Betsey, Aug. 15, 1816.
Moses Williams, s. of Stephen and Julia Emily, June 10, 1829.
Nancy, d. of Gershom and Mary, Feb. 13, 1786.
Nancy, d. of John S. and Polly, Dec. 30, 1811.
Orris Taft, s. of Moses and Betsey, Jan. 27, 1805.
Phineas, Dea., ——, 1769. G.R.1.
Royall, s. of Amiriah and Olive, Dec. 4, 1799.
Ruth Adeline, d. of Moses and Betsey, Oct. 24, 1802.
Salle, d. of Gershom and Mary, Feb. 7, 1781.
Sally, d. of Amiriah and Olive, Sept. 10, 1796.
Sally, d. of John S. and Polly, Dec. 13, 1822.
Samuel, s. of Samuel and Anna, Mar. 12, 1732–3.
Samuel Austin, in Northbridge, Sept. 2, 1811. G.R.1.
Samuel Judson, s. of Phinehas and Eunice, Aug. 27, 1812.
Sarah, d. of Amiriah and Olive, Jan. 21, 1806.
Sarah Maria, d. of Royal and Maria Theresa, Feb. 27, 1822, at 11 o'clock in the morning.
Sarah Richardson, d. of Phinehas and Eunice, Apr. 30, 1800.
Silva, d. of Amiriah and Olive, May 18, 1790.
Stephen, s. of Moses and Betsey, Jan. 4, 1801.
Thomas Hoyt, s. of Bezaleel T. and Martha, Feb. 11, 1838.
W. P. B. Judson, s. of Royal and Maria T., Sept. 27, 1825. G.R.1.

CHAPMAN, Henry, s. of T. and M., ——, 1839. G.R.2.
Samuel, s. of Dea. Samuel and Anna, bp. June 17, 1744. C.R.1.
Thomas, in West Meath, Ire., ——, 1808. G.R.2.

CHASE (see Chace, Chacse), Adam, s. of Eseck and Lucy, Jan. 27, 1787.
Alce, d. of Joseph and Isabel, 30th day, 6th mo. 1793. C.R.4.
Alce, d. of Buffom and Lepha, 26th day, 6th mo. 1815. C.R.4.
Alonzo, s. of Jonathan Jr. and Ruth, 27th day, 4th mo. 1804. C.R.4.
Ambroes, s. of Joseph and Isabel, 29th day, 10th mo. 1787. C.R.4.
Amey, d. of Israel and Matilda, 17th day, 11th mo. 1787. Mendon. C.R.4.
Andrew Patch, s. of Eseck and Lucy, July 10, 1784.
Anna, d. of Nehemiah and Abigail, Dec. 8, 1778.
Anna, d. of Jonathan Jr. and Ruth, 19th day, 3d mo. 1816. C.R.4.

CHASE, Anthoney, s. of Israel and Matilda, 16th day, 6th mo. 1791. C.R.4.
Asa P., s. of Buffom and Lepha, 29th day, 3d mo. 1811. C.R.4.
Betsey, d. of Josiah S. and Charity, Jan. 8, 1827.
Burges Thomas, s. of Joseph and Isabel, 22d day, 7th mo. 1785. C.R.4.
Catharine, d. of Israel and Matilda, 24th day, 8th mo. 1789. Paxton. C.R.4.
Charles Augustus, s. of Anthony and Lydia, 9th day, 9th mo. 1833. C.R.4.
Collins, s. of Buffom and Lepha, 17th day, 9th mo. 1812. C.R.4.
Elisabeth, d. of Jonathan Jr. and Ruth, 13th day, 3d mo. 1803. C.R.4.
Eliza Earl, d. of Anthony and Lydia, 6th day, 5th mo. 1829. C.R.4.
Emeline Bradford, d. of Josiah S. and Charity, Apr. 12, 1821.
Eunice, d. of Joseph and Isabel, 11th day, 9th mo. 1800. C.R.4.
Gardner, Oct. 23, 1805. G.R.1.
Hannah L., d. of Josiah S. and Charity, Mar. 1, 1825.
Homer, s. of Jonathan Jr. and Ruth, 27th day, 3d mo. 1801. C.R.4.
Horace, s. of Jonathan Jr. and Ruth, 8th day, 4th mo. 1818. C.R.4.
Isabel [———], w. of Joseph, 5th day, 6th mo. 1762. C.R.4.
Isabel, d. of Joseph and Isabel, 30th day, 6th mo. 1797. C.R.4.
Israel, 13th day, 9th mo. 1760. Mendon. C.R.4.
Job, s. of Jonathan Jr. and Ruth, 14th day, 12th mo. 1814. C.R.4.
John, s. of Joseph and Isabel, 9th day, 7th mo. 1804. C.R.4.
Jonathan, 11th day, 5th mo. 1729. C.R.4.
Jonathan Jr., 13th day, 8th mo. 1775. C.R.4.
Jonathan, s. of Jonathan Jr. and Ruth, 31st day, 1st mo. 1820. C.R.4.
Joseph, 29th day, 10th mo. 1762. C.R.4.
Joseph, s. of Joseph and Isabel, 2d day, 1st mo. 1790. C.R.4.
Joseph, s. of Jonathan Jr. and Ruth, 18th day, 1st mo. 1806. C.R.4.
Keziah, d. of Joseph and Isabel, 27th day, 2d mo. 1792. C.R.4.
Lepha [———], w. of Buffom, 25th day, 9th mo. 1779. C.R.4.
Liman, s. of Israel and Matilda, 20th day, 7th mo. 1793. C.R.4.
Lucy, d. of Anthony and Lydia, 1st day, 12th mo. 1822. C.R.4.
Lydia, d. of Israel and Matilda, 9th day, 6th mo. 1795. C.R.4.
Lydia [———], w. of Anthony, 24th day, 3d mo. 1798. C.R.4.

CHASE, Mari, d. of Jonathan Jr. and Ruth, 20th day, 1st mo. 1807. c.r.4.
Mary [―――], w. of Jonathan, 5th day, 5th mo. 1736. c.r.4.
Mary, d. of Nehemiah and Abigail, Feb. 6, 1773.
Matilda [―――], w. of Israel, 7th day, 9th mo. 1765. Cumberland, R. I. c.r.4.
Matilda, d. of Jonathan Jr. and Ruth, 22d day, 12th mo. 1808. c.r.4.
Pliny Earl, s. of Anthony and Lydia, 18th day, 8th mo. 1820. c.r.4.
Ruth, d. of Jonathan and Mary, 24th day, 4th mo. 1773. c.r.4.
Ruth [―――], w. of Jonathan, 5th day, 1st mo. 1776. c.r.4.
Sarah, d. of Anthony and Lydia, 29th day, 5th mo. 1836. c.r.4.
Silas, s. of Israel and Matilda, 27th day, 11th mo. 1796. c.r.4.
Susan F. [―――], w. of Gardner, Feb. 1, 1812. g.r.1.
Sylvester, s. of Jonathan and Ruth, 14th day, 7th mo. 1812. c.r.4.
Thomas, s. of Anthony and Lydia, 16th day, 6th mo. 1827. c.r.4.
Waterman, s. of Buffom and Lepha, 16th day, 3d mo. 1807. c.r.4.
William E., s. of Josiah S. and Charity, Apr. 16, 1823.

CHENERY, Adaline M., d. of Elihu and Fanny, July 1, 1847.

CHILSON, Abner, s. of Israal and Joanna, Apr. 2, 1756.
Chloa, d. of Jerimiah and Rachel, May 16, 1768.
David, s. of Jerimiah and Rachel, in Gloucester, Nov. 14, 1757.
Gershom, s. of Beriah and Patience, bp. Apr. 16, 1738. c.r.1.
Hannah, d. of Beriah and Patience, bp. May 6, 1739. c.r.1.
Hephzibah, d. of Beriah and Patience, bp. Aug. 23, 1741. c.r.1.
Leah, d. of Israal and Joanna, June 6, 1758.
Levi, s. of Jerimiah and Rachel, in Gloucester, June 9, 1756.
Margret, d. of Jerimiah and Rachel, in Gloucester, Dec. 27, 1765.
Mercy, d. of Jerimiah and Rachel, in Gloucester, Oct. 31, 1763.
Molly, d. of Jerimiah and Rachel, in Douglas, Nov. 27, 1761.
Nathan, s. of Jerimiah and Rachel, Sept. 10, 1770.
Rachel, d. of Jerimiah and Rachel, Apr. 30, 1777.
Reuben, s. of Jerimiah and Rachel, June 2, 1760.
Rhoda, d. of Jerimiah and Rachel, in Gloucester, Nov. 10, 1758.

CHIPMAN, William Robinson, s. of Stephen and Phebe, Feb. 1, 1831.

CLAPP, Anna, d. of Daniel and Isabella, 1st day, 2d mo. 1800. c.r.4.
Daniel, 27th day, 7th mo. 1784. c.r.4.
David, s. of Daniel and Sarah, 9th day, 7th mo. 1815. c.r.4.
Elizabeth, d. of Daniel and Sarah, 19th day, 3d mo. 1820. c.r.4.
Isabella [———], w. of Daniel, 19th day, 7th mo. 1757. c.r.4.
James, s. of Daniel and Sarah, 3d day, 9th mo. 1817. c.r.4.
Joseph, s. of Daniel and Isabella, 7th day, 11th mo. 1797. c.r.4.
Joseph Dennis, s. of Joseph and Susan D., 19th day, 5th mo. 1828. c.r.4.
Mary E., d. of James and Emily T., 22d day, 8th mo. 1847. c.r.4.
Phebe, d. of Daniel and Isabella, 6th day, 5th mo. 1795. c.r.4.
Phebe Ann, d. of Joseph and Susan D., 16th day, 12th mo. 1833. c.r.4.
Sarah [———], w. of Daniel, 1st day, 10th mo. 1778. c.r.4.
Silas, s. of Daniel and Sarah, 2d day, 8th mo. 1813. c.r.4.
Susan D. [———], w. of Joseph, 10th day, 2d mo. 1799. c.r.4.

CLARK (see Clarke), Annah, d. of Mary Fletcher, May 9, 1761.
Edward, Nov. 22, 1811. g.r.1.
Edward P., Apr. 19, 1844. g.r.1.
Elizabeth Ann, d. of John and Mary, both b. in Ireland, Nov. 19, 1849.
Eunice Pierce [———], w. of Edward, Sept. 20, 1814. g.r.1.
Hiram, June 1, 1802. g.r.1.
James, s. of Joseph dec. and ———, bp. at Mendon, May 14, 1757. c.r.1.
Lucis, s. of Ezekiel and Milley, in Sutton, Sept. 4, 1795.
Lucy, d. of Ichabod and Febey, Sept. 15, 1772.
Nathaniel, s. of Hiram and Susan, bp. Mar. 27, 1836. c.r.2.
Sarah Ann, d. of Hiram and Susan, bp. Mar. 27, 1836. c.r.2.
Susan H. [———], w. of Hiram, Dec. 4, 1804. g.r.1.
Willard Boyd, s. of Ezekiel and Milley, May 18, 1792.

CLARKE (see Clark), Samuel, Rev., in New Boston, N. H., Apr. 21, 1791. g.r.1.
Sophronia, Aug. 21, 1837. g.r.1.

CLEAVELAND (see Clevland), Anna F., d. of Alden B., b. in Franklin, and Sarah, b. in Sutton, Oct. 19, 1849.
Charles B., s. of Alden B. and Sarah, Dec. 29, 1847.
Mary Emma, d. of Alden B. and Sarah, July 17, 1840.
Susan Goddard [———], w. of Charles B., ———, 1849. g.r.1.

CLEMENCE, Ella D., d. of ———— and Ruth D., 15th day, 3d mo. 1847. c.r.4.
George H., s. of ———— and Ruth D., 9th day, 2d mo. 1849. c.r.4.
Ja[me]s A., s. of ———— and Ruth D., 22d day, 1st mo. 1844. c.r.4.
Walter S., s. of ———— and Ruth D., 2d day, 10th mo. 1841. c.r.4.

CLEVLAND (see Cleaveland), Alpheus, s. of Joseph and Jemima, Aug. 21, 1781.
Elisabeth, d. of Joseph and Jemima, Mar. 15, 1771.
Eunice, d. of Joseph and Jemima, Mar. 25, 1788.
Peter, s. of Joseph and Jemima, Oct. 25, 1778.
Phylinder, d. of Joseph and Jemima, Oct. 11, 177-.

CODY, James, s. of Philip and Abigail, bp. June 19, 1763. c.r.1.

COFFIN, Elizabeth, d. of Ebenezer and Mary, Oct. 26, 1786.

COLBURN, Caroline Wing, d. of Charles and Phidelia, Mar. 17, 1843.
Delia Emma, d. of Charles O. and Fidelia, Nov. 11, 1844.
Salley, 21st day, 8th mo. 1782. c.r.4.
Sarah Frances, d. of Charles and Phidelia, Sept. 24, 1840.

COLE, Samuel, s. of Stephen and Hannah, in Sutton, Sept. 6, 1786.
Stephen, s. of Jonathan and Elisabeth, Apr. 8, 1760.

COLEMAN, Mary Jane, d. of Patrick and Ann, both b. in Ireland, Sept. 4, 1849.
Phillip, s. of John and Mary, both b. in Ireland, Nov. 19, 1849.
William, s. of John and Mary, both b. in Ireland, July 17, 1848.

COLLEN (see Collins), Abigail, niece of Mary, w. of Benjamin Thompson, bp. Oct. 9, 1748. c.r.1.

COLLINS (see Collen), ————, s. of John S. and Sarah S., July 26, 1849.
Abby Caroline, d. of John S. and Sarah S., Jan. 20, 1841.
Celia Jane, d. of John S. and Sarah S., Oct. 10, 1842.
Daniel W., s. of John S. and Sarah S., Mar. 7, 1835.
Marline Armington, ch. of John S. and Sarah S., Sept. 28, 1840.
Mary Ann, d. of John S. and Sarah S., Dec. 21, 1836.
Oscar Smith, s. of John S. and Sarah S., Sept. 23, 1844.
Sarah Elizabeth, d. of John S. and Sarah S., Apr. 5, 1838.

COLLY, Rebecca, d. of Ichabod and Mary, bp. Sept. 18, 1763. c.r.1.

COLTON, Ann K. [――――], 2d w. of Samuel H., 24th day, 8th mo. 1816. c.r.4.
John Bowne, s. of Samuel H. and Ann K., his 2d w., 17th day, 11th mo. 1844. c.r.4.
Mary Rodman, d. of Samuel H. and Ann K., his 2d w., 21st day, 10th mo. 1845. c.r.4.
Samuel H., 17th day, 11th mo. 1804. c.r.4.

COMSTOCK (see Cumstock), Ada, d. of Emor and Lucy, Nov. 14, 1843. Twin.
Angela, d. of Emor and Lucy, Nov. 14, 1843. Twin.
Daniel, 28th day, 7th mo. 1768. c.r.4.
Fitz Greene, s. of Gilbert B., b. in Mendon, and Abby G., b. in Smithfield, R. I., Apr. 30, 1849.

CONANT, Emma J., d. of Thomas A. and Julia A., b. in Thompson, Conn., Nov. 7, 1848.

CONGDON, Albert, s. of Joshua and Sarah, 16th day, 9th mo. 1812. c.r.4.
Albert W., s. of William and Lydia H., in Leicester, 20th day, 4th mo. 1817. c.r.4.
Anna B., d. of Joshua and Sarah, 14th day, 9th mo. 1815. c.r.4.
Charles M., s. of William and Lydia H., 1st day, 4th mo. 1824. c.r.4.
Deborah [――――], w. of Joseph, ――――, 1766. c.r.4.
Eliza Ann, d. of William and Lydia H., in Leicester, 8th day, 7th mo. 1818. c.r.4.
Eunice H., d. of William and Lydia H., 11th day, 1st mo. 1821. c.r.4.
George Emerson, s. of William and Lydia H., in Buffalo, N. Y., 4th day, 9th mo. 1826. c.r.4.
Isaac W., s. of Joshua and Sarah, 15th day, 9th mo. 1810. c.r.4.
Jennings C., s. of Joshua and Sarah, 26th day, 4th mo. 1806. c.r.4.
Jesse E., s. of Joshua and Sarah, 14th day, 1st mo. 1798. c.r.4.
Joseph, s. of Joshua and Sarah, 30th day, 1st mo. 1802. c.r.4.
Josiah S., s. of Joshua and Sarah, 14th day, 2d mo. 1809. c.r.4.
Louisa, d. of William and Lydia H., in Leicester, 29th day, 10th mo., 1822. c.r.4.
Sarah [――――], w. of Joshua, 27th day, 4th mo. 1770. c.r.4.
Sarah Ann, d. of William and Lydia H., in Leicester, 30th day, 8th mo. 1819. c.r.4.

CONGDON, Seneca, s. of Joshua and Sarah, 24th day, 7th mo. 1796. Northbridge. c.r.4.
Susan M., d. of William and Lydia H., in Leicester, 2d day, 3d mo. 1825. c.r.4.
Susanna, d. of Joshua and Sarah, 12th day, 5th mo. 1804. c.r.4.
Thomas, s. of Joshua and Sarah, 3d day, 1st mo. 1800. c.r.4.
William, s. of Joshua and Sarah, 7th day, 12th mo. 1793. Providence. c.r.4.

CONKEY, William Church, s. of Isaac G. and Eliza, Sept. 22, 1839.

CONWAY, John, in Ennestymon, County Clare, Ire., May 2, 1822. g.r.2.

COOK (see Cooke), ———, s. of Thomas and ———, bp. at Douglas, Nov. 23, 1746. c.r.1.
Aaron, s. of Alvin and Maria R., June 26, 1837. g.r.16.
Abby Elizabeth, d. of Reuben S. and Rachel L., Dec. 30, 1844.
Abigail, d. of Jonathan and Mehitable, July 26, 1720.
Abigail, d. of Jonathan and Hannah, Jan. 3, 1763. Twin.
Alice Salina, d. of Alvin and Maria R. (Maria R. B., c.r.2), Feb. 26, 1844.
Anne, 17th day, 10th mo. 1750. c.r.4.
Calven, s. of Jonathan and Jerushe, Mar. 17, 1769.
Catharine, d. of Jonathan and Hannah, Mar. 21, 1758.
Cyrus, s. of Stephen and Mary, May 8, 1768.
Daniel, 12th day, 10th mo. 1722. c.r.4.
Edwin Francis, s. of William W. and Abigail D., May 24, 1844.
Francis, s. of Jonathan and Lydia, Mar. 27, 1767.
George, s. of Paskco and Philadelphia, 8th day, 12th mo. 1791. c.r.4.
Hannah, d. of Jonathan and Mehitable, Feb. 14, 1724-5.
Hannah, d. of Jonathan and Hannah, Jan. 3, 1763. Twin.
John, s. of Jonathan and Mehitable, Feb. 19, 1727-8.
John, s. of Jonathan and Hannah, Oct. 28, 1760.
Jonathan, s. of Jonathan and Mehitable, Oct. 31, 1732.
Joseph B., s. of Paskco and Philadelphia, 3d day, 12th mo. 1796. c.r.4.
Joseph S., ———, 1834. g.r.1.
Louis, d. of Jonathan and Lydia, Dec. 16, 1765.
Lucy, d. of Paskco and Philadelphia, 14th day, 4th mo. 1792. c.r.4.
Mary, d. of Jonathan and Mehitable, formerly of Mendon, Jan. 29, 1718-9.

Cook, Mary, d. of Thomas and ———, bp. at New Sherborn, Apr. 4, 1744. c.r.1.
Mary, d. of Jonathan and Lydia, June 11, 1764.
Mary E. Legg [———], w. of Joseph S., ———, 1831. G.R.1.
Mehitable, d. of Jonathan and Mehitable, Jan. 25, 1722-3.
Mehitable, d. of Jonathan and Hannah, Feb. 11, 1754.
Mehitebel, d. of Jonathan (Jr., c.r.1) and Jerushe, in Douglas, Mar. 10, 1765.
Naomi, d. of Jonathan and Mehitable, Oct. 26, 1721.
Nathan, s. of Jonathan and Jerushe, Dec. 26, 1766.
Olive, d. of Jonathan and Hannah, Sept. 22, 1756.
Paskco, 30th day, 5th mo. 1764. c.r.4.
Phebe, d. of Stephen and Mary, June 12, 1770.
Phila, d. of Paskco and Philadelphia, 17th day, 6th mo. 1803. c.r.4.
Philadelphia [———], w. of Paskco, 5th day, 4th mo. 1770. c.r.4.
William, s. of Stephen and Mary, Dec. 14, 1776.
Winfield E., s. of Alvin and Maria, June 21, 1847.

COOKE (see Cook), Ellen Louisa, d. of Alvin and Maria R. B., bp. Sept. 3, 1843. c.r.2.
Samantha Maria, d. of Alvin and Maria R. B., bp. Sept. 3, 1843. c.r.2.

COOMBS, Caleb Seagrave, s. of Reuben and Permela, Aug. 10, 1815.

COOPER, Anna, d. of Nathaniel and Elizeb[e]th, May 14, 1766.
Ezra, s. of Nathaniel and Mary, July 14, 1769.

COPELAND (Danford, G.R.1), s. of Lyman and Phebe, July 26, 1843.
Phebe, d. of Lyman and Phebe, Apr. 21, 1839. G.R.1.

CORARY (see Corrary), Benjamin, s. of Benjamin and Deborah, Jan. 16, 1733-4.
Benjamin, s. of Benjamin and Jerushe, Mar. 14, 1743-4.
Hannah, d. of Benjamin and Jerushe, Feb. 8, 1748-9.
Jerusha, d. of Benjamin and Jerushe, Aug. 28, 1753.
John, s. of Benjamin and Jerushe, July 22, 1742.
Joseph, s. of Benjamin and Deborah, Dec. 6, 1735.
Margret, d. of Benjamin and Jerushe, Feb. 19, 1750-1.
Mary, d. of Benjamin and Deborah, June 1, 1740.
Stephen, s. of Benjamin and Jerushe, Dec. 16, 1746.

CORNWELL, Hannah S. [———], w. of Jacob, ———, 1832. G.R.4.
Jacob, ———, 1830. G.R.4.

CORRARY (see Corary), Chloe, d. of Stephen and Naomi, Apr. 21, 1777.
Joannah, d. of Stephen and Naomi, Feb. 7, 1779.
Phebe, d. of Stephen and Naomi, May 21, 1775.
Polle, d. of Stephen and Naomi, May 13, 1782.
Rachel, d. of Stephen and Naomi, June 18, 1780.
Ruth, d. of Stephen and Naomi, Feb. 18, 1771.
Sarah, d. of Stephen and Naomi, July 21, 1769.
Stephen, s. of Stephen and Naomi, June 1, 1784.
Suliven, s. of Stephen and Naomi, Apr. 18, 1786.

CRAGGIN, Ebenezer, ———, 1778. G.R.1.
Mary Emma, d. of Benjamin (b. in Thompson, Ct., in pencil) and Mary (b. in Pelham, in pencil), Dec. 12, 1839.
Olive [———], w. of Ebenezer, ———, 1783. G.R.1.
Saloma, rep. d. of Timothy Craggin, of Douglas, and real d. of Philena Taft, Feb. 11, 1799.
Samuel, s. of Samuel and Marcy, June 23, 1790.

CRANE, George, s. of George and Philah, 31st day, 3d mo. 1783. C.R.4.
Philah [———], w. of George, 25th day, 6th mo. 1760. C.R.4.

CREATON, George, s. of William and Esther, Sept. 26, 1733.
Sarah, d. of William and Esther, Apr. 28, 1734.

CROCKER, Charles E., s. of Jonathan and Sophronia, May 11, 1847.
George Albert, s. of Jonathan, b. in England, and Sophronia, b. in Medway, Jan. 4, 1849.

CRONEY (see Crowney), Aniel, s. of Daniel and Molley, Aug. 28, 1797.
Catharine, d. of John and Sibel, Oct. 24, 1780.
Francis Willard, s. of Daniel and Molley, Aug. 10, 1795.
Mary Matilda, d. of Sybil, bp. Sept. 27, 1801. C.R.1.
Rosanna, d. of John and Sibel, Dec. 25, 1782.
Sarah, d. of John and Sibel, Oct. 8, 1778.
Timothy, s. of John and Sibel, Aug. 4, 1776.

CROSSWELL, Herbert E., s. of George and Caroline A., ———, 1848. G.R.1.

CROWNEY (see Croney), Daniel, s. of John and Sibel, Jan. 4, 1766.
Elizabeth, d. of John and Sibel, Sept. 21, 1769.
Francis, s. of John and Sibel, Oct. 4, 1774.
John, s. of John and Sibel, June 4, 1772.
Molly, d. of John and Sibel, Oct. 21, 1767.
Sibel, d. of John and Sibel, Dec. 24, 1773.

CROWNINGSHIELD, Elisabeth, d. of ———, May 20, 1759.
Hannah, d. of ———, Mar. 12, 1761.

CRUFF, Charles D., s. of John R. and Mary, Apr. 4, 1846.
John Franklin, s. of John R. and Mary, Dec. 22, 1844.

CUMINGS (see Cummings, Cummins), ———, ch. of Charles and Sarah, Mar. 16, 1845.
Abigail, d. of Samuel and Hannah, Sept. 10, 1743.
Charles H., s. of Charles dec. and Sarah, Nov. 12, 1846.
Chloa, d. of Daniel and Mary, July 24, 1764.
Ebenezer, s. of Samuel (Lieut. Samuel dec., c.r.1), and Sarah, July 4, 1758. (Twin. c.r.1.)
Esther, d. of Samuel and Hannah, bp. Sept. 8, 1738. c.r.1.
Georgianna Elizabeth, d. of Josiah and Celia, Nov. 2, 1831.
Hannah, d. of Samuel and Hannah, Aug. 11, 1745.
Hannah, d. of Samuel and Lucy, Jan. 1, 1764.
Isabella Frances, d. of Josiah and Celia, Oct. 26, 1842.
Isabella Francis, d. of Josiah and Celia, Mar. 27, 1834.
John Fessenden, s. of Charles and Sarah, Aug. 16, 1836.
Judith, d. of Samuel and Lucy, Nov. 26, 1766.
Julius Ames, s. of Charles and Sarah, June 21, 1834.
Leonard, s. of Samuel and Hannah, bp. Aug. 11, 1737. c.r.1.
Lois, d. of Samuel and Hannah, Apr. 2, 1749.
Lois, d. of Samuel and Lucy, Nov. 15, 1771.
Lydia, d. of Samuel and Sarah, Oct. 3, 175-. (Lydia, d. of Samuel and Sarah, bp. May 8, 1757. c.r.1.)
Maria, d. of Mary, ———, 1835. g.r.1.
Mary, d. of Samuel and Hannah, May 5, 1747.
Mary [———], w. of Samuel, July 4, 1813. g.r.1.
Molley, d. of Daniel and Mary, Jan. 27, 1748–9.
Molley, d. of Samuel and Lucy, July 4, 1765.
Pheeby, d. of Samuel and Lucy, Feb. 26, 1770.
Reuben, s. of Samuel and Lucy, May 6, 1768.
Ruth, d. of Daniel and Mary, bp. Aug. 15, 1762. c.r.1.
Samuel, s. of Samuel and Hannah, Mar. 7, 1742.
Samuel, s. of Samuel and Lucy, Dec. 12, 1775.

CUMINGS, Samuel, Mar. 22, 1814. G.R.1.
Sarah, d. of Samuel and Hannah, bp. May 25, 1740. C.R.1.
Sarah Ellen, d. of Paris and Eunice M., Sept. —, 1844.
Sarah Eveline, d. of Joseph and Calista, bp. Sept. 1, 1833. C.R.2.
Sena, d. of Samuel and Lucy, Dec. 16, 1773.
Susanna, d. of Daniel and Mary, Nov. 30, 1760.
Thankfull, d. of Samuel and Sarah, July 4, 175-. (Thankful, d. of Lieut. Samuel dec. and Sarah, bp. July 11, 1758. Twin. C.R.1.)
Thomas, s. of Samuel and Sarah, Sept. 9, 1754.
Thomas, s. of Samuel and Lucy, July 11, 1778.
Walter Chapin, s. of Josiah and Celia, June 22, 1838.

CUMMINGS (see Cumings, Cummins), Charles, s. of Reuben and ———, Jan. 24, 1808.
Gerry Wheeler, s. of Reuben and ———, May 17, 1805.
John Norris, s. of Reuben and ———, Apr. 21, 1810.
Reuben, s. of Reuben and ———, Aug. 12, 1812.

CUMMINS (see Cumings, Cummings), ———, ch. of Reuben and Lois, Oct. 8, 1802.
Josiah, s. of Reuben and Lois, in Grafton, Oct. 9, 1797.
Samuel, s. of Reuben and Lois, in Grafton, May 12, 1795.

CUMSTOCK (see Comstock), David, s. of Samuel and Lucy, 4th day, 8th mo. 1769. C.R.4.
Lucy [———], w. of Samuel, 5th day, 11th mo. 1748. C.R.4.
Martha, d. of Samuel and Lucy, 19th day, 3d mo. 1793. C.R.4.
Nathan, s. of Samuel and Lucy, 24th day, 12th mo. 1776. C.R.4.
Patience, d. of Samuel and Lucy, 2d day, 9th mo. 1774. C.R.4.
Samuel, 29th day, 8th mo. 1736. C.R.4.
Silas, s. of Samuel and Lucy, 28th day, 11th mo. 1771. C.R.4.

CURLIS, Marcus Spring, s. of James and Mary L., June 8, 1846.

CURTIS, Amariah, s. of Noah and Elisabeth, Apr. 11, 1756.
Calvan, s. of Noah and Elizabeth, Mar. 10, 1762.
Luther, s. of Noah and Elizabeth, Sept. 2, 1765.
Molley, d. of Noah and Elisabeth, May 1, 1760.
Noah, s. of Noah and Elisabeth, Sept. 20, 1753.
Samuel, s. of Noah and Elisabeth, July 8, 1751.

CUSHMAN, Isaac, s. of Charl[e]s and Mary, May 24, 1744.
Mary, d. of Charl[e]s and Mary, in Norton, Sept. 9, 1740.

DALEY, Mary Brennan [————], w. of Michael, ———, 1832. G.R.2.
Michael, ———, 1829. G.R.2.

DALRYMPLE (see Derumpel, Derumple), Andrew, s. of David and Susanna, bp. Apr. 10, 1757. C.R.1.
David, s. of David and Susanna, bp. Feb. 11, 1767. C.R.1.
Dorothy, d. of David and Susanna, bp. Feb. 11, 1767. C.R.1.
Edward, s. of David and Susanna, bp. Aug. 30, 1767. C.R.1.
Hannah, d. of David and Susanna, bp. Feb. 11, 1767. C.R.1.

DAMMON, Anna, d. of Joseph and Mary, Apr. 6, 1757.
Ebenezer, s. of Joseph and Mary, Mar. 12, 1746–7.
Ebenezer, s. of (Dea., C.R.1) Joseph and Pat[i]ence, May 28, 1760.
Ebenezer, s. of (Dea., C.R.1) Joseph and Pat[i]ence, Mar. 23, 1762. (Ebenezer, s. of Dea. Joseph dec., bp. May 23, 1762. C.R.1.)
Eunice, d. of Joseph and Mary, Feb. 24, 1744–5.
Eunice, d. of Joseph and Mary, May 14, 1753.
Joseph, s. of Joseph and Mary, Apr. 16, 1740.
Joseph, s. of Joseph and Mary, Nov. 15, 1750.
Mary, d. of Joseph and Mary, June 21, 1738.
Mary, d. of Joseph and Mary, Aug. 4, 1749.
Thomas, s. of Joseph and Mary, May 12, 1742.
Thomas, s. of Joseph and Mary, Apr. 22, 1755.

DANIELS, Abigail, d. of Abraham and Abigail, Dec. 26, 1748.
Abigail, d. of Joseph and Lucy, 17th day, 6th mo. 1799. C.R.4.
Abraham, s. of Abraham and Abigail, June 25, 1742.
Abraham, s. of Abraham and Abigail, May 2, 1751.
Absalom, s. of Nathan and Sarah, 16th day, 4th mo. 1806. C.R.4.
Adaline, d. of Nathan and Mary, Nov. 23, 1843.
Adolphus, s. of David and Ruth, 1st day, 10th mo. 1778. C.R.4.
Alse Fowler [————], w. of Adolphus, 12th day, 6th mo. 1785. C.R.4.
Amy A., ———, 1831. G.R.1.
Anne, d. of Abraham and Abigail, May 29, 1746.
Azor, s. of David and Ruth, 31st day, 3d mo. 1764. C.R.4.
Barsheba, d. of Nathan and Sarah, 19th day, 4th mo. 1800. C.R.4.
Celestaney, d. of Lois Winslow and rep. d. of Peter Daniels, in Sutton, Mar. 20, 1800.

DANIELS, Christopher, s. of Nathan and Sarah, 14th day, 3d mo. 1810. c.r.4.
David, s. of Adolphus and Alice, in Mendon, Aug. 27, 1804.
David H., 8th day, 2d mo. 1805. c.r.4.
Diame, d. of David and Ruth, 24th day, 3d mo. 1774. c.r.4.
Dorcas [―――], w. of Ezekiel (Ezekiel Fowler dup.), 27th day, 4th mo. 1815. c.r.4.
Esther, d. of Joseph and Mary, Aug. 9, 1780.
Ezekiel Fowler, s. of Adolphus and Alice, Nov. 20, 1814.
Ezekiel Fowler, s. of Ezekiel and Dorcas, 20th day, 3d mo. 1842. c.r.4.
George A., ―――, 1828. g.r.1.
Harriet, d. of Adolphus and Alice, Apr. 3, 1810.
Hetta, d. of Nathan and Sarah, 9th day, 4th mo. 1797. c.r.4.
Horace, s. of Adolphus and Alse Fowler, 31st day, 12th mo. 1821. c.r.4.
Huldah, d. of David and Ruth, 17th day, 6th mo. 1776. c.r.4.
James, s. of Ezekiel and Dorcas, 8th day, 8th mo. 1844. c.r.4.
John, s. of Abraham and Abigail, June 16, 1744.
John Milton, s. of Adolphus and Alice, in Mendon, June 14, 1806.
John Milton, s. of Adolphus and Alice, Apr. 10, 1813.
Joseph, s. of Abraham and Abigail, June 23, 1753.
Joseph, s. of David and Ruth, 19th day, 2d mo. 1772. c.r.4.
Josiah, s. of Joseph and Mary, Apr. 9, 1782.
Lucy, d. of David and Ruth, 13th day, 1st mo. 1766. c.r.4.
Marcena, d. of Nathan and Sarah, 31st day, 10th mo. 1807. c.r.4.
Mary Ann, d. of Ezekiel and Dorcas, 12th day, 4th mo. 1839. c.r.4.
Mary Jane, d. of Nathan and Mary, Oct. 14, 1836.
Melissa, d. of Nathan and Mary, Aug. 13, 1834.
Nancy Thompson, d. of Ezekiel and Dorcas, 3d day, 7th mo. 1846. c.r.4.
Nathan, s. of David and Ruth, 12th day, 12th mo. 1769. c.r.4.
Rachel, d. of David and Ruth, 24th day, 12th mo. 1767. c.r.4.
Royal, s. of Adolphus and Alse Fowler, 6th day, 9th mo. 1823. c.r.4.
Ruth [―――], w. of David, 29th day, 6th mo. 1741. c.r.4.
Ruth, d. of Joseph and Lucy, 15th day, 11th mo. 1797. c.r.4.
Ruth, d. of Adolphus and Alse Fowler, 28th day, 9th mo. 1818. c.r.4.
Sarah [―――], w. of Nathan, 27th day, 9th mo. 1773. c.r.4.
Sarah, d. of Nathan and Sarah, 5th day, 8th mo. 1801. c.r.4.

DANIELS, Sarah, d. of Adolphus and Alice, Jan. 15, 1817.
Sarah Fowler, d. of Adolphus and Alice, June 11, 1808.
Silence, d. of Nathan and Sarah, 22d day, 7th mo. 1804. c.r.4.
Urania, d. of Adolphus and Alice, Aug. 27, 1811.
Wait, d. of David and Ruth, 1st day, 12th mo. 1780. c.r.4.

DARCY, Alvina Jannelle [———], w. of F. X., May 18, 1847. g.r.2.
F. X., Sept. 14, 1841. g.r.2.

DARLING, Aaron, s. of Samuel dec. and Sarah, now w. of Thomas Sabin, bp. July 2, 1769. c.r.1.
Allister, ch. of Joshua and Tab[i]tha, Sept. 29, 1803.
Calvin, s. of Joshua and Tab[i]tha, July 16, 1801.
Daniel Franklin, s. of Joshua and Tab[i]tha, Jan. 18, 1799.
Data Ann of Bellingham, Mar. 29, 1779, w. of Ezra Kempton.
Dennis, s. of Samuel dec. and Sarah, now w. of Thomas Sabin, bp. July 2, 1769. c.r.1.
Elnathan, s. of Jesse and Hannah, 8th day, 8th mo. 1793. c.r.4.
Helam, s. of Joshua and Tab[i]tha, Sept. 30, 1786.
Henry, s. of Samuel dec. and Sarah, now w. of Thomas Sabin, bp. July 2, 1769. c.r.1.
Herbert P., s. of Pelatiah and Marietta, b. in Burrillville, R. I., Nov. 2, 1848.
Labiron, ch. of Joshua and Tab[i]tha, Nov. 4, 1796.
Levory, d. of Joshua and Tab[i]tha, May 12, 1790.
Lewis, s. of Joshua and Tab[i]tha, Nov. 2, 1794.
Louisa, d. of Joshua and Sarah, Apr. 21, 1844.
Lyddia, d. of Joshua and Tab[i]tha, Sept. 2, 1793.
Lydia, d. of Samuel dec. and Sarah, now w. of Thomas Sabin, bp. July 2, 1769. c.r.1.
Margus, ch. of Joshua and Tab[i]tha, Nov. 20, 1806.
Maria, d. of Peletiah and Phila, Mar. 22, 1794.
Newbury, s. of Peletiah and Phila, Sept. 18, 1797.
Newton, s. of Peletiah and Phila, Aug. 22, 1791.
Phila, d. of Peletiah and Phila, Sept. 4, 1800.
Polly, d. of Joshua and Tab[i]tha, June 17, 1788.

DAVENPORT, Azubah, d. of William and Sarah, Sept. 19, 1744.
Mary (Mercy, c.r.1), d. of William and Sarah, May 11, 1746.

DAVIS, ———, s. of Amos and ———, bp. Nov. 24, 1734. c.r.1.
Ebenezer H., ———, 1808. g.r.1.
Henry E., s. of Lorenzo and Louisa, b. in Sutton, Feb. 22, 1849.

DAVIS, Julia A., Jan. 22, 1816. G.R.1.
Mary Jane, d. of Alonzo, Oct. 24, 1846.
Polly T. [―――], w. of Ebenezer H., ―――, 1800. G.R.1.
Robert Hague, s. of Ebenezer H. and Polly, May 11, 1837.
Solomon S., July 29, 1818. G.R.1.
Victoria A., d. of Lorenzo D. and Louisa, May 10, 1845.

DAY, Abby E., d. of James W. and Elizabeth, b. in Dudley, Nov. 19, 1849.
Angelina Nelson, d. of Joseph and Nabby, Mar. 15, 1824.
Chloe, d. of David and Susannah, Dec. 15, 1797.
Daniel, s. of Joseph and Nabby, July 22, 1821.
Elizabeth Upham [―――], w. of James W., in Dudley, Feb. 10, 1827. G.R.1.
George Nicholas, s. of Ezekiel and Sabina, Apr. 3, 1828.
James Wellington, s. of Joseph and Nabby, Aug. 4, 1817.
John William, s. of Ezekiel and Sabina, Nov. 29, 1829.
Joseph, in Mendon, Apr. 5, 1791. G.R.1.

DEAN (see Deane), Minerva M., d. of Brigham and Phila B., Mar. 19, 1844.

DEANE (see Dean), Arthur Channing, s. of Francis Jr. and Mary Jane, Sept. 15, 1844.
Francis Brown, s. of Francis and Mary Jane, Apr. 2, 1837.
Frederic Balch, s. of Francis and Mary Jane, Dec. 16, 1840.

DEARNLEY, Mary Carroll [―――], w. of William, ―――, 1838. G.R.1.
William, ―――, 1828. G.R.1.

DEETS, George Champlain Hayward, s. of Daniel and Harriet, Mar. 11, 1845.
Harriot Augusta, d. of Daniel and Harriot, Oct. —, 1837.
Lucretia Sibley, d. of Daniel and Harriot, Nov. —, 1839.
Sylvanus Robbins, d. of Daniel and Harriot, Jan. 16, 1842.

DENNING, Ellen, d. of John and Ann, both b. in Ireland, Mar. 9, 1849.

DENNIS, Amos P., s. of Asa and Sarah, 1st day, 11th mo. 1822. C.R.4.
Asa, s. of Asa and Sarah, 30th day, 8th mo. 1837. C.R.4.
Benjamin C., s. of Asa and Sarah, 22d day, 2d mo. 1829. C.R.4.
Daniel C. Clapp, s. of Obed and Elisabeth, 14th day, 1st mo. 1820. C.R.4.

DENNIS, Elisabeth, d. of Obed and Elisabeth, 8th day, 12th mo. 1788. c.r.4.
Ellen, d. of Asa and Sarah, 21st day, 4th mo. 1835. c.r.4.
George, s. of Obed and Elisabeth, 10th day, 11th mo. 1821. c.r.4.
Gideon, s. of Obed and Elisabeth, 9th day, 9th mo. 1825. c.r.4.
Hannah, d. of Obed and Elisabeth, 19th day, 12th mo. 1815. c.r.4.
John C., s. of Obed and Elisabeth, 28th day, 3d mo. 1827. c.r.4.
Joseph, 3d day, 5th mo. 1759. c.r.4.
Joseph, s. of Obed and Elisabeth, 16th day, 5th mo. 1817. c.r.4.
Mary J., d. of Asa and Sarah, 12th day, 1st mo. 1825. c.r.4.
Obed, 23d day, 3d mo. 1790. c.r.4.
Phebe, d. of Obed and Elisabeth, 15th day, 7th mo. 1823. c.r.4.
Robert, s. of Asa and Sarah, 21st day, 7th mo. 1819. c.r.4.
Sarah [———], w. of Joseph, 7th day, 4th mo. 1754. c.r.4.
Sarah C., d. of Asa and Sarah, 30th day, 1st mo. 1827. c.r.4.
Sarah C., d. of Asa and Sarah, 11th day, 6th mo. 1833. c.r.4.
Sarah Elisabeth, d. of Obed and Elisabeth, 19th day, 6th mo. 1831. c.r.4.
Thomas C., s. of Obed and Elisabeth, 28th day, 6th mo. 1829. c.r.4.
William S., s. of Asa and Sarah, 20th day, 3d mo. 1831. c.r.4.

DERUMPEL (see Dalrymple, Derumple), John Sheperd, s. of David and Susannah, Nov. 16, 1752. (Thomas Shepard, s. of David and Susanna, bp. Feb. 4, 1753. c.r.4.)
William, s. of David and Susannah, June 4, 1751.

DERUMPLE (see Dalrymple, Derumpel), Susanna, d. of David and Susanna, bp. May 4, 1755. c.r.1.

DEVLIN, Bernard, s. of Patrick and Hannah, both b. in Ireland, Sept. 7, 1848.

DE WOLF, Henry, July 30, 1805. g.r.18.

DILLINGHAM, Remember, 26th day, — mo. 1743. c.r.4.

DIX, George, s. of George and Sophronia, Apr. 21, 1833.
Henry, s. of George and Sophronia, Nov. 21, 1831.
Thomas Hatch, s. of George and Sophronia, Jan. 23, 1830.

DODGE, Dorcas [———], w. of Olney, ———, 1800. g.r.1.
Elizabeth O., d. of Olney and Dorcas and w. of Benjamin Guy, Mar. 14, 1833. g.r.1.

DODGE, Hannah T. [———], w. of Henry T., ———, 1816. G.R.1.
Henry T., ———, 1812. G.R.1.
John M., ———, 1837. G.R.1.
Louisa A., d. of Olney and Dorcas, Oct. 26, 1841.
Olney, ———, 1798. G.R.1.

DONOVAN, Rose [———], w. of Dennis, ———, 1832. G.R.2.

DORCY, William, s. of Edward and Bridget, both b. in Ireland, July 6, 1849.

DRAKE, Abigail, d. of Stephen and Abigail, July 8, 1769.
Rachel, d. of Stephen and Abigail, May 26, 1771.

DRAPER, Adolphus, s. of David and Marthew, Aug. 9, 1781.
Adolphus, s. of David and Marthew, Aug. 21, 1789.
Danford, s. of David and Marthew, Apr. 24, 1795.
Darias, s. of David and Marthew, May 31, 1792.
David, s. of David and Elizabeth, Mar. 22, 1742.
David, s. of David and Marthew, Jan. 14, 1775.
Deborah, d. of David and Marthew, June 19, 1784.
Elisabeth, d. of David and Marthew, June 2, 1777.
Elizabeth, d. of David and Elizabeth, bp. May 21, 1738. C.R.1.
Elizabeth, d. of David and Marthew, Nov. 19, 1772.
Emily A., ———, 1840. G.R.1.
Frost, s. of David and Marthew, June 4, 1787.
Harriet M., ———, 1833. G.R.1.
Henry Whitman, s. of Frost and Mary, bp. Mar. 22, 1820. C.R.1.
Jane, ———, 1826. G.R.1.
Josiah, s. of Frost and Mary, bp. July 7, 1815. C.R.1.
Martha, d. of Frost and Mary, bp. July 16, 1819. C.R.1.
Martyn Thayer, s. of Frost and Mary, bp. July 7, 1815. C.R.1.
Mary, d. of David and Elizabeth, bp. Dec. 16, 1750. C.R.1.
Rebecca, d. of David and Elizabeth, bp. Mar. 27, 1748. C.R.1.
Rebecca, d. of David and Marthew, June 18, 1779.
Roxanna [———], w. of Danford, ———, 1799. G.R.1.
Samuel, s. of David and Elizabeth, bp. Mar. 31, 1754. C.R.1.
Sarah, d. of David and Elizabeth, bp. May 6, 1739. C.R.1.
Sarah, d. of David and Elizabeth, bp. Apr. 4, 1745. C.R.1.
Sarah, d. of David and Marthew, Jan. 24, 1771.

DUDLEY, Henry M. (Henry Marchant, C.R.2), s. of Paul W. (Whitin, C.R.2), and Sarah Ann, Aug. 13, 1846.
Molly, d. of William and ———, bp. at Douglas, Oct. 22, 1769. C.R.1.

DUNN, Agneas, d. of John and Jane, Aug. 14, 1749.
David, s. of John and Jane, Apr. 23, 1745.
Elisabeth, d. of John and Jane, Nov. 26, 1746.
James, s. of John and Jane, Aug. 31, 1751.
Samuel, s. of John and Jane, Mar. 3, 1753.
Thomas, s. of John and Jane, June 24, 1748.

EAISMAN, Jerry A., s. of Matthias and Catharine, Sept. 25, 1847.

EARLE, Abigail, d. of Antipas and Mercy, 7th day, 4th mo. 1774.
Amasa, s. of Marmaduke and Elisabeth, 11th day, 3d mo. 1784. C.R.4.
Amos Southgate, s. of Jonah and Elizabeth, 22d day, 4th mo. 1800. C.R.4.
Ann B. [———], w. of Edward, 25th day, 12th mo. 1815. C.R.4.
Ann Buffum, d. of Edward and Ann B., 28th day, 7th mo. 1838. C.R.4.
Ann H., d. of John Milton and Sarah Hussey, 17th day, 4th mo. 1822. C.R.4.
Anna, d. of Silas and Rachel, 26th day, 12th mo. 1797. C.R.4.
Anna K., d. of Timothy and Ruth, 12th day, 10th mo. 1806. C.R.4.
Antipas, 1st day, 6th mo. 1737. C.R.4.
Antipas, s. of Slead and Elisabeth, 13th day, 11th mo. 1787. C.R.4.
Benjamin, s. of Antipas and Mercy, 27th day, 9th mo. 1761. C.R.4.
Candace, d. of Marmaduke and Elisabeth, 31st day, 1st mo. 1792. C.R.4.
Caroline C. [———], 2d w. of Timo[thy] H., 10th day, 4th mo. 1842. C.R.4.
Catharine, 31st day, 3d mo. 1775. C.R.4.
Catherine, d. of John Milton and Sarah Hussey, 24th day, 1st mo. 1828. C.R.4.
Deborah, 1st day, 12th mo. 1716. C.R.4.
Deliverance, d. of Marmaduke and Elisabeth, 10th day, 11th mo. 1779. C.R.4.
Dorothy Ann [———], w. of Timothy, 8th day, 7th mo. 1826. C.R.4.
Edward, s. of Timothy and Sarah, 10th day, 2d mo. 1811. C.R.4.
Elisabeth [———], w. of Marmaduke, 22d day, 6th mo. 1755. C.R.4.
Elisabeth [———], w. of Slead, 8th day, 1st mo. 1765. C.R.4.

EARLE, Elisabeth, d. of Robert Jr. and Sarah, 5th day, 7th mo. 1769. c.r.4.
Elisha, s. of Silas and Rachel, 18th day, 4th mo. 1804. c.r.4.
Eliza, d. of Pliny and Patience, 8th day, 6th mo. 1807. c.r.4.
Elizabeth, d. of John Milton and Sarah Hussey, 4th day, 5th mo. 1824. c.r.4.
Elonar, 6th day, 1st mo. 1800. c.r.4.
Emery, s. of Marmaduke and Esther, 10th day, 9th mo. 1790. c.r.4.
Frances Caroline, d. of John Milton and Sarah Hussey, 2d day, 4th mo. 1840. c.r.4.
George, s. of Silas and Rachel, 17th day, 1st mo. 1800. c.r.4.
Hannah, d. of Robert Jr. and Sarah, 9th day, 4th mo. 1785. c.r.4.
Hannah, d. of Silas and Rachel, 16th day, 3d mo. 1796. c.r.4.
Henry, s. of Robert Jr. and Sarah, 13th day, 3d mo. 1774. c.r.4.
Henry Willard, s. of Henry and Miriam, 18th day, 3d mo. 1810. c.r.4.
Homer, 6th day, 5th mo. 1802. c.r.4.
J. Milton (John Milton dup.), s. of Pliny and Patience, 3d day, 4th mo. 1794. c.r.4.
John, s. of Antipas and Mercy, 13th day, 10th mo. 1777. c.r.4.
John Fry, s. of Henry and Miriam, 29th day, 9th mo. 1812. c.r.4.
John Potter, s. of Jonah and Elizabeth, 11th day, 11th mo. 1795. c.r.4.
Jonah, s. of Robert Jr. and Sarah, 10th day, 3d mo. 1765. c.r.4.
Jonah, s. of Pliny and Patience, 16th day, 11th mo. 1813. c.r.4.
Jonathan, s. of Antipas and Mercy, 22d day, 12th mo. 1767. c.r.4.
Joseph, s. of Slead and Elisabeth, 28th day, 2d mo. 1788. c.r.4.
Lucretia, d. of Marmaduke and Elisabeth, 25th day, 2d mo. 1773. c.r.4.
Lucy, d. of Pliny and Patience, 7th day, 5th mo. 1805. c.r.4.
Lydia, d. of Robert Jr. and Sarah, 16th day, 1st mo. 1776. c.r.4.
Lydia, d. of Pliny and Patience, 24th day, 3d mo. 1798. c.r.4.
Lydia, d. of Henry and Ruth, his 3d w., 11th day, 12th mo. 1821. c.r.4.
Marmaduke, 13th day, 3d mo. 1748. c.r.4.
Martha B., d. of John Milton and Sarah Hussey, 28th day. 12th mo. 1829. c.r.4.
Mary, d. of Silas and Rachel, 9th day, 2d mo. 1802. c.r.4.

EARLE, Mary Bonent, d. of Timothy and Sarah, 5th day, 2d mo. 1819. C.R.4.
Mary Folger, d. of John Milton and Sarah Hussey, 25th day, 7th mo. 1826. C.R.4.
Melissa, d. of Henry and Miriam, 1st day, 4th mo. 1803. C.R.4.
Mercy [———], w. of Antipas, 4th day, 11th mo. 1744. C.R.4.
Miriam [———], w. of Henry, 12th day, 1st mo. 1771. C.R.4.
Narcissa, s. of Henry and Miriam, 3d day, 5th mo. 1800. C.R.4.
Nathaniel Potter, s. of Jonah and Elizabeth, 17th day, 4th mo. 1798. C.R.4.
Oliver Huse, s. of Henry and Ruth, his 3d w., 8th day, 9th mo. 1824. C.R.4.
Persis, d. of Robert Jr. and Sarah, 20th day, 9th mo. 1771. C.R.4.
Persis, 18th day, 12th mo. 1794. C.R.4.
Persis, d. of Timothy and Sarah, 29th day, 8th mo. 1813. C.R.4.
Phebe, 22d day, 6th mo. 1797. C.R.4.
Phebe, d. of Silas and Rachel, 22d day, 3d mo. 1816. C.R.4.
Philip, s. of Marmaduke and Elisabeth, 11th day, 4th mo. 1786. C.R.4.
Pliny, s. of Robert Jr. and Sarah, 17th day, 12th mo. 1762. C.R.4.
Pliny, s. of Pliny and Patience, 31st day, 12th mo. 1809. C.R.4.
Pliny, s. of John Milton and Sarah Hussey, 21st day, 7th mo. 1834. C.R.4.
Rachel, d. of Silas and Rachel, 11th day, 8th mo. 1808. C.R.4.
Rachel, d. of Timothy and Dorothy Ann, 25th day, 10th mo. 1844. C.R.4.
Rebecah, 21st day, 7th mo. 1788. C.R.4.
Richard, s. of Timothy and Sarah, 9th day, 3d mo. 1809. C.R.4.
Robert, s. of Silas and Rachel, 18th day, 5th mo. 1806. C.R.4.
Ruth [———], w. of Timothy, 13th day, 3d mo. 1785. C.R.4.
Samuel, s. of Marmaduke and Elisabeth, 26th day, 12th mo. 1781. C.R.4.
Sam[ue]l Hussey, s. of John Milton and Sarah Hussey, 25th day, 5th mo. 1837. C.R.4.
Sarah [———], w. of Robert Jr., 26th day, 3d mo. 1745. C.R.4.
Sarah, d. of Robert Jr. and Sarah, 1st day, 1st mo. 1781. C.R.4.
Sarah, d. of Pliny and Patience, 8th day, 4th mo. 1800. C.R.4.
Sarah, d. of Henry and Miriam, 8th day, 4th mo. 1805. C.R.4.
Sarah, d. of Timothy and Sarah, 3d day, 1st mo. 1816. C.R.4.
Sarah Folger, d. of John Milton and Sarah Hussey, 8th day, 12th mo. 1831. C.R.4.

EARLE, Sarah Hussey [———], w. of John Milton, 2d day, 8th mo. 1799. C.R.4.
Silas, s. of Robert Jr. and Sarah, 26th day, 5th mo. 1767. C.R.4.
Silas, s. of Silas and Rachel, 29th day, 3d mo. 1811. C.R.4.
Silas, s. of Timothy and Dorothy Ann, 9th day, 4th mo. 1846. C.R.4.
Slead, s. of Antipas and Mercy, 22d day, 11th mo. 1764. C.R.4.
Stephen, s. of Silas and Rachel, 21st day, 4th mo. 1813. C.R.4.
Thomas, s. of Pliny and Patience, 21st day, 4th mo. 1796. C.R.4.
Thomas, s. of Henry and Ruth, his 3d w., 11th day, 1st mo. 1823. Twin. C.R.4.
Timothy, s. of Robert Jr. and Sarah, 22d day, 3d mo. 1778. C.R.4.
Timothy, s. of Silas and Rachel, 14th day, 8th mo. 1820. C.R.4.
Timothy Huse, s. of Henry and Ruth, his 3d w., 11th day, 1st mo. 1823. Twin. C.R.4.
Waldo, s. of Slead and Elisabeth, 11th day, 10th mo. 1796. C.R.4.
William Buffum, s. of Pliny and Patience, 20th day, 12th mo. 1802. C.R.4.
Winthrop, s. of Marmaduke and Elisabeth, 5th day, 5th mo. 1777. C.R.4.

EDDY, Amasa, s. of Thomas and Sarah, 20th day, 12th mo. 1783. C.R.4.
Asa, s. of Thomas and Sarah, 30th day, 7th mo. 1780. C.R.4.
Hannah [———], 2d. w. of Jesse, 9th day, 11th mo. 1781. C.R.4.
Hannah, d. of Jesse and Sarah, 5th day, 8th mo. 1795. C.R.4.
Hannah S., d. of Jesse and Hannah, 30th day, 11th mo. 1811. C.R.4.
Jesse, s. of John, 29th day, 11th mo. 1769. C.R.4.
Jesse, s. of Jesse and Sarah, 18th day, 2d mo. 1801. C.R.4.
Joannah D., d. of Jesse and Hannah, 20th day, 3d mo. 1818. C.R.4.
John, 25th day, 12th mo. 1730. C.R.4.
John, s. of Jesse and Sarah, 18th day, 7th mo. 1799. C.R.4.
Lyman, s. of Thomas and Sarah, 29th day, 8th mo. 1786. C.R.4.
Mary, d. of Jesse and Sarah, 21st day, 8th mo. 1793. C.R.4.
Sarah [———], w. of Thomas, 29th day, 11th mo. 1755. C.R.4.
Sarah [———], w. of Jesse, 5th day, 2d mo. 1762. C.R.4.
Sarah, d. of Jesse and Sarah, 14th day, 5th mo. 1792. C.R.4.
Thomas, 25th day, 1st mo. 1759. C.R.4.

EDWARDS, William H., Aug. 10, 1815. G.R.1.

ELIOT (see Elliot), Amphila, d. of John and Deborah, Mar. 14, 1736–7.
Benjamin, s. of John and Deborah, June 20, 1754.
Deborah, d. of John and Deborah, Aug. 4, 1751.
John, s. of John and Deborah, June 24, 1743.
John, s. of John and Deborah, Mar. 27, 1748.
Peter, s. of John and Deborah, Nov. 25, 1744.

ELLIOT (see Eliot), Daniel, s. of David and Mehitable, Jan. 19, 1742–3.
David, s. of David and Mehitable, Mar. 3, 1744–5.
Hitty, d. of David and Mehitable, Mar. 17, 1752.
Leaban, s. of David and Mehitable, Jan. 4, 1757.
Micajah, s. of David and Mehitable, Oct. 19, 1755.
Prudance, d. of David and Mehitable, Jan. —, 1746–7.
Sarah, d. of David and Mehitable, July 18, 1740.
Sarah, d. of David and Mehitable, Jan. 17, 1750.

ELLIS, Charles Dea., ——, 1804. G.R.1.
Edward Tampling, s. of Thomas and Dorothy, bp. Oct. 14, 1770. C.R.1.
Joseph, s. of Thomas and Dorothy, bp. May 11, 1772. C.R.1.
Ruth Stearns [———], w. of Dea. Charles, ——, 1808. G.R.1.
Sarah Ballard [———], w. of Dea. Charles, ——, 1814. G.R.1.
Stephen, s. of Stephen and Ruth, Oct. 3, 1745.

ELLISON, Adolphus S., Nov. 12, 1812. G.R.1. (Adolphus, s. of Joseph and Lucinda, bp. Oct. 13, 1822. C.R.1.)
Anne, d. of John and Hannah, July 21, 1738.
Charles Willard, s. of Willard and Sylvia, Feb. 17, 1847.
Edward P., s. of Adolphus S. and Julia Ann, Nov. 1, 1847.
Ezekiel, s. of Joseph and Lucinda, bp. Oct. 13, 1822. C.R.1.
George Willard, s. of Joseph and Lucinda, bp. Oct. 13, 1822. C.R.1.
Hannah, d. of John and Hannah, July 24, 1749.
Henry Martin, s. of Adolphus S. and Julia A. (Julia Angelina, C.R.2), July 19, 1844.
Jacob, s. of John and Hannah, July 5, 1746.
John, s. of John and Hannah, Sept. 7, 1736.
Julia A. Hunt [———], w. of Adolphus S., ——, 1821. G.R.1.
Laura, d. of Joseph and Lucinda, bp. Oct. 13, 1822. C.R.1.
Lorena Willard, d. of Joseph and Lucinda, bp. Oct. 13, 1822. C.R.1.
Maria Eliz., d. of Willard and Sylvia, bp. Mar. 3, 1844. C.R.2.
Martha, d. of John and Hannah, Feb. 2, 1752.

ELLISON, Martha Blanchard [———], w. of Adolphus S., Nov. 27, 1817. G.R.1.
Martha Hull, d. of Joseph and Lucinda, bp. Oct. 13, 1822. C.R.1.
Molley, d. of John and Hannah, Apr. 16, 1744.
Sarah, d. of John and Hannah, Nov. 9, 1756.
Silvia Maria, d. of Joseph and Lucinda, bp. Oct. 13, 1822. C.R.1.
Susannah, d. of John and Hannah, Sept. 24, 1732.
Thomas, s. of John and Hannah, Oct. 7, 1734.
Thomas, s. of John and Hannah, Mar. 20, 1740–1.

EMERSON, Abigail, d. of James and Sarah, bp. Sept. 17, 1732. C.R.1.
Abigail, d. of Thomas and Abigail, Apr. 25, 1756.
Amos, s. of Nathaniel Jr. and Polly, Apr. 3, 1798.
Asa, s. of Thomas and Abigail, Aug. 19, 1749.
Chloa, d. of Lyman and Lillis, Dec. 2, 1791.
Daniel, s. of Thomas and Abigail, Apr. 5, 1753.
David, s. of Luke and Ruth, Nov. 20, 1755.
Elisabeth, d. of James and Sarah, Aug. 23, 1735.
Elizabeth, d. of James and Elizabeth, bp. May 23, 1762. C.R.1.
Enoch, s. of Thomas and Abigail, Feb. 26, 1755.
Esther, d. of Thomas and Abigail, June 14, 1751.
Eunice, d. of Thomas and Abigail, Sept. 9, 1761.
Eunice, d. of James D. and Mercy, b. in Smithfield, R. I., Feb. 9, 1849.
Ezekiel, s. of John and Mary, Feb. 14, 1735–6.
Hannah, d. of John and Mary, Mar. 29, 1747.
James, s. of James and Elizabeth, bp. Apr. 27, 1755. C.R.1.
Jason, Apr. 25, 1816. G.R.1.
John, s. of Thomas and Abigail, Oct. 4, 1753.
John, s. of Luke and Ruth, Monday, Mar. 3, 1766, "about 8 o'clock at night."
Jonathan, s. of James and Sarah, Jan. 1, 1728–9.
Jonathan, 25th day, 2d mo. 1753 O. S. C.R.4.
Jonathan, s. of Jonathan and Sarah, in Ipswich, Feb. 25, 1763.
Lillas, d. of Lyman and Lillis, May 9, 1799.
Louis, d. of Luke and Ruth, Feb. 20, 1764, "at 10 o'clock at night of a Monday."
Lucia, d. of Jonathan and Sarah, bp. May 9, 1756. C.R.1.
Luke, s. of John and Mary, Oct. 14, 1733.
Lydia, d. of Jonathan and Molly, Feb. 14, 1784.
Mary, d. of John and Mary, Sept. 17, 1730.
Mary, d. of Thomas and Abigail, Feb. 24, 1757.
Mercy A. [———], w. of Millen, Jan. 14, 1834. G.R.1.

EMERSON, Millen, May 6, 1819. G.R.1.
Molley [———], w. of Jonathan, 4th day, 9th mo. 1752. C.R.4.
Nancy, d. of Nathaniel Jr. and Polly, Apr. 2, 1797.
Oliver S., ———, 1829. G.R.1.
Pheebe, d. of John and Mary, Aug. 17, 1743.
Pheebe, d. of Thomas and Abigail, Nov. 14, 1759.
Philadelphia, d. of Lyman and Lillis, May 4, 1794.
Reuben, s. of James and Elizabeth, bp. Sept. 17, 1758. C.R.1.
Reuben, s. of Lyman and Lillis, Jan. 14, 1790.
Rhoda, d. of Luke and Ruth, Jan. 30, 1763, "of a Sabbath day at three quarters of an hour after 6 o'clock in the morning."
Rhoda, d. of Luke and Ruth, Friday, Mar. 11, 1768, "41 minutes after eight o'clock in the afternoon."
Ruben, s. of Luke and Ruth, Jan. 30, 1763, "of a Sabbath day, about ½ an hour after one of the clock in the afternoon."
Ruth, d. of Luke and Ruth, Feb. 14, 1758.
Salla, d. of Luke and Ruth, Thursday, Jan. 10, 1771, "at eight o'clock in ye morning."
Samuel, s. of Jonathan and Molly, July 20, 1776.
Sarah, d. of John and Mary, Jan. 14 preceding 1740.
Sarah J. Shove [———], w. of Oliver S. ———, 1832. G.R.1.
Silence, d. of Nathanael and ———, bp. July 5, 1747. C.R.1.
Susannah, d. of Luke and Ruth, May 6, 1760, "at 3 o'clock in the afternoon."
Thomas, s. of Luke and Ruth, Friday, Aug. 20, 1773, "at eight o'clock in the morning."
Ursula [———], w. of Jason, July 6, 1814. G.R.1.
Waity, d. of Jonathan and Molly, Jan. 4, 1780.
William, s. of Ebenezer and Elizabeth (Wallcutt), Apr. 9, 1734.
William H., s. of Horace and Azubah, June 10, 1834.

ESTES, Charles, s. of Joseph and Eunice, of Warren, R. I., 14th day, 6th mo. 1849. C.R.4.

ESTY, George H., s. of Harriet L., b. in Attleborough, Oct. —, 1848.

EVERDON, Joseph, s. of Walter and Abigail, July 31, 1768.

EVERETT, Olney W., s. of Silas S. and Almira, June 17, 1845.

FAIRBANKS, Sarah, d. of Jonathan and Esther, bp. July 7, 1745. C.R.1.

FARGUSON, John, s. of Robert and Bridget, both b. in Ireland, May 4, 1848.
Thomas, s. of Robert and Bridget, both b. in Ireland, Nov. 16, 1849.

FARNUM, Abigail, d. of Moses and Abigail, Aug. 19, 1741.
Abigail, d. of Moses (Jr., c.r.4) and Sarah (his 1st w., c.r.4), July 20, 1767.
Abigail, d. of George and Deborah, Jan. 15, 1799.
Abram, s. of Royal and Rozilla, Oct. 25, 1794.
Adaline, d. of Capt. Thomas and Matilda, Sept. 15, 1829.
Adeline (Adeline Louisa, c.r.4), d. of Jonathan and Minerva, b. in Smithfield, R. I., Dec. 5, 1848. (w. of John Breed Daniels. c.r.4.)
Amos, s. of Thomas and Mary, Aug. 14, 1756.
Amos, s. of Thomas and Mary, Oct. 11, 1764.
Amy, d. of Royal and Rozilla, Dec. 1, 1792.
Ann, d. of Moses (Jr., c.r.4) and Sarah, Jan. 19, 1758.
Anna, d. of Moses and Abigail, Sept. 2, 1732. Twin.
Asa Newell, s. of Capt. Thomas and Matilda, Feb. 5, 1821.
Azubah, d. of David and Leah, Aug. 27, 1765.
Bezaleel White, s. of David Jr. and Hopestill, June 26, 1799.
Caleb, s. of Thomas and Mary, Nov. 9, 1753.
Caleb, s. of Caleb and Loice, July 15, 1781.
Caleb, s. of Capt. Thomas and Matilda, May 1, 1823.
Catey, d. of Jonathan and Lettice, Nov. 1, 1793.
Catharina, d. of David and Leah, May 16, 1763.
Charles, s. of Capt. Thomas and Matilda, June 10, 1828.
Charles Augustus, s. of David Jr. and Hopestill, Nov. 5, 1797.
Charles Augustus, s. of Capt. Thomas and Matilda, Nov. 17, 1815.
Charles Edwin, s. of Jonathan and Minerva, 22d day, 10th mo. 1829. c.r.4.
Chloa, d. of Thomas and Mary, June 1, 1750.
Clarissa, d. of John and Paulina, both b. in Canada, Dec. 17, 1849.
Claritsa, d. of Caleb and Loice, Aug. 22, 1784.
D. Mellen, ——, 1808. g.r.1.
Daniel, s. of Moses (Jr., c.r.3) and Sarah, June 4, 1755.
Daniel, s. of David (Jr., c.r.4) and Ruth, Nov. 22, 1784. (29th day, 11th mo. 1784. c.r.4.)
Darius Daniels, s. of Moses and Rachel, Oct. 19, 1798.
Darius Daniels, s. of Jonathan and Minerva, 3d day, 2d mo. 1827. c.r.4.

FARNUM, David, s. of John and Mary, Apr. 6, 1732.
David, s. of Moses and Abigail, June 28, 1745.
David, s. of Moses (Jr., C.R.4) and Sarah, Sept. 29, 1753.
David, s. of David and Leah, July 26, 1770. (12th day, 7th mo. 1770. C.R.4.)
David, s. of Peter and Susannah, Mar. 25, 1796.
David, s. of Capt. Thomas and Matilda, July 20, 1825.
Easman, s. of Caleb and Loice, Dec. 22, 1777.
Elisabeth [———], w. of Moses, — day, 11th mo. 1741. C.R.4.
Elizabeth, d. of George and Sarah, Feb. 28, 1788.
Elizabeth, d. of Peter and Susannah, Mar. 1, 1793.
Elizabeth, d. of George and Deborah, Aug. 10, 1812.
Frost, s. of Royal and Rozilla, Jan. 16, 1799.
George, s. of Moses and Sarah (his 1st w., C.R.4), June 12, 1760.
George, 25th day, 5th mo. 1816. C.R.4.
George Fox, s. of George and Deborah, Jan. 19, 1806.
George W., s. of Whipple and Prudence, Apr. 14, 1832.
Hannah, d. of Moses and Abigail, Sept. 11, 1737.
Hannah, d. of David (Jr., C.R.4) and Ruth, Dec. 22, 1782.
Helen M., d. of Whipple and Prudence, Sept. 10, 1830.
Henry S., s. of Whipple and Lydia A., b. in Barnstable, Sept. 26, 1848.
James M., Apr. 11, 1822. G.R.1.
Jesse, s. of David and Ruth, June 7, 1795.
Job Pitts, s. of George and Deborah, Aug. 17, 1810.
John, s. of Joshua and Margaret, Sept. 20, 1762.
John, s. of Peter and Susannah, Oct. 17, 1790.
Jonathan, s. of John and Mary, Apr. 21, 1739.
Jonathan, s. of Moses and Abigail, June 28, 1745.
Jonathan, s. of David and Leah, Apr. 30, 1760.
Jonathan, s. of Moses and Rachel, Mar. 27, 1804.
Jonathan Backhouse, s. of Jonathan and Minerva, 2d day, 9th mo. 1833. C.R.4.
Joseph, s. of John and Elisabeth, July 17, 1751.
Joseph, s. of John and Polly, Feb. 28, 1848.
Joshua, s. of John and Mary, July 20, 1730.
Joshua, s. of Joshua and Margeret, Feb. 7, 1768.
Lettice [———], w. of Jonathan, 9th day, 6th mo. 1768. C.R.4.
Lois, d. of Caleb and Azubah, July 31, 1799.
Louis, d. of David and Leah, Feb. 15, 1767.
Lucy, d. of Moses and Rachel, Feb. 10, 1795.
Luke S., Jan. 20, 1817. G.R.1.
Luther, s. of Joshua and Margeret, Apr. 29, 1772.
Lydia, d. of Jonathan and Uranah, Oct. 26, 1766.

FARNUM, Marcus, s. of Caleb and Azubah, Nov. 7, 1796.
Marcy, d. of David and Leah, Oct. 22, 1758.
Maria, d. of Jonathan and Lettice, Jan. 26, 1790.
Maria Catherine, d. of Capt. Thomas and Matilda, Apr. 24, 1817.
Mary, d. of Moses and Abigail, Sept. 2, 1732. Twin.
Mary Arnold, d. of Moses and Rachel, Aug. 14, 1808.
Meltiah, d. of David and Leah, Oct. 21, 1761.
Minerva, d. of Jonathan and Minerva, 22d day, 11th mo. 1837. c.r.4.
Minerva Elizabeth, d. of Jonathan and Minerva, 22d day, 11th mo. 1828. c.r.4.
Molley, d. of Thomas and Mary, Jan. 20, 1752.
Molley, d. of Royal and Rozilla, Oct. 16, 1796.
Mordecai, s. of David and Leah, Nov. 11, 1774. (12th day, 11th mo. 1774. c.r.4.)
Moses, s. of Moses and Abigail, Oct. 25, 1730.
Moses, s. of Moses (Jr., c.r.4) and Sarah (his 1st w., c.r.4), Apr. 10, 1770.
Moses, s. of David (Jr., c.r.4) and Ruth, Jan. 29, 1787. (29th day, 11th mo. 1787. c.r.4.)
Moses, s. of Moses and Rachel, Feb. 22, 1802.
Mowry, s. of David and Ruth, Dec. 23, 1799.
Nathan, s. of Royal and Rozilla, Oct. 24, 1802.
Noah, s. of John and Elisabeth, July 21, 1753.
Oliver, s. of Joshua and Margaret, Dec. 2, 1763.
Ophelia S., Dec. 5, 1826. g.r.1.
Paul, s. of Peter and Susannah, Dec. 7, 1788.
Peter, s. of Moses and Sarah (his 1st w., c.r.4), May 22, 1765.
Peter, s. of Peter and Susannah, May 21, 1798.
Phebe, d. of Jonathan and Uranah, July 2, 1769.
Phebe, d. of David (Jr., c.r.4) and Ruth, Apr. 15, 1791.
Pheebe, d. of Thomas and Mary, Nov. 17, 1760.
Rachal [———], w. of Moses, 24th day, 12th mo. 1767. c.r.4.
Rachel, d. of Moses and Abigail, Jan. 13, 1742-3.
Rachel, d. of Moses and Rachel, Mar. 15, 1811.
Rachel, d. of Jonathan and Minerva, 8th day, 2d mo. 1843. c.r.4.
Rhoda, d. of Thomas and Mary, Feb. 3, 1758.
Rhoda, d. of Thomas and Mary, Aug. 24, 1762.
Royal, s. of Caleb and Loice, Nov. 28, 1775.
Royall, s. of Moses and Sarah (his 1st w., c.r.4), Jan. 7, 1763.
Ruth [———], w. of David Jr., 5th day, 3d mo. 1763. c.r.4.
Ruth, d. of David and Leah, Nov. 5, 1768.

FARNUM, Ruth Daniels, d. of Moses and Rachel, Sept. 29, 1800.
Samuel, s. of Jonathan and Minerva, 1st day, 1st mo. 1840.
  c.r.4.
Samuel Judson, s. of David and Ruth, Nov. 8, 1805.
Sarah, d. of John and Mary, July 20, 1736.
Sarah, d. of Joshua and Margaret, June 25, 1764.
Sarah, d. of Moses and Elizabeth (his 2d w., c.r.4), Apr. 7, 1780.
Sarah, d. of George and Deborah, Dec. 17, 1794.
Sarah, d. of George and Deborah, June 5, 1803.
Sarah, d. of Moses and Rachel, Sept. 4, 1805.
Stephen, s. of Moses and Abigail, Sept. 19, 1739.
Susan, d. of Capt. Thomas and Matilda, June 19, 1819.
Susanna [———], w. of Peter, 13th day, 9th mo. 1765. c.r.4.
Thomas, s. of Joshua and Margeret, May 13, 1766.
Thomas, s. of David and Leah, Sept. 6, 1772. (26th day, 8th mo. 1772. c.r.4.)
Thomas, s. of Caleb and Azubah, Aug. 31, 1794.
Wait, d. of Jonathan and Lettice, Oct. 1, 1795.
Warner, s. of Jonathan and Lettice, Mar. 15, 1792.
Welcome, d. of Moses and Rachel, Dec. 18, 1796.
Welcome, d. of Jonathan and Minerva, 3d day, 11th mo. 1835.
  c.r.4.
Whipple, s. of Royal and Rozilla, Nov. 26, 1800.
William Penn, s. of George and Deborah, May 2, 1801.

FARRIS, Daniel P., ———, 1817. g.r.1.

FECHEM, Fidella, d. of Samuel Scarborough and Lydia, Sept. 19, 1801.
Lampetce, d. of Samuel Scarborough and Lydia, Mar. 14, 1798.
Ophelia, d. of Samuel Scarborough and Lydia, Jan. 17, 1808.
Sam[ue]ll, s. of Samuel Scarborough and Lydia, in Waltham, Mar. 30, 1795.
Willard, s. of Samuel Scarborough and Lydia, Sept. 25, 1799.

FERRY, Albert E., Dec. 25, 1846, g.r.1.

FESSENDEN, Henry Austin, s. of Isaac and Olive, June 2, 1843.

FISH, Abel, s. of Nethaniel and Susannah, ——— 14, 1751. (bp. Mar. 24, 1750–1. c.r.1.)
Abigail, d. of Nethaniel and Susannah, Apr. 27, 1761.
Abigail, d. of Nethaniel and Meriam, Nov. 24, 1783.
Benjamin, s. of Stephen and ———, bp. July 1, 1733. c.r.1.
Benjamin, s. of Benjamin and Mary, bp. Mar. 15, 1761. c.r.1.

FISH, Bulah, d. of Benjamin and Sarah, Aug. 3, 1767.
Chloa, d. of Stephen and Mary, June 25, 1751.
Comfort, d. of Nethaniel and Susannah, Apr. 13, 1759.
Deborah, d. of Benjamin and Sarah, Feb. 18, 1766.
Ebenezer, s. of Stephen and Rebeckah, Aug. 11, 1739. (Ebenezer, s. of Stephen and Abigail, bp. Aug. 19, 1739. c.r.1.)
Elisabeth, d. of Nethaniel and Susannah, Feb. 16, 1748-9.
Elizabeth, d. of Stephen and Rebeckah, Aug. 8, 1736.
Experience, d. of Benjamin and Deborah, bp. June 24, 1759. c.r.1.
Ezra, s. of Seth and Louis, in Douglas, Sept. 3, 1773.
Farnum, s. of Nathaniel and Mary, Mar. 5, 1775.
Hannah, d. of Nethaniel and Susannah, May 24, 1757.
Hannah, d. of Nethaniel and Meriam, Sept. 8, 1785.
Isaac, s. of Stephen, bp. July 7, 1734. c.r.1.
Joel, s. of Nethaniel and Meriam, Nov. 30, 1796.
John, s. of Stephen and Ruth, Jan. 26, 1758.
Josiah, s. of Stephen and Mary, Mar. 6, 1754.
Margery, d. of Benjamin and Deborah, Mar. 10, 1754.
Mary, d. of Nethaniel and Meriam, Aug. 24, 1794.
Nathaniel, s. of Nethaniel and Susannah, Mar. 30, 1763.
Nethaniel, s. of Stephen and Mary, Sept. 28, 1748.
Newel, s. of Nethaniel and Meriam, Sept. 5, 1792.
Olive, d. of Benjamin and Deborah, May 22, 1755.
Rebecca, d. of Stephen and Abigail, bp. June 20, 1731. c.r.1.
Reuben, s. of Nethaniel and Susannah, Nov. 28, 1752.
Rhoda, d. of Benjamin and Deborah, Jan. 7, 1757.
Seth, s. of Nethaniel and Susannah, Sept. 25, 1747.
Sophia, d. of Nethaniel and Meriam, Mar. 27, 1789.
Stephen, s. of Benjamin and Mary, bp. Dec. 19, 1762. c.r.1.
Stephen, s. of Nethaniel and Meriam, July 14, 1787.
Susanna, d. of Nethaniel and Susannah, Dec. 13, 1754.
Susannah, d. of Nathaniel and Mary, June 22, 1772.
Susannah, d. of Nethaniel and Meriam, Aug. 11, 1791.
Susannah, d. of Nethaniel and Meriam, Sept. 22, 1799.
Tabatha, d. of Benjamin and Sarah, bp. Sept. 9, 1770. c.r.1.
Thomas, s. of Nathaniel and Mary, Jan. 14, 1770.
Zadock, s. of Nethaniel and Susannah, June 10, 1765.

FISHER, Abba E., d. of Capt. Josiah S. and Alma M., May 3, 1828.
Abba E., d. of Capt. Josiah S. and Alma M., Nov. 15, 1832.
Adaline Wait, d. of Josiah S. and Alma M., Sept. 8, 1845.
Almah, d. of Josiah and Almah M., Jan. 12, 1847.

FISHER, Elias, s. of Nathan and Zilpha, July 10, 1796.
Evalina, d. of Capt. Josiah S. and Alma M., Oct. 1, 1834.
Josiah, s. of Nathan and Zilpha, Feb. 26, 1798.
Josiah, s. of Nathan and Zilpha, Dec. 1, 1801.
Josiah Percy, s. of Capt. Josiah S. and Alma M., May 10, 1839.
Lavinia, d. of Capt. Josiah S. and Alma M., Aug. 14, 1824.
Louisa A., d. of Capt. Josiah S. and Alma M., May 12, 1830.
Mary C., d. of Nathan, Mar. 22, 1806.
Nathan, in Franklin, June 25, 1770. G.R.1.
Nathan, s. of Nathan, Mar. 21, 1811.
Rachal A., d. of Nathan and Zilpha, Jan. 29, 1804.
Zilpha [———], w. of Nathan, July 1, 1772. G.R.1.

FLETCHER, Abraham, s. of Benjamin and Lucy, Dec. 22, 1757.
Charlotte, alias Taft, d. of Mary and rep. d. of ———, Jan. 31, 1773.
Eliza, d. of Stacy and Rachel, 27th day, 5th mo. 1827. C.R.4.
Mary Ann, d. of Stacy and Rachel, 8th day, 7th mo. 1813. C.R.4.
Olive, d. of Stacy and Rachel, 5th day, 3d mo. 1818. C.R.4.
Rachel [———], w. of Stacy, 28th day, 9th mo. 1788. C.R.4.
Stacy, 2d day, 12th mo. 1791. C.R.4.

FLINT, Charles A., May 21, 1835. G.R.21.

FLOOD, Ellen, d. of Patrick and Ellen, Oct. 8, 1844.

FOBES, Charlotte, d. of Abner and Phebe, May 1, 1763.
Thankfull, d. of Abner and Phebe, Apr. 30, 1760.

FOLLET, Curtis Mauran, s. of Samuel W. and Louisa, May 7, 1834.
Ellen Louisa, d. of Samuel W. and Louisa, Sept. 23, 1839.
Samuel D., s. of Samuel W. and Louisa (Ellison in pencil), June 6, 1845.

FORCE, Mary, d. of Benjamin and ———, bp. July 20, 1734. C.R.1.
Zebulon, s. of Benjamin and Jemima, Oct. 7 1729.

FOSTER, Edward, 4th day, 4th mo. 1785. C.R.4.
Edward B., ———, 1821. G.R.1.
George Banfield, s. of Edward and Maranda, Aug. 25, 1809.
Helen R. [———], w. of Edward B., ———, 1824. G.R.1.
Laura Waldo Capron, d. of Edward and Maranda, Dec. 19, 1823.
Lucy Waldo, d. of Edward and Maranda, July 28, 1813 (1815, C.R.4).

FOWLER, Abigail [———], 2d w. of Barnerd, ——, 1775. c.r.4.
Alse, d. of Ezekiel and Sarah, 12th day, 6th mo. 1785. c.r.4.
Bernard, s. of Sam[ue]ll and Hannah, in Warren, R. I., 3d day, 4th mo. 1762. c.r.3.
Caleb, s. of Barnerd and Rebecca, 20th day, 3d mo. 1800. c.r.4.
Charles, s. of Barnerd and Abigail, his 2d w., 17th day, 1st mo. 1815. c.r.4.
David, s. of Ezekiel and Sarah, 3d day, 5th mo. 1791. c.r.4.
Elisabeth, d. of Samuel and Hannah, 2d day, 2d mo. 1768. c.r.3.
Ellen Maria, d. of Edwin D. and Harriet M., Jan. 10, 1837.
Ezekiel, s. of Samuel and Hannah, b. in Warren, R. I., 23d day, 12th mo. 1754. c.r.3.
Ezekiel, s. of Ezekiel and Sarah, 8th day, 5th mo. 1787. c.r.4.
Hannah [———], w. of Samuel, 12th day, 12th mo. 1733. c.r.4.
Hannah, d. of Sam[ue]ll and Hannah, 7th day, 5th mo. 1771. c.r.3.
Huldah [———], w. of John, 17th day, 6th mo. 1776. c.r.4.
Isaac, s. of Samuel and Hannah, in Warren, R. I., 3d day, 8th mo. 1758. c.r.3.
John, s. of Samuel and Hannah, 2d day, 4th mo. 1764. c.r.3.
John Milton, 14th day, 11th mo. 1814. c.r.4.
Martha, d. of Samuel and Hannah, 16th day, 3d mo. 1766. c.r.3.
Mary, d. of Samuel and Hannah, in Warren, R. I., 23d day, 8th mo. 1756. c.r.3.
Mary, d. of Ezekiel and Sarah, 18th day, 6th mo. 1789. c.r.4.
Mary, d. of Barnerd and Rebecca, 12th day, 3d mo. 1791. c.r.4.
Nancy, d. of Barnerd and Abigail, his 2d w., 20th day, 3d mo. 1817. c.r.4.
Olive, d. of Sam[ue]ll and Hannah, in Warren, R. I., 23d day, 6th mo. 1760. c.r.3.
Peace, d. of Sam[ue]ll and Hannah, in Northbridge, 12th day, 5th mo. 1773. c.r.3.
Phebe, d. of Sam[ue]ll and Hannah, in Northbridge, 16th day, 9th mo. 1775. c.r.3.
Phebe, d. of Barnerd and Rebecca, 23d day, 2d mo. 1798. c.r.4.
Rebecah, d. of Barnerd and Abigail, his 2d w., 3d day, 12th mo. 1812. c.r.4.
Robert, s. of Barnerd and Rebecca, 3d day, 8th mo. 1793. c.r.4.

FOWLER, Samuel, 8th day, 12th mo. 1730. c.r.4.
Samuel, s. of Barnerd and Rebecca, 18th day, 5th mo. 1803. c.r.4.
Sarah, d. of Samuel and Hannah, in Swansey, 20th day, 10th mo. 1753. c.r.3.
Sarah [———], w. of Ezekiel, 14th day, 1st mo. 1754. c.r.4.
Sarah, d. of Ezekiel and Sarah, 20th day, 11th mo. 1794. c.r.4.
Thomas, s. of Barnerd and Abigail, his 2d w., 28th day, 11th mo. 1811. c.r.4.
Willis, s. of Barnerd and Rebecca, 22d day, 6th mo. 1795. c.r.4.

FREBORN, Esther [———], w. of Sharp, 26th day, 8th mo. 1733. c.r.4.

FREEMAN, Oscar H., s. of William and Semantha L., Oct. 8, 1847.

FRENCH, Andrew Jackson, s. of Samuel N. and Sarah, June 19, 1845.
Fanny, d. of Jacob and ———, bp. Sept. 1, 1793. c.r.1.
Sarah Files, d. of Jacob and ———, bp. Sept. 1, 1793. c.r.1.
William, s. of Jacob and ———, bp. Sept. 1, 1793. c.r.1.

FROST, Henrietta, d. of Gideon and Henretta, Aug. 16, 1793.

FRY, Abigail, d. of John and Miriam, 6th day, 1st mo. 1784. c.r.4.
Anne, d. of John and Rachel, his 2d w., 21st day, 11th mo. 1792. c.r.4.
James Neal, s. of John and Miriam, 11th day, 7th mo. 1780. c.r.4.
John, 21st day, 1st mo. 1733. c.r.4.
John, s. of John and Miriam, 21st day, 9th mo. 1773. c.r.4.
John, s. of Obadiah and Lydia, 3d day, 2d mo. 1793. c.r.4.
Jonathan, s. of John and Miriam, 22d day, 6th mo. 1777. c.r.4.
Mary, d. of John and Miriam, 1st day, 1st mo. 1769. c.r.4.
Mary, d. of John and Rachel, his 2d w., 4th day, 9th mo. 1788. c.r.4.
Mary, d. of Obadiah and Lydia, 18th day, 3d mo. 1796. c.r.4.
Miriam [———], w. of John, 6th day, 6th mo. 1743. c.r.4.
Miriam, d. of John and Miriam, 12th day, 1st mo. 1771. c.r.4.
Miriam, d. of Obadiah and Lydia, 16th day, 9th mo. 1794. c.r.4.
Obadiah, s. of John and Miriam, 8th day, 11th mo. 1763. c.r.4.

FRY, Rachel [———], 2d w. of John, 26th day, 1st mo. 1751. c.r.4.
Rachel, d. of John and Rachel, his 2d w., 25th day, 5th mo. 1798. c.r.4.
Thomas, s. of John and Rachel, his 2d w., 9th day, 6th mo. 1791. c.r.4.
William, s. of John and Miriam, 9th day, 6th mo. 1766. c.r.4.

FULLER, Elizabeth A. [———], w. of Prentiss L., Jan. 11, 1824. g.r.1.
Prentiss L., Oct. 26, 1819. g.r.1.

GARDINER (see Gardner), Marietta Brown, d. of Emerson and Mary, July 5, 1829.
William Emerson, s. of Emerson, bp. Mar. 1, 1836. c.r.2.

GARDNER (see Gardiner), Jesse, rep. s. of Jesse and real s. of Rachel Chillson, July 10, 1797.

GARSIDE, Albert W., s. of Joshua and Helena, Dec. 3, 1837. g.r.1.
Albert William, s. of Joshua and Helena, June 22, 1843. (June 25, 1843. g.r.1.)
Andrew N., Dec. 3, 1837. g.r.1.
Charles H., s. of Joshua and Hellena, Jan. 7, 1848.
Elizabeth A., ———, 1847. g.r.1.
Henry Augustus, s. of Joshua and Helena, June 5, 1845. (June 2, 1845. g.r.1.)
James A., s. of Joshua and Helena, Sept. 6, 1836. g.r.1.
Kaiara M., d. of Joshua and Helena, Nov. 23, 1833. g.r.1.

GASKIL (see Gaskill), Daniel, s. of Benjamin and Ama, May 9, 1774.
Hosea, s. of Benjamin and Ama, Mar. 9, 1779.
Joseph, s. of Joseph and ———, Aug. 29, 1801.
Lucy, d. of Benjamin and Ama, May 16, 1784.
Nathan, s. of Benjamin and Ama, Aug. 5, 1776.
Patiance, d. of Benjamin and Ama, Feb. 12, 1771 (1772, c.r.4).
Sarah, d. of Benjamin and Ama, June 10, 1781.
Verney, s. of Benjamin and Ama, June 22, 1786.

GASKILL (see Gaskil), Amy [———], w. of Benjamin, 24th day, 11th mo. 1745. c.r.4.
Anna Estella, d. of Asa B. and Melissa M., Sept. 2, 1842.
Anne D., d. of Joseph and Issabella, Mar. 1, 1827.

GASKILL, Asa B., s. of Ezekiel and Elizabeth, 30th day, 6th mo. 1810. C.R.4.
Benjamin, 19th day, 10th mo. 1734. C.R.4.
Caroline Josephine, d. of Joseph and Issabella, June 25, 1840.
Ebenezer, s. of Jonathan and Hannah, 25th day, 6th mo. 1777.
Eliza Ann, d. of Varney and Prisse, 9th day, 12th mo. 1827. C.R.4.
Elizabeth [———], w. of Ezekiel, 12th day, 7th mo. 1775. C.R.4.
Emily Cook, d. of Varney and Prisse, 9th day, 9th mo. 1835. C.R.4.
Eunice, d. of Ezekiel and Elizabeth, Oct. 22, 1807.
Ezekiel, s. of Benjamin and Amy, 12th day, 12th mo. 1769. C.R.4.
Ezekiel Paul, s. of Varney and Prisse, 13th day, 5th mo. 1832. C.R.4.
George Henry, s. of Asa and Melissa, Aug. 22, 1845.
Hannah [———], w. of Jonathan, 12th day, 9th mo. 1739. C.R.4.
Hannah, d. of Jonathan and Hannah, 14th day, 5th mo. 1769. C.R.4.
Hannah, d. of David and Phebe, July 9, 1782.
Isabella [———], w. of Joseph, 12th day, 2d mo. 1805. C.R.4.
Joanna, d. of Benjamin and Amy, 9th day, 1st mo. 1768. C.R.4.
Jonathan, 22d day, 5th mo. 1739. C.R.4.
Joseph, 26th day, 4th mo. 1725. C.R.4.
Joseph, s. of Ezekiel and Elizabeth, Aug. 29, 1801. (29th day, 7th mo. 1800. C.R.4.)
Joseph G., s. of Joseph and Isabella, 14th day, 8th mo. 1845. C.R.4.
Levina, d. of Benjamin and Amy, 27th day, 9th mo. 1765. C.R.4.
Levina, d. of Ezekiel and Elizabeth, June 6, 1805.
Levinia D., d. of Asa B. and Melissa M., Sept. 16, 1846.
Lindley M., s. of Joseph and Isabella, Sept. 17, 1847. (7th day, 4th mo. 1847. C.R.4.)
Loviza, d. of Jonathan and Hannah, 15th day, 6th mo. 1775. C.R.4.
Melissa M. [———], w. of Asa B., 28th day, 8th mo. 1811. C.R.4.
Nathan, s. of Ezekiel and Elizabeth, Apr. 29, 1803.
Olive, d. of Jonathan and Hannah, 6th day, 5th mo. 1771. C.R.4.
Otis, s. of David and Phebe, Dec. 27, 1778.
Patience, d. of Jonathan and Hannah, 18th day, 7th mo. 1781. C.R.4.

GASKILL, Prisse [———], w. of Varney, 3d day, 4th mo. 1794.
C.R.4.
Ruth Elizabeth, d. of Joseph and Issabella, Apr. 28, 1830.
Samuel, s. of Jonathan and Hannah, 30th day, 10th mo. 1763.
C.R.4.
Sarah [———], w. of Joseph, 5th day, 11th mo. 1722. C.R.4.
Silas, s. of Jonathan and Hannah, 22d day, 7th mo. 1773. C.R.4.
Submit, rep. d. of Samuel and real d. of Lydia Keith, May 26, 1783.
Susan Anne, d. of Joseph and Issabella, Oct. 28, 1837.
Tamar, d. of Jonathan and Hannah, 11th day, 7th mo. 1765.
C.R.4.
Varney, s. of Jonathan and Hannah, 14th day, 3d mo. 1767.
C.R.4.
Verney, s. of Ezekiel and Elizabeth, July 20, 1798.

GAUNT, John F., s. of Henry, b. in England, and Mary E., b. in Ireland, in Burrillville, R. I., Feb. 9, 1849.

GEARY, Mary A., ———, 1837. G.R.2.

GERRISH, Polly Draper, d. of John of Providence and Bethiah, bp. at Providence, June 26, 1751. C.R.1.

GIBSON, Mary T. [———], w. of Hiram O., ———, 1834.
G.R.1.

GIFFORD, ———, d. of James W. and Uranah, Mar. 28, 1848. Twin.
———, d. of James W. and Uranah, Mar. 28, 1848. Twin.
Annanias, s. of Seth and Ann, Feb. 27, 1783.
Charles B., s. of James W. and Uranah, July 1, 1845.
Daniel, s. of Seth and Ann, July 10, 1791.
Farnum, s. of Seth and Ann, Aug. 7, 1778.
Joanna, 20th day, 11th mo. 1717. C.R.4.
Joanna, d. of Seth and Ann, Mar. 1, 1789.
John F., s. of Farnum and ———, May 7, 1823.
Joseph, s. of Seth and Ann, Dec. 20, 1787.
Joseph Hiram, s. of Farnum and ———, Oct. 22, 1821.
Mary Ann, d. of Farnum and ———, Apr. 5, 1816.
Mary Ann, d. of Farnum and ———, July 22, 1819.
Moses, s. of Seth and Ann, July 4, 1786.
Prudence, d. of Ananias and Sarah S., Feb. 2, 1825.
Sarah, d. of Seth and Ann, Sept. 6, 1780.
Sarah, d. of Seth and Ann, Feb. 7, 1797.
Seth, s. of Seth and Ann, Apr. 7, 1794.

GIFFORD, Seth B., s. of Farnum and ———, Jan. 9, 1818.
Seth Hastings, s. of Ananias and Sarah S., Feb. 4, 1823.
Susan Ann [———], w. of ———, 2d day, 3d mo. 1826. c.r.4.
Urania Farnum, d. of Farnum and ———, Oct. 18, 1824.
Waity Ann, d. of Ananias and Sarah S., Mar. 8, 1828.

GILES, Mary Ann, d. of Francis and Rosanna, both b. in Ireland, Nov. 17, 1849.

GILPIN, Barbara [———], w. of Edward, ———, 1828. g.r.1.
Edward, ———, 1836. g.r.1.

GLORY, Hannah, d. of Thomas and Ellen, both b. in Ireland, in Northbridge, May 2, 1849.

GOLDTHWAIT (see Goldthwaite, Gouldwait), ———, ch. of Stephen and Patience, bp. July 8, 1764. c.r.1.
Abigail, d. of Joseph and Mary, bp. Aug. 10, 1766. c.r.1.
Benjamin, s. of Joseph and Jerusha, bp. May 26, 1771. c.r.1.
Daniel, s. of Joseph and Mary, bp. Aug. 10, 1766. c.r.1.
Francis J., ———, 1829. g.r.1.
Joseph, s. of Joseph and Mary, bp. Feb. 5, 1769. c.r.1.
Mehitabel, d. of Joseph and Mary, bp. Apr. 5, 1767. c.r.1.
Nathan, s. of Stephen and Patience, bp. Nov. 2, 1766. c.r.1.
Perry Orin, s. of Stephen and Polly, Nov. 12, 1843.
Rebecca, d. of Joseph and Mary, bp. Aug. 10, 1766. c.r.1.
Ruth, d. of Stephen and Patience, bp. Nov. 15, 1761. c.r.1.
Samuel, s. of Stephen and Patience, bp. Nov. 15, 1761. c.r.1.
Sarah, d. of Joseph and Mary, bp. Aug. 10, 1766. c.r.1.
Stephen, s. of Stephen and Patience, bp. May 30, 1762. c.r.1.
Stephen, s. of Stephen and Polly, July 8, 1846.
Thomas, s. of Stephen and Patience, bp. May 14, 1769. c.r.1.

GOLDTHWAITE (see Goldthwait, Gouldwait), Abby Sophia, d. of Stephen and Polly, Aug. 18, 1841.
Ellery M., s. of Stephen and Polly (in Northbridge dup.), Dec. 27, 1837.
Henry M., s. of Stephen and Polly, Sept. 3, 1839.
Merrick, Dec. 29, 1831. g.r.1.

GOODRICH, James C. H. (James Caspar Henry, c.r.2), s. of David W. and Mary L., Oct. 31, 1845.

GORMAN, Daniel, s. of John and Ann, May 4, 1847.

GOULDWAIT (see Goldthwait, Goldthwaite), Ruth, d. of Joseph and Mary, bp. May 2, 1773. c.r.1.

GOULDWRIGHT, Naomi, d. of Stephen and Ruth, bp. Sept. 6, 1772. c.r.1.

GRANT, ———, d. of Harrison and Sarah, Sept. 1, 1845.

GRAVES, Phineas, s. of Joseph and ———, bp. Mar. 2, 1734-5. c.r.1.

GREAVES, John, Aug. 14, 1818. g.r.1.

GREEN (see Greene), Alvin Cook, s. of Samuel H. and Judith, July 17, 1834.
Benjamin, s. of Benjamin and Polly, May 13, 1786.
Benjamin, s. of Israel and Sabra, Nov. 20, 1808.
Dianthia Lorindia, d. of Charles J. and Abigail, Sept. 21, 1826.
Elizabeth, d. of Israel and Sabra, July 18, 1819.
Emily, d. of Israel and Sabra, May 26, 1824.
Hannah, d. of David and Lucy, May 6, 1798.
Henery, s. of Benjamin and Marcy, Jan. 14, 1770.
Israel, s. of Benjamin and Polly, Oct. 13, 1784.
Jabez, s. of David and Lucy, Dec. 20, 1791.
James, s. of David and Lucy, Jan. 15, 1800.
James, s. of Israel and Sabra, Oct. 6, 1811.
John, s. of Benjamin and Polly, Dec. 29, 1788.
Joseph, s. of Israel and Sabra, Jan. 16, 1810.
Judith [———], w. of Samuel H., Apr. 12, 1805. g.r.1.
Lucy [———], w. of David, 22d day, 4th mo. 1767. c.r.4.
Martha Ann, d. of Israel and Sabra, July 25, 1822.
Martha Carpender, d. of Benjamin and Polly, Apr. 14, 1781.
Mary, d. of David and Lucy, in Mendon, Sept. 12, 1788.
Mary Ann, d. of Israel and Sabra, Nov. 5, 1815.
Molley, d. of Benjamin and Marcy, May 28, 1772.
Moses, s. of Israel and Sabra, Aug. 30, 1813.
Nancy (Nancy C., g.r.1), d. of Benjamin and Polly, Jan. 20, 1783.
Olive, d. of Benjamin and Marcy, Sept. 19, 1775.
Stephen, s. of Israel and Sabra, Dec. 13, 1817.
Stephen Carpender, s. of Benjamin and Polly, in Providence, Feb. 6, 1780.
William, s. of David and Margaret, Dec. 5, 1844.

GREENE (see Green), Benjamin Franklin, s. of Merrill and Maria, June 6, 1841.
Ellen Maria, d. of Merrill and Maria, Mar. 7, 1837.
Emma F., d. of Merrill, b. in Burrillville, R. I., and Maria, July 23, 1849.

GREENE, George W., s. of George and Lucy, Dec. 23, 1843.
Merrill, Feb. 12, 1812. G.R.1.
Sarah J., d. of Merrill and Maria, June 8, 1847.
William Merrill, s. of Merrill and Maria, Nov. 2, 1834.
William Merrill, s. of Merrill and Maria, July 21, 1843.

GREGORY, John, Oct. 11, 1826. G.R.1.
Joseph, s. of Edward and Maria, Oct. 13, 1845.
Louisa Adelaide [———], w. of John, May 12, 1830. G.R.1.
Mary E., d. of John, b. in England, and Louisa A., Aug. 17, 1848.

GRISWOLD, Hamilton Byron, s. of Ralph B. and Catharine E., Apr. 28, 1847.

GROUT, Abby R., Dec. 20, 1818. G.R.1.
Cyrus, s. of John and Rhoda, July 13, 1786.
Dorinda, d. of Cyrus and ———, Aug. 19, 1810.
John, s. of John and Rhoda, Nov. 26, 1789.
Nabby Richmond, d. of John and Nabby, Dec. 20, 1818.
Susan (Susanna, C.R.1), Adams, d. of John and Nabby, Feb. 5, 1821.
Waity Arnold, d. of John and Rhoda, June 30, 1779.

GUILD, Eliza I. [———], w. of Oliver A., ———, 1839. G.R.1.
Oliver A., ———, 1840. G.R.1.

GUNN, Ellen Maria, d. of George and Mary E., July 21, 1845.
Eugene A. (Eugene Augustine, C.R.2), s. of George and Mary E., Jan. 19, 1847.
George, ———, 1817. G.R.1.
Mary E. Baylies [———], w. of George, ———, 1825. G.R.1.

HADWEN, Charles, 4th day, 1st mo. 1797. C.R.4.
Mary R. [———], w. of Charles, 1st day, 10th mo. 1806. C.R.4.
Obadiah B., — day, 8th mo. 1824. C.R.4.

HAGERTY, John, s. of Patrick and Hanora, both b. in Ireland, Apr. 29, 1849.

HAIGHT, Lydia, 3d day, 1st mo. 1823. C.R.4.

HALE, Elisha, s. of Sarah Morss, May 1, 1773.
Mason, s. of Elisha and Mary, Nov. 20, 1768.

HALL, ———, s. of Alvah and Charlotte, Apr. 25, 1845.
———, d. of Isaac and Polly, ———, 1848.
Abbie A., ———, 1840. G.R.1.
Abbie Williams [———], w. of William, ———, 1835. G.R.1.

HALL, Abigail, d. of Nathan and Keziah, Jan. 9, 1781.
Abijah, s. of Edward and Lydia, June 7, 1754.
Alonzo, s. of Andrew and Maranda, Dec. 2, 1819.
Alvah, s. of Nehemiah and Hannah, Oct. 2, 1806.
Andrew, s. of Nehemiah and Hannah, Apr. 2, 1793.
Anne Mowry Saben, [———], w. of Chandler, ———, 1826. G.R.I.
Arthur H., s. of John L., b. in Maine, and Lucy, b. in Leominster, Oct. 10, 1848.
Barna, s. of Baxter and Lydia, Dec. 19, 1784.
Baxter, s. of Nehemiah and Hannah, July 18, 1801.
Baxtor, s. of Nehemiah and Sarah, Oct. 10, 1757.
Bette, d. of Edward and Lydia, July 5, 1768.
Calven, s. of Nathan and Keziah, Sept. 13, 1791.
Chandler, s. of Baxter and Lydia, Mar. 28, 1787.
Chandler, s. of Andrew and Maranda, Sept. 30, 1824.
Charles, s. of Andrew and Maranda, Aug. 13, 1840.
Charles E., s. of Benjamin F., b. in Temple, Me., and Caroline M., b. in Lincoln, Me., July 5, 1848.
Chloe, d. of David and Deborah, Mar. 4, 1789.
Claritsa (Clarissa, C.R.1), d. of Daniel and Deborah, Jan. 22, 1791.
Clark, s. of David and Deborah, Feb. 20, 1797.
Darias, s. of Edward and Lydia, Aug. 19, 1772.
David, s. of Nehemiah and Sárah, Oct. 2, 1762.
Deborah, d. of Hez[e]kiah and Deborah, June 21, 1763.
Edward, s. of Edward and Lydia, Oct. 4, 1760.
Elisabeth, d. of Hez[e]kiah and Deborah, Jan. 6, 1754.
Ellis, s. of David and Deborah, Nov. 16, 1795.
Emely, d. of Alva and Charlotte T., May 27, 1837.
Eunice, d. of Nehemiah and Hannah, Mar. 10, 1791.
Eunice, d. of Andrew and Maranda, May 20, 1831.
Ezekiel, s. of Edward and Lydia, Feb. 5, 1752.
Ezra, s. of Edward and Lydia, June 20, 1770.
Fanny, d. of Baxter and Lydia, July 7, 1799.
Fanny, d. of Andrew and Maranda, June 23, 1816.
Ferrington, s. of Baxter and Lydia, June 20, 1791.
George, s. of Alva and Charlotte T., June 23, 1841.
George Franklyn, s. of Elijah and Elizabeth Louisa, bp. Jan. 5, 1840. Colored. C.R.2.
Hannah, d. of Edward and Lydia, Sept. 30, 1749.
Han[n]ah, d. of Hez[e]kiah and Deborah, Dec. 2, 1758. Twin.
Hannah, d. of Nehemiah and Sarah, Oct. 10, 1759.
Hannah, d. of Nehemiah and Sarah, Mar. 19, 1768.

HALL, Hannah, d. of Nehemiah and Hannah, July 11, 1797.
Hopa, d. of Nehemiah and Hannah, June 11, 1787.
Isaac, s. of Hez[e]kiah and Deborah, Dec. —, 1752. Twin.
James, s. of Edward and Lydia, Apr. 19, 1757.
John, s. of Nehemiah and Sarah, Oct. 3, 1751.
John, s. of Nehemiah and Sarah, June 30, 1755.
John, s. of Edward and Lydia, Feb. 14, 1763.
John, s. of Nathan and Keziah, May 26, 1782.
John Milton, s. of Alva and Charlotte T., Mar. 19, 1834.
Jonathan, s. of Nehemiah and Sarah, Sept. 18, 1770.
Joseph Carpenter, s. of Alva and Charlotte T., May 11, 1839.
Laura Jane, d. of Andrew and Maranda, Feb. 14, 1833.
Levi, s. of Nehemiah and Hannah, Jan. 7, 1805.
Levi Augustus, s. of Baxter and Sarah Ann, Mar. 22, 1831.
Lincoln, s. of Baxter and Lydia, Oct. 29, 1782.
Louisa, d. of Andrew and Maranda, Feb. 11, 1827.
Lucinda, d. of Jonathan and Hepzibah, Dec. 9, 1796. Twin.
Luther, s. of Nathan and Keziah, Jan. 25, 1790.
Lydia, d. of Edward and Lydia, July 10, 1765.
Marcy, d. of Hez[e]kiah and Deborah, Apr. 14, 1765.
Mary, d. of Hez[e]kiah and Deborah, Jan. 29, 1751.
Mary Ann, d. of Otis and Emeline B., Sept. 9, 1844.
Minerva, d. of Andrew and Maranda, Apr. 5, 1829.
Miranda, d. of Baxter and Lydia, Sept. 29, 1797.
Mirick Eaton, s. of Andrew and Maranda, Apr. 11, 1835.
Moses, s. of Nathan and Keziah, Apr. 14, 1785.
Nathan, s. of Nehemiah and Sarah, Aug. 26, 1753.
Nathan Weeb, s. of Nathan and Keziah, June 19, 1794.
Nehemiah, s. of Nehemiah and Sarah, Dec. 7, 1764.
Newell, s. of Baxter and Lydia, Dec. 8, 1788.
Otis, s. of Nehemiah and Hannah, Apr. 13, 1789.
Otis, s. of Andrew and Maranda, Apr. 20, 1818.
Paris, s. of Nehemiah and Hannah, in Douglas, Mar. 17, 1795. Twin.
Perrey, s. of Nehemiah and Hannah, in Douglas, Mar. 17, 1795. Twin.
Rebeckah, d. of Hez[e]kiah and Deborah, Dec. —, 1752. Twin.
Rebekah, d. of Hez[e]kiah and Deborah, Apr. 14, 1756.
Resvilla Maria, d. of Andrew and Maranda, Apr. 14, 1838.
Rosetta Elizabeth, inf. d. of Elijah and E. L., bp. Feb. 28, 1841. c.r.2.
Salle, d. of David and Deborah, Sept. 4, 1785.
Samuel, s. of Jonathan and Hepzibah, Mar. 22, 1794.
Samuel, s. of David and Deborah, Aug. 25, 1794.

HALL, Samuel Judson, s. of Alva and Charlotte T., Sept. 8, 1832.
Sarah, d. of Hez[e]kiah and Deborah, Dec. 2, 1758. Twin.
Sena, d. of Jonathan and Hepzibah, Dec. 9, 1796. Twin.
Stephen Carpenter, s. of Alvah and Charlotte, Aug. 11, 1843.
Submit, d. of David and Deborah, Nov. 20, 1798.
Thomas Ocington, s. of Baxter and Lydia, June 12, 1790.
Welcom, s. of Baxter and Lydia, Dec. 31, 1792.
Welcome, s. of Andrew and Maranda, July 20, 1822.
Willard, s. of Baxter and Lydia, Sept. 24, 1794.
William, ———, 1834. G.R.1.
William Henry, s. of Alva and Charlotte T., Jan. 3, 1831.

HALLOCK, Sam[ue]l P., 23d day, 9th mo. 1844. C.R.4.
Sarah Jane [———], w. of Sam[ue]l P., 19th day, 9th mo. 1847. C.R.4.

HAMILTON, Elizabeth Westcott [———], w. of George J., ———, 1830. G.R.1.
George J., ———, 1825. G.R.1.

HANDY, Abigail, d. of Benjamin and Mary, Sept. 9, 1783.
Almy, s. of Benjamin and Mary, Jan. 9, 1781.
Amme [———], w. of Paul, 8th day, 3d mo. 1739. C.R.4.
Benjamin, 21st day, 12th mo. 1745. C.R.4.
Benjamin, s. of Caleb and Prudence, Dec. 30, 1796.
Caleb, s. of Caleb and Prudence, June 17, 1798.
Charles, s. of Benedict A. and Caroline, Feb. 1, 1848. G.R.18.
Dinah, d. of Paul and Amme, 20th day, 1st mo. 1768. C.R.4.
George, s. of Paul and Amme, 10th day, 5th mo. 1775. C.R.4.
Lillis, d. of Paul and Amme, 1st day, 3d mo. 1779. C.R.4.
Lucy, d. of Paul and Amme, 22d day, 12th mo. 1766. C.R.4.
Margaret, d. of Paul and Amme, 26th day, 11th mo. 1772. C.R.4.
Mary [———], w. of Benjamin, 12th day, 10th mo. 1749. C.R.4.
Mary, d. of Benjamin and Mary, Nov. 12, 1787.
Paul, 1st day, 4th mo. 1737. C.R.4.
Prudence, d. of Paul and Amme, 29th day, 8th mo. 1777. C.R.4.
William, s. of Joseph and ———, Dec. 6, 1810.

HAPGOOD, Horace, ———, 1846. G.R.1.

HARBACH, Estus Warren, s. of Rufus H. and Susan S., Sept. 21, 1836.

HARDY, John A., ———, 1824. G.R.1.
Keziah [———], w. of John A., ———, 1824. G.R.1.

HARKNESS, Buffum, s. of Nathan, 23d day, 2d mo. 1772. c.r.4.
Elijah, s. of Nathan, 15th day, 9th mo. 1777. c.r.4.
Elijah, s. of James and Sarah, 28th day, 7th mo. 1805. c.r.4.
George, s. of Nathan, 7th day, 1st mo. 1782. c.r.4.
James, s. of Nathan, 4th day, 11th mo. 1775. c.r.4.
James, 28th day, 11th mo. 1810. c.r.4.
John, s. of Nathan, 14th day, 8th mo. 1767. c.r.4.
Moses, s. of James and Sarah, 20th day, 1st mo. 1799. c.r.4.
Nathan, 4th day, 9th mo. 1745. c.r.4.
Nathan, s. of Nathan, 24th day, 8th mo. 1769. c.r.4.
Nathan, s. of James and Sarah, 28th day, 2d mo. 1801. c.r.4.
Obed, s. of Nathan, 16th day, 2d mo. 1784. c.r.4.
Sarah, d. of Nathan, 30th day, 9th mo. 1779. c.r.4.
Sarah [———], w. of James, 7th day, 4th mo. 1780. c.r.4.

HARRINGTON, Anne [———], w. of Jeremiah, ———, 1800. g.r.2.
Asenath, d. of Asa and Asenah, in Worcester, June 1, 1779.
Eunice, d. of Asa and Asenah, Nov. 19, 1791.
Jeremiah, ———, 1796. g.r.2.
John Adams, s. of Uriah and Patty, Oct. 18, 1798.
Noah, s. of Asa and Asenah, in Gloucester, R. I., July 19, 1789.
Panthea, d. of Asa and Asenah, Jan. 18, 1795.
Sally, d. of Asa and Asenah, in Worcester, June 2, 1782.
Steward, s. of Asa and Asenah, in Gloucester, R. I., Sept. 21, 1787.

HARRIS, ———, d. of Almon and Charlotte, Aug. 1, 1845. Twin.
———, s. of Almon and Charlotte, Aug. 1, 1845. Twin.

HARVEY, Abby Maria, d. of John P. and Martha Ann, in Alton, N. H., Mar. 2, 1844.

HARWOOD, Amharst, s. of Nathan and Huldah, Dec. 29, 1765.
Ebenezer, s. of John and Hannah, Jan. 22, 1740.
Ebenezer, s. of John and Hannah, Feb. 8, 1745–6.
Elisabeth, d. of John and Margret, Nov. 4, 1759.
Eunice, d. of John and Margret, Sept. 10, 1773.
Ezra, s. of John and Margret, Nov. 26, 1761.
Francies, s. of Nathan and Huldah, Aug. 14, 1763.
Hannah [———], w. of John, in Mendon, June 2, 1704.
Hannah, d. of John and Hannah, Mar. 23, 1735.
Hannah, d. of John and Hannah, July 30, 1751.
Jason, s. of John (Jr., c.r.1) and Margret, Feb. 7, 1758.

HARWOOD, Jerusha, d. of Peter and Mary, Nov. 17, 1761.
John, in Concord, Apr. 28, 1703.
John, s. of John and Hannah, in Mendon, July 31, 1730.
John (Jr., c.r.1), s. of John and Margret, July 19, 1769.
Lydia, d. of Ebenezer and Margret, Sept. 29, 1772.
Marvil, s. of John (Jr., c.r.1) and Margret, Aug. 30, 1756.
Mary, d. of John and Hannah, Mar. 26, 1733.
Mary, d. of John and Hannah, Mar. 10, 1738.
Mary, d. of John and Hannah, Sept. 8, 1743.
Mary, d. of John and Margret, Jan. 1, 1764.
Mehitable, d. of Peter and Mary, July 30, 1758.
Nathan, s. of John and Hannah, Feb. 22, 1736–7.
Nathan, s. of Nathan and Huldah, Aug. 15, 1768.
Nathanel, s. of John and Margret, July 1, 1771.
Oliver, s. of Peter and Mary, Dec. 16, 1763.
Pamela, d. of Nathan and Huldah, Mar. 23, 1761.
Peter, s. of John and Hannah, in Mendon, Oct. 26, 1727.
Ruth, s. of Peter and Mary, Feb. 16, 1760.
Tristan, s. of John and Margret, Jan. 29, 1766.
Webb, s. of Peter and Mary, Jan. 2, 1757.

HATHAWAY, Elizabeth Bowen, d. of Wesson and Mercy Ann, 29th day, 3d mo. 1814. c.r.4.
Mercy Ann [———], w. of Wesson, 16th day, 11th mo. 1791. c.r.4.
Nancy A., d. of Wesson and Mercy Ann, 29th day, 6th mo. 1818. c.r.4.
Sarah Ann, d. of Wesson and Mercy Ann, 20th day, 3d mo. 1816. c.r.4.
Thomas Smith, s. of Wesson and Mercy Ann, 25th day, 9th mo. 1822. c.r.4.
Wesson, 30th day, 4th mo. 1787. c.r.4.
William, s. of Wesson and Mercy Ann, 11th day, 7th mo. 1820. c.r.4.

HAWKINS, Jimna, s. of John and Sarah, bp. Aug. 19, 1770. c.r.1.
Mary, d. of John and Sarah, bp. ———, 1775. c.r.1.
Phebe, d. of John and Sarah, bp. Aug. 19, 1770. c.r.1.
Samuel, s. of John and Sarah, bp. Aug. 19, 1770. c.r.1.
Sylva, d. of John and Sarah, bp. Apr. 28, 1771. c.r.1.

HAYWARD, A. Dora Lovett [———], w. of ———, ———, 1847. g.r.1.
Artimus, s. of Samuel and Rachel, Jan. 26, 1773.

HAYWARD, Ebenezer W., in Braintree, May 22, 1798. G.R.1.
Ellis Taft, s. of Elisha and Nancy, May 16, 1843.
Ester, d. of Josiah and Molle, Nov. 25, 1773.
Esther, d. of Dependance and Esther, Apr. 21, 1765.
Fila, d. of Samuel and Rachel, Dec. 1, 1774.
Jacob, s. of Dependance and Esther, Aug. 10, 1761.
Molley, d. of Dependance and Esther, Apr. 18, 1763.
Olive, d. of Samuel and Rachel, Sept. 18, 1776.
Ruth, d. of Josiah and Molle, Mar. 10, 1772.
Susan B. [———], w. of Ebenezer W., in Boston, Aug. 12, 1796. G.R.1.

HAZARD, Samuel, s. of Samuel and Olive, Jan. 22, 1846.

HAZELTINE, Daniel, s. of Peter and Mary, Mar. 21, 1766.

HAZLEHURST, Elizabeth G., d. of George and Almira, Feb. 15, 1846.

HEKNEY, ———, d. of James and Mary, Nov. 18, 1847.

HEMENWAY, William Davis, s. of David and Susannah, Oct. 3, 1828.
William Henry, s. of Henry and Ann, Jan. 1, 1844.

HENDRAKE, Hannah Foster, adopted d. of Edward and Maranda Foster, Feb. 22, 1808.

HENRY, Albert F., ———, 1842. G.R.1.
Alice J. Holbrook [———], w. of Albert F., ———, 1848. G.R.1.
Andrew F., s. of Richard and Lucy, Mar. 9, 1844.
Richard, s. of Richard and Lucy, Oct. 17, 1846.

HEWETT, Deborah, d. of William and Patiance, June 3, 1780.
Eli, s. of William and Patiance, Apr. 6, 1782.
Hammond, s. of William and Patiance, Aug. 19, 1786.
Patiance, d. of William and Patiance, in Norton, Feb. 26, 1777.
Rhoda, d. of William and Patiance, June 17, 1784.
William, s. of William and Patiance, in Gloucester, June 30, 1778.

HICKEY, William, s. of Catharine, b. in Ireland, Dec. 24, 1848.

HILL, Harriet Frances, d. of Paul D. and Angeline, Mar. 23, 1845.
Jacob, s. of Ralph and ———, bp. at Upton, July —, 1737. C.R.1.
Jonah, s. of Ephraim and Hannah, bp. May 15, 1737. C.R.1.

HILL, Joseph, s. of Ralph and Hannah, Apr. 2, 1732.
Marion Algeline, d. of Halsey and Ophelia, Nov. 11, 1826.
Micah Whitney, s. of Caleb and Elizabeth, June 19, 1795.
Minerva Letetia Romaline, d. of Halsey and Ophelia, June 15, 1828.
Sarah, d. of Ralph and Hannah, Apr. 22, 1734.

HIXON, Frank E., Nov. 8, 1849. G.R.1.
Harriet A., d. of Edwin and Arantha M., Jan. 12, 1845.

HOBBS, Asaana N., July 23, 1842. G.R.1.
George W., Mar. 22, 1839. G.R.1.

HOLBROOK, Abigail, d. of Samuel and Lydia, Mar. 14, 1752.
Abigail, d. of Selvanus and Thankfull, Sept. 13, 1765.
Adaline, d. of Capt. Willard and Alice, Sept. 8, 1823.
Allice, d. of William and Hopstil, Nov. 9, 1728.
Allice, d. of William and Hopstil, Apr. 26, 1734.
Amanda C., d. of Capt. Willard and Alice, May 6, 1826.
Amariah, s. of John and Zilpah, Mar. 2, 1747.
Annah, d. of William and Hopstil, June 11, 1737.
Annah, d. of Daniel and Catharina, in Mendon, Apr. 2, 1754.
Bethiah, d. of Josiah and Bethiah, Sept. 6, 1744.
Cata, d. of John and Rhoda, July 3, 1781.
Catharina, d. of John and Zilpah, ———, 1752.
Catharina, d. of Daniel and Catharina, in Mendon, Apr. 29, 1752.
Chloa, d. of Samuel and Lydia, May 13, 1762.
Chloe, d. of Moses and Annor, Nov. 18, 1799.
Chloe, d. of Stephen and Hopestill, Aug. 13, 1801.
Chloe Malvina, d. of Ellery and Hannah, Dec. 17, 1839.
Comfort, d. of Selvanus and Thankfull, Mar. 12, 1756.
Daniel, s. of Daniel and Catharina, Mar. 12, 1758.
Daniel S., s. of Capt. Willard and Alice, Feb. 20, 1829.
David, s. of Micah and Rhoda, Sept. 4, 1767.
Deborah, d. of William and Hopstil, Feb. 24, 1731–2.
Eber, s. of John and Rhoda, Feb. 12, 1773.
Eliza, d. of Ellery and Hannah, Feb. 27, 1832.
Ellery, s. of Stephen and Hopestill, June 26, 1810.
Ellery Channing, s. of Ellery and Hannah, Dec. 14, 1837.
Enos, s. of Micah and Rhoda, Dec. 16, 1772.
Eunice, d. of Peter and Lydia, Apr. 4, 1762.
Ezekiel, s. of Selvanus and Mary, Apr. 18, 1777.
Ezra, s. of John and Rhoda, Aug. 17, 1776.
Franklin, s. of Henry and Sarah, Nov. 25, 1829.

HOLBROOK, Hannah, d. of Samuel and Lydia, Apr. 17, 1754.
Hannah C. [———], w. of Ellery, Oct. 21, 1806. G.R.1.
Henery, s. of Selvanus and Thankfull, Feb. 11, 1768.
Henry, s. of Stephen and Hopestill, Apr. 19, 1804.
Job, s. of Daniel and Catharina, in Mendon, Mar. 17, 1751.
John, s. of John and Zilpah, June —, 1748.
John, s. of John and Rhoda, Dec. 16, 1774.
John 2d, s. of John and Rhoda, Sept. 12, 1778.
John W., s. of Henry and Sarah, July 9, 1833.
Jonathan, s. of Samuel and Hannah, Aug. 12, 1732.
Jonnath, s. of Samuel and Lydia, June 29, 1760.
Joseph, s. of Selvanus and Mary, Nov. 6, 1781.
Lucy, d. of Selvanus and Thankfull, Sept. 13, 1770.
Lydia, d. of Samuel and Lydia, May 27, 1756.
Lydia, d. of Samuel and Lydia, Apr. 11, 1758.
Margret, d. of Selvanus and Thankfull, Aug. 14, 1757.
Martha, d. of Micah and Mary, Jan. 30, 1784.
Micah, s. of John and Zilpah, Mar. 11, 1744.
Molley, d. of Selvanus and Thankfull, Feb. 1, 1762.
Moses, s. of John and Rhoda, June 21, 1771.
Paul, s. of Daniel and Catharina, in Mendon, Jan. 29, 1756.
Peter, s. of Samuel and Hannah, Aug. 3, 1740.
Pheebe, d. of Selvanus and Mary, Feb. 16, 1773.
Phinehas, s. of Daniel and Catharina, Apr. 8, 1760.
Rachel, d. of Selvanus and Thankfull, Nov. 6, 1753.
Rachel, d. of Stephen and Hopestill, Apr. 22, 1789.
Rhoda, d. of John and Zilpah, June —, 1750.
Rhoda, d. of Micah and Mary, Sept. 6, 1781.
Rhoday, d. of John and Hannah, June 6, 1798.
Ruth, d. of William and Hopstil, Sept. 6, 1729.
Ruth, d. of Selvanus and Thankfull, Aug. 10, 1751.
Samuel, s. of Samuel and Hannah, Sept. 27, 1730.
Samuel, s. of Moses and Annor, June 2, 1795.
Sarah, d. of Micah and Rhoda, Apr. 7, 1769.
Selvanus, s. of Selvanus and Thankfull, Apr. 21, 1750.
Seth, s. of Isaac and Mary, Feb. 24, 1752.
Silence, d. of Isaac and Mary, Nov. 21, 1756. (Silence, d. of Isaac dec. and Mary, bp. May 14, 1757. C.R.1.)
Silvanus, s. of Stephen and Hopestill, July 28, 1792.
Stephen, s. of Selvanus and Thankfull, June 19, 1764.
Stephen, s. of Henry and Sarah, Nov. 4, 1831.
Thankfull, d. of Selvanus and Thankfull, Feb. 23, 1760.
Thayer, s. of John and Rhoda, Feb. 20, 1784.
Thomas, s. of William and Hopstil, Aug. 11, 1738.

HOLBROOK, Wilder, s. of Stephen and Hopestill, Apr. 7, 1795. Twin.
Willard, s. of Stephen and Hopestill, Apr. 7, 1795. Twin.
William E., s. of Ellery and Hannah, Feb. 29, 1836.

HOLDER, Daniel, s. of Thomas and Sarah, 14th day, 8th mo. 1787. C.R.4.
Daniel, s. of Thomas and Sarah, 19th day, 5th mo. 1791. C.R.4.
David, s. of Thomas and Sarah, 12th day, 9th mo. 1788. C.R.4.
Hannah, d. of Thomas and Sarah, 16th day, 6th mo. 1782. C.R.4.
Joseph, s. of Thomas and Sarah, 13th day, 5th mo. 1785. C.R.4.
Phebe, d. of Thomas and Sarah, 25th day, 4th mo. 1779. C.R.4.
Sarah [———], w. of Thomas, 12th day, 8th mo. 1759. C.R.4.
Thomas, 28th day, 9th mo. 1754. C.R.4.
Thomas, s. of Thomas and Sarah, 6th day, 6th mo. 1794. C.R.4.

HOLROYD, Mary Ann Tillinghast, d. of Samuel T. and Mary, Apr. 5, 1818. Samuel T. was a native of Providence and died at sea a few months before the birth of this child.

HOLT, Ella, d. of William and Jane, Sept. 13, 1847.
Matilda Emma, d. of William and Jane, Dec. 7, 1843.

HOPKINS, Catherine, ———, 1835. G.R.2.

HORTON, Andrew Jackson, s. of Edward and Serena, Apr. 5, 1834.
Eliza Esther, d. of Edward and Serena, Sept. 3, 1837. Twin.
Harriet Elizabeth, d. of Edward S. and Serena, Nov. 1, 1844.
Henry Clay, s. of Edward and Serena, July 27, 1842.
James K., s. of Edward S. and Serena, Mar. 28, 1846.
Jerome, s. of Edward and Serena, Sept. 3, 1837. Twin.
Jerome Bonapart, s. of Edward and Serena, June 6, 1831.
Ruth Eliza, d. of Edward and Serena, Apr. 18, 1840.

HOUGHTON, Jane E., d. of Charles, b. in Keene, N. H., and Elvira, b. in Richmond, N. H., Dec. 20, 1849.

HOW, Polley, d. of Samuel and Salley, Apr. 27, 1797.

HOWARD, Lucy B., Mar. 31, 1817. G.R.1.
Rosannah Dorcas, d. of Joshua L. and Lucy B., Sept. 2, 1843.

HOYLE, Richard, 11th day, 5th mo. 1752. C.R.4.

HUBBARD, Mary A. W., ———, 1820. G.R.1.

HUDSON, Samuel, ———, 1822. G.R.1.

HUGGS, Susan Lettice, d. of Samuel and Maria, Mar. 24, 1846.

HULL, Elias, s. of William and Martha, Oct. 7, 1797.
Elias, s. of William and Martha, Sept. 16, 1806.
Jabesh, s. of William and Martha, Oct. 25, 1789.
Jesse, s. of James and Rebekah, Oct. 16, 1769.
Joel, s. of James and Rebekah, Aug. 29, 1771.
Joel, s. of William and Martha, May 19, 1802.
Mary, d. of James and Rebekah, Apr. 29, 1775.
Nancy, d. of William and Martha, Sept. 24, 1791.
Nancy, d. of William and Martha, Dec. 22, 1808.
Paris, s. of William and Martha, July 29, 1795.
Paty, d. of William and Martha, Sept. 11, 1793.
William, s. of James and Rebekah, Apr. 6, 1767.
William, s. of William and Martha, Feb. 9, 1800.
William, s. of William and Martha, July 23, 1804.

HUMES, Experance, d. of Nicholas and Darcos, May 27, 1750.
Josiah, s. of Samuel and Martha, July 11, 1744.
Margret, d. of Richard and Sarah, Dec. 5, 1753.
Rachel, d. of Nicholas and Margret, Aug. 24, 1735.
Robart, s. of Nicholas and Margrat, June 18, 1731.
Ruth, d. of Richard and Sarah, Dec. 8, 1751.
Samuel, s. of Nicholas and Margaret, bp. Sept. 5, 1731. C.R.1.
Stephen, s. of Richard and Sarah, Feb. 18, 1756.
Tabitha, d. of Thomas and Silance, June 17, 1774.
Thomas, s. of Nicholas and Darcos, June 29, 1746.

HUNT, Ann, d. of John and Ann, July 4, 1756.
Daniel of Gloucester, 15th day, 7th mo. 1751. C.R.4.
Polly, d. of Daniel, 26th day, 8th mo. 1799. C.R.4.
Sarah, d. of John and Ann, Sept. 5, 1754.
Selenda, rep. d. of Daniel and real d. of Jerusa Corarry, May 21, 1787.
William, s. of Ezekiel and Eunice, Jan. 12, 1764.

HUSE, Glaudus, s. of Alfred and Abigail, Dec. 3, 1798.
Sarah, d. of Alfred and Abigail, Dec. 6, 1801.
Sylva, d. of Alfred and Abigail, Mar. 30, 1800.

HUTCHINSON, Ellen, ——, 1845. G.R.1.
Hattie [——], w. of James, ——, 1844. G.R.1.
James, ——, 1839. G.R.1.
Margaret, ——, 1842. G.R.1.
Martha [——], w. of Robert, ——, 1800. G.R.1.
Robert, ——, 1794. G.R.1.

HYLAND, Richard, ———, 1845. G.R.2.

INGERSOLL, George B., June 10, 1809. G.R.1.
James D., June 17, 1808. G.R.1.
Sarah [———], w. of Capt. James D. of Boston, Feb. 3, 1782. G.R.1.

INMAN, Almira, d. of George and Ruth, 30th day, 4th mo. 1802. C.R.4.
Ann [———], w. of Samuel, 27th day, 11th mo. 1751. C.R.4.
Ann Buffum, d. of James and Nancy, 29th day, 6th mo. 1832. C.R.4.
Anna, d. of Samuel and Ann, 23d day, 3d mo. 1793. C.R.4.
Betsey, d. of James and Nancy, 19th day, 9th mo. 1824. C.R.4.
Buffum, s. of Samuel and Ann, 17th day, 2d mo. 1783. C.R.4.
Buffum, s. of George and Ruth, — day, 4th mo. 1800. C.R.4.
Charles Burns, s. of James and Nancy, 5th day, 10th mo. 1838. C.R.4.
Daniel, s. of Samuel and Ann, 15th day, 1st mo. 1773. C.R.4.
Dorcas, d. of James and Nancy, 27th day, 4th mo. 1815. C.R.4.
Edna Paine [———], w. of M. Arnold, ———, 1843. G.R.1.
Edward, s. of Samuel and Ann, 11th day, 9th mo. 1789. C.R.4.
Elisha, ———, 1802. G.R.1.
Eliza Ann, d. of George and Ruth, 12th day, 4th mo. 1807. C.R.4.
Estey, ch. of George and Ruth, 26th day, 6th mo. 1813. C.R.4.
Ethalina, d. of George and Ruth, 9th day, 4th mo. 1810. C.R.4.
Francis Henry, s. of James and Nancy, 19th day, 4th mo. 1817. C.R.4.
George, s. of Samuel and Ann, 18th day, 9th mo. 1774. C.R.4.
George, s. of George and Ruth, 23d day, 12th mo. 1818. C.R.4.
Hannah, d. of Samuel and Ann, 22d day, 9th mo. 1779. C.R.4.
Hyrena, d. of Daniel and Abigail, 12th day, 10th mo. 1803. C.R.4.
Hyrena Paine, d. of James and Nancy, 24th day, 9th mo. 1819. C.R.4.
James, s. of Samuel and Ann, 13th day, 1st mo. 1785. C.R.4.
James Orsborn, s. of James and Nancy, 4th day, 7th mo. 1829. C.R.4.
M. Arnold, ———, 1826. G.R.1.
Mary, d. of James and Nancy, 7th day, 3d mo. 1822. C.R.4.
Mary Elizabeth, d. of Elisha and Mary, May 3, 1844.
Mary G., d. of George and Ruth, 11th day, 8th mo. 1811. C.R.4.
Nancy [———], w. of James, 4th day, 3d mo. 1791. C.R.4.

INMAN, Nathaniel, s. of George and Ruth, 10th day, 1st mo. 1799. C.R.4.
Nelly, d. of George and Ruth, 31st day, 1st mo. 1804. C.R.4.
Oliver, s. of James and Nancy, 2d day, 6th mo. 1826. C.R.4.
P. Jane Bullock [———], w. of M. Arnold, ———, 1833. G.R.1.
Ruth [———], w. of George, 1st day, 9th mo. 1776. C.R.4.
Ruth, d. of George and Ruth, 20th day, 5th mo. 1808. C.R.4.
Ruth [———], w. of George, 6th day, 6th mo. 1822. C.R.4.
Samuel, 22d day, 4th mo. 1746. C.R.4.
Samuel, s. of George and Ruth, 19th day, 4th mo. 1805. C.R.4.
Urania, d. of Daniel and Abigail, 16th day, 6th mo. 1805. C.R.4.
William Albert, s. of James and Nancy, 21st day, 7th mo. 1812. C.R.4.
Witham Henry, s. of James and Nancy, 27th day, 8th mo. 1810. C.R.4.

IRONS, Edwin, s. of Francis D. and Uranah, Sept. 25, 1845.

JACKSON, Lucy Ann, d. of John and Sarah, Dec. 2, 1846.

JACOBS, Benjamin, s. of William and Comfort, May 25, 1781.
Betsey, d. of William and Comfort, Mar. 27, 1785.
Dolphios, s. of William and Comfort, Mar. 11, 1789.
John, s. of William and Comfort, May 23, 1787.
Joseph, s. of William and Comfort, May 30, 1796.
Martha, d. of William and Comfort, Sept. 2, 1793.
Sally, d. of William and Comfort, Mar. 18, 1798.
Susanah, d. of William and Comfort, Sept. 13, 1791.
William, s. of William and Comfort, Sept. 2, 1802.

JEFFERSON (see Jepardson, Jeperson, Jepherson), Sarah G., ———, 1828. G.R.1.
Susan G., ———, 1804. G.R.1.

JENNE (see Jenny), Bezaleel, s. of Seth and Abigal, Sept. 27, 1768.
Lydia, d. of Seth and Abigal, Mar. 27, 1773.
Uri, s. of Seth and Abigal, Apr. 6, 1771.

JENNY (see Jenne), Abigail [———], w. of Seth, 28th day, 10th mo. 1740. C.R.4.
Dorcas, d. of Seth and Abigail, 26th day, 6th mo. 1780. C.R.4.
Mary, d. of Seth and Abigail, 8th day, 3d mo. 1777. C.R.4.
Pruda, d. of Seth and Abigail, 5th day, 6th mo. 1775. C.R.4.
Seth, 18th day, 1st mo. 1746. C.R.4.

JEPARDSON (see Jefferson, Jeperson, Jepherson), ———, s. of ———, bp. June 20, 1736. c.r.1.
John, s. of Thomas and ———, bp. Aug. 12, 1733. c.r.1.

JEPERSON (see Jefferson, Jepardson, Jepherson), Benoni, s. of wid. Deborah, July 31, 1751.
Elisabeth, d. of William and Elisabeth of New Sherborn, Dec. 10, 1741.
Margret, d. of Thomas and Susannah, Oct. 12, 1730.
William, s. of William and Elisabeth, Dec. —, 1743.

JEPHERSON (see Jefferson, Jepardson, Jeperson), Adolphas, s. of John and Mary, Nov. 11, 1791.
Alpheus, s. of John and Mary, Sept. 20, 1802.
Amy Ann, d. of Joseph and Susan, Aug. 13, 1831.
Azubah, d. of Joseph and Ruth, Sept. 10, 1779.
Edwin S., s. of Reuben M. and Phebe, Aug. 2, 1847.
Emily, d. of Royal and Harriet B., Jan. 29, 1832.
Frank J., s. of Royal and Harriet, b. in Fitzwilliam, N. H., Oct. 29, 1848.
George Henry, s. of Adolphus and Pamela, Nov. 18, 1830.
Hannah Elizabeth, d. of Royal and Harriet B., Feb. 20, 1844.
Hellen Marantha, d. of Royal and Harriet B., Jan. 7, 1830.
Henrieta, d. of John and Mary, Dec. 11, 1812.
John, s. of John and Mary, Oct. 26, 1789.
Joseph, s. of John and Mary, Feb. 11, 1794.
Laura Amanda, d. of Royal and Harriet B., Sept. 15, 1828.
Marianna, d. of Adolphus and Pamela, Sept. 25, 1832.
Martin Van Buren, s. of Adolphus and Pamela, May 19, 1834.
Mary Eddy, d. of Joseph and Susan, Oct. 8, 1833.
Mary W., d. of Reuben and Phebe, Sept. 11, 1845.
Otis, s. of John and Mary, Feb. 10, 1788.
Phebe M., d. of Reuben M. and Phebe, b. in Barnstable, June 21, 1849.
Polly, d. of John and Mary, Feb. 13, 1807.
Royal, s. of John and Mary, Mar. 20, 1800.
Royal Lee, s. of Joseph and Susan, Sept. 23, 1829.
William Milton, s. of Royal and Harriet B., July 23, 1834.

JESSEMAN, Alexander, s. of George and Jemima, Oct. 3, 1768.
Chloe, d. of George and Jemima, June 2, 1784.
Elisabeth, d. of George and Jemima, Monday, Oct. 8, 1770.
Faithfull, d. of George and Jemima, May 21, 1782.
George, s. of George and Jemima, July 20, 1766.
Jemima, d. of George and Jemima, Wednesday, Feb. 26, 1777.

JESSEMAN, Mary, d. of George and Jemima, Sunday, Dec. 25, 1774.
Solomon, s. of George and Jemima, Wednesday, May 10, 1780.

JEWEL, Elisabeth, d. of Nathaniel and Elisabeth, May 18, 1739.
Samuel, s. of Nathanael and Elizabeth, bp. May 10, 1741. c.r.1.

JILLSON, Paul, 6th day, 12th mo. 1752. c.r.4.
Rachel, d. of Paul, 19th day, 11th mo. 1778. c.r.4.
Sarah, d. of Paul, 13th day, 8th mo. 1780. c.r.4.
Silas, s. of Paul, 15th day, 4th mo. 1784. c.r.4.

JOHNSON, Bety, d. of William and Huldah, Apr. 12, 1738.
Hannah, d. of William and Huldah, Sept. 7, 1733.
Lucy Ann, d. of Hiram and Susan, Jan. 26, 1845.
Molly, d. of William and Huldah, Sept. 16, 1735.
Molly, d. of William Jr. and Ama, in Batemans Precinct, N. Y., July 13, 1766.
Stephen G., Dec. 12, 1839. g.r.1.
William, s. of William and Huldah, Aug. 4, 1743.
William, s. of William Jr. and Ama, Sept. 30, 1769.

JONES, Simeon, s. of Benjamin and ———, bp. Mar. 29, 1752. c.r.1.
Thankfull, d. of Benjamin and Ruth, July 15, 1749.

JOSLIN, Benjamin, 22d day, 6th mo. 1753. c.r.4.
Susanna [———], w. of Benjamin, 12th day, 8th mo. 1757. c.r.4.

JUDSON, Elizabeth Ann, d. of Rev. Sam[ue]ll and Sally, Nov. 6, 1803.
Mary Chapin [———], w. of Willard, June 30, 1803. g.r.1.
Samuel, Rev., Dec. —, 1767 (b. in Woodbury, Conn., Dec. 8, 1767, g.r.1).
Samuel Hubert, s. of Rev. Sam[ue]ll and Sally, Oct. 3, 1801.
Sarah [———], w. of Rev. Samuel, Apr. 20, 1770. g.r.1.
Sarah, d. of Rev. Sam[ue]ll and Sally, May 17, 1805.
Walter Bartlet, s. of Rev. Sam[ue]ll and Sally, Apr. 19, 1798.
Walter Price Bartlet, 2d s. of Rev. Sam[ue]ll and Sally, Jan. 30, 1800.
Willards, s. of Rev. Sam[ue]ll and Sally, Jan. 18, 1807.

KEEGAN, James H. L., ———, 1846. g.r.1.

KEEN, Avis [———], w. of Josiah, — day, 4th mo. 1781.
C.R.4.
Benjamin F., s. of Josiah and Avis [no date]. c.r.4.
Elizabeth H., d. of Josiah and Avis [no date]. c.r.4.
George, s. of Josiah and Avis, 11th day, 2d mo. 1815. c.r.4.
Joseph, s. of Josiah and Avis [no date]. c.r.4.
Josiah, 20th day, 9th mo. 1781. c.r.4.
Josiah H., s. of Josiah and Avis, 16th day, 1st mo. 1805. c.r.4.
Lydia Gardner, d. of Josiah and Avis, 24th day, 12th mo. 1816.
C.R.4.

KEITH, ———, d. of Lyman M. and Lydia R., b. in Union, Conn., Sept. 6, 1849.
Aaron, s. of James and Lydia, Mar. 12, 1771.
Abigail, d. of James and Comfort, May 3, 1730.
Abigail, d. of Comfort and Deborah, July 9, 1772.
Abigail, d. of Job and Elizabeth, in Sutton, Jan. 7, 1785.
Abijah, s. of Comfort and Deborah, June 20, 1770.
Albert, s. of Lyman and ———, May 20, 1827.
Amos, s. of David and Ruth, June 17, 1768.
Andrew, s. of Lyman and ———, May 25, 1834.
Artemas, s. of Gershom and Lydia, July 14, 1776.
Artemas, s. of Artemas and Urania, Apr. 28, 1803.
Asaal, s. of Artemas and Urania, Mar. 27, 1797.
Barak, s. of Peter and Hannah, Aug. 25, 1762.
Betsey, d. of Job and Elizabeth, in Sutton, Oct. 9, 1782.
Calvin J., s. of Chapin and Elisabeth, Apr. 12, 1801.
Chapin, s. of Noah and Deborah, May 16, 1771.
Cheaney, s. of Chapin and Elisabeth, Jan. 3, 1798.
Chloa, d. of Garshom and Mary, Mar. 2, 1735–6.
Chloa, d. of Noah and Deborah, June 14, 1764.
Chloe, d. of David and Ruth, Oct. 24, 1766.
Chloe Ann, d. of Lyman and ———, Aug. 18, 1831.
Comfort, d. of James and Comfort, Mar. 6, 1742–3.
Cyrus A., Oct. 23, 1841. G.R.1.
Daniel Thurber, s. of Lyman and ———, May 12, 1825.
David, s. of Garshom and Mary, Jan. 21, 1744–5.
David, s. of Artemas and Urania, Nov. 24, 1798.
Deborah, d. of Israil and Deborah, Jan. 14, 1736–7.
Deborah, d. of Noah and Deborah, Aug. 26, 1750.
Deborah, d. of Peter and Hannah, May 2, 1751.
Deborah, d. of Artemas and Urania, Feb. 12, 1805.
Debororah, d. of Comfort and Jerusha, his 2d w., Mar. 26, 1779.
Elizabeth, d. of Israel and ———, bp. July 8, 1733. c.r.1.

KEITH, Emergene Bremer (Imogene B., G.R.1), d. of Joseph C. and Mary, b. in Northbridge, Oct. 17, 1849.
Erasmus, s. of Chapin and Elisabeth, July 28, 1792.
Esther, d. of Peter and Hannah, Jan. 23, 1758.
Eunice, d. of Comfort and Deborah, Aug. 24, 1768.
Eunice, d. of Moses and Mary, Feb. 25, 1771.
Eunice, d. of Noah Jr. and Rhoda, Jan. 27, 1778.
Francis, s. of Abijah and Polly, Mar. 25, 1796.
Garshom, s. of Garshom and Mary, Dec. 20, 1741.
George, s. of Comfort and Jerusha, his 2d w., Mar. 29, 1785.
Gershom, s. of Gershom and Lydia, Aug. 26, 1782.
Grindall, s. of Noah and Deborah, Sept. 10, 1760.
Grindall, s. of Noah and Deborah, Aug. 19, 1762.
Hannah, d. of Peter and Hannah, July 17, 1753.
Hannah, d. of Henery and Hannah, his 1st w., Oct. 29, 1766.
Hopestill, d. of James and Lydia, June 22, 1782.
Ichabod, s. of Noah and Deborah, Aug. 10, 1755.
James, s. of James and Comfort, Mar. 9, 1733-4.
James, s. of James and Comfort, Mar. 31, 1740.
James D., s. of Artemas and Urania, May 20, 1816.
Jemima, d. of Noah and Deborah, Nov. 5, 1748.
Jemima, d. of Noah and Deborah, Oct. 29, 1758.
John, s. of Garshom and Mary, Oct. 1, 1738.
Jonathan, s. of Garshom and Mary, May 5, 1732.
Jonathan R., s. of Jonathan R. and Sally, June 30, 1812.
Joseph, s. of Peter and Hannah, July 20, 1749.
Joseph Comstock, s. of Lyman and ———, Mar. 8, 1814.
Josiah, s. of James and Lydia, Sept. 29, 1766.
Kezia, d. of James and Comfort, Nov. 4, 1731.
Leonard, s. of Chapin and Elisabeth, July 15, 1795.
Lois, d. of Comfort and Jerusha, his 2d w., Mar. 13, 1782.
Lois, d. of Abijah and Polly, Aug. 21, 1791.
Lois, d. of Comfort and Jerusha, his 2d w., June 6, 1793.
Louis Winslow, ch. of Job and Elizabeth, in Sutton, June 10, 1780.
Lucinda, d. of Artemas and Urania, Aug. 19, 1813.
Luther, s. of Noah Jr. and Rhoda, June 2, 1774.
Lydia, d. of Moses and Mary, Nov. 12, 1767.
Lyman, s. of Comfort and Jerusha, his 2d w., Mar. 24, 1788.
Lyman, s. of Warren and Susan, Dec. 2, 1830.
Lyman Madison, s. of Lyman and ———, May 10, 1818.
Margret, d. of Garshom and Mary, June 1, 1733.
Marshal, s. of Peter and Hannah, May 4, 1765.
Martin, s. of Abijah and Polly, Feb. 23, 1800. Twin.

KEITH, Mary, d. of Garshom and Mary, Dec. 11, 1729.
Mary, d. of Peter and Hannah, Sept. 17, 1755.
Mary, d. of Noah and Deborah, May 18, 1766.
Mary, d. of Abijah and Polly, Apr. 12, 1803.
Miller, s. of Abijah and Polly, Feb. 23, 1800. Twin.
Miriam, d. of Noah and Deborah, Nov. 26, 1769.
Molley, d. of James and Lydia, Mar. 29, 1773.
Moses, s. of Garshom and Mary, Apr. 17, 1748.
Moses, s. of Moses and Mary, Feb. 20, 1773.
Moses B., s. of Artemas and Urania, Feb. 5, 1811.
Nathan, s. of James and Comfort, Nov. 8, 1737.
Nathan, s. of James and Lydia, June 11, 1785.
Nathaniel, s. of Nathan and Abigail, Dec. 21, 1768.
Nelson, s. of Comfort and Jerusha, his 2d w., Aug. 18, 1783.
Noah, s. of James and Comfort, in Mendon, June 11, 1723.
Noah, s. of Noah and Deborah, Feb. 5, 1746–7.
Olive Mariah, d. of Jonathan R. and Sally, Apr. 12, 1815.
Pacience, d. of James and Lydia [no date, bet. 1773 and 1779].
Patience, d. of Comfort and Deborah, Nov. 27, 1774.
Peter, s. of Peter and Hannah, May 3, 1760.
Pheeby, d. of Garshom and Mary, Dec. 15, 1739.
Pheeby, d. of Garshom and Mary, Aug. 6, 1751.
Phinehes, s. of Henery and Hannah, his 1st w., Mar. 26, 1761.
Rachel, d. of James and Comfort, Apr. 4, 1728.
Rachel, d. of James and Comfort, Jan. 20, 1745–6.
Rachel, d. of James and Lydia, Sept. 28, 1779.
Rhoda, d. of Israil and Deborah, Aug. 26, 1735.
Rhoda, d. of Gershum and Susanna, Dec. 11, 1769.
Rhoda, d. of Noah Jr. and Rhoda, July 6, 1772.
Rhoda, d. of Artemas and Urania, Feb. 24, 1809.
Rowsel Read, s. of Chapin and Elisabeth, Nov. 28, 1790.
Royal, s. of Comfort and Jerusha, his 2d w., Aug. 1, 1786.
Ruel, s. of Moses and Mary, May 30, 1769.
Russell, s. of Job and Elizabeth, in Sutton, Apr. 15, 1788.
Ruth, d. of Gershom and Lydia, Mar. 27, 1778.
Sarah Josephine, d. of Joseph C. and Mary A., Apr. 14, 1844.
Silance, d. of James and Comfort, Mar. 3, 1734–5.
Silance, d. of Noah and Deborah, Sept. 22, 1753.
Silence, d. of Israel and Deborah, bp. Sept. 14, 1740. C.R.1.
Silva, d. of Comfort and Jerusha, his 2d w., Dec. 5, 1776.
Simeon Dagget, s. of Warren and Susan, July 7, 1829.
Stephen, s. of Israil and Deborah, Oct. 12, 1731.
Stephen, s. of Peter and Hannah, Aug. 24, 1768.
Susanna, d. of James and Comfort, Mar. 5, 1726–7.

KEITH, Susanna, d. of Gershum and Susanna, Sept. 5, 1773.
Susanna, d. of Artemas and Urania, Jan. 3, 1801.
Sylvia, d. of Lyman and ———, Mar. 9, 1816.
Thomas, s. of James and Lydia, Apr. 5, 1769.
Urania, d. of Artemas and Urania, Feb. 18, 1807.
Walter Channing, s. of Joseph C. and Mary A., Mar. 17, 1847.
Warren, s. of Comfort and Jerusha, his 2d w., Feb. 10, 1778.
Warren, s. of Comfort and Jerusha, his 2d w., June 8, 1780.
Wellington, s. of Lyman and ———, Apr. 4, 1820.
Willard, s. of Comfort and Jerusha, his 2d w., May 18, 1790.
William Eustis, s. of Lyman and ———, Aug. 30, 1822.
Willis, s. of Abijah and Polly, Sept. 4, 1792.

KELLY, Abbie, d. of Albert and Deborah Inman, 15th day, 6th mo. 1847. c.r.4.
Albert Wing, s. of Albert and Deborah Inman, 16th day, 1st mo. 1842. c.r.4.
Benedict Arnold, s. of Daniel and Dorcas, 3d day, 3d mo. 1802. c.r.4.
Daniel, 23d day, 7th mo. 1777. c.r.4.
Daniel Jr., s. of Daniel and Dorcas, 5th day, 10th mo. 1806. c.r.4.
Deborah Inman [———], w. of Albert, 7th day, 4th mo. 1815. c.r.4.
Diame, w. of Wing, 24th day, 3d mo. 1774. c.r.4.
Dorcas [———], w. of Daniel, 14th day, 10th mo. 1775. c.r.4.
Elvira, d. of Daniel and Dorcas, 29th day, 10th mo. 1805. c.r.4.
Hannah Dennis, d. of Albert and Deborah Inman, 15th day, 11th mo. 1843. c.r.4.
Oliver Arnold, s. of Daniel and Dorcas, 30th day, 4th mo. 1804. c.r.4.
Seth, s. of Albert and Deborah Inman, 1st day, 8th mo. 1845. c.r.4.

KEMPTON (see Kympton), Abram Willson, s. of Ezra and Data Ann Darling of Bellingham, in Northbridge, Aug. 23, 1811.
Amasa Dudley, s. of Ezra and Data Ann Darling of Bellingham, in Northbridge, Sept. 15, 1819.
Bethiah, d. of John and Bethiah, bp. Mar. 6, 1742-3. c.r.1.
Data Ann, d. of Ezra and Data Ann Darling of Bellingham, June 30, 1813.
Deliverance, d. of Ezra and Data Ann Darling of Bellingham, Dec. 31, 1806.

KEMPTON, Eben, s. of Ezra and Data Ann Darling of Bellingham, June 18, 1804.
Ezra, s. of George, Oct. 17, 1776.
Ezra, s. of Ezra and Data Ann Darling of Bellingham, Apr. 9, 1808.
George, s. of Ezra and Data Ann Darling of Bellingham, Feb. 8, 1799.
Hannah, d. of Ezra and Data Ann Darling of Bellingham, May 21, 1802.
Samuel, s. of John and Bethiah, bp. May 27, 1753. c.r.1.

KENDALL, Anna Maria, d. of Abijah and Waity Arnold, June 14, 1819. g.r.1.
Elizabeth Jane [———], w. of William H., June 21, 1817. g.r.1.
Frances Arnold, d. of Abijah and Waity Arnold, July 22, 1814. g.r.1.
Mary Ann H., d. of Abijah and Waity Arnold, Nov. 20, 1816. g.r.1.

KENNEDY, Alonzo David, s. of William and Sally B., Feb. 8, 1832.
Mary Ann, d. of William and Sally B., Oct. 3, 1833.
Michael, ———, 1836. g.r.2.

KEYES, Amasa, s. of Abijah and Jane, Sept. 12, 1771.
Betsey, d. of Oren and Lois, Apr. 12, 1801.
Lois, d. of Oren and Lois, Dec. 14, 1793.
Olive Willard, d. of Oren and Lois, Dec. 1, 1796.
Permely, d. of Oren and Lois, Aug. 10, 1791.
Polley, d. of Oren and Lois, Mar. 3, 1785.
Rebekah, d. of Titus and Esther, Jan. 8, 1765.
Salley, d. of Oren and Lois, Dec. 15, 1788.
Wolter, s. of Abijah and Jane, Nov. 22, 1769.

KILTY, Mary, d. of James and Catharine, Oct. 10, 1844.

KING, Rhoda, — day, 6th mo. 1736. c.r.4.

KNAP (see Knapp, Knop), Anna, d. of Joshua and Hannah, bp. Oct. 5, 1760. c.r.1.
Elizabeth, d. of Joshua and Hannah, bp. Apr. 9, 1749. c.r.1.
James, s. of Joshua and Hannah, bp. Sept. 8, 1751. c.r.1.
Joshua, s. of Joshua and Hannah, bp. June 23, 1745. c.r.1.
Thankful, d. of Joshua and Hannah, bp. Oct. 5, 1760. c.r.1.

KNAPP (see Knap, Knop), Eunice, ——, 1789. G.R.1.
Joel, s. of —— and Sybil, bp. Nov. 3, 1805. C.R.1.
William M., ——, 1788. G.R.1.

KNIGHT, Ella Gertrude, d. of William, b. in Connecticut, and Minerva W., Aug. 4, 1849.
George William, s. of William and Minerva W., Feb. 20, 1841.
Walter Edward, s. of William and Minerva, Mar. 26, 1844.

KNOP (see Knap, Knapp), Abigail, d. of Joshua and Hannah, May 28, 1743.
Hannah, d. of Joshua and Hannah, Aug. 3, 1740.
Lemual, s. of Joshua and Hannah, July 15, 1733.
Molley, d. of Joshua and Hannah, Sept. 7, 1736.
Samuel, s. of Joshua and Anne, Aug. 22, 1730.
Sarah, d. of Joshua and Hannah, July 15, 1735.
Susannah, d. of Joshua and Hannah, Jan. 24, 1737–8.

KNOWLS, David, 7th day, 5th mo. 1766. C.R.4.
Samuel, 11th day, 5th mo. 1764. C.R.4.

KNOWLTON, Josiah S., ——, 1829. G.R.1.

KYMPTON (see Kempton), Abigail, d. of Ephraim and Hannah, Apr. 4, 1764.
Bethiah, d. of John and Bethiah, Apr. 6, 1757.
Ephraim, s. of Ephraim and Abigail, Dec. —, 1741.
Ephraim, s. of John and Bethiah, Mar. 2, 1755.
Ephraim, s. of Ephraim and Hannah, Mar. 23, 1770.
George, s. of John and Bethiah, Mar. 3, 1751–2.
Hannah, d. of John and Bethiah, July 27, 1748.
Hannah, d. of Ephraim and Hannah, Mar. 17, 1776.
Jeremiah, s. of Ephraim and Hannah, Mar. 7, 1766.
John, s. of John and Bethiah, Dec. 12, 1735.
Joseph, s. of Ephraim and Abigail, Aug. 4, 1745.
Joseph, s. of Ephraim and Hannah, Mar. 26, 1772.
Mary, d. of Ephraim and Abigail, July 9, 1748.
Mary, d. of Ephraim and Hannah, Mar. 29, 1774.
Rufus, s. of Ephraim and Hannah, Sept. 2, 1762.
Ruth, d. of John and Bethiah, Sept. 11, 1745.
Sarah, d. of John and Bethiah, Jan. 17, 1741–2.
Stephen, s. of Ephraim and Abigail, Feb. 22, 1743–4.
Susanna, d. of Ephraim and Hannah, Sept. 3, 1766.
Thomas, s. of Ephraim and Hannah, July 21, 1778.

LACKEY, Ellen Maria, d. of Warren and Susan C., Feb. 22, 1844. (w. of Mark H. Wood. G.R.1.)
Samuel W., s. of Warren and Susan C., Apr. 2, 1846.
Susan G. [———], w. of Dea. Warren, Sept. 24, 1814. G.R.1.
Susan S., d. of Warren, b. in Northbridge, and Susan C., Sept. 9, 1849.
Warren, Dea., Jan. 3, 1814. G.R.1.

LAIGHTON, Henrietta Augusta, d. of George E. R. and Sarah J., Oct. 31, 1843.

LAMB, Charles F., s. of Emory, b. in Charlton, and Phebe Ann, b. in Exeter, R. I., Sept. 14, 1849.

LAMBY (see Lemey), James, s. of Patrick and Mary, Aug. 3, 1845.
John, s. of Patrick and Mary, Mar. 31, 1847.
William, s. of Patrick and Mary, both b. in Ireland, Apr. 19, 1849.

LANGDON, Caroline Hibbard, d. of ———, now of Smithfield, bp. Jan. 20, 1814. C.R.1.

LAPHAM, Abigail, d. of Jethro and Sarah, 10th day, 9th mo. 1763. C.R.4.
Amasa, s. of Levi, 7th day, 8th mo. 1796. C.R.4.
Amey, d. of Levi, 2d day, 9th mo. 1786. C.R.4.
Elisabeth [———], w. of ———, — day, 6th mo. 1695. C.R.4.
Jesse, s. of Jethro and Sarah, 6th day, 7th mo. 1765. C.R.4.
Job, s. of Levi, 6th day, 3d mo. 1794. C.R.4.
Levi, s. of Jethro and Sarah, 27th day, 12th mo. 1767. C.R.4.
Lusine, d. of Levi, 25th day, 4th mo. 1792. C.R.4.
Richard, s. of Levi, 19th day, 3d mo. 1790. C.R.4.

LAPOINT, ———, s. of Ambos and Maria, Mar. 31, 1848.

LARNARD, Lurana, rep. d. of ——— Larnard, and real d. of Mary Draper, Jan. 1, 1777.

LASURE (see Lesuer, Lesure), Laura, d. of Thomas and Anna, Dec. 8, 1810.
Polly, d. of Gideon and ———, bp. Aug. 13, 1809. C.R.1.

LATAILLE, Delina [———], w. of Oliver, ———, 1841. G.R.2.
Oliver, ———, 1842. G.R.2.

LATHAM, Amy Mowry [――], w. of George W., ――, 1829. G.R.1.
George W., ――, 1829. G.R.1.

LAW, Mary, d. of Richard and ――, bp. Oct. 1, 1751. C.R.1.

LAWLER, Joseph Henry, s. of James and Sally, Apr. 14, 1831.

LAWTON, Deliverence Peck, d. of William and ――, Jan. 28, 1804.
George H., s. of John, b. in Connecticut, and Susannah C., b. in Douglas, June 10, 1849.
Henrietta Frost, d. of William and Lydia, Feb. 22, 1801.
Henry, Aug. 15, 1835. G.R.2.
Joseph Stodder, s. of William and Lydia, Oct. 31, 1798.
Julian Newman, d. of William and Lydia, May 22, 1802.
Samuel Newman, s. of William and Lydia, Dec. 6, 1799.

LEACH, Lydia Atwood Sears, d. of Benjamin M. and Hannah, Aug. 13, 1846.

LEE, Albert, s. of Briggs and Ruth, May 6, 1831.
Benjamin, s. of Benjamin and Sarah, May 7, 1771.
Chapman, s. of Benjamin and ――, bp. June 25, 1777. C.R.1.
Clara Caroline, d. of Newell and Clara Caroline, July 11, 1826.
Clementine Smith, d. of Newell and Clara Caroline, Nov. 21, 1823.
Diancy Maria, d. of Briggs and Ruth, May 22, 1829.
Experance, d. of Benjamin and Sarah, July 1, 1764.
Faithfull, d. of Benjamin and Sarah, Oct. 7, 1766.
George Taft, s. of Newell and Clara Caroline, July 20, 1828.
Henry, s. of Briggs and Ruth, Jan. 9, 1826.
Joel, s. of Benjamin and Sarah, Feb. 21, 1760.
Mary, d. of Benjamin and Sarah, Mar. 25, 1762.
Noah, s. of Briggs and Ruth, Sept. 14, 1827.
Sarah, d. of Benjamin and Sarah, May 16, 1774. Twin.
Smith J., s. of Welcome and Persis, Jan. 8, 1844.
Solomon, s. of Benjamin and Sarah, May 16, 1774. Twin.

LEGG, Abigail, d. of David and Margery, in Mendon, Feb. 5, 1782.
Adna, s. of David and Comfort, Jan. 1, 1796.
Angelina M. (Angeline Maria, C.R.2), d. of Peter, b. in Holliston, and Sarah W., b. in Northbridge, Aug. ―, 1848.

LEGG, Asa, s. of David and Comfort, in Mendon, May 7, 1792.
Basley, s. of David and Margery, in Mendon, May 9, 1783.
Edna Isidore, d. of Lyman and Hannah, Sept. 25, 1846.
Eliza P., d. of Peter and Sarah W., Nov. 15, 1838.
George W. (George Willard, c.r.2), s. of Peter and Sarah W., Sept. 6, 1834.
Hannah, d. of William and Elizabeth and niece of Abigail, w. of Moses White, bp. Sept. 22, 1754. c.r.1.
Harriet H., d. of Bailey and Mary, June 14, 1817.
Henry Holbrook, s. of Peter and Sarah W., Apr. 31, 1832.
Lucy, d. of David and Comfort, Feb. 26, 1798.
Mary, d. of David and Margery, in Mendon, Mar. 17, 1785.
Mary Elizabeth, d. of Peter and Sarah W., Apr. 8, 1831.
Mary H., d. of Bailey and Mary, July 7, 1815.
Olive Emma, d. of Peter and Sarah W., Aug. 15, 1844. (w. of Samuel W. Lackey. g.r.1.)
Samuel Adams, s. of Peter and Sarah, Aug. 31, 1843.
Sarah A. [————], w. of Peter, Nov. 7, 1803. g.r.2.
Sarah J. (Sarah Jane, c.r.2), d. of Peter and Sarah W. (Sarah A., c.r.2), July 2, 1836.
Sophia, d. of Abijah and Loies, Sept. 1, 1791.
Sylvanus B., s. of Bailey and Mary, in Mendon, June 20, 1813.

LEMEY (see Lamey), Mary Ann, d. of Patrick and Mary, Feb. 1, 1844.

LESUER (see Lasure, Lesure), Edward, s. of Edward and Chloe, Sept. 24, 1772.
Melletier, d. of Edward and Chloe, Aug. 15, 1764.
Prudence, d. of Edward and Chloe, Aug. 29, 1767.
Samuel, s. of Edward and Chloe, Nov. 1, 1762.
Willard, s. of Edward and Chloe, Apr. 1, 1770.

LESURE (see Lasure, Lesuer), Allen, s. of Gideon and Rhoda, July 18, 1795.
Chloe, d. of Gideon and Rhoda, Aug. 30, 1787.
David, s. of David and Lucinda, b. in Winchendon, in Holden, Jan. 25, 1849.
David Dunn, s. of Gideon and Rhoda, Aug. 12, 1799.
Eunice, d. of Isaiah and Rachel, Jan. 29, 1759.
Eunice, d. of Isaiah and Rachel, Feb. 17, 1763.
Eunice, d. of Gideon and Rhoda, Mar. 18, 1784.
Hannah, d. of Isaiah and Rachel, Dec. 16, 1756.
John, s. of Isaiah and Rachel, May 8, 1749.
Louis, d. of Isaiah and Rachel, May 13, 1761.

LESURE, Lucinda, d. of William and Eliza, June 29, 1845.
Mary, d. of Isaiah and Rachel, Jan. 6, 1755.
Rachel, d. of Isaiah and Rachel, —— 30, 1751.
Rhoda, d. of Gideon and Rhoda, Mar. 28, 1785.
Richard, s. of Gideon and Rhoda, May 24, 1792.
Samuel, s. of Gideon and Rhoda, May 9, 1797.
Simeon, s. of Gideon and Rhoda, Aug. 9, 1789.

LEWIS, Almy, s. of Robert and Alless, in Gloucester, R. I., Aug. 26, 1796.
Denby, s. of Robert and Alless, in Brookfield, Mar. 3, 1795.
Orton, s. of Robert and Alless, Feb. 6, 1802.
Timothy Hall, s. of Robert and Alless, May 3, 1799.

LIVERMORE, Abigail, d. of Jonas and Esther, bp. Aug. 21, 1748. C.R.1.
Elisabeth, d. of Jonas and Esther, Sept. 22, 1745.
Jonas, s. of Jonas and Esther, Dec. —, 1741.
Mary, d. of Jonas and Esther, Jan. 8, 1743-4.

LOVEL (see Lovell), Clara Ann, d. of Owen, b. in Smithfield, R. I., and Clarissa M., b. in Millbury, July 14, 1848.

LOVELL (see Lovel), H. Milton of Houston, Tex., ——, 1833. G.R.1.
Mary F. Thwing [——], w. of H. Milton, ——, 1835. G.R.1.

LOVEWELL, Baron P., May 31, 1841. G.R.1.
Louise, Sept. 30, 1840. G.R.1.

LOWELL, ——, s. of John T. and Elizabeth, Apr. 2, 1846.
Lucius, s. of John T. and Elizabeth, May 24, 1843.

LUTHER, Elisabeth, d. of William and Mary, 1st day, 3d mo. 1789. C.R.4.
James, 3d day, 11th mo. 1803. C.R.4.
Kiziar, d. of William and Mary, 28th day, 11th mo. 1782. C.R.4.
Mary [——], w. of William, 3d day, 1st mo. 1757. C.R.4.
Mary, d. of Luther and Mary, 7th day, 1st mo. 1797. C.R.4.
Sarah, d. of William and Mary, 2d day, 9th mo. 1794. C.R.4.
Susannah, d. of William and Mary, 18th day, 5th mo. 1787. C.R.4.
William, 6th day, 4th mo. 1753. C.R.4.
William, s. of William and Mary, 6th day, 3d mo. 1791. C.R.4.

LYNCH, Anne [———], w. of William, ———, 1837. G.R.2.
Ellen [———], w. of Paul, ———, 1835. G.R.2.
Paul, ———, 1839. G.R.2.

MACFARLANE, Elizabeth, ———, 1825. G.R.1.
Jane [———], w. of John, ———, 1794. G.R.1.
Jane, ———, 1829. G.R.1.

MACK, Dennis, ———, 1819. G.R.2.
Johanna [———], w. of Dennis, ———, 1828. G.R.2.

MACNEMARA, Hannah, d. of Timothy and Martha, Feb. 25, 1742–3.
Hopstil, d. of Timothy and Silance, Mar. 3, 1762.
Hugh, s. of Timothy and Silance, Aug. 22, 1759.
Martha, d. of Timothy and Martha, Mar. 11, 1745–6.

MACOMBER, Charles Lee, s. of J. Mason and Sarah A. L., ———, 1840. G.R.1.
J. Mason, ———, 1811. G.R.1.
Sarah A. L. [———], w. of J. Mason, ———, 1809. G.R.1.
William H., s. of William H., b. in Dorchester, and Mary E., b. in Hardwick, Mar. 11, 1849.

MADDEN (see Maden), Mical, rep. s. of Timothy and real s. of Elisabeth Thurston, Apr. 23, 1740.

MADEN (see Madden), Molley, d. of Timothy and Abigail, Aug. 10, 1769.
Timothy, s. of Timothy and Abigail, Apr. 11, 1772.

MAGEE, Elizabeth J., ———, 1810. G.R.1.
Johnson, ———, 1808. G.R.1.

MAHONY, Margaret, d. of Timothy and Ellen, both b. in Ireland, in Burrillville, R. I., Jan. 10, 1849.

MALLEY, Hannah [———], w. of Michael, ———, 1835. G.R.2.
Michael, ———, 1825. G.R.2.

MALONY, Eugene R., s. of John and Bridget A., Jan. 1, 1847.
John, s. of Daniel and Catharine, both b. in Ireland, Nov. 1, 1848.

MANCHESTER, Angenett J., d. of Asa, b. in Tiverton, R. I., and Angenett, b. in Smithfield, R. I., Nov. 9, 1849.

MANLEY (see Manly), Henry Clinton, s. of Michael, b. in Ireland, and Lydia W., b. in Coventry, R. I., June 30, 1849.

MANLY (see Manley), John S., s. of Michael and Lydia W., Jan. 3, 1847.

MANN, Albinus, Mar. 20, 1824. g.r.1.
Gideon, 1st day, 9th mo. 1735. c.r.4.
Mary Lavina [——], w. of Albinus, Dec. 20, 1823. g.r.1.

MARSH, Abigail, d. of Lieut. Joseph and Abigail, bp. June 1, 1760. c.r.1.
Albert Hamilton, s. of Aaron and Sylvia, Apr. 29, 1840. Twin.
Alfred Harrison, s. of Aaron and Sylvia, Apr. 29, 1840. Twin.
Avis K., d. of Joel and Betsey, 27th day, 8th mo. 1815. c.r.4.
Betsey [——], w. of Joel, 13th day, 4th mo. 1779. c.r.4.
Cornelius Judson, s. of Aaron and Sylvia, May 25, 1837.
Douglass, s. of Joel and Betsey, 18th day, 6th mo. 1813. c.r.4.
Francis Emerson, s. of Eli Cooley and Tamsen, Nov. 25, 1832.
Jasper, s. of Lieut. Joseph and Abigail, bp. Aug. 24, 1760. c.r.1.
Joel, ——, 1777. c.r.4.
Joseph, s. of Lieut. Joseph and Abigail, bp. June 1, 1760. c.r.1.
Kezia, d. of Lieut. Joseph and Abigail, bp. June 1, 1760. c.r.1.
Meltiah, d. of Joel and Betsey, 20th day, 1st mo. 1818. Twin. c.r.4.
Phebe [——], 2d w. of Joel, 9th day, 7th mo. 1794. c.r.4.
Rachel, d. of Joel and Betsey, 20th day, 1st mo. 1818. Twin. c.r.4.
Sibyl, d. of Lieut. Joseph and Abigail, bp. June 1, 1760. c.r.1.
Sylvia Jane, d. of (Dea., c.r.2) Aaron and Sylvia, Jan. 31, 1847.
Welcome, s. of Joel and Betsey, 27th day, 5th mo. 1811. c.r.4.

MARSHAL (see Marshall), Mary Jane, d. of Henry and Uranah, May 12, 1835.

MARSHALL (see Marshal), Ezra Aldis, s. of Richard, b. in Hudson, N. H., and Mary, b. in Winchester, N. H., Nov. 12, 1848.
Horace G., s. of Richard and Mary, Jan. 12, 1845.

MARTIN (see Martyn), Elizabeth [——], w. of James, ——, 1803. g.r.2.
James, ——, 1795. g.r.2.
Jemima [——], w. of Sanford M., Oct. 15, 1832. g.r.1.

MARTIN, John, 15th day, 8th mo. 1710. C.R.4.
Jonathan, s. of John and Margery, July 28, 1750.
Rachel, d. of John and Margery, May 15, 1748.
Sanford M., Oct. 4, 1825. G.R.1.
Sarah B., d. of David T. and Catharine S., Sept. 13, 1845.
Zilpha, d. of John and Margery, Sept. 17, 1753.

MARTYN (see Martin), William, s. of Isaac and Sarah, bp. at Douglas, July 2, 1766. C.R.1.

MASON, Lucy A., Mar. 1, 1844. G.R.2.

MATHEWSON, Arthur H., ——, 1843. G.R.1.
Philip, ——, 1817.
Ruth E. Horton [——], w. of Arthur H., ——, 1840. G.R.1.

McANIFF, Charles, s. of John and Betsey, both b. in Ireland, Sept. 4, 1849.

McARTHUR, Walter S., s. of Matthew and Jane, May 14, 1845.

McBRIDE, Phebe, 7th day, 5th mo. 1758. C.R.4.

McCAIG, Neil, ——, 1815. G.R.1.

McCALLUM, David S., ——, 1830. G.R.1.
Janet MacFarlane [——], w. of David S., ——, 1823. G.R.1.

McCARTHY, Matthew, ——, 1841. G.R.2.

McDONALD, Ellen [——], w. of John, ——, 1829. G.R.2.
John, ——, 1828. G.R.2.

McGLAFLIN, Benjamin F., s. of Hiram and Lucy, Jan. 17, 1848.

McINTIRE (see McIntyre), Phebe, 5th day, 4th mo. 1750. C.R.4.

McINTYRE (see McIntire), Orrin A., s. of Jeremiah S. and Jerusha, May 26, 1847.

McKNIGHT, William, s. of John and Polly, July 26, 1843.

McNAY, James, ——, 1819. G.R.1.

MEADE, Margaret, ——, 1832. G.R.2.

MELLENDY, Ebenezer, s. of John and Lydia, Feb. 2, 1757. Twin.
James, s. of John and Lydia, Sept. 18, 1761.
John, s. of John and Lydia, Jan. 11, 1753.
John, s. of John and Lydia, Feb. 2, 1757. Twin.
Lydia, d. of John and Lydia, Aug. 14, 1754.
William, s. of John and Lydia, July 4, 1760.

MERRIFIELD, Newel Goodel, rep. s. of Marcus and real s. of Levina Lusure, June 16, 1801.

MERRILL, John G., ———, 1820. G.R.1.
Sophronia A. [———], w. of John G., ———, 1820. G.R.1.

MESSENGER (see Messinger), Charles A., Aug. 11, 1811. G.R.21.

MESSINGER (see Messenger), Charles H., s. of Austin and Emeline F., Dec. 18, 1847.
Hannah Churchill, d. of Rev. Roswell and w. of William J. Held, in York, Me., Oct. 6, 1812. G.R.1.

METCALF, Lucy Seagrave [———], w. of Aaron B., ———, 1822. G.R.1.
Mary E. [———], w. of W. H., ———, 1847. G.R.1.
William H., s. of Aaron B. and Lucy of East Douglas, June 25, 1846.

MILES, George Mastin, s. of Mastin and Mary, Sept. 11, 1844.

MILLER, Nathan, s. of William and Anna, Oct. 28, 1797.

MINOT (see Minott), Charles Thayer, s. of Lois, bp. May 26, 1831. C.R.1.
Francis, s. of Francis and Mary V., both b. in Canada, Aug. 8, 1849.
Maria, d. of Buckley and Clarissa, Aug. 10, 1832.
Mary Wood, d. of Buckley and Clarissa, Feb. 1, 1829.

MINOTT (see Minot), Clara M. Dyke [———], w. of W. Henry, Nov. 18, 1844. G.R.1.
W. Henry, Nov. 6, 1829. G.R.1.

MITCHEL, Thomas Kelly, rep. s. of Richard of Gloucester, R. I., and real s. of Mary Chase [no date].

MOOR (see Moore), Jonathan, 30th day, 4th mo. 1704. C.R.4.
Mary [———], w. of Jonathan, 1st day, 2d mo. 1710. C.R.4.

MOORE (see Moor), Amelia, d. of Thomas and Susan M., Oct. 25, 1846.

MORRIS, Peter, ——, 1830. G.R.2.

MORSE (see Morss), Betsey, d. of Marvel and ——, Jan. 11, 1824.
Deborah Wheelock, d. of Nahum and Olive, in Western, N. Y., Apr. 2, 1799.
Jacob, s. of Marvel and ——, June 11, 1815.
Jesse, rep. s. of Jesse Jr. and real s. of Philadelphia Emerson, Mar. 23, 1782.
Lucretia Buckman, d. of Timothy H. and Lucy, Sept. 12, 1831.
Maria, d. of Marvel and ——, Feb. 12, 1813.
Marvel, s. of Marvel and ——, Aug. 28, 1821.
Mercy W., d. of Marvel and ——, Nov. 3, 1819.
Nahum J., s. of Marvel and ——, July 24, 1833.
Rebecca, d. of Marvel and ——, in Douglas, Nov. 18, 1807.
Samuel Read, s. of Timothy H. and Lucy, Dec. 23, 1833.
William Gilbert, s. of Timothy H. and Lucy, Feb. 7, 1829.

MORSS (see Morse), Abigail, d. of Jesse and Marcy, Mar. 3, 1783.
Anne, d. of Nathan and Mary, Aug. 7, 1754.
Betsey, d. of Jesse and Marcy, Mar. 4, 1787.
Comfort, d. of Abijah and Lydia, Nov. 7, 1752.
Cynthia, d. of Joseph and Olive, Nov. 12, 1792.
Ebenezer, s. of Jesse and Rachel, Feb. 7, 1757.
Ebenezer, s. of Jesse and Rachel, Mar. 6, 1763.
Elisha, s. of Sarah, May 1, 1773.
Eunes, d. of Jesse and Rachel, Apr. 9, 1771.
Eunice, d. of Samuel and Jane, Feb. 27, 1745–6.
Eunice, d. of Joseph and Olive, Nov. 13, 1794.
Gidean, s. of Samuel and Jane, Feb. 7, 1735–6.
Gidean, s. of Samuel and Jane, Nov. 30, 1741.
Gidean, s. of Jesse and Rachel, Mar. 8, 1765.
Hannah, d. of Samuel and Deborah, May 2, 1764.
Jesse, s. of Samuel and Jane, Jan. 13, 1729–30.
Jesse, s. of Jesse and Rachel, Aug. 18, 1758.
Joseph, s. of Jesse and Rachel, Apr. 3, 1761.
Joshua, s. of Samuel and Jane, May 19, 1733.
Levi, s. of Nathan and Elisabeth, May 1, 1763.
Lois, d. of Jesse and Rachel, Aug. 20, 1755.
Marjera, d. of Jesse and Rachel, Apr. 22, 1773.
Marthew, d. of Jesse and Rachel, Feb. 11, 1769.

MORSS, Marvel, s. of Jesse and Marcy, Apr. 18, 1784.
Mary, d. of Jesse and Rachel, Dec. 4, 1766.
Mercy, d. of Jesse and Marcy, Apr. 25, 1797.
Molley, d. of Nathan and Elisabeth, Nov. 14, 1761.
Nahum, s. of Samuel and Deborah, Aug. 29, 1765.
Nansy, d. of Joseph and Olive, Mar. 7, 1788.
Olive, d. of Samuel and Deborah, Mar. 15, 1763.
Polley, d. of Joseph and Olive, Mar. 11, 1785.
Samuel, s. of Samuel and Deborah, June 2, 1769.
Sarah, d. of Samuel and Jane, Aug. 8, 1731.
Sarah, d. of Samuel and Jane, Aug. 21, 1744.
Silis, s. of Samuel and Deborah, Mar. 12, 1767.
Willirad, s. of Joseph and Olive, Dec. 27, 1786.

MOSHER, Abiel, s. of Joseph and Meribah, 2d day, 4th mo. 1773. c.r.4.
Allen, 29th day, 5th mo. 1755. c.r.4.
Deborah, d. of Joseph and Meribah, 6th day, 3d mo. 1758. c.r.4.
Elizabeth [———], 2d w. of Joseph, 12th day, 1st mo. 1747. c.r.4.
George, s. of Joseph and Meribah, 12th day, 11th mo. 1775. c.r.4.
Hannah, d. of Joseph and Meribah, 10th day, 4th mo. 1768. c.r.4.
Job, s. of Joseph and Meribah, 22d day, 12th mo. 1770. c.r.4.
Jonathan, s. of Joseph and Meribah, 1st day, 11th mo. 1765. c.r.4.
Joseph, 12th day, 5th mo. 1732. c.r.4.
Mary, d. of Joseph and Elizabeth, 29th day, 3d mo. 1783. c.r.3.
Meribah [———], 1st w. of Joseph, 16th day, 1st mo. 1739. c.r.4.
Paulina, d. of Joseph and Meribah, 11th day, 5th mo. 1763. c.r.4.

MOTT, Eugene Rockwell, s. of Minor and Polly, Apr. 29, 1847.

MOWRY, Amey, d. of Richard and Huldah, Feb. 2, 1785.
Anna, d. of Aaron and Mary, Nov. 6, 1789.
Anne D. [———], 2d w. of Gideon, 24th day, 10th mo. 1787. c.r.4.
Arnold, s. of Gardner and Chloe Ann, Nov. 27, 1836.
Caroline, d. of Gideon and Ruth, Apr. 12, 1814.
Charels Sayles, s. of Aaron and Mary, Aug. 12, 1795.

MOWRY, Charlotta, d. of Warton and Mary, Feb. 13, 1794.
Clarinda [———], w. of Caleb, Feb. 28, 1789. G.R.1.
David, 23d day, 9th mo. 1745. C.R.4.
David, s. of David and Elizabeth, 10th day, 7th mo. 1778. C.R.4.
Duty, s. of Warton and Mary, Aug. 26, 1788.
Elizabeth [———], w. of David, 13th day, 2d mo. 1751. C.R.4.
Elizabeth, d. of David and Elizabeth, 29th day, 6th mo. 1788. C.R.4.
Emeline Maxwell, d. of Jonathan and Hannah B., 19th day, 2d mo. 1826. C.R.4.
Gideon, s. of Richard and Huldah, July 7, 1778.
Hannah B. [———], w. of Jonathan, 27th day, 8th mo. 1800. C.R.4.
Hellen Francelia, d. of Richard D. and Lucy M., May 9, 1840.
Henry, Mar. 10, 1802. G.R.1.
Huldah [———], w. of Richard, 25th day, 5th mo. 1745. C.R.4.
Huldah, d. of Richard and Huldah, in Scituate, Dec. 30, 1775.
Huldah Harris, d. of Gideon and Anna, Sept. 15, 1824.
Isabella, d. of Gideon and Ruth, 12th day, 2d mo. 1805.
Issabel [———], w. of Richard, 19th day, 9th mo. 1760. C.R.4.
Jonathan, s. of Gideon and Ruth, Feb. 2, 1801.
Lucetta, d. of Gideon and Ruth, 2d day, 1st mo. 1803.
Lucy M., ———, 1817. G.R.1.
Meriba, d. of David and Elizabeth, 14th day, 1st mo. 1784. C.R.4.
Molisia (Melissa, C.R.4), d. of Gideon and Ruth, Aug. 28, 1811.
Phebe, d. of Richard and Huldah, Aug. 8, 1780. (6th day, 8th mo. 1780. C.R.4.)
Phebe, d. of Gideon and Ruth, Sept. 19, 1808.
Polley, d. of Warton and Mary, Sept. 14, 1791.
Richard, 11th day, 2d mo. 1749. C.R.4.
Richard Dennis, s. of Gideon and Anna, Sept. 17, 1819.
Russell, s. of Aaron and Mary, Sept. 30, 1791.
Ruth [———], w. of Gideon, 4th day, 10th mo. 1780. C.R.4.
Ruth, d. of Warton and Mary, Dec. 25, 1798.
Ruth Wheeler, d. of Jonathan and Hannah B., 6th day, 6th mo. 1822. C.R.4.
Sarah, d. of Richard and Huldah, Aug. 14, 1788.
Sarah, d. of Warton and Mary, Dec. 31, 1795.
Sarah E., d. of Richard D. and Lucy M., b. in Charlton, Sept. 18, 1849.
Sarah J., d. of Horatio F. and Ann A., Mar. 22, 1848.
Sarah W., Aug. 1, 1820. G.R.1.

MOWRY, Sayles, s. of Aaron and Mary, Oct. 18, 1793.
Seth, s. of David and Elizabeth, 17th day, 7th mo. 1772. c.r.4.
Susan Lydia, d. of Gideon and Anna, Jan. 21, 1822.
Wait, d. of Richard and Huldah, Feb. 4, 1783.
William Augustus, s. of Jonathan and Hannah B., 13th day, 8th mo. 1829. c.r.4.

MULLIGAN, Matthew, ——, 1839. g.r.2.

MURDOCK, Abba Eliza, d. of Fuller and Esther, Nov. 13, 1808.
Albert, s. of Warren and Charlotte, Mar. 27, 1826.
Anne, d. of John and Bethiah, July 23, 1767.
Benjamin, s. of Benjamin and Mary, Mar. 31, 1736.
Benjamin, s. of John and Bethiah, Dec. 9, 1757.
Betsey, d. of Elisha and Hannah, Apr. 5, 1785.
Bezaleel White, s. of Hezekiah and Mary, Nov. 22, 1798.
Caleb, s. of John and Bethiah, Sept. 4, 1759.
Caleb, s. of Fuller and Esther, Feb. 16, 1817.
Chapin, s. of Elisha and Hannah, Apr. 21, 1793.
Chapin, s. of Fuller and Esther, June 20, 1823.
Charles, s. of Fuller and Esther, Feb. 11, 1815.
Cyrus Grout, s. of Moses and Dorinda, June 16, 1833.
Elisha, s. of John and Bethiah, Nov. 25, 1755.
Fuller, s. of Samuel and Zeporah, Aug. 5, 1774.
Fuller, s. of Elisha and Hannah, Feb. 19, 1781.
George T., s. of George T. and Abby A., July 4, 1846.
George Taft, s. of Fuller and Esther, Mar. 18, 1819.
Gilbert Deblois, s. of Warren and Charlotte, May 30, 1824.
Harriet, d. of Fuller and Esther, Feb. 6, 1821.
Hezekiah, s. of Samuel and Zeporah, June 30, 1776.
Jesse, s. of John and Bethiah, Sept. 13, 1762.
John, s. of John and Bethiah, Nov. 14, 1753.
John, s. of Fuller and Esther, Sept. 9, 1812.
Lewis, s. of Elisha and Hannah, Aug. 1, 1788.
Lewis Henry, s. of Moses and Dorinda, Mar. 17, 1835.
Lucius Walter, s. of Moses T. and Dorinda, Apr. 11, 1846.
Lucretia, d. of Warren and Charlotte, Mar. 6, 1828.
Luther, s. of Benjamin and Hannah, Feb. 9, 1783.
Luther Oscar, s. of Chapin and Julia A., b. in Smithfield, R. I., Oct. 6, 1848.
Mary, d. of Benjamin and Mary, Jan. 3, 1742-3.
Mary, d. of John and Bethiah, June 15, 1764.
Mary Ann, d. of Fuller and Esther, June 18, 1825.
Moses Taft, s. of Fuller and Esther, Sept. 12, 1810.

MURDOCK, Philena, d. of Fuller and Esther, Aug. 26, 1807.
Royall, s. of Benjamin and Hannah, Jan. 1, 1786.
Samuel, s. of John and Bethiah, Mar. 7, 1752-3.
Samuel J., s. of Moses T. and Dorinda, May 13, 1848.
Sarah A. Aldrich [———], w. of Cyrus G., ———, 1831. G.R.1.
Sophia, d. of Caleb and Mary, Nov. 19, 1792.
Warren, s. of Elisha and Hannah, Feb. 18, 1795.

MURPHY, Abigail S. [———], w. of Jeremiah, Dec. 31, 1815. G.R.1.
Amanda M., Feb. 13, 1815. G.R.1.
Catharine Amanda, d. of Isaac R. and Fanny, Sept. 16, 1846.
Emma Frances, d. of Jeremiah and Abigail L., Apr. 17, 1846.
Fanny Seagrave [———], w. of Isaac Ramsdell, Apr. 13, 1815. G.R.1.
Henry Clinton, s. of Isaac R. and Fanny S., Dec. 6, 1838. G.R.1.
Isaac Ramsdell, Jan. 12, 1808. G.R.1.
Jeremiah, Mar. 1, 1812. G.R.1.
Jeremiah, s. of John and Ellen, Feb. 8, 1846.
Owen, s. of John and Ellen, both b. in Ireland, Oct. 8, 1848.

NEWELL, Charlotte, d. of Ezbon C. and Patience, Apr. 29, 1829.
John Taft, s. of Ezbon C. and Patience, July 22, 1830.

NEWTON, Delia, d. of Guy S. and Dorothy, 25th day, 12th mo. 1815. C.R.4.
Dorothy [———], w. of Guy S., 29th day, 2d mo. 1788. C.R.4.
Dorothy Ann, d. of Guy S. and Dorothy, 7th day, 8th mo. 1826. C.R.4.
Elizabeth, d. of Guy S. and Dorothy, 29th day, 1st mo. 1831. C.R.4.
George, s. of Guy S. and Dorothy, 7th day, 6th mo. 1818. C.R.4.
George, s. of Guy S. and Dorothy, 17th day, 3d mo. 1820. C.R.4.
Isaac, s. of Guy S. and Dorothy [no date]. C.R.4.
Issabella, d. of Guy S. and Dorothy, 19th day, 10th mo. 1823. C.R.4.
James, s. of Guy S. and Dorothy, 29th day, 1st mo. 1825. C.R.4.
Lucy, d. of Guy S. and Dorothy, 11th day, 1st mo. 1822. C.R.4.
W[illia]m Stafford, s. of Guy S. and Dorothy, 16th day, 8th mo. 1828. C.R.4.
Zelotee, d. of Guy S. and Dorothy, 23d day, 3d mo. 1814. C.R.4.

NICHOLS, Catherine, ——, 1841. G.R.2.
George Henry, s. of Nelson and Lavina, May 19, 1843.

NUTTING, Sarah, d. of Jonas and Ruth S., Nov. 15, 1844.

O'BRIEN, ——, d. of Morris, ——, 1847.
Bridget Chapman [——], w. of Martin, ——, 1840. G.R.2.
Martin, ——, 1838. G.R.2.
Richard, s. of James and Nancy, both b. in Ireland, in Blackstone, Mar. 5, 1849.

OKELL, Amanda M., Oct. 3, 1832. G.R.1.
Joseph H., May 27, 1822. G.R.1.

OWEN, Ruth, 17th day, 12th mo. 1754. C.R.4.
Thomas, 14th day, 5th mo. 1707. C.R.4.

OWNSLEY (see Ownsly), Elizabeth, d. of Judson and Dolly, Feb. 6, 1848.
Josephine, d. of Judson and Dolly, Oct. 27, 1846.

OWNSLY (see Ownsley), Elizabeth Bowers, d. of Willis A. R. and Harriet Newell, Dec. 7, 1846.
Emma Wyman, d. of Willis A. R. and Harriet Newell, Apr. 6, 1848.

PAGE, Clarissa, in South Walpole, May 2, 1822. G.R.1.

PAINE, Chloe Ellen, d. of Dea. David D. and Jemima, Nov. 28, 1834.
David D., Dea., ——, 1788. G.R.1.
Elizabeth Grovesner, d. of Dea. David D. and Jemima, June 21, 1832.
George Francis, s. of Dea. David D. and Jemima, Aug. 30, 1837.
James Solon, s. of Dea. David D. and Jemima, Dec. 28, 1828.
Jemima F. [——], w. of Dea. David D., ——, 1800. G.R.1.
John, s. of Dea. David D. and Jemima, Nov. 19, 1823.
Mary Draper, d. of Dea. David D. and Jemima, June 11, 1825.
Morris Lee, s. of Dea. David D. and Jemima, Jan. 24, 1831.
Nathaniel Baker, s. of Dea. David D. and Jemima, Jan. 17, 1827.
Stephen, Mar. 28, 1780. G.R.1.

PAIRPOINT, Thomas, s. of Thomas and Mary, July 13, 1737.

PALMER, Paul Taylor, 16th day, 1st mo. 1826. C.R.4.
Silas, s. of Samuel and Rachel, Feb. —, 1753.

PARK, Eleanor, d. of Nathan and Sarah, bp. July 12, 1741. c.r.1.
Martha, d. of Nathan and Sarah, bp. May 14, 1744. c.r.1.
Nathan, s. of Nathan and Sarah, bp. June 11, 1738. c.r.1.
William, s. of Nathan and Sarah, bp. Dec. 17, 1749. c.r.1.

PARKER, Annie S., July 21, 1829. g.r.1.
Augustin Eugene, s. of Horace and Julia, Mar. 11, 1844.
Charles, s. of W[illia]m and Eunice, Sept. 3, 1793.
Ester, d. of W[illia]m and Eunice, Aug. 30, 1787.
John Herbert, s. of Horace and Julia, Dec. 19, 1845.
Joseph, 29th day, 2d mo. 1751. c.r.4.
Julia F. [――――], w. of Horace N., June 6, 1808. g.r.1.
Permela, d. of W[illia]m and Eunice, Mar. 17, 1790.

PARKIS, Emily Ann, d. of Ira and Emily, Feb. 8, 1844.
Emily Lawton [――――], w. of Ira, Aug. 19, 1817. g.r.1.
Ira, Feb. 13, 1806. g.r.1.
Ira H., Aug. 25, 1840. g.r.1.
S. L., ――――, 1836. g.r.1.
Sarah J., d. of Ira and Emily, Oct. 26, 1847.

PARSON, Anne, d. of William and Sarah, Aug. 31, 1761.
George, s. of William and Sarah, Oct. 24, 1757.
James, s. of William and Sarah, June 11, 1764.
John, s. of William and Sarah, Sept. 20, 1759.
Rachel, d. of William and Sarah, July 12, 1766.
Sarah, d. of William and Sarah, Apr. 12, 1768.
Thankful, d. of William and Sarah, Jan. 29, 1771.

PARTRIDGE, Abigail, d. of Lovett and Sarah, Feb. 24, 1775.
Dolly, d. of Lovett and Sarah, Dec. 4, 1776.

PECK, Abraham, s. of Simon and Sarah, Jan. 14, 1723-4.
Anna, d. of Simon and Sarah, Apr. 22, 1732.
Ebenezer, s. of Simon and Sarah, Nov. 28, 1720.
Hannah, d. of Ebenezer and Sarah, June 22, 1743.
John, s. of Simon and Sarah, Dec. 30, 1726.
Mary, d. of Simon and Sarah, Aug. 7, 1738.
Nathan, s. of Ebenezer and Sarah, Nov. 7, 1745.
Rachel, d. of Ebenezer and Sarah, Feb. 11, 1747-8.
Samuel, s. of Ebenezer and Sarah, Mar. 5, 1740-1.
Sarah, d. of Simon and Sarah, Oct. 18, 1729.
Sarah, d. of Simon and Sarah, Aug. 24, 1735.

PEES, Josiah, s. of Josiah and ――――, bp. at Upton, June 29, 1735. c.r.1.

PENIMAN (see Penniman), Adnah, s. of Jonathan and Elisabeth, Oct. 5, 1752.
Adnah, s. of Jonathan and Elisabeth, July 24, 1755.
Ann, d. of Jonathan and Elisabeth, Aug. 26, 1749.
Bethiah, d. of Jonathan and Elisabeth, Nov. 12, 1758.
Jonathan, s. of Jonathan and Elisabeth, Mar. 21, 1744.
Mary, d. of Jonathan and Elisabeth, Oct. 27, 1746.
Nathan, s. of Jonathan and Elisabeth, Nov. 26, 1766.

PENNIMAN (see Peniman), Aldis, s. of Jesse and Louis, Apr. 5, 1785.
Elkana, d. of Jesse and Louis, Jan. 14, 1782.
Pearlley, d. of Jesse and Louis, Jan. 30, 1780.

PERKINS, Catharine A. (Catherine A. Solomon, G.R.1), d. of John K., b. in New Hampshire, and Jane (Jane Seagraves, G.R.1), Jan. 1, 1849.
Helen S., d. of John K. and Mariamne, Sept. 8, 1841.
Mariamne C. (Mariamne C. Johnson, G.R.1), d. of John K. and Jane (Seagrave, G.R.1), July 7, 1846.
Sarah S., d. of John K. and Mariamne, Apr. 7, 1843.

PERRY, ———, s. of Dr. Adams and Jemima, Aug. 9, 1847.
Benjamin D., Sept. 16, 1834. G.R.1.
Charles Hartshorne, s. of Joseph Hartshorne and Mary, Sept. 14, 1824.
Experience, d. of Joseph Hartshorne and Mary, Jan. 13, 1821.
Frances Lombard, d. of Dr. Adams and Jemima W., Aug. 24, 1845.
George Williams, s. of Joseph Hartshorne and Mary, June 20, 1822.
James D., in Milford, Apr. 14, 1823. G.R.1.
Josephine, d. of Horace D. and Eliza Ann, Dec. 13, 1845.
Mary J. [———], w. of Benjamin D., June 7, 1834. G.R.1.

PERSONS, Allen W. (Allen Wright, C.R.2), s. of Nathaniel and Sophia, Aug. 14, 1847.
Amarintha Aldrich, d. of Nathaniel and Sophia, Sept. 8, 1826.
Bennet, s. of John and Lydia, Mar. 30, 1797.
Chandler, s. of Paul and Nancy, Oct. 11, 1809.
Eber, s. of John and Lydia, Mar. 25, 1785.
Elias F., s. of Paul and Nancy, Sept. 5, 1804.
Elias Frost, s. of Nathaniel and Sophia, Feb. 22, 1828.
Emila, d. of Paul and Nancy, May 11, 1813.
George Patterson, s. of George and Molly, in Northbridge, Oct. 2, 1807.

PERSONS, Henry Albert, s. of Nathaniel and Sophia, July 21, 1824.
Horis, s. of John and Lydia, Mar. 31, 1795.
John, s. of John and Lydia, Apr. 7, 1790.
John Davis, s. of Nathaniel and Sophia, Nov. 18, 1834.
Juleyan, d. of Paul and Nancy, Mar. 31, 1817.
Lyddia Whitmore, d. of George and Molly, Feb. 9, 1806.
Matilda Lion, d. of George and Molly, Nov. 13, 1802.
Nathaniel, s. of John and Lydia, Oct. 11, 1799.
Nathaniel, s. of Paul and Nancy, Oct. 21, 1820.
Olive W., d. of Paul and Nancy, Dec. 20, 1805.
Orris, s. of Paul and Nancy, Jan. 12, 1815.
Paul, s. of Paul and Nancy, Feb. 8, 1807.
Phebe, d. of Paul and Nancy, Dec. 24, 1818.
Samuel W., s. of Paul and Nancy, July 16, 1811.
Sarah, d. of John and Lydia, July 24, 1787.
William, s. of John and Lydia, June 21, 1792.

PETERS, Alexander, s. of Moses and Eleanor, Feb. 4, 1785.
Mary, 30th day, 3d mo. 1752. c.r.4.
Polley, d. of Moses and Eleanor, May 17, 1787.
Royal, s. of Moses and Eleanor, Jan. 12, 1783.

PHELAN, Bridget Hyland [———], w. of Patrick, Feb. 1, 1849. G.R.2.
Patrick, Mar. 9, 1846. G.R.2.

PHELPS, Amiel E., 24th day, 12th mo. 1833. c.r.4.
Lydia A. [———], w. of Amiel E., 21st day, 2d mo. 1830. c.r.4.

PHILIPS (see Phillips), Abraham, 16th day, 10th mo. 1757. c.r.4.
Abraham, s. of Abraham and Lucy, 27th day, 11th mo. 1785. c.r.4.
Amey, d. of Israel and Ammati, 3d day, 11th mo. 1763. c.r.4.
Ammati [———], w. of Israel, 5th day, 6th mo. 1737. c.r.4.
Ammiti, d. of Israel and Ammati, 17th day, 3d mo. 1771. c.r.4.
Annanias, s. of Israel and Ammati, 6th day, 6th mo. 1768. c.r.4.
Deborah, d. of Abraham and Lucy, 8th day, 3d mo. 1784. c.r.4.
Dinah, d. of Abraham and Lucy, 10th day, 8th mo. 1787. c.r.4.
Enoch, s. of Israel and Ammati, 15th day, 10th mo. 1764. c.r.4.

PHILIPS, Isaac, s. of Abraham and Lucy, 3d day, 11th mo. 1782. c.r.4.
Israel, 8th day, 1st mo. 1737. c.r.4.
Israel, s. of Israel and Ammati, 4th day, 4th mo. 1766. c.r.4.
Lucy [———], w. of Abraham, 15th day, 2d mo. 1761. c.r.4.
Lucy, d. of Israel and Ammati, 28th day, 3d mo. 1778. c.r.4.
Lucy, d. of Abraham and Lucy, 23d day, 2d mo. 1789. c.r.4.
Reuben, s. of Israel and Ammati, 28th day, 4th mo. 1772. c.r.4.

PHILLIPS (see Philips), Adaline Eliza, d. of Aaron and Harriet, Apr. 30, 1835. Twin.
Caroline Elizabeth, d. of Aaron and Harriet, Apr. 30, 1835. Twin.
Charles Barney, s. of George V. and Lois, Sept. 14, 1817.
George Henry, s. of Aaron and Harriet, June 30, 1833.
Martha Sales, d. of Aaron, bp. Mar. 1, 1840. c.r.2.
Sarah Dorrington, d. of Aaron and Harriet, Aug. 2, 1837.

PICKERING, Sarah Louisa, d. of Sylvester and Hannah, Feb. 18, 1839.

PIERCE, Benjamin Holbrook, s. of Timothy and Rhoda, Aug. 28, 1801.
Richard, s. of Timothy and Rhoda, June 18, 1799.

PIKE, Artimus, s. of Benjamin and Ab[b]y, Sept. 23, 1767.
Benjamin, s. of Benjamin and Ab[b]y, Sept. 28, 1769.
Jarvis, s. of Benjamin and Ab[b]y, Oct. 5, 1765.

PITTS, ———, s. of Seth S. and Susan L., Jan. 15, 1845. g.r.16.
———, s. of Seth S. and Susan L., Feb. 6, 1846. g.r.16.
Abner, s. of Job and Lois, May 9, 1778.
Amos Wood, s. of Capt. Esek and Abigail, Feb. 14, 1804.
Daniel, s. of Job Jr. and Mary, Aug. 23, 1797.
David Miles, s. of Esek and Bathsheba, Oct. 11, 1829.
Dennis M., s. of Seth S., b. in Millbury, and Susan L., Sept. 10, 1849.
Ellen Louisa, d. of Joseph S., b. in Millbury, and Caroline A., b. in Smithfield, R. I., Sept. 11, 1849.
Esek, s. of Job Jr. and Mary, Apr. 28, 1799.
Henry Adelbert, s. of Joseph S. and Caroline A., Sept. 30, 1847.
Job, Aug. 24, 1815. g.r.1.
Louisa, d. of Capt. Esek and Abigail, Oct. 30, 1805.
M. Anginette [———], w. of Job, July 29, 1823. g.r.1.
Nathaniel Daniels, s. of Esek and Bathsheba, July 1, 1827.
Seth F., s. of Seth S. and Susan L., July 14, 1847.

PLIMTON (see Plympton), Maria Malvina, d. of Silas W. and Louis, Sept. 17, 1833.

PLYMPTON (see Plimton), George H., s. of Alden B., b. in Boylston and Lydia E., b. in Athol, in Millbury, Feb. 12, 1849.

POND, Ella A. [———], w. of Fred A., ———, 1842. G.R.1.
Fred A., ———, 1844. G.R.1.

POTTER, Asa, 1st day, 7th mo. 1755. C.R.4.
Eunice [———], w. of Asa, 1st day, 3d mo. 1756. C.R.4.
Joseph, s. of William and Hephzibah, bp. May 18, 1755. C.R.1.
Mary, d. of William and He[p]sibah, Aug. 28, 1745.

POWERS, Mary Cullen [———], w. of Michael, ———, 1845. G.R.2.
Michael, ———, 1843. G.R.2.

PRATT, Benjamin Wheeler, rep. s. of Benjamin and real s. of Mary Taft, Nov. 7, 1826.
Daniel, ———, 1820. G.R.1.

PRENTICE (see Prentis, Prentiss), Josiah, s. of Jonas and Abigail, bp. Mar. 17, 1771. C.R.1.
Luther, s. of James and ———, bp. ———, 1774. C.R.1.

PRENTIS (see Prentice, Prentiss), Ellepir, d. of Jonah and Abigail, Jan. 19, 1765.
Hannah, d. of Jonah and Abigail, June 6, 1763.
Javan, s. of Jonah and Abigail, Aug. —, 1775. (bp. July 30, 1775. C.R.1.)
Samuel, s. of Jonah and Abigail, Nov. 8, 1767.
Thaddeus, s. of Jonah and Abigail, Aug. 8, 1772.
William, s. of Jonah and Abigail, Feb. 27, 1762.

PRENTISS (see Prentice, Prentis), Calvin, s. of James and ———, bp. July 5, 1772. C.R.1.

PRESTON, Ameriah, s. of Ameriah and Elisabeth, Feb. 5, 1758.
Chloe, d. of Wilson and Susanna, Aug. 2, 1771.
Daniel, s. of Wilson and Susanna, Nov. 10, 1766.
Elisabeth, d. of Amariah and Elisebeth, June 13, 1779.
Ezekiel, s. of Amariah and Susanna, Mar. 10, 1765.
Lovice, d. of Amariah and Susanna, May 27, 1770.
Otis, s. of Amariah and Susanna, Oct. 22, 1772.

PRESTON, Polly, d. of Amariah and Elisebeth, Dec. 12, 1780.
Sally, d. of Amariah and Elizabeth, bp. Dec. 2, 1787. C.R.1.
Submit, d. of Wilson and Susanna, Apr. 25, 1769.
Warren, s. of Ameriah and Elisabeth, Oct. 6, 1759.
Warren, s. of Amariah and Elisebeth, Dec. 21, 1782.
Willard, s. of Amariah and Elisebeth, May 29, 1785.
Winifred, d. of Amariah and Susanna, Oct. 1, 1762.

PRIBBEL, Uriah, s. of Joseph and Abigail, Apr. 24, 1769.

PRIEST, William, ———, 1830. G.R.1.

PUBLICOVER, Angeline, ———, 1841. G.R.1.

RANDALL, Abraham, 24th day, 11th mo. 1731. C.R.4.
Reuben, s. of Abraham, 27th day, 1st mo. 1760. C.R.4.

RAWSON, Abigail, d. of Thom[a]s and Eunice, Dec. 13, 1756.
Abner, s. of Edmond and Elisabeth, Apr. 27, 1721.
Abner, s. of Edward and Lucy, May 15, 1796.
Abner H., s. of Charles and Salley, Oct. 25, 1805.
Allen, s. of Seth and Deborah, Nov. 11, 1788.
Alpheus, s. of Charles and Salley, Mar. 31, 1797.
Amery, s. of Seth and Deborah, Jan. 25, 1793.
Ary Venner, s. of Isaac and Polley, June 5, 1795.
Asa, s. of Joel and Molley, May 4, 1775.
B. A., Feb. 3, 1818. G.R.1.
Bala (Bela Gardener, C.R.1), s. of Thom[a]s and Eunice, Aug. 14, 1760.
Calven, s. of Timothy and Chloe, June 4, 1783.
Calvin, s. of Seth and Deborah, May 13, 1797.
Chancey, s. of Timothy and Chloe, Oct. 23, 1770.
Charl[e]s, s. of Silas and Sarah, Oct. 29, 1768.
Charles Buffington, s. of Simon and Levina, Dec. 18, 1810.
Charles Clark, s. of Abner H. and Eveline, Apr. 26, 1831.
Charles Mason, s. of Charles and Salley, Apr. 26, 1803.
Charles Newton, s. of Charles B. and Mary A., Oct. 28, 1836.
Charlotte Emeline, d. of Otis and Mary, Apr. 9, 1811.
Cynthia, d. of John and Lydia, June 19, 1794.
Cynthia, d. of John and Lydia, Nov. 28, 1795.
Daniel Johnson, s. of Abner and Martha, in Shrewsbury, Nov. 25, 1820.
Daniel Ward, s. of John and Lydia, July 21, 1792.
Dearing Jones, s. of Edward and Lucy, Aug. 8, 1798.
Delia Ann, d. of Asa and ———, Oct. 10, 1807.
Dolley, d. of Timothy and Chloe, Mar. 10, 1768.

RAWSON, Edmand, s. of Edmand and Martha, Dec. 29, 1744.
Edmond, s. of Edmond and Elisabeth, Aug. 16, 1718.
Edmund, s. of Edmand and Martha, June 2, 1751.
Edward, s. of Nathan and Mary, June 17, 1773.
Elisabeth, d. of Nathan and Mary, his 2d w., Jan. 8, 1765.
Elsey Mowrey, d. of Grindal and Mary, Aug. 23, 1812.
Eunice, d. of Thom[a]s and Eunice, Mar. 5, 1765.
Ezbon Newell, s. of Abner and Martha, May 21, 1822.
Garner, s. of Thom[a]s and Eunice, Aug. 23, 1762.
George Clinton, s. of Charles B. and Mary A., July 8, 1835.
George Washington, s. of Edward and Lucy, Sept. 8, 1803.
Gerry Wheelor, s. of John and Lydia, Oct. 22, 1797.
Grindal, s. of John and Mary, Apr. 23, 1735.
Grindal, s. of Joel and Molley, Oct. 27, 1769.
Hannah, d. of Edmund and Sarah, Jan. 28, 1771.
Hannah Park, d. of Asa and ———, Sept. 23, 1811.
Hooker, s. of John and Mary, Dec. 3, 1738.
Horace, s. of Otis and Mary, Sept. 26, 1807.
Isaac, s. of Nathan and Mary, his 2d w., Apr. 23, 1767.
James, s. of Nathan and Mary, his 2d w., Dec. 22, 1775.
James Augustus, s. of James and Polly, Dec. 24, 1819.
James Maddison, s. of Asa and ———, July 6, 1809.
Jane Augusta, d. of Charles B. and Mary A., Jan. 10, 1840.
John, s. of Nathan and Mary, his 2d w., Apr. 26, 1769.
John Aldrich, s. of Simon Jr. and Roxalana, July 1, 1837.
Jonah, s. of John and Mary (Mercy, C.R.1), Mar. 30, 1736.
Joseph, s. of Edmand (Jr., C.R.1) and Martha, Sept. 21, 1756.
Joseph, s. of Otis and Mary, Mar. 20, 1817.
Keith Wood, s. of John and Lydia, July 29, 1799.
Levina, d. of Simon and Levina, June 24, 1807.
Louisa J. [———], w. of James A., Mar. 31, 1826. G.R.1.
Lucretia, d. of Otis and Mary, Apr. 22, 1819.
Lucy, d. of Timothy and Chloe, Dec. 23, 1775.
Luther, s. of Timothy and Chloe, Dec. 13, 1780.
Lydia, d. of Thom[a]s and Eunice, Aug. 19, 1758.
Lymon, s. of Thom[a]s and Eunice, June 28, 1772.
Marcy, d. of Silas and Sarah, Nov. 10, 1770.
Martha, d. of Seth and Deborah, Sept. 4, 1786.
Martha Relief, d. of Abner and Martha, Sept. 27, 1823.
Mary, d. of John and Mary, Feb. 1, 1739-40.
Mary, d. of Nathan and Mary, his 2d w., Mar. 22, 1771.
Mary, d. of Charles and Salley, July 1, 1808.
Mary Almira, d. of James A. and Louisa J., Sept. 11, 1845.
Mary Ann, d. of James and Polly, June 17, 1809.

RAWSON, Mary J. [———], w. of B. A., Aug. 27, 1820. G.R.1.
Merrit, s. of James and Polly, June 18, 1805.
Mille, d. of Silas and Sarah, Dec. 23, 1772.
Molly, d. of John and Mary (Mercy, C.R.1), Apr. 2, 1741.
Nathan, s. of Edmond and Elisabeth, Aug. 4, 1724.
Nathan, s. of Nathan and Mary, Dec. 10, 1762.
Nathan, s. of Edward and Lucy, Jan. 20, 1801.
Olive, d. of Thom[a]s and Eunice, May 23, 1769.
Otis, s. of Joel and Molley, Aug. 19, 1780.
Otis Newel, s. of Otis and Mary, June 17, 1821.
Parly, d. of Timothy and Chloe, May 9, 1773.
Perliney, d. of Timothy and Chloe, Mar. 20, 1787.
Permela, d. of Seth and Deborah, June 3, 1790.
Polly, rep. d. of Seth and real d. of Deborah Torry, May 4, 1781.
Prisalla, d. of William and Deziah, Apr. 16, 1763.
Prude, d. of William and Desiar, May 16, 1764.
Rachel, d. of Edmand (Jr., C.R.1) and Martha, Sept. 21, 1753.
Rachel, d. of William and Desiar, June 17, 1768.
Rachel Parn, d. of Joel and Molley, Apr. 3, 1764.
Rebeka, d. of Samuel and Molley, Sept. 30, 1785.
Rhoda, d. of Abner and Mary, Oct. 4, 1749.
Rhoda, d. of Joel and Molley, Nov. 22, 1777.
Salley, d. of Timothy and Chloe, Jan. 6, 1778.
Sally D., d. of James and Polly, Jan. 10, 1807.
Samuel, s. of Edmand (Jr., C.R.1) and Martha, May 20, 1746.
Samuel Read, s. of Thom[a]s and Eunice, Mar. 27, 1767.
Sarah Hale, d. of Abner H. and Eveline, Feb. 18, 1836.
Seth, s. of Edmand and Martha, Nov. 20, 1748.
Seth, s. of Edmand and Martha, Oct. 2, 1759.
Silas, s. of Abner and Mary, July 26, 1746.
Silas, s. of Simon and Levina, Mar. 24, 1802.
Silvia, d. of Otis and Mary, Mar. 16, 1813.
Simon, s. of Silas and Sarah, Apr. 9, 1775.
Simon, s. of Simon and Levina, Apr. 3, 1812.
Simon Putnam, s. of Simon Jr. and Roxalana, Aug. 27, 1838.
Sophe, d. of Charles and Salley, Oct. 21, 1798.
Stephen, s. of Joel and Molley, Dec. 18, 1772.
Susannah, d. of Joel and Molley, Mar. 25, 1767.
Thomas, s. of William and Desiar, Aug. 6, 1766.
Timothy, s. of Abner and Mary, Oct. 2, 1747.
Warren, s. of Seth and Deborah, May 7, 1795.
William, s. of William and Desiar, June 12, 1765.
Zepporah, d. of William and Deziah, in Upton, Aug. 27, 1761.

RAY, George E., Dec. 3, 1825. G.R.1.
Rexavilla M. Hall [———], w. of George E., Apr. 14, 1838. G.R.1.

RAYMER, James, 2d day, 2d mo. 1733. C.R.4.

READ (see Reed), Abigail, d. of Samuel and Ruth, Dec. 12, 1736.
Abigail, d. of Daniel and Mary, Jan. 22, 1769.
Abigail Murdock, d. of Samuel and Nancy, July 12, 1796.
Azubah, d. of Moses and Mary, bp. Oct. 12, 1731. C.R.1.
Benjamin, s. of Ebenezer (Jr., C.R.1) and Hannah, Jan. 21, 1739–40.
Betsa Hunt, d. of Thaddeus and Hannah, Oct. 3, 1781.
Catharina, d. of Samuel and Ruth, in Mendon, Feb. 23, 1739–40.
Cheney, s. of Joseph and Eunice, Sept. 9, 1758.
Comfort, d. of Samuel Jr. and Abigail, bp. Oct. 25, 1767. C.R.1.
Daniel, s. of Daniel and Sarah, June 3, 1743.
David, s. of David and Thankful, Nov. 14, 1744.
David, s. of David and Patience, bp. at New Sherborn, May 7, 1746. C.R.1.
Ebenezer, s. of Ebenezer and Hannah, Aug. 24, 1741.
Ebenezer, s. of David and Thankful, bp. Dec. 1, 1760. C.R.1.
Elezabeth, d. of John Sr. and Elizabeth, bp. Sept. 12, 1731. C.R.1.
Elizabeth, d. of Thomas and Ruth, Oct. 19, 1769.
Elizabeth Hill, d. of Samuel and Nancy, Sept. 18, 1798.
Esther, d. of John Sr. and Elizabeth, bp. Sept. 12, 1731. C.R.1.
Esther, d. of Ebenezer and Hannah, Aug. 24, 1739.
Eunice, d. of Samuel and Ruth, Oct. 27, 1733.
Eunice, d. of Joseph and Eunice, Dec. 26, 1755.
Ezra, s. of Daniel and Sarah, June 28, 1737.
George W., s. of Seth and Hannah, Mar. 24, 1782.
Hannah, d. of Moses and Mary, bp. June 14, 1741. C.R.1.
Hannah, d. of Joseph and Eunice, July 24, 1762.
Henery, s. of David and Thankful, Jan. 7, 1734–5.
Henry Joseph, s. of Seth and Hannah, Dec. 20, 1779.
James Jordan, s. of (Dea., C.R.1) Samuel and Elisabeth, his 2d w., July 18, 1750.
James Manning, s. of Seth and Hannah, Jan. 6, 1770.
Japhet, s. of David and Thankful, Sept. 6, 1736.
John, s. of John Sr. and Elizabeth, bp. Sept. 12, 1731. C.R.1.
John, s. of John and Lucy, June —, 1742–3.
John, s. of Seth and Hannah, Dec. 23, 1771.
John Taft, s. of John (Jr., C.R.1) and Hannah, Mar. 4, 1769.

READ, Joseph, s. of John and Lucy, Mar. 6, 1731-2.
Joseph, s. of Joseph and Eunice, Sept. 1, 1760.
Josiah, s. of John and Lucy, July 23, 1753.
Lydia, d. of David and Thankful, Nov. 8, 1738.
Lydia, d. of Samuel and Ruth, Jan. 10, 1741-2.
Lydia, d. of Samuel and Abigail, Feb. 4, 1759.
Martha, d. of Thomas and Martha, Feb. 15, 1765.
Mary, d. of David and Thankful, Oct. 14, 1740.
Mary, d. of Moses and Mary, bp. June 14, 1741. C.R.I.
Mary, d. of Daniel and Mary, Feb. 5, 1767.
Mary Green, d. of Samuel and Nancy, Oct. 22, 1800.
Moses, 2d, s. of Moses and Mary, bp. June 14, 1741. C.R.I.
Nancy Whitney, d. of Samuel and Nancy, Aug. 3, 1794.
Nathan, s. of Joseph and Eunice, Dec. 9, 1754.
Nathan, s. of John (Jr., C.R.I) and Hannah, Jan. 24, 1766.
Peter, s. of John and Lucy, Nov. 13, 1735.
Phila, d. of John (Jr., C.R.I) and Hannah, Dec. 13, 1763.
Polley, d. of Seth and Hannah, Apr. 19, 1784.
Rachel, d. of John Sr. and Elizabeth, bp. Sept. 12, 1731. C.R.I.
Ruth, d. of Samuel and Ruth, Apr. 8, 1732.
Ruth, d. of Samuel (Jr., C.R.I) and Abigail, Nov. 3, 1764.
Sally, d. of Thaddeus and Hannah, Feb. 28, 1784.
Sally Adams, d. of Seth and Hannah, Nov. 1, 1777.
Samuel, s. of Samuel and Ruth, Apr. 12, 1730.
Samuel, s. of Samuel and Abigail, Jan. 10, 1756.
Samuel, s. of Samuel (Jr., C.R.I) and Abigail, Dec. 12, 1769.
Sarah, d. of John and Lucy, Oct. 24, 1729.
Sarah, d. of Moses and Mary, bp. Oct. 12, 1731. C.R.I.
Sarah, d. of Daniel and Sarah, bp. Feb. 4, 1738-9. C.R.I.
Sarah, d. of Daniel and Sarah, Jan. 23, 1739-40.
Sarah, d. of Thomas and Martha, Sept. 22, 1768.
Seth, s. of John (John 2d, C.R.I) and Lucy, Mar. 6, 1745-6.
Seth, s. of Seth and Hannah, Oct. 16, 1775.
Silance, d. of David and Thankful, Nov. 4, 1742.
Sophia, d. of Seth and Hannah, Sept. 26, 1773.
Submit, d. of Samuel and Abigail, Aug. 23, 1761.
Submit, d. of Samuel and Abigail, June 21, 1763.
Thaddeus, s. of (Dea., C.R.I) Samuel and Elisabeth, his 2d w., Apr. 19, 1752.
Thankful, d. of David and Thankful, bp. Oct. 31, 1762. C.R.I.
Thomas, s. of Daniel and Sarah, May 31, 1741.
Thomas, s. of (Dea., C.R.I) Samuel and Ruth, July 11, 1746.
Thomas, s. of Thomas and Martha, Oct. 8, 1766.

REED (see Read), Harriet E., d. of Jehiel H. and Eliza, Nov. 30, 1846.
Jonathan, s. of Daniel, 14th day, 11th mo. 1764. c.r.4.
Mary, d. of Daniel, 22d day, 1st mo. 1772. c.r.4.
Moses, s. of Daniel, 26th day, 4th mo. 1763. c.r.4.
Rachel, d. of Daniel, 26th day, 5th mo. 1766. c.r.4.
Sarah, d. of Daniel, 31st day, 12th mo. 1769. c.r.4.

REILLY, Mary Ann Dempsey [———], w. of Michael, ———, 1841. g.r.2.

REMINGTON, Severett L., s. of Thomas W. and Susan, May 28, 1847.

RHODES, ———, s. of George and Almira D. R., July 23, 1844. Twin.
———, s. of George and Almira D. R., July 23, 1844. Twin.
———, d. of George W. and Elmira D. R., Mar. 12, 1846.
Frances Louisa, d. of Salmon and Phebe, bp. Apr. 3, 1843. c.r.2.
Geo[rge] C. Taft, s. of Salmon and Phebe, bp. Apr. 3, 1843. c.r.2.
George Washington, s. of Zebulon and Abigail, Oct. 7, 1820.
Georgiaette A., d. of George W. and Elmira D. R., Apr. 11, 1848.
Zebulon, Aug. —, 1790. g.r.1.

RICE, Charles Luther, s. of Matthias and Hannah, Aug. 28, 1834.
Dolle, d. of Asahel and Mary, July 14, 1763.
G. S., May 8, 1838. g.r.2.
Philomene [———], w. of G. S., Sept. 20, 1839. g.r.2.

RICH, Dinah, d. of James and Hannah, 29th day, 4th mo. 1794. c.r.4.
James, s. of James and Hannah, 17th day, 7th mo. 1796. c.r.4.
Sarah, d. of James and Hannah, 19th day, 1st mo. 1790. c.r.4.
Stephen, s. of James and Hannah, 13th day, 1st mo. 1792. c.r.4.

RICHARDSON, Amanda, Oct. 12, 1835. g.r.19.
Anan, July 21, 1818. g.r.14.
Ann Maria, d. of Anan and Sarah A., Aug. 6, 1844.
Anna M. Waterman [———], w. of W[illia]m B., ———, 1849. g.r.14.

RICHARDSON, Beulah, d. of Bethiah, lately Woodward, bp. July 2, 1758. c.r.1.
Bezaleel, Sept. 23, 1823. g.r.1.
Caleb Taft, s. of Joseph Jr. and Roby, Feb. 9, 1813.
David, s. of Joseph Jr. and Roby, Dec. 31, 1808.
Dextor, s. of Joseph and Molley, Apr. 12, 1787.
Joseph, s. of Joseph and Molley, Sept. 2, 1785. (Sept. 3, 1784. g.r.14.)
Joseph, s. of Simon and Martha Taft, May 5, 1825. g.r.19.
Joseph, s. of David and Almira, June 10, 1834.
Levi, s. of Joseph Jr. and Roby, Nov. 5, 1817.
Margaret M., Mar. 1, 1833. g.r.19.
Mary Malvina, d. of David and Almira, Feb. 8, 1831.
Mowrey, s. of Joseph Jr. and Roby, Apr. 17, 1810.
Phebe [———], w. of Caleb T., Feb. 26, 1823. g.r.14.
Roby [———], w. of Joseph, Oct. 22, 1790. g.r.14.
Sarah, d. of Joseph and Molley, July 21, 1791.
Sarah A. [———], w. of Anan, Jan. 1, 1822. g.r.14.
Simon, s. of Joseph and Molley, Feb. 19, 1800.
Sumner Smith, s. of Anan and Sarah, July 25, 1846.
Susannah, d. of Joseph and Molley, June 19, 1796.
William Bainbridge, s. of Joseph Jr. and Roby, Apr. 28, 1815.
William Benjamin, s. of Caleb and Phebe, June 15, 1843.

RICKARD, Louisa, in Cornish, N. H., Mar. 8, 1807. g.r.1.
Truman, Dr., in Cornish, N. H., Feb. 12, 1814. g.r.1.

RIEDEL, Henry, s. of George and Roseana, Nov. 8, 1844.

RILEY, Robert, s. of Hugh and Harriet, Dec. 22, 1829.

RIST, ———, d. of Luther and Betsey, Apr. 20, 1844.
Amos, s. of Thomas and Sarah, July 5, 1754.
Amos, s. of Thaddius and Polly, Sept. 17, 1822.
Anna, d. of Joseph and Rachel, May 10, 1772.
Caleb, s. of Joseph and Rachel, Dec. 18, 1769.
Calvin, s. of Thaddius and Polly, May 21, 1817.
Charles Thomas, s. of Thaddius and Polly, Apr. 28, 1805.
Cutler, s. of Joseph and Rachel, Apr. 16, 1787.
Daniel W., s. of Ezbon and Emeline W. Taylor, ———, 1839. g.r.1.
Daniel Waldo, s. of Thaddius and Polly, Apr. 14, 1811.
Emeline W. Taylor [———], w. of Ezbon, ———, 1816. g.r.1.
Ezbon, s. of Thaddius and Polly, May 27, 1814.
Ezra, s. of Thomas and Lois, Sept. 14, 1764.

RIST, Frederick A., s. of Ezbon and Emeline, b. in Corinth, Vt., Oct. 5, 1848.
Joseph, s. of Thomas and Sarah, Sept. 28, 1740.
Levi, s. of Joseph and Rachel, May 14, 1784.
Marcy, d. of Thomas and Sarah, Jan. —, 1744–5.
Nathan, s. of Thomas and Sarah, June 25, 1742.
Sarah, d. of Thomas and Sarah, Mar. 1, 1750–1.
Smith Capron, s. of Thaddius and Polly, Sept. 26, 1808.
Susannah, d. of Joseph and Rachel, Nov. 13, 1767.
Thaddeus, s. of Joseph and Rachel, Apr. 18, 1775.
Thomas, s. of Thomas and Mary, Dec. 18, 1736.

ROBBINS, Alvin Cook, s. of Horace B. and Chloe, May 12, 1828.
Edward, 5th day, 11th mo. 1789. C.R.4.
Elizabeth, d. of Lemuel and ———, bp. Apr. 4, 1745. C.R.1.
Manasseh, 31st day, 10th mo. 1794. C.R.4.
Stephen, s. of Lemuel and ———, bp. July 5, 1747. C.R.1.

ROBERTSON, Joseph Nelson, s. of Maria, Jan. 22, 1844.

ROBINSON, Diana, d. of Stephen Updike and Ann Robinson, Apr. 27, 1846.
Elizabeth M. Cobb [———], w. of Ethan A., ———, 1835. G.R.1.
Ethan A., ———, 1837. G.R.1.
Josiah, s. of Josiah and Anna, Nov. 27, 1739.
Simeon, s. of Peter and ———, bp. Sept. 2, 1744. C.R.1.

ROCHE, Gady, ———, 1817. G.R.2.
Johannah [———], w. of Thomas, Dec. 25, 1823. G.R.2.
Mary Hension [———], w. of Gady, ———, 1837. G.R.2.
Thomas, Jan. 2, 1821. G.R.2.

ROCKWOOD, Calvin R., 15th day, 3d mo. 1820. C.R.4.

ROGERS, Annie [———], w. of Ja[me]s S., 28th day, 7th mo. 1838. C.R.4.

ROGERSON, Elizabeth Slater, in Boston, Oct. 24, 1823. G.R.1.
Minerva B., d. of Robert and Mary Ann Jr., Oct. 22, 1847.
William B., s. of Robert and Mary A., Sept. 11, 1845.

ROOKS, Daniel, s. of John and Deliverance, Mar. 26, 1765. (Daniel Powers, s. of John and Deliverance dec., bp. Jan. 21, 1767. C.R.1.)
Ezekiel, s. of John and Deliverance, June 8, 1763.

ROSS, Andrew J., ———, 1839. G.R.1.

ROURKE, Francis, s. of Patrick and Bridget, June 17, 1846.

RUSSELL, Harriot Carolina, d. of James and Hannah, Dec. 4, 1792.
Sylvia Abby, d. of James and Hannah, July 20, 1795.

RUTTER, John, s. of Jesse and Abigail, June 22, 1773.

SABEN (see Sabin, Sabine), Lydia J. Albee [———], w. of Israel, ———, 1841. G.R.1.

SABIN (see Saben, Sabine), Alfred, s. of Israel and Beulah, 15th day, 1st mo. 1775. C.R.4.
Anna Mowry, d. of Israel, 11th day, 6th mo. 1826. C.R.4.
Benedict, s. of Israel and Beulah, 6th day, 5th mo. 1792. C.R.4.
Beulah [———], w. of Israel, 26th day, 9th mo. 1749. C.R.4.
Beulah, d. of Israel and Beulah, 11th day, 6th mo. 1786. C.R.4.
Chloe, d. of Israel and Beulah, 19th day, 10th mo. 1772. C.R.4.
Darling, d. of Israel and Beulah, 14th day, 9th mo. 1778. C.R.4.
Elisabeth, d. of Israel and Beulah, 4th day, 4th mo. 1784. C.R.4.
Gideon Mowry, s. of Israel, 9th day, 2d mo. 1819. C.R.4.
Huldah, d. of Israel, 23d day, 11th mo. 1830. C.R.4.
Israel, 14th day, 9th mo. 1749. C.R.4.
Israel, s. of Israel and Beulah, 5th day, 5th mo. 1790. C.R.4.
Israel, s. of Israel, 8th day, 1st mo. 1821. C.R.4.
Lucy, d. of Israel and Beulah, 4th day, 4th mo. 1788. C.R.4.
Lucy, d. of Israel, 1st day, 4th mo. 1824. C.R.4.
Lydia, d. of Israel and Beulah, 25th day, 9th mo. 1776. C.R.4.
Mary, d. of Israel and Beulah, 18th day, 11th mo. 1780. C.R.4.
Moses, s. of Israel and Beulah, 24th day, 8th mo. 1782. C.R.4.
Richard M., s. of Gideon M. and Mary, May 23, 1847.
Richard Mowry, s. of Israel, 7th day, 10th mo. 1811. C.R.4.
Sarah, d. of Israel, 7th day, 9th mo. 1828. C.R.4.
Timothy, s. of Israel and Beulah, 12th day, 3d mo. 1771. C.R.4.

SABINE (see Saben, Sabin), Elisabeth, d. of Thomas and Sarah, Jan. 5, 1765.

SADLER, Lydia, d. of Joseph and Sarah, Aug. 27, 1746.
Lydia, d. of Joseph and Sarah, July 27, 1751.
Mary, d. of Joseph and ———, bp. Feb. 3, 1744–5. C.R.1.
Mary, d. of Joseph and Sarah, Sept. 28, 1748.

SANDERS, Temperance, d. of Ebenezer of Mendon and ———, bp. July 20, 1735. C.R.1.

SANGOR, Abigail, d. of Isaac and Mary, Dec. 9, 1743.
Elisabeth, d. of Isaac and Mary, in Worcester, Feb. 28, 1730–1.
Isaac, s. of Isaac and Mary, Mar. 21, 1735–6.
John, s. of Isaac and Mary, in Shrewsbury, Dec. 20, 1733.
Lydia, d. of Isaac and Mary, Aug. 16, 1746.
Mary, d. of Isaac and Mary, in Weston, Feb. 19, 1726–7.
Pheeby, d. of Isaac and Mary, Aug. 7, 1738.
Phinahas, s. of Isaac and Mary, Oct. 19, 1741.

SANTURN, Charles Lesley, s. of Joseph and Mary, Mar. 27, 1847.
Ellen J., d. of Joseph and Mary, Mar. 12, 1848.
George, s. of Joseph, b. in Canada, and Mary, b. in New York State, Nov. 24, 1849.

SAWYER, Philinia T., d. of Leander, b. in Burrillville, R. I., and Huldah, Sept. 23, 1848.

SAYLES, Albert, Sept. 28, 1814. G.R.1.
Amasa, Nov. 18, 1788. G.R.1.
Andrew J., s. of Richard, b. in Gloucester, and Sarah E., b. in Northbridge, Sept. 19, 1849.
Caroline M. [———], w. of Horatio, Jan. 26, 1812. G.R.1.
Emilie H. [———], w. of Renselaer, Aug. 26, 1841. G.R.1.
Herbert R., Aug. 11, 1847. G.R.1.
Iscah H. [———], w. of Renselaer, Aug. 27, 1825. G.R.1.
John E., s. of Amasa and Mary, Nov. 13, 1825. G.R.1.
Louisa J., d. of Horatio and Caroline M., June 28, 1835. G.R.1.
Lucy Anna, d. of Horatio and Caroline M., Nov. 3, 1844.
Maria [———], w. of Albert, Oct. 31, 1817. G.R.1.
Mary [———], w. of Amasa, Jan. 10, 1794. G.R.1.
Mary E., d. of Horatio and Caroline M., July 22, 1837. G.R.1.
Renselaer, June 2, 1823. G.R.1.
Richard, Sept. 13, 1819. G.R.1.
Sarah E. [———], w. of Richard, Oct. 14, 1822. G.R.1.
William, s. of Amasa and Mary, Nov. 18, 1815. G.R.1.
William F., s. of Renselaer and Iscah H., June 14, 1847. G.R.1.

SCOTT, Abigail Boyd, d. of Manly and ———, Sept. 15, 1821.
Ann E. Chilson [———], w. of Orlando, ———, 1837. G.R.1.
Anne Gray, d. of Manly and ———, Sept. 14, 1812.
Anne Gray, d. of Manly and ———, Apr. 16, 1818.
Asaanna N., d. of Samuel W. and Susan Farnum, July 23, 1842.
Charles Amos, s. of Manly and ———, May 17, 1811.
Charlotte Louisa, d. of Manly and ———, Mar. 2, 1825. Twin.

Scott, Crysa Arrora, d. of Manly and ———, May 5, 1823. Twin.
Crysus Tallamacus, d. of Manly and ———, May 5, 1823. Twin. (w. of Eddy G. Smith. G.R.1.)
Ellen Maria, d. of Samuel W. and Susan (Farnum in pencil), May 29, 1845.
Emma Matilda, d. of Samuel W. and Susan (Farnum in pencil), Oct. 15, 1846.
Eunice [———], w. of Job, 8th day, 7th mo. 1760. C.R.4.
George Nahum, s. of Manly and ———, Mar. 2, 1825. Twin.
Henrietta T. [———], w. of Manly, June 22, 1790. G.R.1.
James, s. of Job and Eunice, 7th day, 4th mo. 1788. C.R.4.
Job, — day, 10th mo. 1751. C.R.4.
John Van Rensselaer, s. of Manly, Oct. 16, 1829.
Lois Amanda, d. of Manly, Feb. 14, 1827.
Lydia, d. of Job and Eunice, 28th day, 9th mo. 1782. C.R.4.
Manly, Oct. 9, 1775. G.R.1.
Maria Catharine, d. of Manly and ———, May 18, 1816. (w. of Rev. Moses P. Webster. G.R.1.)
Marion Adalade, d. of Manly, Mar. 19, 1831.
Mary, d. of Job and Eunice, 7th day, 1st mo. 1786. C.R.4.
Mary Capron, d. of Learned and Joana, Sept. 16, 1824.
Orlando, ———, 1830. G.R.1.
Oziel, s. of Job and Eunice, 16th day, 4th mo. 1780. C.R.4.
Samuel White, s. of Manly and ———, Oct. 16, 1819.
Sarah, d. of Job and Eunice, 1st day, 7th mo. 1784. C.R.4.
Sarah Green [———], w. of Charles A., ———, 1811. G.R.1.
Sir George St. Clair Prevost, s. of Manly and ———, Feb. 27, 1814.
Susan F. [———], w. of Samuel W., June 19, 1819. G.R.1.
Walter P., s. of Samuel W. and Susan Farnum, May 29, 1845.

SCRIBNER, ———, d. of Cinkler and Rosanna, Apr. 18, 1846.
Abbie S. Goldthwaite [———], w. of Addison C., ———, 1841. G.R.1.
Addison C., ———, 1841. G.R.1.

SCULLY, James, ———, 1819. G.R.2.
Margaret Quaan [———], w. of James, ———, 1836. G.R.2.

SEAGRAVE (see Seagraves, Segrave), ———, d. of Josiah T. and Angeline P., Apr. 29, 1845.
Abigail, d. of Dorrington and Jerusha, in Northbridge, Sept. 10, 1810.
Alma Eliza, d. of Sullivan and Annjanett B., Feb. 15, 1843.

SEAGRAVE, Alpheus Mason, s. of George W. and Mary (Rawson in pencil) Seagrave, July 20, 1844.
Amey, d. of Beazeel and Mary, Jan. 19, 1796.
Ann Eliza, d. of Scott and Eliza Ann, Apr. 27, 1833.
Annjanett B. Beals [——], w. of Sullivan, ——, 1815. G.R.I.
Arthur Amasa, s. of John 2d and Almina, July 25, 1841.
Austin Ross, s. of John 2d and Almina, in Northbridge, Jan. 4, 1835.
Axalana, d. of Dorrington, in Northbridge, Mar. 7, 1822.
Bezaleel, s. of Edward and Louis, Dec. 14, 1766.
Bezaleel, s. of John and Sarah, Nov. 30, 1787.
Caleb, s. of Edward and Louis, Mar. 14, 1771. (Caleb, s. of Edward and Eunice, bp. June 23, 1771. C.R.I.)
Calista, d. of Samuel and Betsey, Sept. 29, 1814.
Caroline E., d. of Edward F. and Sarah R., May 26, 1847.
Caroline Selah, d. of John Jr. and (Mary, C.R.I), Jan. 31, 1806.
Carophalia, d. of Scott and Eliza Ann, Jan. 1, 1839.
Chapin Murdock, s. of Samuel and Betsey, May 15, 1824.
Charles Augustus, s. of Bezaleel Jr. and Lucy, Sept. 27, 1819.
Charles Edwin, s. of John Jr. and ——, Oct. 1, 1825.
Charles Stowe, s. of Scott and Eliza Ann, Dec. 1, 1836.
Clinton, s. of Beazeel and Mary, Sept. 28, 1812.
Clinton, s. of Washington and Mary, May 8, 1839.
Daniel, s. of John and Sarah, Nov. 2, 1795.
Daniel, s. of Dorrington, Oct. 21, 1826.
Daniel, s. of Daniel and Mary, Sept. 5, 1831.
Edward, s. of Edward and Louis, Nov. 9, 1776.
Edward, s. of Beazeel and Mary, Aug. 6, 1793.
Edward Foster, s. of John Jr. and (Mary, C.R.I), Aug. 13, 1817.
Edward Pembroke, s. of Seth and Mary, Jan. 13, 1819.
Edwin C., s. of Charles E. and Abigail, b. in Pawtucket, R. I., Feb. 18, 1849.
Fanny, d. of Beazeel and Mary, Apr. —, 1815.
George Edward, s. of Edward and Hannah, Sept. 4, 1838.
George Leonard, s. of Daniel and Mary, Mar. 12, 1837.
George Washington, s. of Dorrington and Jerusha, in Northbridge, Mar. 24, 1812.
Gilbert Henry, s. of Saul S. and Mary Almira, Apr. 23, 1834.
Hannah, d. of Beazeel and Mary, Aug. 28, 1791.
Hannah, d. of Samuel and Betsey, May 22, 1809.
Harriot, d. of Dorrington and Jerusha, June 8, 1808.
Hellen Mariah, d. of Daniel and Mary, Sept. 19, 1842. Twin.
Hellen Ross, d. of Saul S. and Mary Almira, Oct. 3, 1838.
Henry Martin, s. of John 2d and Almina, June 21, 1836.

SEAGRAVE, Henry Martyn, s. of Edward F. and Sarah, Jan. 16, 1840.
Henry Merritt, s. of Daniel and Mary, Sept. 19, 1842. Twin.
Horatio, s. of Samuel and Betsey, Apr. 2, 1807.
Ida R., d. of Sullivan and Anngenett, Nov. 22, 1846. Removed to Medway.
James Carter, s. of John Jr. and (Mary, C.R.1), Apr. 14, 1821.
James Edward, s. of Edward P. and Mary, June 18, 1843.
James Richmond (Redmond dup.), s. of Edward F. and Sarah (Sarah R., C.R.2), Dec. 3, 1844 (Dec. 2, 1844 dup.).
Jane, d. of Beazeel and Mary, Mar. 26, 1819.
John, s. of Edward and Louis, Nov. 6, 1757.
John, s. of John Jr. and (Mary, C.R.1), Jan. 20, 1808.
John Dorrington, s. of Dorrington and Jerusha, in Northbridge, Feb. 28, 1814.
Joseph, s. of Edward and Louis, Dec. 21, 1761.
Joseph Day, s. of Dorrington, July 26, 1824.
Josephine Victoria, d. of Lewis and Elizabeth B. W., Oct. 17, 1845. (w. of Bezaleel Taft. G.R.1.)
Josiah, s. of Edward and Louis, Oct. 14, 1773.
Keith White, s. of Seth and Mary, Mar. 20, 1816.
Laura Elizabeth, d. of Samuel and Betsey, Sept. 25, 1826.
Lawson Alexander, d. of Bezaleel Jr. and Lucy, Jan. 24, 1814.
Levina, d. of Dorrington and Jerusha, Feb. 17, 1818.
Lewis, s. of Samuel and Betsey, Oct. 1, 1812.
Louis, d. of Edward and Louis, Nov. 5, 1759.
Louisa, d. of Beazeel and Mary, Oct. 25, 1809.
Lucy, d. of Bezaleel Jr. and Lucy, Mar. 9, 1822.
Maria, d. of Bezaleel Jr. and Lucy, Feb. 7, 1812.
Mary, d. of Edward and Louis, Apr. 1, 1764.
Mary, d. of Samuel and Betsey, Mar. 16, 1805.
Mary, d. of Dorrington, in Northbridge, May 19, 1820.
Mary, d. of Daniel and Mary, Sept. 22, 1839.
Mary Aldrich, d. of Beazeel and Mary, May 10, 1811.
Mary Elizabeth, d. of John and Almina, Mar. 19, 1846.
Mary Lucinda, d. of Saul S. and Mary Almira, Apr. 11, 1836.
Melinda, d. of Daniel and Mary, July 13, 1834.
Moses Taft, s. of Bezaleel Jr. and Lucy, Aug. 18, 1817.
Nancy, d. of Bezaleel Jr. and Lucy, Nov. 5, 1815.
Nancy Ann, d. of John 2d and Almina, Mar. 30, 1839. (Nancy Ross, d. of John 2d, bp. June —, 1839. C.R.2.)
Olive, d. of Edward and Louis, Apr. 17, 1779.
Orville Barton, s. of John 2d and Almina, Oct. 26, 1837.

SEAGRAVE, Richard A., s. of Edward F. and Sarah R., b. in Burrillville, R. I., Aug. 25, 1849.
Sally, d. of Dorrington and Jerusha, Dec. 4, 1806.
Saloma, d. of Seth and Mary, June 5, 1812.
Samuel, s. of Edward and Louis, Feb. 3, 1782. (Samuel, s. of Edward dec. and Lois, bp. May 26, 1793. c.r.1.)
Samuel W., s. of Lewis and Elizabeth [1847 or 1848].
Sarah, d. of Edward and Louis, Dec. 31, 1768. (Sarah, d. of Edward and Eunice, bp. Mar. 19, 1769. c.r.1.)
Sarah, d. of Beazeel and Mary, Aug. 9, 1798.
Sarah, d. of Bezaleel Jr. and Lucy, Aug. 27, 1825.
Sarah D. [————], w. of John, in Boston, Apr. 7, 1755. g.r.1.
Sarah H., d. of Washington and Mary, Jan. 21, 1837.
Saul Scott, s. of John Jr. and (Mary, c.r.1), Mar. 3, 1810.
Scott, s. of Dorrington and Jerusha, July 25, 1805.
Selah, d. of Dorrington and Jerusha, in Northbridge, Dec. 26, 1815.
Selissa Scott (Celista Scot, c.r.1), d. of John Jr. and (Mary, c.r.1), Apr. 14, 1812.
Seth, s. of Beazeel and Mary, Sept. 23, 1789.
Silas Bamfield, s. of Scott and Eliza Ann, July 16, 1831.
Sophia, d. of George W. and Mary, Feb. 5, 1847.
Sullivan, s. of Beazeel and Mary, Mar. 6, 1817.
Susan, d. of Beazeel and Mary, Sept. 13, 1821.
Sylvanus, s. of Beazeel and Mary, Aug. 26, 1800.
Waity, d. of Beazeel and Mary, Aug. 14, 1802.
Washington, s. of Beazeel and Mary, Dec. 28, 1807.
W[illia]m Henry, s. of John Jr. and (Mary, c.r.1), Jan. 6, 1815.
William Henry, s. of Edward F. and Sarah, Apr. 21, 1843.

SEAGRAVES (see Seagrave, Segrave), Caleb, s. of Josiah and Lois, Feb. 8, 1815.
Edward, s. of Josiah and Lois, Sept. 3, 1807.
Ezbon, s. of Josiah and Lois, Dec. 28, 1818.
George Augustus, s. of Josiah and Lois, Jan. 6, 1823.
Henrietta, d. of Josiah and Lois, Dec. 1, 1803.
Jacob Taft, s. of Josiah and Lois, Apr. 8, 1802.
Josiah, s. of Josiah and Lois, May 24, 1811.
Louis T., s. of Josiah and Lois, Apr. 13, 1809.
Lucy [————], w. of Bezaleel, Apr. 24, 1795. g.r.1.
Malvina, d. of Josiah and Lois, Apr. 2, 1813.
Mary Ann, d. of Josiah and Lois, Nov. 17, 1799.
Samuel, s. of Caleb and Eunice, Jan. 9, 1803.
Waity Grout, d. of Josiah and Lois, Sept. 23, 1805.

SEGRAVE (see Seagrave, Seagraves), Dorrington, s. of John S. and Sarah, Sept. 25, 1781.
Harriet, d. of John S. and Sarah, Feb. 28, 1792.
John, s. of John S. and Sarah, Dec. 1, 1783.
Polley, d. of John S. and Sarah, Dec. 8, 1779.

SESSIONS, Harvey G., ———, 1846. G.R.1.

SEVERANCE (see Sevrence), Sarah R., d. of Martin and Elizabeth, May 28, 1847.

SEVERY, Elisabeth, d. of Reuben and Lucy, July 18, 1787.
Georg[e] Carayl, s. of Reuben and Lucy, May 27, 1790.
Haman, s. of Reuben and Lucy, in Douglas, June 22, 1782.
Marshel, s. of Reuben and Lucy, Mar. 13, 1779.
Rhozanna, d. of Reuben and Lucy, Jan. 17, 1784.

SEVRENCE (see Severance), Mary Sophia, d. of Martin and Elizabeth, July 17, 1844.

SHAUGHNESSY, Alice [———], w. of Thomas, ———, 1834. G.R.2.
Thomas, ———, 1832. G.R.2.

SHAW, Elizabeth H., 10th day, 10th mo. 1810. C.R.4.
Ellen Mariah, d. of John and Persis B., July 14, 1840.

SHEEHAN, Annie E. Lynch [———], w. of John H., Apr. 10, 1845. G.R.2.
Ellen Cronin [———], w. of James, ———, 1822. G.R.2.
James, ———, 1831. G.R.2.

SHERBURN, ———, s. of Barney and Bridget, Oct. 18, 1847.

SHERLOCK, John, s. of Rebecca, bp. July 24, 1743. C.R.1.
Jonathan, s. of Rebecca, bp. July 24, 1743. C.R.1.
Sarah, d. of Rebecca, bp. July 24, 1743. C.R.1.

SHERMAN, Ann A., d. of Albert and Lucy, Dec. 31, 1847.
John D., s. of Albert, b. in Lincoln, and Lucy, b. in Charlton, Oct. 7, 1849.

SHOVE, Alvin, s. of James M. and Bashaba, Feb. 22, 1833.
Avis [———], 2d w. of Josiah, 10th day, 8th mo. 1756. C.R.4.
Baxtor, s. of Thomas B. and Hannah, May 30, 1788.
Benedict, s. of Thomas B. and Hannah, May 17, 1802.
Calven, s. of Thomas B. and Hannah, Jan. 6, 1797.
Charlotte Brown, d. of Luther and Pamela, Nov. 4, 1824.

SHOVE, Dextor, s. of Thomas B. and Hannah, Aug. 12, 1790.
Eliza, 2d day, 10th mo. 1814. c.r.4.
Esther, d. of Thomas B. and Hannah, Nov. 25, 1792.
George, s. of Thomas B. and Hannah, Nov. 12, 1805.
Hannah, d. of Josiah and Joanna, 9th day, 11th mo. 1781. c.r.4.
Isaac, s. of Josiah and Joanna, 16th day, 7th mo. 1795. c.r.4.
James Madison, s. of Thomas B. and Hannah, Apr. 7, 1808.
Joanna [―――], w. of Josiah, 14th day, 11th mo. 1755. c.r.4.
Joanna, d. of Josiah and Joanna, 31st day, 10th mo. 1791. c.r.4.
Jonathan Marble, s. of Josiah and Joanna, 17th day, 1st mo. 1787. c.r.4.
Josiah, 18th day, 4th mo. 1756. c.r.4.
Josiah, s. of Josiah and Joanna, 9th day, 4th mo. 1783. c.r.4.
Laura Ann, d. of Luther and Pamela, July 12, 1830.
Luther, s. of Thomas B. and Hannah, Sept. 10, 1794.
Marvel, s. of Josiah and Joanna, 9th day, 5th mo. 1793. c.r.4.
Mary [―――], w. of Jonathan Marble, 11th day, 2d mo. 1796. c.r.4.
Mary Elizabeth, d. of Luther and Pamela, Nov. 24, 1826.
Mary Spring, d. of Jonathan Marble and Mary, 30th day, 6th mo. 1814. c.r.4.
Reuben, s. of Josiah and Ruth, 8th day, 4th mo. 1785. c.r.4.
Samuel, s. of Josiah and Joanna, 2d day, 2d mo. 1789. c.r.1.
Sarah [―――], 3d w. of Josiah, 7th day, 5th mo. 1755. c.r.4.
Sarah, d. of Josiah and Joanna, 3d day, 9th mo. 1779. c.r.4.
Sarah M. [―――], w. of Thomas M., ――, 1818. g.r.11.
Squire, s. of Thomas B. and Hannah, May 10, 1800.
Thomas Merrick, s. of Thomas B. and Hannah, Jan. 13, 1812.

SIBLEY, Almira, d. of Joel and Lois [no date; entered between 1795 and 1799].
Anna Maria Porter, d. of Royal and Lucretia, Nov. 3, 1822.
Chloa, d. of Stephen and Thankfull, Nov. 23, 1780.
Dorrance, s. of Peter and Mary, Aug. 24, 1791.
Emmery (Amory, c.r.1), s. of Joel and Lois, Jan. 20, 1792.
George Henry, s. of Royal and Lucretia, in Augusta, Ga., Jan. 5, 1821. (George Henry, s. of wid. Lucretia, bp. Sept. 18, 1831. c.r.1.)
George Nightingale, s. of Joel and Lois, Aug. 12, 1810.
Hannah, d. of John and Abigail, in Sutton, Sept. 26, 1742.
Hannah, d. of Stephen and Thankfull, June 30, 1785.
Joel, s. of Stephen and Thankfull, Friday, Apr. 25, 1766, at 2 o'clock in the morning.

SIBLEY, John, s. of Peter and Mary, June 1, 1789.
Josiah, s. of Joel and Lois, Apr. 1, 1808.
Keith, s. of Peter and Mary, June 15, 1787.
Lydia, d. of John and Abigail, June 28, 1745.
Lydia, d. of Stephen and Thankfull, Apr. 2, 1769, Sabbath day, at half after nine in the morning.
Martha, d. of Joel and Lois, Dec. 31, 1804.
Mary, d. of John and Abigail, Jan. 20, 1751.
Mary, d. of Joel and Lois, Dec. 28, 1802.
Molly, d. of Stephen and Thankfull, Nov. 24, 1775.
Nabe, d. of Stephen and Thankfull, Jan. 2, 1774.
Nabby, d. of Joel and Lois, July 29, 1799. Twin.
Nancy, d. of Joel and Lois, July 29, 1799. Twin.
Olive, d. of Peter and Mary, Apr. 12, 1782.
Peter, s. of John and Abigail, Sept. 16, 1749.
Royal, s. of Joel and Lois, ———, 1795.
Salley, d. of Peter and Mary, Sept. 16, 1784.
Stephen, s. of John and Abigail, in Sutton, July 12, 1741.

SILVESTER (see Sylvester), Horace Earl, s. of Deborah, 31st day, 3d mo. 1804. c.r.4.
Peter, 6th day, 4th mo. 1755. c.r.4.

SIMONS, Benjamin, s. of Benjamin and Sarah, Apr. 2, 1753.
Elisabeth, d. of Benjamin and Sarah, Jan. 13, 1755.
Sibbulah, d. of Benjamin and Sarah, Dec. 27, 1758.

SLADE (see Slead), Asenath Purinton, d. of Howland and Mary, 7th day, 9th mo. 1809. c.r.4.
Benjamin Bowers, s. of Howland and Mary, 1st day, 7th mo. 1807. c.r.4.
George Willard, s. of Howland and Mary, 3d day, 3d mo. 1805. c.r.4.
Mary Jane, Nov. 19, 1820. g.r.1.
Mary Shepard, d. of Howland and Mary, 27th day, 4th mo. 1803. c.r.4.
Sarah Ballou, d. of Howland and Mary, 3d day, 6th mo. 1811. c.r.4.
Stephen H., s. of Stephen S. and Mary Jane, Mar. 4, 1848.
Stephen S., Mar. 10, 1820. g.r.1.

SLATER, Emily Carpenter [———], w. of Henry P., Dec. 16, 1823. g.r.1.
Henry P., Dec. 28, 1822. g.r.1.

SLEAD (see Slade), Anthony, s. of Henry and Naomy, 18th day, 10th mo. 1779. c.r.4.
Naomy [———], w. of Henry, 17th day, 7th mo. 1752. c.r.4.

SMITH, Asa, 14th day, 2d mo. 1751. c.r.4.
Asa of Gloucester, ———, 1752. c.r.4.
Betsey E. Wood [———], w. of Seymour, Feb. 22, 1817. g.r.1.
Bezalleel White, s. of Moses and Sally, June 23, 1806.
Chloe, d. of Victerious and Susanna, June 9, 1773.
Dillwyn, ch. of James, 19th day, 11th mo. 1777. c.r.4.
Drusilla, d. of James, 18th day, 6th mo. 1789. c.r.4.
Eddy G., Dec. 7, 1818. g.r.1.
Harriet Amelia, d. of Samuel and Harriet, May 26, 1844.
James, 23d day, 10th mo. 1752. c.r.4.
Job, s. of James, 5th day, 4th mo. 1787. c.r.4.
John R., ———, 1809. g.r.4.
Jonah, s. of James, 16th day, 9th mo. 1779. c.r.4.
Katharine [———], w. of Asa, 16th day, 1st mo. 1756. c.r.4.
Lydia [———], w. of Ephraim, June 20, 1794. g.r.1.
Mary, d. of Asa and Katharine, 18th day, 5th mo. 1781. c.r.4.
Mary Chapin, d. of Moses and Sally, Nov. 25, 1804.
Nancy, 21st day, 9th mo. 1770. c.r.4.
Rhoda, d. of James, 9th day, 1st mo. 1782. c.r.4.
Rufus, s. of James, 22d day, 5th mo. 1776. c.r.4.
Samuel, s. of Victerious and Susanna, June 20, 1776.
Sarah Mariah, d. of Samuel and Harriet, Mar. 21, 1834.
Seymour, Mar. 29, 1815. g.r.1.
Thomas, s. of Asa and Katharine, 12th day, 11th mo. 1783. c.r.4.
Warner, s. of James, 5th day, 11th mo. 1784. c.r.4.
W[illia]m Henry, s. of Moses and Sally, Apr. 24, 1808.
Woodbury C., s. of Samuel and Harriet, Dec. 5, 1836.

SOUTHWICK, ———, d. of Thomas and Lavinia, ———, 1847.
———, s. of Israel M. and Lucy H., Mar. 29, 1848.
Abigail, d. of Enoch and Mary, 2d day, 3d mo. 1784. c.r.4.
Alice [———], w. of Joseph, 5th day, 2d mo. 1756. c.r.4.
Amanda Malvina, d. of Daniel and Hannah, 16th day, 10th mo. 1820. c.r.4.
Amasa, s. of John and Chloe, 5th day, 3d mo. 1778. c.r.4.
Amasa, 13th day, 11th mo. 1778. c.r.4.
Amey, d. of Enoch and Mary, 26th day, 7th mo. 1793. c.r.4.
Ann H. [———], w. of Edward, 17th day, 4th mo. 1822. c.r.4.
Arnold, s. of Joseph and Alice, 14th day, 2d mo. 1798. c.r.4.

SOUTHWICK, Asa, 3d day, 8th mo. 1766. c.r.4.
Betsey Willard [———], w. of Andre, ———, 1816. G.R.1.
Betty, d. of Enoch and Mary, 20th day, 2d mo. 1782. c.r.4.
Catharine, d. of Daniel and Hannah, 10th day, 11th mo. 1826. c.r.4.
Chad, ch. of Lawrance and Hannah, 1st day, 10th mo. 1774. c.r.4.
Chloe [———], w. of John, 4th day, 8th mo. 1757. c.r.4.
Chloe, d. of John and Chloe, 14th day, 12th mo. 1779. c.r.4.
Chloe Bartlet, d. of Daniel and Hannah, 24th day, 3d mo. 1822. c.r.4.
Cyntha, d. of Enoch and Mary, 17th day, 6th mo. 1779. c.r.4.
Daniel, 6th day, 5th mo. 1769 (1767 dup.). c.r.4.
Daniel, s. of George and Judith, May 28, 1780.
Daniel, s. of David and Elisabeth, 2d day, 6th mo. 1793. c.r.4.
Daniel B., s. of John and Chloe, 11th day, 11th mo. 1791. c.r.4.
David, 21st day, 3d mo. 1754. c.r.4.
David, s. of Edward and Elisabeth, 4th day, 2d mo. 1776. c.r.4.
David, s. of David and Elisabeth, 11th day, 1st mo. 1787. c.r.4.
David, s. of Jacob and Sarah, 6th day, 1st mo. 1789. Twin. c.r.4.
David, s. of David and Lucretia, 30th day, 7th mo. 1819. Twin. c.r.4.
Dorcas, d. of Lawrance and Hannah, 12th day, 8th mo. 1770. c.r.4.
Duty, s. of Joseph and Alice, 15th day, 7th mo. 1794. c.r.4.
Eber, s. of John and Chloe, 27th day, 11th mo. 1768. c.r.4.
Edward, 19th day, 3d mo. 1740. c.r.4.
Edward, s. of Lawrance and Hannah, 2d day, 11th mo. 1769. c.r.4.
Edward, s. of Amasa and Polly, 31st day, 5th mo. 1812. c.r.4.
Elisabeth [———], w. of Edward, 18th day, 2d mo. 1746. c.r.4.
Elisabeth [———], w. of David, 29th day, 6th mo. 1760. c.r.4.
Elisabeth, d. of George and Judith, Oct. 2, 1785.
Elisabeth, d. of Amasa and Polly, 27th day, 1st mo. 1814. c.r.4.
Elisha, s. of Lawrance and ———, 17th day, 2d mo. 1757 (19th day, 2d mo. 1757 dup.). c.r.4.
Elisha, s. of David and Elisabeth, 31st day, 3d mo. 1795. c.r.4.
Elisha, s. of Royal and Phebe, Apr. 4, 1809.
Elisha Arnold, s. of Enoch and Wait, 31st day, 5th mo. 1805. c.r.4.
Eliza, d. of Amasa and Elce, 8th day, 5th mo. 1801. c.r.4.

SOUTHWICK, Elizabeth, d. of Joseph and Alice, 23d day, 3d mo. 1785. c.r.4.
Elizabeth, d. of David and Elisabeth, 11th day, 1st mo. 1791. c.r.4.
Elizabeth, d. of Enoch and Mary, 24th day, 3d mo. 1795. c.r.4.
Elizabeth A. Pitts [———], w. of Edward L., Sept. 7, 1838. g.r.1.
Elizabeth A. S., d. of Arnold and Patience, July 24, 1833. g.r.21.
Emeline Farnum, d. of Jonathan F. and Chloe, Nov. 29, 1825.
Enoch, 4th day, 4th mo. 1753. c.r.4.
Enoch (s. of John and Chloe, c.r.4), June 7, 1776. g.r.1.
Enoch, s. of Enoch and Mary, 12th day, 3d mo. 1797. c.r.4.
Esther, d. of Jacob and Sarah, 28th day, 12th mo. 1783. c.r.4.
Ezra, s. of Joseph and Alice, 22d day, 2d mo. 1780. c.r.4.
Ezra, s. of Jacob and Sarah, 14th day, 4th mo. 1782. c.r.4.
Ezra, s. of Edward and Elisabeth, 25th day, 7th mo. 1782. c.r.4.
Farnum, s. of Royal and Phebe, 14th day, 9th mo. 1801. c.r.4.
Farnum, 21st day, 9th mo. 1813. c.r.4.
George, 14th day, 10th mo. 1747. c.r.4.
George, s. of John and Chloe, 28th day, 2d mo. 1784. c.r.4.
George, s. of George and Judith, Jan. 11, 1789. Twin.
George, s. of David and Elisabeth, 10th day, 4th mo. 1789. c.r.4.
George, s. of David and Lucretia, 25th day, 10th mo. 1817. c.r.4.
Geo[rge] S., 28th day, 2d mo. 1813. c.r.4.
Hannah [———], w. of Lawrance, 10th day, 2d mo. 1741. c.r.4.
Hannah, d. of Edward and Elisabeth, 14th day, 10th mo. 1773. c.r.4.
Hannah, d. of Lawrance and Hannah, 3d day, 7th mo. 1778. c.r.4.
Hannah, d. of David and Elisabeth, 20th day, 2d mo. 1785. c.r.4.
Hannah, d. of Enoch and Mary, 29th day, 8th mo. 1789. c.r.4.
Hannah, d. of Jacob and Sarah, 29th day, 5th mo. 1791. c.r.4.
Hannah [———], w. of Daniel, 6th day, 8th mo. 1798. c.r.4.
Hannah, d. of David and Lucretia, 11th day, 8th mo. 1812. c.r.4.
Hannah D., d. of James and Ruth, July 10, 1810.
Hannah Smith, d. of Daniel and Hannah, 30th day, 4th mo. 1828. c.r.4.

SOUTHWICK, Hannah T., d. of James and Ruth, 10th day, 7th mo. 1810. c.r.4.
Hepsabah, d. of Amasa and Elce, 19th day, 7th mo. 1807. c.r.4.
Huldah, d. of David and Elisabeth, 6th day, 4th mo. 1783. c.r.4.
Isaac, 13th day, 12th mo. 1767. c.r.4.
Isaac, s. of Jacob and Sarah, 1st day, 5th mo. 1785. c.r.4.
Israel Mowry, s. of Enoch and Wait, 22d day, 8th mo. 1809. c.r.4.
Jacob, 5th day, 4th mo. 1751. c.r.4.
Jacob, s. of Jacob and Sarah, 17th day, 1st mo. 1793. c.r.4.
James, s. of George and Judith, Jan. 11, 1789. Twin.
James, s. of Royal and Phebe, Oct. 7, 1789.
James, s. of George and Judith, Sept. 1, 1795.
James, s. of Amasa and Elce, 19th day, 3d mo. 1803. c.r.4.
James Comstock, s. of Daniel and Hannah, 12th day, 12th mo. 1824. c.r.4.
Jane L., d. of David and Lucretia, 13th day, 1st mo. 1837. c.r.4.
Jesse, s. of Lawrance and Hannah, 5th day, 12th mo. 1772. c.r.4.
Jesse, s. of Enoch and Mary, 14th day, 12th mo. 1785. c.r.4.
Jesse E., s. of David and Lucretia, 30th day, 10th mo. 1814. c.r.4.
John, 6th day, 7th mo. 1754. c.r.4.
John, s. of John and Chloe, 29th day, 8th mo. 1771. c.r.1.
John, s. of David and Lucretia, 3d day, 9th mo. 1827. c.r.4.
Jonathan, s. of Jacob and Sarah, 19th day, 6th mo. 1786. c.r.4.
Jonathan, s. of Jacob and Sarah, 6th day, 1st mo. 1789. Twin. c.r.4.
Jona[than], s. of David and Lucretia, 30th day, 7th mo. 1819. Twin. c.r.4.
Jonathan F., s. of Royal and Phebe, Dec. 14, 1799.
Joseph, 21st day, 12th mo. 1745. c.r.4.
Joseph, s. of Joseph and Alice, 2d day, 3d mo. 1793. c.r.4.
Joseph, 31st day, 12th mo. 1817. c.r.4.
Joseph B., s. of Enoch and Waity, Nov. 7, 1823. g.r.1.
Judith [———], w. of George, 23d day, 10th mo. 1757. c.r.4.
Judith, d. of George and Judith, July 21, 1791.
Lawrance, 11th day, 11th mo. 1731. c.r.4.
Leroy D., s. of Israel M. and Lucy H., Mar. 29, 1848. g.r.1.
Levina, d. of John and Chloe, 26th day, 1st mo. 1786. c.r.4.
Louisa, d. of David and Lucretia, 1st day, 11th mo. 1834. c.r.4.

SOUTHWICK, Lucretia [———], w. of David, 29th day, 7th mo. 1790. c.r.4.
Lucy, d. of John and Chloe, 22d day, 4th mo. 1767. c.r.4.
Lucy, d. of Jacob and Sarah, 4th day, 5th mo. 1797. c.r.4.
Lucy H. [———], w. of Israel M., July 12, 1817. g.r.1.
Luke, s. of Joseph and Alice, 11th day, 9th mo. 1789. c.r.4.
Lyddia Capron, d. of Royal and Phebe, Apr. 20, 1807.
Lydia, d. of Lawrance and Hannah, 5th day, 5th mo. 1781. c.r.4.
Lydia, d. of George and Judith, Apr. 11, 1800.
Lydia, d. of Enoch and Waity, Sept. 10, 1810. g.r.1.
Lydia Anna, d. of Daniel and Hannah, 19th day, 2d mo. 1836. c.r.4.
Lydia C., d. of Royal and Phebe, 20th day, 4th mo. 1807. c.r.4.
Lydia Morse, d. of Jonathan F. and Chloe, June 29, 1829. (d. of Jonathan F. and Chloe Holbrook and w. of Edwin S. Thayer, June 28, 1829. g.r.21.)
Margaret [———], w. of Elisha, 16th day, 8th mo. 1758. c.r.4.
Marianne, d. of Elisha and Delia, Jan. 16, 1838.
Mary [———], w. of Enoch, 11th day, 5th mo. 1758. c.r.4.
Mary, d. of Jacob and Sarah, 30th day, 7th mo. 1779. c.r.4.
Mary, d. of Joseph and Alice, 15th day, 7th mo. 1787. c.r.4.
Mary, d. of Enoch and Mary, 20th day, 9th mo. 1791. c.r.4.
Mary, d. of David and Elisabeth, 23d day, 4th mo. 1797. c.r.4.
Mary, d. of David and Elisabeth, 27th day, 10th mo. 1798. c.r.4.
Mary Martha, d. of Daniel and Hannah, 8th day, 11th mo. 1830. c.r.4.
Mary Urania Farnum, d. of Jonathan F. and Chloe, May 29, 1833.
Mercy, d. of Edward and Elisabeth, 18th day, 10th mo. 1779. c.r.4.
Moses, s. of Joseph and Alice, 6th day, 5th mo. 1783. c.r.4.
Moses D., ———, 1805. c.r.4.
Muzzy, s. of George and Judith, Mar. 17, 1778.
Nancy, d. of Enoch and Mary, 18th day, 8th mo. 1780. c.r.4.
Nancy, d. of David and Lucretia, 15th day, 9th mo. 1816. c.r.4.
Nancy M., d. of David and Lucretia, 8th day, 5th mo. 1823. c.r.4.
Nathan, s. of Amasa and Polly, 30th day, 1st mo. 1818. c.r.4.
Nathaniel, 2d day, 5th mo. 1752. c.r.4.

SOUTHWICK, Olive, d. of Edward and Elisabeth, 2d day, 7th mo. 1780. C.R.4.
Olive, d. of Jacob and Sarah, 20th day, 9th mo. 1787. C.R.4.
Patience [———], w. of Arnold, Jan. 30, 1803. G.R.21.
Phebe [———], w. of Royal, July 2, 1769.
Phebe, d. of Jacob and Sarah, 9th day, 7th mo. 1794. C.R.4.
Phebe, d. of Royal and Phebe, Sept. 15, 1797.
Phebe F., d. of James and Ruth, 28th day, 7th mo. 1814. C.R.4.
Philadelphia, d. of John and Chloe, 5th day, 4th mo. 1770. C.R.4.
Polly [———], w. of Amasa, — day, 9th mo. 1781. C.R.4.
Royal (s. of Lawrance and Hannah, C.R.4), Dec. 6, 1760.
Royal, s. of Royal and Phebe, Sept. 9, 1795.
Royal A., s. of Israel M. and Lucy H., May 21, 1841. G.R.1.
Ruth, d. of Lawrance and Hannah, 5th day, 3d mo. 1763. C.R.4.
Ruth, d. of George and Judith, Nov. 22, 1782.
Ruth [———], w. of James, 3d day, 12th mo. 1783. C.R.4.
Ruth M., d. of Daniel and Mary Farnum, Aug. 29, 1819. G.R.1.
Samuel, s. of Jacob and Sarah, 10th day, 12th mo. 1780. C.R.4.
Samuel, s. of Daniel and Jemima, 11th day, 2d mo. 1793. C.R.4.
Sarah [———], w. of Jacob, 20th day, 1st mo. 1753. C.R.4.
Sarah, d. of Lawrance and ———, 27th day, 4th mo. 1754. C.R.4.
Sarah, d. of Joseph and Alice, 2d day, 7th mo. 1781. C.R.4.
Sarah Elizabeth, 19th day, 2d mo. 1825. C.R.4.
Stephen, s. of Enoch and Mary, 2d day, 2d mo. 1788. C.R.4.
Stephen H., s. of Jonathan F. and Chloe, Aug. 15, 1827.
Stephen Swett, s. of David and Elisabeth, 12th day, 7th mo. 1781. C.R.4.
Susan, d. of Ezra and Chloe, and w. of Col. Silas A. Comstock, Feb. 10, 1810. G.R.18.
Sylvanus H., s. of Jonathan F. and Chloe, Feb. —, 1835.
Thamisin, d. of David and Elisabeth, 19th day, 3d mo. 1780. C.R.4.
Thomas, s. of Amasa and Polly, 28th day, 4th mo. 1816. C.R.4.
Thomas Mussey, s. of Enoch and Wait, 9th day, 3d mo. 1812. C.R.4.
Urana, d. of Royal and Phebe, Feb. 1, 1792.
Urana F., d. of James and Ruth, 19th day, 10th mo. 1817. C.R.4.
Wait, d. of John and Chloe, 10th day, 1st mo. 1782. C.R.4.
Waity [———], w. of Enoch, Nov. 12, 1780. G.R.1.
Weaty, d. of Elisha and Margaret, 14th day, 2d mo. 178-. C.R.4.

SOUTHWICK, Willet S. C., s. of Elisha A., b. in Smithfield, R. I., and Athaline, b. in Burrillville, R. I., July 1, 1848.
Zadock, s. of Lawrance and Hannah, 8th day, 5th mo. 1765. c.r.4.

SOUTHWORTH, George Willard, s. of Josiah and Nancy, Sept. 19, 1812.

SPALDING (see Spaulding), Amanda W., Feb. 14, 1819. g.r.1.
Girdon R., July 24, 1816. g.r.1.
Irene C., Feb. 19, 1809. g.r.1.
James H., Mar. 25, 1846. g.r.1.
Josiah, s. of Rev. Josiah and Mary, bp. July 29, 1787. c.r.1.
Mary, d. of Rev. Josiah and Mary, bp. Apr. 24, 1785. c.r.1.

SPAULDING (see Spalding), Henry, in Killingly, Conn., Mar. 22, 1809. g.r.1.
Pamelia [―――], w. of Henry, in Monson, June 3, 1807. g.r.1.

SPRAGUE, Albert A., s. of George W., b. in Thompson, Conn., and Harriet D., b. in Bellingham, Aug. 15, 1849.
Albion, 19th day, 12th mo. 1812. c.r.4.
Amay, d. of John and Elisabeth, in Smithfield, R. I., 3rd day, 11th mo. 1765. c.r.3.
Anna L., ―――, 1849. g.r.1.
Elias, 1st day, 10th mo. 1786. c.r.4.
Elisabeth, d. of John and Elisabeth, in Richmond, N. H., 1st day, 7th mo. 1770. c.r.3.
George W., ―――, 1824. g.r.1.
Hannah [―――], w. of Albion, 9th day, 9th mo. 1811. c.r.4.
Harriet D., ―――, 1824. g.r.1.
Hosea, 17th day, 4th mo. 1805. c.r.4.
Jane F., d. of George W. and Harriet D., May 22, 1847.
Marcus Le Roy, s. of Ebenezer and Mary, Mar. 24, 1844.
Mercy, 23d day, 10th mo. 1745 (29th day, 10th mo. 1745 dup.). c.r.4.
Michael, s. of John and Elisabeth, 12th day, 7th mo. 1767. c.r.3.
Sarah [―――], 2d w. of Zebulon, 17th day, 1st mo. 1793. c.r.4.
Silama [―――], w. of Zebulon, 13th day, 8th mo. 1778. c.r.4.
Sina, 20th day, 12th mo. 1789. c.r.4.

SPRING, Abby W., ―――, 1813. g.r.1.
Abigail, d. of John and Hannah, Apr. 4, 1774.

UXBRIDGE BIRTHS.

SPRING, Abigail 2d, d. of John and Hannah, Jan. 4, 1778.
Abigal White, d. of John and Sarah, June 30, 1739. Twin.
Adolphus, s. of John and Hannah, May 13, 1772.
Adolphus, s. of John Jr. and Mary, bp. Oct. 5, 1783. C.R.I.
Avery, s. of John and Hannah, Mar. 23, 1776.
Calvin, s. of Ephraim and Eunice, Aug. 4, 1791.
Charles Carter, s. of Luther and Nancy, Mar. 24, 1824.
Elkanah, s. of John and Hannah, Feb. 6, 1768.
Elkanah, s. of Ephraim and Eunice of Northbridge, Sept. 17, 1780.
Emily Augusta, d. of Luther and Nancy, Dec. 21, 1827.
Ephraim, s. of John and Sarah, July 21, 1750.
Ephraim, s. of Ephraim and Eunice, Apr. 6, 1796.
Ephraim, s. of George C. and Sabrina, Oct. 16, 1846.
Eunice, d. of Ephraim and Eunice, Aug. 13, 1789.
Frances Elizabeth, d. of George C. and Sabrina, Dec. 2, 1843.
Frances Elizabeth, d. of George C. and Sabrina, Jan. 5, 1845.
Franklin Henry, s. of Luther and Nancy, Mar. 3, 1838.
George, s. of Calvin and Hannah, Jan. 25, 1819.
George Whitney, s. of Luther and Nancy, Oct. 15, 1830.
Hannah Maria, d. of George and Sabrina, in Needham, Oct. 19, 1840.
Joanna, d. of Ephraim and Eunice, Aug. 14, 1800.
John, s. of John and Sarah, Aug. 30, 1736.
John, s. of John and Sarah, June 10, 1741.
John, s. of Calvin and Hannah, Jan. 26, 1818.
John Calvin, s. of George and Sabrina, Feb. 19, 1842.
Josiah, s. of Ephraim and Eunice of Northbridge, June 11, 1778.
Josiah, s. of Ephraim and Eunice, Nov. 2, 1784.
Luther, s. of Ephraim and Eunice, Oct. 12, 1787.
Luther, ——, 1812. G.R.I.
Lydia, d. of Ephraim and Eunice of Northbridge, July 23, 1782.
Maria, d. of Calvin and Hannah, Aug. 30, 1824.
Margaret, ——, 1807. G.R.I.
Mary, d. of John and Sarah, Dec. 19, 1743.
Mary, d. of John and Hannah, Jan. 17, 1770.
Mary E., d. of Daniel and Orra, Mar. 16, 1829. G.R.I.
Mary Elizabeth, d. of Luther and Nancy, July 22, 1822.
Marya, d. of Ephraim and Eunice, Oct. 19, 1793.
Nancy Jane, d. of Luther and Nancy, Aug. 17, 1835.
Samuel, s. of John and Sarah, Feb. 27, 1745-6.
Samuel Read, s. of Luther and Nancy, Sept. 7, 1819.
Sarah, d. of Ephraim and Eunice of Northbridge, late of Uxbridge, Feb. 5, 1776.

SPRING, Sarah, d. of Calvin and Hannah, Nov. 14, 1822.
Sophrona, d. of Ephraim and Eunice, July 26, 1798.
Thomas Read, s. of John and Sarah, June 30, 1739. Twin.
William Luther, s. of Luther and Nancy, Oct. 25, 1832.

STANLEY, Joseph Burgess, s. of Wells, bp. Mar. 27, 1836. c.r.2.

STAPLES, Albert, s. of Nahor and Elizabeth, in Brunswick, N. Y., Sept. 3, 1831.
Benjamin Franklin, s. of Nahor and Elizabeth, June 20, 1839.
Charles Edwin, s. of Charles and Melatiah, Feb. 14, 1821.
Esther Chilson, d. of Nahor and Elizabeth, Mar. 13, 1827.
Ezra F., s. of Ezra and Cynthia, Aug. 27, 1822. g.r.1.
Henry Clay, s. of Charles and Melatiah, Oct. 8, 1831.
Maria, d. of Charles and Melatiah, Mar. 27, 1829. Twin.
Mary, d. of Charles and Melatiah, Mar. 27, 1829. Twin.
Sarah Angeline, d. of Charles and Melatiah, Jan. 4, 1825.
Seth, s. of Ezra, in Mendon, Mar. 18, 1815. g.r.1.
Susan Ann, d. of Nahor and Elizabeth, in Norway, N. Y., Sept. 1, 1834.

STARBUCK, ———, s. of Uriah, 5th day, 12th mo. 1800. c.r.4.
George, s. of Uriah, 13th day, 11th mo. 1801. c.r.4.
John, s. of Uriah, 8th day, 3d mo. 1806. c.r.4.
Paul, s. of Uriah, 14th day, 5th mo. 1809. c.r.4.
Thomas Howse, s. of Uriah, 18th day, 4th mo. 1804. c.r.4.

STEARNS, David, s. of Ebenezer and Chloe, May 24, 1776.
George, s. of Ebenezer and Chloe, Apr. 15, 1772.
Jonah, s. of Ebenezer and Chloe, May 15, 1781.
Marcy, d. of Ebenezer and Chloe, Feb. 16, 1774. Twin.
Micah, s. of Ebenezer and Chloe, Feb. 16, 1774. Twin.
Moses, s. of Ebenezer and Chloe, Nov. 28, 1778.
Thomas, s. of Ebenezer and Chloe, June 9, 1770.

STEERE, Anna W., Sept. 4, 1840. g.r.1.
Marquis D. F., ———, 1822. g.r.1.

STEPHENS (see Stevens), Sarah, d. of William and Jemima, Sept. 29, 1753.

STETSON, Lucy G. Taft [———], w. of Lyman J., May 12, 1826. g.r.1.
Lyman J., Apr. 6, 1817. g.r.1.

STEVENS (see Stephens), Harriet Grout [———], w. of James, ———, 1804. G.R.1.
James, ———, 1819. G.R.1.
Mary H. Hoxsie [———], w. of James, ———, 1830. G.R.1.

STEWART, Mary [———], w. of William, ———, 1841. G.R.1.
William, ———, 1831. G.R.1.

STONE, ———, s. of Almon, b. in Coventry, R. I., and Sarah, b. in Upton, Dec. 26, 1849.
Ezra, 31st day, 3d mo. 1736. C.R.4.
Fanny A., d. of Charles H. and Catharine B., Jan. 25, 1846.
Freelove [———], w. of Ezra, 29th day, 2d mo. 1737. C.R.4.
Lydia, d. of Ebenezer and ———, bp. Jan. 18, 1756. C.R.1.
William E., s. of Charles H., b. in Coventry, R. I., and Catharine R., b. in Newport, R. I., in Douglas, Oct. 22, 1849.

STOW, Charles Augustus, s. of Silas W. and Rhoda, May 1, 1810.
Eliza Ann, d. of Silas W. and Rhoda, Apr. 17, 1808.

SWEET, Abigail, d. of Jonathan and Amme, 17th day, 1st mo. 1772. C.R.4.
Amme [———], w. of Jonathan, 9th day, 11th mo. 1733. C.R.4.
Amme, d. of Jonathan and Amme, 8th day, 11th mo. 1766. C.R.4.
Arnold S., ———, 1827. G.R.1.
Elisabeth, d. of Jonathan and Amme, 13th day, 4th mo. 1769. Twin. C.R.4.
Hannah, d. of Jonathan and Amme, 12th day, 4th mo. 1776.
Jonathan, 28th day, 7th mo. 1732. C.R.4.
Lucy Wheelock [———], w. of Arnold S., ———, 1836. G.R.1.
Mary, d. of Jonathan and Amme, 13th day, 4th mo. 1769. Twin. C.R.4.

SWETT, Hannah [———], w. of Stephen, — day, 9th mo. 1710. C.R.4.
Huldah [———], w. of Stephen, 14th day, 4th mo. 1726. C.R.4.
Stephen, 20th day, 11th mo. 1698. C.R.4.
Stephen, 4th day, 2d mo. 1728. C.R.4.

SWIFT, Daniel Wheeler, 12th day, 6th mo. 1840.
Emma C. [———], w. of Henry D., 22d day, 12th mo. 1844. C.R.4.
Henry D., 21st day, 5th mo. 1834. C.R.4.
Sarah Jane [———], w. of Daniel Wheeler, 16th day, 11th mo. 1847. C.R.4.

SYKES, John C., s. of Joseph and Annis, both b. in England, in Woonsocket, R. I., Nov. 12, 1848.

SYLVESTER (see Silvester), Joseph, 18th day, 7th mo. 1761. c.r.4.

TAFT, ———, s. of Oliver and Laura Ann, July 7, 1844. Twin.
Aaron, s. of Lieut. Joseph and Elisabeth, Apr. 12, 1727.
Aaron, s. of Peter and Elisabeth, May 28, 1743.
Abba Caroline, d. of Robert G. and Julia Ann, July 16, 1833.
Abbie E. R., ———, 1832. g.r.1.
Abby, d. of Frederick and Abigail and w. of Joseph Day, June 7, 1793. g.r.1.
Abi, d. of Nathan and Ruth, Nov. 11, 1781.
Abigail, 6th day, 3d mo. 1753. c.r.4.
Abigail, d. of Jacob and Esther, Oct. 5, 1754.
Abigail, d. of Ephraim and Abigail, Apr. 12, 1772.
Abigail, d. of Silas and Elisabeth, Nov. 20, 1777.
Abigail, d. of Bezaleel and Sarah, Dec. 5, 1777.
Abigail, d. of Robart and Chloe, Aug. 17, 1778.
Abigail [———], w. of Zadock, in Smithfield, R. I., July 23, 1779. g.r.1.
Abigail, d. of James and Esther, Jan. 24, 1791.
Abigail Caroline, d. of Zadock and Abigail, Apr. 21, 1807.
Abigail Wood, d. of Samuel Jr. and Sarah, Dec. 7, 1810.
Abner, s. of Moses and Priscilla, Dec. 28, 1736.
Abner, s. of Moses and Nancy, Jan. 5, 1782.
Abner, s. of Moses and Judith, bp. Oct. 3, 1802. c.r.1.
Adaline Emery, d. of Eber and Lurana, Nov. 29, 1839.
Adelbert Mortimer, s. of Jason and ———, July 28, 1838.
Adeline, d. of David and Sena, Apr. 13, 1806.
Adna, s. of Darias and Anna, May 8, 1786.
Adna, s. of Darias and Loies, Nov. 28, 1801.
Adolphas, s. of Stephen and Anna, Oct. 3, 1791.
Adolphus, s. of Timothy and Abigail, July 10, 1784.
Adolphus, s. of Marvel and Ruth, bp. Oct. 2, 1803. c.r.1.
Adolphus Baylies, s. of Orsmus and Margeret, June 2, 1832.
Albert, s. of Newell and Hannah G., Aug. 28, 1823.
Alice Bradford, d. of Augustine C. and Deborah M., Oct. 26, 1841.
Alonzo Merrick, s. of Squire and Mary, Nov. 28, 1836.
Alpheus, s. of Daniel and Hopestill, bp. Apr. 3, 1757. c.r.1.

TAFT, Amanda, d. of Luther and Deborah, Aug. 29, 1804.
Amanda Maria, d. of Eber and Lurana, Mar. 18, 1838.
Amanda Newell, d. of Jason and ———, July 21, 1819.
Amariah, s. of Oliver and Chloe, Sept. 19, 1807.
Amay, d. of Thaddeus and Silance, Oct. 8, 1778.
Amos, s. of Daniel and Hopestill, bp. Apr. 25, 1745. c.r.1.
Amos Craggin, s. of Willis and Margara, July 15, 1787.
Andre, s. of Josiah and Margery, June 25, 1792.
Andrew Jackson, s. of Eber and Lurana, Jan. 29, 1833.
Anna, d. of Ephraim and Anna, Apr. 4, 1748.
Anna, d. of Aaron (Jr., c.r.1) and Rhoda, Aug. 20, 1777.
Anna, d. of William and Anna, Mar. 30, 1779.
Anna, d. of Stephen and Anna, Nov. 29, 1784.
Anna, d. of Darias and Loies, Aug. 23, 1791.
Anne, d. of Silas and Mary, Dec. 29, 1755.
Anne Cecila, d. of Samuel Jr. and Sarah, Sept. 5, 1807.
Arba (Arba Legg dup.), s. of Worner and Mary, May 25, 1824.
Ariadne [———], w. of Henry G., ———, 1837. G.R.1.
Arnold, s. of Aaron and Marcy, May 4, 1756.
Arnold, s. of Thaddeus and Silance, Mar. 8, 1784.
Artemas, s. of Ezra and Mary, May —, 1828.
Asa, s. of Gidean and Elisabeth, May 8, 1747.
Asa, rep. s. of Asa and real s. of Bashaby Jackson, July 17, 1766.
Asa, s. of Silas and Elisabeth, Apr. 29, 1774.
Asahael, s. of Josiah and Lydia, Apr. 23, 1740.
Asahel, s. of Joseph (2d, c.r.1) and Elisabeth, July 30, 1752.
Asenath Cumings, d. of Timothy and ———, July 29, 1819.
Asenath Cumings, d. of David and Henrietta, June 29, 1833.
Asenath Thayer, d. of Willard and Marietta, Sept. 21, 1820.
Augustine Calvin, s. of Chandler and Nabby, May 11, 1817.
Augustus Richardson, s. of Bezaleel Esq., and Margaret, Sept. 17, 1809.
Aurilia Blue, d. of Bailey and Relief, Nov. 14, 1827.
Austin, s. of Ezra and Mary, Mar. 1, 1822.
Aves, d. of William and Anna, Mar. 19, 1784.
Azuba, d. of Willis and Margara, June 25, 1803.
Azubah Craggin, d. of Adna and Emma, Apr. 13, 1837.
Bashaba White [———], w. of Benjamin, ———, 1803. G.R.1.
Benjamin, s. of Stephen and Mary, Feb. 8, 1734-5.
Benjamin, s. of Oliver and Molle, Dec. 23, 1771.
Benjamin, s. of Josiah and Margery, Aug. 3, 1784.
Benjamin, s. of Marvel and Ruth, Feb. 12, 1791.
Benjamin, s. of Cummings and Marcy, Aug. 10, 1798.
Benjamin, s. of Cummings and Marcy, May 6, 1800.

TAFT, Benjamin Clark, s. of Calvin and Molley, May 17, 1790.
Benjamin Lorin or Lorin B., s. of Benjamin and Bashaba, June 25, 1823.
Bethiah, d. of John and Hannah, Aug. 9, 1747.
Bethiah, d. of (Capt., c.r.1) John and Deborah, July 5. 1762.
Betsa, d. of Reuben and Faithfull, Mar. 24, 1776.
Betsy Smith, d. of Bailey and Relief, Mar. 12, 1824.
Beulah, d. of Daniel and Hopestill, bp. Apr. 25, 1745. c.r.1.
Bezaleel, s. of Josiah and Lydia, Nov. 3, 1750.
Bezalcel, s. of Bezaleel and Sarah, Sept. 8, 1780.
Bezaleel, s. of Samuel 2d and Dorcas, Apr. 8, 1838.
Caleb, s. of Josiah and Lydia, Jan. 15, 1738–9.
Caleb, s. of Caleb and Susannah, Apr. 14, 1757.
Caleb, s. of Bezaleel and Sarah, Dec. 20, 1786.
Calista, d. of Frederic and Abigail, Jan. 31, 1787.
Calista Clinara, d. of Samuel Jr. and Sarah, Mar. 17, 1813.
Calvin, s. of Gershom and Abigail, Nov. 17, 1765.
Caroline, d. of Reuben and Nancy, Feb. 3, 1806.
Cata, d. of William and Anna, Sept. 24, 1780.
Catharina, d. of Paul and Mehitable, Feb. 26, 1753.
Catharine, d. of Squire and Mary, July 27, 1829.
·Catherine Aldrich, ———, 1783. G.R.3.
Chandler, s. of Calvin and Molley, May 29, 1792.
Charles, s. of Luther and Deborah, Jan. 15, 1806.
Charles Augustus, s. of Timothy and ———, Nov. 12, 1825.
Charlotta, d. of Noah and Margret, June 10, 1768.
Charlotte, d. of Noah and Margret, Aug. 27, 1774. (Charlotte, d. of Noah and Deborah, bp. ———, 1774. c.r.1.)
Charlotte, d. of Micajah and Phebe, Oct. 21, 1791.
Charlotte, d. of Sweeting and Marcy, Dec. 6, 1794.
Charlotte, d. of Jacob and Mary, bp. Jan. 15, 1809. c.r.1.
Charlotte Arnold, d. of Noah and Eliza, bp. June 22, 1834. c.r.2.
Charlotte Elizabeth, d. of Orsmus and Margeret, July 31, 1825.
Charlotte Isabelle, d. of Mellens and Maria, bp. Sept. 18, 1831. c.r.1.
Cheany, s. of Marvel and Ruth, Dec. 8, 1787.
Cheny, s. of Gershom and Abigail, May 3, 1771.
Cheny, s. of Henry C. and Elizabeth Catharine, Aug. 10, 1842.
Chloa, d. of Josiah and Lydia, June 7, 1753.
Chloa, d. of Noah and Margret, Nov. 25, 1763.
Chloa, d. of Easman and Hannah, July 7, 1785.
Chloe, d. of Nathan and Ruth, Apr. 19, 1784.
Chloe, d. of Bezaleel and Sarah, Mar. 10, 1793.

TAFT, Chloe, d. of David and Sena, Dec. 21, 1811.
Chloe Ann, d. of Samuel 2d and Dorcas, Aug. 23, 1827.
Chloe Elizabeth, d. of David and Henrietta, July 25, 1842.
Chloe Jane, d. of Oliver and Laura Ann, Nov. 25, 1849.
Chloe M., d. of Luke and Nancy, Feb. 5, 1823.
Chole, d. of Robart and Chloe, Jan. 20, 1786.
Clarinda, d. of Frederic and Abigail, Feb. 28, 1789.
Clarisa W., d. of Luke and Nancy, May 3, 1810.
Clirana, d. of Samuel Jr. and Sarah, Apr. 12, 1822.
Comfort, d. of Daniel and Hopestill, bp. Dec. 16, 1744. C.R.1.
Cruff, s. of Silas and Elisabeth, May 12, 1784.
Cummings, s. of Joseph and Elisabeth, Aug. 27, 1770. (Cummings, s. of Joseph Jr. and Elizabeth dec., bp. Sept. 4, 1770. C.R.1.)
Cynthia, d. of Aaron (Jr., C.R.1) and Rhoda, Aug. 17, 1773.
Dan, s. of Silas and Elisabeth, May 6, 1769.
Dandridge, s. of Samuel and Experiance, Aug. 1, 1787.
Dandridge Gordon, s. of Warner and Mary, Feb. 18, 1828.
Daniel, s. of Daniel and Hopestill, bp. July 28, 1751. C.R.1.
Daniel, s. of Stephen and Marcy, Nov. 11, 1763.
Daniel Farnum, s. of Squire and Mary, Sept. 10, 1828.
Daniel Waldo, s. of Orsmus and Margeret, July 26, 1833.
Darius, s. of Abner and Tryal, Sept. 29, 1763.
David, s. of Nathaniel, 3d day, 8th mo. 1770. C.R.4.
David, s. of Noah and Margret, Aug. 14, 1770.
David, s. of Ephraim and Abigail, Feb. 11, 1774.
David, s. of David and Sena, Jan. 13, 1801.
David 3d, s. of Dutee and Judy, Sept. 19, 1825.
Deborah, d. of Joseph Jr. and ———, bp. May 11, 1735. C.R.1.
Deborah, d. of Joseph and Hannah, Mar. 12, 1744–5.
Deborah, d. of Daniel and Hopestill, bp. May 24, 1747. C.R.1.
Deborah, d. of Noah and Margret, Sept. 30, 1753.
Delamount, s. of Sweeting and Marcy, May 23, 1785.
Deriues, s. of Silas and Mary, Feb. 14, 1763.
Diana, d. of Reuben and Faithfull, Sept. 4, 1767.
Dolphus, s. of Marvel and Ruth, Jan. 30, 1789.
Duty, s. of Leonard and Asenath, June 30, 1796.
Easeman, s. of Jacob and Esther, June 16, 1763.
Easman, s. of Easman and Chloa, May 2, 1783.
Eben, s. of Sweeting and Marcy, Feb. 24, 1787.
Ebenezer, s. of Lieut. Joseph and Elisabeth, Aug. 8, 1732.
Ebenezer, s. of Josiah and Lydia, Aug. 20, 1735.
Edward A. (Edward Augustine dup.), s. of Dr. Augustus C. and Deborah M. (b. in Boston dup.), Apr. 8, 1845.

TAFT, Edward C., s. of Calvin and Eliza, Jan. 29, 1846.
Edward Cheney, s. of Henry C. and Elizabeth Catharine, June 29, 1841.
Edwin Augustus, s. of Adna and Emma, Feb. 27, 1824.
Elethan, ch. of Mijamin and Sarah, June 16, 1777.
Elinor Relief, d. of Bailey and Relief, Feb. 14, 1830.
Elisabeth, d. of Lieut. Joseph and Elisabeth, Oct. 30, 1724.
Elisabeth, d. of Gideon and Elisabeth, ——, 1746.
Elisabeth, d. of Gideon and Elisabeth, Mar. 1, 1750.
Elisabeth, d. of Esther, Sept. 14, 1755.
Elisabeth, d. of Joseph and Elisabeth, July 2, 1756.
Eliza (Elizabeth, c.r.1), d. of Calvin and Molley, July 20, 1805.
Eliza Maria, d. of Zadock and Abigail, Apr. 11, 1810.
Elizabeth, d. of Gershom and Abigail, May 13, 1769.
Elizabeth, d. of Joseph (Jr., c.r.1) and Abigail, June 9, 1774. Twin.
Elizabeth Southwick [——], w. of Charles A., ——, 1834. G.R.1.
Ellen Maria, d. of Samuel 2d and Dorcas, Dec. 8, 1836.
Ellis C., ——, 1831. G.R.1.
Emeline Newell, d. of Timothy and ——, Apr. 25, 1822.
Emma Azubah, d. of Adna and Emma, Nov. 21, 1840.
Emma C. [——], w. of Adna, May 12, 1799. G.R.1.
Emory, s. of Ephraim and Abigail, Apr. 8, 1779.
Ephraim, s. of Elisabeth Printes, Sept. 26, 1739.
Ephraim, s. of Ephraim and Mary, Sept. 27, 1743.
Ephraim, s. of Silas and Mary, July 14, 1749.
Ephraim, s. of Stephen and Anna, Aug. 18, 1780.
Esther, d. of Mijamin and Sarah, Nov. 23, 1734.
Esther, d. of Jacob and Esther, Jan. 9, 1747–8.
Esther, d. of James and Esther, Aug. 5, 1786.
Eunice, d. of John and Hannah, June 18, 1735.
Eunice, d. of Joseph (Jr., c.r.1) and Elisabeth, Feb. 11, 1761.
Eunice, d. of Oliver and Molle, Mar. 29, 1773.
Eunice, d. of Bezaleel and Abigail, Jan. 28, 1775.
Eunice, d. of Jesse and Hannah, Aug. 19, 1776.
Eunice, d. of Ephraim and Abigail, Oct. 17, 1784.
Everlina Holbrook, d. of Thaddeus and Silence, bp. Aug. 1, 1801. c.r.1.
Experance, d. of Joseph and Hannah, Apr. 7, 1733.
Experiance, d. of Samuel and Experiance, Dec. 10, 1791.
Ezekiel, s. of James and Esther, Jan. 21, 1777.
Ezra, s. of Joseph (Jr., c.r.1) and Hannah, Apr. 15, 1731.
Ezra, s. of Joseph (Jr., c.r.1) and Elisabeth, Dec. 22, 1752.

TAFT, Ezra, s. of Easman and Hannah, Mar. 6, 1793.
Ezra, s. of Cummings and Marcy, May 13, 1797.
Ezra Wood, s. of Frederic and Abigail, Aug. 26, 1800.
Fanny Adams, d. of Adna and Emma, June 25, 1826.
Fraderick, s. of Samuel and Mary, June 8, 1759.
Francis Amariah, s. of Amariah and Mary, Sept. 18, 1847.
Francis Merrick, s. of Eber and Lurana, July 12, 1835.
Frederic, s. of Samuel Jr. and Sarah, in Belchertown, Apr. 18, 1815.
Frederic Augustus, s. of Frederic and Abigail, Apr. 7, 1791.
Frederick E., s. of John R. and Irene W., June 21, 1848. G.R.1.
Garshom, s. of Peter and Elisabeth, Oct. 20, 1739.
George, s. of Ephraim and Abigal, Jan. 25, 1774.
George Burrows, s. of Thaddeus and Silance, Sept. 4, 1797.
George Carpenter, s. of Mellen and Maria, Aug. 22, 1824.
George Spring, s. of Bezaleel Jr., Esq. and Hannah (Spring), Sept. 14, 1822.
George Spring, s. of Bezaleel Jr., Esq. and Hannah (Spring), Dec. 26, 1826.
George Washington, s. of Samuel and Mary, May 1, 1783.
George Washington, s. of Oliver and Chloe, May 13, 1823.
George Willard, s. of Willard and Marietta, Aug. 27, 1816.
Gershum, s. of Noah and Margret, Mar. 25, 1772. Twin.
Gidean, s. of Gidean and Elisabeth, Nov. 10, 1738.
Gidean, s. of (Capt., C.R.1) John and Deborah, Sept. 3, 1764.
Gravenor, s. of Stephen and Anna, Feb. 17, 1773.
Guilford Hodges, s. of Josiah and Margery, Jan. 1, 1799.
Hannah, d. of John and Hannah, July 4, 1737.
Hannah, d. of John and Hannah, June 5, 1744.
Hannah, d. of Stephen and Mary, Aug. 17, 1750.
Hannah, d. of Jesse and Lydia, Nov. 1, 1763.
Hannah, d. of Joseph (Jr., C.R.1) and Elisabeth, Mar. 12, 1764.
Hannah, d. of Robart and Chloe, Mar. 12, 1772.
Hannah, d. of Mijamin and Sarah, Apr. 16, 1773.
Hannah, d. of Nathaniel, 3d day, 2d mo. 1774. C.R.4.
Hannah, d. of Joseph and Hannah, Sept. 29, 1789.
Hannah, d. of Cummings and Marcy, May 18, 1802.
Hannah [———], w. of Henry, June 19, 1810. G.R.1.
Hannah Jane, d. of Ezra and Mary, Nov. 17, 1839.
Hannah Tillinghast, d. of Willis and Margara, May 4, 1790.
Hannah Tillinghast, d. of Zadock and Abigail, Jan. 28, 1803.
Harriet Jerusha, d. of Jason and ———, July 28, 1827.
Harriet Maria, d. of Warner and Mary, July 28, 1832.
Harriet Whiting, d. of Noah and Eliza, bp. June 22, 1834. C.R.2.

TAFT, Harriot, d. of Frederic and Abigail, July 25, 1795.
Hazelton, s. of Stephen and Anna, Jan. 6, 1769.
Hellen Sophronia, d. of William H. and Arrina, Apr. 28, 1839.
Henery, s. of Peter and Elisabeth, Feb. 17, 1736–7.
Henrietta Aldrich, d. of John R. and Irene W., ——, 1846. G.R.1.
Henry, Sept. 13, 1819. G.R.1.
Henry Gordon, s. of Bezaleel Jr., Esq. and Hannah (Spring), Apr. 3, 1832.
Henry Lortin (Henry Lawton dup.), s. of Eber and Hannah, Mar. 8, 1822.
Hephzibah, d. of Daniel and Hopestill, bp. Apr. 25, 1745. C.R.1.
Hiram Allen, s. of Eber and Lurana, Dec. 8, 1828.
Hopa or Hopestill, d. of David and Sena, May 12, 1794.
Hopestill, d. of Daniel and Hopestill, bp. July 9, 1749. C.R.1.
Horace Loring, s. of William H. and Arrina, Apr. 4, 1835.
Huldah, d. of John and Mary, Apr. 7, 1770.
Huldah, d. of Joseph and Hannah, Feb. 17, 1775.
Huldah, d. of Joseph and Hannah, May 21, 1780.
Irena, d. of James and Esther, Oct. 25, 1774.
Irene, d. of Luke and Nancy, Sept. 19, 1816.
Irene W. [———], w. of John R., ——, 1828. G.R.1.
Isaac Dexter, s. of Eber and Lurana, Feb. 11, 1832.
Israel, s. of Oliver and Molle, Aug. 19, 1779.
Israel, s. of Josiah and Margery, July 30, 1782.
Israel Mowry, s. of Samuel Jr. and Sarah, Dec. 6, 1803.
Israiel, s. of Jacob and Esther, Mar. 1, 1761.
Jacob, s. of Jacob and Esther, Dec. 1, 1751.
Jacob, May 19, 1823. G.R.1.
James, s. of Moses and Priscilla, Apr. 9, 1738.
James, s. of James and Esther, June 13, 1780.
James, s. of Luke and Nancy, ——, 1830.
James Madison 2d, s. of Dutee and Judy, Dec. 27, 1827.
James Whitman, s. of Calvin and Molley, Jan. 21, 1809.
James Woodbury, s. of Orsmus and Margeret, July 17, 1830.
Jason, s. of Webb and Lucy, June 5, 1796.
Jehosheba, d. of Daniel and Hopestill, bp. May 11, 1755. C.R.1.
Jemima, d. of Gidean and Elisabeth, Sept. 8, 1736.
Jemima, d. of Gidean and Elisabeth, Jan. 26, 1752.
Jemima, d. of Caleb and Susannah, Aug. 15, 1755.
Jesse, s. of John and Hannah, June 8, 1742.
Jesse, s. of Nathan and Sarah, in Smithfield, Apr. 2, 1767.
Jesse, s. of Robart and Chloe, Feb. 3, 1781.

TAFT, Jesse, s. of Robart and Chloe, Apr. 30, 1783.
Jesse, s. of Abner Jr. and Abigail, Feb. 16, 1806.
Joanna, d. of Moses and Priscilla, June 26, 1756.
Joanna, d. of Nahum and Rachel, Aug. 2, 1769.
Joanna, d. of Ephraim and Abigail, June 8, 1782.
Joanna Bennett, d. of Zadock and Abigail, Oct. 13, 1805.
Job, s. of Stephen and Mary, Dec. 25, 1740.
Job, s. of Silas and Elisabeth, Feb. 2, 1772.
Joel, s. of Josiah and Lydia, Aug. 15, 1742.
Joel, s. of Peter and Elisabeth, May 28, 1747.
Joel, s. of Josiah and Lydia, Feb. 19, 1747-8.
John, s. of Stephen and Mary, June 19, 1737.
John, s. of John and Hannah, Jan. 2, 1740.
John, s. of Jesse and Hannah, July 11, 1771.
John, s. of Jacob and Mary, bp. Jan. 15, 1809. C.R.1.
John Aborn, s. of Otis and Mary Ann, Sept. 25, 1819.
John Brooks, s. of Adna and Emma, July 28, 1819.
John Read, s. of Orsmus and Margeret, Apr. 21, 1826.
John Sullivan, s. of Thaddeus and Silance, Nov. 30, 1803.
Joseph, s. of Lieut. Joseph and Elisabeth, Apr. 19, 1722.
Joseph, s. of Moses and Priscilla, July 6, 1751.
Joseph, s. of Noah and Margret, Mar. 25, 1772. Twin.
Joseph, s. of Leonard and Asenath, Oct. 14, 1793.
Joseph K., s. of Oliver and Laura Ann, Sept. 25, 1846.
Josiah, s. of Josiah and Margery [no date].
Josiah, s. of Josiah and Lydia, May 10, 1733.
Josiah, s. of Mijamin and Sarah, Oct. 28, 1752.
Josiah, s. of John and Hannah, bp. Nov. 29, 1752. C.R.1.
Josiah, s. of Moses and Priscilla, Oct. 17, 1758.
Josiah, s. of Capt. John and Deborah, bp. Nov. 18, 1759. C.R.1.
Josiah, s. of Josiah dec. and Lydia, and gr. s. of wid. Lydia, bp. Dec. 5, 1762. C.R.1.
Josiah, s. of Jesse and Hannah, May 28, 1768.
Josiah, s. of Reuben and Faithfull, Monday, June 26, 1769, at two o'clock in the morning.
Josiah, s. of Robart and Chloe, July 6, 1776.
Josiah, s. of Abner Jr. and Abigail, Oct. 31, 1807.
Jotham, s. of Caleb and Susanna, Jan. 3, preceding the year 1748.
Judson, s. of Josiah and Margery, Feb. 14, 1793.
Julia Ann, d. of Israel and Ann, Apr. 15, 1810.
Julia Emily, d. of Darias and Loies, ———, 1807.
Keith, s. of Noah and Margret, May 5, 1761.
L. Herbert, ———, 1846. G.R.1.

TAFT, Lamon, s. of Marvel and Ruth, May 1, 1796.
Laura Ann, d. of Ezra and Mary, June —, 1824.
Laura Ann Maria, d. of Oliver and Laura Ann, July 7, 1844. Twin.
Laura Matilda, d. of Jason and ———, Feb. 26, 1830.
Lenord, s. of Joseph (Jr., C.R.1) and Elisabeth, Mar. 29, 1767.
Levi, s. of Silas and Mary, Mar. 28, 1751.
Levina, d. of Aaron and Bethiah, Jan. 30, 1746–7.
Levina, d. of Abner Jr. and Abigail, Feb. 9, 1805.
Lewes, s. of Silas and Elisabeth, Apr. 19, 1781.
Lewis Spring, s. of Bezaleel Jr., Esq. and Hannah (Spring), Apr. 5, 1820.
Lewis W., s. of Bridgham and Eliza, July 8, 1845.
Lois [———], w. of Darius, Nov. 15, 1771. G.R.1.
Louis, d. of Gidean and Elisabeth, July —, 1756.
Louis, d. of Jacob and Esther, Apr. 28, 1757.
Louisa Josephine, d. of Jason and ———, Dec. 1, 1833.
Louisa Margaret, d. of Bezaleel Esq. and Margaret, Apr. 7, 1811.
Lovice, d. of Stephen and Anna, July 1, 1783.
Lucinda, d. of Weeb and Lucy, Nov. 22, 1793.
Lucinda, d. of Ezra and Mary, Mar. 15, 1826.
Lucy, d. of Joseph (3d, C.R.1) and Elisabeth, Mar. 5, 1745–6.
Lucy, d. of James and Esther, Nov. 22, 1769.
Lucy, d. of Joseph (Jr., C.R.1) and Abigail, June 9, 1774. Twin.
Lucy, d. of Moses and Judith, Apr. 24, 1795.
Lucy Ann, d. of Jason and ———, Sept. 3, 1824.
Lucy Caroline, d. of Warner and Mary, May 12, 1826.
Lucy Scott, d. of Seth and Eliza L., b. in Stratton, Vt., July 8, 1849.
Luke, s. of Moses and Priscilla, Aug. 10, 1754.
Luke, s. of James and Esther, June 3, 1783.
Luke Herbert, s. of Moses 2d and Sylvia Ann (Wheelock in pencil), Nov. 9, 1846.
Lurana Jane, d. of Eber and Lurana, Jan. 9, 1842.
Luther, s. of Ephraim and Abigail, Nov. 10, 1775.
Luther, s. of Paris T. and Julia, May 22, 1833.
Lydia, d. of Caleb and Susanna, July 17, 1749.
Lydia, d. of Mijamin and Sarah, Sept. 18, 1751.
Lydia, d. of Jesse and Lydia, June 26, 1765.
Lydia, d. of Stephen and Anna, Oct. 13, 1766.
Lydia, d. of Ephraim and Abigal, Nov. 17, 1771.
Lydia, d. of Jesse and Hannah, Mar. 15, 1774.
Lydia, d. of Robart and Chloe, May 22, 1774.

TAFT, Lydia, d. of Marvel and Ruth, June 23, 1798.
Lydia [———], w. of Sullivan H., Feb. 6, 1825. G.R.1.
Lydiah, d. of Silas and Mary, Feb. 26, 1767.
Marcy, d. of Mijamin and Sarah, May 22, 1747.
Marcy, d. of Jacob and Esther, Mar. 5, 1758.
Marcy, d. of Paul and Mehitable, June 26, 1763. Twin.
Marcy, d. of Stephen and Marcy, Jan. 14, 1765.
Marcy, d. of Samuel and Mary, Apr. 23, 1765.
Marcy, d. of Reuben and Faithfull, Aug. 11, 1771.
Marcy, d. of Timothy and Priscillah, Sept. 28, 1771.
Marcy, d. of Samuel and Mary, Jan. 26, 1772.
Marcy, d. of Stephen and Anna, Sept. 5, 1775.
Marcy, d. of Thaddeus and Silance, Nov. 27, 1791.
Marcy, d. of Israel and Ann, June 2, 1812.
Margaret, d. of Frederic and Abigail, May 31, 1806.
Margaret Amy, d. of Orsmus and Margeret, Oct. 11, 1841. Twin.
Margaret Smith [———], w. of Orsmus, July 29, 1801. G.R.1.
Margaret Stoddard, d. of Bezaleel and Margaret, at 2 P.M., May 21, 1816.
Margaret Stoddard, d. of Bezaleel Jr., Esq. and Hannah (Spring), Nov. 14, 1818.
Margary Ann, d. of Andre and Sally, May 4, 1818.
Margery, d. of John and Mary, Aug. 21, 1767.
Margret, d. of Lieut. Joseph and Elisabeth, Feb. 9, 1729-30.
Margret, d. of Moses and Priscilla, Feb. 19, 1743.
Margret, d. of Paul and Mehitable, Nov. 14, 1751.
Margret, d. of Noah and Margret, Dec. 20, 1756.
Maria, d. of Robart and Chloe, Jan. 10, 1791.
Maria, d. of Micajah and Phebe, Mar. 19, 1801.
Marinda T., d. of Bailey and Relief, Jan. 12, 1820.
Mary, d. of Stephen and Mary, July 24, 1742.
Mary, d. of Daniel and Hopestill, bp. Dec. 16, 1744. C.R.1.
Mary, d. of Moses and Priscilla, July 17, 1747.
Mary, d. of Caleb and Susannah, Jan. 17, 1754.
Mary, d. of John and Hannah, Feb. 14, 1758.
Mary, d. of Moses and Priscilla, July 19, 1761.
Mary, d. of Paul and Mehitable, June 26, 1763. Twin.
Mary, d. of Abner and Tryal, Oct. 12, 1767.
Mary, d. of Jacob and Mary, Mar. 16, 1786. G.R.1.
Mary, d. of Silas and Elisabeth, Apr. 1, 1786.
Mary, d. of Sweeting and Marcy, Aug. 20, 1799.
Mary, d. of Calvin and Molley, Aug. 25, 1803.

TAFT, Mary A., d. of Willis and Margara, June 18, 1792.
Mary Ann, d. of Frederic and Abigail, Sept. 11, 1803.
Mary Ann, d. of Henry C. and Elizabeth Catharine, June 3, 1840.
Mary Augusta, d. of Warner and Mary, Jan. 21, 1830.
Mary B. [――――], w. of Robert, Aug. 8, 1819. G.R.1.
Mary Burn, d. of Bailey and Relief, Dec. 25, 1822.
Mary Eliza, d. of Noah and Eliza, bp. June 22, 1834. C.R.1.
Mary Elizabeth, d. of Amariah and Mary, May 23, 1843.
Mary M. Brown [――――], w. of Zadock A., Aug. 29, 1815. G.R.1.
Maryan, d. of Oliver and Chloe, July 9, 1814.
Mehitable, d. of Sweeting and Marcy, May 5, 1790.
Mellen, s. of Samuel and Maria, Apr. 22, 1834.
Mercy, d. of Jacob and Esther, bp. May 7, 1759. C.R.1.
Merret, ch. of Samuel and Mary, Jan. 26, 1769.
Micajah, s. of Noah and Margret, Mar. 8, 1766.
Mijamin, s. of Mijamin and Sarah, June 13, 1740.
Millens, s. of Calvin and Molley, Oct. 18, 1799.
Milley, d. of Aaron (Jr., C.R.1) and Rhoda, July 29, 1769.
Minerva Lucretia, d. of Orsmus and Margeret, Aug. 10, 1839.
Minerva Slater, d. of Orsmus and Margeret, July 24, 1835.
Miranda, d. of Ephraim and Abigail, Sept. 21, 1792.
Molley, d. of Mijamin and Sarah, Oct. 10, 1756.
Molley, d. of Noah and Margret, Nov. 10, 1777.
Moses, s. of Moses and Priscilla, Dec. 21, 1742.
Moses, s. of Silas and Mary, Mar. 2, 1758.
Moses, s. of Abner and Tryal, Sept. 29, 1760.
Moses, s. of James and Esther, July 14, 1788.
Moses (Moses Holbrook, C.R.1), s. of Willis and Margara, Feb. 13, 1795.
Moses, s. of Luke and Nancy, Jan. 26, 1812.
Nabba, d. of Frederic and Abigail, June 7, 1793.
Nabby, d. of Micajah and Phebe, Mar. 24, 1793.
Nahum, s. of Moses and Priscilla, Aug. 17, 1745.
Nancy, d. of Reuben and Faithfull, July 9, 1763.
Nancy, d. of Moses and Judith, Mar. 10, 1787.
Naomi G. [――――], w. of Royal K., May 19, 1814. G.R.1.
Nathan, s. of Mijamin and Sarah, Dec. 11, 1738.
Nathan, s. of Gidean and Elisabeth, July 24, 1742.
Nathan, s. of Daniel and Hopestill, bp. May 27, 1753. C.R.1.
Nathan, s. of Joseph (Jr., C.R.1) and Elisabeth, June 3, 1758.
Nathan, s. of (Capt., C.R.1) John and Deborah, Oct. 20, 1766.
Nathan, s. of Nathan and Ruth, Mar. 21, 1773.

TAFT, Nathaniel, s. of Nathaniel, 18th day, 4th mo. 1772. C.R.4.
Nelson, s. of Samuel 2d and Dorcas, Nov. 17, 1829.
Nethaniel, s. of Mijamin and Sarah, Oct. 28, 1742.
Newell, s. of Calvin and Molley, Feb. 13, 1788.
Newell, s. of Moses and Judith, July 28, 1804.
Noah, s. of Noah and Margret, Jan. 14, 1758.
Olive, d. of John and Mary, Apr. 11, 1765.
Olive, d. of Jacob and Esther, Apr. 16, 1770.
Olive, d. of Oliver and Chloe, Mar. 1, 1806.
Olive Maria, d. of Samuel and Maria, June 10, 1831.
Oliver, s. of Aaron and Marcy, Feb. 4, 1750.
Oliver, s. of Abner and Tryal, May 1, 1758.
Oliver, s. of Joseph and Hannah, Nov. 6, 1777.
Oliver, s. of Oliver and Chloe, June 16, 1812.
Ophelia Adams, d. of Amariah and Mary, Jan. 23, 1841.
Orsamus, s. of Jacob and Mary, Jan. 1, 1795.
Orsmus Agustine, s. of Orsmus and Margeret, Oct. 11, 1841. Twin.
Orson, s. of Marvel and Ruth, Apr. 9, 1793.
Oscar A., s. of Bridgham and Eliza Ann, Jan. 17, 1847.
Oscar Fitzallen, s. of Jason and ———, Jan. 21, 1837.
Otice, s. of Samuel and Mary, Oct. 29, 1771.
Otis, s. of Thaddeus and Silance, Sept. 1, 1788.
Pamelia, d. of Darius and Lois, Dec. 13, 1795. G.R.1.
Parla Parilla, d. of Frederic and Abigail, Mar. 5, 1798.
Parley Perilah, d. of Samuel Jr. and Sarah, Feb. 20, 1820.
Parly, d. of Samuel and Mary, Mar. 24, 1774.
Parn, d. of Aaron and Marcy, May 4, 1769.
Patiance, d. of Aaron and Marcy, Sept. 1, 1761.
Patiance, d. of Thaddeus and Silance, Mar. 7, 1781.
Patience, d. of Capt. Daniel dec. and Hopestill, bp. Apr. 25, 1762. C.R.1.
Patience, d. of Mijamin and Sarah, July 8, 1768.
Paul, s. of William and Anna, June 16, 1782.
Peggy, d. of Joseph Sr. and Elizabeth, bp. July 20, 1766. C.R.1.
Peleg, 9th day, 4th mo. 1769. C.R.4.
Perley, d. of Samuel and Mary, Jan. 20, 1768.
Permela, d. of Darias and Loies, Dec. 13, 1795.
Peter, s. of Peter and Elisabeth, Aug. 26, 1741.
Peter, s. of Joseph and Hannah, Apr. 24, 1786.
Peter Rawson, s. of Aaron and Rhoda, Apr. 14, 1785.
Pheebe, d. of Joseph (Jr., C.R.1) and Elisabeth, Nov. 26, 1760.
Phila, d. of Nahum and Rachel, Jan. 4, 1772.
Phila, d. of Gershom and Abigail, July 4, 1775.

TAFT, Phila, d. of Samuel and Mary, Mar. 11, 1781.
Phila, d. of Calvin and Molley, Mar. 25, 1796.
Phila, d. of Eber and Lurana, Jan. 2, 1820.
Phila W., d. of Dexter and Louis, Jan. 11, 1846.
Phin[e]as, s. of Gidean and Elisabeth, Jan. 29, 1754.
Phineas Smith, s. of Bailey and Relief, Feb. 15, 1815.
Phinehas, s. of Silas and Mary, —— 20, 1753.
Phinehas, s. of Ephraim and Abigail, Oct. 3, 1780.
Polley, d. of Reuben and Faithfull, June 9, 1773.
Polley, d. of Timothy and Abigail, Jan. 20, 1780.
Polley, d. of Samuel and Experiance, Mar. 18, 1794.
Polly, d. of Stephen and Anna, Sept. 18, 1777.
Polly, d. of Aaron (Jr., c.r.1) and Rhoda, July 12, 1783.
Polly, d. of David and Sena, Jan. 11, 1800.
Polly, d. of Samuel Jr. and Sarah, June 21, 1809.
Presarved, s. of Silas and Mary, Mar. 15, 1765.
Prisella, d. of Moses and Priscilla, July 30, 1749.
Pruda, d. of William and Anna, Mar. 15, 1778.
Prudance, d. of Paul and Mehitable, Nov. 10, 1756.
Rachel, d. of Silas and Mary, Sept. 18, 1760.
Rawson, s. of Aaron and Rhoda, Oct. 15, 1775.
Read, s. of Marvel and Ruth, Apr. 28, 1785.
Reed, s. of Gershom and Abigail, Mar. 13, 1780.
Reuben, s. of Joseph and Elisabeth, Oct. 21, 1742.
Reuben, s. of Moses and Nancy, Jan. 15, 1784.
Rhoda, d. of Aaron and Marcy, Feb. 4, 1753.
Rhoda, d. of Mijamin and Susanna, Dec. 6, 1780.
Rhoda Grout, d. of Zadock and Abigail, Apr. 24, 1815.
Rhoxanna, d. of Reuben and Faithfull, Aug. 14, 1765.
Richard, s. of Nathan and Ruth, in Smithfield, Aug. 10, 1771.
Robart, s. of John and Hannah, July 21, 1749.
Robert, s. of Robart and Chloe, Nov. 26, 1788.
Robert, s. of John and Lucretia, May 27, 1819.
Robert G. (Robert Gibbs, c.r.1), s. of Willis and Margara, July 29, 1799.
Royal, s. of Mijamin and Sarah, Nov. 18, 1779.
Royal Chapin, s. of Orsmus and Margeret, Feb. 14, 1823.
Royal Kimbal, s. of Bailey and Relief, Mar. 1, 1817.
Rufus, s. of Oliver and Molle, Jan. 4, 1775.
Rufus, s. of Mijamin and Sarah, Sept. 25, 1775.
Russell White, s. of Benjamin and Bashaba, Jan. 23, 1826.
Ruth, d. of Moses and Priscilla, Feb. 19, 1740.
Ruth, d. of Joseph (Sr., c.r.1) and Elisabeth, May 13, 1763.
Ruth, d. of Gershom and Abigail, Feb. 23, 1773.

TAFT, Ruth, d. of Reuben and Faithfull, July 5, 1778.
Ruth, d. of Mijamin and Susanna, July 26, 1782.
Sally, d. of Bezaleel and Sarah, Nov. 2, 1783.
Sally Rhodes, d. of Otis and Mary Ann, June 12, 1821.
Samuel, s. of Mijamin and Sarah, May 5, 1749.
Samuel, s. of (Capt., c.r.1) John and Deborah, Feb. 6, 1769.
Samuel, s. of Moses and Judith, Sept. 24, 1790.
Samuel, s. of Worner and Mary, Jan. 23, 1822.
Samuel H., June 25, 1828. G.R.1.
Samuel Judson, s. of Aaron (Jr., c.r.1) and Rhoda, Nov. 6, 1791.
Samuel Judson, s. of Aaron (Jr., c.r.1) and Rhoda, Oct. 4, 1794.
Sarah, d. of Lieut. Joseph and Elisabeth, Mar. 9, 1719-20.
Sarah, d. of Mijamin and Sarah, Sept. 22, 1736.
Sarah, d. of Stephen and Mary, Feb. 11, 1747-8.
Sarah, d. of Joseph (2d, c.r.1) and Elisabeth, Mar. 8, 1750.
Sarah, d. of Nathan and Ruth, Sept. 19, 1775.
Sarah, d. of Sweeting and Mary, Apr. 18, 1802.
Sarah, d. of Luke and Nancy, Jan. 15, 1815.
Sarah Congdon, d. of Samuel Jr. and Sarah, Oct. 4, 1823.
Sarah E. Bowen [———], w. of Charles A., ———, 1825. G.R.1.
Sarah Frances, d. of Warner and Mary, Mar. 11, 1835.
Sarah Marsh, d. of Timothy and ———, Feb. 12, 1821.
Sarah Smith, d. of Zadock A. and Mary M., Apr. 17, 1846.
Sarah Wood, d. of Moses 2d and Sylvia Ann, Jan. 6, 1838.
Savillia Maria, d. of Noah and Eliza, bp. June 22, 1834. C.R.2.
Selina, d. of Aaron (Jr., c.r.1) and Rhoda, Feb. 20, 1771.
Serepta Martin, d. of Squire and Mary, Mar. 5, 1831.
Serrne, ch. of Abner Jr. and Abigail, Mar. 22, 1809 (Apr. 22, 1809 dup.).
Seth, s. of Stephen and Mary, Sept. 14, 1739.
Seth, s. of Willis and Margara, Apr. 8, 1797.
Shayes, s. of William and Anna, Dec. 31, 1785.
Shem, s. of Caleb and Susannah, Oct. 28, 1751.
Sibbel, d. of Samuel and Mary, Aug. 19, 1760.
Sibley, s. of Jesse and Hannah, Mar. 29, 1780.
Silas, s. of Stephen and Mary, June 10, 1744.
Silas, s. of Joseph and Elisabeth, Nov. 22, 1747.
Silas, s. of Silas and Elisabeth, Jan. 2, 1779.
Smith, s. of Mijamin and Sarah, Mar. 22, 1784.
Sophia, d. of Aaron (Jr., c.r.1) and Rhoda, Dec. 30, 1787.
Squire, s. of Sweeting and Marcy, July 2, 1797.
Stephen, s. of Mijamin and Sarah, June 9, 1744.
Stephen, s. of Stephen and Mary, July 23, 1754.

TAFT, Stephen, s. of Stephen and Anna, Dec. 12, 1787.
Stephen Decator, s. of Bridgham A. and Eliza Ann, b. in Canada, Aug. 3, 1848.
Stephen Keith, s. of Samuel 2d and Dorcas, Oct. 25, 1831.
Submit, d. of Ephraim and Abigail, Apr. 1, 1790.
Sullivan, s. of Timothy and Abigail, Sept. 4, 1781.
Sullivan H., Aug. 23, 1822. G.R.1.
Susan Hortense, d. of Moses 2d and Sylvia Ann, Jan. 5, 1843.
Susan Margery, d. of Robert G. and Julia Ann, in Grafton, Feb. 19, 1827.
Susan Wadsworth, d. of Calvin and Eliza, Feb. 22, 1842.
Susanna, d. of Reuben and Faithfull, Dec. 27, 1761.
Susannah, d. of John and Mary, Mar. 6, 1763.
Susannah, d. of Nathan and Ruth, Sept. 24, 1777.
Susannah, d. of Samuel Jr. and Sarah, in Fletcher, Vt., Sept. 12, 1805.
Susannah Smith, d. of Willard and Marietta, June 3, 1818.
Sweeting, s. of Mijamin and Sarah, Nov. 26, 1753.
Sylvenus, s. of Sweeting and Marcy, July 5, 1792.
Sylvia, d. of Moses and Judith, Aug. 23, 1810. (Sylva, d. of Moses and Lois, bp. Nov. 21, 1810. C.R.1.)
Sylvia [———], w. of Moses, ———, 1815. G.R.1.
Sylvia Cordelia, d. of Samuel 2d and Dorcas, May 10, 1826.
Tabbarah, d. of Ephraim and Mary, Sept. 4, 1745.
Thaddeus, s. of Aaron and Marcy, Dec. 13, 1757.
Thaddeus, s. of Thaddeus and Silance, Nov. 13, 1794.
Thankfull, d. of Peter and Elisabeth, May 25, 1745.
Thankfull, d. of Caleb and Susannah, Mar. 15, 1762.
Thomas, s. of Joseph (Jr., C.R.1) and Elisabeth, Aug. 19, 1754.
Timothy, s. of Gidean and Elisabeth, Sept. 10, 1740.
Timothy, s. of Jacob and Esther, Apr. 3, 1750.
Timothy, s. of Noah and Margret, Feb. 16, 1755.
Timothy, s. of David and Sena, Nov. 22, 1796.
Timothy Foster, s. of Reuben and Nancy, Jan. 16, 1808.
Trial, d. of Abner and Tryal, Apr. 13, 1777.
Uranah, d. of Ezra and Mary, Jan. 25, 1831.
Viana O., d. of Dexter dec. and Lois, Mar. 20, 1848.
Wait, d. of Mijamin and Sarah, Nov. 30, 1771.
Walter Adolphus, s. of Orsmus and Margeret, Feb. 1, 1844.
Warner, s. of Samuel and Experiance, Sept. 15, 1789.
Washington, s. of Samuel and Mary, Sept. 16, 1775.
Wate Mariah, d. of Samuel Jr. and Sarah, Oct 19, 1817.
Watee E. Wood [———], w. of Samuel H., May 8, 1836. G.R.1.
Webb, s. of Abner and Tryal, Mar. 26, 1772.

TAFT, Whitman, s. of Calvin and Molly, bp. Mar. 22, 1809. C.R.I.
Willard, s. of Leonard and Asenath, Aug. 25, 1791.
Willerd, s. of Samuel and Mary, Oct. 30, 1766.
William Hathaway, s. of Adna and Emma, Feb. 27, 1831.
William Henry, s. of Paris T. and Julia, Jan. 3, 1835.
William Holroyd, s. of Willis and Margara, Aug. 27, 1808.
William Nelson, s. of Squire and Mary, Dec. 23, 1834.
William Nelson, s. of William H. and Arrina, May 27, 1837.
Willis, s. of Aaron and Marcy, Aug. 13, 1765.
Zadoc, s. of Daniel and Comfort, bp. May 7, 1759. C.R.I.
Zadock, s. of Aaron and Marcy, Aug. 15, 1763.
Zadok Arnold, s. of Zadock and Abigail, Nov. 11, 1817.
Zerviah, d. of Aaron (Jr., C.R.I) and Rhoda, Nov. 21, 1779.
Zilpha, d. of James and Esther, July 1, 1772.

TAMPLING, Edward, s. of William and Sarah, bp. Feb. 22, 1740–1. C.R.I.

TANCRED, Olive Ann, d. of James and Sarah, both b. in Dublin, Aug. 24, 1848.

TAYLOR, Abraham, s. of James and Lydia, bp. Feb. 26, 1748–9. C.R.I.
Annah, d. of James and Lydia, Feb. 10, preceding the year 1748.
Ellen [————], w. of James, June 29, 1820. G.R.I.
James, Mar. 19, 1819. G.R.I.
Jane McCaig [————], w. of John, ————, 1820. G.R.I.
John, Nov. 13, 1820. G.R.I.
Lydia, d. of James and Lydia, Sept. 24, 1749.

TEMPSE, Alice, ————, 1839. G.R.2.

THAYER, Alexander, s. of William and ————, bp. at Mendon Apr. 1, 1744. C.R.I.
Alonzo, s. of George and Betta, June 5, 1785.
Amos, s. of Samuel and Sarah, Aug. 19, 1757.
Amos, s. of Grindal and Amy, Jan. —, 1788.
Andrew Jackson, s. of Asa and Chloe, Jan. 19, 1829.
Anna, d. of Isaac and Marcy, June 20, 1757.
Asa, s. of Samuel and Sarah, Oct. 4, 1761.
Asa, s. of Asa and Mary, Sept. 2, 1799.
Asena, d. of Grindal and Amy, Feb. 10, 1797.
Betty, d. of Micah and Sarah, bp. July 5, 1761. C.R.I.
Catharine, d. of Royal and Hannah, Jan. 21, 1813.

THAYER, Charles Augustus, s. of Asa and Chloe, July 29, 1830.
Charles R., Dec. 28, 1825. G.R.1.
Charlotte Augusta, d. of Royal and Hannah, Sept. 18, 1817.
Chloe, ——, 1793. G.R.1.
Clinton, s. of Asa and Mary, Apr. 27, 1784.
Collins, s. of Asa and Mary, Apr. 7, 1790.
Daniel, s. of Reuben and Experence, May 22, 1770.
David, s. of Isaac and Marcy, Apr. 11, 1761.
Deborah, d. of Isaac and Marcy, Apr. 18, 1763.
Deborah [——], w. of Chapin, May 9, 1814. G.R.20.
Dennis, s. of Reuben and Experence, June 2, 1767.
Edward Carrington, s. of Joseph and Chloe, May 10, 1828.
Elizabeth, d. of Micah and Sarah, bp. Mar. 12, 1758. C.R.1.
Emery, s. of Asa and Mary, Feb. 19, 1794.
Eunice, d. of Samuel and Sarah, Jan. 19, 1768.
Ezekiel, s. of Isaac and Marcy, July 12, 1759.
Francis Henry, s. of Asa and Chloe, June 8, 1832.
George, s. of George and Betta, June 14, 1783.
George Dilwin, s. of Alonzo and Wait, 25th day, 6th mo. 1808. C.R.4.
Grindel, rep. s. of Grindel and real s. of Abigail Bolster, Tuesday afternoon, June 16, 1767.
Hamulet, d. of Jeremiah and Allice, July 20, 1762.
Hannah, d. of Reuben and Experence, May 16, 1765.
Hannah, d. of Grindal and Amy, Jan. 27, 1801.
Hannah Adaline, d. of Royal and Hannah, Mar. 28, 1822.
Harriet Lydia, d. of Sullivan and Ruth, May 3, 1839.
Herbert Morton, s. of Sullivan and Ruth, Feb. 18, 1843.
Isaac, s. of Isaac and Marcy, Nov. 20, 1754.
Israel, s. of Micah and Sarah, bp. June 19, 1763. C.R.1.
James, s. of George and Betta, June 21, 1787.
Joseph, ——, 1790. G.R.1.
Julia Ball, ——, 1835. G.R.1.
Levi Lincoln, ——, 1823. G.R.1.
Levi Lincoln, ——, 1824. G.R.1.
Levi Lincoln, s. of Joseph and Chloe, Nov. 10, 1825.
Loies, d. of Samuel and Sarah, Feb. 15, 1764.
Louis, d. of Asa and Mary, Oct. 3, 1796.
Louisa Augusta, d. of Joseph and Chloe, Sept. 10, 1834.
Lovisa, d. of Asa and Mary, Apr. 4, 1806.
Lovisey, d. of Samuel and Sarah, Apr. 23, 1774.
Lydia, d. of Grindal and Amy, Dec. 18, 1789.
Maria S. [——], w. of William W., ——, 1831. G.R.1.
Mary, d. of Isaac and Marcy, June 15, 1750.

THAYER, Mary, d. of Asa and Mary, Sept. 4, 1803.
Mary Aldrich, d. of Royal and Hannah, Mar. 14, 1830.
Mary E. G., d. of Fisher E., b. in Mendon, and Achsah, b. in Northbridge, Aug. 8, 1849.
Mehetabel, d. of Micah and Sarah, bp. Sept. 1, 1765. c.r.1.
Mowry, s. of Alonzo and Wait, 22d day, 7th mo. 1806. c.r.4.
Nancy, d. of Asa and Mary, Apr. 15, 1786.
Nancy, d. of Grindal and Amy, Oct. 28, 1794.
Olive, d. of Asa and Mary, Aug. 10, 1782.
Polley, d. of Samuel and Sarah, Feb. 18, 1766.
Reuben, s. of Reuben and Abigail, Oct. 6, 1786.
Royal, s. of Asa and Mary, Mar. 19, 1788.
Royal, s. of Royal and Hannah, Dec. 18, 1832.
Salley, d. of Reuben and Abigail, in Boston, Feb. 9, 1790.
Sally, d. of Grindal and Amy, Mar. 8, 1792.
Samuel, s. of Samuel and Judith, Apr. 30, 1784.
Sarah Ann, d. of Royal and Hannah, Oct. 7, 1814.
Sarah Richardson, d. of Joseph and Chloe, July 17, 1819.
Silas, s. of Experiance, Sept. 29, 1774.
Stephen, s. of Stephen and Sarah, July 9, 1767.
Stephen, s. of Samuel and Judith, Feb. 10, 1783.
Sullivan, s. of Asa and Mary, Apr. 3, 1792.
Susan Smith, d. of Joseph and Chloe, Apr. 15, 1821.
Susannah, d. of George and Betta, in Ward, Aug. 22, 1781.
Sylvia Wheaton, d. of Royal and Hannah, Mar. 8, 1824.
Turner, s. of Asa and Mary, Feb. 2, 1802.
Wait [———], w. of Alonzo, 4th day, 2d mo. 1783. c.r.4.
William Walter, s. of Royal and Hannah, May 1, 1827.

THOMAS (see Thomass), Augustus N., s. of Sylvester and Anna, b. in Hampton, Conn., Oct. 24, 1849. Colored.

THOMASS (see Thomas), George Washington, s. of Thomas and Sabria, Feb. 23, 1809.
Leander, s. of Thomas and Sabria, July 5, 1803.
William Whitaker, s. of Thomas and Sabria, Oct. 13, 1806.

THOMPSON (see Thomson), Abigail, d. of Elisha and Sarah, Jan. 27, 1784.
Benjamin, s. of Benjamin and Eunice, Feb. 5, 1795.
Cynthia, d. of Stephen and Cynthia, Feb. 14, 1817.
Duty, s. of Stephen and Cynthia, Oct. 13, 1800.
Eber, s. of Benjamin and Eunice, Mar. 17, 1793.
Elisabeth, d. of Joseph and Martha, Mar. 18, 1745. (Elizabeth, d. of Joseph and Jemima, bp. Mar. 5, 1744–5. c.r.1.)

THOMPSON, Elisha, s. of Woodland and ———, bp. Apr. 22, 1733. c.r.1.
Ellis, s. of Ellis and Mary, Jan. 23, 1831.
Emery, s. of Benjamin and Eunice, Apr. 19, 1792.
Fanny Maria, d. of Duty and Rachel, Mar. 21, 1846.
George Goodale, s. of Everett and Eliza Ann, Oct. 6, 1837.
Gerry, s. of Stephen and Cynthia, Dec. 23, 1809.
Hannah, d. of Benjamin and Eunice, Mar. 12, 1791.
Jemima, d. of Joseph and Martha, Oct. 14, 1732.
Joel, s. of Stephen and Cynthia, Nov. 29, 1798.
John, s. of Stephen and Cynthia, Jan. 26, 1803.
Josephine G., d. of Alexander, b. in Douglas, and Watee Ann, in Blackstone, Apr. 6, 1849.
Kezia, d. of Joseph and Martha, June 28, 1739.
Levi, s. of Benjamin and Eunice, Apr. 17, 1797.
Lydia, d. of Elisha and Sarah, Feb. 15, 1786.
Lyman, s. of Elisha and Sarah, Feb. 23, 1788.
Margara, d. of Benjamin and Eunice, Mar. 7, 1794.
Margaret, d. of Woodland and ———, bp., Apr. 22, 1733. c.r.1.
Mary, d. of Woodland and ———, bp. Apr. 22, 1733. c.r.1.
Moses E., s. of Levi and Eliza, Oct. 28, 1843.
Nahum W., s. of Ellis and Mary, May 20, 1820.
Patty, d. of Benjamin and Eunice, Apr. 18, 1796.
Pelina, d. of Stephen and Cynthia, Nov. 5, 1815.
Perlina Frances, d. of Duty and Rachel, May 14, 1844.
Peter, s. of Elisha and Sarah, May 20, 1782.
Phebe, d. of Stephen and Cynthia, Sept. 1, 1807.
Rachel, d. of Ellis and Mary, Jan. 4, 1822.
Rachel Daniels, d. of Woodland and Sarah, bp. May 1, 1743. c.r.1.
Robert Edgar, s. of Alexander and Waity Ann, June 1, 1846.
Sarah, d. of Woodland and ———, bp. Apr. 22, 1733. c.r.1.
Sarah H., d. of Elbridge G. and Julia A., May 5, 1844.
Smith, s. of Stephen and Cynthia, Mar. 22, 1812.
Stephen, s. of Joel and Susannah, Jan. 1, 1780.
Stephen, s. of Stephen and Cynthia, Feb. 12, 1805.
Winfield Scott, s. of Everett and Eliza Ann, Oct. 8, 1838.

THOMSON (see Thompson), A[a]ron, s. of Moses and Mary, Oct. 27, ———. (bp. Dec. 25, 1743. c.r.1.)
Benjamin, s. of Elishua and Abigail, Oct. 5, 1760.
Benjamin, s. of Samuel, June 22, 1763.
Bulah, d. of Samuel and Rhoda, June 28, 1765.

THOMSON, Comfort R., ———, 1818. G.R.1.
Elijah, s. of Moses and Mary, Aug. 26, 1742.
Elisha, s. of Elishua and Abigail, Dec. 9, 1748.
Hannah, d. of Elishua and Abigail, Aug. 29, 1755.
Joel, s. of Elishua and Abigail, Dec. 28, 1746.
John, s. of William and Mehitable, Jan. 9, 1743-4.
John, s. of John and Lucy, Sept. 23, 1765.
Joseph, s. of William and Mehitable, Dec. 22, 1752. Twin.
Louisa M. [———], w. of Comfort, ———, 1825. G.R.1.
Mary, d. of Moses and Mary, May 23, 1751.
Mary, d. of William and Mehitable, Dec. 22, 1752. Twin.
Moses, s. of Moses and Mary, Apr. —, 1745.
Peter, s. of Elishua and Abigail, Apr. 27, 1750.
Phinehas, s. of Moses and Mary, Oct. 8, 1747.
Sarah, d. of Moses and Mary, Oct. 7, 1749.
Submit, d. of Moses and Mary, Apr. 1, 1753. (Submit, d. of Moses dec. and Mary, bp. May 20, 1753. C.R.1.)
Susannah, d. of Woodlan and Sarah, Nov. 23, 1737.
William, s. of William and Mehitable, Jan. 13, 1741-2.

THORNTON, Joshua, adopted s. of Jonathan Penniman, bp. May 6, 1764. C.R.1.

THURBER, Rachel, 22d day, 1st mo. 1749. C.R.4.

THURSTON, Benjamin, s. of Benjamin and Elisabeth, Jan. 2, 1747-8. (Benjamin, s. of Benjamin and Mary, bp. Mar. 20, 1747-8. C.R.1.)
Elisabeth, d. of Benjamin and Elisabeth, June 26, 1743.
John, s. of Benjamin and Elisabeth, Mar. 2, 1741.
Levi, s. of Benjamin and Elisabeth, July 30, 1751. (Levi, s. of Benjamin and Mary, bp. Aug. 4, 1751. C.R.1.)
Lucy, d. of David and Abigail, Apr. 28, 1745.
Lydia, d. of Daniel and Meriam, Aug. 26, 1735.
Michael, s. of Elizabeth, bp. June 22, 1740. C.R.1.
Moses, s. of Daniel and Meriam, Sept. 17, 1733.
Nathan, s. of David and Abigail, Nov. —, 1747.
Peter, s. of Benjamin and Elisabeth, Sept. 17, 1745.

THWING (see Twing), Albert, s. of Benjamin Jr. and Anna, Jan. 2, 1800.
Almon, s. of Benjamin Jr. and Anna, July 21, 1808.
Anna [———], w. of Benjamin Jr., in Gloucester, Sept. 30, 1779.
Anna, d. of Benjamin and Anna, Dec. 23, 1814.
Benjamin, in Mendon, May 25, 1732.

THWING, Benjamin, s. of Benjamin and Molley, Jan. 31, 1777.
Benjamin 3d, s. of Benjamin Jr. and Anna, Feb. 4, 1802.
Charles Augustus, s. of Benjamin Jr. and Anna, Aug. 24, 1806.
Edwin Augustus, s. of Charles A. and Uranah, Dec. 22, 1829.
Else Rawson, d. of B., Oct. 25, 1820.
Hannah, d. of Benjamin and Mary, Apr. 1, 1765.
Hannah, d. of B., Jan. 1, 1817.
Hellen, d. of Almon and Sarah Ann, Mar. 20, 1845.
Luther, s. of Benjamin and Molley, Sept. 7, 1778.
Marcy, d. of Benjamin and Mary, Aug. 16, 1763.
Mary [———], w. of Benjamin, in Sutton, June 22, 1736.
Mary, d. of Charles A. and Uranah, June 29, 1835.
Mary Mowry, d. of Benjamin Jr. and Anna, Aug. 21, 1810.
Minerva Wheaton, d. of B., Oct. 17, 1818.
Molley, d. of Benjamin and Mary, in Sutton, May 12, 1758.
Nathaniel, s. of Benjamin and Mary, Mar. 18, 1760.
Sabra, d. of Benjamin and Molley, May 10, 1775.
Sally, d. of Benjamin Jr. and Anna, Oct. 5, 1812.
Samuel, s. of Benjamin and Mary, Nov. 29, 1760.
Sarah, d. of Benjamin and Mary, Sept. 14, 1767.
Silvia Willard, d. of B., June 26, 1824.
Susan Aldrich, d. of Benjamin Jr. and Anna, June 12, 1804.
Uranah [———], w. of Charles A., ———, 1807. G.R.1.

TILLEY, Elisabeth, d. of James and Elisabeth, July 26, 1782.
John, s. of James and Elisabeth, Jan. 20, 1781.

TILLINGHAST, Daniel Hopkins, s. of Capt. John and Hannah, Apr. 15, 1804 (Apr. 16 dup.).
George, s. of Capt. John and Hannah, June 15, 1812.
Hannah [———], w. of John, Sept. 15, 1769. G.R.1.
Hannah Gibbs, d. of Robert Gibbs and Patience, Mar. 24, 1782.
John, s. of Capt. John and Hannah, Dec. 17, 1807.
John, s. of Capt. John and Hannah, Dec. 15, 1808.
Mary Matilda, rep. d. of John and real d. of Sibbel Croney of Northbridge, Feb. 22, 1797.
Samuel Willard, s. of Paris Jenckes and Elizabeth, Feb. 29, 1796.
Sarah Scott, d. of Capt. John and Hannah, Mar. 17, 1806.
William Holroyd, s. of Paris Jenckes and Elizabeth, Feb. 7, 1794.

TINKAM, Jacob, s. of Jacob dec. and Judith, bp. Sept. 2, 1733. C.R.1.
Lydia, d. of Jacob dec. and Judith, bp. Sept. 2, 1733. C.R.1.

TIRRELL, Joseph, s. of Edward and Maria, Oct. 6, 1847.

TOBEY, Jane Eliza, d. of Merchant and Maria, Mar. 2, 1828.
Lucy Ann, d. of Merchant and Maria, bp. June 22, 1828. c.r.1.
Maria Antoninette, d. of Merchant and Maria, Sept. 26, 1824.
Sarah, d. of Silvanus and Ruth, Jan. 16, 1786.
Sarah Ann, d. of Merchant and Maria, Dec. 23, 1819.
William Merchant, s. of Merchant and Maria, Jan. 9, 1822.

TOURTELOTTE, ———, ch. of George and Caroline, Oct. —, 1843.

TRASK, Lydia, 5th day, 12th mo. 1752. c.r.4.

TUCKER, Alsie H., Mar. 25, 1806. g.r.1.
Arnold, s. of Benjamin and Lydia, Oct. 26, 1809.
Arnold, s. of Jonathan and Esther, Sept. 13, 1825.
Benjamin, s. of Benjamin and Lydia, Jan. 31, 1799.
Caroline Capron, d. of Benjamin Jr. and Mary, Apr. 23, 1836.
Chilon, s. of Benjamin and Lydia, Dec. 9, 1791.
Derias, s. of Nathan and Abigal, June 26, 1771.
Eliza Issabella, d. of Benjamin Jr. and Mary, July 7, 1838.
Esther, d. of Jonathan and Esther, Nov. 23, 1836.
George Farnum, s. of Benjamin Jr. and Mary, Feb. 10, 1828.
Isaac, s. of Benjamin and Lydia, May 27, 1804.
Jonathan, s. of Benjamin and Lydia, Sept. 16, 1787.
Joseph, s. of Benjamin and Lydia, Oct. 8, 1796.
Lydia, d. of Benjamin and Lydia, July 19, 1811.
Martha, d. of Nathan and Abigal, Nov. 24, 1768.
Mary, d. of Benjamin and Lydia, Aug. 26, 1789.
Newell, s. of Jonathan and Esther, May 13, 1819.
Pemela, d. of Benjamin and Lydia, Dec. 27, 1801. Twin.
Phebe, d. of Benjamin and Lydia, Dec. 27, 1801. Twin.
Royal, s. of Benjamin and Lydia, Apr. 17, 1794.
Sarah Maria, d. of Benjamin Jr. and Mary, Aug. 29, 1829.
Silas, s. of Nathan and Abigal, Oct. 25, 1773.
Uranah, d. of Benjamin and Lydia, May 8, 1807.

TURNER, Ellen M., d. of Joseph and Mary Ann, Sept. 17, 1847.
Mary Elizabeth, d. of James and Mary, Sept. 10, 1845.

TUTTLE, David, s. of John and ———, bp. Mar. 21, 1730-1. Twin. c.r.1.
Dorothy, d. of John and ———, bp. May 23, 1736. c.r.1.
Jonathan, s. of John and ———, bp. Mar. 21, 1730-1. Twin. c.r.1.

TWICHEL (see Twitchel), Abner, 23d day, 12th mo. 1753. c.r.4.
Daniel, s. of Abner, 26th day, 11th mo. 1779. c.r.4.
Joanna, 16th day, 2d mo. 1744. c.r.4.

TWING (see Thwing), Anna, d. of Benjamin and ———, bp. July 9, 1775. c.r.1.
Patience, d. of Benjamin and ———, bp. Oct. 12, 1780. c.r.1.

TWITCHEL (see Twichel), Jonah, s. of Daniel and Keziah, Feb. 4, 1744-5.
Nathan, s. of Daniel and Keziah, Jan. 12, 1742-3.

TYLER, Amery, s. of Solomon and Mary, Aug. 30, 1792.
Benjamin, s. of Joseph and Mary, July 28, 1759.
Benjamin, s. of Nathan, bp. May 23, 1779. c.r.1.
Benjamin, s. of Solomon and Mary, Feb. 22, 1796.
Bette Read, d. of Joseph and Ruth, Sept. 1, 1766.
Elizabeth, d. of Nathan and ———, bp. May or June, 1776. c.r.1.
Emory, ch. of Solomon and Mary, bp. July 20, 1794. c.r.1.
Joseph, s. of Joseph and Mehitable, May 21, 1738.
Joseph, s. of Solomon and Mary, Jan. 8, 1782.
Kelita, d. of Solomon and Mary, Feb. 5, 1784.
Lydia, d. of Joseph and Ruth, Aug. 7, 1762.
Mary, d. of Solomon and Mary, Oct. 25, 1797.
Mary, d. of Solomon and Mary, Apr. 17, 1804.
Mehitable, d. of Joseph and Mehitable, Dec. —, 1744.
Melinda, d. of Solomon and Mary, Feb. 7, 1786.
Minerva, d. of Newell and Sybil, July 9, 1847.
Newel, s. of Solomon and Jerusha, bp. May 25, 1810. c.r.1.
Parker, s. of Solomon and Mary, Nov. 14, 1790.
Polly Weels, d. of Nathan and Nancy, Apr. 2, 1792.
Royal, s. of Solomon and Mary, Aug. 2, 1788.
Ruth, d. of Joseph and Mehitable, Feb. 7, preceding the year 1751.
Solomon, s. of Joseph and Mary, Sept. 23, 1757.
Solomon, s. of Solomon and Mary, July 18, 1802.
Timothy, s. of Joseph and Mehitable, June 2, 1735.
Timothy, s. of Joseph and Mehitable, May 17, 1742.
Timothy, s. of Solomon and Mary, July 16, 1799.
Zaccheus, s. of Joseph and Ruth, May 1, 1764.

USHER, Annah J., d. of Joseph, b. in Smithfield, R. I., and Susan R., b. in Temple, Me., July 6, 1848.
Mary E., d. of John and Susan R., Aug. 5, 1847.

VARNEY, Daniel, 15th day, 4th mo. 1799. c.r.4.

VORCE, ———, s. of Benjamin, bp. Apr. 9, 1732. c.r.1.

WADSWORTH, David, 25th day, 1st mo. 1741. c.r.4.
Susannah, d. of David, 13th day, 9th mo. 1765. c.r.4.

WAKEFIELD, Ellen Carpenter [———], w. of John T., ———, 1835. g.r.1.

WALKER, Abraham, s. of Walter and Thankful, 9th day, 1st mo. 1776. c.r.4.
Anna, d. of Walter and Thankful, 13th day, 1st mo. 1787. c.r.4.
Cynthia, d. of Nathaniel and Martha, 21st day, 8th mo. 1789. c.r.4.
Elisabeth, d. of Walter and Thankful, 25th day, 5th mo. 1789. c.r.4.
Emery Arnold, s. of Timothy and Olive, Mar. 23, 1794.
John, 12th day, 4th mo. 1726. c.r.4.
Joseph, s. of Levi and Kezia, Apr. 2, 1761.
Keziah, d. of Nathaniel and Martha, 4th day, 8th mo. 1797. c.r.4.
Lydia, d. of Reuben and Mary, Apr. 15, 1765.
Margaret [———], w. of John, 7th day, 7th mo. 1725. c.r.4.
Margaret, d. of Walter and Thankful, 1st day, 7th mo. 1774. c.r.4.
Martha [———], w. of Nathaniel, 7th day, 8th mo. 1763. c.r.4.
Mary, d. of John and Margaret, 11th day, 3d mo. 1768. c.r.4.
Mary, d. of Reuben and Mary, Sept. 12, 1780.
Mehitabel, d. of John and Margaret, 1st day, 5th mo. 1748. c.r.4.
Nathaniel, 30th day, 1st mo. 1754. c.r.4.
Ruth, d. of Nathaniel and Martha, 23d day, 11th mo. 1795. c.r.4.
Salle, d. of Reuben and Mary, June 7, 1771.
Sarah, d. of Nathaniel and Martha, 4th day, 3d mo. 1792. c.r.4.
Stephen, s. of Levi and Kezia dec., bp. June 10, 1770. c.r.1.
Summers, ch. of Walter and Thankful, 7th day, 11th mo. 1779. c.r.4.
Thankful [———], w. of Walter, 15th day, 7th mo. 1756. c.r.4.
Timothy, s. of Reuben and Mary, Mar. 2, 1767.
Timothy, s. of Levi and Kezia dec., bp. June 10, 1770. c.r.1.
Walter, 21st day, 12th mo. 1749. c.r.4.
Wing, ch. of Walter and Thankful, 29th day, 7th mo. 1784. c.r.4.

WALKUP, Ruth, d. of Henderson and Susannar, July 13, 1798.

WALL, Caleb A., 6th day, 11th mo. 1820. c.r.3.
Louisa, d. of George and Mary, Oct. 3, 1813.
Marianna, d. of George and Mary, Mar. 3, 1812.
Sarah [―――], w. of Caleb, 7th day, 4th mo. 1780. c.r.4.
Thomas, s. of Caleb and Sarah, 2d day, 6th mo. 1808. c.r.4.

WALLING, Adeline A. Morse [―――], w. of Willard, ―――, 1828. g.r.17.
Nancy Louisa, d. of Willard and Adeline A. Morse, July 18, 1849. g.r.17.

WALSH, Catherine [―――], w. of Thomas, June 10, 1844. g.r.2.
Thomas, Mar. 12, 1840. Native of Bilerough, Kilworth, County Cork, Ire.

WARD, Abigail, d. of Elijah and Hannah, Aug. 5, 1753.
Caleb, s. of Elijah and Hannah, in Mendon, Nov. 5, 1751.
Hannah, d. of Elijah and Hannah, bp. June 12, 1757. c.r.1.
Judith, d. of Elijah and Hannah, bp. July 18, 1759. c.r.1.
Nahum, s. of Elijah and Hannah, bp. May 11, 1755. c.r.1.
Sarah, d. of Elijah and Hannah, in Mendon, Mar. 3, 1750.

WARE, Abby Richmond, d. of Albert O. and Mahetabel, Sept. 17, 1838.
Ellen Eliza, d. of Albert O. and Mahetabel, July 29, 1840.
Polly Maria, d. of Albert O. and Mahetabel, Sept. 20, 1836.

WARFIELD (see Wharfield), Lydia E., ―――, 1835. g.r.1.
Marius H., ―――, 1810. g.r.1.
Mary A., ―――, 1802. g.r.1.

WARNER, Albert, s. of Daniel and Mary Jane, Jan. 30, 1834.
Patience E., d. of David E. and Ruth S., June 28, 1840.

WARREN, Jason, s. of Samuel and ―――, bp. at Upton, Dec. 9, 1739. c.r.1.

WATSON, Elisabeth, d. of Thomas and Mary, 19th day, 7th mo. 1789. c.r.4.
Emily, d. of Mary Buxton, Nov. 27, 1848.
Hannah, d. of Thomas and ―――, 2d day, 5th mo. 1783. c.r.4.
Joseph, s. of Thomas and ―――, 16th day, 9th mo. 1781. c.r.4.

WATSON, Mary [———], w. of Thomas, 5th day, 7th mo. 1754. C.R.4.
Nancy, d. of Thomas and Mary, 11th day, 10th mo. 1790. C.R.4.
Thomas, 5th day, 5th mo. 1753. C.R.4.

WEBB, Daniel, s. of Daniel and Betsey, July 3, 1800.

WEBSTER, Elizabeth, d. of Thomas and Elizabeth, Jan. 27, 1755.
Mehitable, d. of Thomas and Elizabeth, Nov. 29, 1752.

WETHERELL, Ellen Augusta, d. of Horace R. and Sarah, Mar. 12, 1842.
George K., ———, 1848. G.R.1.

WHALER (see Wheeler), Amos, s. of Levi and Mary, 27th day, 12th mo. 1792. C.R.4.
Mary [———], w. of Levi, 4th day, 8th mo. 1770. C.R.4.
Mary, d. of Levi and Mary, 12th day, 8th mo. 1798. C.R.4.
Peregreen, s. of Levi and Mary, 12th day, 10th mo. 1796. C.R.4.

WHARFIELD (see Warfield), Amanda Maria, d. of John C. and Louisa, Apr. 4, 1846.

WHEATON, Hannah LeBaron, d. of George and Fanny, Apr. 21, 1821.

WHEELER (see Whaler), Abigail [———], w. of George B., 17th day, 4th mo. 1820. C.R.4.
Abraham, 19th day, 11th mo. 1750. C.R.4.
Abraham, s. of Abraham and Naomi, 24th day, 6th mo. 1781. C.R.4.
Ann [———], w. of Obadiah Jr., 13th day, 9th mo. 1752. C.R.4.
Ann Buffum, d. of George B. and Abigail, 2d day, 7th mo. 1847. C.R.3.
Anne, d. of Obadiah Jr. and Ann, 20th day, 8th mo. 1774. C.R.4.
Asa, s. of Obadiah and Hannah, 9th day, 4th mo. 1761. C.R.4.
Benjamin, s. of Stephen and Meriam, 27th day, 11th mo. 1780. C.R.4.
Benjamin, s. of Obadiah Jr. and Ann, 24th day, 2d mo. 1786 (21st day, 2d mo. 1786 dup.). C.R.4.
Benjamin Franklin, s. of Benjamin and Rhoda, 26th day, 10th mo. 1824. C.R.4.
Buffum, s. of Jonathan Jr. and Mary, 2d day, 11th mo. 1791. C.R.4.

WHEELER, Buffum, s. of Jonathan Jr. and Mary, 3d day, 4th mo. 1795. c.r.4.
Caleb B., s. of Obediah Jr. and Phila, 10th day, 9th mo. 1815. c.r.4.
Caleb Watson, s. of Caleb B. and Lucy A., May 3, 1844.
Charles, s. of Obediah Jr. and Phila, 12th day, 8th mo. 1810. c.r.4.
Charles Henry, s. of Caleb B. (Caleb Buffum, b. in Northbridge dup.) and Lucy A. (b. in Northampton dup.), Apr. 24, 1843.
Content, d. of Jonathan Jr. and Mary, 11th day, 6th mo. 1793. c.r.4.
Daniel, s. of Jonathan Jr. and Mary, 1st day, 11th mo. 1776. c.r.4.
Daniel, s. of George B. and Abigail, 2d day, 12th mo. 1843. c.r.4.
David, s. of Abraham and Naomi, 18th day, 8th mo. 1786. c.r.4.
Dinah, d. of Jonathan, 10th day, 6th mo. 1761. c.r.4.
Eleanor, d. of Obadiah Jr. and Ann, 26th day, 10th mo. 1781. c.r.4.
Elisabeth, d. of Jonathan Jr. and Mary, 1st day, 1st mo. 1779. c.r.4.
Elisabeth, d. of Obadiah Jr. and Ann, 23d day, 9th mo. 1779. c.r.1.
George Buffum, s. of Benjamin and Rhoda, 10th day, 9th mo. 1812. c.r.4.
George Washington, s. of Asa and ———, June 15, 1826.
Hannah [———], w. of Obadiah, 16th day, 11th mo. 1718. c.r.4.
Hannah, d. of Abraham and Naomi, 9th day, 2d mo. 1779. c.r.4.
Hannah, d. of Jonathan Jr. and Mary, 2d day, 12th mo. 1782. c.r.4.
Hannah, d. of Moses and Sarah, 11th day, 2d mo. 1787. c.r.4.
Hannah, d. of Obadiah Jr. and Ann, 27th day, 7th mo. 1791. c.r.4.
Holder, ch. of Moses and Sarah, 11th day, 9th mo. 1788. c.r.4.
John Brown, s. of Benjamin and Rhoda, 8th day, 5th mo. 1822. c.r.4.
Jonathan, 3d day, 7th mo. 1720. c.r.4.
Jonathan Jr., 6th day, 4th mo. 1752. c.r.4.
Jonathan, s. of Stephen and Miriam, 16th day, 2d mo. 1783. c.r.4.

WHEELER, Jonathan, s. of Jonathan Jr. and Mary, 13th day, 5th mo. 1787. C.R.4.
Joseph, s. of Stephen and Meriam, 22d day, 12th mo. 1794. C.R.4.
Joseph, s. of Obadiah Jr. and Ann, 2d day, 5th mo. 1796. C.R.4.
Joseph, s. of Obadiah Jr. and Ann, 4th day, 5th mo. 1798. C.R.4.
Levi, s. of Jonathan, 29th day, 4th mo. 1768. C.R.4.
Levi of Richmond, 26th day, 4th mo. 1802. C.R.4.
Lucy, 13th day, 11th mo. 1803. C.R.4.
Luther Collins, s. of Benjamin and Rhoda, 24th day, 2d mo. 1829. C.R.4.
Lydia, d. of Abraham and Naomi, 16th day, 9th mo. 1783. C.R.4.
Mary, d. of Jonathan, 5th day, 7th mo. 1754. C.R.4.
Mary [――――], w. of Jonathan Jr., 3d day, 4th mo. 1757. C.R.4.
Mary, d. of Obadiah and Ann, 12th day, 12th mo. 1770. C.R.4.
Mary, d. of Jonathan Jr. and Mary, 1st day, 2d mo. 1785. C.R.4.
Meriam, d. of Stephen and Meriam, 22d day, 7th mo. 1787. C.R.4.
Meriam, d. of Benjamin and Rhoda, 13th day, 8th mo. 1809. C.R.4.
Miriam [――――], w. of Stephen, 21st day, 4th mo. 1761. C.R.4.
Miriam, d. of Obadiah Jr. and Ann, 25th day, 5th mo. 1794. C.R.4.
Moses, 17th day, 8th mo. 1752. C.R.4.
Moses, s. of Moses and Sarah, 8th day, 10th mo. 1790. C.R.4.
Naomi [――――], w. of Abraham, 25th day, 8th mo. 1748. C.R.3.
Obadiah, 22d day, 12th mo. 1716. C.R.4.
Obadiah Jr., 10th day, 11th mo. 1744. C.R.4.
Obadiah, s. of Obadiah Jr. and Ann, 24th day, 3d mo. 1784. C.R.4.
Obediah, s. of Abraham and Zeresh, 23d day, 11th mo. 1794. C.R.4.
Paul, s. of Stephen and Susanna, 17th day, 2d mo. 1813. C.R.4.
Paul A., s. of Obadiah Jr. and Phila, 10th day, 7th mo. 1821. C.R.4.
Peregreen, s. of Jonathan, 4th day, 7th mo. 1759. C.R.4.
Phebe, d. of Abraham and Zeresh, 25th day, 9th mo. 1792. C.R.4.
Phila [――――], w. of Obediah Jr., 23d day, 4th mo. 1787. C.R.4.

WHEELER, Rhoda [———], w. of Benjamin, 17th day, 2d mo. 1786. c.r.4.
Rufus, s. of Stephen and Susanna, 6th day, 2d mo. 1818. c.r.4.
Ruth, d. of Jonathan Jr. and Mary, 4th day, 10th mo. 1780. c.r.4.
Ruth, d. of Obediah Jr. and Phila, 12th day, 10th mo. 1812. c.r.4.
Sally T., 2d day, 8th mo. 1794. Pomfret. c.r.4.
Salome C., 12th day, 2d mo. 1834. c.r.4.
Samuel Aldrich, s. of Benjamin and Rhoda, 29th day, 4th mo. 1815. c.r.4.
Sarah [———], w. of Moses, 21st day, 8th mo. 1760. c.r.4.
Sarah, d. of Moses and Sarah, 23d day, 7th mo. 1793. c.r.4.
Sarah Ann, d. of Benjamin and Rhoda, 7th day, 11th mo. 1826. c.r.4.
Stephen, 13th day, 3d mo. 1756. c.r.4.
Stephen, s. of Stephen and Meriam, 15th day, 2d mo. 1785. c.r.4.
Stephen, s. of Obadiah Jr. and Ann, 26th day, 1st mo. 1788. c.r.4.
Stephen, s. of Stephen and Susanna, 1st day, 12th mo. 1815. c.r.4.
Stephen Sweat, s. of Benjamin and Rhoda, 7th day, 4th mo. 1818. c.r.4.
Susanna [———], w. of Stephen, 27th day, 4th mo. 1789. c.r.4.
Susanna A., d. of Obediah Jr. and Phila, 3d day, 12th mo. 1825. c.r.4.
Thankful, d. of Jonathan Jr. and Mary, 12th day, 7th mo. 1789. c.r.4.
Thankful, d. of Jonathan Jr. and Mary, 28th day, 10th mo. 1790. c.r.4.
Thomas, s. of Obadiah Jr. and Ann, 17th day, 3d mo. 1792. c.r.4.
Tryphena, d. of Abraham and Zeresh, 6th day, 5th mo. 1797. c.r.4.
Zeresh [———], 2d w. of Abraham, 22d day, 11th mo. 1768. c.r.4.

WHEELOCK, Abba, d. of Elias and Abba, bp. Sept. 18, 1831. c.r.1.
Abba Elizabeth, d. of Jerry and Sukey, Sept. 20, 1832.
Abby Ann, d. of Elias and Sarah, Jan. 14, 1826.
Alice Augusta, d. of Charles A. and Nancy, Sept. 18, 1845.

WHEELOCK, Alice Augusta, d. of Silas M. and Irene, Jan. 22, 1849.
Alpheus, s. of Paul and Lydia, Sept. 18, 1764.
Charles Augustus, s. of Jerry and Sukey, Feb. 27, 1812.
Daniel, s. of Daniel and Deborah, Aug. 13, 1744.
Deborah, d. of Daniel and Deborah, bp. June 17, 1753. C.R.1.
Elias, Feb. 4, 1794.
Elizabeth, d. of Elias and Abba, bp. Sept. 18, 1831. C.R.1.
Ellen Maria, d. of Silas M. and Irene, Sept. 2, 1842.
Eugene Augustine, s. of Silas M. and Irene, Feb. 15, 1846.
Eunice, d. of Simeon and Deborah, Feb. 13, 1764.
Gerrey, s. of Simeon and Deborah, Sept. —, 1782.
Hannah, d. of Daniel and Deborah, Dec. 13, 1741.
Hannah, d. of Simeon and Deborah, Oct. 16, 1771.
Hellen C., d. of Dennis, b. in Mendon, and Lucy Ann, b. in Greenwich, R. I., July 4, 1849.
Herbert W., s. of William and Caroline E., Feb. 12, 1848.
Lucretia Elizabeth, d. of Elias and Sarah, June 5, 1820.
Lucy Sefrona, d. of Charles A. and Nancy, June 25, 1836.
Maria Issabella, d. of Jerry and Sukey, July 7, 1821.
Maria Issabella, d. of Jerry and Sukey, Mar. 8, 1824.
Mary, d. of Daniel and Deborah, Jan. 14, 1733-4.
Mary, d. of Daniel and Deborah, Sept. 20, 1746.
Mary Antoinette, d. of Charles A. and Nancy, Mar. 27, 1835.
Nancey, d. of Simeon and Deborah, Nov. 19, 1781.
Olive, d. of Paul and Deborah, Apr. 21, 1790.
Paul, s. of Daniel and Deborah, Feb. 9, preceding the year 1739.
Phyletus, s. of Paul and Lydia, June 14, 1769.
Polley, d. of Simeon and Deborah, Mar. 11, 1779.
Rachel, d. of Simeon and Deborah, June 10, 1774.
Rhoda, d. of Daniel and Deborah, bp. Apr. 15, 1750. C.R.1.
Rodah, d. of Daniel and Deborah, Dec. 28, 1758.
Rowena, d. of Paul and Lydia, Dec. 28, 1766.
Royall, s. of Simeon and Deborah, July 16, 1766.
Sarah Elizabeth, d. of Charles A. and Nancy, Jan. 21, 1839.
Silas, s. of Simeon and Deborah, Mar. 26, 1769.
Silas Mandeville, s. of Jerry and Sukey, Nov. 11, 1818.
Sylvia Ann, d. of Jerry and Sukey, Feb. 3, 1815.

WHIPPEL (see Whipple), Olive Williard, d. of Jonathan and Mary, Aug. 3, 1795.
Patty, d. of Jonathan and Mary, July 10, 1793.
Polley, d. of Jonathan and Mary, June 16, 1791.

WHIPPLE (see Whippel), George M., s. of Independance and Sophia, July 25, 1826.
Horace, s. of Jonathan and Mary, bp. Dec. 10, 1797. c.r.1.
Liberty, s. of Independence and Sophia, Jan. 26, 1825.

WHITE, Abi, d. of Noah and Rebecca, 29th day, 8th mo. 1762. c.r.4.
Abigail, d. of Samuel and Elisabeth, Apr. 4, 1734.
Abigail, d. of Seth and Abigail, Dec. 16, 1748.
Abigail, d. of Ebenezer and Elisabeth, Sept. 9, 1752.
Abigail, d. of Moses and Mary, Oct. 1, 1758.
Abigail, d. of Joseph and Deborah, Mar. 18, 1780.
Abigail, d. of Solomon and Esther, Oct. 28, 1790.
Abigail Read, d. of Nathan Jr. and Elizabeth H., Mar. 9, 1827.
Abner, s. of Moses and Abigail, bp. May, 27, 1753. c.r.1.
Abner, s. of Joseph and Judith, Apr. 5, 1758.
Abner, s. of Levi and Margaret, Nov. 25, 1778.
Adam, s. of Samuel and Mary, Oct. 17, 1752.
Alexander, s. of Seth and Jemima, Jan. 13, 1780.
Alexander, s. of Seth and Jemima, Feb. 9, 1791.
Alpheus, s. of Thomas and Ellenor, Feb. 1, 1752.
Ama [———], w. of Simon, 2d day, 9th mo. 1786. g.r.13.
Amariah, s. of Moses and Mary, bp. Mar. 14, 1762. c.r.1.
Amariah, s. of Moses and Mary, Dec. 11, 1763.
Amos, s. of Joseph and Judith, Oct. 26, 1748.
Asa, s. of Seth and Abigail, Feb. 13, 1741–2.
Asa, s. of Ezekiel and Amity, Jan. 18, 1743–4.
Asa, s. of Joseph and Judith, bp. Aug. 4, 1754. c.r.1.
Asa, s. of Josiah and Mary, his 2d w., May 21, 1769.
Avery, s. of Jonathan and Abigail, June 26, 1793.
Barzillai, s. of Peter and Chloe, Nov. 10, 1767.
Benjamin, s. of Levi and Margaret, Sept. 5, 1776.
Benjamin, s. of Alpheus and Lyddia, June 25, 1806.
Bethane, d. of Thomas and Ellenor, May 31, 1769.
Bethany, d. of Benjamin and Naomi, Aug. 2, 1756.
Bethiah, d. of Peter and Jemima, bp. Mar. 1, 1740–1. c.r.1.
Bethiah, d. of Joseph and Deborah, Dec. 7, 1767.
Betsey Taft, d. of Alpheus and Lyddia, in Petersham, Sept. 14, 1816.
Beulah, d. of Benjamin and Naomi, Mar. 6, 1762. Twin.
Charles, s. of Alpheus and Lyddia, Feb. 19, 1814.
Charles, ———, 1824. g.r.1.
Chloa, d. of Daniel and Hannah, Nov. 6, 1757.

WHITE, Chloe, d. of Moses and Mary, Feb. 11, 1769.
Chloe, d. of Jonathan and Abigail, Oct. 9, 1800.
Clarissa D., ——, 1824. G.R.1.
Claritsa, d. of Solomon and Esther, Aug. 12, 1786.
Comfort, d. of Seth and Abigail, Feb. 13, 1744.
Comfort, d. of Seth and Abigail, Sept. 5, 1758. (Comfort, d. of Seth dec. and Abigail, bp. Oct. 15, 1758. C.R.1.)
Dauphin, s. of Solomon and Esther, Sept. 17, 1788.
David, s. of Ezekiel and Amity, Nov. 7, 1734.
David Farnum, s. of Ezra and Chloe, May 26, 1788.
Deborah, d. of Samuel and Elisabeth, Nov. 4, 1737.
Deborah, d. of Moses and Mary, May 9, 1764.
Deborah, d. of Joseph and Deborah, July 14, 1778.
Diadame, d. of Thomas and Ellenor, Nov. 19, 1765.
Diana, d. of William and Deborah, Feb. 24, 1800.
Dolla, d. of Joseph and Deborah, Apr. 9, 1771.
Dorcas, d. of John and Rachel, Sept. 9, 1750.
Ebenezer, s. of Joseph and Prudance, in Mendon, Nov. 20, 1726.
Edward, s. of Joseph and Judith, June 5, 1756.
Elijah, s. of Samuel and Elisabeth, June 12, 1732.
Elisabeth, d. of Samuel and Elisabeth, Mar. 27, 1743.
Elisabeth, d. of Peter and Jemima, Dec. 13, 1743.
Elisabeth, 9th day, 1st mo. 1749. C.R.4.
Eliza, d. of Seth and Jemima, Mar. 5, 1800. Twin.
Ellis, s. of Ebenezer and Elisabeth, Oct. 13, 1748.
Emeline Buffum [———], w. of George, Sept. 20, 1827. G.R.1.
Enoch, s. of John and Rachel, Nov. 22, 1732.
Ervin, s. of Anan and Anna, both b. in Burrillville, R. I., June 8, 1849.
Esther, d. of Samuel and Louis, Apr. 25, 1767.
Eunice, d. of Benjamin and Eunice, Dec. 9, 1736.
Eunice, d. of Joseph and Judith, Nov. 1, 1741.
Eunice, d. of Levi and Margaret, Mar. 14, 1768.
Eunice, d. of Nathan and Eunice, Feb. 15, 1782.
Eunice, d. of Jonathan and Abigail, Feb. 16, 1789.
Ezekiel, s. of Ezekiel and Amity, Dec. 30, 1730.
Ezra, s. of Moses and Mary, Feb. 1, 1765.
Ezra, s. of Ezra and Chloe, Apr. 2, 1804.
Farnum, s. of Seth and Abigail, Feb. 22, 1751.
Farnum, s. of Seth and Jemima, June 9, 1781.
Francis, s. of Seth and Jemima, Feb. 23, 1789.
Frebun, s. of Seth and Jemima, Feb. 15, 1785.
George, s. of Alpheus and Lyddia, Feb. 10, 1808.

WHITE, George, Dec. 23, 1827. G.R.1.
Gidean, s. of Benjamin and Naomi, Oct. 18, 1755.
Hannah, d. of Benjamin and Eunice, July 12, 1738.
Hannah, d. of Levi and Margaret, Sept. 22, 1766.
Hannah, d. of Jonathan and Abigail, Oct. 25, 1786.
Hannah Maria, d. of Jonathan and Mary, Aug. 30, 1835.
Henery, s. of Joseph and Deborah, May 19, 1765.
Henery, s. of Joseph and Deborah, Dec. 15, 1774.
Hepzibah, d. of Benjamin and Naomi, Mar. 6, 1762. Twin.
Ichabod, s. of John and Rachel, Feb. 28, 1729.
Jael, d. of Thomas and Ellenor, Nov. 25, 1761.
Jasper, s. of Solomon and Esther, Sept. 8, 1784.
Jemima, d. of Peter and Jemima, Dec. 15, 1750.
Jesse, s. of John and Rachel, Sept. 2, 1744.
Jesse, s. of Joseph and Judith, June 12, 1754.
Joel, s. of Joseph and Judith, Oct. 4, 1751.
John, Mar. 13, 1702.
John, s. of John and Rachel, Jan. 11, 1731.
John, s. of Ezekiel and Amity, Aug. 31, 1742.
John B., Jan. 16, 1820. G.R.1.
John C., s. of Aaron and Sarah, May 4, 1844.
Jonah, s. of Ezekiel and Amity, Jan. 19, 1738.
Jonathan, s. of Benjamin and Naomi, Oct. 30, 1752.
Jonathan, s. of Samuel and Mary, May 15, 1754.
Jonathan, s. of Jonathan and Abigail, Sept. 2, 1795.
Jonathan, s. of Jonathan and Abigail, Feb. 15, 1798.
Joseph, s. of Peter and Jemima, June 25, 1738.
Joseph, s. of Joseph and Judith, May 4, 1744.
Joseph, s. of Joseph and Deborah, Mar. 15, 1773.
Josiah, s. of Alpheus and Lyddia, July 6, 1804.
Josiah Gould, s. of Josiah and Hannah, Aug. 13, 1767.
Judith, d. of Joseph and Judith, Dec. 1, 1746.
Judson, s. of Josiah Gould and Marcy, Mar. 9, 1793.
Julia A. Roper [———], w. of John B., Dec. 13, 1835. G.R.1.
Keith, s. of Seth and Jemima, Mar. 17, 1783.
Keith, s. of Keith and Betsey, Apr. 8, 1810.
Keith, s. of Keith and ———, bp. Apr. 1, 1838. C.R.2.
Keith Wood, s. of Ameriah and Pheebe, Oct. 5, 1801.
Levi, s. of Benjamin and Naomi, Jan. 30, 1743-4.
Levi, s. of Simon and Ama, 3d day, 5th mo. 1807. G.R.13.
Levina, d. of Ezra and Chloe, Nov. 22, 1795.
Lilly, d. of Paul and Martha, June 7, 1782.
Lorane, d. of Thomas and Ellenor, June 9, 1758.
Louies, d. of Samuel and Louis, Sept. 6, 1769.

WHITE, Louis, d. of Joseph and Judith, Aug. 25, 1739.
Lucinda Taft [———], w. of Charles, ———, 1826. G.R.1.
Lucine, d. of Samuel and Louis, Nov. 1, 1771.
Lucreta, d. of Thomas and Ellenor, Feb. 20, 1755.
Lydia, d. of Samuel and Elisabeth, Aug. 21, 1749.
Lydia, d. of John and Rachel, Feb. 20, 1753.
Lydia, d. of Samuel and Mary, June 7, 1756.
Lydia Wallis [———], w. of Charles, ———, 1827. G.R.1.
Maranda Harkness [———], w. of John B., July 26, 1824. G.R.1.
Marcy Taft, d. of Alpheus and Lyddia, Feb. 10, 1811.
Marvel, s. of Josiah and Mary, June 26, 1780.
Mary, d. of John and Rachel, Mar. 13, 1726.
Mary, d. of Benjamin and Eunice, Oct. 16, 1735. (Mary, d. of wid. Eunice, bp. Sept. 20, 1741. C.R.1.)
Mary, d. of Samuel and Elisabeth, Apr. 8, 1741.
Mary, d. of Moses and Mary, Mar. 11, 1760.
Mary, d. of Alpheus 2d or Jr. and Rhoda, Feb. 8, 1805.
Mary B., ———, 1837. G.R.1.
Melatiah, d. of Ebenezer and Elizabeth, bp. May 18, 1766. C.R.1.
Merril, s. of Alpheus 2d or Jr. and Rhoda, May 3, 1803.
Molley, d. of Benjamin and Naomi, Feb. 19, 1747-8.
Moses, s. of Moses and Abigail, July 24, 1751.
Moses, s. of Joseph and Judith, Aug. 3, 1759.
Moses, s. of Ameriah and Pheebe, Apr. 26, 1790.
Nahum, s. of Moses and Mary (Mercy, C.R.1), Feb. 18, 1774.
Nancey, d. of Seth and Jemima, Mar. 5, 1800. Twin.
Nathan, s. of Samuel and Elisabeth, Aug. 1, 1739.
Nathan, s. of Ezekiel and Amity, bp. Dec. 10, 1746. C.R.1.
Nathan, s. of John and Rachel, Oct. 21, 1748.
Nathan, s. of Peter and Jemima, June 10, 1755.
Noah, s. of John and Rachel, Oct. 1, 1724. (12th day, 10th mo. 1724. C.R.4.)
Noah, s. of Noah and Rebecca, 5th day, 12th mo. 1767. C.R.4.
Obediah, s. of Joseph and Judith, Sept. 8, 1753.
Olive, d. of Moses and Mary, Mar. 7, 1767.
Olive, d. of Samuel and Louis, Mar. 4, 1778.
Orpah, d. of Levi and Margaret, Apr. 30, 1770.
Orpha, d. of Jonathan and Abigail, Sept. 29, 1790.
Otis, s. of Levi and Margaret, Oct. 28, 1774.
Paul, s. of John and Rachel, Dec. 25, 1736.
Paul, s. of Samuel and Elisabeth, Dec. 1, 1744.
Paul, s. of Benjamin and Naomi, Sept. 18, 1746.

WHITE, Peter, s. of Peter and Jemima, Oct. 19, 1746.
Peter, s. of Joseph and Deborah, Feb. 13, 1785.
Pheeby, d. of Thomas and Deborah, Aug. 22, 1730.
Pheeby, d. of Thomas and Deborah, Oct. 8, 1737.
Philadelphia, d. of Ebenezer and Elisabeth, Oct. 6, 1760.
Polly, d. of Seth and Jemima, Nov. 28, 1786.
Polly, d. of Seth and Jemima, Nov. 4, 1802.
Prudence, d. of Joseph and Prudance, Sept. 4, 1729.
Prudence, d. of William and Deborah, Sept. 4, 1801.
Rachel [———], w. of John, Dec. 25, 1708.
Rachel, d. of Joseph and Prudance, Nov. 14, 1732.
Rachel, d. of John and Rachel, Mar. 10, 1738.
Rebecca [———], w. of Noah, — day, 6th mo. 1730. c.r.4.
Roxelane, d. of Thomas and Ellenor, Aug. 11, 1763.
Ruth, d. of Ezekiel and Amity, Jan. 28, 1731-2.
Ruth, d. of Samuel and Elisabeth, Jan. 6, 1746-7.
Ruth, d. of Ebenezer and Elisabeth, Sept. 6, 1758.
Salley, d. of Nathan and Eunice, Dec. 2, 1779.
Sally, d. of Solomon and Esther, Nov. 24, 1782.
Sally, d. of Ameriah and Pheebe, Apr. 20, 1788. Twin.
Samuel, s. of Samuel and Louis, Feb. 5, 1781.
Sarah, d. of Joseph and Prudance, in Mendon, Nov. 8, 1724.
Sarah, d. of Joseph and Judith, Sept. 4, 1735.
Sarah, d. of Silas and Margaret, bp. May 8, 1757. c.r.1.
Seth, s. of Seth and Abigail, Apr. 18, 1756.
Silas, s. of Samuel and Elisabeth, Oct. 30, 1735.
Silas, s. of John and Rachel, May 4, 1742.
Silvest, d. of Aaron, Mar. 8, 1758.
Simon, 10th day, 2d mo. 1783. g.r.13. (1784. c.r.4.)
Smith, s. of Ebenezer and Elisabeth, Oct. 9, 1755.
Solomon, s. of Seth and Abigail, Apr. 28, 1754.
Sophia, d. of Seth and Jemima, Aug. 1, 1792.
Stephen, s. of Ezekiel and Amity, Apr. 15, 1737.
Stephen, s. of Moses and Abigail, bp. Sept. 22, 1754. c.r.1.
Stephen, s. of Ebenezer and Elisabeth, May 12, 1763.
Suky, d. of Ameriah and Pheebe, Apr. 20, 1788. Twin.
Susannah, d. of Alpheus 2d or Jr. and Rhoda, May 13, 1807.
Sylvia Huse, adopted d. of Amariah and Phebe, bp. Aug. 27, 1809. c.r.1.
Thomas, s. of Thomas and Ellenor, Sept. 26, 1749.
Tryal, d. of Joseph and Judith, May 8, 1737.
Tryal, d. of Daniel and Hannah, Sept. 14, 1759.
Tryphena, d. of Seth and Abigail, May 12, 1747.
Turner, s. of Ebenezer and Elisabeth, Dec. 4, 1750.

WHITE, Weltha, d. of Noah and Rebecca, 27th day, 7th mo. 1756. C.R.4.
William, s. of Noah and Rebecca, 2d day, 2d mo. 1772. C.R.4.
William Wallace, s. of Jonathan and Mary, Feb. 21, 1828.

WHITING, Caroline Augusta, d. of Prentis and Harriet, Apr. 20, 1842.
Ellen Martha, d. of Prentis and Harriet, June 25, 1835.
George Augustus, s. of Prentis and Harriet, July 12, 1833.
George H., s. of Nelson, b. in Wrentham, and Rhoda, b. in Easton, in Cumberland, R. I., Oct. 23, 1848.
Harriet Frances, d. of Prentis and Harriet, June 17, 1839.
Nelson, Aug. 10, 1823. G.R.1.
Prentiss Mellen, s. of Prentis and Harriet, June 13, 1837.

WHITMORE (see Whittemore), Caroline F. [――――], w. of Harrison C., Aug. 3, 1827. G.R.1.
Hannibal, Feb. 14, 1834. G.R.1.
Harrison C., July 5, 1822. G.R.1.

WHITNEY, Anna Wyett, d. of Moses and Hannah, Apr. 18, 1787.
Benjamin, s. of Joshua and Pheeby, Mar. 14, 1743.
Hannah, d. of Joshua and Pheeby, Feb. 4, 1746.
Hannah, d. of Aaron and Margret, Sept. 28, 1760.
Hannah Tillinghast, d. of Moses and Nancy, Feb. 7, 1800.
Jennet, d. of Ezekiel and Jennet, bp. Oct. 12, 1746. C.R.1.
Jennet, d. of Ezekiel and Jennet, bp. Sept. 10, 1749. C.R.1.
John Andrews, s. of Moses and Hannah, Jan. 10, 1789.
Joseph, s. of Joshua and Pheeby, Mar. 21, 1739-40.
Joshu[a], s. of Joshua and Pheeby, Feb. 27, 1738-9.
Julian Mann, d. of Moses and Nancy, June 25, 1798.
Margaret, d. of Ezekiel and Jennet, bp. Aug. 18, 1751. C.R.1.
Margett, d. of Ezekiel and Jennet, bp. Sept. 11, 1748. C.R.1.
Mary, d. of Joshua and Hannah, Oct. 27, 1732.
Nancy Wyett, d. of Moses and Nancy, Apr. 4, 1797.
Pheeby, d. of Joshua and Pheeby, July 25, 1745. (Phebe, d. of Joshua and Phebe, bp. Sept. 2, 1744. C.R.1.)
Samuel, s. of Aaron and Margret, May 23, 1764.
Samuel, s. of Moses and Hannah, Dec. 18, 1791.
Susanna, d. of Ezekiel and Jane, bp. Oct. 13, 1745. C.R.1.

WHITTEMORE (see Whitmore), Isaac P., Jan. 5, 1807. G.R.1.
Mary Lawrence [――――], w. of Isaac P., June 21, 1813. G.R.1.

WILBUR, Lydia, 5th day, 3d mo. 1757. C.R.4.

WILCOX, Augustus, s. of Jirea and Bathsheba, 11th day, 11th mo. 1770. c.r.1.
Bathsheba [———], w. of Jirea, 5th day, 5th mo. 1738. c.r.4.
Charles Henry, s. of Otis and Mary, July 1, 1833.
Edwin Augustus, s. of Otis and Mary, Dec. 29, 1829.
Elisabeth, d. of Jirea and Bathsheba, 11th day, 6th mo. 1762. c.r.4.
Emma M. [———], w. of Gilbert H., Oct. 14, 1846. g.r.1.
Emma Sylvia, d. of Otis and Mary, Dec. 2, 1846.
Gilbert Hamilton, s. of Otis and Mary, Apr. 2, 1839.
Herbert Lovell, s. of David and Mary J., Oct. 10, 1846.
Lewis Gilbert, s. of Otis and Mary, Mar. 24, 1836.
Mary, d. of Jirea and Bathsheba, 3d day, 6th mo. 1773. c.r.4.
Mary J.; Mar. 3, 1825. g.r.1.
Phebe, d. of Jirea and Bathsheba, 27th day, 3d mo. 1777. c.r.4.
Samuel, s. of Willard and Evalina, Dec. 28, 1831.
Walter A., s. of Otis and Mary, Sept. 2, 1841.
William, s. of Jirea and Bathsheba, 2d day, 10th mo. 1764. c.r.4.

WILLARD, Abijah, s. of Samuel and Olive, Feb. 16, 1782.
Agnes Frederica Herresshoff, d. of Dr. George and Sylvia, May 17, 1823.
Emeline, d. of Dr. George and Sylvia, Oct. 25, 1815.
Emeline Chapin, d. of Dr. George and Sylvia, June 4, 1818.
George, s. of Samuel and Olive, Oct. 8, 1787, at 9 o'clock in the morning.
George Wheaton, s. of Dr. Abijah and Fanny, Feb. 21, 1811.
Isaac Davis, s. of Bezaleel P. and Rebecca, b. in Webster, June 28, 1848. Colored.
Lemira Francis Ann Maria, d. of Dr. Abijah and Fanny, Apr. 23, 1813.
Louis Capet, rep. s. of Cato and real s. of Lucy Brown, Aug. 20, 1796.
Samuel Towsand, s. of Dr. Abijah and Fanny, Oct. 14, 1808.
Sylvia C. [———], w. of Dr. George, May 18, 1790. g.r.1.

WILLIAMS, Abigail, d. of Stephen and Nancy, Jan. 7, 1823.
Alice Amelia, d. of Nelson and Mary D., Aug. 1, 1848.
Augustus, ———, 1840. g.r.1.
Betsey, d. of Stephen and Nancy, Nov. 8, 1810.
Catherine Learned, d. of Charles W. and Frances Elizabeth, Nov. 4, 1840.

WILLIAMS, Charles Henry, s. of Charles W. and Frances Elizabeth, May 24, 1843.
Chester, s. of Stephen and Lydia, Sept. 26, 1767.
Chester Draper, s. of Chester and Sarah, Apr. 10, 1803.
Edward F., s. of George and Delilah, July 22, 1832.
Eleanor, d. of Stephen and Nancy, Feb. 18, 1815.
Eliza Bruce, d. of Chester and Sarah, July 13, 1807.
Emily Angeline, d. of George and Delilah, June 30, 1843.
Frederick G., s. of Nelson and Mary, May 16, 1847.
George, s. of Stephen and Nancy, Jan. 21, 1804.
Gustavus B., s. of George and Delilah, Oct. 28, 1834.
Horace W., s. of George and Delilah, July 10, 1840.
James H., s. of George and Delilah, May 14, 1838.
John, s. of Stephen and Lydia, Jan. 19, 1769.
John, s. of Stephen and Nancy, Dec. 23, 1819.
John Capron, inf. s. of Ch[arle]s W. and Frances E., bp. June 18, 1848. c.r.2.
John D., s. of Chester and Sarah, June 20, 1812.
Lyddia, d. of Chester and Sarah, May 22, 1805.
Martha, d. of Chester and Sarah, Jan. 14, 1801.
Nancy, d. of Stephen and Nancy, Oct. 27, 1812.
Nelson, s. of Stephen and Nancy, Jan. 31, 1806.
Nicholas, s. of Stephen and Nancy, Sept. 22, 1825.
Ruth, d. of ——— of New Sherborn, bp. Oct. 14, 1739. c.r.1.
Sarah, d. of Stephen and Lydia, May 31, 1771.
Sarah, d. of Chester and Sarah, Mar. 22, 1799.
Sarah, d. of Stephen and Nancy, Sept. 21, 1808.
Sarah Aldrich [———], w. of Stephen, ———, 1819. g.r.1.
Stephen, s. of Stephen and Sarah, Sept. 8, 1779.
Stephen, s. of Stephen and Nancy, Sept. 11, 1817.

WILLMARTH, William H., ———, 1832. g.r.1.

WILSON, Elizabeth, d. of Samuel, Sept. 14, 1771. Twin.
Elizabeth B., 29th day, 3d mo. 1814. c.r.4.
Jonas, Aug. 7, 1818. g.r.1.
Rachel, d. of Samuel, Sept. 18, 177-.
Samuel, s. of Samuel, Nov. 23, 1769.
Susannah, d. of Samuel, Sept. 14, 1771. Twin.
Tryfene, d. of Samuel, Sept. 21, 1768.

WING, Albert F., ———, 1818. g.r.1.
Anna, d. of Joseph and Dinah, 18th day, 7th mo. 1774. c.r.1.
Caroline, d. of Paul and Mercy Ann, 30th day, 7th mo. 1811. c.r.4.

WING, Charles, ——, 1816. G.R.1.
Charles Hamilton, s. of Charles and Mary G., June 18, 1843.
Deborah, d. of John and Margaret, 1st day, 8th mo. 1774.
  C.R.4.
Dinah [———], w. of Joseph, 11th day, 7th mo. 1746. C.R.4.
Edgar Taft, s. of Albert F. and Emeline N., Dec. 16, 1847.
Emeline Henshaw, d. of Albert F. and Emeline N., Jan. 5, 1843.
Emeline N. Taft [———], w. of Albert F., ——, 1822. G.R.1.
Francis Carpenter, s. of Charles and Mary G., Apr. 13, 1845.
Hannah, d. of Joseph and Dinah, 26th day, 6th mo. 1769.
  C.R.4.
Hattil, ch. of Joseph and Dinah, 28th day, 12th mo. 1780.
  C.R.4.
Hellen Louisa, d. of Charles and Mary G., Sept. 4, 1840.
Henry T., s. of Albert F. and Emeline N., Sept. 11, 1845.
Hiram, 27th day, 10th mo. 1799. C.R.4.
Huldah, d. of John and Margaret, 8th day, 2d mo. 1780. C.R.4.
Jabez, s. of Joseph and Dinah, 24th day, 6th mo. 1783. C.R.4.
Joseph, 23d day, 6th mo. 1747. C.R.4.
Joseph, s. of Joseph and Dinah, 3d day, 8th mo. 1776. C.R.4.
Margaret [———], w. of John, 23d day, 11th mo. 1755. C.R.4.
Mary Brown [———], w. of Hiram, 12th day, 1st mo. 1803.
  C.R.4.
Mary G. [———], w. of Charles, ——, 1820. G.R.1.
Mercy Ann, 16th day, 12th mo. 1791. C.R.4.
Paul, 6th day, 6th mo. 1787. C.R.4.
Suvery, ch. of Joseph and Dinah, 28th day, 9th mo. 1771.
  C.R.4.
William, s. of John and Margaret, 20th day, 2d mo. 1776.
  C.R.4.

WINSLOW, Albert, s. of Ebenezer and Lucy, July 24, 1797.
Alvin, s. of Ebenezer and Lucy, Aug. 27, 1801.
Claramond, d. of Ebenezer and Lucy, Feb. 19, 1799.

WINTER (see Wintor), Rebecca, d. of Christopher and Zeruiah,
  Mar. 30, 1772.

WINTOR (see Winter), Abigail, d. of Christophar and Ruth,
  Nov. 20, 1738.
Christophar, s. of Christophar and Ruth, Apr. 10, 1740.
David, s. of Christophar and Ruth, May 23, 1759.
Ebenezer, s. of Timothy and Rachel, Mar. 22, 1765.
Hannah, d. of Christophar and Ruth, May 23, 1751.

WINTOR, John, s. of Christophar and Ruth, July 24, 1749.
Penellipy, d. of Christophar and Ruth, Jan. 6, 1756.
Rachel, d. of Christophar and Ruth, Nov. 11, 1741.
Ruth, d. of Christophar and Ruth, Apr. 10, 1746.
Sarah, d. of Christophar and Ruth, July 15, 1747.
Thadeus, s. of Timothy and Rachel, Jan. 30, 1767.
Timothy, s. of Christophar and Ruth, Apr. 17, 1744.
William, s. of Christophar and Ruth, Aug. 18, 1757.

WOOD, ———, d. of Josiah and Zipporah, bp. Aug. —, 1776. C.R.I.
Abigail, d. of Ezekiel and Mary, Mar. 28, 1742.
Abigail, d. of Josiah and Zipporah, Aug. 30, 1759.
Abigail, d. of (Dr., C.R.I) Joshua and Rachel, June 29, 1765.
Abigail, d. of Ezekiel and Marthew, Nov. 8, 1781.
Abigail, d. of Samuel and Rachel, Apr. 16, 1813.
Amariah Albee, s. of Samuel and Rachel, Nov. 2, 1802.
Amaza, s. of Solomon and Hannah, June 3, 1769.
Amos, s. of Dexter and ———, bp. ———, 1775. C.R.I.
Amos, s. of David and Molle, Dec. 23, 1783.
Amos, s. of Ezekiel and Sarah, Jan. 22, 1798.
Amos, s. of Samuel and Rachel, Dec. 18, 1804.
Anna, d. of Ezra and Anna, ——— 14, 1753.
Anna, d. of Dextor and Deborah, Oct. 5, 1774.
Anna, d. of Samuel and Rachel, Mar. 19, 1797.
Annah I., d. of Amariah A. and Sarah T., Aug. 18, 1848.
Arthur Eugene, s. of David F. and Harriet, Jan. 20, 1844.
Benjamin, s. of Solomon and Hannah, Sept. 30, 1778.
Betsy [———], w. of George H., ———, 1798. G.R.I.
Caleb, s. of Simeon and M[a]rgery, June 2, 1767.
Caroline Roxellana, d. of Whitney and Esther, June 5, 1810.
Charles Dexter, s. of Ezekiel and Eunice, Jan. 20, 1830.
Charles Olney, s. of Wheelock and Hannah, Nov. 6, 1821.
Charles Phineas, s. of Phineas and Harriet M., Aug. 3, 1837.
Chloa, d. of James and Esther, Sept. 21, 1742.
Chloa, d. of Jonah and Rachel, Apr. 19, 1771.
Chloe, d. of David and Molle, Nov. 10, 1770.
Clarissa, d. of David and Molle, Dec. 27, 1794.
Clarissa F. [———], w. of Phineas, in Barre, Vt., Feb. 14; 1807. G.R.I.
Cynthia, d. of Dextor and Deborah, Oct. 30, 1779.
Cyrus, s. of Reuben and Sally, Nov. 12, 1819.
Daniel, s. of Josiah and Zipporah, bp. Apr. 15, 1770. C.R.I.
Daniel, s. of Jonah and Rachel, June 21, 1773.

WOOD, David, s. of Obediah and Esther, Aug. 11, 1748.
David, s. of David and Molle, Nov. 6, 1792.
David, s. of Reuben and Sally, Feb. 16, 1818.
Deborah, d. of Dextor and Deborah, Nov. 1, 1767.
Dextor, s. of Ezekiel and Mary, Sept. 22, 1733.
Easther, d. of Henery and Sarah, Mar. 15, 1773.
Elisabeth, d. of Solomon and Hannah, Apr. 15, 1776.
Elizabeth, d. of Obadiah and Esther, Aug. 4, 1735.
Emery, s. of Josiah and Zipporah, bp. Mar. 27, 1768. C.R.1.
Emily M., d. of Riley and Rosana, Aug. 22, 1847.
Esther, d. of Obediah and Esther, Aug. 11, 1741.
Eunice, d. of Joshua and Rachel, May 17, 1762.
Eunice, d. of Simeon and M[a]rgery, Apr. 11, 1773. Twin.
Eunice, d. of David and Molle, Jan. 4, 1781.
Eunice, d. of Reuben and Sally, Oct. 12, 1822.
Ezekiel, s. of Ezekiel and Mary, Feb. 5, 1743–4.
Ezekiel, s. of Dextor and Deborah, Apr. 15, 1772.
Ezekiel, s. of Henery and Sarah, Dec. 19, 1777.
Ezekiel, Mar. 6, 1783. G.R.1.
Ezekiel, s. of Ezekiel and Sarah, Mar. 8, 1788.
Ezekiel, s. of Ezekiel 3d and Barshaba, Mar. 16, 1804.
Farnum, s. of David and Molle, Dec. 22, 1772. Twin.
Francis, s. of Mark and Rachel, Apr. 8, 1798.
George H., ———, 1813. G.R.1.
Hannah, d. of (Dr., C.R.1) Joshua and Rachel, Jan. 4, 1769.
Hannah, d. of Solomon and Hannah, May 5, 1784.
Haward, s. of David and Molle, Jan. 3, 1777.
Henery, s. of James and Esther, Apr. 3, 1737.
Jabesh, s. of Ezekiel and Sarah, Aug. 12, 1784.
Jemima, d. of Solomon and Faithfull, Feb. 16, 1740.
Jerusha, d. of Simeon and M[a]rgery, June 28, 1765.
Jesse, s. of Simeon and M[a]rgery, Aug. 29, 1775.
Jeudah, d. of Henery and Sarah, Oct. 2, 1775.
John, s. of Ezekiel and Mary, Oct. 20, 1737. Twin.
John, s. of Joshua and Rachel, Dec. 15, 1754.
John, s. of Solomon and Hannah, June 3, 1781.
Jonah, s. of James and Esther, Sept. 10, 1731.
Joshua, s. of Ezekiel and Mary, Dec. 23, 173–. (bp. Jan. 2, 1731–2. C.R.1.)
Joshua, s. of Dr. Joshua and Rachel, bp. Mar. 9, 1755. C.R.1.
Joshua, s. of Joshua and Rachel, July 16, 1758.
Josiah, s. of Josiah and Zipporah, Apr. 24, 1764.
Josiah, s. of Ezekiel and Sarah, Dec. 22, 1793.
Keith, s. of David and Molle, Dec. 22, 1772. Twin.

WOOD, Levicy, d. of Jonah and Rachel, Dec. 7, 1765.
Loeis, d. of Josiah and Zipporah, bp. Jan. 26, 1772. C.R.1.
Lois, d. of Simeon and M[a]rgery, Apr. 11, 1773. Twin.
Louies, d. of Ezekiel (Jr., C.R.1) and Marthew, June 24, 1767.
Louis, d. of Ezekiel and Mary, June 2, 1746.
Lucenda, d. of Ezekiel and Marthew, Nov. 9, 1774.
Lucenda, d. of Ezekiel and Marthew, Mar. 29, 1777.
Lydia, d. of Joshua and Rachel, bp. Aug. 22, 1773. C.R.1.
Lyman (Lyman W., G.R.1), s. of Reuben and Sally, Feb. 27, 1825.
Margret, d. of Ezra and Anna, Mar. 16, 1751.
Marie, Oct. 31, 1812. G.R.1.
Mark, s. of Henery and Sarah, Feb. 26, 1766.
Martha, d. of Solomon and Faithfull, Jan. 12, 1729–30.
Martha, d. of Ezekiel (Jr., C.R.1) and Marthew, Mar. 10, 1770.
Mary, d. of James and Esther, Aug. 15, 1729.
Mary, d. of Ezekiel and Mary, Mar. 3, 1734–5.
Mary, d. of Henry and Sarah, Dec. 2, 1759.
Mary, d. of Dextor and Deborah, Nov. 21, 1760.
Mary, d. of Dextor and Deborah, Dec. 10, 1761.
Mary, d. of Henery and Sarah, Dec. 7, 1770.
Mary, d. of Samuel and Rachel, Nov. 8, 1800.
Mary Baylies, d. of Amariah A. and Sarah, Apr. 29, 1847.
Mary E. Rawson [———], w. of Samuel T., ———, 1845. G.R.1.
Merrit, s. of Howard and Waity, Nov. 27, 1805.
Minerva E., d. of Emory and Elisabeth, Apr. 24, 1847.
Miranda, d. of David and Molle, Mar. 6, 1791.
Molley, d. of Jonah and Rachel, Apr. 14, 1769.
Nancy, d. of David and Molle, Feb. 6, 1787.
Nathan, s. of Simeon and M[a]rgery, July 24, 1771.
Obediah, s. of Obediah and Esther, May 9, 1737.
Obediah, s. of Solomon and Hannah, Mar. 16, 1773.
Olive, d. of David and Molle, Mar. 19, 1775.
Olive Adams, d. of Reuben and Sally, June 12, 1831.
Olive D. Seagraves [———], w. of Samuel T., ———, 1842. G.R.1.
Oliver, s. of Dr. Joshua and Rachel, bp. Oct. 27, 1771. C.R.1.
Patiance, d. of Ezekiel and Marthew, Oct. 25, 1772.
Pheebe, d. of David and Molle, Jan. 8, 1769.
Phinehas, s. of Solomon and Hannah, Mar. 15, 1767.
Phinehas, s. of Mark and Rachel, Apr. 19, 1800.
Phines, s. of Henery and Sarah, Aug. 19, 1768.
Polley, d. of David and Molle, Jan. 27, 1779.
Rachel, d. of James and Esther, Mar. 16, 1733–4.
Rachel, d. of (Dr., C.R.1) Joshua and Rachel, Mar. 24, 1760.

WOOD, Rachel, d. of Samuel and Rachel, Oct. 4, 1806.
Reuben, ——, 1787. G.R.1.
Rhoda, d. of Simeon and M[a]rgery, May 25, 1763.
Rhoda, d. of Ezekiel and Marthew, Aug. 19, 1779.
Ruth, d. of James and Esther, Aug. 26, 1745.
Salley, d. of David and Molle, Mar. 15, 1785.
Salley, d. of Ezekiel and ——, bp. Aug. 13, 1786. C.R.1.
Salley, d. of David and Molle, Mar. 29, 1789.
Sally [——], w. of Reuben, ——, 1789. G.R.1.
Samuel, s. of Dextor and Deborah, Nov. 10, 1764.
Samuel T., s. of Amariah A. and Sarah T., Oct. 4, 1841.
Sarah, d. of Solomon and Faithfull, July 6, 1735.
Sarah, d. of Obediah and Esther, Aug. 18, 1739.
Sarah, d. of Ezekiel and Sarah, Feb. 1, 1790.
Sarah, d. of Samuel and Rachel, Sept. 24, 1798.
Sarah, d. of Mark and Rachel, Nov. 27, 1808.
Sarah H. Emma, d. of Manning and Sarah H., Mar. 15, 1844.
Sibbel, d. of Henery and Sarah, July 7, 1761.
Silvia, Apr. 19, 1815. G.R.1.
Simeon, s. of Solomon and Faithfull, Jan. 7, 1732-3.
Solomon, s. of Solomon and Faithfull, Oct. 27, 1727.
Solomon, s. of Obediah and Esther, May 25, 1744.
Stephen, s. of Simeon and M[a]rgery, Oct. 14, 1761.
Sumner, s. of Josiah and Zipporah, May 28, 1762.
Susan A., Aug. 22, 1822. G.R.1.
Susanna, d. of Ezekiel and Mary, Jan. 7, 1739-40.
Susanna, d. of Solomon and Hannah, Sept. 24, 1770.
Sylvia A. [——], w. of Phineas, in Douglas, Sept. 26, 1818. G.R.1.
Thomas, s. of Ezekiel and Mary, Oct. 20, 1737. Twin.
Thomas, s. of (Dr., C.R.1) Joshua and Rachel, Oct. 24, 1756.
Timothy, s. of Henery and Sarah, Feb. 17, 1763.
Timothy, s. of (Dr., C.R.1) Joshua and Rachel, Aug. 31, 1766.
Tryal, d. of James and Esther, Jan. 4, 1739.
Warfield, s. of Obediah and Esther, Feb. 1, 1733-4.
Wheelock, s. of Josiah and Zipporah, bp. Mar. 2, 1766. C.R.1.
Whitney, s. of Ezekiel and Sarah, Jan. 28, 1783.
Willard, s. of Jonah and Rachel, June 24, 1767.
William W., Sept. 30, 1819. G.R.1.
Willis, s. of Simeon and M[a]rgery, July 14, 1769.
Zipporah, d. of Josiah and Zipporah, bp. ——, 1774. C.R.1.

WOODIS, John M., ——, 1815. G.R.1.
Sarah J. [——], w. of John M., ——, 1830. G.R.1.

WOODWARD, Moses, s. of Bethiah, bp. Oct. 19, 1741. c.r.1.

WORK, Sarah, d. of ———, bp. at Upton, Apr. 25, 1737. c.r.1.

YATES, Abner, s. of James and Tabbaroh, Aug. 12, 1746.
Amariah, s. of James and Tabbaroh, Feb. 28, 1749.
Barzleel, s. of James and Elisabeth, Oct. 12, 1757.
Elisabeth, d. of James and Tabbaroh, Dec. 13, 1736.
Gilberd, s. of James and Tabbaroh, Nov. 16, 1751.
James, s. of James and Tabbaroh, Dec. 11, 1743.
James, s. of James and Elisabeth, May 15, 1755.
John, s. of James and Tabbaroh, Dec. 17, 1734.
Marcy, d. of James and Tabbaroh, Apr. 3, 1741.
Paul, s. of James and Tabbaroh, Jan. 11, 1738-9.

YOUNG, George B., s. of George B. and Catharine, Nov. 5, 1847.
John E., s. of Joseph, b. in Vermont, and Susan, b. in Canada, in Wrentham, Dec. 6, 1848.

NEGRO AND UNIDENTIFIED.

———, William, apprentice boy of Asa Blake, bp. Feb. 13, 1786. c.r.1.
Brister, s. of Dinah, a negro woman, bp. Dec. 8, 1775. c.r.1.

UXBRIDGE MARRIAGES.

UXBRIDGE MARRIAGES.

To the year 1850.

ADAMES (see Adams), Nathaniel and Lucy Woods of Southboro, int. Dec. 8, 1768.

ADAMS (see Adames), Abigail, wid., of Northbridge, and Dea. Nicholas Baylies, int. Sept. 24, 1804.
Abner of Sutton, and Lucy Holbrook, Nov. 4, 1795.
Andrew of Northbridge, and Betsy Chapin, Nov. 4, 1790.
Ann A., d. of Leonard and Maria, a. 17 y., and Ezra F. Staples, s. of Ezra and Cynthia, a. 24 y., Apr. 6, 1848.
Benja[min] and Betsey Craggin, Jan. 19, 1794.
Benjamin Esq. and Susanna Richmond of Providence, R. I., int. Jan. —, 1809.
Cyrus of Northbridge, and Olive Wood, Oct. 4, 1798.
Dolly and Henry Bond of Northbridge, int. Sept. 25, 1846.
George and Angelina N. Day, May 26, 1841.
Hannah and Caleb Hill, both of New Sherborn, Dec. 22, 1740.*
John Jr. and Elizabeth Newton (Nuten, int.) of Sutton, in Sutton, Nov. 28, 1768.
Jonathan of Sutton, and Sarah Fish, int. Feb. 20, 1774.
Joseph and Elisabeth Draper, Oct. 14, 1756.
Joseph and Abigal Perrien of Woodstock, int. June 8, 1776.
Josiah of Mendon, and Sarah Read, Dec. 27, 1750.
Laura and Horatio Cogswell, Jan. 25, 1844.
Leonard and Maria Chilson, Aug. 30, 1829.
Lyman and Cynthia S. Smith, Apr. 11, 1837.
Mary and Joseph C. Keith, Oct. 19, 1836.
Mary and Elisha Inman, Jan. 23, 1843.
Mowry and Abiah Pingree, Oct. 3, 1831.
Nancy L. and W[illia]m S. Fogg, both of Mendon, Aug. 16, 1836.*
Nathaniel and Emeline Buffum, Nov. 15, 1837.
Polly and Warren Rawson, both of Mendon, July 3, 1803.*

* Intention not recorded.

ADAMS, Rebecca, d. of Fleming and Rebecca, a. 23 y., and Silas H. Metcalf of Wrentham, s. of Silas and Nancy, a. 21 y., Mar. 20, 1845.
Ruth of Braintree, and Rev. Nathan Webb, in Braintree, Nov. 23, 1751 (int. Oct. 30, 1731).
Samuel and Susannah Rist, int. Sept. 25, 1790.
Sarah of Northbridge, and Peter Legg, int. May 3, 1829.
William and Mary Cousens of Sherborn, in Sherborn, Aug. 19, 1730.*
William H. of Northbridge, s. of Fleming and Rebecca, a. 21 y., and Julia Pressey of Northbridge, d. of Phineas and Harriet, a. 20 y., Apr. 20, 1846.*

ADDEY, Dorcas and Joseph Plumbly, July 30, 1747.*

ALBB (see Albee, Allbee), Benjamin of Gloucester, R. I., and Sarah Taft, int. Aug. 1, 1768.

ALBEE (see Albb and Allbee), Abial and David Wallis of Douglas, int. Oct. 25, 1778.
Abigail of Mendon, and Nathan Keith, in Mendon, Oct. 7, 1762.
Abigail and Stephen Drake, int. July 12, 1768.
Alpheus and Hannah Goldthwait, int. Mar. 3, 1822.
Betsey and Timothy Alexander of Mendon, int. Aug. 24, 1807.
Bulah and Iseral Saben, Sept. 27, 1770.
Eleazor and Mary Shippee of Smithfield, County of Providence, int. July 30, 1743.
Eliza, d. of Ellis and Lavinia, a. 17 y., and Obed P. Thayer of Mendon, s. of Otis and Mercy of Mendon, a. 21 y., Nov. 14, 1844.
Ellis and Eliza Buxton of Smithfield, R. I., int. Nov. 23, 1817.
Ellis and Lavina Southwick of Mendon, int. Oct. 23, 1827.
Emily M. and George W. Cook of Mendon, int. July 7, 1839.
Eunice and Smith White, int. Oct. 14, 1781.
Hepsebah and Jonathan Hall, May 29, 1793. C.R.1.
Hopa and Stephen Holbrook, Sept. 11, 1788.
James and Prudence White of Mendon, in Mendon, Jan. 21, 1745 [prob. 1745–6] (int. Aug. 23, 1745).
James Jr. and Ruth White of Mendon, in Mendon, Feb. 29, 1776.
James and Rachael Darling of Mendon, in Mendon, Feb. 1, 1787.
James and Betsy Tourtelott of Mendon, int. Feb. 11, 1821.
Jesse and Rachel Benson of Mendon, int. Nov. 27, 1803.

* Intention not recorded.

ALBEE, Joseph and Ruth Darling of Mendon, int. Oct. 17, 1744.
Lavinia S. of Mendon, and Stephen A. Aldrich, Dec. 25 [1835].*
Lucy M. of Oxford, and Richard D. Mowry, int. July 31, 1838.
Mary and Jonathan White, Oct. 12, 1823.
Naum C. and Charlotte Blake, Jan. 19, 1829.
Nelly and Henry Holbrook, int. Nov. 15, 1812.
Phila and Enos Taft of Mendon, in Mendon, Nov. 7, 1799.
Rachel of Mendon, and Samuel Wood, in Mendon, June 22, 1794.
Ruth of Gloucester, and Douglas White, int. June 10, 1771.
Sarah of Mendon, and Ezekiel Wood, int. Mar. 18, 1782.
Silvia of Milford, and Willard Ellison, int. Mar. 7, 1830.
Susanah and Ebenezer Read, Feb. 27, 1792.
Sylvia and Willis Southwick of Smithfield, R. I., int. Nov. 10, 1816.

ALBRO, Amasa and Lucy Parkes of Scituate, R. I., int. Apr. 17, 1836.

ALDEN, Lydia B. of Walpole, and Seth R. Aldrich, int. Sept. 19, 1841.

ALDRICH, Aaron and Tarzah Thayer of Douglas, Jan. 23, 1769.
Abel and Elisabeth Aldrich of Mendon, int. July 29, 1732.
Abel and Uranna Sprig of Smithfield, int. Oct. 17, 1741.
Abel and Olive Lovel, Jan. 7, 1773.
Abel and Elizabeth Rawson, in Northbridge, June 21, 1791.
Abel Jr. and Phebe Comstock, int. Dec. 10, 1820.
Abial and William Carpenter, Apr. 12, 1795. c.r.1.
Abigail and Alexander Aldrich, int. July 22, 1766.
Abigail and Seth Jenne, int. Mar. 14, 1768.
Abner of Smithfield, R. I., and Susan S. Taft, Feb. 29, 1844.
Abraham of Mendon, and Levina Taft, in Mendon, Mar. 31, 1768.*
Abraham and Martha Martin, Dec. 1, 1808.
Ahaz and Joanna Scout of Bellingham, int. Mar. 17, 1792.
Ahaz and Mary Arnold of Bellingham, int. May 6, 1821.
Alexander and Abigail Aldrich, int. July 22, 1766.
Alma M. and Josiah S. Fisher, Jan. 18, 1824.
Amos of Douglas, and Rhoda Keith, int. June 11, 1788.
Ann H. and Willard Taft, int. Dec. 30, 1832. Banns forbid by Ann H. Aldrich, Dec. 31, 1832.
Anna and Willard Morse, July 16, 1809.
Anna and David Sibley of Oxford, int. July 20, 1828.

* Intention not recorded.

ALDRICH, Anna of Mendon, and Osborn Aldrich, int. July 26, 1829.
Armelia and Willis Thompson, Dec. 1, 1803.
Arnold and Polly Rawson, int. July, Aug. 1808.
Arnold Jr. and Diana Cass of Mendon, int. Sept. 2, 1832.
Artemas and Clarissa Wood, Mar. 7, 1824.
Asael and Susanna Aldrich, int. Mar. 8, 1773.
Asahel and Olive Daniels of Mendon, int. Feb. 27, 1803.
Asahel and Ruth Southwick, int. Oct. 28, 1816.
Asahel 2d and Scheherezade Cumings of Douglas, int. Aug. 14, 1831.
Barnabas and Prudence Allbee, Apr. 9, 1766.
Bathsheba and John Marsh of Killingly, Conn., Dec. 27, 1781.*
Benjamin, s. of Abel, and Lydia Twist, d. of Lydia of Salem, 6th day, 9th mo., called September, 1759. C.R.3.*
Betsey and Josiah Colburn (2d, C.R.1) of Dracut, Jan. 8, 1832.
Catharine, d. of Nathaniel and Rachel, a. 51 y., and Elkanah Taft, widr., s. of Nathaniel and Abigail of Mendon, a. 63 y., Mar. 24, 1847.
Chauncey, s. of Willard and Azubah, a. 34 y., and Mary B. York, d. of Hannah of Farmington, Me., a. 27 y., May 21, 1848.
Chauncy and Elvira Holbrook of Milford, int. Feb. 21, 1841.
Chole and Peleg Buxton, int. July 24, 1795.
Clarrissa and Buckley Minot of Northbridge, Jan. 18, 1827. C.R.1.
Cromwell of Grafton, and Rosina Morse of Upton, May 14, 1822.*
Daniel, s. of Jacob, and Tamzen Southwick, d. of Caleb of Salem, 1st day, 5th mo., called May, 1755. C.R.3.*
Daniel, s. of Jacob and Mary Cook, formerly of Smithfield, R. I., now residing in Mendon, d. of Seth, 2d day, 9th mo., called September, 1762. C.R.3.*
Daniel and Marcy Pitts, int. Feb. 23, 1788.
Daniel H. of Northbridge, s. of Samuel and Sarah of Northbridge, a. 33 y., and Cyrena R. Munyon, d. of Miranda, a. 22 y., Apr. 9, 1846.*
David and Mary Brown, int. Mar. 30, 1784.
David and Chloe Hall of Ashford, Conn., int. Feb. 8, 1807.
Deborah and John Eliot, Oct. 2, 1736.
Deborah and Thomas Jeperson of New Sherborn, int. Sept. 5, 1745 (May 26, 1744 dup.).
Delphina B. and Daniel Crossman of Mendon (of Waterford, int.), June 3, 1838.

* Intention not recorded.

ALDRICH, Desire and William Rawson (of Mendon, int.), Mar. 12, 1760.
Dinah and Edward Aldrich, int. Mar. 7, 1731-2.
Dutee and Eliza Ann Taft of Sutton, in Douglas, May 8, 1837.
Edward and Dinah Aldrich, int. Mar. 7, 1731-2.
Edward of Douglas, and Elisabeth Aldrich, int. Sept. 6, 1761.
Elexander and Abigail Clark, Aug. 21, 1766.*
Elisabeth of Mendon, and Abel Aldrich, int. July 29, 1732.
Elisabeth and Noah Curtis of Oxford Gore, int., Apr. 11, 1750.
Elisabeth and Edward Aldrich of Douglas, int., Sept. 6, 1761.
Eliza E., d. of Ahaz and Mary, a. 22 y., and James M. Williams of Burrillville, R. I., s. of George W. and Ruth of Burrillville, R. I., a. 22 y., Mar. 2, 1846.
Elizabeth and Ezra Hatherway, int. Feb. —, 1815.
Ellener of Douglas, and Pellatiah White, int. June 3, 1804.
Ellis and Hannah Gould White, Mar. 3, 1803.
Ellis of Northbridge, and Sarah Parsons (Persons, int.), Jan. 7, 1830.
Enoch and Deborah Wheelock of Gloucester, int. Oct. 21, 1774.
Enoch Jr. and Sabra Scot of Bellingham, int. Mar. 6, 1798.
Enoch and Phebe Buffum, int. Apr. 30, 1843.
Ephraim, s. of Ephraim and Dorcas, and Lydia Blanchard of Foster, R. I., d. of Caleb and Betsy, at Coventry, R. I., Dec. 24, 1826.
Ezekiel and Miriam Wadkins of Hopkinton, in Hopkinton, Feb. 20, 1794.
George and Meriam Pitts of Orring, int. May 6, 1793.
Gerusha of Mendon, and Comfort Keith, int. Mar. 3, 1776.
Grosvenor and Joanna H. Smith of Farmington, Me., int. July 29, 1849.
— Hannah and John Elison, Apr. 11, 1732.
Hannah, wid., and Richard Estes of Cumberland, R. I., 5th day, 6th mo. 1778. c.r.3.*
Hannah and Artemas Keith, int. Oct. 14, 1796.
Hannah and Stephen Howland, both of Douglas, May 3, 1809.*
Hannah of Douglas, and Calvin B. Hacket, int. Sept. 13, 1835.
Hitty and John McGrath, int. Sept. 6, 1829.
Hopestill and David Bowin (of Warren, int.), Mar. 8, 1764.
Horatio and Laura Harris, int. Jan. 14, 1838.
Hosea and Rachel Carary (Chorarey, int.), Nov. 22, 1798.
Hosea of Grafton, and Mary Eliza Chard of Upton, Nov. 28, 1817.*
Hosea and Mary Ann Taft, May 25, 1834.
Huldah and William Johnson, in Mendon, June 16, 1731.*

* Intention not recorded.

ALDRICH, Huldah and David Dunn, both of Northbridge, Jan. 3, 1805.*
Isaac and Zilphah Fisk, Jan. 26, 1763.*
Isaac and Susannah Aldrich, Mar. 16, 1773.*
Israel and Philadelphia Emerson, int. Oct. 2, 1784.
Issabella and Isaac Blanchard (of Mendon, int.), Aug. 31, 1815.
Jacob and Joanna Bartlet, int. July 3, 1731.
Jacob and Hannah Brown, wid. of Joseph of Gloucester, R. I., 26th day, 2d mo., called February, 1768. C.R.3.*
Jacob and Mehitebel Gefford, int. Oct. 16, 1769.
Jacob and Mary Blanchard of Foster, R. I., June 1, 1814.
Jacob and Mrs. Hannah C. Underwood of Charlestown, Nov. 29, 1838.
Jane and Abijah Keyes, June 8, 1769.
Jemima and Bezaleel Seagrave, int. Dec. 7, 1806.
Jeremiah and Hanna Plumbly, int. ——, 1732.
Jesse of New Salem, and Rachel Brown, in Douglas, Dec. 3, 1772.
Jesse and Susannah Keith, Dec. 30, 1793.
Jesse of Northbridge, and Deborah Brown, Feb. 4, 1798.
Jesse, Capt., and wid. Waity Wood of Northbridge, int. Nov. 15, 1840.
Joana and Jonas Twitchel, int. Feb. 1, 1768.
Joanna and Ziba Cook of Bellingham, int. Dec. 3, 1787.
John and Mary Hill, June 1, 1748.*
John Jr. of Northbridge, and Betsy Keyes, Jan. 1, 1821.
John A. of Worcester, s. of Joseph and Harriet, a. 21 y., and Emeline W. Hall, d. of Isaac and Polly, a. 18 y., Jan. 13, 1848.
Joseph and Elisabeth Prentice, Jan. 2, 1740–1.
Joseph of Gloucester, R. I., and Abigail Fish, Mar. 19, 1750–1.*
Joseph and Harriot Seagraves, Jan. 11, 1811.
Juliah and James H. Morse, May 28, 1823.
Justus and Permelia Arnold (of Bellingham, int.), Jan. 6, 1831.
Katharine and Joseph Newell of Richmond, int. Mar. 26, 1770.
Katherina and Samuel Kempton, int. Feb. 21, 1777.
Layman and Cynthia Fay, Apr. 20, 1831.
Louis and David (Daniel, int.) Shermon of Burrillville, R. I., Mar. 8, 1812.
Lovina and John A. (John Arnold, int.) Smith of Burrillville, R. I., Nov. 9, 1828.
Lucinda and Marvel Thayer of Douglas, Apr. 27, 1820.
Lucy G. and Richard Henry of Worcester, Dec. 9, 1838.
Lydia and Jonathan Cook, Oct. 20, 1763.

* Intention not recorded.

ALDRICH, Lydia of Northbridge, and Jennings B. Congdon, int. Feb. 26, 1832.
Lyman Jr. of Northbridge, and Abigail W. Taft, May 28, 1828.
Manson A., s. of Ahaz and Mary, a. 21 y., and Delia A. Brooks, d. of George and Betsey of Farmington, Me., a. 19 y., Jan. 5, 1846.
Margery and John Martin of Bolton, int. Nov. 3, 1739.
Maria of Burrillville, R. I., and Samuel R. Spring, int. Aug. 31, 1845.
Marinda and James Howard of Upton, Apr. 13, 1813.
Martha and Nathan Aldrich, June 4, 1815.
Martin and Dulcinia Larned, Mar. 24, 1836.
Mary, d. of Jacob, and John Bennet, 4th day, 12th mo., called December, 1760. c.r.3.*
Mary, d. of Joseph, and Seth Aldrich, s. of Jacob, 3d day, 11th mo., called November, 1763. c.r.3.*
Mary and Stephen Cook of Gloucester, R. I., int. June 4, 1764.
Mary and Nathaniel Cooper, Dec. 19, 1765.
Mary and Willard Taft, Aug. 10, 1841.
Mary Ann, Mrs., and Briggs Lee, Mar. 29, 1836.
Mary H. of Mendon, and Otis Aldrich, int. Apr. 8, 1838.
Mary J., d. of Ahaz and Mary, a. 19 y., and Jeremiah S. McIntire, s. of Jeremiah and Nancy, a. 22 y., Jan. 5, 1846.
Mehetabel and David Eliot of Oblong [Duchess County, N. Y.], int. Dec. 29, 1739.
Milton of Mendon, s. of Samuel and Delila, a. 21 y., and Eliza A. Gardner of Mendon, d. of Thomas and Nancy, a. 26 y., June 20, 1849.*
Molley and Joseph Baker of Mendon, int. May 9, 1773.
Molly and Bezaleel Seagrave, Feb. 19, 1789.
Molly (or Polly, int.) and Royal Taft, Dec. 19, 1805.
Moses and Hannah Hill, int., Feb. 10, 1783.
Mowry of Douglas (Gloucester, R. I., int.), and Mary (Polly, int.), Paine, June 11, 1801.
Nancy and George Colson of Bellingham, Jan. 18, 1802.
Nathan and Martha Aldrich, June 4, 1815.
Nathan 2d and Maria Fowler of Northbridge, int. Dec. 12, 1824.
Nathan and Mrs. Martha Britton, Jan. 1, 1843.
Nathan 2d, widr., s. of Obediah and Judith, a. 52 y., and Eunice Robbins, wid., d. of Ezekiel and Elizabeth Gaskill, a. 36 y., July 8, 1845.

* Intention not recorded.

ALDRICH, Nathan, widr., s. of Seth and Amey, a. 58 y., and Sarah
    Chase, d. of Josiah and Charity, a. 28 y., July 5, 1846.
Nathaniel, s. of Joseph and Elisabeth, and Rachel Aldrich, d.
    of Jacob, 18th day, 6th mo. 1773. c.r.3.*
Nehemiah, s. of Jacob dec., and Anna Gaskill, d. of Ebenezer
    of Mendon, 5th day, 6th mo. 1777. c.r.3.*
Nehemiah and Polly Morse, int. Jan. 31, 1806.
Obadiah and Judith Chase, of Gloucester, int. Nov. 17, 1787.
Olive and Prince Parker, int. Feb. 26, 1795.
Omar and Mary Ann Fay, Mar. 3, 1825.*
Osborn and Anna Aldrich of Mendon, int. July 26, 1829.
Otis and Judith Southwick Jr., int. Feb. 18, 1827.
Otis and Mary H. Aldrich of Mendon, int. Apr. 8, 1838.
Otis, widr., of Blackstone, s. of Enoch and Deborah, a. 59 y.,
    and wid. Hannah W. Darling of Blackstone, d. of Mr.
    Luther, July 29, 1847.*
Paine of Worcester, and Mrs. Sophia W. Capron, June 24, 1841.
Pardon and Rachel Drake, both of Mendon, May 8, 1796.*
Patience and Cornelius Gibson, Oct. 21, 1804.
Penelap and Thomas Bowin (of Warren, int.), Jan. 24, 1765.
Peter Jr. and Esther Comstock of Providence, int. Feb. 8,
    1745–6.
Phebe and Joel Whiting, int. July 25, 1819.
Rachel and Daniel Wood, int. Mar. 20, 1755.
Rachel, d. of Jacob, and Nathaniel Aldrich, s. of Joseph, 18th
    day, 6th mo. 1773. c.r.3.*
Rachel and Stasa Fletcher of Charlton, int. Jan 5, 1812.
Rachel, d. of William of Mendon, and Hannah, and Richard
    Battey, s. of Jesse of Burrillville, R. I., and Nancy dec.,
    6th day, 5th mo. 1829. c.r.3.*
Rachel P. of Northbridge, and Charles Taft, int. Nov. 7, 1847.
Rhoda and Thomas Morrey (Moore, int.) of Smithfield, R. I.,
    in Mendon, Sept. 14, 1769.
Rhoda and Dr. Enoch Thayer of Gloucester, R. I., int. May
    3, 1801.
Rhozilla of Cumberland, R. I., and Royal Farnum, int. Oct. 15,
    1792.
Richard and Abigail Thompson, int. Nov. 22, 1801.
Roxalana of Douglas, and Simon Rawson Jr., int. May 1, 1836.
Royal and Mary Trask, int. Mar. 16, 1828.
Ruth and Christopher Winter, Jan. 28, 1737–8. (Jan. 18,
    1737–8. c.r.1.)
Ruth and Moses Marten of Richmond, int. Jan. 27, 1772.
Ruth and W[illia]m Livermore of Spencer, Aug. 18, 1839.
Ruth K. and Royal Cumings of Douglas, int. June 28, 1829.

* Intention not recorded.

ALDRICH, Sally and Jeremiah Larned of Sutton, Oct. 25, 1810.
Samuel, s. of Seth dec., and Huldah Hill, d. of David of Bellingham, 21st day, 1st mo., called March, 1745. c.r.3.*
Sarah and Isaac Richerson of Smithfield, County of Providence, int. June 27, 1732.
Sarah and Israel Cook of Gloucester, County of Providence, Oct. 6, 1768.
Sarah and George Farnum, int. Apr. 6, 1787.
Sarah and Job Jenckes of Wrentham, Sept. 4, 1794.
Sarah and Horace R. Witherell of Taunton, Nov. 3, 1840.
Sarah A. and Tyler D. Aldrich of Pelham, Oct. 31, 1843.
Seth, s. of Jacob and Mary Aldrich, d. of Joseph, 3d day, 11th mo., called November, 1763. c.r.3.*
Seth and Ama Cook of Cumberland, int. June 22, 1767.
Seth Jr. of Douglas, and Ruth Lasure, int. Feb. 24, 1811.
Seth R. and Lydia B. Alden of Walpole, int. Sept. 19, 1841.
Silas of Mendon, and Elizabeth Brown, in Mendon, June 30, 1757.*
Silas and Mehetible Thayer of Mendon, Aug. 9, 1774.
Solomon and Amphila Elot, int. Mar. 25, 1755.
Solomon and Elisabeth Jones of Mendon, int. May 31, 1756.
Sophia and Amasa L. Howard, both of Northbridge, Jan. 1, 1824.*
Stephen and Mary Brown, int. Jan. 20, 1761.
Stephen A. and Lavinia S. Albee of Mendon, Dec. 25 [1835].*
Susanna and Sam[ue]l Balch, in Douglas, Jan. 14, 1761.*
Susanna and Wilson Preston, Oct. 30, 1765.
Susanna and Asael Aldrich, int. Mar. 8, 1773.
Susanna and Joseph Richardson, int. Jan. 9, 1780.
Susannah and Isaac Aldrich, Mar. 16, 1773.*
Susannah and Samuel Orel, in Mendon, Apr. 12, 1773.
Susannah and Benjamin H. G. Blanchard of Foster, R. I., int. Mar. 3, 1822.
Sussan[n]a and John Willy of Oxford, int. Nov. 25, 1732.
Sylvia of Douglas, and Phineas Wood, int. July 28, 1849.
Thomas J. and Lydia Varney, Mar. 29, 1836.
Timothy and Abigail Winter, Jan. 30, 1760.
Tirzah of Douglas, and Stephen Paine, int. May 17, 1801.
Tyler D. of Pelham, and Sarah A. Aldrich, Oct. 31, 1843.
Valentine M., s. of Jacob and Mary B., a. 29 y., and Abigail Williams, d. of Stephen and Nancy, a. 21 y., July 2, 1844.
Welcome and Maria Rawson of Northbridge, Feb. 21, 1830.
Wheeler and Polly Thayer of Mendon, int. Sept. 12, 1841.
Willis and Ruth Keith, June 20, 1799.

* Intention not recorded.

ALEXANDER (see Elexanders), Dan and Abigail Thayer, int. Oct. 28, 1838.
David of Mendon, and Molly Blake, int. Aug. 17, 1765.
Elijah of Mendon, and Elisabeth Taft, Oct. 31, 1765.
Isaac, s. of Samuel and Polly, a. 21 y., and Mary Jane Thayer, d. of Wiles and Polly, a. 19 y., May 28, 1846.
Leonard and Sarah Rhodes, both of Upton, Apr. 29, 1807.*
Samuel and Mrs. Betsey Ingly of Franklin, int. Dec. 13, 1840.
Simon (Simeon, int.) of Mendon, and Martha White, in Mendon, May 21, 1786.
Timothy Jr. of Mendon, and Betsey Albee, int. Aug. 24, 1807.

ALGER, Bethany and Job Archer, int. Sept. 1, 1761.
John of Rehoboth, and Elisabeth Humes, int. June 20, 1773.

ALLBEE (see Albb, Albee), Eleaz[e]r and Dorcas Daniels, Aug. 27, 1767.
Prudence and Barnabas Aldrich, Apr. 9, 1766.
Rachel and Na[h]um Taft, Feb. 19, 1767.

ALLEN, Amos C. of North Kingston, and Harriet Kempton, int. May 28, 1843.
Caleb N. of Mendon, and Nancy Wheelock, Jan. 17, 1807. (Jan. 11, 1807. c.r.1.)
Diarca (of Medway, int.) and Joanna Spring, June 20, 1822.
Emery and Lydia Crocker, Mar. 29, 1821.
James, widr., of Northbridge, s. of Simeon and Elizabeth of Thompson, Conn., a. 33 y., and Sarah E. Brigham of Worcester, d. of Jabez and Sophia of Grafton, a. 26 y., June 6, 1849.*
Joann of Barrington, R. I., and Benjamin J. White, int. May 11, 1834.
John and Abigail Goldthwaight of Northbridge, int. Nov. 8, 1778.
John (Jr., int.) of Sutton, and Azuba Taft, Oct. 28, 1828.
Jonathan and Ruth Newcomb, Dec. 11, 1760.
Leah of Medway, and David Farnum, in Medway, Jan. 25, 1758.
Lydia B., d. of Walter of Smithfield, R. I., and Lucy dec., and Effingham L. Capron, s. of John and Asenath dec., 5th day, 5th mo. 1831. c.r.3.*
Martha of Medway, and Edmund Rawson (Jr., int.), Jan. 12, 1743–4.
Mary of Medway, and Abner Rawson, in Medway, May 17, 1745.
Mary (of Sutton, int.) and Joseph Manning, Jan. 15, 1760.

* Intention not recorded.

ALLEN, Rac[h]el and Is[a]iah Lesure of Mendon, Aug. 5, 1744.
Rachel of Medway, and Jesse Morse, in Medway, Nov. 28, 1754.
Samuel and Mary Rogers of New London, Conn., int. Dec. 17, 1743.
Samuel and Mary Benham, Jan. 21, 1744 [prob. 1744-5] (int. Dec. 8, 1744).
Samuel of Milford, and Bethany White, Apr. 26, 1785.
Sarah and Ebenezer Peck, June 19, 1739. (June 29, 1739. c.r.1.)
Sarah of Medway, and Henry Wood, in Medway, Aug. 1, 1759.
Timothy and Sarah Powers, int. Mar. 27, 1769.
Whipple of Milford, and Amanda N. Taft, June 7, 1843.

AMBLEY, Christopher and Sarah Hunt, int. Aug. 11, 1805.

AMIDOWN (see Ammidown), Philip and Submit Bullard, July 28, 1731.

AMMIDOWN (see Amidown), Samuel of Douglas, and Ruth Wood, Mar. 3, 1768.

AMOS, Sarah and James Nuttien, Apr. 20, 1758.

ANDREUS (see Andrew, Andrews), Hannah E. and William H. Baker, int. Dec. 6, 1829.

ANDREW (see Andreus, Andrews), Catharine and Warren Murdock, Aug. 5, 1832.
Hannah of Douglas, and George Kempton 2d, int. Sept. 12, 1824.

ANDREWS (see Andreus, Andrew), Pamela of Northbridge, and Ezra T. Benson, int. Dec. 11, 1831.

ANGEL, Jemima of Smithfield, and Seth Taft, int. Feb. 21, 1761.

ANSON, Esther and Asa Burlingame of Burrillville, R. I., int. Mar. —, 1807.
John, Dr., of Dudley, and Ester Wood, Nov. 11, 1798.
Manning W. and Susan A. Thwing, Apr. 1, 1827. c.r.1.

ANTHONY, Abigail of Gloucester, R. I., and Nathan White, in Mendon, Mar. 6, 1793.
Ruth Eliza and Silas Lewis of Burrillville, R. I., int. Oct. 23, 1831.
Sally of Douglas, and Nathan Moore, int. Mar. 19, 1848.
Sarah Ann, d. of Elisha, a. 28 y., and Augustus W. Monroe of New Bedford, 2d m., s. of Turner, a. 36 y., Jan. 5, 1848.
William and Elizabeth Warmsly, int. July 15, 1832.

APPLIN, John of Swansey, and Molle Sabein, int. Sept. 10, 1775.

ARCHER, Benjamin and Elisabeth Thayer of New Sherborn, Nov. 28, 1739.
Benjamin and Mary Holbrook, Mar. 15, 1759.
Benjamin and wid. Deborah Hull, May 8, 1766.
David and Mary Benson of Gloucester, R. I., int. Apr. 12, 1764.
Elisabeth and Jesse White, int. Feb. 7, 1764.
Job and Bethany Alger, int. Sept. 1, 1761.
Mary and Solomon Tyler, int. Dec. 4, 1780.

ARMSBY, Edwin of Northbridge, and H. Adaline Thayer, Nov. 30, 1842.

ARMSTRON (see Armstrong), Rachal of Gloucester, R. I., and Alpheus Wheelock, int. Nov. 28, 1785.

ARMSTRONG (see Armstron), Elmira of Burrillville, R. I., and James N. Carlton, int. Mar. 23, 1844.
Mary (resident of Mendon, int.) and Isaac Holbrook, Oct. 28, 1750.
Seth and Maria C. Farnum, Oct. 6, 1839.

ARNOLD, Alfred and Sarah Tenney, Nov. 13, 1833.
Almira of Burrillville, R. I., and David Richardson, int. Sept. 20, 1829.
Anne and John Carpenter, May 11, 1815.
Charles and Lorinda Sibley, Nov. 6, 1833.
Charlotta of Gloucester, R. I., and Noah Taft Jr., int. Jan. 30, 1790.
Eber of Gloucester, and Rachel Green, Dec. 30, 1790.
Eber and Charlotte Tyler, Mar. 13, 1831.
Elisha of Gloucester, and Theodate Mussey, int. Apr. 24, 1774.
Israel and Abigail Daniels, of Mendon, int. Jan. 13, 1805.
John C., s. of Welcome and Rebecca, a. 23 y., and Mary E. Shove, d. of Luther and Pamela, a. 19 y., Apr. 2, 1846.
Lucia (of Smithfield, R. I., c.r.1) and Samuel G. Arnold (of Providence, R. I., c.r.1), Dec. 10, 1818.*
Maning of Burrillville, R. I., and Laura Ann Richardson, int. Jan. 30, 1831.
Marcy of Gloucester, County of Providence, and Aaron Taft, int. Oct. 28, 1749.
Maria and Walter Brown, int. Dec. 28, 1828.
Mary of Gloucester, R. I., and Peter Taft, June 4, 1767.
Mary of Bellingham, and Ahaz Aldrich, int. May 6, 1821.

* Intention not recorded.

ARNOLD, Mary S. and Seba (Bela, int.) Carpenter of Seekonk, Feb. 25, 1836.
Mercy and Willard Sales of Smithfield, R. I., Apr. 24, 1821.
Noah of Gloucester, County of Providence, and Elenor Whipple, int. Dec. 1, 1743.
Olive and Timothy Walker, in Mendon, Nov. 5, 1793.
Patience and Ezbon C. Newell, int. Mar. 26, 1826.
Permelia (of Bellingham, int.) and Justus Aldrich, Jan. 6, 1831.
Richard of Smithfield, R. I., and Lydia Emerson, Apr. 9, 1809.
Ruth and Briggs Lee, int. Aug. 24, 1823.
Samuel G. (of Providence, R. I., c.r.1) and Lucia Arnold (of Smithfield, R. I., c.r.1), Dec. 10, 1818.*
Sarah and Ebenezer Torrey Esq. of Fitchburg, Dec. 25, 1832.
Smith R. of Burrillville, R. I., and Sally Richardson, Oct. 21, 1841.
Welcome Jr., s. of Welcome and Rebecca, a. 21 y., and Charlotte B. Shove, d. of Luther and Pamelia, a. 21 y., Dec. 18, 1845.

ATWOOD, Jesse and Hannah Fletcher of Smithfield, R. I., int. Dec. 13, 1829.

AUSTIN, Stilman and Rhoda Stockwell Munyan of Mendon, int. Sept. 7, 1828.

AVERIC, Joseph and Abigail Marsh of Bellingham, int. Jan. 29, 1742-3.

AVOY, Valentine and Mary Dorry, int. June 4, 1843.

AYERS, Calvin of Dover, s. of Fisher and Sarah, a. 21 y., and Rebecca Cady of Blackstone, b. in Blackstone, d. of Atwood and Uranah, a. 24 y., Sept. 26, 1848.*

BACHELDER (see Batchelder, Batcheler, Batcheller), David of Northbridge, and Abigail Bacon, int. Sept. 21, 1772.
Jonathan and Thankfull Whitney of Upton, int. Dec. 26, 1768.

BACON, Abigail and Ezra Hamilton of Brookfield, int. July 16, 1770.
Abigail and David Bachelder of Northbridge, int. Sept. 21, 1772.
Abigail, wid., and George Martin of Richmond, N. H., int. Nov. 7, 1799.
Almira and John W. Baker, int. Feb. 12, 1832.
Elizabeth of Dudley, and Amariah Preston, in Dudley, Nov. 18, 1777.

* Intention not recorded.

BACON, James and Olive Persons, Oct. 21, 1827.
Jonathan and Martha Wood, Jan. 1, 1750–1.
Miles of Smithfield, R. I., and wid. Louis Daily, int. Oct. 5, 1817.
Ruth of Sutton, and David Keith, in Sutton, Nov. 5, 1765.
Zipporah and Samuel Morduck, Apr. 22, 1773.

BAGGS, Noble and Mary Darling of Mendon, in Mendon, Nov. 30, 1768.*

BAKER, Amos, now residing in Gloucester, R. I., s. of John and Abigail, and Rachal Richardson, d. of Isaac dec. and Bethiah, 7th day, 2d mo. 1783. c.r.3.*
Chloe T. and Daniel W. Williams, July 13, 1835.
David J. of Worcester, and Diana R. Davol, May 20, 1841.
Elizabeth of Oxford, and Peter Thompson of Douglas, Feb. 26, 1807.*
Elizabeth of Smithfield, R. I., and Joseph Hamer, int. Oct. 22, 1815.
Elizabeth and John T. Lowell, May 22, 1836.
Hannah of Douglas, and Samuel White, int. Jan. 7, 1801.
John of Scituate, R. I., and Elenor Handy, int. Aug. 9, 1821.
John W. and Almira Bacon, int. Feb. 12, 1832.
Joseph of Mendon, and Molley Aldrich, int. May 9, 1773.
Lydia of Douglas, and Micah Stearns, int. Feb. 27, 1796.
Manasseh and Lois Benson of Mendon, in Mendon, June 4, 1795.
Manasseth and Sarah Williams, in Northbridge, May 31, 1792.
Maria and Benjamin Evans Jr. of Smithfield, R. I., int. Dec. 11, 1836.
Mary W. of Grafton, and Andrew E. Turner, int. Sept. 9, 1832.
Rachel of Medfield, resident in Douglas, and Mark Wood, in Douglas, Sept. 1, 1796.
Sally and Andre Taft, Aug. 27, 1815.
Timothy D. and Caroline S. Cook, Jan. 1, 1835.
William H. and Hannah E. Andreus, int. Dec. 6, 1829.

BALCH, Sam[ue]l and Susanna Aldrich, in Douglas, Jan. 14, 1761.*

BALCOM (see Balkam, Bolcum), Deborah and Benjamin Corary, both of New Sherborn, Mar. 21, 1732–3.
Elijah and Caroline Ramsdell of Mendon, in Mendon, May 13, 1777.
Harriet of Douglas, and Abner P. Taft, int. Nov. 8, 1836.

* Intention not recorded.

BALCOM, Mary of Douglas, and Robert Taft, int. May 23, 1841.
Phebe of New Sherborn, and William Barter, May 19, 1737.*
Sarah and Joseph Thayer of Mendon or Bellingham, int. Feb. 27, 1740-1.
Sibil of Douglas, and Nahum Cook, int. Feb. 17, 1822.
Sophia and Aaron Smith of Providence, Jan. 1, 1816.
Susan (Susan F., int.) and Gardiner Chase, May 24 [1835].

BALKAM (see Balcom, Bolcum), Aaron of Douglas, and Phebe Taft, in Douglas, Jan. 18, 1781.*

BALL, Mary A. and Robert Rogerson Jr., Mar. 26, 1838.

BALLARD, Sarah of Charlestown, and Charles Ellis, int. Apr. 21, 1844.

BALLOU, Chloe and Levin Jilson, int. Jan. 24, 1802.
Rufus of Smithfield, R. I., and Hannah Darling, int. Nov. 30, 1842.
Welcome Jr. of Burrillville, R. I., s. of Welcome and Lavinia, a. 26 y., and Sarah M. Tucker, d. of Benjamin and Mary, a. 18 y., July 23, 1848.
Wilcome of Smithfield, and Aurilla Taft of Mendon, Jan. 10, 1802.*

BANCROFT, Joseph B., s. of Samuel and Mary, a. 23 y., and Sylvia W. Thwing, d. of Benjamin and Anna, a. 20 y., Sept. 11, 1844.
William and Mary Daniels, Sept. 29, 1763.

BANISTER, Huldah of Brookfield, and Nathan Harwood, int. Feb. 16, 1760.
Ruth of Marlboro, and Nathan Park, int. Nov. 19, 1763.

BARDEN (see Bardens, Bardins), James and Tryphena White, May 5, 1763.

BARDENS (see Barden, Bardins), Elisabeth and Nathaniel Wallis (of Douglas, int.), Dec. 9, 1758.
James and Meribah Comstock of Smithfield, County of Providence, int. Feb. 29, 1752-3.
James and Mary Sanders of Needham, in Needham, May 17, 1753.

BARDINS (see Barden, Bardens), Jerusha and Jonathan Cook of Douglas, June 4, 1764.

* Intention not recorded.

BARDS, Meritea (Maritta Boyd, int.) of Burrillville, R. I., and Willard Taft, Mar. 3, 1816.

BARNES, Mary E. of Smithfield, R. I., and William B. Johnson, int., July 28, 1839.
Mary L. of Northbridge, and Haskett D. P. Bigelow, May 19, 1836.

BARRETT, Daniel and Mary Ann Hoyle, int. Aug. 23, 1835.

BARRON, Susan of Wrentham, and George Bliss, int. Dec. 12, 1830.

BARTER, William and Phebe Balcom of New Sherborn, May 19, 1737.*

BARTLET (see Bartlett), Joanna and Jacob Aldrich, int. July 3, 1731.

BARTLETT (see Bartlet), Sally of Salem, and Rev. Samuel Judson, in Salem, May 28, 1797.
Sally L. of Douglas, and Albert Taft, int. Feb. 27, 1848.
William O. of Worcester, s. of Otis of Smithfield, R. I., a. 25 y., and Agnes E. H. Willard, d. of George and Sylvia, a. 22 y., Oct. 23, 1845.

BARTON, Anna of Leicester, and Josiah Roberson (Robinson, int.), June 28, 1738.
Mary of Sutton, and Obadiah Brown, in Sutton, Apr. 3, 1766.

BASCOM, Catharine and Joel N. Blake, Oct. 18, 1832.
Mary and Benjamin F. Lesure, Feb. 16, 1831.

BASSETT, Ephraim, s. of Joseph and Rachel, and Mercy Comstock, d. of Woodbury dec., late of North Providence, R. I., and Hannah, 6th day, 11th mo. 1811. c.r.3.*
Ephraim, s. of Joseph and Rachel, and Mary Smith, d. of Samuel of Mendon, and Hannah, 2d day, 5th mo. 1827. c.r.3.*
Jaazaniah, s. of John dec. and Lucy of Killingly, Conn., and Rhoda Read, d. of John and Hannah of Smithfield, R. I., 4th day, 5th mo. 1780. c.r.3.*

BATCHELDER (see Bachelder, Batcheler, Batcheller), Mary E. and Joseph T. Bowen of Worcester, int. Feb. 26, 1849.

BATCHELER (see Bachelder, Batchelder, Batcheller), Lydia of Douglas, and Turner Thayer, int. Jan. 11, 1824.

* Intention not recorded.

BATCHELLER (see Bachelder, Batchelder, Batcheler), Aaron of Northbridge, and Sarah Thwing, in Northbridge, Dec. 10, 1789.

Roxana and Charles Young, int. Apr. 8, 1832.

BATES, Catharine F. of Blackstone, and Samuel Hudson, int. Feb. 18, 1849.

Chloe of Dudley, and Amos Craggin Taft, int. Sept. —, 1808.

Eli of Mendon, and Louisa Hall, int. July 30, 1848.

BATTEY, Richard, s. of Jesse of Burrillville, R. I., and Nancy dec., and Rachel Aldrich, d. of William of Mendon, and Hannah, 6th day, 5th mo. 1829. c.r.3.*

BATTLES, Edward of Mendon, and Ruth Kimton, Nov. 26, 1766.

Hannah (of Mendon, int.) and Ephraim Kimpton, Nov. 18, 1761.

BAXTER, Joseph and Jemima Thayer of Mendon, in Mendon, Aug. 14, 1734.

BAYLIES, Abigail and Henry Chapin, Feb. 19, 1794. (Feb. 27, 1794. c.r.1.)

Adolphus and Mary Wood, Mar. 9, 1825. c.r.1.

Alpheus and Sarah Spring of Northbridge, in Northbridge, Apr. 24, 1794.

Ephraim and Henrietta Whitney, Feb. 19, 1823.

Mary (Polley, int.) and Rufus Knap of Douglas, Oct. 16, 1794. c.r.1.

Mary E., d. of Ephraim, a. 19 y., and George Gunn, s. of Samuel and Mary, a. 27 y., Sept. 5, 1844.

Nancy and Stephen Williams (Jr., int.), June 21, 1803. (June 24, 1803. c.r.1.)

Nicholas and Elisabeth Park of Newton, int. Oct. 21, 1738.

Nicholas, Dea., and Hannah Elliot of Sutton, in Sutton, Dec. 8, 1789.

Nicholas, Dea., and wid. Abigail Adams of Northbridge, int. Sept. 24, 1804.

Nicholas (a. 83 y., int.) and Olive Taft of Sutton (wid., a. 40 y., int.), July 3, 1823.

Nicolas and Abigail Wood, Apr. 24, 1760.

Sarah and Welcome Wilmarth of Brooklyn, Conn., int. Apr. 24, 1831.

Submit and James T. (James Taylor, int.) Elliot of Sutton, Jan. 25, 1810.

Sukey (Susannah, int.) and Charles Brigham of Grafton, Oct. 20, 1797.

* Intention not recorded.

BEALS, Anngenett B. of Slaterville, R. I., and Sullivan Seagrave, int. Dec. 20, 1841.
Phila B. of Smithfield, R. I., and Brigham Deane of Sutton, Jan. 8, 1838 (Jan. 22, 1838 dup.).*
Priscilla G. and Lawson (Lawson A., int.), Seagrave, Oct. 24, 1834.

BEAMAN (see Beman), Henry T. and Wealthy Keith, May 17, 1836.

BECKWITH, Lucy A. and Rawson Tilt, both of Mendon, Apr. 30, 1837.*

BELEW, Abner and Bulah Thayer, Sept. 5, 1750.*

BELLOWS, Elvira and Charles Chids Coburn of Mendon, int. Oct. 3, 1819.
Martha (Belles, int.) and John Hunt, Mar. 17, 1757.

BEMAN (see Beaman), Betsey and Robert Rogerson, both of Boston, Jan. 7, 1832.*

BEMIS, Lucretia M. of Spencer, and Simon P. Taft, int. Sept. 14, 1834.

BENHAM, Mary and Samuel Allen, Jan. 21, 1744 [prob. 1744-5] (int. Dec. 8, 1744).
Patience and Samuel Dennis of Sutton, in Sutton, Mar. 27, 1754.

BENJAMIN, Elisha and Hanna[h] Taft, Sept. 9, 1747.*

BENNET (see Bennett), Abigail of Northbridge, and Zadok Taft, int. Oct. 2, 1800.
John and Mary Aldrich, d. of Jacob, 4th day, 12th mo., called December, 1760. C.R.3.*
Rufus of Northbridge, and Polly Wood, June 10, 1802.
Sally of Douglas, and George Kempton, int. Mar. 7, 1830.
Sarah and William Parsons, Dec. 23, 1756.

BENNETT (see Bennet), Alonzo W., Dr., s. of James and Parna of Rindge, N. H., a. 29 y., and Margaret L. Taft, d. of Bezaleel and Hannah, a. 30 y., Nov. 30, 1848.
Elizabeth and Leonard Morrison of Johnston, R. I., Apr. 8, 1827. C.R.1.
Semantha and Cheny Snow of Spencer, Mar. 10, 1833.

* Intention not recorded.

BENSON, Abba A. and Calvin Rawson, Apr. 3, 1827. C.R.I.
Abigail of Mendon, and Jonathan Holbrook, int. Nov. 23, 1783.
Abner of Mendon, and Expearence Muxscom, int. Feb. 28, 1771.
Amasa B. of Northbridge, s. of Amasa and Sarah, a. 29 y., and Eunice S. Wood, d. of Reuben and Sally, a. 22 y., May 28, 1845.
Baruch of Gloucester, R. I., and Sarrah Buxton, int. Feb. 11, 1776.
Benjamin of Mendon, and Martha McNamara, in Mendon, Feb. 15, 1769.
Benoni of Mendon, and Prudence White, Sept. 3, 1739.
Benoni of Mendon, and Ruth Holbrook, in Mendon, Dec. 6, 1770.
Charlotte T. and Moses Dyer of Northbridge, Nov. 26, 1840.
Eliza T. (Elsa T., int.) of Mendon, and Lewis Browning, May 4, 1836.
Ezra T. and Pamela Andrews of Northbridge, int. Dec. 11, 1831.
Hannah of Gloucester, R. I., and Samuel Buxton, int. Feb. 11, 1776.
Hannah T. and Henry Dodge of Smithfield, R. I., Apr. 5, 1836.
Henry Staples of Mendon, and Lydia Sibley, May 6, 1793.
Joanna of Mendon, and Daniel Holbrook, Jan. 9, 1785.
John, Lieut., of Mendon, and Mary Holbrook, int. Sept. 17, 1780.
John (Jr., int.) of Mendon, and Chloe Taft, Dec. 19, 1805.
John (Lieut., int.) and (wid., int.) Lucretia Taft, Mar. 13, 1831.
Joseph of Mendon, and Susanna Bolster, Apr. 16, 1754.
Lois of Mendon, and Manasseh Baker, in Mendon, June 4, 1795.
Maria R. of Mendon, and Alvin Cook, Sept. 7, 1828.
Mary of Gloucester, R. I., and David Archer, int. Apr. 12, 1764.
Mellen and Mary Peck, both of Mendon, July 13, 1842.*
Moses of Mendon, and Eunice Holbrook, May 26, 1753.
Phila of Mendon, and Phineas Tyler, in Mendon, Jan. 29, 1788.
Polly of Mendon, and Stephen Kimpton, int. Dec. 21, 1799.
Rachel of Mendon, and Jesse Albee, int. Nov. 27, 1803.

BIGELOW, Haskett D. P. and Mary L. Barnes of Northbridge, May 19, 1836.
Lucy of Worcester, and Amos Robbins, int. Oct. 3, 1830.

BILLINGS, Ruth Hartwell of Dedham, and Avery White, int. Feb. 14, 1813.

* Intention not recorded.

BILLS, Davis, widr., s. of Samuel and Susan, a. 42 y., and Julia E. Bills, d. of Jason and Margaret of Hope, Me., a. 20 y., Aug. 24, 1845.
Julia E., d. of Jason and Margaret of Hope, Me., a. 20 y., and Davis Bills, widr., s. of Samuel and Susan, a. 42 y., Aug. 24, 1845.
Samuel and Susanna Wood of Mendon, Mar. 6, 1803.

BILSLOOK, Mary of Boston, and Leues Crips, int. Aug. 29, 1768.

BISBEE, Samantha L., d. of William O. and Charlotte Barrett, a. 16 y., and William H. Freeman, s. of Thomas J. and Rebecca, a. 23 y., Jan. 15, 1846.

BISHOP, Ebenezer and Abigail Haywood, int. Jan. 28, 1745-6.

BLACK, Edwin M. and Maria E. Voss, Mar. 31, 1828.
James and Rhoda Howard of Mendon, int. Sept. 28, 1772.
Simeon (Blake, int.) and Sarah Wheler of Sutton, in Sutton, Nov. 4, 1779.

BLACKBURN, Sarah M. (Blackman, int.) and Thomas M. Shove of Douglas, May 13, 1839.

BLACKMAN, Amelia and Samuel Thayer of Douglas, Apr. 28, 1816.
Harriet and Samuel Smith, July 6, 1829.

BLAKE, Asa and Joanah Nye of Douglas, in Douglas, Dec. 10, 1778.
Benjamin and Sarah Kimton, May 8, 1760.
Charlotte and Naum C. Albee, Jan. 19, 1829.
Daniel Souther of Mendon, and Sally Smith, int. Sept. 13, 1801.
Hannah and (Lieut. int.) Peletiah Thayer of Mendon, Mar. 21, 1793.
Hellen R., d. of Thomas and Abigail, a. 24 y., and Edward B. Foster of Northbridge, s. of Hinsdale and Hannah F., a. 28 y., Aug. 29, 1849.
Joel N. and Catharine Bascom, Oct. 18, 1832.
Molley and Daniel Bullard of Bellingham, int. May 17, 1776.
Molly and David Alexander of Mendon, int. Aug. 17, 1765.
Polly and Otis Rawson, int. July 5, 1807.

BLANCHAR (see Blanchard), Edward and Abigail Hayward of Sutton, int. Feb. 18, 1743-4.

BLANCHARD (see Blanchar), Benjamin H. G. of Foster, R. I., and Susannah Aldrich, int. Mar. 3, 1822.
Isaac (of Mendon, int.) and Issabella Aldrich, Aug. 31, 1815.
Lydia of Foster, R. I., d. of Caleb and Betsy, and Ephraim Aldrich, s. of Ephraim and Dorcas, at Coventry, R. I., Dec. 24, 1826.
Mary of Foster, R. I., and Jacob Aldrich, June 1, 1814.
Nabby D. (of Sutton, int.) and Lemuel Walker, Apr. 3, 1835.

BLASDELL, Sergeant of Smithfield, R. I., and Amelia Shippa, int. Dec. 10, 1810.

BLISS, George and Susan Barron of Wrentham, int. Dec. 12, 1830.

BLODGETT, Charles P., widr., s. of Nehemiah and Sarah A., a. 30 y., and wid. Harriet E. Esty, d. of Abigail Newton, a. 25 y., June 10, 1848.

BLOOD, Abigail and Elnathan Wight, both of Bellingham, Aug. 13, 1754.*
Patty of Charlton, and Nathan Harris, int. Nov. 2, 1828.

BLY, Mary of Leicester, and Benjamin Thomson, int. Aug. 10, 1732.
Otis W. of Smithfield, R. I., and Lydia Esten, int. Nov. 22, 1835.

BOLCUM (see Balcom, Balkam), Mary of Douglas, and Paul White, int. Jan. 25, 1768.

BOLSTAR (see Bolster), Abigail and Ephraim Kimton (Kympton, int.), Oct. 29, 1740.

BOLSTER (see Bolstar), Abigail and Joseph Prebble of Old York, int. Jan. 23, 1769.
Anna and John Gage of Smithfield, R. I., int. Feb. 20, 1814.
Isaac and Hipzebah Waite of Sutton, June 4, 1735. (May 4, 1735. C.R.1.)*
Isaac and Susannah Smith of Leicester, in Leicester, Feb. 4, 1742.
Isaac Jr. and Thankful Smith Inman, int. Mar. and Apr. 1811.
Jemima and Aaron Brown, int. Dec. 18, 1774.
Jesse and Lucretia Inman, int. Apr. 15, 1811.
Jesse and Nancy Inman, int. Mar. 24, 1816.
Jesse and Nancy Farnum, Dec. 18, 1816.
Joel of Upton, and Sarah Seagrave, in Mendon, July 30, 1789.

* Intention not recorded.

BOLSTER, John and Abigail Keith, June 2, 1752.
Keziah and Benjamin Clemmens of Upton, Mar. 15, 1774.
Nathan and Chloe Keith, int. Dec. 23, 1781.
Susanna and Joseph Benson of Mendon, Apr. 16, 1754.
Washington and Phebe Ann Sage, int. Mar. 20, 1831.

BOND, Henry of Northbridge, and Dolly Adams, int. Sept. 25, 1846.

BONHAM, Sarah and John Hopkins, Oct. 13, 1771.

BOON, Francis of Upton, and Mary Wallis, June 10, 1786.

BOWDISH, Crawford T., s. of Asa and Patience, a. 23 y., and Mary Jane McLellen, d. of Andrew and Mary, a. 19 y., Apr. 20, 1845.

BOWEN (see Bowin), Charles and Sarah G. Kincum, int. Dec. 10, 1843.
Elisha A. and Caroline A. Campbell of Providence, R. I., int. June 15, 1845.
Horatio F., s. of Benjamin and Nancy, a. 21 y., and Amey A. Mowry, d. of Israel and Phila, a. 19 y., May 28, 1846.
John A. and Mary M. Waters, Apr. 18, 1844.
Joseph T. of Worcester, and Mary E. Batchelder, int. Feb. 26, 1849.
Lydia, d. of Benjamin and Nancy, a. 23 y., and Lyman Keith of Northbridge, s. of Lyman and Chloe, a. 28 y., Oct. 17, 1846.*
Mary (Brown, int.) of Rehoboth, and John Peck, in Rehoboth, Dec. 23, 1750.
Sarah E. of Worcester, and Charles A. Taft, int. Aug. 29, 1847.

BOWIN (see Bowen), David (of Warren, int.) and Hopestill Aldrich, Mar. 8, 1764.
Hezekiah of Gloucester, R. I., and Molley Wood, int. May 29, 1791.
Thomas (of Warren, int.) and Penelap Aldrich, Jan. 24, 1765.

BOWKER, Abigail of Hopkinton, and Jonathan White, in Hopkinton, Jan. 21, 1785.

BOYCE, Bethiah and Josiah Holbrook, Mar. 28, 1744.
Bethiah and Moses Comstock, Apr. 19, 1764.*
Katherine of Mendon, and Stephen Kimpton, in Mendon, Apr. 15, 1762.

* Intention not recorded.

BOYD, Sophia of Burrillville, R. I., and Joseph Taft 3d, at Burrillville, R. I., Aug. 19, 1821.

BRADY, Mary Ann of Lowell, and Stephen Phillips, int. July 2, 1843.

BRAMAN, Leonard, s. of Hannah, a. 22 y., and Rosetta C. Marsh, d. of Aaron and Lydia, a. 19 y., Oct. 22, 1845.
S. W. (W. S., int.) and Sylvia Keith, Oct. 28, 1840.
Whitman P., s. of Hannah, a. 26 y., and Elizabeth J. Rice of Blackstone, d. of Stephen and Joanna, a. 21 y., May 28, 1846.

BRANCH, Henrietta M. A. and Luther Capron, May 31, 1828.
Nath[anie]l and Rachel Wheelock, Mar. 8, 1799.
Ophelia and Halsey Hill, Apr. 9, 1826. c.r.1.

BRASTOW, Abagail and Joel Thayer of Boston, Nov. 17, 1808.
Abigail and John Capron, int. Sept. 8, 1811.
David and Abigail Penniman of Mendon, in Mendon, Apr. 18, 1779.
Sally and Capt. James D. (James Dalton, c.r.1) Ingersoll of Boston, Aug. 20, 1807.

BRATON, Lydia of Smithfield, R. I., and Cato Willard, int. Jan. 3, 1802.

BREADY, James and Ann Quillen, int. Aug. 27, 1848.

BRIGHAM, Charles of Grafton, and Sukey (Susannah, int.) Baylies, Oct. 20, 1797.
Dulcena of Grafton, and John Thacher, int. Dec. 22, 1816.
Sarah E. of Worcester, d. of Jabez and Sophia of Grafton, a. 26 y., and James Allen, widr., of Northbridge, s. of Simeon and Elizabeth of Thompson, Conn., a. 33 y., June 6, 1849.*

BRITTON, Charles and Anna Dickeson (Deckerson, int.), Mar. 30, 1758.
Martha, Mrs., and Nathan Aldrich, Jan. 1, 1843.

BROCK, Hannah A. of Mendon, and Charles C. Chapin, int. Aug. 8, 1841.

BRONETT, Martha S. of Marshpee, and Benjamin Roberts, Apr. 12, 1835.

* Intention not recorded.

BROOKS, Delia A., d. of George and Betsey of Farmington, Me., a. 19 y., and Manson A. Aldrich, s. of Ahaz and Mary, a. 21 y., Jan. 5, 1846.

BROWN, Aaron and Jemima Bolster, int. Dec. 18, 1774.
Abigail and Ephraim Taft, int. Jan. 21, 1771.
Abigail and Thomas Nolen, Jan. 27, 1833.
Alpheus and Patty Martha Rawson, int. July 26, 1807.
Amory R. and Amanda Chamberlain, Dec. 3, 1835.
Andrus and Hannah Jacobs, int. Jan. 1, 1819.
Caroline M., d. of Ephraim, a. 20 y., and Benjamin Hall, s. of John P., a. 21 y., July 4, 1847.*
Chloe of Mendon, and Nellson Keith, int. Feb. 25, 1806.
Clarissa H. and James A. McKoy of Worcester, Feb. 4, 1838.
Daniel and Ann Dudley of Douglas, int. July 25, 1768.
Daniel and Elizabeth Cook of Mendon, int. Sept. 20, 1800.
Deborah and Jesse Aldrich of Northbridge, Feb. 4, 1798.
Derick P. and Harriet Merchant of Smithfield, R. I., int. Aug. 24, 1834.
Elenor and Thomas White, Oct. 29, 1747.
Elihu and Mercy Thwing, in Mendon, Dec. 30, 1789.
Elizabeth and Silas Aldrich of Mendon, in Mendon, June 30, 1757.*
Hannah, wid. of Joseph of Gloucester, R. I., and Jacob Aldrich, 26th day, 2d mo., called February, 1768. c.r.3.*
Hannah of Douglas, and David Draper Jr., int. Mar. 14, 1798.
Hannah (Hannah T., int.) and Hinsdale Foster of Sturbridge (Southbridge, int.), Apr. 9, 1820.
Israel of Gloucester, R. I., and Elisabeth Chilson, int. Dec. 6, 1778.
John and Sarah Brown, Jan. 5, 1742–3.
John Jr. of Douglas, and Rebekah Draper, May 12, 1807.
John B. of Wilmington, and Sarah Taft, June 29, 1807.
John C. of Smithfield, R. I., and Sabrina Hall, int. July 7, 1829.
Josiah and Mary Holebrook, Dec. 10, 1744.
Levina of Douglas, and Simon Rawson, int. Mar. 14, 1798.
Lydia of Leicester, and Edward Hall, in Leicester, Aug. 17, 1747.
Lydia and James Keith, Oct. 30, 1765.
Maria A., wid., d. of William and Hannah Arnold, a. 47 y., and John M. Sabin, widr., of Woodstock, Conn., s. of Silas and Prudence, a. 60 y., Apr. 16, 1848.
Martin S. and Clara L. Roberts of Grafton, int. Feb. 28, 1847.
Mary and Ezekiel Wood, Mar. 25, 1732.*

*Intention not recorded.

BROWN, Mary and Stephen Aldrich, int. Jan. 20, 1761.
Mary and Ichabode Carly, Oct. 8, 1761.
Mary of Leicester, and Daniel Read, in Leicester, Dec. 19, 1765.
Mary and Elisha Hale, Nov. 5, 1767.
Mary and David Aldrich, int. Mar. 30, 1784.
Mary B. and Zadock Goldthwait, June 2, 1831.
Mary Jane of Charlestown, and Francis Deane Jr., int. May 8, 1836.
Mary M., d. of George and Sarah of Burrillville, R. I., a. 29 y., and Zadok A. Taft, s. of Zadock and Abigail, a. 27 y., Jan. 17, 1845.
Nelson and Mary R. Mann [no date; year preceding Apr. 21, 1834].*
Obadiah and Lucy Hull, Mar. 5, 1761.
Obadiah and Mary Barton of Sutton, in Sutton, Apr. 3, 1766.
Olive and Arnold Mowry, both of Mendon, Dec. 19, 1802.*
Olive of Burrillville, R. I., and Dexter Richardson, int. June, July, 1808.
Pamela and Luther Shove, Mar. 20, 1822. (Apr. 20, 1822. c.r.1.) (Mar. 24, 1822, int.)
Pemberton and Abba Eliza Murdock, int. Mar. 11, 1827.
Pemberton, Capt., and Paulina Whitmore, Sept. 25, 1838.
Phebe and David Gaskill of Mendon, int. Jan. 7, 1776.
Rachel and Jesse Aldrich of New Salem, in Douglas, Dec. 3, 1772.
Robe of Smithfield, R. I., and Farnum Gifford, int. Aug. 6, 1815.
Ruth of Mendon, and Samuel Read, in Mendon, Jan. 21, 1728–9.*
Sarah and Nathan Park, Nov. 10, 1736.*
Sarah and John Brown, Jan. 5, 1742–3.
Thankfull and Abel Fish, Sept. 6, 1770.
Theophilus S. of Douglas, and Lydia Tucker, int. Aug. 4, 1833.
Walter of Oxford, and Phila Jepherson, int. Jan. 20, 1811.
Walter and Maria Arnold, int. Dec. 28, 1828.
William and Mary Jones, Nov. 25, 1760.
Willis and Thankful H. Harvey, Sept. 20, 1832.
Willis and Charlotte Staples of Mendon, int. Nov. 2, 1834.

BROWNING, Edwin, widr., of Utica, N. Y., s. of Ephraim and Clarinda, a. 29 y., and Harriet Pierce, wid., d. of Thomas and Martha Page of Paxton, a. 29 y., Nov. 13, 1845.
Lewis and Eliza T. (Elsa T., int.) Benson of Mendon, May 4, 1836.

* Intention not recorded.

BRUMFIELD, Lydia and David Pate, Jan. 31, 1744.*

BRYANT, Lydia I. of Blackstone, d. of Luther and Betsey, a. 18 y., and William H. Putnam of Manchester, N. H., s. of William and Susan, a. 24 y., Feb. 14, 1847.*

BUCK, Leddol and Experience Page, int. Jan. 15, 1736–7.

BUCKNAM, Elizabeth and Asa Taft, Mar. 5, 1767.
Josiah Jr. of Bethel, Vt., and Annah Twing, Jan. 9, 1794. c.r.1.*

BUFFUM, Abigail and Seth Sumner of Taunton, int. Mar. 26, 1791.
Benjamin of Smithfield, R. I., s. of Benjamin dec. and Ann Farnum, d. of Moses, 6th day, 5th mo., called July, 1749. c.r.3.*
Benjamin Jr. of Douglas, and Olive Wheelock, int. May —, 1810.
Benjamin and Hannah Taft, May 5, 1822.
Benjamin Jr. (of Douglas, int.), and Rosamond Sprague, Nov. 14, 1830.
Benjamin of Douglas, and Sophia Wheelock, int. Nov. 18, 1849.
Daniel of Douglas, and Mary Kempton, Apr. 4, 1839.
Emeline and Nathaniel Adams, Nov. 15, 1837.
Jedediah of Smithfield, R. I., and Sarah Taft, int. Aug. 18, 1757.
Jedediah and Ruth Buxton, Jan. 8, 1815.
Mary and Abner C. Read, int. Oct. 2, 1831.
Phebe and Caleb T. Richardson, int. Nov. 21, 1841.
Phebe and Enoch Aldrich, int. Apr. 30, 1843.
Sarah and Thomas Buxton of Mendon, July 3, 1839.
Tyla of Smithfield, R. I., and Wilder Holbrook, int. Apr. 12, 1818.

BUGBEE, Edna L., d. of Charles and Lucy of Waterford, Vt., a. 23 y., and George S. Russell of Northbridge, s. of Job and Martha of Northbridge, a. 22 y., Nov. 4, 1845.*

BULLARD, Daniel of Bellingham, and Molley Blake, int. May 17, 1776.
John D. and Emily M. Wilde of Wrentham, int. Nov. 10, 1844.
Luther and Hannah Dudley (of Northbridge, int.), Dec. 8, 1814.
Mary of Holliston, and Michael Madden, int. Oct. 31, 1761.
Submit and Philip Amidown, July 28, 1731.

* Intention not recorded.

BULLOCK, Susan M. and Royal Tucker, Mar. 8, 1831.

BURDON, Sarah M. of Blackstone, and William A. Dodge, int. Oct. 27, 1849.

BURGESS, Hannah of Douglas, and Wells Stanley Jr., int. June 8, 1823.
Julia Ann and Paris (Paris T., int.) Taft, Mar. 5, 1833.
Phebe H. and Nathan W. Heath of Douglas, int. Feb. 27, 1831.

BURKS, Abigail (Burke, int.) and David Thurstun, June 5, 1744.

BURLING, William and Clarrisa I. T. Howard, int. Nov. 13, 1831.

BURLINGAME, Asa of Burrillville, R. I., and Esther Anson, int. Mar. —, 1807.
James of Burrillville, R. I., and (wid., int.) Barshba Wood, May 31, 1808.
Jane of Smithfield, R. I., and John M. Fowler, int. Apr. 6, 1840.

BURMAN, Isaiah (Buckman, int.) of Bethel, Vt., and Hannah Thwing, Jan. 7, 1794.

BURNAP, John of Hopkinton, and Anna Wheat, May 1, 1755.

BURNHAM, Catharine, d. of Andrew, a. 22 y., and Francis G. Cook, s. of George, a. 27 y., Nov. 4, 1844.
Martha M. (Arantha M., int.) and Edwin Hixon, Oct. 13, 1839.

BURRILL, Marcisus E. and Harriet N. Lane, int. Oct. 5, 1834.

BURROUGHS, Elinor of Mendon, and Nathan Darling Jr. of Sturbridge, Aug. 19, 1830.*

BURT, Samuel and Molly Cooke of Douglas, int. Apr. 1, 1821.

BURTUON, David and Ruth Putnam of Salem, int. Sept. 10, 1743.

BUTTLER, Lydia of Upton, and Thomas Wilson, Sept. 27, 1769.

BUXTON, Eliza of Smithfield, R. I., and Ellis Albee, int. Nov. 23, 1817.
Henry of Gloucester, R. I., and Lydia Buxton, int. May 7, 1778.
James of Smithfield, R. I., and Esther Southwick, int. June 3, 1771.

* Intention not recorded.

BUXTON, Joanna and Augustus Hicks, int. Jan. 16, 1820.
Jonathan of Mendon, and Mrs. Sally Packard, int. Dec. 6, 1829.
Joseph and Marcy Trask of Mendon, int. Mar. 3, 1805.
Judith and Rufus Buxton of Smithfield, R. I., int. May 30, 1802.
Leonard and Sally Cady of Northbridge, int. May 18, 1823.
Lydia and Henry Buxton of Gloucester, R. I., int. May 7, 1778.
Lydia and Nelson Miller of Smithfield, R. I., int. June 24, 1838.
Peleg and Chole Aldrich, int. July 24, 1795.
Rufus of Smithfield, R. I., and Judith Buxton, int. May 30, 1802.
Ruth and Jedediah Buffum, Jan. 8, 1815.
Samuel and Hannah Benson of Gloucester, R. I., int. Feb. 11, 1776.
Sarrah and Baruch Benson of Gloucester, R. I., int. Feb. 11, 1776.
Thomas of Mendon, and Sarah Buffum, July 3, 1839.

CABLE, James of Vermont (a transient person, c.r.1), and Lucy Read of Northbridge, Jan. 31, 1803.*

CADY, Rebecca of Blackstone, b. in Blackstone, d. of Atwood and Uranah, a. 24 y., and Calvin Ayers of Dover, s. of Fisher and Sarah, a. 21 y., Sept. 26, 1848.*
Sally of Northbridge, and Leonard Buxton, int. May 18, 1823.

CAHOON, Christopher Olny and Emily Palmer Coats, Oct. 14, 1832.

CALLUM, Lyman of Smithfield, R. I., and Cynthia Wood, Nov. 15, 1829.

CAMBELL (see Campbell), Ezra B. (Campbell, int.) of Sutton, and Elizabeth B. Chamberlain, Oct. 1, 1835.

CAMPBELL (see Cambell), Caroline A. of Providence, R. I., and Elisha A. Bowen, int. June 15, 1845.

CAPRON, Asenath C. (Asenath Cargill, int.) and Josiah Chapin, Nov. 20, 1815.
Celia of Mendon, and Josiah Cumings, int. June 27, 1830.
Charles S. (Charles Scott, int.) and Sophia White, June 27, 1816.
Dordana and Willis Kelley of Mendon, int. Nov. 21, 1795.

* Intention not recorded.

CAPRON, Effingham L., s. of John and Asenath dec., and Lydia B. Allen, d. of Walter of Smithfield, R. I., and Lucy dec., 5th day, 5th mo. 1831. c.r.3.*
Elizabeth Read, d. of John W. and Abigail M., a. 27 y., and Dr. Truman Rickard of Woburn, s. of Lemuel and Abigail S. of Hanover, N. H., a. 34 y., Apr. 26, 1848.
John and Abigail Brastow, int. Sept. 8, 1811.
John W. and Abigail M. Read, Jan. 4, 1820.
John W. (Col., c.r.1) and Catharine B. Messenger, Oct. 30, 1831.
Luther and Henrietta M. A. Branch, May 31, 1828.
Maranda and Edward Foster, Nov. 20, 1808.
Phebe and Elkanah Spring, June 6, 1805.
Polly (Mary, c.r.1) and John S. Chapin, Oct. 21, 1806.
Sally and Murdock Taft, June 9, 1808.
Sophia W., Mrs., and Paine Aldrich of Worcester, June 24, 1841.
William C. and Chloe Day, Oct. 29, 1821.

CAPUT, Lewis and Maria Glases of Griswold, Conn., int. Dec. 4, 1825.

CARARY (see Corary, Corrary, Corray), Rachel (Chorarey, int.) and Hosea Aldrich, Nov. 22, 1798.

CAREY, Hannah (Corrary, int.), d. of Benjamin and Esek Comstock, s. of Jeremiah, Mar. 20, 1770.

CARLTON, James N. and Elmira Armstrong of Burrillville, R. I., int. Mar. 23, 1844.

CARLY, Ichabode and Mary Brown, Oct. 8, 1761.

CARPENTER, Charles V. and Esther French, Apr. 16, 1826. c.r.1.
Charlotte and Alva Hall, July 5, 1829.
Clarra C. (Clara Caroline, int.) and Newell Lee, Sept. 10, 1822.
Daniel and Eunice Wood of Northbridge, in Northbridge, Feb. 12, 1797.
Daniel G. (George D., int.) and Waity T. Seagrave, June 27, 1820. (June 29, 1820. c.r.1).
Edwin R. and Delphia F. Meriam, Jan. 1, 1840.
George, Capt., and Charlotte Taft, Nov. 5, 1818.
Hannah and Calvin Spring, May 18, 1817.
Henry, Dr. (Jr., int.), of Upton, and Harriet L. Hazard, June 1, 1841.

* Intention not recorded.

CARPENTER, John and Anne Arnold, May 11, 1815.
Joseph and Julia Ann Howard, int. Oct. 25, 1829.
Levi of Mendon, and Eunas Taft, Nov. 25, 1804.
Maria T. (Maria Theresa, int.) and Royal Chapin, May 16, 1821.
Martha Ann and William S. Merrill of Lowell, May 30, 1832.
Mary G. and Charles Wing, Dec. 5, 1839.
Mary T. and Tyler Howard of Northbridge, July 21, 1841.
Nancy and Alvin Carter of Thompson, Conn., Aug. 26, 1804.
Polly and Benja[min] Green Jr., int. June 27, 1779.
Sarah and Easman Taft Jr., Apr. 11, 1805.
Seba (Bela, int.) of Seekonk, and Mary S. Arnold, Feb. 25, 1836.
Sophia and Henry Cushing, Apr. 13, 1826. c.r.1.
Stephen and Hannah Taft, Jan. 30, 1801.
William and Abial Aldrich, Apr. 12, 1795. c.r.1.

CARREL (see Carriel, Carryl), Jesse and Mary Mann, int. Jan. 24, 1785.

CARRIEL (see Carrel, Carryl), Ruth of Sutton, and Thomas Read Jr., Dec. 29, 1768.

CARRYL (see Carrel, Carriel), George, Dr., and Permela Martin, Nov. 17, 1790.

CARTER, Abigail of Lunenburg, and Charles E. Seagrave, int. May 14, 1848.
Alvin of Thompson, Conn., and Nancy Carpenter, Aug. 26, 1804.
Lucretia and Royal Sibley, Oct. 28, 1819.

CARY, Lydia and Nicholas Hicks, int. Jan. 2, 1741–2.
Lydia and Jonathan Montague, Oct. 6, 1743.

CASS, Abigail S. and Jeremiah Murphy, Sept. 3, 1838.
Diana of Mendon, and Arnold Aldrich Jr., int. Sept. 2, 1832.
Hannah, d. of Daniel of Richmond, N. H., and Nathaniel Taft, s. of Mijamin, 4th day, 2d mo., called February, 1768. c.r.3.*
John of Richmond, and Lydia Taft, int. Sept. 21, 1767.

CHACE (see Chase), Abigail and Thomas Killy, June 23, 1782.*
Charles of Sutton, and Lorena Ellison, Apr. 4, 1838.
Ebenezer and Mary Triphel, June 30, 1768.
Hannah and Jacob Martin, Oct. 30, 1766.*

* Intention not recorded.

CHACE, Hannah and Jacob Elison, both of Northbridge, Oct. 26, 1772.*
Hennery and Hipsibah Walker, int. Feb. 8, 1766.
Mary and Nathan Rawson, Mar. 24, 1764.
Sarah and Elisha Thompson Jr., int. Oct. 21, 1781.
Thomas and Hannah Knap (Knop, int.), Jan. 15, 1766.

CHADWICK, John W. and Hannah Welch, Sept. 4, 1836.

CHAMBERLAIN (see Chamberlin), Amanda and Amory R. Brown, Dec. 3, 1835.
Elizabeth B. and Ezra B. Cambell (Campbell, int.) of Sutton, Oct. 1, 1835.
Rebecca of Dudley, and Edmand Farnum, int. Dec. 21, 1799.

CHAMBERLIN (see Chamberlain), Henry H. of Worcester, and Charlotte R. Clarke, Aug. 19, 1839.

CHAMBERS, Thomas P. and Prudence Frazier of Providence, R. I., int. Mar. 30, 1845.

CHAPEN (see Chapin), Deborah and Dexter Wood, Mar. 3, 1757.
Garshom of Mendon, and Betsy Johnson, Mar. 9, 1758.
Jesse and Eunice Wheelock, Nov. 20, 1783.
Joseph and Ruth Taft, Mar. 9, 1758.
Shem of Springfield, and Anna Clark, Jan. 4, 1753.*

CHAPIN (see Chapen), Abagail and Josiah Spring, June 15, 1815.
Adelia, d. of John S. and Polly, a. 38 y., and Josiah Spring, widr., s. of Ephraim and Eunice, a. 62 y., Dec. 9, 1846.
Ameriah and Olive Taft, Jan. 4, 1787.
Betsey T. and Parley Gould, Oct. 29, 1832.
Betsy and Andrew Adams of Northbridge, Nov. 4, 1790.
Caleb T. and Clarissa W. Taft, Nov. 1, 1830.
Charles C. and Hannah A. Brock of Mendon, int. Aug. 8, 1841.
Charles F. of Milford, and Sarah T. Spring, Jan. 6, 1842.
Chloe (Chloe T., int.) and Asa Thayer Jr., Sept. 24, 1827.
Dianna Maria and Richard Waterman of Warwick, R. I., Feb. 15, 1831.
Eliza B. and Laban M. Wheaton of Norton, June 25, 1829.
Ely of Worcester, and Margarett Taft, int. Mar. 29, 1778.
Eunice of Worcester, and Nathan White, in Worcester, Jan. 14, 1779.

* Intention not recorded.

CHAPIN, Gersham and Mary (Sarah, int.) Sherman of Grafton, in Grafton, Nov. 5, 1778.
Hannah and Elisha Murdock, int. Jan. 10, 1779.
Henry and Abigail Baylies, Feb. 19, 1794. (Feb. 27, 1794. c.r.1.)
Henry Esq. and Sarah R. Thayer, Oct. 7, 1839.
John S. and Polly (Mary, c.r.1), Capron, Oct. 21, 1806.
Joseph, Col., and wid. Abigail Holbrook of Thompson, Conn., int. May 23, 1802.
Joseph and Louisa Veaux (Voax, int.), Aug. 12, 1824.
Josiah and Asenath C. (Asenath Cargill, int.) Capron, Nov. 20, 1815.
Julia E., wid., d. of Darius and Lois Taft, a. 40 y., and Bezaleel Seagrave, widr., s. of John and Sarah, a. 60 y., Jan. 4, 1848.
Laurinda and Ezra W. Fletcher of Northbridge, Mar. 25, 1819.
Lois and Abijah Legg., Dec. 5, 1790.
Margaret A. and Ephraim S. Fletcher of Solon, Me., Oct. 24, 1828. (Oct. 26, 1828. c.r.1.)
Mary and Willard Judson, int. Mar. 9, 1828.
Mary W. and Samuel B. Halliday (of New York, int.), Mar. 21, 1833.
Moses and Betsey Taft, Dec. 15, 1796.
Moses W., s. of Stephen and Julia E., a. 19 y., and Catharine Lackey, d. of Joel and Arispa, a. 19 y., Feb. 1, 1849.
Nancy and Obed Goldthwait of Northbridge, Dec. 7, 1809.
Phila and Elijah Taft of Mendon, int. Oct. 8, 1789.
Phineas and Eunice Taft, Sept. 3, 1795.
Polly and John Warren of Grafton, May 20, 1797. (Aug. 20, 1797. c.r.1.) (July 30, 1797, int.)
Royal and Maria T. (Maria Theresa, int.) Carpenter, May 16, 1821.
Ruth A. and (Dr., int.) William Thornton of Grafton, May 17, 1830.
Sally and Moses Smith, Oct. 6, 1803.
Sally and Paris Hill of Savannah, Ga., Aug. 21, 1827.
Samuel and Beulah Taft of Mendon, in Mendon, Feb. 26, 1761.
Sarah R. and Paul Whitin Jr. of New York, Aug. 26, 1822.
Stephen of Milford, and Julia E. Taft, Mar. 19, 1826. c.r.1.
Sylvia and (Dr., int.) George Willard, Dec. 21, 1809.

CHAPMAN, Hezekiah, Rev., and Chloe Flynt of Windham, Conn., int. May 24, 1778.
Perly of Woodstock, Conn., and Thankful Persons, Feb. 24, 1803.

CHAPPEL, Sarah and Simon Paine, int. May 1, 1825.

CHARD, Mary Eliza of Upton, and Hosea Aldrich of Grafton, Nov. 28, 1817.*

CHASE (see Chace), Abigail and Daniel Owen, Nov. 18, 1751.*
Abigail and Solomon Chase, Mar. 14, 1764.*
Anna and Aaron Keith, May 1, 1799.
Charity, wid., d. of James and Sally Tilly, a. 56 y., and John D. Williams, widr., s. of Chester and Sarah, a. 46 y., Mar. 6, 1848.
Ede and James Knop, int. Mar. 16, 1772.
Gardiner and Susan (Susan F. int.) Balcom, May 24 [1835].
Hannah of Sutton, and Joshua Kop (Knap, int.), Sept. 26, 1732.
Isaac and Rachel Harris, int. July 2, 1757.
Jam[e]s and Olive Farnam, int. Apr. 16, 1770.
Joshua Knop and Dorcas Hewett, Nov. 27, 1788.
Judith of Gloucester, R. I., and Obadiah Aldrich, int. Nov. 17, 1787.
Lydia of Sutton, and John Rawson, in Sutton, Oct. 20, 1791.
Sarah and Jonathan Elliot Jr. of Sutton, in Sutton, Oct. 17, 1771.
Sarah, d. of Josiah and Charity, a. 28 y., and Nathan Aldrich, widr., s. of Seth and Amey, a. 58 y., July 5, 1846.
Solomon and Abigail Chase, Mar. 14, 1764.*
Solomon and Anna Patch of Dudley, int. Aug. 28, 1786.
Timothy G. of Northbridge, s. of Charles and Polly, a. 28 y., and Martha H. Ellison, d. of Joseph, a. 33 y., Oct. 5, 1847.
William E. and Hannah B. Reynolds of North Kingston, R. I., int. Sept. 22, 1848.

CHEENEY (see Cheney), Andrew and Mary M. Worden, July 25, 1839.

CHENEY (see Cheeney), Elizabeth of Medfield, and Peter Taft, in Medfield, Apr. 20, 1736.
Hannah (of Medfield, int.) and John Taft, in Boston, Apr. 11, 1734.
Norman M. and Sally Williston, both of Newton, Nov. 9, 1841.*

CHESON, Jerimiah Jr. and Mary Thayer, int. Oct. 19, 1750.

CHESSMAN, Nathaniel and Ann Perry of Milford, int. Apr. 24, 1831.

* Intention not recorded.

CHILD, W[illia]m G. of North Woodstock, Conn., and Mary Jane Simson, Dec. 14, 1840.

CHILLSON (see Chilson), Eliza W. and Jehiel H. Reed of Upton, int. Oct. 28, 1838.
Hipzebah and William Potter of Upton, Mar. 1, 1742–3.*
Margery, Mrs., of Smithfield, R. I., and Silvanus Taft, int. Dec. 29, 1822.

CHILSON (see Chillson), Abner of Gloucester, R. I., and Rhoda Farnum, int. May 20, 1781.
Beriah and Patiance Gansey (Gernsey, int.), Apr. 7, 1736.
Elisabeth and Israel Brown of Gloucester, R. I., int. Dec. 6, 1778.
Eliza Ann of Smithfield, R. I., and Everett Thompson, Sept. 1, 1834.
Israel and Jonna Humes, int. Mar. 3, 1755.
Jerimiah of Gloucester, R. I., and Rachel Humes, int. Oct. 13, 1755.
Maria and Leonard Adams, Aug. 30, 1829.
Molly and John Smith of Sutton, Oct. 20, 1784.
Rhoda and Gideon Lesure, Dec. 11, 1783.
Rufus and Ruth Hill, in Mendon, Dec. 23, 1773.
Ruth and Levi Morse of Douglas, Mar. 21, 1808.

CLAFLIN, Hannah and Ezra Cumstock of Mendon, int. Apr. 20, 1834.

CLAPP, William A., Rev., and Lois S. Starkey of Providence, R. I., int. May 30, 1841.

CLARK (see Clarke), Abigail and Elexander Aldrich, Aug. 21, 1766.*
Anna and Shem Chapen of Springfield, Jan. 4, 1753.*
Everline W. of New Salem, and Abner H. Rawson, int. Jan. 31, 1830.
Ezekiel and Milley Taft, Mar. 26, 1792.
Griffin of Douglas, and Sarah S. Tillinghast, Apr. 1, 1832.
Henry and Mary Fletcher, int. May 11, 1761.
Joanna of Mendon, and Jason Marsh, in Mendon, Mar. 12, 1795.
Judith and Joseph White Jr., Dec. 4, 1734.
Mary of Gloucester, R. I., and Mijamin Taft, int. May 5, 1787.
Robart and Aannah Taft, int. Oct. 6, 1739.

CLARKE (see Clark), Charlotte R. and Henry H. Chamberlin of Worcester, Aug. 19, 1839.

* Intention not recorded.

CLARKEN, Ellen of Blackstone, and Peter Smith, int. Aug. 31, 1845.

CLEAVELAND (see Cleveland), Joseph and Jemima White, May 24, 1770. (Joseph Clenelan and Jemima White, int. Dec. 18, 1769.)
Philander and Samuel Read Rawson, Jan. 17, 1795.

CLEMANS (see Clemmens), William C. P., s. of James* dec. of Burrillville, R. I., and Ruth, and Ruth Daniels, d. of Adolphus of Mendon, and Alcy dec., 5th day, 11th mo. 1840. c.r.3.*

CLEMMENS (see Clemans), Benjamin of Upton, and Keziah Bolster, Mar. 15, 1774.

CLEVELAND (see Cleaveland), Alden B. and Sarah Metcalf, Oct. 19, 1836.

COATS, Emily Palmer and Christopher Olny Cahoon, Oct. 14, 1832.

COBURN (see Colburn), Charles Chids of Mendon, and Elvira Bellows, int. Oct. 3, 1819.

CODY, Philip and Abigail Emerson, in Hopkinton, Nov. 12, 1754.

COFFIN, Charlottee and Sam[ue]l Mather Crocker of Douglas, int. Aug. 4, 1811.
Ebenezer (of Boston, int.) and Mary Thayer, May 28, 1786.

COGSWELL, Benja[min] and Susanna Houghton of Sutton, int. May 31, 1778.
Horatio and Laura Adams, Jan. 25, 1844.
Rebecca B. and Benjamin Darling, Apr. 5, 1835.

COIT, Isaac Esq. of Plainfield, and Elizabeth Webb, Nov. 15, 1773.

COLBURN (see Coburn), Josiah (2d, c.r.1) of Dracut, and Betsey Aldrich, Jan. 8, 1832.

COLE, Albert, Rev., of Bluehill, Me., and Sarah Judson, May 9, 1838.
Asa of Grafton, and Sarah Pitts, Sept. 3, 1829.
Jonathan and Elisabeth Crowningshield, Sept. 12, 1759.
Stephen of Sutton, and Hannah Hewitt, int. Aug. 8, 1785.

* Intention not recorded.

COLINS, Mathew and Jane Trifle, Oct. 31, 1765.

COLSON, George of Bellingham, and Nancy Aldrich, Jan. 18, 1802.

COLWELL, Charles of Gloucester, R. I., and Anna Taft, int. Aug. 26, 1762.

COMBS, Martha and Nathan White of Douglas, Mar. 16, 1770.*

COMEY, Hannah of Peterboro, N. H., and Alonzo C. Rounds, int. June 8, 1845.

COMINGS, Samuel (Cummings, int.) and Hannah Read, Oct. 7, 1736.

COMSTOCK (see Cumstock), Deborah of Gloucester, R. I., and William White, int. Nov. 12, 1799.
Deborah of Framingham, and George Haskell, Mar. 10, 1828. c.r.1.*
Esek, s. of Jeremiah and Hannah Carey (Corrary, int.), d. of Benjamin, Mar. 20, 1770.
Esther of Providence, R. I., and Peter Aldrich Jr., int. Feb. 8, 1745–6.
Hannah of Smithfield, R. I., and John Whipple, int. June 26, 1742.
Hannah and Wheelock Wood, int. Nov. 26, 1820.
Martha of Smithfield, R. I., and John Farnum, int. July 24, 1756.
Mercy, d. of Woodbury dec., late of North Providence, R. I., and Hannah, and Ephraim Bassett, s. of Joseph and Rachel, 6th day, 11th mo. 1811. c.r.3.*
Meribah of Smithfield, County of Providence, and James Bardens, int. Feb. 29, 1752–3.
Moses and Bethiah Boyce, Apr. 19, 1764.*
Olive and Nahum Morse, int. Feb. 9, 1793.
Patiance of Gloucester, R. I., and Ebenezer Handy, int. Oct. 10, 1794.
Phebe and Abel Aldrich Jr., int. Dec. 10, 1820.
Polly and Thaddeus Rist, Apr. 24, 1803.
Sarah of Smithfield, County of Providence, and Moses Farnum Jr., int. ——, 1752.
William G. of Blackstone, b. in Mendon, s. of William and Abida of Blackstone, a. 22 y., and Elma A. Cook, b. in Mendon, d. of Joseph B. and Thankful, a. 22 y., Oct. 17, 1849.

* Intention not recorded.

CONANT, Eliza D. of Harvard, and Otis Jepherson, int. Apr. 21, 1822.

CONGDON, Jennings B. and Lydia Aldrich of Northbridge, int. Feb. 26, 1832.
Sarah Ann and Henry M. Hathaway of New Bedford, Feb. 21, 1842.

CONNEDY, John and Martha Thomson, Aug. 11, 1730.*

CONVERSE, Jacob Jr. of Thompson, Conn., and Meriam Keith, in Northbridge, Apr. 12, 1792.

COOK (see Cooke), Aaron and Asenath Jepherson of Douglas, int. Jan. 3, 1802.
Abigail and Elisha Thomson, Feb. 20, 1745–6.
Abigail and Job Hill, Aug. 8, 1766.*
Albert L. and Olive C. Kelley, both of Bellingham, Nov. 13, 1839.*
Almira and Albert Jencks of Cumberland, R. I., Feb. 17, 1831.
Alvin and Maria R. Benson of Mendon, Sept. 7, 1828.
Ama of Cumberland, and Seth Aldrich, int. June 22, 1767.
Caroline S. and Timothy D. Baker, Jan. 1, 1835.
Daniel G. and Lydia A. Darling of Blackstone, int. July 13, 1845.
Elisha of Burrillville, R. I., and Mary Handy, int. Jan. 28, 1810.
Elizabeth of Mendon, and Daniel Brown, int. Sept. 20, 1800.
Elma A., b. in Mendon, d. of Joseph B. and Thankful, a. 22 y., and William G. Comstock of Blackstone, b. in Mendon, s. of William and Abida of Blackstone, a. 22 y., Oct. 17, 1849.
Francis G., s. of George, a. 27 y., and Catharine Burnham, d. of Andrew, a. 22 y., Nov. 4, 1844.
George W. of Mendon, and Emily M. Albee, int. July 7, 1839.
Hannah and Oliver Thayer of Mendon, Sept. 25, 1753.
Israel of Gloucester, County of Providence, and Sarah Aldrich, Oct. 6, 1768.
Jonathan (Jr., int.) and Hannah Thayer of Mendon, in Mendon, Mar. 21, 1754.
Jonathan and Jane Dunzemere (Jan Dunsmor, int.) of Mendon, Aug. 6, 1754.
Jonathan and Lydia Aldrich, Oct. 20, 1763.
Jonathan of Douglas, and Jerusha Bardins, June 4, 1764.
Margaret and William Rawson Jr. of Mendon, in Mendon, May 13, 1731.

* Intention not recorded.

Cook, Mary, formerly of Smithfield, R. I., now residing in Mendon, d. of Seth, and Daniel Aldrich, s. of Jacob, 2d day, 9th mo., called September, 1762. c.r.3.*
Mary, d. of Ebenezer of Mendon, and Levi Taft, s. of Silas, 2d day, 6th mo. 1775. c.r.3.*
Mehitable and Paul Taft, May 10, 1750.*
Nahum and Sibil Balcom of Douglas, int. Feb. 17, 1822.
Naoma and Benjamin White, Apr. 28, 1743.*
Nathan of Gloucester, R. I., and Almy Handy, int. Sept. 26, 1802.
Stephen of Gloucester, R. I., and Mary Aldrich, int. June 4, 1764.
William W. and Abigail Draper of Saugus, int. Jan. 9, 1842.
Ziba of Bellingham, and Joanna Aldrich, int. Dec. 3, 1787.
Ziba and Miranda Saddler of Upton, int. June 13, 1829.

COOKE (see Cook), Molly of Douglas, and Samuel Burt, int. Apr. 1, 1821.

COOMBS, Carrol (of Smithfield, R. I., int.) and Cloe Lesure, July 22, 1810.
Reuben (Jr., c.r.1) of Holden, and Permela Keyes, June 28, 1815.

COOPER (see Coopper), Abner of Northbridge, and Patience Taft, int. Sept. 18, 1803.
Elisabeth and David Dunn, Oct. 24, 1769.
Ezra and Ruth Winter, Nov. 7, 1765.
Hepsibah and Timothy Winter, both of Northbridge, Oct. 19, 1773.*
John and Penellope Winter, int. Nov. 21, 1771.
John L. of Northbridge, and Sarah Lippitt of Smithfield, R. I., Oct. 31, 1836.*
Nathaniel and Mary Aldrich, Dec. 19, 1765.

COOPPER (see Cooper), Mary of Gloucester, R. I., and Nathan Taft, int. Nov. 22, 1758.

COPLAND, Rebeckah and Isaac Parks of Pomfret, County of Windham, May 14, 1740.

CORARY (see Carary, Corrary, Corray), Benjamin and Deborah Balcom, both of New Sherborn, March 21, 1732–3.
Benjamin (Crary, int.) and Jerusha Thayer of Mendon, Mar. 30, 1741.
Margrit and Samuel Parker, int. June 13, 1768.
Mary and Samuel Shearman of Gloucester, R. I., int. Apr. 15, 1758.

* Intention not recorded.

CORBAN, Henry and Jemima Vial of Upton, July 27, 1826.

CORBET, Jesse and Mary Woodwell, in Hopkinton, May 28, 1755.

CORRARY (see Carary, Corary, Corray), Ruth and Asa Horton of Danby, Conn., int. Apr. 18, 1789.
Sarah and Benjamin Pain of Gloucester, R. I., int. Dec. 29, 1787.

CORRAY (see Carary, Corary, Corrary), S[t]ephen and Naomi Thayer of Mendon, int. Jan. 23, 1769.

COUSENS (see Cozens), Mary of Sherborn, and William Adams, in Sherborn, Aug. 19, 1730.*

COY, Silas and Elizabeth White of Douglas, int. Mar. 15, 1801.

COZENS (see Cousens), Elisabeth (Cuzans, int.) and Samuel White, Sept. 23, 1731.

CRAGEN (see Craggin, Cragin), Deborah of Mendon, and Benjamin Fish, Oct. 2, 1753.

CRAGGIN (see Cragen, Cragin), Anna and Moses Holbrook, both of Mendon, Mar. 20, 1794.*
Benjamin 3d and Mary Sibley, Mar. 6, 1836.
Betsey and Benja[min] Adams, Jan. 19, 1794.
Cynthia and Pitts A. Learned, both of Sutton, Aug. 1, 1838.*
Elizabeth and A. R. (Addison, int.) Flint of Canton, Conn., Mar. 25, 1840.
Elmira of Northbridge, and Isaac R. Murphy, int. Oct. 3, 1830.
Emma of Douglas, and Adna Taft, int. May 31, 1818.
Marcy and Robert Hale of Douglas, June 28, 1804.
Margare of Mendon, and Willis Taft, in Mendon, Dec. 14, 1786.
Timothy of Douglas, and Philena Taft, June 6, 1799.

CRAGIN (see Cragen, Craggin), Mary of Mendon, and Moses White, int. Nov. 5, 1757.

CRATON (see Creaton), Esther (Createn, int.) and Jonathan Fairbanks of New Sherborn, Aug. 5, 1741.
Sarah of Douglas, and Adam White, Feb. 10, 1771.

CRAWFORD, Silas B. (Elias B. of Grafton, int.) and Jane T. Taft [no date] (int. Mar. 9, 1834).

CREATON (see Craton), William and Esther White, int. Mar. 11, 1730–1.

* Intention not recorded.

CRIPS, Leues and Mary Bilslook of Boston, int. Aug. 29, 1768.

CROCKER, Jonathan, s. of Edmund and Ann, a. 25 y., and Sophronia Stoddard, d. of Joanna, a. 17 y., Oct. 30, 1845.
Lydia and Emery Allen, Mar. 29, 1821.
Samuel M. (Jr., int.) and Cornelia Wilcox, Mar. 9, 1834.
Sam[ue]l Mather of Douglas, and Charlottee Coffin, int. Aug. 4, 1811.

CRONEY, Catharina and Simeon Wheelock of Northbridge, int. Sept. 16, 1804.
Elizabeth and Abijah Hazard of South Kingston, R. I., int. Jan. 9, 1797.
John and Elisabeth Smith, int. May 12, 1764.
Polly and Jonas Hemenway of Worcester, int. Jan. 10, 1797.

CROSBY, Hannah of Upton, and John Spring, int. Apr. 13, 1767.
Sarah and Jonathan Wood Jr., both of Upton, Feb. 20, 1750.*

CROSMAN, (see Crossman), Harriet of Northbridge, and Hugh Riley, int. Oct. 8, 1826.

CROSSMAN (see Crosman), Daniel of Mendon (of Waterford, int.), and Delphina B. Aldrich, June 3, 1838.

CROWNINGSHIELD, Elisabeth and Jonathan Cole, Sept. 12, 1759.
Sarah and David Harwood Jr. of Sutton, int. Aug. 17, 1783.

CRUFF, Elisabeth, d. of Samuel of Smithfield, R. I., and Silas Taft, s. of Stephen, Dec. 4, 1768.

CULLIS, James and Rebeckah Southworth of Douglas, int. Aug. 16, 1807.

CUMING (see Comings, Cumings, Cumming, Cummings), Judith (Juda Cummings, int.) and Moses Taft Jr., May 26, 1785.

CUMINGS (see Comings, Cuming, Cumming, Cummings), Charles and Sarah Fessenden of Charlton, int. Nov. 14, 1830.
Elisabeth and Joseph Taft 3d (minor, int.), Feb. 12, 1752-3.
Josiah and Celia Capron of Mendon, int. June 27, 1830.
Mary and Moses Keith, Jan. 22, 1767.
Royal of Douglas, and Ruth K. Aldrich, int. June 28, 1829.

* Intention not recorded.

CUMINGS, Samuel and Mrs. Mary Hervey, May 3, 1842.
Scheherezade of Douglas, and Asahel Aldrich 2d, int. Aug. 14, 1831.

CUMMING (see Comings, Cuming, Cumings, Cummings), Hannah and Samuel Leshuer, Aug. 17, 1785.

CUMMINGS (see Comings, Cuming, Cumings, Cumming), Abigail and Jonah Prentis, Nov. 25, 1760.
Hanna[h] and Henery Keith, Jan. 16, 1766.
Lois and Seth Fish, Dec. 10, 1772.
Lois and Darius Taft, in Mendon, Dec. 23, 1790.
Molley and Ezekiel Philips of Gloucester, R. I., May 22, 1788.
Phebe and Michajah Taft, int. July 30, 1790.
Samuel and Sarah Emerson, formerly of Ipswich, int. Nov. 10, 1753.
Samuel and Lucy Taft, Dec. 9, 1762.
Samuel and Bethany French of Douglas, in Douglas, Sept. 8, 1796.
Seena and David Taft, Nov. 20, 1793.
Thomas and Jane Shepherd, int. Mar. 19, 1848.

CUMSTOCK (see Comstock), Allis M. of Burrillville, R. I., and Ens. Willard Holbrook, int. July 7, 1822.
Ezra of Mendon, and Hannah Claflin, int. Apr. 20, 1834.
Rachel of Smithfield, R. I., and Samuel Taft Jr., int. Jan. 20, 1777.
Stephen and Olive Pickering of Mendon, int. Mar. 15, 1829.

CUNNINGHAM, Julia A. of Grafton, and George W. Ellison, int. May 2, 1847.

CURLES (see Curless), James of Burrillville, R. I., and Lydia Willard, Thursday, Apr. 28, 1842.

CURLESS (see Curles), James and Mary Locke of Cumberland, R. I., int. Dec. 8, 1844.

CURTICE (see Curtis), John of Dudley, and Pheeby Keith, Apr. 19, 1770.

CURTIS (see Curtice), Noah of Oxford Gore, and Elisabeth Aldrich, int. Apr. 11, 1750.
Ruth of Gloucester, R. I., and Peter Wooding, int. Aug. 29, 1785.

CUSHING, Henry and Sophia Carpenter, int. Apr. 13, 1826.
C.R.1.

CUTLER, Jerush of Medway, and Joseph Rist, in Medway, May 27, 1779.

DAILEY (see Daily, Daley), David of Concord, N. H., and Louis Pitts, Oct. 25, 1804.

DAILY (see Dailey, Daley), Louis, wid., and Miles Bacon of Smithfield, R. I., int. Oct. 5, 1817.

DALEY (see Dailey, Daily), David of Smithfield, R. I., and Molley Harris, int. July 6, 1772.

DALRUMPEL (see Dalrumple, Darumple, Derumple), William and Mary Straight, int. Dec. 24, 1770.

DALRUMPLE (see Dalrumpel, Darumple, Derumple), Susanna of Northbridge, and Seth Holbrook, May 24, 1774.

DAMON, Joseph, Dea., and wid. Patience Whitney of Sherborn, May 13, 1759.
Joseph and Silance Keith, int. Sept. 28, 1772.

DANIEL (see Daniels, Danils), Joseph Jr. of Needham, and Mary Keith (the younger, int.), in Needham, Nov. 27, 1777.

DANIELS (see Daniel, Danils), Abigail of Mendon, and Israel Arnold, int. Jan. 13, 1805.
Abraham of Mendon, and Hannah Whitney, int. Aug. 30, 1735.
Anne of Mendon, and Joshua Knap, in Mendon, Mar. 17, 1729–30.*
Bathsheba of Mendon, and Esek Pitts, int. Aug. 17, 1823.
Deborah of Mendon, and Hezekiah Hall, int. Nov. 2, 1749.
Dorcas and Eleaz[e]r Allbee, Aug. 27, 1767.
Elbridge G. of Mendon, and Charlotte Taft, int. Dec. 3, 1815.
Lydia of Holliston, and Dea. Edmond Rawson, Mar. 5, 1761.
Mary and William Bancroft, Sept. 29, 1763.
Moses (Jr., int.) of Mendon, and Charlotte Taft, Sept. 20, 1818.
Olive of Mendon, and Asahel Aldrich, int. Feb. 27, 1803.
Ruth, d. of Adolphus of Mendon, and Alcy dec., and William C. P. Clemans, s. of James dec., of Burrillville, R. I., and Ruth, 5th day, 11th mo. 1840. c.r.3.*

DANILS (see Daniel, Daniels), Sarah of Mendon, and Woodlan Thomson, Jan. 16, 1734–5.

* Intention not recorded.

DARLIN (see Darling), Mathew of Mendon, and Hannah Emerson, Oct. 29, 1767.

DARLING (see Darlin), Adah of Mendon, and Abram Farnum, int. Dec. 30, 1827.
Benjamin and Rebecca B. Cogswell, Apr. 5, 1835.
Cortis (Curtis, int.), and Hannah A. Staples, May 20, 1829.
Data of Cumberland, R. I., and Ezra Kimpton, int. Nov. 12, 1798.
Deborah of Mendon, and Daniel Wheelock, in Mendon, Mar. 30, 1732.
Eliza and Otis Marsh of Smithfield, R. I., int. Mar. 16, 1834.
Hannah and Rufus Ballou of Smithfield, R. I., int. Nov. 30, 1842.
Hannah W., wid., of Blackstone, d. of Mr. Luther, and Otis Aldrich, widr., of Blackstone, s. of Enoch and Deborah, a. 59 y., July 29, 1847.*
Joanna and Hiram Wilmarth of Smithfield, R. I., Sept. 23, 1829.
Lydia of Mendon, and Peter Holbrook, in Mendon, May 27, 1761.
Lydia, d. of Daniel of Mendon, and Gershom Keath, s. of Gershom, Nov. 9, 1775.
Lydia A. of Blackstone, and Daniel G. Cook, int. July 13, 1845.
Maria and Leonard White of Bellingham, Jan. 31, 1836.
Mary of Mendon, and Noble Baggs, in Mendon, Nov. 30, 1768.*
Mary of Mendon, and Jonathan Emerson, int. Nov. 21, 1774.
Mary of Mendon, and Daniel Kimpton, int. May 6, 1811.
Mehetible and Joseph How of Sutton, Apr. 12, 1770.
Nathan Jr. of Sturbridge, and Elinor Burroughs of Mendon, Aug. 19, 1830.*
Peter, s. of Samuel and Sibel Thayer, d. of Uriah, June 24, 1776.
Rachael of Mendon, and James Albee, in Mendon, Feb. 1, 1787.
Ruth of Mendon, and Joseph Albee, int. Oct. 17, 1744.
Ruth and William H. Luther, both of Sutton, May 24, 1841.*
Sarah of Mendon, and Thomas Seaben (Sabens, int.), in Mendon, Dec. 22, 1768.
Sarah Ann and Almon Thwing, int. Aug. 19, 1832.
Seviah and Elisha Thompson Jr. of Douglas, int. May 30, 1813.
William of Mendon, and Rachel White, int. May 14, 1757.

DARUMPLE (see Dalrumpel, Dalrumple, Derumple), David and Susannah Ellison, Dec. 20, 1750.

DAVENPORT, Abigail and Steward Easty, Mar. 13, 1753.*

* Intention not recorded.

DAVIS, Ebenezer H. and Polly Taft, May 11, 1836.
Eliza J. and Amos Dean Esq. of Albany, N. Y., Sept. 14, 1842.
Eunice of Mendon, and John Sanger, Jan. 28, 1767.
Lorenzo and Louisa Hammond, July 16, 1837.
Samuel and Sarah Ann Kinnicum, Dec. 10, 1838.

DAVOL, Diana R. and David J. Baker of Worcester, May 20, 1841.

DAY, Angelina N. and George Adams, May 26, 1841.
Chloe and William C. Capron, Oct. 29, 1821.
James W., s. of Joseph and Abby, a. 29 y., and Elizabeth Upham, d. of Danforth and Watee, a. 19 y., Nov. 25, 1846.
Joseph and Abagail Taft, May 29, 1816.
Judson of Sutton, and Mary Learned, Mar. 20, 1834.
Nathaniel of Smithfield, R. I., and Eliza Southwick, int. May 31, 1812.
Sukey and Jerry Wheelock, Jan. 24, 1811.

DEAN (see Deane), Amos Esq. of Albany, N. Y., and Eliza J. Davis, Sept. 14, 1842.
Lucina and Luke Lesure of Mendon, Sept. —, 1803 (int., Aug. 7, 1803).

DEANE (see Dean), Brigham of Sutton, and Phila B. Beals of Smithfield, R. I., Jan. 8, 1838 (Jan. 22, 1838 dup.).*
Francis Jr. and Mary Jane Brown of Charlestown, int. May 8, 1836.

DEIRK, Henry and Amelia Keith of Smithfield, R. I., int. Mar. 1, 1846.

DENNIS, Samuel of Sutton, and Patience Benham, in Sutton, Mar. 27, 1754.

DERUMPLE (see Dalrumpel, Dalrumple, Darumple), Sarah and William Tamplen, Nov. 27, 1739.

DICKE, Barshaba and Benj[ami]n Taft, Jan. 14, 1762.

DICKESON, Anna (Deckerson, int.) and Charles Britton, Mar. 30, 1758.

DODD, Caroline of Holden, and Benedict A. Handy, int. June 13, 1830.

* Intention not recorded.

DODGE (see Doge), Henry of Smithfield, R. I., and Hannah T. Benson, Apr. 5, 1836.
James and Hannah Hill, int. Jan. 2, 1769.
Mary of Charlton, and Thomas J. Fletcher, int. Apr. 29, 1832.
Mary J., d. of Olney and Dorcas, a. 19 y., and David Wilcox, s. of Willard and Hannah of Mendon, a. 23 y., Dec. 12, 1844.
William A. and Sarah M. Burdon of Blackstone, int. Oct. 27, 1849.

DOGE (see Dodge), Nathaniel and Sarah Doge of Brookfield, int. Jan. 26, 1763.
Sarah of Brookfield, and Nathaniel Doge, int. Jan. 26, 1763.

DORR, Katherine of Mendon, and Ezekiel Emerson, in Mendon, Mar. 27, 1760.

DORRINTON, Sarah and John Seagrave, int. Oct. 25, 1778.

DORRY, Mary and Valentine Avoy, int. June 4, 1843.

DOTY, Mahala and Horace Eaton, both of Mendon, Nov. 29, 1836.*

DOW, Sarah W. and Daniel Leonard, int. Sept. 30, 1832.

DOWN, Ann S. and Erasmus B. Metcalf of Franklin, Mar. 31, 1841.

DOWSE, Betsey of Sherborn, and Jonathan Ryan, int. Mar. 1, 1812.

DOYLE, Maria and James Galan, int. Dec. 14, 1845.

DRAKE, Rachel and Pardon Aldrich, both of Mendon, May 8, 1796.*
Stephen and Abigail Albee, int. July 12, 1768.

DRAPER, Abigail of Saugus, and William W. Cook, int. Jan. 9, 1842.
Danforth and Roxana Morse, Sept. 13, 1822.
David (see David Dupee).
David Jr. and Martha Hull, Feb. 15, 1770.
David Jr. and Hannah Brown of Douglas, int. Mar. 14, 1798.
Ebenezer D. and Anna Thwing, Sept. 11, 1834.
Elisabeth and Joseph Adams, Oct. 14, 1756.
Frost and Mary Thayer of Amherst, int. Sept. 13, 1812.
George of Palmer, and Hannah B. Thwing, Wednesday, Mar. 6, 1839.

* Intention not recorded.

DRAPER, Lydia of Saugus, and John Edmands, int. Jan. 18, 1835.
Mary of Roxbury, and Joseph Tyler, int. Aug. 30, 1756.
Mary and Lecester Paine of Woodstock, Conn., Oct. 25, 1781.
Rebecca and James Hull, Sept. 15, 1766.
Rebekah and John Brown Jr. of Douglas, May 12, 1807.
Rhoda and Samuel Printis, Nov. 19, 1745.*
Sally and Chester Williams of Northbridge, June 13, 1797.
Samuel, formerly of Roxbury, and Pheebe Rist, int. Oct. 13, 1739.
Sarah and Silas Rawson, Mar. 17, 1768.

DRESSER, Isaac of Charlton, and Susanna Taft, int. Dec. 4, 1780.

DREW, Lucy of Dedham, and William Johnson, int. June 8, 1834.

DUDLEY (see Dudly), Ann of Douglas, and Daniel Brown, int. July 25, 1768.
Hannah (of Northbridge, int.) and Luther Bullard, Dec. 8, 1814.
Lydia and Benjamin Wallis, both of Douglas, Nov. 9, 1747.*
Otis of Harpers Ferry, Va., and Elizabeth Richardson, Aug. 18, 1825. C.R.I.
P. W. and Sarah A. Toby of Worcester, int. Sept. 11, 1842.

DUDLY (see Dudley), Samuel Esq. and Sarah Shepherd, Nov. 25, 1747.*

DUN (see Dunn), Elisabeth (Margret, int.) and Daniel McFarling of Rutland, Oct. 8, 1747.
Elizabeth and Samuel Stodderd of Grafton, Dec. 6, 1770.

DUNN (see Dun), David and Elisabeth Cooper, Oct. 24, 1769.
David and Huldah Aldrich, both of Northbridge, Jan. 3, 1805.*

DUNZEMERE, Jane (Jan Dunsmor, int.) of Mendon, and Jonathan Cook, Aug. 6, 1754.

DUPEE, David (Draper, int.) and Elizabeth Simons, in Bedford, Feb. 21, 1733.

DYER, Lydia (of Hopkinton, int.) and William Thompson, in Hopkinton, Jan. 10, 1769.
Moses of Northbridge, and Charlotte T. Benson, Nov. 26, 1840.

EASTY (see Estey, Esty), Steward and Abigail Davenport, Mar. 13, 1753.*

* Intention not recorded.

EATON, Horace and Mahala Doty, both of Mendon, Nov. 29, 1836.*

EDDY, Arnold and Sarah Nicholls [no date] (int. Apr. 7, 1833).
Mary of Mendon, and Philander White, int. Oct. 17, 1824.
Sarah and Lyman Wood, Feb. 4, 1836.

EDMANDS (see Edmonds, Edmunds), John and Lydia Draper of Saugus, int. Jan. 18, 1835.

EDMONDS (see Edmands, Edmunds), Elvira S. and Laban Tucker of Winchendon, Oct. 7, 1831.
John and Elenor Morris (of Mendon, int.), June 7, 1744.

EDMUNDS (see Edmands, Edmonds), Harriet of Dudley, and Ivory Stephens, int. Oct. 8, 1826.

EGAN, Charlotte M., d. of George and Charlotte of Pittston, Me., a. 18 y., and Ward B. Hager, s. of Abraham and Dolly of West Boylston, a. 19 y., Mar. 1, 1846.

ELEXANDERS (see Alexander), William and Sarah Lenerd, int. Sept. 24, 1770.

ELIOT (see Elliot, Elot), Benjamin and Elisabeth Wallis of New Sherborn, Sept. 29, 1737.
David of Oblong [Duchess Co., N. Y.], and Mehetabel Aldrich, int. Dec. 29, 1739.
John and Deborah Aldrich, Oct. 2, 1736.
Mary and Moses Thomson, Nov. 12, 1741.

ELISON (see Ellison), Jacob and Hannah Chace, both of Northbridge, Oct. 26, 1772.*
John and Hannah Aldrich, Apr. 11, 1732.

ELKINS, Mary (Mary E., int.) and Reuben Nichols, Oct. 15 [1835].
Ruth B. and Ebenezer Graves of Marblehead, int. Jan. 5, 1845.

ELLIOT (see Eliot, Elot), Asahel and Amey Gaskill, int. Mar. 23, 1817.
Hannah of Sutton, and Dea. Nicholas Baylies, in Sutton, Dec. 8, 1789.
James T. (James Taylor, int.) of Sutton, and Submit Baylies, Jan. 25, 1810.
Jonathan Jr. of Sutton, and Sarah Chase, in Sutton, Oct. 17, 1771.

* Intention not recorded.

ELLIS, Charles and Sarah Ballard of Charlestown, int. Apr. 21, 1844.
Elisabeth and Ebenezer White (of Mendon, int.), Apr. 21, 1748.
Joseph S. and Henrietta Jones of Lunenburg, int. Mar. 20, 1836.
Ruth and John Thayer of Mendon, int. July 8, 1749.
Willard and Eliza Pierce (of Bellingham, int.), Sept. 18, 1832.

ELLISON (see Elison), Adolphus S. and Julia A. Hunt of Springfield, int. Sept. 15, 1839.
Anna and Mark Williams of Bateman's Precinct, N. Y., int. Nov. 3, 1764.
Edward of Northbridge, and Polly Pierce, in Northbridge, Feb. 28, 1793.
George W. and Julia A. Cunningham of Grafton, int. May 2, 1847.
John and Mary Tamplin of Dighton, int. Mar. 17, 1764.
Joseph of Northbridge, and Lucinda Wood, Nov. 27, 1798.
Lorena and Charles Chace of Sutton, Apr. 4, 1838.
Louisa and Samuel M. Follett [no date] (int. Aug. 25, 1833).
Maria (Sylvia M., int.) and Augustus Thayer, Oct. 5, 1837.
Martha H., d. of Joseph, a. 33 y., and Timothy G. Chase of Northbridge, s. of Charles and Polly, a. 28 y., Oct. 5, 1847.
Susannah and David Darumple, Dec. 20, 1750.
Thomas and Dorithy Tamplen, Dec. 6, 1768.
Willard and Silvia Albee of Milford, int. Mar. 7, 1830.

ELOT (see Eliot, Elliot), Amphila and Solomon Aldrich, int. Mar. 25, 1755.

EMERSON (see Emmerson) ———, and John Herlbut, int. Dec. 1, 1759.
Abigail and Philip Cody, in Hopkinton, Nov. 12, 1754.
Daniel and Judeth Gaill of Sutton, int. Apr. 6, 1772.
Ebenezer and Elizabeth Wallcutt (of Attleborough, County of Bristol, alias Smithfield, County of Providence, int.), in Smithfield, R. I., last of March or beginning of April, 1733.
Elisabeth and Nathan Morss, Oct. 18, 1759.
Esther and Stephen Partridge of Medway, Feb. 27, 1772.
Ezekiel and Katherine Dorr of Mendon, in Mendon, Mar. 27, 1760.
Hannah and Mathew Darlin of Mendon, Oct. 29, 1767.
James Jr. and Bulah Marsh, int. July 22, 1776.

EMERSON, James D. and Rebecca W. Fisher of Wrentham, int. Dec. 12, 1830.
John and Marcy Wood, Feb. 27, 1745–6.*
John and Lucy Haden of Hopkinton, int. Apr. 17, 1769.
Jonathan and Sarah Marshall of Ipswich, in Ipswich, Dec. 20, 1752.
Jonathan and Mary Darling of Mendon, int. Nov. 21, 1774.
Jonathan and Eunice Selinda Jans of Brimfield, int. Mar. 23, 1834.
Joseph and Phebe Thayer, Dec. 3, 1767.*
Joseph and Sally Wood of Gloucester, R. I., int. Apr. 12, 1798.
Lois (of Gloucester, R. I., int.) and Samuel White, May 8, 1766.
Luke and Ruth Emerson, Apr. 30, 1755.
Lydia and Richard Arnold of Smithfield, R. I., Apr. 9, 1809.
Lyman and Lillie Hall, Nov. 18, 1789.
Molley and Gideon Morse, int. Dec. 25, 1788.
Nathaniel and Mary Jepherson, Apr. 15, 1762.*
Nathaniel Jr. and Polley Thompson, Jan. 27, 1797.
Philadelphia and Israel Aldrich, int. Oct. 2, 1784.
Rhoda and Ebenezer Morse, Apr. 30, 1789.
Ruth and Luke Emerson, Apr. 30, 1755.
Ruth of Douglas, and Abner Yates, int. Apr. 30, 1770.
Ruth and Joseph Jepherson of Killingly, Conn., int. Mar. 14, 1779.
Samuel and Eunice Whipple of Dana, int. Jan. 23, 1803.
Sarah, formerly of Ipswich, and Samuel Cummings, int. Nov. 10, 1753.
Sarah and Micah Thayer, Mar. 2, 1757.
Sarah and Tho[ma]s Saben (of Mendon, int.), Jan. 17, 1763.
Sarah and John Hawkins of Providence, R. I., Nov. 29, 1764.
Susanna and Jedediah Jepherson, int. Oct. 28, 1781.
Thomas and Abigail Marsh, Nov. 29, 1748.
Waity and Howard Wood, Apr. 22, 1804.

EMMERSON (see Emerson), Elizabeth of Ipswich, and James Emmerson, in Ipswich, Nov. 27, 1752.
James and Elizabeth Emmerson of Ipswich, in Ipswich, Nov. 27, 1752.

ENNIS, Allice, Mrs., and John Johnson Jr., int. Dec. 2, 1849.

ESTEN, Lydia and Otis W. Bly of Smithfield, R. I., int. Nov. 22, 1835.

ESTES, Richard of Cumberland, R. I., and wid. Hannah Aldrich, 5th day, 6th mo. 1778. c.r.3.*

* Intention not recorded.

ESTEY (see Easty, Esty), Abigail (of Mendon, int.) and Manariah Kelley, Jan. 7, 1837.

ESTY (see Easty, Estey), Harriet E., wid., d. of Abigail Newton, a. 25 y., and Charles P. Blodgett, widr., s. of Nehemiah and Sarah A., a. 30 y., June 10, 1848.

EVANS, Benjamin Jr. of Smithfield, R. I., and Maria Baker, int. Dec. 11, 1836.
Martha and Paul White (Jr., int.) in Hopkinton, June 18, 1778.

EVERETT, Preston F. and Jerusha A. Nicholas of Pawtucket, R. I., int. Mar. 27, 1836.

FAIRBANKS, Charles, s. of Silas and Millia of Medway, a. 30 y., and Charlotte L. Scott, d. of Manley and Henrietta, a. 21 y., Dec. 8, 1846.
Cynthia of Bellingham, and Joel Hammond, int. July 11, 1844.
David and Sally Hall, Nov. 6, 1803.
Jonathan of New Sherborn, and Esther Craton (Createn, int.), Aug. 5, 1741.
Lydia of Sherborn, and Abijah Morse, in Sherborn, Oct. 10, 1751.*
Mary of Sherborn, and Samuel White Jr., int. Apr. 1, 1748.

FAIRFIELD, Abraham of Gloucester, R. I., and Abiel White, int. Apr. 10, 1798.

FALES, Emerson and Deborah Snow of Franklin, int. Jan. 29, 1832.

FARNAM (see Farnum), Olive and Jam[e]s Chase, int. Apr. 16, 1770.

FARNSWORTH, Mary A. of Mendon, and Gideon M. Saben, int. Aug. 24, 1845.

FARNUM (see Farnam), Abigail and Seth White, Aug. 20, 1740–1.
Abigail and David Harris of Smithfield, R. I., int. Feb. 26, 1761.
Abram and Adah Darling of Mendon, int. Dec. 30, 1827.
Amos and Lydia Penniman, int. Mar. 18, 1793.
Amy and Eben Kempton of Mendon, int. Aug. 2, 1829.
Ann, d. of Moses and Benjamin Buffum of Smithfield, R. I., s. of Benjamin dec., 6th day, 5th mo., called July, 1749. C.R.3.*

* Intention not recorded.

FARNUM, Azubah and (Lieut., int.) Caleb Farnum, in Mendon, Sept. 16, 1793.
Caleb (Lieut., int.) and Azubah Farnum, in Mendon, Sept. 16, 1793.
Caroline of Ashford, Conn., and Keith W. White, int. Oct. 25, 1829.
Chloe and Peter White Jr., Dec. 4, 1766.
Clarrissa and Phineas Wood, July 31, 1839.
Daniel Jr. and Mary Southwick, int. Dec. 30, 1810.
Daniel and Mary Smith of Burrillville, R. I., int. June 1, 1823.
David and Leah Allen of Medway, in Medway, Jan. 25, 1758.
David, s. of Moses and Sarah dec., and Ruth Southwick, d. of Lawrence and Hannah, 7th day, 12th mo. 1781. C.R.3.*
David Jr. and Hopestill Taft of Mendon, in Mendon, Jan. 21, 1796.
Edmand and Rebecca Chamberlain of Dudley, int. Dec. 21, 1799.
George and Sarah Aldrich, int. Apr. 6, 1787.
George and Deborah Pitts, int. Mar. 6, 1790.
Hannah, d. of Moses and John Reed, s. of Jonathan of Smithfield, R. I., 24th day, 4th mo., called April, 1755. C.R.3.*
Hannah and Humphry Taylor, int. Oct. 19, 1828.
Harriet S. of Blackstone, and Stephen H. Southwick, int. Sept. 16, 1849.
James M. of Northbridge, s. of Daniel and Mary, a. 25 y., and Ophelia Stoddard, d. of Lott and Joanna, a. 20 y., May 6, 1847.
John, Cornet, and Abigail Marsh of Bellingham, int. Oct. 30, 1733.
John, s. of Moses, and Elisebeth Gaskill, d. of Sam[ue]ll of Mendon, 3d day, 3d mo., called May, 1750. C.R.3.*
John and Martha Comstock of Smithfield, R. I., int. July 24, 1756.
Jonathan (Joshua, int.) and Margaret Thayer of Mendon, in Mendon, Nov. 16, 1752.
Jonathan and Uranah Harris of Smithfield, R. I., int. Aug. 31, 1765.
Jonathan, s. of David dec. and Leah, and Lettice Kelly, d. of Seth of Mendon, and Molly, 5th day, 2d mo. 1789. C.R.3.*
Joshua and Margaret Legg (of Mendon, int.), Dec. 17, 1761.
Luke S. of Northbridge, s. of Daniel and Mary, a. 32 y., and Chloe M. Taft, d. of Luke and Nancy, a. 26 y., Mar. 7, 1849.
Maria C. and Seth Armstrong, Oct. 6, 1839.

* Intention not recorded.

FARNUM, Mary and Silas Taft, int. Dec. 30, 1748.
Mary and Nathaniel Fish, Apr. 13, 1769.
Molla and David Wood, June 23, 1768.
Moses Jr. and Sarah Comstock of Smithfield, County of Providence, int. —— 1752.
Moses and Elisabeth Southwick, d. of Lawrance of Mendon, 2d day, 5th mo. 1777. c.r.3.*
Nancy and Jesse Bolster, Dec. 18, 1816.
Rachel, d. of Moses and Daniel Read, s. of Jonathan of Smithfield, R. I., 7th day, 2d mo., called February, 1760. c.r.3.*
Rhoda and Abner Chilson of Gloucester, R. I., int. May 20, 1781.
Royal and Rhozilla Aldrich of Cumberland, R. I., int. Oct. 15, 1792.
Ruth and Henry Green, in Mendon, Mar. 16, 1794.
Sarah and Samuel Thayer 3d of Mendon, May 9, 1754.
Susan and Samuel W. Scott, Oct. 12, 1841.
Thomas and Mary Keith, May 31, 1749.
Thomas and Matilda Newell, June 28, 1815.
Whipple and Prudence Staples, Nov. 29, 1829.
Whipple, widr., s. of Royal and Rosetta, a. 46 y., and Lydia A. Sears, d. of Thomas and Lydia A., a. 36 y., Nov. 4, 1847.

FAY, Cynthia and Layman Aldrich, Apr. 20, 1831.
Mary Ann and Omar Aldrich, Mar. 3, 1825.*
Mary K. and Samuel F. Meriam, May 18, 1836.
Nahum W. of Berlin, s. of Dexter and Zilpha, a. 23 y., and Emily R. Thompson, d. of Adams and Charity, a. 27 y., Sept. 12, 1844.

FERRY, William G. of Grafton, s. of Darias and Philena of Grafton, a. 23 y., and Charlotte Parmiter, d. of Jonas and Charlotte, Apr. 6, 1845.*

FESSENDEN, Louisa B., d. of Isaac and Olive, a. 19 y., and William Howard of Framingham, s. of William and Susannah of Canton, a. 27 y., Jan. 27, 1845.
Sarah of Charlton, and Charles Cumings, int. Nov. 14, 1830.

FISH, Abel and Thankfull Brown, Sept. 6, 1770.
Abigail and Moses White, int. Feb. 7, 1746-7.
Abigail and Joseph Aldrich, of Gloucester, R. I., Mar. 19, 1750-1.*
Abigail and Ichabod Keith, Apr. 1, 1783.
Benjamin and Deborah Cragen of Mendon, Oct. 2, 1753.
Benjamin and Sarah Wood, Feb. 16, 1764.
Chloey and Timothy Rawson, Dec. 3, 1767.

* Intention not recorded.

FISH, Deborah of Mendon, and Joseph White, in Mendon, Mar. 15, 1759.
Elisabeth and Roger Thomson of Smithfield, R. I., Jan. 12, 1769.
Hannah of Mendon, and Solomon Wood, in Mendon, Oct. 1, 1765.
Joseph of Douglas, s. of Charles and Louisa of the Province of Canada, a. 24 y., and Susan Matthew, d. of Peter and Victoria R., a. 15 y., Apr. 26, 1845.
Lydia of Mendon, and Ebenezer Lewis, int. Jan. 23, 1740-1.
Lydia and Samuel Gage, June 8, 1769.
Mary and Joseph Hammon Esq. of Swanzey, Oct. 21, 1784.
Nathaniel and Susanna Keith, Dec. 2, 1746.
Nathaniel and Mary Farnum, Apr. 13, 1769.
Sarah and Jonathan Adams of Sutton, int. Feb. 20, 1774.
Seth and Lois Cummings, Dec. 10, 1772.
Simeon of Mendon, and Tabitha Taft, Nov. 10, 1768.
Stephen and Ruth Hayward of Mendon, Mar. 10, 1757.
Susanna of Mendon, and Timothy Tyler, Dec. 10, 1774.

FISHER, Alfred and Mary Ann Oliver of Framingham, int. Mar. 26, 1826.
Ellen and Nathan Paine, int. Nov. 10, 1843.
Josiah S. and Alma M. Aldrich, Jan. 18, 1824.
Laura Ann of Holliston, and Albert Thwing, int. May 16, 1824.
Louisa A., d. of Josiah S. and Alma M., a. 17 y., and John Gregory of Burrillville, R. I., s. of Daniel and Elizabeth, a. 21 y., Oct. 13, 1847.
Nathan of Mendon, and Zilpah Taft, Dec. 20, 1795.
Rachel Adaline and Moses D. Southwick of Mendon, int. May 6, 1830.
Rebecca W. of Wrentham, and James D. Emerson, int. Dec. 12, 1830.
Susan of Wrentham, d. of Hosea and Amanda, a. 20 y., and Albert Green of Blackstone, s. of Sarah A., a. 22 y., Oct. 13, 1846.*

FISK, Molley of Mendon, and Benjamin Thwing, int. Nov. 20, 1770.
Zilphah and Isaac Aldrich, Jan. 26, 1763.*

FLAG (see Flagg), James and Anna Penniman, Jan. 10, 1775.

FLAGG (see Flag), Josiah F., Dr., and Mary Wait of Boston, int. Sept. 20, 1818.
Sarah G. of Needham, and Lewis S. White, int. Mar. 6, 1825.

* Intention not recorded.

FLETCHER, Abraham of Mendon, and Harriet E. Taft, Aug. 21, 1839.*
Alpha of Mendon, and Samuel Willson, int. Feb. 17, 1805.
Ephraim S. of Solon, Me., and Margaret A. Chapin, Oct. 24, 1828. (Oct. 26, 1828. c.r.1.)
Ezra W. of Northbridge, and Laurinda Chapin, Mar. 25, 1819.
Hannah of Smithfield, R. I., and Jesse Atwood, int. Dec. 13, 1829.
Mary and Henry Clark, int. May 11, 1761.
Samuel of Northbridge, and Lyddia Spring, May 5, 1803.
Stasa of Charlton, and Rachel Aldrich, int. Jan. 5, 1812.
Thomas J. and Mary Dodge of Charlton, int. Apr. 29, 1832.

FLINT (see Flynt), A. R. (Addison, int.) of Canton, Conn., and Elizabeth Craggin, Mar. 25, 1840.

FLYNT (see Flint), Chloe of Windham, Conn., and Rev. Hezekiah Chapman, int. May 24, 1778.

FOGG, W[illia]m S. and Nancy L. Adams, both of Mendon, Aug. 16, 1836.*

FOLLET (see Follett), Robert and Mary Walkup, May 14, 1820.

FOLLETT (see Follet), Nancy and Zebulon Rhodes, Dec. 10, 1837.
Samuel M. and Louisa Ellison [no date] (int. Aug. 25, 1833).

FORBUSH, Curtis of Grafton, and Rhoda G. Taft, int. Sept. 1, 1839.

FOSTER, Alpheus (of Sturbridge, int.) and Ruth Haywood, Apr. 22, 1811.
Alpheus and Mrs. Polly P. Inman of Blackstone, int. May 17, 1846.
Edward and Maranda Capron, Nov. 20, 1808.
Edward B. of Northbridge, s. of Hinsdale and Hannah F., a. 28 y., and Hellen R. Blake, d. of Thomas and Abigail, a. 24 y., Aug. 29, 1849.
Hinsdale of Sturbridge (Southbridge, int.), and Hannah (Hannah T., int.) Brown, Apr. 9, 1820.
Nancy of Dudley, and Reuben Taft, int. Jan. 13, 1805.

FOWLER, Edwin D. and Harriet M. Sprague of Leicester, int. Apr. 10, 1836.
John M. and Jane Burlingame of Smithfield, R. I., int. Apr. 6, 1840.

* Intention not recorded.

FOWLER, Maria of Northbridge, and Nathan Aldrich 2d, int. Dec. 12, 1824.
Mary of Lebanon, County of Windham, and Thomas Rist, int. Oct. 11, 1735.

FRAZIER, Prudence of Providence, R. I., and Thomas P. Chambers, int. Mar. 30, 1845.

FREEMAN, Deborah L. of Lowell, and Nathiel W. Keith, int. Mar. 26, 1837.
William H., s. of Thomas J. and Rebecca, a. 23 y., and Samantha L. Bisbee, d. of William O. and Charlotte Barrett, a. 16 y., Jan. 15, 1846.

FRENCH, Benjamin and Olive Sprague, Oct. 18, 1807.
Benjamin and Mrs. Lois Taft of Sutton, int. Dec. 14, 1834.
Bethany of Douglas, and Samuel Cummings, in Douglas, Sept. 8, 1796.
Esther and Charles V. Carpenter, Apr. 16, 1826. c.r.1.
Jemima and David D. Paine, Oct. 3, 1822.

FROST, Gideon of Wells, and Henrietta Thayer, int. Mar. 11, 1781.
Henrietta and Brigham Morse, Apr. 6, 1835.
Olive of Mendon, and Dr. Samuel Willard, in Mendon, Nov. 3, 1774.

FULLAR (see Fuller), Rachel and Rev. William Phipps of Douglas, int. Oct. 12, 1751.

FULLER (see Fullar), Bethiah of Newton, and John Murdock, in Newton, Jan. 24, 1750.
Brigham of East Douglas, and Mary L. Jencks, int. Feb. 26, 1837.
Jeduthan and Huldah M. Saunders, Apr. 6, 1835.
Nancy and Jesse Whiting, int. Nov. 19, 1826.
Rufus of Cumberland, R. I., and Julia M. Keith, July 31, 1836.
Thomas and Sarah Wheeler of Sutton, in Sutton, Feb. 6, 1749-50.

GAGE, John of Smithfield, R. I., and Anna Bolster, int. Feb. 20, 1814.
Samuel and Lydia Fish, June 8, 1769.

GAILL, Judeth of Sutton, and Daniel Emerson, int. Apr. 6, 1772.

GALAN, James and Maria Doyle, int. Dec. 14, 1845.

GANSEY (see Garnsey), Patiance (Gernsey, int.) and Beriah Chilson, Apr. 7, 1736.

GARDNER, Eliza A. of Mendon, d. of Thomas and Nancy, a. 26 y., and Milton Aldrich of Mendon, s. of Samuel and Delila, a. 21 y., June 20, 1849.*

GARNSEY (see Gansey), Thankful and David Read, May 29, 1734.

GARSIDE, Joshua of Mendon, and Helena Lowell of Millbury, Mar. 24, 1833.

GARY, Samuel (of Pomfret, County of Windham, int.), and Martha Thurston, Nov. 10, 1752.

GASKIL (see Gaskill), Sarah and Jesse Morse 3d, int. Mar. 6, 1803.

GASKILL (see Gaskil), Amey and Asahel Elliot, int. Mar. 23, 1817.
Anna, d. of Ebenezer of Mendon, and Nehemiah Aldrich, s. of Jacob dec., 5th day, 6th mo. 1777. c.r.3.*
David of Mendon, and Phebe Brown, int. Jan. 7, 1776.
Elisebeth, d. of Sam[ue]ll of Mendon, and John Farnum, s. of Moses, 3d day, 3d mo., called May, 1750. c.r.3.*
Sarah, d. of Ebenezer and Hannah of Mendon, and Thomas Holder, s. of Daniel dec. of Lynn, and Hannah, 6th day, 11th mo. 1777. c.r.3.*

GATES, Louisa and Jonas Livermore, Apr. 19, 1827. c.r.1.
Mary and Alexander Havens (Jr., int.) of Warwick, R. I., Nov. 20, 1825. c.r.1.

GAULT, William (Capt., c.r.1) and (wid., int.) Anne Kelly, Apr. 17, 1831.

GEFFORD (see Gifford), Mehitebel and Jacob Aldrich, int. Oct. 16, 1769.

GIBSON, Cornelius and Patience Aldrich, Oct. 21, 1804.
John of Hopkinton, and Olive Green, Jan. 1, 1801.
Rebecca of Fitchburg, and Galen G. Lamb, int. July 16, 1837.
Richard B., s. of Richard and Ann of Ware, a. 20 y., and Susan A. Tripp, d. of David and Nancy, a. 19 y., Feb. 26, 1846.

* Intention not recorded.

GIFFORD (see Gefford), Ananias and Sarah S. Thayer of Douglas, int. Mar. 24, 1822.
Daniel and Amelia Langley, int. Mar. 19, 1848.
Elisabeth, d. of Annanias and David Mowry, 2d day, 5th mo., called May, 1771. c.r.3.*
Farnum and Robe Brown of Smithfield, R. I., int. Aug. 6, 1815.
Farnum and Mary Ann Tift (Taft, int.), Oct. —, 1834.
James W. and Uranah F. Gifford, int. Mar. 23, 1844.
Seth Jr. and Thankful Jeptherson, int. Feb. 28, 1816.
Uranah F. and James W. Gifford, int. Mar. 23, 1844.
Watee Ann, d. of Ananias, a. 17 y., and Alexander Thompson, s. of Elisha, a. 23 y., Apr. 10, 1845.

GILES, Thomas W. and Amarintha A. Persons, int. Dec. 2, 1849.

GILLMORE, Charles T. and Hannah S. Slade of Pawtucket, int. Aug. 9, 1829.

GLASES, Maria of Griswold, Conn., and Lewis Caput, int. Dec. 4, 1825.

GOLDTHWAIGHT (see · Goldthwait, Gouldthwait, Gouldthwight), Abigail of Northbridge, and John Allen, int. Nov. 8, 1778.

GOLDTHWAIT (see Goldthwaight, Gouldthwait, Gouldthwight) Abram W. and Agnes P. Pendleton of Mendon, int. Oct. 8, 1843.
Hannah and Alpheus Albee, int. Mar. 3, 1822.
Josiah M. and Cynthia Lackey of Sutton, int. June 18, 1837.
Obed of Northbridge, and Nancy Chapin, Dec. 7, 1809.
Zadock and Mary B. Brown, June 2, 1831.

GOODWIN, Sarah of Reading, and Thomas Rist, int. Sept. 1, 1739.

GORTON, Mary and David R. Wilcox, Oct. 10, 1839.

GOULD, Bershaba and Paris Hall, Sept. —, 1815.
Ezra of Douglas (Millbury, int.), and Amy Swasey, Sept 16, 1821.
Hannah of Sutton, and Josiah White, in Sutton, Nov. 14, 1765.
Parley and Betsey T. Chapin, Oct. 29, 1832.
Phebe and Foster Lewis, Apr. 16, 1835.

* Intention not recorded.

GOULDTHWAIT (see Goldthwaight, Goldthwait, Gouldthwight), Eunice and Thomas Legg, Feb. 4, 1768.*

GOULDTHWIGHT (see Goldthwaight, Goldthwait, Gouldthwait), Prince and Thankfull Sneal, int. Sept. 10, 1786.

GRANT, John and Rhoda Taft, int. Sept. 21, 1776.

GRAVES, Ebenezer of Marblehead, and Ruth B. Elkins, int. Jan. 5, 1845.

GREEN (see Greene), Albert of Blackstone, s. of Sarah A., a. 22 y., and Susan Fisher of Wrentham, d. of Hosea and Amanda, a. 20 y., Oct. 13, 1846.*
Anna of Coventry, R. I., and Isaac Jordan, int. Apr. 6, 1794.
Benja[min] Jr. and Polly Carpenter, int. June 27, 1779.
Hannah and George Wilson, July 25, 1833.
Henry and Ruth Farnum, in Mendon, Mar. 16, 1794.
Henry and Catharine Southerland of Upton, int. Dec. 6, 1829.
Israel and Saberry Whitman of North Providence, R. I., int. Nov. 1, 1807.
Marcy and Cummings Taft, June 2, 1796.
Margree and Josiah Taft, int. Mar. 2, 1777.
Maria and Andrew A. Williams, Sept. 23, 1824.
Mary of Mendon, and Josiah White, in Mendon, Jan. 26, 1769.
Olive and John Gibson of Hopkinton, Jan. 1, 1801.
Rachel and Eber Arnold of Gloucester, R. I., Dec. 30, 1790.
Reuben and Mary Taft, int. Oct. 25, 1829.
Samuel and Salley Oxx, Mar. 7, 1791.
Samuel H. and wid. Judith Taft [no date] (int. Jan. 19, 1834).
Silvia and Lewis Taft, Aug. 25, 1822.

GREENE (see Green), Merrill and Maria Seagrave, Nov. 28, 1833.
Molly and Dr. Timothy Wood, int. Mar. 30, 1806.

GREGORY, Jeremiah and Betsey I. McLellen of Grafton, int. Aug. 17, 1845.
John of Burrillville, R. I., s. of Daniel and Elizabeth, a. 21 y., and Louisa A. Fisher, d. of Josiah S. and Alma M., a. 17 y., Oct. 13, 1847.

GRIFFIN, Silas and Maria Martin of Douglas, int. Apr. 5, 1835.

* Intention not recorded.

GROUT, Cyrus and Sally Wood, July 15, 1810.
Dorinda W. and Moses T. Murdock, Sept. 9, 1832.
John (Capt., int.) and Nabby Richmond, Jan. 1, 1818.
Sally and Reuben Wood, Feb. 2, 1817.*
Waity A. (Waity Arnold, int.) and Abijah Kendal of Medford, Dec. 1, 1808.

GROVESNOR, David A., Rev., and Sally Whitney of Worcester, int. Apr. 5, 1835.

GUILD, Calvin of Hookset, N. H., and Margaret Taft, May 19, 1836.
Loring C. and Harriet (Harriet B., int.) Warner, Sept. 28, 1836.

GUNN, George, s. of Samuel and Mary, a. 27 y., and Mary E. Baylies, d. of Ephraim, a. 19 y., Sept. 5, 1844.

HACKET, Calvin B. and Hannah Aldrich of Douglas, int. Sept. 13, 1835.

HADEN, Lucy of Hopkinton, and John Emerson, int. Apr. 17, 1769.
Oliver of Grafton, and Sarah Wood, int. May 1, 1808.

HADLOCK, Deborah and Samuel Morss, Dec. 16, 1762.

HAGER, Ward B., s. of Abraham and Dolly of West Boylston, a. 19 y., and Charlotte M. Egan, d. of George and Charlotte of Pittston, Me., a. 18 y., Mar. 1, 1846.

HALE, Elisha and Mary Brown, Nov. 5, 1767.
Hannah C. of Northbridge, and Elery Holbrook, int. Apr. 7, 1831.
Robert of Douglas, and Marcy Craggin, June 28, 1804.
Salley of Douglas, and Charles Rawson, int. July 11, 1794.

HALL, Alva and Charlotte Carpenter, July 5, 1829.
Andrew and Maranda Hall, July 7, 1816. (Jan. 7, 1816. c.r.1.)
Baxter and Lydia Marsh, int. Dec. 3, 1780.
Benjamin, s. of John P., a. 21 y., and Caroline M. Brown, d. of Ephraim, a. 20 y., July 4, 1847.*
Chloe of Ashford, Conn., and David Aldrich, int. Feb. 8, 1807.
David and Deborah White, Apr. 28, 1785.
Edward and Lydia Brown of Leicester, in Leicester, Aug. 17, 1747.

* Intention not recorded.

HALL, Elijah and Louisa E. (Louisa Elizabeth, int.) Williams, Sept. 5, 1838.
Emeline W., d. of Isaac and Polly, a. 18 y., and John A. Aldrich of Worcester, s. of Joseph and Harriet, a. 21 y., Jan. 13, 1848.
Eunice and Reuben Ide Jr. of Douglas, June 6, 1821.
Eunice M., d. of Andrew and Miranda, a. 18 y., and Thomas Read of Southboro, s. of Noah and Lucy, a. 26 y., Sept. 5, 1849.
Fanny and Charles Thayer, June 25, 1837.
Hannah and Ezekiel Powers, Jan. 28, 1767.
Hannah and Solomon Smith, int. Feb. 15, 1790.
Hannah and Moses Perry of Worcester, Apr. 2, 1791.
Hannah F., d. of Isaac and Polly, a. 19 y., and Daniel Usher, Jr., s. of Daniel and Freelove, a. 22 y., Dec. 16, 1847.
Hezekiah and Deborah Daniels of Mendon, int. Nov. 2, 1749.
Joanna and William Miller of Cumberland, R. I., int. Feb. 8, 1791.
John and Catharine Taft, int. May 2, 1795.
Jonathan and Hepsebah Albee, May 29, 1793. C.R.I.
Lillie and Lyman Emerson, Nov. 18, 1789.
Louisa and Eli Bates of Mendon, int. July 30, 1848.
Maranda and Andrew Hall, July 7, 1816. (Jan. 7, 1816. C.R.I.)
Nehemiah and Sarah Hayward, Oct. 30, 1750.
Nehemiah (Jr., int.) and Hannah White, June 1, 1786.
Paris and Bersheba Gould, Sept. —, 1815.
Sabrina and John C. Brown of Smithfield, R. I., int. July 7, 1829.
Sally and David Fairbanks, Nov. 6, 1803.
Stephen of Sutton, and Sarah Read, int. Mar. 23, 1744–5.
Susan, b. in Temple, Me., d. of John P. and Ann, a. 23 y., and Joseph Usher, b. in Smithfield, R. I., s. of Daniel and Freelove, a. 25 y., Dec. 25, 1845.
Welcome of Cumberland, R. I., s. of Andrew and Maranda, a. 23 y., and Chloe A. Taft, d. of Samuel and Dorcas, a. 18 y., Nov. 27, 1845.
William and Martha Wood, int. June 6, 1789.
William (of Sutton, int.) and Joanna Spring [no date] (int. May 12, 1833).

HALLIDAY, Samuel B. (of New York, int.) and Mary W. Chapin, Mar. 21, 1833.

HAMER, Joseph and Elizabeth Baker of Smithfield, R. I., int. Oct. 22, 1815.

HAMILTON, Ezra of Brookfield, and Abigail Bacon, int. July 16, 1770.

HAMMON (see Hammond), Abigail of Swanzey, and Ichabod Keith, int. May 1, 1786.
Joseph Esq. of Swanzey, and Mary Fish, Oct. 21, 1784.

HAMMOND (see Hammon), Joel and Cynthia Fairbanks of Bellingham, int. July 11, 1844.
John C. of Douglas, s. of John and Nancy of Douglas, a. 20 y., and Lucy J. Thayer of Douglas, d. of Turner and Lydia of Douglas, a. 21 y., Feb. 9, 1846.*
Louisa and Lorenzo Davis, July 16, 1837.

HANDY, Almy and Nathan Cook of Gloucester, R. I., int. Sept. 26, 1802.
Avis of Gloucester, R. I., and Philetas Wheelock, int. Nov. 10, 1790.
Benedict A. and Caroline Dodd of Holden, int. June 13, 1830.
Benjamin 2d and Mary Peck of Smithfield, R. I., int. Aug. 10, 1817.
Caleb and Prudence White, int. May 12, 1796.
Ebenezer and Jemima Tefft of Smithfield, R. I., int. Feb. 4, 1764.
Ebenezer and Patiance Comstock of Gloucester, R. I., int. Oct. 10, 1794.
Elenor and John Baker of Scituate, R. I., int. Aug. 9, 1821.
Kezia and Simon Harris of Smithfield, R. I., int. Apr. 12, 1791.
Mary and Elisha Cook of Burrillville, R. I., int. Jan. 28, 1810.

HARBACK, Rufus A. (of Grafton, int.) and Susan S. Keith, Oct. 21 [1835].

HARRES (see Harris), Anna of Gloucester, R. I., and Joktan Putnam, int. Feb. 19, 1770.

HARRINGTON, Stephen N. and Charlotte S. Mellen of Thompson, Conn., int. Nov. 12, 1826.

HARRIS (see Harres), Almon and Charlotte Sage, int. Sept. 8, 1833.
Amaziah of Blackstone, Mendon, and Emily Howard, int. Mar. 12, 1843.
Amy and Alanson Mowry, int. Nov. 2, 1828.
Anna of Gloucester, R. I., and William Taft, int. Feb. 8, 1777.

* Intention not recorded.

HARRIS, David of Smithfield, R. I., and Abigail Farnum, int. Feb. 26, 1761.
John Jr. and Marcy Raymond of Gloucester, R. I., June 8, 1781.
Laura and Horatio Aldrich, int. Jan. 14, 1838.
Mary and Willard A. Mowry of Mendon, Mar. 23, 1843.
Molley and David Daley of Smithfield, R. I., int. July 6, 1772.
Nathan and Patty Blood of Charlton, int. Nov. 2, 1828.
Rachel and Isaac Chase, int. July 2, 1757.
Sarah and Ephraim Kympton, Jr., int. Mar. 18, 1777.
Simon of Smithfield, R. I., and Kezia Handy, int. Apr. 12, 1791.
Uranah of Smithfield, R. I., and Jonathan Farnum, int. Aug. 31, 1765.

HARRISON, Lydia of Cumberland, R. I., and George Holroyd, int. May 4, 1834.

HART, Ann E. and Robert Rogerson (2d, int.), Feb. 5, 1832.

HARVEY (see Hervey), Hannah and Daniel Man, Nov. 23, 1758.*
Sarah H. and Manning Wood, int. July 1, 1832.
Thankful H. and Willis Brown, Sept. 20, 1832.

HARWOOD, David Jr. of Sutton, and Sarah Crowningshield, int. Aug. 17, 1783.
Ebenezer and Margaret Willson of Killingly, Conn., int. Oct. 2, 1769.
John and Margaret Marvil, Dec. 4, 1755.
Mary and John Taft, Nov. 25, 1762.
Nathan and Huldah Banister of Brookfield, int. Feb. 16, 1760.
Peter and Mary Webb, Apr. 22, 1756.

HASKELL, Ann and Ephraim Taft [no date] (int. Mar. 17, 1833).
George and Deborah Comstock of Framingham, Mar. 10, 1828. c.r.1.*
W[illia]m and Betsey Tilley, Oct. 5, 1805.*
William and Amy Seagrave, Mar. 20, 1828. (Mar. 26, 1828. c.r.1.)

HASTINGS, Lemuel (Lemuel G., int.), s. of Nahum and Ann of West Boylston, a. 22 y., and Martha Ann Stone, d. of John S. and Emeline of Boston, a. 21 y., May 19, 1844.

HATHAWAY (see Hatherway), Henry M. of New Bedford, and Sarah Ann Congdon, Feb. 21, 1842.
Lucy of Sutton, and John Persons Jr., Nov. 4, 1813.

* Intention not recorded.

HATHERWAY (see Hathaway), Ezra and Elizabeth Aldrich, int. Feb. —, 1815.

HAVENS, Alexander (Jr., int.) of Warwick, R. I., and Mary Gates, Nov. 20, 1825. c.r.1.

HAWKINS, John of Providence, R. I., and Sarah Emerson, Nov. 29, 1764.

HAWS, Mehetabel of Cumberland, R. I., and Albert O. Ware, int. Apr. 26, 1835.

HAYNES, Lovisa and Maj. Artemas Keith, int. Aug. 28, 1831.

HAYWARD (see Haywood), Abigail of Sutton, and Edward Blanchar, int. Feb. 18, 1743-4.
Charles of Millbury, s. of Samuel and Sally of Hopkinton, a. 22 y., and Louisa A. Williams, d. of Levi and Mahitable of Newton, a. 22 y., Feb. 10, 1846.
Dependence of Mendon, and Esther Wood, Nov. 27, 1760.
Elisabeth of Bridgewater, and Edmund Rawson of Mendon, May 22, 1717.*
Elizabeth of Mendon, and Benjamin Thurston, in Mendon, Oct. 26, 1739.
Esther of Mendon, and Obadiah Wood, int. Jan. 27, 1732-3.
Experience of Mendon, and Obadiah Wood, in Mendon, Nov. 22, 1759.
Joseph of Mendon, and Ruth Jones, Dec. 28, 1749.
Ruth of Mendon, and Stephen Fish, Mar. 10, 1757.
Samuel (Howard, int.) of Mendon, and Rachel Rawson, Oct. 12, 1772.
Sarah and Nehemiah Hall, Oct. 30, 1750.
William of Mendon, and Kesiah Taft, in Mendon, Nov. 11, 1741.

HAYWOOD (see Hayward), Abigail and Ebenezer Bishop, int. Jan. 28, 1745-6.
Ruth and Alpheus Foster (of Sturbridge, int.), Apr. 22, 1811.

HAZARD, Abijah of South Kingston, R. I., and Elizabeth Croney, int. Jan. 9, 1797.
Eliza and William Leishuer of Mendon, int. Oct. 23, 1844.
Hannah and Olney Phillipps, int. Mar. 23, 1845.
Harriet L. and Dr. Henry Carpenter (Jr., int.) of Upton, June 1, 1841.
Rufus and Elethea Jonah, int. Jan. 22, 1843.
Samuel and Mrs. Mary Smith of Mendon, int. Jan. 21, 1849.

* Intention not recorded.

HAZLETINE, Marcy and Stephen Taft, Apr. 14, 1763.

HEATH, Calvin Butler, Rev., and Eliza T. Peck of Mendon, May 20, 1839.*
Nathan W. of Douglas, and Phebe H. Burgess, int. Feb. 27, 1831.

HEMENWAY, Jonas of Worcester, and Polly Croney, int. Jan. 10, 1797.

HENDRICK, Will[ia]m and Mary Pulsipher of Douglas, int. Dec. 4, 1803.

HENRY, Lydia of Northbridge, and William Lewis, in North Providence, R. I., Apr. 25, 1830.
Richard of Worcester, and Lucy G. Aldrich, Dec. 9, 1838.
Sarah A. of Grafton, d. of Samuel and Dorcas B., a. 22 y., and Samuel B. Parmenter of Worcester, s. of Jonas and Charlotte, a. 23 y., Nov. 25, 1847.*

HERLBUT, John and ——— Emerson, int. Dec. 1, 1759.

HERVEY (see Harvey), Hiram H. and Mary Tenney, Aug. 20, 1833.
Mary, Mrs., and Samuel Cumings, May 3, 1842.

HEWES (see Huse), Daniel (of Mendon, int.), and Abigail Holebrook, Aug. 30, 1747.
James of Gloucester, R. I., and Mary Taft, int. Aug. 6, 1785.

HEWET (see Hewett, Hewitt, Huet), William and Luvina (Lurana, int.) Larned, Jan. 17, 1802.

HEWETT (see Hewet, Hewitt, Huet), Dorcas and Joshua Knop Chase, Nov. 27, 1788.

HEWITT (see Hewet, Hewett, Huet), Hannah and Stephen Cole of Sutton, int. Aug. 8, 1785.

HIBBARD, Jonathan and Experance Warfield, Apr. 1, 1742.

HICKS, Augustus and Joanna Buxton, int. Jan. 16, 1820.
Jonathan of Batemans Precinct, Duchess County, N. Y., and Eunice Holbrook, int. Feb. 1, 1752–3.
Lydia of Sutton, and Stephen Williams, Oct. 16, 1766.
Nicholas and Lydia Cary, int. Jan. 2, 1741–2.

* Intention not recorded.

HILL, Caleb of New Sherborn, and Bathiah Taft of Mendon, int. Nov. 24, 1739.
Caleb and Hannah Adams, both of New Sherborn, Dec. 22, 1740.*
Halsey and Ophelia Branch, Apr. 9, 1826. c.r.1.
Hannah and James Dodge, int. Jan. 2, 1769.
Hannah and Moses Aldrich, int. Feb. 10, 1783.
Huldah, d. of David of Bellingham, and Samuel Aldrich, s. of Seth dec., 21st day, 1st -mo., called March, 1745. c.r.3.*
Job and Abigail Cook, Aug. 8, 1766.*
Juley of Grafton, and Ezekiel Johnson, int. Dec. 18, 1800.
Martha and John Pickett, Apr. 7, 1833.
Mary of Holliston, and Sam[ue]ll Thompson, int. Jan. 28, 1745-6.
Mary and John Aldrich, June 1, 1748.*
Matthew of Mendon, and Elisabeth Rice, Jan. 28, 1746-7.*
Nancy of Grafton, and George Washington Taft, int. July 17, 1803.
Paris of Savannah, Ga., and Sally Chapin, Aug. 21, 1827.
Paul D. and Angeline Rice of Sutton, Feb. 27, 1844.
Ruth and Rufus Chilson, in Mendon, Dec. 23, 1773.

HILLARD, Mehitable of Hadley, and William Thomson, Oct. 25, 1740.*

HIXON, Edwin and Martha M. (Arantha M., int.) Burnham, Oct. 13, 1839.
Edwin and Christina Whitehill, int. Nov. 16, 1845.

HODGES, Fanny of Norton, and Dr. Abijah Willards of Norton, int. Oct. 25, 1807.

HOIT, Laura and Genery Taft Jr. of Upton, int. Mar. 31, 1833.

HOLBROOK (see Holebrook), Abagail and Nathaniel Taft of Mendon, in Mendon, May 31, 1768.*
Abigail of Mendon, and Moses White, in Mendon, Dec. 12, 1749.
Abigail, wid., of Thompson, Conn., and Col. Joseph Chapin, int. May 23, 1802.
Allice and Jeremiah Thayer, Apr. 21, 1748.
Amariah and Keziah Nye of Douglas, in Douglas, Nov. 20, 1777.
Catharina and Daniel Holbrook of Mendon, Sept. 29, 1743.
Chloe and Jonathan F. Southwick, Nov. 14, 1822.
Daniel of Mendon, and Catharina Holbrook, Sept. 29, 1743.
Daniel and Joanna Benson of Mendon, Jan. 9, 1785.
Elery and Hannah C. Hale of Northbridge, int. Apr. 7, 1831.

* Intention not recorded.

HOLBROOK, Elvira of Milford, and Chauncy Aldrich, int. Feb. 21, 1841.
Eunice and Jonathan Hicks of Batemans Precinct, Duchess County, N. Y., int. Feb. 1, 1752-3.
Eunice and Moses Benson of Mendon, May 26, 1753.
Ezra of Townsend, and Mehetable Tyler, Nov. 18, 1771.
Hannah of Mendon, and John Kempton, int. May 27, 1771.
Hannah of Smithfield, R. I., and Percival Taylor, in West Boylston, June 13, 1838.
Hannah C., wid., d. of Robert and Mary Hale, a. 42 y., and Charles J. Stratford, widr., of Webster, s. of Samuel and Lucy, a. 53 y., May 1, 1849.
Henry and Barbara Thayer of Mendon, in Mendon, Sept. 22, 1791.
Henry and Nelly Albee, int. Nov. 15, 1812.
Isaac and Mary Armstrong (resident of Mendon, int.), Oct. 28, 1750.
John and Zilpah Thayer of Mendon, in Mendon, Mar. 11, 1732 (int. Jan. 13, 1742-3).
John and Lydia Holbrook of Bellingham, in Mendon, Jan. 13, 1762.
John and Rhoda Thayer of Mendon, in Mendon, Dec. 6, 1770.
John and Hannah Prince of Swansea, int. Apr. 13, 1797.
Jonathan and Abigail Benson of Mendon, int. Nov. 23, 1783.
Josiah and Bethiah Boyce, Mar. 28, 1744.
Keziah and Daniel Twitchel, July 12, 1742.
Lucy and Abner Adams of Sutton, Nov. 4, 1795.
Lydia of Bellingham, and John Holbrook, in Mendon, Jan. 13, 1762.
Margarett and Thaddeus Thayer of Douglas, int. May 24, 1778.
Mary and Benjamin Archer, Mar. 15, 1759.
Mary and Lieut. John Benson of Mendon, int. Sept. 17, 1780.
Micah and Rhoda Thayer (of Douglas, int.), Nov. 27, 1766.
Micah and Mary Thompson of Smithfield, R. I., int. May 30, 1779.
Moses and Anna Craggin, both of Mendon, Mar. 20, 1794.*
Naomi and Benj[ami]n Taft, Jan. 4, 1753.
Otis and Leah Willson of Mendon, int. May 20, 1810.
Peter and Lydia Darling of Mendon, in Mendon, May 27, 1761.
Phebe of Douglas, and Keith Taft, int. June 18, 1790.
Rachal and Jonathan Staples of Mendon, int. Dec. 29, 1777.
Rachel and Foster Verry of Mendon, int. Apr. 25, 1810.
Rachel C. of Sturbridge, and Joseph D. Seagrave, int. Oct. 10, 1847.

* Intention not recorded.

HOLBROOK, Rhoda and Nathan Wood, int. July 22, 1771.
Ruth and Benoni Benson of Mendon, in Mendon, Dec. 6, 1770.
Ruth and John Thwing of District of Conway, Oct. 6, 1771.
Sarah and Aaron White, int. Apr. 19, 1738.
Sarah and Peter Thayer of Mendon, in Mendon, June 12, 1740.
Seth and Susanna Dalrumple of Northbridge, May 24, 1774.
Silance and Timothy McNamarrah, Feb. 2, 1759.
Silence and Thadeous Taft, int. Apr. 8, 1777.
Silvanus and Thankful Thayer of Mendon, in Mendon, Oct. 25, 1748.
Silvenes and Molley Thayer, int. Jan. 20, 1772.
Stephen and Hopa Albee, Sept. 11, 1788.
Stephen Jr. of Bellingham, and Mary Penniman, int. July 30, 1790.
Thankful and David Legg, Apr. 4, 1802.
Wilder and Tyla Buffum of Smithfield, R. I., int. Apr. 12, 1818.
Willard, Ens., and Allis M. Cumstock of Burrillville, R. I., int. July 7, 1822.

HOLDER, Thomas, s. of Daniel dec. of Lynn, and Hannah, and Sarah Gaskill, d. of Ebenezer and Hannah of Mendon, 6th day, 11th mo. 1777. C.R.3.*

HOLEBROOK (see Holbrook), Abigail and Daniel Hewes (of Mendon, int.), Aug. 30, 1747.
Alice and Elijah Ward, Sept. 16, 1762.
Mary and Josiah Brown, Dec. 10, 1744.

HOLLON, Mary of Mendon, and Joseph Rasey, in Mendon, May 6, 1757.

HOLMAN, Elijah of Millbury, and Experience Taft, Oct. 25, 1820.
Jonathan of Sutton, and Hannah Siblay, Nov. 3, 1763.

HOLROYD, George and Lydia Harrison of Cumberland, R. I., int. May 4, 1834.
Mary Ann of Pawtuxet, R. I., and Capt. Otis Taft, int. Oct. 15, 1818.
Mary A. and Angel Sweet of Upton, Apr. 28, 1825. C.R.1.
W[illia]m of Providence, R. I., and Patience Tillinghast, Nov. 28, 1805.

HOOPPER, David and Deborah Taft of Killingly, Conn., int. May 31, 1778.

* Intention not recorded.

HOOTON (see Houghton), Charlotte P. and Elkanah Taft, int. Feb. 12, 1843.

HOPCINS (see Hopkins), Susan[n]ah and Edward Martin, Apr. 4, 1765.

HOPKINS (see Hopcins), John and Sarah Bonham, Oct. 13, 1771.

HORN, Mary Jane and Daniel Warner, Mar. 17, 1833.

HORTON, Asa of Danby, and Ruth Corrary, int. Apr. 18, 1789.

HOUGHTON (see Hooton), Abel and Mary Ann Packard, May 21, 1838.
Susanna of Sutton, and Benja[min] Cogswell, int. May 31, 1778.

HOW (see Howe), Joseph of Sutton, and Mehetible Darling, Apr. 12, 1770.

HOWARD, Alanson of New York City, and Ruth K. Whitney, Apr. 24, 1838.
Amasa L. and Sophia Aldrich, both of Northbridge, Jan. 1, 1824.*
Clarrisa I. T. and William Burling, int. Nov. 13, 1831.
Emily and Amaziah Harris of Blackstone, Mendon, int. Mar. 12, 1843.
James of Upton, and Marinda Aldrich, Apr. 13, 1813.
Julia Ann and Joseph Carpenter, int. Oct. 25, 1829.
Polly and James T. Sweet, both of Northbridge, Mar. 11, 1833.*
Rhoda of Mendon, and James Black, int. Sept. 28, 1772.
Tyler of Northbridge, and Mary T. Carpenter, July 21, 1841.
William of Framingham, s. of William and Susannah of Canton, a. 27 y., and Louisa B. Fessenden, d. of Isaac and Olive, a. 19 y., Jan. 27, 1845.

HOWE (see How), Zara and Miranda White, Oct. 14, 1822.

HOWLAND, Phebe of Douglas, and John W. Thompson, int. July 24, 1825.
Sarah and Aaron White, Nov. 29, 1838.
Stephen and Hannah Aldrich, both of Douglas, May 3, 1809.*

HOYLE, Mary Ann and Daniel Barrett, int. Aug. 23, 1835.

HUDSON, Samuel and Catharine F. Bates of Blackstone, int. Feb. 18, 1849.

* Intention not recorded.

HUET (see Hewet, Hewett, Hewitt), Alanson and Brooksey Sprague, int. Mar. 6, 1831.

HUGS, Samuel and wid. Maria Robinson, int. July 13, 1845.

HULL, Deborah, wid., and Benjamin Archer, May 8, 1766.
James and Rebecca Draper, Sept. 15, 1766.
James and Anna Putnam of Sutton, int. Apr. 21, 1777.
John and Martha Terry (Torry, int.), Oct. 25, 1773.
Lucy and Obadiah Brown, Mar. 5, 1761.
Martha and David Draper Jr., Feb. 15, 1770.
Mary and Joel Rawson, Feb. 17, 1763.
Mary and Simeon Lee of Douglas, May 24, 1798.
Sarah and Edmund Rawson, int. July 10, 1770.

HUMES, Elisabeth and John Alger of Rehoboth, int. June 20, 1773.
Experiance and Samuel Taft, Jan. 9, 1786.
Jonna and Israel Chilson, int. Mar. 3, 1755.
Josiah and Lydia Wallis, Dec. 7, 1767.*
Nicholas and Dorcas Williams of New Sherborn, Mar. 28, 1744.
Rachel and Jerimiah Chilson of Gloucester, R. I., int. Oct. 13, 1755.
Richard and Sarah Williams, Mar. 14, 1750–1.
Richard and Keziah Marsh of Douglas, int. Oct. 29, 1757.
Samuel and Marthay Thayer of New Sherborn, Dec. 7, 1743.*
Samuel Jr. and Marcy Thompson, both of Douglas, Apr. 5, 1769.*
Thomas and Silance Read, int. Mar. 1, 1773.

HUNT, John and Ann Peck, Feb. 26, 1753.
John and Martha Bellows (Belles, int.), Mar. 17, 1757.
Juda of Northbridge, and Stephen Trask, in Northbridge, Aug. 2, 1785.
Julia A. of Springfield, and Adolphus S. Ellison, int. Sept. 15, 1839.
Levina and Seth Wheelock of Gloucester, R. I., Feb. 17, 1796.
Miranda A. (Miranda Angenette, int.), d. of Demas and Nancy Ann, a. 24 y., and Job Pitts of Blackstone, s. of Esek and Abigail, a. 31 y., May 18, 1847.
Otis and Sarah Taft, Feb. 20, 1796.
Sarah and Christopher Ambley, int. Aug. 11, 1805.
Washington of Burrillville, R. I., and Mehittabelle Taft, Aug. 17, 1809.
William and Esther Trask, in Douglas, Dec. 13, 1787.

* Intention not recorded.

HUSE (see Hewes), Alfred and Abigail Keith, Aug. 16, 1798.
Sarah Taft and Morris Lee of Oxford, Apr. 2, 1823.*
Silvia and Aaron Marsh of Douglas, Dec. 25, 1822.

HYDE, Charles and Abby Jane Richards of Burrillville, R. I., int. May 18, 1845.

HYLORD, John (Hillyard, int.) and Mehetabel Thomson, Feb. 14, 1765.

IDE, Reuben Jr. of Douglas, and Eunice Hall, June 6, 1821.

INGERSOLL, James D. (James Dalton, c.r.1), Capt., of Boston, and Sally Brastow, Aug. 20, 1807.

INGLY, Betsey, Mrs., of Franklin, and Samuel Alexander, int. Dec. 13, 1840.

INMAN, Alpheus and Sylvia Swift, int. Mar. 2, 1817.
Arnold of Douglas, and Anna Lesure, Dec. 11, 1814.
Athalina of Burrillville, R. I., and Elisha A. Southwick, int. Nov. 14, 1830.
Elisha and Mary Adams, Jan. 23, 1843.
Harkless of Seekonk, and Joanna B. Rawson, int. Jan. 13, 1828.
Lucretia and Jesse Bolster, int. Apr. 15, 1811.
Nancy and Jesse Bolster, int. Mar. 24, 1816.
Polly P., Mrs., of Blackstone, and Alpheus Foster, int. May 17, 1846.
Sarah and Sweeting Taft, Nov. 25, 1829.
Thankful Smith and Isaac Bolster Jr., int. March and April, 1811.

JACKSON, Francis of Mt. Washington, Ky., s. of Isaac and Betsey, a. 36 y., and Mary A. C. Riedel, d. of George C. and Amy S., a. 27 y., Sept. 22, 1845.
Joseph (of Mendon, int.) and Bathsheba Thayer of Mendon (of Uxbridge, int.), May 8, 1760.

JACOBS, Benjamin and Sophia Wood, Oct. 8, 1820.
Hannah and Andrus Brown, int. Jan. 1, 1819.
Hulday and Daniel Read of Northbridge, June 16, 1799.
Martha and David Walker of New Salem, May 28, 1812.
William and Harriet Swasey, Apr. 2, 1823.

JAHA, Rebecca and Bezaleel Willard, int. Mar. 21, 1841.

JANS, Eunice Selinda of Brimfield, and Jonathan Emerson, int. Mar. 23, 1834.

* Intention not recorded.

JEFFERSON (see Jeperson, Jepherson, Jepsson, Jeptherson), Laura A., d. of Royal and Harriet, a. 19 y., and Daniel Pratt, s. of Caleb and Sarah W. of Boston, a. 27 y., Nov. 22, 1847.

JENCKES (see Jencks), Job of Wrentham, and Sarah Aldrich, Sept. 4, 1794.

JENCKS (see Jenckes), Albert of Cumberland, R. I., and Almira Cook, Feb. 17, 1831.
Mary L. and Brigham Fuller of East Douglas, int. Feb. 26, 1837.
Nelson of Cumberland, R. I., and Deborah W. (Deborah Wheelock, c.r.1) Morse, Jan. 1, 1822.

JENNE, Seth and Abigail Aldrich, int. Mar. 14, 1768.

JENNISON, William and Barbara Ramsdil of Mendon, int. Nov. 18, 1799.

JEPERSON (see Jefferson, Jepherson, Jepsson, Jeptherson), Hannah of New Sherborn, and Samuel Taft, Apr. 12, 1739.
Thomas of New Sherborn, and Deborah Aldrich, int. Sept. 5, 1745 (May 26, 1744 dup.).

JEPHERSON (see Jefferson, Jeperson, Jepsson, Jeptherson), Adolphus and Permila Tucker, Mar. 26, 1826.
Asenath of Douglas, and Aaron Cook, int. Jan. 3, 1802.
Henrietta and David Taft, in Mendon [no date] (int. Apr. 7, 1833).
Jedediah and Susanna Emerson, int. Oct. 28, 1781.
John of Gloucester, R. I., and Mary Morse, int. Oct. 6, 1787.
Joseph of Killingly, Conn., and Ruth Emerson, int. Mar. 14, 1779.
Mary and Nathaniel Emerson, Apr. 15, 1762.*
Mary and Otis Wilcox, Apr. 29, 1828.
Mary Jane and Barnabas A. Rawson, Nov. 25, 1841.
Otis and Eliza D. Conant of Harvard, int. Apr. 21, 1822.
Phila and Walter Brown of Oxford, int. Jan. 20, 1811.
Rachel and Joseph Thayer, Oct. 11, 1764.*
Reuben and Mary Joslen of Gloucester, R. I., int. Apr. 15, 1781.
Reuben and Polly Mowry, July 13, 1809.
Royal and Harriet B. Jones of Winchendon, int. June 8, 1828.

JEPSSON (see Jefferson, Jeperson, Jepherson, Jeptherson), William and Sarah Thayer, both of New Sherborn, int. Aug. 1, 1740.

* Intention not recorded.

JEPTHERSON (see Jefferson, Jeperson, Jepherson, Jepsson), Thankful and Seth Gifford Jr., int. Feb. 28, 1816.

JESSEMAN, George and Jemima Wood, Dec. 5, 1765.

JILLSON (see Jilson), Stephen C. and Mary A. Taft of Mendon, int. Jan. 24, 1847.

JILSON (see Jillson), Levin and Chloe Ballou, int. Jan. 24, 1802.

JOHNSON (see Jonson), Betsy and Garshom Chapen of Mendon, Mar. 9, 1758.
Clarisa S. and Arnold Lee, int. Jan. 21, 1821.
Eliseb[e]th and John Seagrave, int. Dec. 30, 1757.
Ezekiel and Juley Hill of Grafton, int. Dec. 18, 1800.
Hannah and Samuel Pond of Wrentham, Jan. 10, 1753.
John Jr. and Mrs. Allice Ennis, int. Dec. 2, 1849.
Mary and Joshua Taft of Mendon, in Mendon, Apr. 24, 1757.
William and Huldah Aldrich, in Mendon, June 16, 1731.*
William and Lucy Drew of Dedham, int. June 8, 1834.
William B. and Mary E. Barnes of Smithfield, R. I., int. July 28, 1839.

JONAH, Elethea and Rufus Hazard, int. Jan. 22, 1843.

JONES, Bezleel of Mendon, and Mary Nuttin, Feb. 28, 1759.
Elisabeth of Mendon, and Solomon Aldrich, int. May 31, 1756.
Harriet B. of Winchendon, and Royal Jepherson, int. June 8, 1828.
Henrietta of Lunenburg, and Joseph S. Ellis, int. Mar. 20, 1836.
Leucy and Edward Rawson, int. Dec. 11, 1795.
Mary and William Brown, Nov. 25, 1760.
Nancy and Paul Persons, Feb. 2, 1803.
Ruth and Joseph Hayward of Mendon, Dec. 28, 1749.
Sybel L., d. of John and Sylvia of Newton, a. 21 y., and Edwin R. Knapp, s. of William M. and Eunice P., a. 24 y., Aug. 19, 1845.
Thankfull and Bezaleel Snell, int. May 2, 1779.

JONSON (see Johnson), John and Sarah White, both of Providence, R. I., Dec. 29, 1729.*

JORDAN, Elisabeth of Rehoboth, County of Bristol, and Dr. Samuel Read, int. Aug. 6, 1749.
Isaac and Anna Green of Coventry, R. I., int. Apr. 6, 1794.

* Intention not recorded.

JOSLEN, Mary of Gloucester, R. I., and Reuben Jepherson, int. Apr. 15, 1781.
Thomas of Smithfield, R. I., and Sarah Taft, int. Jan. 26, 1767.

JUDSON, Samuel, Rev., and Sally Bartlett of Salem, in Salem, May 28, 1797.
Sarah and Rev. Albert Cole of Bluehill, Me., May 9, 1838.
Willard and Mary Chapin, int. Mar. 9, 1828.

KEATH (see Keith), Gershom, s. of Gershom and Lydia Darling, d. of Daniel of Mendon, Nov. 9, 1775.
Hannah and Joseph Taft, 3d, Feb. —, 1773.

KEECH, Calista of Burrillville, R. I., and Whipple Walling of Providence, R. I., May 15, 1843.*

KEITH (see Keath), Aaron and Anna Chase, May 1, 1799.
Ab[b]y and Benjamin Pyke (Pike, int.), Feb. 21, 1765.
Abigail and John Bolster, June 2, 1752.
Abigail and Alfred Huse, Aug. 16, 1798.
Abigail and Anderson Scott of Bellingham, Jan. 17, 1806.
Abigal and Moses White, int. Mar. 4, 1748-9.
Abijah and Polly Legg, int. Apr. 20, 1791.
Amelia of Smithfield, R. I., and Henry Deirk, int. Mar. 1, 1846.
Artemas and Hannah Aldrich, int. Oct. 14, 1796.
Artemas, Maj., and Lovisa Haynes, int. Aug. 28, 1831.
Asahel and Sarah Mowry, Apr. 28, 1818.
Chapin and Elisabeth Taft, June 26, 1790 (June 24 dup.).
Chloe and Nathan Bolster, int. Dec. 23, 1781.
Comfort and Deborah Nelson of Mendon, in Mendon, Oct. 31, 1765.
Comfort and Gerusha Aldrich of Mendon, int. Mar. 3, 1776.
David and Ruth Bacon of Sutton, in Sutton, Nov. 5, 1765.
Deborah and Lyman Rawson of Townsend, int. Oct. 19, 1794.
Deborah and Luther Taft, Oct. 16, 1803.*
Deborah and Beala Thayer, both of Mendon, Oct. 4, 1838.*
Dorcas of Ward, and Samuel Taft 2d, int. Nov. 21, 1824.
Eleazer of Thompson, Conn., and Kilita Tyler, Oct. 8, 1801.
Garshom and Susanna Wiley, int. Aug. 17, 1765.
Gershom and Deborah Smith, int. May 31, 1794.
Gershom Jr. and Sarah Southwick, int. July 17, 1803.
Hannah and Thomas Shove, int. Nov. 29, 1787.
Henery and Hannah Wheelock of Gloucester, R. I., int. Sept. 27, 1760.
Henery and Hanna[h] Cummings, Jan. 16, 1766.

* Intention not recorded.

KEITH, Ichabod and Abigail Fish, Apr. 1, 1783.
Ichabod and Abigail Hammon of Swanzey, int. May 1, 1786.
Israel and Elizabeth Thayer, both living at New Sherborn, int. May 13, 1741.
James and Comfort Thayer, May 17, 1722.*
James and Lydia Brown, Oct. 30, 1765.
Jemima and Seth White, int. May 23, 1779.
John M. and Mary Ann Whipple of Pelham, int. Sept. 1, 1833.
Jonathan Russell and Sally Page of New Marlborough, N. H., int. June 15, 1811.
Joseph C. and Mary Adams, Oct. 19, 1836.
Julia M. and Rufus Fuller of Cumberland, R. I., July 31, 1836.
Lydia B. of Milford, and William Sprague, int. June 15, 1834.
Lyman of Northbridge, s. of Lyman and Chloe, a. 28 y., and Lydia Bowen, d. of Benjamin and Nancy, a. 23 y., Oct. 17, 1846.*
Margret and Noah Taft, Nov. 23, 1752.
Mary and Thomas Farnum, May 31, 1749.
Mary (the younger, int.) and Joseph Daniel Jr. of Needham, in Needham, Nov. 27, 1777.
Mary of Killingly, Conn., and Peter Sibley, int. Sept. 3, 1780.
Meriam and Jacob Converse Jr. of Thompson, Conn., in Northbridge, Apr. 12, 1792.
Molly and Elisha Thayer of Douglas, int. May 16, 1812.
Moses and Mary Cumings, Jan. 22, 1767.
Nathan and Abigail Albee of Mendon, in Mendon, Oct. 7, 1762.
Nathan (Lieut. int.) and Phebe Wheelock of Mendon, in Mendon, Jan. 10, 1788.
Nathiel W. and Deborah L. Freeman of Lowell, int. Mar. 26, 1837.
Nellson and Chloe Brown of Mendon, int. Feb. 25, 1806.
Noah and Deborah Taft of Mendon, int. Aug. 3, 1745.
Noah and Mary Legg of Mendon, in Mendon, June 13, 1771.
Peter and Hannah Taft, Aug. 11, 1748.
Pheeby and John Curtice of Dudley, Apr. 19, 1770.
Rachel and Joseph Rist, Dec. 18, 1766.
Rhoda and Amos Aldrich of Douglas, int. June 11, 1788.
Ruth and Willis Aldrich, June 20, 1799.
Silance and Joseph Damon, int. Sept. 28, 1772.
Simeon and Rebeckah Leland of Grafton, int. Apr. 11, 1764.
Susan and Ezra Taft, Mar. 20, 1823.
Susan S. and Rufus A. Harback (of Grafton, int.), Oct. 21 [1835].
Susan[n]a and Abner Rawson, int. Nov. 17, 1744.
Susanna and Nathaniel Fish, Dec. 2, 1746.

* Intention not recorded.

KEITH, Susannah and Jesse Aldrich, Dec. 30, 1793.
Sylvia and S. W. (W. S., int.) Braman, Oct. 28, 1840.
Uraniah and Charles A. Thwing, Oct. 5, 1828.
Wealthy and Henry T. Beaman, May 17, 1836.
Wellington and Almeda B. Preston of Cumberland, R. I., int. Aug. 23, 1846.
William E. and Harriet Treadway of Salem, Conn., int. July 26, 1846.

KELLEY (see Kelly, Killy), Manariah and Abigail Estey (of Mendon, int.), Jan. 7, 1837.
Olive C. and Albert L. Cook, both of Bellingham, Nov. 13, 1839.*
Willis of Mendon, and Dordana Capron, int. Nov. 21, 1795.

KELLY (see Kelley, Killy), Anne (wid., int.) and (Capt., c.r.1) William Gault of Oakham, Apr. 17, 1831.
Lettice, d. of Seth of Mendon and Molly, and Jonathan Farnum, s. of David dec. and Leah, 5th day, 2d mo. 1789. c.r.3.*

KEMPTON (see Kimpton, Kimton, Kympton, Kymton), Eben of Mendon, and Amy Farnum, int. Aug. 2, 1829.
George 2d and Hannah Andrew of Douglas, int. Sept. 12, 1824.
George and Sally Bennet of Douglas, int. Mar. 7, 1830.
Harriet and Amos C. Allen of North Kingston, int. May 28, 1843.
John and Hannah Holbrook of Mendon, int. May 27, 1771.
Mary and Daniel Buffum of Douglas, Apr. 4, 1839.
Samuel and Katherina Aldrich, int. Feb. 21, 1777.

KENDAL, Abijah of Medford, and Waity A. (Waity Arnold, int.) Grout, Dec. 1, 1808.

KENNEY (see Kenny), Hannah F. and John Whiting, int. Jan. 9, 1831.

KENNY (see Kenney), Isreal of Grafton, and Sibbel Lealand, int. Oct. 24, 1761.

KEYES, Abijah and Jane Aldrich, June 8, 1769.
Betsy and John Aldrich Jr. of Northbridge, Jan. 1, 1821.
Olive W. and William Minot, Nov. 4, 1824. c.r.1.*
Oren of Northbridge, and Louis Seagrave, Sept. 7, 1783.
Permela and Reuben Coombs (Jr., c.r.1) of Holden, June 28, 1815.
Sally (Sarah B. int.) and Judson Taft, Nov. 12, 1816.

* Intention not recorded.

KIBBEY, Abigail of Medway, and Timothy Madden, in Medway, Nov. 10, 1768.

KIDDER, Ezra of Alsted, N. H., and Calista Taft, Sept. 9, 1806.

KILBURN, Marcy and Asa Rawson, int. Feb. 22, 1801.

KILLY (see Kelley, Kelly), Thomas and Abigail Chace, June 23, 1782.*

KIMBAL (see Kimball), Joab of Peacham, and Betsey Read of Danville, Vt., Jan. 23, 1799.*

KIMBALL (see Kimbal), Relief of Milford, and Phinehas Taft, int. Mar. —, 1808.

KIMPTON (see Kempton, Kimton, Kympton, Kymton), Daniel and Mary Darling of Mendon, int. May 6, 1811.
Ephraim and Hannah Battles (of Mendon, int.), Nov. 18, 1761.
Ezra and Data Darling of Cumberland, R. I., int. Nov. 12, 1798.
Hannah and Nathan Twichel, Dec. 18, 1766.
John and Susannah Washburn of Mendon, in Mendon, Dec. 1, 1768.
Sarah of Gloucester, R. I., and Nathan Taft Jr., int. Aug. 25, 1798.
Stephen and Katherine Boyce of Mendon, in Mendon, Apr. 15, 1762.
Stephen and Polly Benson of Mendon, int. Dec. 21, 1799.
Susanah and Champlin Round, int. May 9, 1824.

KIMTON (see Kempton, Kimpton, Kympton, Kymton), Ephraim (Kympton, int.), and Abigail Bolstar, Oct. 29, 1740.
Ruth and Edward Battles of Mendon, Nov. 26, 1766.
Sarah and Benjamin Blake, May 8, 1760.

KINCUM (see Kinnicum), Sarah G. and Charles Bowen, int. Dec. 10, 1843.

KING, Isaac and Rosalinda Stockwell of Sutton, int. Sept. 14, 1845.

KINGSBURY, Ephraim of Oxford, and Abigail Taft, Aug. 14, 1814.
Polly and Alanson Taft, int. Oct. 13, 1822.

KINNICUM (see Kincum), Sarah Ann and Samuel Davis, Dec. 10, 1838.

* Intention not recorded.

KNAP (see Knapp, Knop, Kop), Hannah (Knop, int.) and Thomas Chace, Jan. 15, 1766.
Joshua and Anne Daniels of Mendon, in Mendon, Mar. 17, 1729–30.*
Rufus of Douglas, and Mary (Polley, int.) Baylies, Oct. 16, 1794. C.R.1.

KNAPP (see Knap, Knop, Kop), Edwin R., s. of William M. and Eunice P., a. 24 y., and Sybel L. Jones, d. of John and Sylvia of Newton, a. 21 y., Aug. 19, 1845.
Harriet D., d. of William and Eunice of Mendon, a. 21 y., and George W. Sprague, s. of Daniel and Eveline, a. 22 y., July 22, 1846.

KNIGHT, William and Minerva Thwing, Oct. 22, 1839.*

KNOP (see Knap, Knapp, Kop), James and Ede Chase, int. Mar. 16, 1772.
Ruth of Douglas, and Ezra Whitney Esq., int. Nov. 8, 1795.

KNOWLTON, Freeman and Hannah Murphy, both of Northbridge, Oct. 9, 1825.*
Hannah of Wrentham, and John Shearlock, in Smithfield, R. I., Jan. 1, 1760.

KOP (see Knap, Knapp, Knop), Joshua (Knap, int.) and Hannah Chase of Sutton, Sept. 26, 1732.

KYMPTON (see Kempton, Kimpton, Kimton, Kymton), Bethiah and Prince Nye of Douglas, int. Dec. 19, 1777.
Ephraim Jr. and Sarah Harris, int. Mar. 18, 1777.

KYMTON (see Kempton, Kimpton, Kimton, Kympton), George and Deliverance Nye of Douglas, in Douglas, Mar. 13, 1775.

LACKEY, Catharine, d. of Joel and Arispa, a. 19 y., and Moses W. Chapin, s. of Stephen and Julia E., a. 19 y., Feb. 1, 1849.
Cynthia of Sutton, and Josiah M. Goldthwait, int. June 18, 1837.
Warren and Susan C. Stowe, Nov. 24, 1842.

LAKE, James G. and Susan A. Pierce of Cumberland, R. I., int. Oct. 24, 1844.

* Intention not recorded.

LAMB, Diantha and Luke A. Meriam, int. Mar. 23, 1845.
Emery, s. of Jesse and Mary, a. 23 y., and Phebe Ann Richmond, d. of Edward and Mercy, a. 21 y., May 16, 1844.
Galen G. and Rebecca Gibson of Fitchburg, int. July 16, 1837.

LANE, Harriet N. and Marcisus E. Burrill, int. Oct. 5, 1834.

LANGLEY, Amelia and Daniel Gifford, int. Mar. 19, 1848.

LAPHAM, Amey of Gloucester, R. I., and Simon White, int. Mar. 17, 1805.
Maranda of Burrillville, R: I., and Joseph Southwick, int. Nov. 26, 1820.
Patience of Burrillville, R. I., and Arold Southwick, int. Feb. 11, 1827.

LARNED (see Learned), Dulcinia and Martin Aldrich, Mar. 24, 1836.
Jeremiah of Sutton, and Sally Aldrich, Oct. 25, 1810.
Luvina (Lurana, int.) and William Hewet, Jan. 17, 1802.

LASHURE (see Lasure, Leishuer, Leshuer, Leshure, Lesuer, Lesure), Sally and Nathan Starnes of Douglas, int. April, May, 1809.

LASURE (see Lashure, Leishuer, Leshuer, Leshure, Lesuer, Lesure), Amos and Sarah Persons, Feb. 22, 1807.
Eunice and Benjamin Lee, Aug. 7, 1806.
Ruth and Seth Aldrich Jr. of Douglas, int. Feb. 24, 1811.
Thomas of Smithfield, R. I., and Anna Murdock, int. July 15, 1810.

LATHROP, Mary of Canterbury, and George E. Willard, in Westminster, Conn., Apr. 16, 1837.

LAW, Sally, wid., and James M. Taft, int. June 21, 1829.

LAWLER, James and Mrs. Sally Taft, Dec. 4, 1830.

LAWRANCE (see Lawrence), Harriet N., d. of Chandler, a. 20 y., and Daniel C. Mowry, s. of Israel and Phyla, a. 21 y., Aug. 13, 1846.
Mary of Holliston, and Nathan Morss, int. June 22, 1753.
Sarah of Millbury, d. of Thomas, a. 23 y., and Brigham Morse of Douglas, s. of Ezra and Zilpha, a. 24 y., Aug. 13, 1846.*

LAWRENCE (see Lawrance), David and Lucy Moore of Somersworth, N. H., int. Sept. 18, 1831.
Susan R. and John Usher, int. Jan. 25, 1846.

* Intention not recorded.

LEALAND (see Leland), Sibbel and Isreal Kenney of Grafton, int. Oct. 24, 1761.

LEARNED (see Larned), Mary and Judson Day of Sutton, Mar. 20, 1834.
Pitts A. and Cynthia Craggin, both of Sutton, Aug. 1, 1838.*

LEATHE, Asa of Grafton, and Priscilla Rawson, int. July 15, 1786.

LEAVANS (see Levens), Keziah Ann and Brown Richardson, Mar. 5, 1835.

LEDWICK, Sarah and James Tancred, int. Nov. 10, 1847.

LEE, Arnold and Clarisa S. Johnson, int. Jan. 21, 1821.
Benjamin and Sarah Wood, Oct. 17, 1759.
Benjamin and Eunice Lasure, Aug. 7, 1806.
Briggs and Ruth Arnold, int. Aug. 24, 1823.
Briggs and Mrs. Mary Ann Aldrich, Mar. 29, 1836.
Cynthia and Asa Spooner, int. May 8, 1825.
Ephraim of Mendon, and Nancy Nichols, int. Oct. 8, 1826.
John of Smithfield, R. I., and Lydia Lee, int. Oct. 12, 1828.
Lydia and John Lee of Smithfield, R. I., int. Oct. 12, 1828.
Morris of Oxford, and Sarah Taft Huse, Apr. 2, 1823.*
Newell and Clarra C. (Clara Caroline, int.) Carpenter, Sept. 10, 1822.
Samuel and Anna Trask, int. Dec. 3, 1820.
Simeon of Douglas, and Mary Hull, May 24, 1798.
Welcome and Percis Nye of Sutton, int. Sept. 29, 1833.
William of Douglas, and Mary Wood, int. Sept. 3, 1791.
William and Louisa M. Taft, int. May 15, 1836.

LEGG, Abigail and John Sterns of Milford, Mar. 27, 1822.
Abijah and Lois Chapin, Dec. 5, 1790.
Almira (Elmira, int.) and Stephen Taft, Dec. 2, 1819.
Amy of Mendon, and William Wood, int. May 5, 1839.
David of Mendon, and Comfort White, int. June 18, 1791.
David and Thankful Holbrook, Apr. 4, 1802.
Lyman and Hannah Thayer of Blackstone, int. June 15, 1845.
Margaret (of Mendon, int.) and Joshua Farnum, Dec. 17, 1761.
Mary of Mendon, and Noah Keith, in Mendon, June 13, 1771.
Mary of Upton, and Warner Taft, int. Jan. 21, 1821.
Peter and Sarah Adams of Northbridge, int. May 3, 1829.
Polly and Abijah Keith, int. Apr. 20, 1791.
Thomas and Eunice Gouldthwait, Feb. 4, 1768.*

* Intention not recorded.

LEIGHTON, George E. R. and Sarah J. Randall, both of Easton, Sept. 18, 1841.*

LEISHUER (see Lashure, Lasure, Leshuer, Leshure, Lesuer, Lesure), William of Mendon, and Eliza Hazard, int. Oct. 23, 1844.

LELAND (see Lealand), Rebeckah of Grafton, and Simeon Keith, int. Apr. 11, 1764.

LENERD (see Leonard), Sarah and William Elexanders, int. Sept. 24, 1770.

LEONARD (see Lenerd), Daniel and Sarah W. Dow, int. Sept. 30, 1832.
Louisa of Worcester, and Nathan Moore, int. June 27, 1830.
Phillip, 2d m., b. in Middleboro, s. of Ephraim, a. 54 y., and Lucy L. Newton, 3d m., b. in Cumberland, R. I., d. of Wanton Tower, a. 58 y., Nov. 13, 1849.

LESHUER (see Lashure, Lasure, Leishuer, Leshure, Lesuer, Lesure), Samuel and Hannah Cumming, Aug. 17, 1785.

LESHURE (see Lashure, Lasure, Leishuer, Leshuer, Lesuer, Lesure), Chloe and Paul White, int. Nov. 19, 1777.

LESUER (see Lashure, Lasure, Leishuer, Leshuer, Leshure, Lesure), David and Sarah Peirce, July 21, 1761.
Edward and Cloe Taft, July 1, 1762.
Joseph of Upton, and Persis Whitney, int. Aug. 15, 1768.

LESURE (see Lashure, Lasure, Leishuer, Leshuer, Leshure, Lesuer), Anna and Arnold Inman of Douglas, Dec. 11, 1814.
Benjamin F. and Mary Bascom, Feb. 16, 1831.
Cloe and Carrol Coombs (of Smithfield, R. I., int.), July 22, 1810.
Gideon and Rhoda Chilson, Dec. 11, 1783.
Is[a]iah of Mendon, and Rac[h]el Allen, Aug. 5, 1744.
Julia Ann and Emory Miller, July 1, 1832.
Laura and Phinehas Smith Taft, int. Feb. 16, 1834.
Lovina of Douglas, and Charles S. Whitman, int. Nov. 21, 1830.
Luke of Mendon, and Lucina Dean, Sept. —, 1803 (int. Aug. 7, 1803).

LEVENS (see Leavans), Rosamond of Burrillville, R. I., and Joseph Richardson, int. Mar. 17, 1822.

* Intention not recorded.

LEWIS, Amy G. and Andrew J. Varney, Nov. 29, 1836.
Ebenezer and Lydia Fish of Mendon, int. Jan. 23, 1740-1.
Foster and Phebe Gould, Apr. 16, 1835.
John and Hannah Staples, June 15, 1748.*
Mary of New Sherborn, and Stephen Taft, int. Feb. 15, 1733-4.
Silas of Burrillville, R. I., and Ruth Eliza Anthony, int. Oct. 23, 1831.
William and Lydia Henry of Northbridge, in North Providence, R. I., Apr. 25, 1830.

LINKON, Hannah of Taunton, and Ritchard Low, int. Jan. 31, 1761.

LION (see Lyon), Elisabeth of Woodstock, and John Rawson, int. Jan. 8, 1753-4.

LIPPITT, Sarah of Smithfield, R. I., and John L. Cooper of Northbridge, Oct. 31, 1836.*

LIVERMORE, Jonas and Louisa Gates, Apr. 19, 1827. c.r.1.
W[illia]m of Spencer, and Ruth Aldrich, Aug. 18, 1839.

LOCKE, Mary of Cumberland, R. I., and James Curless, int. Dec. 8, 1844.

LOCKWOOD, Gratia A. of Northbridge, d. of Amasa and Henrietta, a. 19 y., and Ambrose C. Wheeler of Northbridge, s. of Ephraim and Charlotte, a. 21. y., Oct. 11, 1848.*

LOGE, Arrina of Burrillville, R. I., and William H. Taft, int. Oct. 7, 1832.

LOVEL, Olive and Abel Aldrich, Jan. 7, 1773.

LOW, Ritchard and Hannah Linkon of Taunton, int. Jan. 31, 1761.

LOWELL, Helena of Millbury, and Joshua Garside of Mendon, Mar. 24, 1833.
John T. and Elizabeth Baker, May 22, 1836.

LUTHER, William H. and Ruth Darling, both of Sutton, May 24, 1841.*

LYON (see Lion), Aaron of Woodstock, Conn., and Mary Marsh, Oct. 9, 1735.
Polly and George Persons, Apr. —, 1802 (int. Mar. 22, 1802).

* Intention not recorded.

MacNEMARA (see McNamara, McNamarrah), Hannah and Abner Palmer of Upton, int. Oct. 6, 1766.

MADDEN, Michael and Mary Bullard of Holliston, int. Oct. 31, 1761.
Timothy and Abigail Kibbey of Medway, in Medway, Nov. 10, 1768.

MAGILL, Susan and Paul Persons Jr., Dec. 23, 1827.

MALSTON, Susannah and Abram Mintoo, int. Jan. 5, 1789.

MAN (see Mann), Daniel and Hannah Harvey, Nov. 23, 1758.*
Nancy of Wrentham, and Nathan Tyler, int. Dec. 12, 1788.

MANCHESTER, Thomas A. of Millbury, and Nancy Taft, int. Apr. 9, 1843.

MANLEY, Michael and Lydia W. Morse of Coventry, R. I., int. Feb. 15, 1846.

MANN (see Man), James, Dr., of Wrentham, and Patty Tyler, int. Dec. 12, 1788.
Mary and Jesse Carrel, int. Jan. 24, 1785.
Mary R. and Nelson Brown [no date; year preceding Apr. 21, 1834].*

MANNING, Joseph and Mary Allen (of Sutton, int.), Jan. 15, 1760.

MANTON, Joseph (Marston, int.) of Johnston, R. I., and Mary Whipple, May 6, 1812.
Sophia of Providence, R. I., and Independence Whipple, int. Jan. 4, 1824.

MARBLE, Lucy and Albert Sherman, int. Aug. 28, 1836.

MARCEY, Prudence and Stephen Thompson, Feb. 6, 1834.

MARSH, Aaron of Douglas, and Silvia Huse, Dec. 25, 1822.
Abigail of Bellingham, and Cornet John Farnum, int. Oct. 30, 1733.
Abigail of Bellingham, and Joseph Averic, int. Jan. 29, 1742-3.
Abigail and Thomas Emerson, Nov. 29, 1748.
Abigail and Joseph Taft, int. Oct. 19, 1772.
Allice and Joseph Rist, int. Mar. 17, 1791.
Ann and Silas Waickfield, Feb. 17, 1767.*

* Intention not recorded.

MARSH, Bulah and James Emerson Jr., int. July 22, 1776.
Eli C. and Tamson F. Sprague of Douglas, int. Dec. 11, 1831.
Esther and Jacob Taft, Feb. 13, 1745-6.
James and Keziah Marsh, both of New Sherborn, Jan. 4, 1743-4.
Jason and Joanna Clark of Mendon, in Mendon, Mar. 12, 1795.
John of Killingly, Conn., and Bathsheba Aldrich, Dec. 27, 1781.*
Keziah and James Marsh, both of New Sherborn, Jan. 4, 1743-4.
Keziah of Douglas, and Richard Humes, int. Oct. 29, 1757.
Laura of Oxford, and John W. Thompson, int. Jan. 19, 1823.
Lydia and Baxter Hall, int. Dec. 3, 1780.
Mary and Aaron Lyon of Woodstock, Conn., Oct. 9, 1735.
Otis of Smithfield, R. I., and Eliza Darling, int. Mar. 16, 1834.
Polly of Douglas, and Timothy Taft, int. May 31, 1818.
Rosetta C., d. of Aaron and Lydia, a. 19 y., and Leonard Braman, s. of Hannah, a. 22 y., Oct. 22, 1845.
Sarah and Asher Prentice, int. Sept. 12, 1779.

MARSHAL (see Marshall), Henry of Saco, Me., and Uranah Farnum Tucker, int. June 2, 1833.

MARSHALL (see Marshal), Sarah of Ipswich, and Jonathan Emerson, in Ipswich, Dec. 20, 1752.

MARTEN (see Martin), Moses of Richmond, and Ruth Aldrich, int. Jan. 27, 1772.

MARTIN (see Marten), Benjamin and Sarah Meller of Mendon, Oct. 1 [1835].*
Edward and Susan[n]ah Hopcins, Apr. 4, 1765.
Esther of Douglas, and Jonathan Tucker, int. Oct. 26, 1817.
George of Richmond, N. H., and wid. Abigail Bacon, int. Nov. 7, 1799.
Jacob and Hannah Chace, Oct. 30, 1766.*
James and Mary McDermot, int. Apr. 9, 1843.
John of Bolton, and Margery Aldrich, int. Nov. 3, 1739.
John of Richmond, and Sarah Winter, Nov. 7, 1765.*
Maria of Douglas, and Silas Griffin, int. Apr. 5, 1835.
Martha and Abraham Aldrich, Dec. 1, 1808.
Permela and Dr. George Carryl, Nov. 17, 1790.

MARVELL (see Marvil), Peter of Providence, R. I., and Elizabeth Taft, in Boston, Dec. 6, 1727.*

* Intention not recorded.

MARVIL (see Marvell), Margaret and John Harwood, Dec. 4, 1755.

MASON, Anna and Jesse White of Northbridge, int. Mar. 28, 1777.

MATTHEW, Susan, d. of Peter and Victoria R., a. 15 y., and Joseph Fish of Douglas, s. of Charles and Louisa of the Province of Canada, a. 24 y., Apr. 26, 1845.

MATTHEWSON, Mason of Killingly, Conn., and Margaret Taft, Aug. 28, 1808.

McBRIDE, Sarah E. of Northbridge, and Richard Sayles, int. Dec. 7, 1845.

McCLAREN, Mary of Sutton, and John Prentice, Jan. 29, 1756.

McCRILLIS, Joseph E. of Grafton, and Abigail Rist, Apr. 11, 1832.

McDERMOT, Mary and James Martin, int. Apr. 9, 1843.

McFARLING, Daniel of Rutland, and Elisabeth (Margret, int.) Dun, Oct. 8, 1747.

McGRATH, John and Hitty Aldrich, int. Sept. 6, 1829.

McINTIRE, Jeremiah S., s. of Jeremiah and Nancy, a. 22 y., and Mary J. Aldrich, d. of Ahaz and Mary, a. 19 y., Jan. 5, 1846.

McKOY, James A. of Worcester, and Clarissa H. Brown, Feb. 4, 1838.

McLELLAN (see McLellen), Harriet of Portland, Me., and Handel Rogerson, int. Jan. 21, 1833.

McLELLEN (see McLellan), Betsey I. of Grafton, and Jeremiah Gregory, int. Aug. 17, 1845.
Mary Jane, d. of Andrew and Mary, a. 19 y., and Crawford T. Bowdish, s. of Asa and Patience, a. 23 y., Apr. 20, 1845.

McNAMARA (see MacNemara, McNamarrah), James and Mary Taft, int. May 9, 1830.
Martha and Benjamin Benson of Mendon, in Mendon, Feb. 15, 1769.

McNAMARRAH (see MacNemara, McNamara), Timothy and Silance Holbrook, Feb. 2, 1759.

MELLEN, Charlotte S. of Thompson, Conn., and Stephen N. Harrington, int. Nov. 12, 1826.

MELLER (see Miller), Sarah of Mendon, and Benjamin Martin, Oct. 1 [1835].*

MERCHANT, Harriet of Smithfield, R. I., and Derick P. Brown, int. Aug. 24, 1834.

MERIAM (see Merriam), Delphia F. and Edwin R. Carpenter, Jan. 1, 1840.
Luke A. and Diantha Lamb, int. Mar. 23, 1845.
Samuel F. and Mary K. Fay, May 18, 1836.

MERRIAM (see Meriam), Samuel and Philena Murdock, Dec. 15, 1833.

MERRILL, William S. of Lowell, and Martha Ann Carpenter, May 30, 1832.

MESSENGER (see Messinger), Catharine B. and (Col., c.r.1) John W. Capron, Oct. 30, 1831.

MESSINGER (see Messenger), Charles A., s. of David and Polly, a. 32 y., and Emeline F. Southwick, d. of Jonathan F. and Chloe, a. 21 y., May 14, 1846.
Frances E. and Charles W. Williams, Apr. 30, 1840.

METCALF, Aaron B. of Leicester, and Lucy Seagrave, Sept. 29, 1841.
Erasmus B. of Franklin, and Ann S. Down, Mar. 31, 1841.
Sarah and Alden B. Cleveland, Oct. 19, 1836.
Silas H. of Wrentham, s. of Silas and Nancy, a. 21 y., and Rebecca Adams, d. of Fleming and Rebecca, a. 23 y., Mar. 20, 1845.

MILLER (see Meller), Emory and Julia Ann Lesure, July 1, 1832.
Evelina of Mendon, and Willard Wilcox, int. Nov. 21, 1830.
Nelson of Smithfield, R. I., and Lydia Buxton, int. June 24, 1838.
William of Cumberland, R. I., and Joanna Hall, int. Feb. 8, 1791.

MINOT, Buckley of Northbridge, and Clarrissa Aldrich, Jan. 18, 1827. c.r.1.
William and Olive W. Keyes, Nov. 4, 1824. c.r.1.*

* Intention not recorded.

MINTOO, Abram and Susannah Malston, int. Jan. 5, 1789.

MITCHEL, Amy and Grindal Thayer, int. Oct. 6, 1787.
Hannah of Burrillville, County of Providence, d. of John Esten Esq., and Joel Thompson, s. of Stephen of Smithfield, in said county, Oct. 24, 1819.*
Lydia and Samuel Willison, int. Apr. 4, 1790.

MONROE, Augustus W. of New Bedford, 2d m., s. of Turner, a. 36 y., and Sarah Ann Anthony, d. of Elisha, a. 28 y., Jan. 5, 1848.

MONTAGUE, Jonathan and Lydia Cary, Oct. 6, 1743.

MOORE, Catharine of Holden, and Cyrus B. Snow, int. Mar. 17, 1833.
Jack and Silva Pierce, in Douglas, Nov. 20, 1788.*
Lucy of Somersworth, N. H., and David Lawrence, int. Sept. 18, 1831.
Nathan and Louisa Leonard of Worcester, int. June 27, 1830.
Nathan and Sally Anthony of Douglas, int. Mar. 19, 1848.

MORDUCK (see Murdock, Murdocks), Samuel and Zipporah Bacon, Apr. 22, 1773.

MORREY (see Mowry), Thomas (Moore, int.) of Smithfield, R. I., and Rhoda Aldrich, in Mendon, Sept. 14, 1769.

MORRIS, Elenor (of Mendon, int.) and John Edmonds, June 7, 1744.

MORRISON, Leonard of Johnston, R. I., and Elizabeth Bennett, Apr. 8, 1827. c.r.1.

MORSE (see Morss), Abigail and Abner Taft (Abner 2d, int.), Dec. 8, 1803.
Abijah and Lydia Fairbanks of Sherborn, in Sherborn, Oct. 10, 1751.*
Adeline and Willard W. Walling of Providence, R. I., int. Sept. 25, 1848.
Betsey of Douglas, and Marvel Morse, int. Aug. —, 1808.
Brigham and Henrietta Frost, Apr. 6, 1835.
Brigham of Douglas, s. of Ezra and Zilpha, a. 24 y., and Sarah Lawrance of Millbury, d. of Thomas, a. 23 y., Aug. 13, 1846.*
Daniel, Capt., and Lydia Southwick, int. Jan. 5, 1823.

* Intention not recorded.

MORSE, Deborah and Paul Wheelock, Aug. 30, 1784.
Deborah W. (Deborah Wheelock, c.r.1) and Nelson Jencks of Cumberland, R. I., Jan. 1, 1822.
Delilah and George Williams, Mar. 27, 1831. (Mar. 29, 1831. c.r.1.)
Ebenezer and Rhoda Emerson, Apr. 30, 1789.
Eunice and Benja[min] Thompson, int. Mar. 2, 1791.
Ezekiel of Sutton, and Mary Tyler, Feb. 18, 1785.
Gideon and Molley Emerson, int. Dec. 25, 1788.
James H. and Juliah Aldrich, May 28, 1823.
Jesse and Rachel Allen of Medway, in Medway, Nov. 28, 1754.
Jesse Jr. and Marcy White, int. Apr. 8, 1782.
Jesse 3d and Sarah Gaskil, int. Mar. 6, 1803.
Joseph and Olive White, Jan. 13, 1785.
Levi of Douglas, and Ruth Chilson, Mar. 21, 1808.
Lydia and Joseph Stoddard, both of Douglas, Dec. 28, 1807.*
Lydia W. of Coventry, R. I., and Michael Manley, int. Feb. 15, 1846.
Marcy and Ellis Thompson, int. Feb. 6, 1820.
Maria and George S. Southwick, int. Apr. 14, 1833.
Marvel and Betsey Morse of Douglas, int. Aug. —, 1808.
Mary and John Jepherson of Gloucester, R. I., int. Oct. 6, 1787.
Nahum and Olive Comstock, int. Feb. 9, 1793.
Patty and Nathan Stevanns of Douglas, int. Oct. 15, 1797.
Philena of Warwick (Philenda of Norwich, int.), and Benjamin White, in Warwick, May 28, 1786.
Polly and Nehemiah Aldrich, int. Jan. 31, 1806.
Rosina of Upton, and Cromwell Aldrich of Grafton, May 14, 1822.*
Roxana and Danforth Draper, Sept. 13, 1822.
Silas and Orpah White, Feb. 15, 1791.
Willard and Anna Aldrich, July 16, 1809.

MORSS (see Morse), Lois and Simeon Sheppard of Douglas, int. Sept. 21, 1776.
Nathan and Mary Lawrance of Holliston, int. June 22, 1753.
Nathan and Elisabeth Emerson, Oct. 18, 1759.
Samuel and Deborah Hadlock, Dec. 16, 1762.

MOSELY, Joseph of Sutton, and Susannay Young, Apr. 19, 1784.

MOTT, Miner of Lebanon, Conn., and Polly Sibley, Feb. 28, 1843.

* Intention not recorded.

MOULTON, David of Hardwick, and Mary Seagrave, Apr. 7, 1840.
Fanny of Hopkinton, and William Phipps, int. Aug. 19, 1810.

MOWRY (see Morrey), Alanson and Amy Harris, int. Nov. 2, 1828.
Alanson and Mrs. Lucinda Mowry of Marlboro, int. Aug. 9, 1840.
Amey A., d. of Israel and Phila, a. 19 y., and Horatio F. Bowen, s. of Benjamin and Nancy, a. 21 y., May 28, 1846.
Anna of Mendon, and Benjamin Thwing Jr., May 10, 1798.
Anna (Mary, int.) of Mendon, and Grindal Rawson, Jan. 15, 1801.
Arnold and Olive Brown, both of Mendon, Dec. 19, 1802.*
Caleb of Mendon, and Clarinda Taft, Sept. 30, 1813.
Candace of Smithfield, R. I., and Samuel S. Mowry, int. Apr. 1, 1827.
Caroline and Dr. David P. White, Sept. 7, 1837.
Charlotte and Sullivan Thayer, Sept. 6, 1814.
Chloe Ann and Lyman W. Thayer of Bellingham, int. Mar. 19, 1848.
Daniel C., s. of Israel and Phila, a. 21 y., and Harriet N. Lawrance, d. of Chandler, a. 20 y., Aug. 13, 1846.
David and Elisabeth Gifford, d. of Annanias, 2d day, 5th mo., called May, 1771. c.r.3.*
Emma of Mendon, and Seth Partridge, int. Apr. 19, 1835.
Gardner and Chloe Ann Taft of Mendon, Jan. 7, 1836.
Lavinia B. of Warwick, R. I., and Thomas M. Southwick, int. Jan. 20, 1839.
Lucinda, Mrs., of Marlboro, and Alanson Mowry, int. Aug. 9, 1840.
Maria and Samuel Taft, Apr. 27, 1828.
Meribah of Douglas, and Chilion Tucker, int. July 20, 1816.
Philip (Jr., int.) of Smithfield, R. I., and Clarisa Pitts, Apr. 27, 1817.
Polly and Reuben Jepherson, July 13, 1809.
Rachel of Smithfield, R. I., and David Taft, int. Feb. 18, 1791.
Richard D. and Lucy M. Albee of Oxford, int. July 31, 1838.
Roby of Smithfield, R. I., and Joseph Richardson Jr., int. Nov. 26, 1807.
Samuel S. and Candace Mowry of Smithfield, R. I., int. Apr. 1, 1827.
Samuel S. and Lucinda Temple of Marlborough, int. Sept. 4, 1831.

* Intention not recorded.

MOWRY, Sarah of Mendon, and Samuel Taft 2d, Aug. 25, 1803.
Sarah and Asahel Keith, Apr. 28, 1818.
Susan L. and Seth S. Pitts, Nov. 3, 1841.
Willard A. of Mendon, and Mary Harris, Mar. 23, 1843.

MUNYAN (see Munyon), Rhoda Stockwell of Mendon, and Stilman Austin, int. Sept. 7, 1828.

MUNYON (see Munyan), Cyrena R., d. of Miranda, a. 22 y., and Daniel H. Aldrich of Northbridge, s. of Samuel and Sarah of Northbridge, a. 33 y., Apr. 9, 1846.*

MURDOCK (see Morduck, Murdocks), Abba Eliza and Pemberton Brown, int. Mar. 11, 1827.
Abigail and Samuel Read, Apr. 12, 1753.
Anna and Darias Taft, int. Sept. 20, 1784.
Anna and Thomas Lasure of Smithfield, R. I., int. July 15, 1810.
Benjamin and Katherine Read, May 20, 1760.
Benja[mi]n and Hannah Taft, int. Apr. 8, 1782.
Betsey and Samuel Seagrave, Sept. 13, 1804.
Caleb and Mary Wood, Apr. 11, 1786.
Charles and Ann (Mary Ann, int.) Weightman of Springfield, Vt., Oct. 18, 1842.
Elisha and Hannah Chapin, int. Jan. 10, 1779.
Fuller and Esther Taft, Nov. 22, 1805.
George T. and Abby A. Robinson of Mansfield, int. Aug. 24, 1845.
Harriet of Townsend, Vt., and Phineas Wood, int. Oct. 3, 1830.
Harriet and David Wood, Mar. 18, 1841.
Hezekiah and Polly Taft (Dolley, int.), Feb. 7, 1798. (Feb. 13, 1798. C.R.1.)
Jesse and Selina Taft, Mar. 12, 1793.
John and Bethiah Fuller of Newton, in Newton, Jan. 24, 1750.
Mary and Samuel White, Feb. 12, 1752–3.
Mary and Asa Thayer, int. Apr. 19, 1782.
Molley and Calvin Taft, June 1, 1786.
Moses T. and Dorinda W. Grout, Sept. 9, 1832.
Philena and Samuel Merriam, Dec. 15, 1833.
Ruth and Marvel Taft of Northbridge, Apr. 29, 1784.
Warren and Charlotte Thayer of Sutton, int. May 25, 1823.
Warren and Catharine Andrew, Aug. 5, 1832.

MURDOCKS (see Morduck, Murdock), Mary and Samuel Taft, int. Dec. 16, 1758.

* Intention not recorded.

MURPHY, Hannah and Freeman Knowlton, both of Northbridge, Oct. 9, 1825.*
Isaac R. and Elmira Craggin of Northbridge, int. Oct. 3, 1830.
Isaac R. (of Sutton, int.) and Fanny Seagrave, Aug. 12, 1838.
Jeremiah and Lucy Welch, Aug. 3, 1834.
Jeremiah and Abigail S. Cass, Sept. 3, 1838.

MUSSEY, Theodate and Elisha Arnold of Gloucester, R. I., int. Apr. 24, 1774.

MUXSCOM, Expearence and Abner Benson of Mendon, int. Feb. 28, 1771.

NEFF, Pamelia C. and Nathaniel W. Quint, both of Northbridge, Dec. 25, 1836.*

NELSON, Deborah of Mendon, and Comfort Keith, in Mendon, Oct. 31, 1765.
Sarah of Upton, and Stephen Williams, int. June 14, 1778.

NEWCOMB, Ruth and Jonathan Allen, Dec. 11, 1760.

NEWELL, Asa of Providence, R. I., and Asenath A. Taft, Sept. 10, 1826. c.r.1.
Ezbon C. and Patience Arnold, int. Mar. 26, 1826.
Jerusha of Dudley and Solomon Tyler, int. May —, 1809.
Jerusha and Jason Taft, Dec. 24, 1818.
Joseph of Richmond, and Katharine Aldrich, int. Mar. 26, 1770.
Lucretia and John Taft, Sept. 9, 1818.
Matilda and Thomas Farnum, June 28, 1815.

NEWMAN, Daniel, s. of Daniel and Nancy, a. 25 y., and Mary Ann Soule of Northbridge, d. of Orra and Nancy, a. 23 y., Nov. 3, 1847.

NEWTON, Elizabeth (Nuten, int.) of Sutton, and John Adams Jr., in Sutton, Nov. 28, 1768.
Lucy L., 3d m., b. in Cumberland, R. I., d. of Wanton Tower, a. 58 y., and Phillip Leonard, 2d m., b. in Middleboro, s. of Ephraim, a. 54 y., Nov. 13, 1849.

NICHOLAS, Jerusha A. of Pawtucket, R. I., and Preston F. Everett, int. Mar. 27, 1836.

NICHOLLS (see Nichols), Charlotte and Thomas B. Wright (Thomas D. of Pawtucket, int.) [no date] (int. Apr. 7, 1833).
Sarah and Arnold Eddy [no date] (int. Apr. 7, 1833).

* Intention not recorded.

NICHOLS (see Nicholls), Nancy and Ephraim Lee of Mendon, int. Oct. 8, 1826.
Reuben and Mary (Mary E. int.) Elkins, Oct. 15 [1835].

NICKERSON, Freeman and Mary M. Thwing, Oct. 21, 1830.

NOLEN, Thomas and Abigail Brown, Jan. 27, 1833.

NUTTIEN (see Nuttin, Nutting), James and Sarah Amos, Apr. 20, 1758.

NUTTIN (see Nuttien, Nutting), Mary and Bezleel Jones of Mendon, Feb. 28, 1759.

NUTTING (see Nuttien, Nuttin), Jonas and Ruth S. Taft of Mendon, int. Apr. 12, 1840.
Lydia and Josiah Peas of Upton, int. Apr. 2, 1757.

NYE, Deliverance of Douglas, and George Kymton, in Douglas, Mar. 13, 1775.
Joanah of Douglas, and Asa Blake, in Douglas, Dec. 10, 1778.
Keziah of Douglas, and Amariah Holbrook, in Douglas, Nov. 20, 1777.
Percis of Sutton, and Welcome Lee, int. Sept. 29, 1833.
Prince of Douglas, and Bethiah Kympton, int. Dec. 19, 1777.

OLIVER, Mary Ann of Framingham, and Alfred Fisher, int. Mar. 26, 1826.

O'NEIL, James and Elenor Taft, Feb. 13, 1831.

ONION, Asa F. of Bellingham, and Asenath Thwing, int. Oct. 23, 1819.

OREL (see Orrel), Samuel and Susannah Aldrich, in Mendon, Apr. 12, 1773.

ORREL (see Orel), Susanna and Joseph White of Smithfield, R. I., int. July 2, 1780.

OWEN, Daniel and Abigail Chase, Nov. 18, 1751.*
Ruth of Mendon, and Elijah Tylor of Upton, Sept. 14, 1749.*

OXX, Salley and Samuel Green, Mar. 7, 1791.

PACKARD, Allen and Frances Thayer, Jan. 1, 1839.
Mary Ann and Abel Houghton, May 21, 1838.
Olive and Joshua Waters of Leverett, Apr. 26, 1819. (Joshua Waters of Leverett, and Ellis Packard, int. Nov. 30, 1818.)
Sally, Mrs., and Jonathan Buxton of Mendon, int. Dec. 6, 1829.

* Intention not recorded.

PAGE, Experience and Leddol Buck, int. Jan. 15, 1736–7.
Sally of New Marlborough, N. H., and Jonathan Russell Keith, int. June 15, 1811.

PAIN (see Paine, Pane), Benjamin of Gloucester, R. I., and Sarah Corrary, int. Dec. 29, 1787.
Molley of Gloucester, R. I., and Joseph Richardson, int. Nov. 1, 1784.
Simon of Gloucester, R. I., and Molle Taft, int. Dec. 5, 1774.

PAINE (see Pain, Pane), David D. and Jemima French, Oct. 3, 1822.
Lecester of Woodstock, Conn., and Mary Draper, Oct. 25, 1781.
Mary (Polly, int.) and Mowry Aldrich of Douglas (Gloucester, R. I., int.), June 11, 1801.
Mary D., d. of David D. and Jemima, a. 20 y., and Nelson Williams, s. of Stephen and Nancy, a. 39 y., Jan. 21, 1846.
Molly and Rufus Wallace of Douglas (Sutton, int.), Jan. 18, 1827. c.r.1.
Nathan and Ellen Fisher, int. Nov. 10, 1843.
Sarah and Duty Southwick, int. Dec. 23, 1832.
Simon and Sarah Chappel, int. May 1, 1825.
Stephen and Tirzah Aldrich of Douglas, int. May 17, 1801.

PALMER, Abner of Upton, and Hannah MacNemara, int. Oct. 6, 1766.

PANE (see Pain, Paine), Elisabeth of Gloucester, R. I., and John White, int. Dec. 24, 1777.

PARK, Elisabeth of Newton, and Nicholas Baylies, int. Oct. 21, 1738.
Nathan and Sarah Brown, Nov. 10, 1736.*
Nathan and Ruth Banister of Marlboro, int. Nov. 19, 1763.

PARKAS (see Parkes, Parks, Perks), Susanna (Parkes, int.) and Paul White, Dec. 5, 1771.

PARKER, John D. and Caroline G. Wait, int. Oct. 13, 1839.
Leonard (Leonard M., int.) and Paulina Thwing, Jan. 10, 1829.
Prince of Douglas, and Olive Aldrich, int. Feb. 26, 1795.
Samuel and Margrit Corary, int. June 13, 1768.

PARKES (see Parkas, Parks, Perks), Lucy of Scituate, R. I., and Amasa Albro, int. Apr. 17, 1836.

PARKHURST, Ziba of Milford, and Sophronia Spring, Oct. 4, 1821.

* Intention not recorded.

PARKS (see Parkas, Parkes, Perks), Isaac of Pomfret, County of Windham, and Rebeckah Copland, May 14, 1740.
Marth[a] and Thomas Read, Dec. 14, 1763.

PARMENTER (see Parmiter), Samuel B. of Worcester, s. of Jonas and Charlotte, a. 23 y., and Sarah A. Henry of Grafton, d. of Samuel and Dorcas B., a. 22 y., Nov. 25, 1847.*

PARMITER (see Parmenter), Charlotte, d. of Jonas and Charlotte, and William G. Ferry of Grafton, s. of Darias and Philena of Grafton, a. 23 y., Apr. 6, 1845.*

PARSONS (see Persons), Sarah (Persons, int.) and Ellis Aldrich of Northbridge, Jan. 7, 1830.
William and Sarah Bennet, Dec. 23, 1756.

PARTRIDGE, Seth and Emma Mowry of Mendon, int. Apr. 19, 1835.
Stephen of Medway, and Esther Emerson, Feb. 27, 1772.

PASSMORE, Susanna and Victorious Smith, Nov. 21, 1771.

PATCH, Anna of Dudley, and Solomon Chase, int. Aug. 28, 1786.

PATE, David and Lydia Brumfield, Jan. 31, 1744.*

PATTERSON, Frederick W. of Rochester, N. Y., and Louisa M. Taft, Sept. 16, 1834.
Jenet of Mendon, and Ezekiel Whitney, int. Mar. 31, 1743.

PEAS, Josiah of Upton, and Lydia Nutting, int. Apr. 2, 1757.

PECK, Ann and John Hunt, Feb. 26, 1753.
Ebenezer and Sarah Allen, June 19, 1739. (June 29, 1739. c.r.1.)
Eliza T. of Mendon, and Rev. Calvin Butler Heath, May 20, 1839.*
John and Mary Bowen (Brown, int.) of Rehoboth, in Rehoboth, Dec. 23, 1750.
Mary of Smithfield, R. I., and Benjamin Handy 2d, int. Aug. 10, 1817.
Mary and Mellen Benson, both of Mendon, July 13, 1842.*

PEIRCE (see Pierce), L. and John W. Ruegger, July 8, 1841.*
Sarah and David Lesuer, July 21, 1761.

* Intention not recorded.

PELTON, Joseph and Submit Wood, Nov. 1, 1828.

PENDLETON, Agnes P. of Mendon, and Abram W. Goldthwait, int. Oct. 8, 1843.

PENNEMAN (see Penniman, Penyman), Jonathan and Elisabeth Taft, Sept. 19, 1743.

PENNIMAN (see Penneman, Penyman), Abigail and David Brastow of Mendon, in Mendon, Apr. 18, 1779.
Anna and James Flag, Jan. 10, 1775.
Eleonor of Mendon, and Moses Peters, int. Mar. 18, 1782.
Jesse Ware and Maria Bradfoot Robinson, both of Mendon, Aug. 16, 1836.*
Lydia and Amos Farnum, int. Mar. 18, 1793.
Mary and Stephen Holbrook Jr. of Bellingham, int. July 30, 1790.
Samuel of Mendon, and Deborah Taft, Oct. 25, 1770.
Thomas of Plainfield, N. H., and Dorinda Wood, Jan. 4, 1814. (Jan. 30, 1814. c.r.1.)

PENYMAN (see Penneman, Penniman), Jesse of Mendon, and Lois Wood, Dec. 8, 1763.

PERKINS, John K., widr., s. of John and Susan, a. 28 y., and Jane Seagrave, d. of Bezaleel and Jemima, a. 25 y., May 8, 1845.

PERKS (see Parkas, Parkes, Parks), May (Mercy Parkes, int.) of Hardwick, and Josiah (Isaiah, int.) White, in Hardwick, Sept. 20, 1798.

PERRIEN, Abigal of Woodstock, and Joseph Adams, int. June 8, 1776.

PERRY, Adams, Dr., widr., s. of Adams and Anna, a. 54 y., and Selissa S. Seagrave, d. of John and Mary, a. 35 y., Oct. 26, 1847.
Ann of Milford, and Nathaniel Chessman, int. Apr. 24, 1831.
Joseph H. and Mary Taft, Feb. 16, 1820.
Moses of Worcester, and Hannah Hall, Apr. 2, 1791.
Olive of Milford, and Ezekiel F. Tewksbury, int. Mar. 23, 1835.

PERSONS (see Parsons), Amarintha A. and Thomas W. Giles, int. Dec. 2, 1849.
George of Northbridge, and Abigail Rawson, in Northbridge, Mar. 19, 1789.

* Intention not recorded.

PERSONS, George and Polly Lyon, Apr. —, 1802 (int. Mar. 22, 1802).
George and Esther Wood, Apr. 5, 1818.
James and Thankfull Read, Apr. 13, 1796.
John Jr. and Lucy Hathaway of Sutton, Nov. 4, 1813.
John and wid. Asenath Thwing, Feb. 20, 1827. c.r.1.
Olive and James Bacon, Oct. 21, 1827.
Paul and Nancy Jones, Feb. 2, 1803.
Paul Jr. and Susan Magill, Dec. 23, 1827.
Sarah and Amos Lasure, Feb. 22, 1807.
Thankful and Perly Chapman of Woodstock, Conn., Feb. 24, 1803.

PETERS, Moses and Eleonor Penniman of Mendon, int. Mar. 18, 1782.

PHETEPLACE, Hosea and Sarah Ann H. White of Sutton, int. Apr. 30, 1837.

PHILIPS (see Phillipps, Phillips, Philps), Ezekiel of Gloucester, R. I., and Molley Cummings, May 22, 1788.
Molley and Jonathan Wood of Gloucester, R. I., int. Mar. 28, 1779.

PHILLIPPS (see Philips, Phillips, Philps), Olney and Hannah Hazard, int. Mar. 23, 1845.

PHILLIPS (see Philips, Phillipps, Philps), Andrew of Gloucester, R. I., and Ruth ———, int. Jan. —, 1783.
Stephen and Mary Ann Brady of Lowell, int. July 2, 1843.
Thomas of Barclay, and Louis Pitts, int. Mar. 4, 1795.

PHILPS (see Philips, Phillipps, Phillips), Elias (Philips, int.) of Milford, and Lois Thayer, July 1, 1790.

PHIPPS, William, Rev., of Douglas, and Rachel Fullar, int. Oct. 12, 1751.
William and Fanny Moulton of Hopkinton, int. Aug. 19, 1810.

PICKERING, Mary of Mendon, and Squire Taft, int. Sept. 2, 1827.
Olive of Mendon, and Stephen Cumstock, int. Mar. 15, 1829.
Sylvester of Mendon, and Hannah C. Wood, Sept. 3, 1835.
Uranah of Mendon, and Eber Taft, int. Mar. 28, 1819.

PICKETT, John and Martha Hill, Apr. 7, 1833.

PIERCE (see Peirce), Eliza (of Bellingham, int.) and Willard Ellis, Sept. 18, 1832.
Harriet, wid., d. of Thomas and Martha Page of Paxton, a. 29 y., and Edwin Browning, widr., of Utica, N. Y., s. of Ephraim and Clarinda, a. 29 y., Nov. 13, 1845.
Polly and Edward Ellison of Northbridge, in Northbridge, Feb. 28, 1793.
Silva and Jack Moore, in Douglas, Nov. 20, 1788.*
Susan A. of Cumberland, R. I., and James G. Lake, int. Oct. 24, 1844.

PINGREE, Abiah and Mowry Adams, Oct. 3, 1831.

PITTS, Abner and Polly Simmons, Dec. 25, 1814.
Clarisa and Philip Mowry (Jr., int.) of Smithfield, R. I., Apr. 27, 1817.
Deborah and George Farnum, int. Mar. 6, 1790.
Esek (Lieut., int.) and Abigail Wood, Apr. 5, 1803.
Esek and Bathsheba Daniels of Mendon, int. Aug. 17, 1823.
Job Jr. and Mary Read, Nov. 10, 1796.
Job and wid. Lydia Pitts of Ward, int. Feb. 19, 1815.
Job of Blackstone, s. of Esek and Abigail, a. 31 y., and Miranda A. (Miranda Angenette, int.) Hunt, d. of Demas and Nancy Ann, a. 24 y., May 18, 1847.
Louis and Thomas Phillips of Barclay, int. Mar. 4, 1795.
Louis and David Dailey of Concord, N. H., Oct. 25, 1804.
Lydia, wid., of Ward, and Job Pitts, int. Feb. 19, 1815.
Marcy and Daniel Aldrich, int. Feb. 23, 1788.
Meriam of Orring, and George Aldrich, int. May 6, 1793.
Sarah and Asa Cole of Grafton, Sept. 3, 1829.
Seth S. and Susan L. Mowry, Nov. 3, 1841.

PLUMBLY, Hanna and Jeremiah Aldrich, int. ——, 1732.
Joseph and Dorcas Addey, July 30, 1747.*

PLYMPTON, Silas W. and Louis T. Seagrave, June 24, 1829.

POND, John, Dr., of Mendon, and Phebe Southwick, int. Mar. 15, 1818.
Samuel of Wrentham, and Hannah Johnson, Jan. 10, 1753.

POTTER, Nathan[ie]ll (of Leecester, int.) and Mary Thompson, Dec. 2, 1755.
William of Upton, and Hipzebah Chillson, Mar. 1, 1742-3.*

* Intention not recorded.

POWERS, Deliverance and John Rook (Rokes, int.), July 26, 1759.
Ezekiel and Hannah Hall, Jan. 28, 1767.
Lydia and Jonah Stow of Grafton, int. Oct. 17, 1768.
Prudance and Garshom Ward of Grafton, Sept. 1, 1768.
Sarah and Timothy Allen, int. Mar. 27, 1769.
Stephen and Rachel Winter, Apr. 2, 1762.

PRATT, Daniel, s. of Caleb and Sarah W. of Boston, a. 27 y., and Laura A. Jefferson, d. of Royal and Harriet, a. 19 y., Nov. 22, 1847.
Elisabeth of Medfield, and Rev. Nathan Webb, int. Nov. 12, 1763.

PREBBLE, Joseph of Old York, and Abigail Bolster, int. Jan. 23, 1769.

PRENTICE (see Prentis, Printis), Asher and Sarah Marsh, int. Sept. 12, 1779.
Eleanor of Northbridge, and Charles C. Spring, Feb. 15, 1844.
Elisabeth and Joseph Aldrich, Jan. 2, 1740-1.
John and Mary McClaren of Sutton, Jan. 29, 1756.

PRENTIS (see Prentice, Printis), Hannah of Hopkinton, and Franklin A. Sawyer, int. Sept. 8, 1833.
Jonah and Elisabeth Smith of Bellingham, int. July 8, 1754.
Jonah and Abigail Cummings, Nov. 25, 1760.
Mary D. of Northbridge, and Alpheus Rawson, int. Mar. 4, 1821.

PRESSEY, Julia of Northbridge, d. of Phineas and Harriet, a. 20 y., and William H. Adams of Northbridge, s. of Fleming and Rebecca, a. 21 y., Apr. 20, 1846.*

PRESTON, Almeda B. of Cumberland, R. I., and Wellington Keith, int. Aug. 23, 1846.
Amariah and Elisabeth Warren, int. Aug. 26, 1757.
Amariah and Elizabeth Bacon of Dudley, in Dudley, Nov. 18, 1777.
Ameriah and Susanna Wood, Sept. 21, 1760.
Wilson and Susanna Aldrich, Oct. 30, 1765.
Winositt and William Taft, int. Feb. 21, 1779.

PRINCE, Hannah of Swansea, and John Holbrook, int. Apr. 13, 1797.
Job of Gloucester, County of Providence, and Sarah Wiles, int. Feb. 20, 1743-4.

* Intention not recorded.

PRINTIS (see Prentice, Prentis), Samuel and Rhoda Draper, Nov. 19, 1745.*

PROVENDER, Joseph and Abigail Winter, int. Aug. 19, 1737.

PULSIPHER, Mary of Douglas, and Will[ia]m Hendrick, int. Dec. 4, 1803.
Sarah of Douglas, and Moses Southwick, int. Dec. 9, 1804.

PURINTON, Delia of Monson, and Elisha Southwick, int. Dec. 28, 1834.

PUTNAM, Anna of Sutton, and James Hull, int. Apr. 21, 1777.
Cornelius, widr., of Oxford, s. of David and Elizabeth of Sutton, a. 62 y., and Rachel Rist, d. of Caleb and Betsey, a. 32 y., Oct. 30, 1844.
Eli of Spencer, and Betsey Rist, int. Aug. 27, 1826.
Joktan and Anna Harres of Gloucester, R. I., int. Feb. 19, 1770.
Nabby of Sutton, and Lieut. Simon Rawson, int. Dec. 15, 1804.
Ruth of Salem, and David Burtuon, int. Sept. 10, 1743.
Susanna of Sutton, and Thomas White, int. Aug. 2, 1778.
William H. of Manchester, N. H., s. of William and Susan, a. 24 y., and Lydia I. Bryant of Blackstone, d. of Luther and Betsey, a. 18 y., Feb. 14, 1847.*

PYKE, Benjamin (Pike, int.) and Ab[b]y Keith, Feb. 21, 1765.

QUILLEN, Ann and James Bready, int. Aug. 27, 1848.

QUINT, Eliza H. of Sanford, Me., and William C. Walker, int. Nov. 11, 1832.
Nathaniel W. and Pamelia C. Neff, both of Northbridge, Dec. 25, 1836.*

RAMSDELL (see Ramsdil), Caroline of Mendon, and Elijah Balcom, in Mendon, May 13, 1777.

RAMSDIL (see Ramsdell), Barbara of Mendon, and William Jennison, int. Nov. 18, 1799.

RANDALL, Sarah J. and George E. R. Leighton, both of Easton, Sept. 18, 1841.*

RASEY, Joseph and Mary Hollon of Mendon, in Mendon, May 6, 1757.

* Intention not recorded.

RAWSON (see Roson), Abigail and George Persons of Northbridge, in Northbridge, Mar. 19, 1789.
Abner and Susan[n]a Keith, int. Nov. 17, 1744.
Abner and Mary Allen of Medway, in Medway, May 17, 1745.
Abner H. and Everline W. Clark of New Salem, int. Jan. 31, 1830.
Allen and Sophia Rawson of Montague, int. Feb. 28, 1816.
Alpheus and Mary D. Prentis of Northbridge, int. Mar. 4, 1821.
Asa and Marcy Kilburn, int. Feb. 22, 1801.
Barnabas A. and Mary Jane Jepherson, Nov. 25, 1841.
Calvin and Abba A. Benson, Apr. 3, 1827. c.r.1.
Charles and Salley Hale of Douglas, int. July 11, 1794.
Charles B. and Mary A. Seagrave, Aug. 31, 1834.
Dolly (Polley, int.) and Mason Whitney, in Mendon, Mar. 29, 1792.
Edmond, Dea., and Lydia Daniels of Holliston, Mar. 5, 1761.
Edmund of Mendon, and Elisabeth Hayward of Bridgewater, May 22, 1717.*
Edmund (Jr., int.) and Martha Allen of Medway, Jan. 12, 1743–4.
Edmund and Sarah Hull, int. July 10, 1770.
Edmund (Ens., int.), and Rebecca Turner of Medfield, in Medfield, Mar. 21, 1782.
Edward and Leucy Jones, int. Dec. 11, 1795.
Elizabeth and Abel Aldrich, in Northbridge, June 21, 1791.
Grindal and Anna (Mary, int.), Mowry of Mendon, Jan. 15, 1801.
Hannah and Henry Taft, int. Sept. 7, 1845.
Isaac and Polly Ward of Sutton, int. Mar. 29, 1794.
James and Polly Seagrave, Oct. 4, 1804.
James A., s. of James and Polly, a. 24 y., and Louisa J. Scott of Mendon, d. of Emery and Watee of Mendon, a. 18 y., June 14, 1844.
Joanna B. and Harkless Inman of Seekonk, int. Jan. 13, 1828.
Joel and Mary Hull, Feb. 17, 1763.
John and Elisabeth Lion of Woodstock, Conn., int. Jan. 8, 1753–4.
John and Lydia Chase of Sutton, in Sutton, Oct. 20, 1791.
John N. of Northbridge, and Mary Ann Rawson, Aug. 7, 1836.
Lyman of Townsend, and Deborah Keith, int. Oct. 19, 1794.
Margaret of Mendon, and Benjamin Walker, Nov. 15, 1773.
Maria of Northbridge, and Welcome Aldrich, Feb. 21, 1830.
Mary and Daniel Ward of Sutton, in Mendon, Sept. 20, 1792.

* Intention not recorded.

RAWSON, Mary and Jared Thayer, both of Mendon, Jan. 16, 1803.*
Mary of Quincy, and Beza Soule, int. July 30, 1815.
Mary and George W. Seagrave, Mar. 27, 1836.
Mary Ann and John N. Rawson of Northbridge, Aug. 7, 1836.
Nathan and Mary White, Feb. 18, 1762.
Nathan and Mary Chace, Mar. 24, 1764.
Otis and Polly Blake, int. July 5, 1807.
Pamela and Benjamin Sadler of Upton, June 23, 1825. c.r.1.
Patty Martha and Alpheus Brown, int. July 26, 1807.
Polly and Arnold Aldrich, int. July, August, 1808.
Priscilla and Asa Leathe of Grafton, int. July 15, 1786.
Rachel and Samuel Hayward (Howard, int.) of Mendon, Oct. 12, 1772.
Rachel Paine and Ebenezer Whitney of Montague, Dec. 28, 1776.
Rhoda and Aaron Taft Jr., June 1, 1769 (int., June 5, 1769).
Rhoda and Alpheus White of Mendon, Oct. 14, 1802.
Samuel and Molley Thwing, June 23, 1785.
Samuel Read and Philander Cleaveland, Jan. 17, 1795.
Sarah and Mowry Taft of Burrillville, R. I., Nov. 28, 1816. (Mowry Taft of Burrillville, R. I., and Sarah Richardson, int. Oct. 26, 1816.)
Seth and Deborah Torry, int. Nov. 20, 1780.
Silas and Sarah Draper, Mar. 17, 1768.
Silas and Sally White of Sullivan, N. H., int. Feb. 6, 1826.
Simon and Levina Brown of Douglas, int. Mar. 14, 1798.
(Simon, c.r.1) and (Abigail, c.r.1) Wood, Mar. (28, c.r.1), 1804 (both of Mendon, c.r.1).*
Simon, Lieut., and Nabby Putnam of Sutton, int. Dec. 15, 1804.
Simon Jr. and Roxalana Aldrich of Douglas, int. May 1, 1836.
Sophia of Montague, and Allen Rawson, int. Feb. 28, 1816.
Sophia and Lewis Wood of Mendon, Oct. 20, 1833.
Thomas and Eunice Read, May 6, 1756.
Timothy and Chloey Fish, Dec. 3, 1767.
Warren and Polly Adams, both of Mendon, July 3, 1803.*
Warren and Augusta Sadler of Upton, int. Mar. 9, 1823.
William Jr. of Mendon, and Margaret Cook, in Mendon, May 13, 1731.
William (of Mendon, int.) and Desire Aldrich, Mar. 12, 1760.

RAY, Samuel S. of Slatersville, R. I., s. of Samuel and Susan of Slatersville, R. I., a. 20 y., and Semantha White, d. of John and Cynthia, a. 19 y., Aug. 4, 1846.

* Intention not recorded.

RAYMOND, Marcy of Gloucester, R. I., and John Harris Jr., June 8, 1781.

READ (see Reed), Abigail and Thomas Starns (Stern, int.) of Littleton, Apr. 28, 1743.
Abigail and Garshom Taft, Mar. 22, 1764.
Abigail M. and John W. Capron, Jan. 4, 1820.
Abner C. and Mary Buffum, int. Oct. 2, 1831.
Anna of Smithfield, County of Providence, and Ephraim Taft, int. June 13, 1747.
Benjamin of Smithfield, R. I., and Elisabeth Yates, int. Nov. 4, 1755.
Benjamin and Comfort Taft of Mendon, May 27, 1762.
Betsey of Danville, Vt., and Joab Kimbal of Peacham, Jan. 23, 1799.*
Daniel and Sarah Taft, Jan. 28, 1735-6.
Daniel, s. of Jonathan of Smithfield, R. I., and Rachel Farnum, d. of Moses, 7th day, 2d mo., called February, 1760. c.r.3.*
Daniel and Mary Brown of Leicester, in Leicester, Dec. 19, 1765.
Daniel of Northbridge, and Hulday Jacobs, June 16, 1799.
David and Unice Taft, int. Sept. 5, 1732.
David and Thankful Garnsey, May 29, 1734.
David Jr. and Lydia Saben, int. Apr. 21, 1776.
Eben[eze]r and Hannah Torrey of Mendon, int. Dec. 23, 1738.
Ebenezer and Susanah Albee, Feb. 27, 1792.
Elizabeth (Elizabeth H., int.) and Nathan White Jr. of Worcester, Oct. 31, 1822.
Eunice and Thomas Rawson, May 6, 1756.
Hannah and Samuel Comings (Cummings, int.), Oct. 7, 1736.
John and Hannah Taft, June 23, 1763.
Joseph and Eunice Taft, Nov. 22, 1753.
Katherine and Benjamin Murdock, May 20, 1760.
Lucy of Northbridge, and James Cable (a transient person, c.r.1) of Vermont, Jan. 31, 1803.*
Mary and Reuben Walker, Nov. 28, 1764.
Mary and Job Pitts Jr., Nov. 10, 1796.
Nancy and Luther Spring, Dec. 29, 1814.
Rhoda, d. of John and Hannah of Smithfield, R. I., and Jaazaniah Bassett, s. of John dec. and Lucy of Killingly, Conn., 4th day, 5th mo. 1780. c.r.3.*
Ruth and Joseph Tyler, Apr. 2, 1761.
Samuel and Ruth Brown of Mendon, in Mendon, Jan. 21, 1728-9.*

* Intention not recorded.

READ, Samuel, Dr., and Elisabeth Jordan of Rehoboth, County of Bristol, int. Aug. 6, 1749.
Samuel and Abigail Murdock, Apr. 12, 1753.
Samuel Jr. and Marcy Whitney of Douglas, int. June 10, 1792.
Samuel Esq. and Mrs. Charlotte Wigglesworth, Nov. 2, 1836.
Sarah and Stephen Hall of Sutton, int. Mar. 23, 1744-5.
Sarah and Josiah Adams of Mendon, Dec. 27, 1750.
Silance and Thomas Humes, int. Mar. 1, 1773.
Submit and Israel Taft, Nov. 26, 1782.
Thankfull and James Persons, Apr. 13, 1796.
Thomas and Marth[a] Parks, Dec. 14, 1763.
Thomas Jr. and Ruth Carriel of Sutton, Dec. 29, 1768.
Thomas of Southboro, s. of Noah and Lucy, a. 26 y., and Eunice M. Hall, d. of Andrew and Miranda, a. 18 y., Sept. 5, 1849.

REED (see Read), Ebenezer (Jr. int.) and Esther Webb of Braintree, in Braintree, Jan. 26, 1736-7.
Jehiel H. of Upton, and Eliza W. Chillson, int. Oct. 28, 1838.
John, s. of Jonathan of Smithfield, R. I., and Hannah Farnum, d. of Moses, 24th day, 4th mo., called April, 1755. c.r.3.*
Josiah, A.M., and Elizabeth Taylor of Douglas, in Douglas, Apr. 21, 1782.
Thaddeus (Lieut., int.) and Hannah Taylor of Grafton, in Grafton, May 24, 1780.

REMICK, August and Ann Elizabet[h] Niles Tift, int. Dec. 27, 1840.

REYNOLDS, Hannah B. of North Kingston, R. I., and William E. Chase, int. Sept. 22, 1848.

RHOADES (see Rhodes), Elizabeth F. of Dedham, and John C. Robbins, int. Dec. 30, 1849.

RHODES (see Rhoades), George W. of Northbridge, and Elmira D. R. Taft, Nov. 30, 1843.
Salmon (Solomon, c.r.1) of Mendon (of Thompson, Conn., int.), and Phebe Tucker, Feb. 27, 1831.
Sarah and Leonard Alexander, both of Upton, Apr. 29, 1807.*
Zebulon and Abagail Taft, Nov. 17, 1816.
Zebulon and Nancy Follett, Dec. 10, 1837.

RICE, Angeline of Sutton, and Paul D. Hill, Feb. 27, 1844.
Comfort of Milbury, and Lucinda Wood, int. Jan. 4, 1824.
Elisabeth and Matthew Hill of Mendon, Jan. 28, 1746-7.*

* Intention not recorded.

RICE, Elizabeth J. of Blackstone, d. of Stephen and Joanna, a. 21 y., and Whitman P. Braman, s. of Hannah, a. 26 y., May 28, 1846.
Lucy of Upton, and Thomas Walker, int. Feb. 8, 1766.
Mary (Rist, int.) and James Taylor of Sutton, in Sutton, Nov. 21, 1781.
Rachel and Obediah Wheelock, int. June 17, 1765.
Samuel Jr. and Eliza M. Shepherd, Apr. 28, 1825. c.r.1.
Silas of Lancaster, and Elizabeth Taft, int. Dec. 31, 1775.

RICHARDS, Abby Jane of Burrillville, R. I., and Charles Hyde, int. May 18, 1845.

RICHARDSON (see Richerson), Anan and Sarah Arnold Wood of Burrillville, R. I., int. Dec. 13, 1840.
Brown and Keziah Ann Leavans, Mar. 5, 1835.
Caleb T. and Phebe Buffum, int. Nov. 21, 1841.
David and Almira Arnold of Burrillville, R. I., int. Sept. 20, 1829.
Dexter and Olive Brown of Burrillville, R. I., int. June, July 1808.
Elizabeth and Otis Dudley of Harpers Ferry, Va., Aug. 18, 1825. c.r.1.
Isaac of Gloucester, R. I., and Bethiah Woodward, Mar. 30, 1758.
Joseph and Susanna Aldrich, int. Jan. 9, 1780.
Joseph and Molley Pain of Gloucester, R. I., int. Nov. 1, 1784.
Joseph Jr. and Roby Mowry of Smithfield, R. I., int. Nov. 26, 1807.
Joseph and Rosamond Levens of Burrillville, R. I., int. Mar. 17, 1822.
Laura Ann and Maning Arnold of Burrillville, R. I., int. Jan. 30, 1831.
Mary and Amariah Taft, Apr. 29, 1840.*
Mowry and Arilla Thayer of Douglas, int. Nov. 23, 1834.
Rachal, d. of Isaac dec. and Bethiah, and Amos Baker, now residing in Gloucester, R. I., s. of John and Abigail, 7th day, 2d mo. 1783. c.r.3.*
Sally and Smith R. Arnold of Burrillville, R. I., Oct. 21, 1841.
Sarah and Bezaleel Taft, Jan. 2, 1777.
Sarah and Oliver Taft Jr., Nov. 8, 1843.
Simon and Martha Taft of Burrillville, R. I., int. Mar. 5, 1820.

RICHERSON (see Richardson), Isaac of Smithfield, County of Providence, and Sarah Aldrich, int. June 27, 1732.

* Intention not recorded.

RICHMOND, Nabby and (Capt. int.) John Grout, Jan. 1, 1818.
Phebe Ann, d. of Edward and Mary, a. 21 y., and Emery Lamb, s. of Jesse and Mary, a. 23 y., May 16, 1844.
Polly, d. of Edward and Mercy, a. 27 y., and Seth Staples, s. of Ezra and Cynthia, a. 31 y., Oct. 8, 1846.
Susanna of Providence, R. I., and Benjamin Adams Esq., int. Jan. —, 1809.

RICKARD, Truman, Dr., of Woburn, s. of Lemuel and Abigail S. of Hanover, N. H., a. 34 y., and Elizabeth Read Capron, d. of John W. and Abigail M., a. 27 y., Apr. 26, 1848.

RIEDEL (see Riedell), Mary A. C., d. of George C. and Amy S., a. 27 y., and Francis Jackson of Mt. Washington, Ky., s. of Isaac and Betsey, a. 36 y., Sept. 22, 1845.

RIEDELL (see Riedel), Henry and Sarah Ann Thayer, Sept. 26, 1837.

RILEY, Hugh and Harriet Crosman of Northbridge, int. Oct. 8, 1826.

RIST, Abigail and Joseph E. McCrillis of Grafton, Apr. 11, 1832.
Anna and Josiah Taft Jr., int. June 10, 1791.
Betsey and Eli Putnam of Spencer, int. Aug. 27, 1826.
Ezbon and Emeline W. Taylor of Ludlow, int. Apr. 10, 1836.
Joseph and Rachel Keith, Dec. 18, 1766.
Joseph and Jerusha Cutler of Medway, in Medway, May 27, 1779.
Joseph and Allice Marsh, int. Mar. 17, 1791.
Luther and Betsy Sibley of Cumberland, R. I., int. Apr. 12, 1829.
Pheebe and Samuel Draper, formerly of Roxbury, int. Oct. 13, 1739.
Rachel and Nathan White, Jan. 21, 1801.
Rachel, d. of Caleb and Betsey, a. 32 y., and Cornelius Putnam, widr., of Oxford, s. of David and Elizabeth of Sutton, a. 62 y., Oct. 30, 1844.
Sarah and John Wright, Jan. 2, 1783.
Susannah and Samuel Adams, int. Sept. 25, 1790.
Thaddeus and Polly Comstock, Apr. 24, 1803.
Thomas and Mary Fowler of Lebanon, County of Windham, int. Oct. 11, 1735.
Thomas and Sarah Goodwin of Reading, int. Sept. 1, 1739.

* Intention not recorded.

RITE (see Wright), Abigail of Upton, and Timothy Taft Jr., int. Oct. 10, 1779.

ROBBINS (see Robins), Amos and Lucy Bigelow of Worcester, int. Oct. 3, 1830.

Eunice, wid., d. of Ezekiel and Elizabeth Gaskill, a. 36 y., and Nathan Aldrich 2d, widr., s. of Obediah and Judith, a. 52 y., July 8, 1845.

John C. and Elizabeth F. Rhoades of Dedham, int. Dec. 30, 1849.

ROBERSON (see Robinson), Josiah (Robinson, int.) and Anna Barton of Leicester, June 28, 1738.

ROBERTS, Benjamin and Martha S. Bronett of Marshpee, Apr. 12, 1835.

Clara L. of Grafton, and Martin S. Brown, int. Feb. 28, 1847.

ROBINS (see Robbins), Susanna of Douglas, and Mijamin Taft, int. Dec. 12, 1779.

ROBINSON (see Roberson), Abby A. of Mansfield, and George T. Murdock, int. Aug. 24, 1845.

Erastus, Dr., of Northbridge, and Chloe Stone, int. Jan. 23, 1845.

James K. of Smithfield, R. I. (Slatersville, R. I., int.), s. of Gurdon and Clarissa of Mansfield, Conn., a. 27 y., and Abigail W. White, d. of John and Cynthia, a. 23 y., June 17, 1845.

Maria, wid., and Samuel Hugs, int. July 13, 1845.

Maria Bradfoot and Jesse Ware Penniman, both of Mendon, Aug. 16, 1836.*

ROGERS, Mary of New London, Conn., and Samuel Allen, int. Dec. 17, 1743.

ROGERSON, Handel and Harriet McLellan of Portland, Me., int. Jan. 21, 1833.

Robert and Betsey Beman, both of Boston, Jan. 7, 1832.*
Robert (2d, int.) and Ann E. Hart, Feb. 5, 1832.
Robert Jr. and Mary A. Ball, Mar. 26, 1838.

ROOK (see Rooks), John (Rokes, int.) and Deliverance Powers, July 26, 1759.

ROOKS (see Rook), John and Elisabeth Thomson, int. Feb. 1, 1768.

ROSON (see Rawson), Marcy (Rawson, int.) and Josiah Gould White, in Sutton, June 5, 1793.

ROSS, Alminna of Cumberland, R. I., and John Seagrave 3d, int. Jan. 19, 1834.
Sarah and Edward F. Seagrave, Oct. 31, 1838.

ROUND (see Rounds), Champlin and Susanah Kimpton, int. May 9, 1824.

ROUNDS (see Round), Alonzo C. and Hannah Comey of Peterboro, N. H., int. June 8, 1845.
Judy and Duty Taft, int. May 1, 1825.

RUEGGER, John W. and L. Peirce, July 8, 1841.*

RUGGELS, Edward of Pomfret, Conn., and Sibbel Taft, Feb. 14, 1786.

RUSSEL (see Russell), James and Hannah Shearman, int. Aug. 26, 1791.

RUSSELL (see Russel), George S. of Northbridge, s. of Job and Martha of Northbridge, a. 22 y., and Edna L. Bugbee, d. of Charles and Lucy of Waterford, Vt., a. 23 y., Nov. 4, 1845.*
Hannah and (Capt., int.) John Tillinghast, Aug. 7, 1803.

RUTTER, Job of Northbridge, and Sarah Trusdel of Leicester, Apr. 15, 1774.*

RYAN, Jonathan and Betsey Dowse of Sherborn, int. Mar. 1, 1812.

SABEIN (see Saben, Sabin, Seaben), Molle and John Applin of Swansey, int. Sept. 10, 1775.

SABEN (see Sabein, Sabin, Seaben), Gideon M. and Mary A. Farnsworth of Mendon, int. Aug. 24, 1845.
Iseral and Bulah Albee, Sept. 27, 1770.
Lydia and David Read Jr., int. Apr. 21, 1776.
Tho[ma]s (of Mendon, int.) and Sarah Emerson, Jan. 17, 1763.

SABIN (see Sabein, Saben, Seaben), John M., widr., of Woodstock, Conn., s. of Silas and Prudence, a. 60 y., and Maria A. Brown, wid., d. of William and Hannah Arnold, a. 47 y., Apr. 16, 1848.

* Intention not recorded.

SADDLER (see Sadler), Miranda of Upton, and Ziba Cook, int. June 13, 1829.

SADLER (see Saddler), Augusta of Upton, and Warren Rawson, int. Mar. 9, 1823.
Benjamin of Upton, and Pamela Rawson, June 23, 1835. c.r.1.

SAGE, Charlotte and Almon Harris, int. Sept. 8, 1833.
Phebe Ann and Washington Bolster, int. Mar. 20, 1831.

SALBURY, Nicholas of Gloucester, R. I., and Roena Wheelock, int. Oct. 1, 1786.
William of Gloucester, R. I., and Phebe Taft, int. Nov. 27, 1784.

SALES (see Sayles), Willard of Smithfield, R. I., and Mercy Arnold, Apr. 24, 1821.

SANDERS (see Saunders), Mary of Needham, and James Bardens, in Needham, May 17, 1753.

SANFORD, Giles and Mrs. Sally Ann Smith, int. Apr. 12, 1829.

SANGER, John and Eunice Davis of Mendon, Jan. 28, 1767.

SAUNDERS (see Sanders), Huldah M. and Jeduthan Fuller, Apr. 6, 1835.

SAVERY (see Severy), Haman and Jemima Walker of Union, Conn., int. Feb. 27, 1803.

SAWYER, Franklin A. and Hannah Prentis of Hopkinton, int. Sept. 8, 1833.

SAYLES (see Sales), Edwin C. of Burrillville, R. I., and Nancy J. Tenny, Feb. 23, 1843.
Lucy H. of Gloucester, R. I., and Israel M. Southwick, int. May 3, 1840.
Richard and Sarah E. McBride of Northbridge, int. Dec. 7, 1845.

SCOT (see Scott, Scout), Sabra of Bellingham, and Enoch Aldrich Jr., int. Mar. 6, 1798.

SCOTT (see Scot, Scout), Anderson of Bellingham, and Abigail Keith, Jan. 17, 1806.
Charlotte L., d. of Manley and Henrietta, a. 21 y., and Charles Fairbanks, s. of Silas and Millia of Medway, a. 30 y., Dec. 8, 1846.

SCOTT, Crysa A., d. of Manly, a. 26 y., and Eddy C. Smith of Cumberland, R. I., s. of John of Cumberland, R. I., a. 28 y., Oct. 23, 1849.
Eliza S., d. of Ira and Sophronia, a. 30 y., and Seth Taft, s. of Willis and Margery, a. 51 y., July 6, 1848.
Jerusha of Bellingham, and Dorrinton Seagrave, int. Oct. 7, 1804.
Louisa J. of Mendon, d. of Emery and Watee of Mendon, a. 18 y., and James A. Rawson, s. of James and Polly, a. 24 y., June 14, 1844.
Manly of Mendon, and Henrietta Thayer, int. Mar. —, 1810.
Mary of Bellingham, and John Seagrave Jr., int. Feb. 18, 1805.
Samuel W. and Susan Farnum, Oct. 12, 1841.

SCOUT (see Scot, Scott), Joanna of Bellingham, and Ahaz Aldrich, int. Mar. 17, 1792.

SCRIBNER, Cinkler, widr., s. of Iddo and Phebe, a. 37 y., and Caroline S. Seagrave, d. of John and Mary, a. 43 y., Apr. 25, 1849.

SEABEN (see Sabein, Saben, Sabin), Thomas (Sabens, int.) and Sarah Darling of Mendon, in Mendon, Dec. 22, 1768.

SEAGRAVE (see Seagraves, Segrave), Abigail S. and Abiel Thayer of Mendon, June 5, 1836.
Achsah Lana, d. of Dorrington and Jerusha, a. 26 y., and Fisher E. Thayer, s. of Jonathan W. and Polly, a. 24 y., Oct. 5, 1848.
Amy and William Haskell, Mar. 20, 1828. (Mar. 26, 1828. c.r.1.)
Ann (Mary Ann, int.) and George Tiffany of Douglas, Sept. 6, 1820.
Bezaleel and Molly Aldrich, Feb. 19, 1789.
Bezaleel and Jemima Aldrich, int. Dec. 7, 1806.
Bezaleel, widr., s. of John and Sarah, a. 60 y., and wid. Julia E. Chapin, d. of Darius and Lois Taft, a. 40 y., Jan. 4, 1848.
Caleb and Eunace Wood, June 20, 1802.
Caroline S., d. of John and Mary, a. 43 y., and Cinkler Scribner, widr., s. of Iddo and Phebe, a. 37 y., Apr. 25, 1849.
Charles E. and Abigail Carter of Lunenburg, int. May 14, 1848.
Daniel and Mary Weld of Charlton, int. Jan. 31, 1830.

SEAGRAVE, Daniel and wid. Elmira Whipple of Douglas, int. Mar. 26, 1845.
Dorrinton and Jerusha Scott of Bellingham, int. Oct. 7, 1804.
Edward and Louis White, Jan. 6, 1757.
Edward F. and Sarah Ross, Oct. 31, 1838.
Fanny and Isaac R. Murphy (of Sutton, int.), Aug. 12, 1838.
George W. and Mary Rawson, Mar. 27, 1836.
George W., 2d m., s. of Bezaleel, a. 41 y., and Louisa T. Tiffany, b. in Attleboro, d. of Joseph, a. 38 y., Nov. 8, 1849.
Hannah and Newell Taft, Dec. 31, 1843.
Horatio and Bethiah Ward of Pelham, int. Apr. 6, 1834.
Jane, d. of Bezaleel and Jemima, a. 25 y., and John K. Perkins, widr., s. of John and Susan, a. 28 y., May 8, 1845.
John and Eliseb[e]th Johnson, int. Dec. 30, 1757.
John and Sarah Dorrinton, int. Oct. 25, 1778.
John Jr. and Mary Scott of Bellingham, int. Feb. 18, 1805.
John 3d and Alminna Ross of Cumberland, R. I., int. Jan. 19, 1834.
Joseph D. and Rachel C. Holbrook of Sturbridge, int. Oct. 10, 1847.
Lawson (Lawson A., int.) and Priscilla G. Beals, Oct. 24, 1834.
Lewis and Elizabeth B. Williams, Oct. 15, 1840.
Louis and Oren Keyes of Northbridge, Sept. 7, 1783.
Louis T. and Silas W. Plympton, June 24, 1829.
Lucy and Aaron B. Metcalf of Leicester, Sept. 29, 1841.
Maria and Merrill Greene, Nov. 28, 1833.
Mary and David Moulton of Hardwick, Apr. 7, 1840.
Mary A. and Charles B. Rawson, Aug. 31, 1834.
Nancy and Charles A. Wheelock, Apr. 20, 1834.
Polly and James Rawson, Oct. 4, 1804.
Samuel and Betsey Murdock, Sept. 13, 1804.
Sarah and Joel Bolster of Upton, in Mendon, July 30, 1789.
Saul S. and Mary A. Tyler [no date] (int. Mar. 3, 1833).
Scott (Capt., int.) and Eliza Ann Stow, Mar. 21, 1828 (1830, c.r.1) (int. Feb. 28, 1830).
Selissa S., d. of John and Mary, a. 35 y., and Dr. Adams Perry, widr., s. of Adams and Anna, a. 54 y., Oct. 26, 1847.
Sullivan and Anngenett B. Beals of Slatersville, R. I., int. Dec. 20, 1841.
Waity G. and Danford Upham of Dudley, Dec. 2, 1830.
Waity T. and Daniel G. (George D., int.) Carpenter, June 27, 1820. (June 29, 1820. c.r.1.)
William H., s. of John dec. and ———, a. 29 y., and Lucretia E. Wheelock, d. of Elias and Sarah, a. 23 y., Apr. 3, 1844.

SEAGRAVES (see Seagrave, Segrave), Bezaleel (Jr., int.) and Lucy Taft, Jan. 4, 1811.
Hannah and Royal Thayer, June 21, 1812.
Harriot and Joseph Aldrich, Jan. 11, 1811.
Josiah and Lois Taft, Dec. 25, 1798.
Seth and Polly Taft, Feb. 21, 1810. (Feb. 11, 1810. c.r.1.)

SEARS, Lydia A., d. of Thomas and Lydia A., a. 36 y., and Whipple Farnum, widr., s. of Royal and Rosetta, a. 46 y., Nov. 4, 1847.

SEGRAVE (see Seagrave, Seagraves), Olive and Stephen Sprage of Douglas, Sept. 25, 1796.

SEVERY (see Savery), George and Chloe Wood, int. Apr. 21, 1811.

SHEARLOCK, John and Hannah Knowlton of Wrentham, in Smithfield, R. I., Jan. 1, 1760.

SHEARMAN (see Sherman, Shermon), Hannah and James Russel, int. Aug. 26, 1791.
Samuel of Gloucester, R. I., and Mary Corary, int. Apr. 15, 1758.

SHEPHERD (see Sheppard), Eliza M. and Samuel Rice Jr., Apr. 28, 1825. c.r.1.
Jane and Thomas Cummings, int. Mar. 19, 1848.
Sarah and Samuel Dudly Esq., Nov. 25, 1747.*

SHEPPARD (see Shepherd), Simeon of Douglas, and Lois Morss, int. Sept. 21, 1776.

SHERMAN (see Shearman, Shermon), Albert and Lucy Marble, int. Aug. 28, 1836.
James of Mendon, and Marcia C. Stoddard, Apr. 25, 1842.
Mary (Sarah, int.) of Grafton, and Gersham Chapin, in Grafton, Nov. 5, 1778.

SHERMON (see Shearman, Sherman), David (Daniel, int.) of Burrillville, R. I., and Louis Aldrich, Mar. 8, 1812.

SHIPPA (see Shippee), Amelia and Sergeant Blasdell of Smithfield, R. I., int. Dec. 10, 1810.

SHIPPEE (see Shippa), Mary of Smithfield, County of Providence, and Eleazor Albee, int. July 30, 1743.
Nathan of Smithfield, County of Providence, and Mary White, int. Dec. 12, 1743.

* Intention not recorded.

SHOVE, Charlotte B., d. of Luther and Pamelia, a. 21 y., and Welcome Arnold Jr., s. of Welcome and Rebecca, a. 21 y., Dec. 18, 1845.
Esther and Michael Starnes of Smithfield, R. I., int. Aug. 25, 1816.
James M. of Burrillville, R. I., and Barshaba Taft, int. July 15, 1832.
Luther and Pamela Brown, Mar. 20, 1822. (Apr. 20, 1822. c.r.1.) (Mar. 24, 1822, int.)
Mary E., d. of Luther and Pamela, a. 19 y., and John C. Arnold, s. of Welcome and Rebecca, a. 23 y., Apr. 2, 1846.
Thomas and Hannah Keith, int. Nov. 29, 1787.
Thomas M. of Douglas, and Sarah M. Blackburn (Blackman, int.), May 13, 1839.

SIBLAY (see Sibley), Hannah and Jonathan Holman of Sutton, Nov. 3, 1763.

SIBLEY (see Siblay), Betsy of Cumberland, R. I., and Luther Rist, int. Apr. 12, 1829.
David of Oxford, and Anna Aldrich, int. July 20, 1828.
Ezra of Sutton, and Mary (Marcy, int.) Taft, June 1, 1815.
Joel and Lois Wood, int. May 22, 1790.
Lorinda and Charles Arnold, Nov. 6, 1833.
Lydia and Jesse Taft, May 12, 1763.
Lydia and Henry Staples Benson of Mendon, May 6, 1793.
Mary and Daniel Taft, Nov. 22, 1770.
Mary and Benjamin Craggin 3d, Mar. 6, 1836.
Peter and Mary Keith of Killingly, Conn., int. Sept. 3, 1780.
Polly and Miner Mott of Lebanon, Conn., Feb. 28, 1843.
Royal and Lucretia Carter, Oct. 28, 1819.
Stephen and Thankfull Taft, May 30, 1765.
Timothy of Sutton, and Mary Wood, May 27, 1752.

SIMMONS (see Simons), Polly and Abner Pitts, Dec. 25, 1814.

SIMONS (see Simmons), Elizabeth and David Dupee (Draper, int.), in Bedford, Feb. 21, 1733.

SIMSON, Mary Jane and W[illia]m G. Childs of North Woodstock, Conn., Dec. 14, 1840.

SLADE, Hannah S. of Pawtucket, and Charles T. Gillmore, int. Aug. 9, 1829.

SMITH, Aaron of Providence, R. I., and Sophia Balcom, Jan. 1, 1816.
Asa, s. of Caleb and Deborah of Oxford, and Katharine Steere, d. of Thomas of Smithfield, R. I., 6th day, 4th mo. 1780. c.r.3.*
Betsey of Grafton, and Philip Wing, int. Apr. 1, 1821.
Cynthia S. and Lyman Adams, Apr. 11, 1837.
Deborah and Gershom Keith, int. May 31, 1794.
Dolly E. of Providence, R. I., and Samuel Judson Warmsly, int. Nov. 20, 1842.
Eddy C. of Cumberland, R. I., s. of John of Cumberland, R. I., a. 28 y., and Crysa A. Scott, d. of Manly, a. 26 y., Oct. 23, 1849.
Elisabeth of Bellingham, and Jonah Prentis, int. July 8, 1754.
Elisabeth and John Croney, int. May 12, 1764.
James H. of Grafton, s. of Henry and Louisa, a. 23 y., and Sylvia W. Wilson, d. of Samuel and Celia, a. 18 y., Mar. 28, 1848.
Joanna H. of Farmington, Me., and Grosvenor Aldrich, int. July 29, 1849.
John of Sutton, and Molly Chilson, Oct. 20, 1784.
John A. (John Arnold, int.) of Burrillville, R. I., and Lovina Aldrich, Nov. 9, 1828.
Margaret of Mendon, and Orsamus Taft, int. Oct. 14, 1821.
Mary of Burrillville, R. I., and Daniel Farnum, int. June 1, 1823.
Mary, d. of Samuel of Mendon, and Hannah and Ephraim Bassett, s. of Joseph and Rachel, 2d day, 5th mo. 1827. c.r.3.*
Mary, Mrs., of Mendon, and Samuel Hazard, int. Jan. 21, 1849.
Mary D. and William W. Wood of Northbridge, int. Sept. 18, 1842.
Moses and Sally Chapin, Oct. 6, 1803.
Origen and Anne C. Taft, Dec. 20, 1829.
Permelia and Joseph Whiston of Medway, int. Mar. 5, 1800.
Peter and Ellen Clarken of Blackstone, int. Aug. 31, 1845.
Robart Jr. of Bellingham, and Rhoda Taft, int. June 19, 1774.
Rufus of Gloucester, County of Providence, and Mercy Taft, int. Sept. 28, 1751.
Rufus of Smithfield, R. I., and Mary Taft, int. July 9, 1763.
Sabina W. of Mendon, and Lawson Tyler, int. Mar. 8, 1835.
Sally and Daniel Souther Blake of Mendon, int. Sept. 13, 1801.
Sally Ann, Mrs., and Giles Sanford, int. Apr. 12, 1829.
Samuel and Harriet Blackman, July 6, 1829.
Seymore and Betsey E. Wood of Northbridge, int. Feb. 4, 1838.

* Intention not recorded.

SMITH, Solomon and Hannah Hall, int. Feb. 15, 1790.
Susannah of Leicester, and Isaac Bolster, in Leicester, Feb. 4, 1742.
Victorious and Susanna Passmore, Nov. 21, 1771.
William Jr. of Dudley, and Ruth Taft, Sept. 22, 1797.

SNEAL (see Snell), Thankful and Prince Gouldthwight, int. Sept. 10, 1786.

SNELL (see Sneal), Bezaleel and Thankfull Jones, int. May 2, 1779.

SNOW, Cheny of Spencer, and Semantha Bennett, Mar. 10, 1833.
Cyrus B. and Catharine Moore of Holden, int. Mar. 17, 1833.
Deborah of Franklin, and Emerson Fales, int. Jan. 29, 1832.

SOULE, Beza and Mary Rawson of Quincy, int. July 30, 1815.
Mary Ann of Northbridge, d. of Orra and Nancy, a. 23 y., and Daniel Newman, s. of Daniel and Nancy, a. 25 y., Nov. 3, 1847.

SOUTHERLAND, Catharine of Upton, and Henry Green, int. Dec. 6, 1829.

SOUTHWICK, Arold and Patience Lapham of Burrillville, R. I., int. Feb. 11, 1827.
Benjamin F. (of Cumberland, R. I., int.) and Mary Ann Wilber, July 27, 1825.
Daniel and Luvina Thayer of Mendon, int. Oct. 4, 1801.
Duty and Sarah Paine, int. Dec. 23, 1832.
Elisabeth, d. of Lawrance of Mendon, and Moses Farnum, 2d day, 5th mo. 1777. c.r.3.*
Elisha and Delia Purinton of Monson, int. Dec. 28, 1834.
Elisha A. and Athalina Inman of Burrillville, R. I., int. Nov. 14, 1830.
Eliza and Nathaniel Day of Smithfield, R. I., int. May 31, 1812.
Emeline F., d. of Jonathan F. and Chloe, a. 21 y., and Charles A. Messinger, s. of David and Polly, a. 32 y., May 14, 1846.
Esther and James Buxton of Smithfield, R. I., int. June 3, 1771.
Ezra and Chloe Taft, int. May 1, 1803.
Ezra and Suse Taft, int. Oct. 17, 1814.
Ezra and wid. Nancy Taft of Gloucester, R. I., int. Nov. 26, 1837.
George S. and Maria Morse, int. Apr. 14, 1833.

* Intention not recorded.

SOUTHWICK, Israel M. and Lucy H. Sayles of Gloucester, R. I., int. May 3, 1840.
Jonathan F. and Chloe Holbrook, Nov. 14, 1822.
Joseph and Maranda Lapham of Burrillville, R. I., int. Nov. 26, 1820.
Judith Jr. and Otis Aldrich, int. Feb. 18, 1827.
Lavina of Mendon, and Ellis Albee, int. Oct. 23, 1827.
Lydia and Capt. Daniel Morse, int. Jan. 5, 1823.
Mary and Daniel Farnum Jr., int. Dec. 30, 1810.
Moses and Sarah Pulsipher of Douglas, int. Dec. 9, 1804.
Moses D. of Mendon, and Rachel Adaline Fisher, int. May 6, 1830.
Phebe and Dr. John Pond of Mendon, int. Mar. 15, 1818.
Ruth, d. of Lawrence and Hannah, and David Farnum, s. of Moses and Sarah dec., 7th day, 12th mo. 1781. c.r.3.*
Ruth and Asahel Aldrich, int. Oct. 28, 1816.
Sarah and Gershom Keith Jr., int. July 17, 1803.
Stephen H. and Harriet S. Farnum of Blackstone, int. Sept. 16, 1849.
Tamzen, d. of Caleb of Salem and Daniel Aldrich, s. of Jacob, 1st day, 5th mo., called May, 1755. c.r.3.*
Thomas M. and Lavinia B. Mowry of Warwick, R. I., int. Jan. 20, 1839.
William of Mendon, and Abir Trask, int. Sept. 29, 1822.
Willis of Smithfield, R. I., and Sylvia Albee, int. Nov. 10, 1816.

SOUTHWORTH, Josiah and Nancy Taft, Nov. 30, 1806.
Rebeckah of Douglas, and James Cullis, int. Aug. 16, 1807.

SPALDING (see Spaulding), Josiah, Rev., and Mary Williams of Taunton, int. Dec. 28, 1783.

SPAULDING (see Spalding), Girdon R. (of Thompson, Conn., int.), and Irene Taft, May 24, 1843.

SPOONER, Asa and Cynthia Lee, int. May 8, 1825.

SPRAGE (see Sprague), John of Smithfield, R. I., and Elisabeth Titus, Nov. 29, 1764.
Stephen of Douglas, and Olive Segrave, Sept. 25, 1796.

SPRAGUE (see Sprage), Brooksey and Alanson Huet, int. Mar. 6, 1831.
George W., s. of Daniel and Eveline, a. 22 y., and Harriet D. Knapp, d. of William and Eunice of Mendon, a. 21 y., July 22, 1846.

* Intention not recorded.

SPRAGUE, Harriet M. of Leicester, and Edwin D. Fowler, int. Apr. 10, 1836.
Olive and Benjamin French, Oct. 18, 1807.
Rosamond and Benjamin Buffum Jr. (of Douglas, int.), Nov. 14, 1830.
Tamson F. of Douglas, and Eli C. Marsh, int. Dec. 11, 1831.
William and Lydia B. Keith of Milford, int. June 15, 1834.

SPRIG, Uranna of Smithfield, R. I., and Abel Aldrich, int. Oct. 17, 1741.

SPRING, Adolphus Esq. and Mrs. Harriet Thurber, int. Aug. 4, 1839.
Calvin and Hannah Carpenter, May 18, 1817.
Charles C. and Eleanor Prentice of Northbridge, Feb. 15, 1844.
Elkanah and Phebe Capron, June 6, 1805.
Ephraim of Northbridge, and Eunice Taft, Aug. 25, 1774.
Eunice and Ezekiel Wood, Nov. 22, 1827.
George of Charleston, S. C., and Louisa Margaret Taf, int. Sept. 13, 1829.
Hannah of Northbridge, and Bezaleel Taft Jr., Esq., int. Nov. 30, 1817.
Joanna and Diarca Allen (of Medway, int.), June 20, 1822.
Joanna and William Hall (of Sutton, int.) [no date] (int. May 12, 1833).
John and Hannah Crosby of Upton, int. Apr. 13, 1767.
Josiah and Abagail Chapin, June 15, 1815.
Josiah, widr., s. of Ephraim and Eunice, a. 62 y., and Adelia Chapin, d. of John S. and Polly, a. 38 y., Dec. 9, 1846.
Luther and Nancy Read, Dec. 29, 1814.
Luther and Abby Wood, Oct. 23, 1838.
Lyddia and Samuel Fletcher of Northbridge, May 5, 1803.
Margaret S. of Newburyport, and Bezaleel Taft Jr., int. June 13, 1807.
Maria and Merchant Toby (of Northbridge, int.), Mar. 26, 1818. (Mar. 25, 1818. C.R.1.)
Mary and Edward Thurbar of Providence, R. I., Nov. 21, 1765.
Mary and Thomas Taft Jr. of Mendon, in Mendon, Jan. 30, 1777.
Samuel R. and Maria Aldrich of Burrillville, R. I., int. Aug. 31, 1845.
Sarah of Northbridge, and Alpheus Baylies, in Northbridge, Apr. 24, 1794.
Sarah T. and Charles F. Chapin of Milford, Jan. 6, 1842.
Sophronia and Ziba Parkhurst of Milford, Oct. 4, 1821.

STANLEY (see Stanly), Wells Jr. and Hannah Burgess of Douglas, int. June 8, 1823.

STANLY (see Stanley), William and Susan H. Verney of Spencer, int. Sept. 12, 1841.

STAPLES, Abraham of Mendon, and Lydia White, Oct. 1, 1740.*
Charlotte of Mendon, and Willis Brown, int. Nov. 2, 1834.
Ezra F., s. of Ezra and Cynthia, a. 24 y., and Ann A. Adams, d. of Leonard and Maria, a. 17 y., Apr. 6, 1848.
Hannah and John Lewis, June 15, 1748.*
Hannah A. and Cortis (Curtis, int.) Darling, May 20, 1829.
Jonathan of Mendon, and Rachal Holbrook, int. Dec. 29, 1777.
Prudence and Whipple Farnum, Nov. 29, 1829.
Seth, s. of Ezra and Cynthia, a. 31 y., and Polly Richmond, d. of Edward and Mercy, a. 27 y., Oct. 8, 1846.

STARKEY, Lois S. of Providence, R. I., and Rev. William A. Clapp, int. May 30, 1841.

STARNES (see Starns, Stearns, Sterns), Michael of Smithfield, R. I., and Esther Shove, int. Aug. 25, 1816.
Nathan of Douglas, and Sally Lashure, int. April, May, 1809.

STARNS (see Starnes, Stearns, Sterns), Thomas (Stern, int.) of Littleton, and Abigail Read, Apr. 28, 1743.

STEADLY, Sally (Studley, int.) of Sutton, and Asa White, in Sutton, May 28, 1793.

STEARNS (see Starnes, Starns, Sterns), Azuba and William Tray of Worcester, in Worcester, Apr. 6, 1783.*
Micah and Lydia Baker of Douglas, int. Feb. 27, 1796.

STEERE, Katharine, d. of Thomas of Smithfield, R. I., and Asa Smith, s. of Caleb and Deborah of Oxford, 6th day, 4th mo. 1780. c.r.3.*

STEPHENS (see Stevanns), Ivory and Harriet Edmunds of Dudley, int. Oct. 8, 1826.
William and Jimima Thomson, int. Dec. 23, 1752.

STERNS (see Starnes, Starns, Stearns), Ebenezer and Chloe Wood, int. Oct. 16, 1769.
John of Milford, and Abigail Legg, Mar. 27, 1822.

* Intention not recorded.

STEVANNS (see Stephens), Nathan of Douglas, and Patty Morse, int. Oct. 15, 1797.

STOCKWELL, Olive of Sutton, and Luther Thwing, int. Sept. 26, 1802.
Rosalinda of Sutton, and Isaac King, int. Sept. 14, 1845.

STODDARD (see Stodderd), Joseph and Lydia Morse, both of Douglas, Dec. 28, 1807.*
Levi M. of Douglas, and Mary B. Tanner, int. Jan. 27, 1833.
Marcia C. and James Sherman of Mendon, Apr. 25, 1842.
Ophelia, d. of Lott and Joanna, a. 20 y., and James M. Farnum of Northbridge, s. of Daniel and Mary, a. 25 y., May 6, 1847.
Sophronia, d. of Joanna, a. 17 y., and Jonathan Crocker, s. of Edmund and Ann, a. 25 y., Oct. 30, 1845.

STODDERD (see Stoddard), Samuel of Grafton, and Elizabeth Dun, Dec. 6, 1770.

STONE, Chloe and Dr. Erastus Robinson of Northbridge, int. Jan. 23, 1845.
Ezra Jr. of Gloucester, R. I., and Lucina Whit, int. Jan. 6, 1793.
Martha Ann, d. of John S. and Emeline of Boston, a. 21 y., and Lemuel (Lemuel G. int.) Hastings, s. of Nahum and Ann of West Boylston, a. 22 y., May 19, 1844.

STOW (see Stowe), Eliza Ann and (Capt. int.) Scott Seagrave, Mar. 21, 1828 (1830, c.r.1) (int. Feb. 28, 1830).
Jonah of Grafton, and Lydia Powers, int. Oct. 17, 1768.
Silas W. of Boston, and Rhoda Wood, Apr. 7, 1807.

STOWE (see Stow), Susan C. and Warren Lackey, Nov. 24, 1842.

STRAIGHT, Mary and William Dalrumpel, int. Dec. 24, 1770.

STRATFORD, Charles J., widr., of Webster, s. of Samuel and Lucy, a. 53 y., and Hannah C. Holbrook, wid., d. of Robert and Mary Hale, a. 42 y., May 1, 1849.

SUMNER, Clark, Maj., of Milford, and Mary M. Thayer, Sept. 3, 1833.
Luc[e]na and James Usher, Oct. 19, 1837.
Seth of Taunton, and Abigail Buffum, int. Mar. 26, 1791.

* Intention not recorded.

SWASEY, Amy and Ezra Gould of Douglas (Millbury, int.), Sept. 16, 1821.
Harriet and William Jacobs, Apr. 2, 1823.

SWEET, Angel of Upton, and Hannah T. Taft, Nov. 27, 1817.
Angel of Upton, and Mary A. Holroyd, Apr. 28, 1825. C.R.1.
James T. and Polly Howard, both of Northbridge, Mar. 11, 1833.*

SWEETING, Sarah of Providence, and Mijamin Taft, int. Mar. 6, 1733-4.

SWIFT, Nancy and Samuel Willson, Nov. 27, 1806.
Sylvia and Alpheus Inman, int. Mar. 2, 1817.

TAF (see Taft, Tift), Louisa Margaret and George Spring of Charleston, S. C., int. Sept. 13, 1829.

TAFT (see Taf, Tift), Aannah and Robart Clark, int. Oct. 6, 1739.
Aaron and Marcy Arnold of Gloucester, County of Providence, int. Oct. 28, 1749.
Aaron Jr. and Rhoda Rawson, June 1, 1769 (int. June 5, 1769).
Abagail and Joseph Day, May 29, 1816.
Abagail and Zebulon Rhodes, Nov. 17, 1816.
Abigail and Barzillai Taft, in Mendon, Dec. 17, 1772.
Abigail and Ephraim Kingsbury of Oxford, Aug. 14, 1814.
Abigail and Chandler Taft, int. May 9, 1815.
Abigail W. and Lyman Aldrich Jr. of Northbridge, May 28, 1828.
Abner and Tryal White, Nov. 25, 1756.
Abner (Abner 2d, int.) and Abigail Morse, Dec. 8, 1803.
Abner P. and Harriet Balcom of Douglas, int. Nov. 8, 1836.
Adna and Emma Craggin of Douglas, int. May 31, 1818.
Alanson and Polly Kingsbury, int. Oct. 13, 1822.
Albert and Sally L. Bartlett of Douglas, int. Feb. 27, 1848.
Almira of Douglas, and Collins Thayer, int. Aug. 9, 1819.
Amanda N. and Whipple Allen of Milford, June 7, 1843.
Amariah and Mary Richardson, Apr. 29, 1840.*
Amos Craggin and Chloe Bates of Dudley, int. Sept. —, 1808.
Andre and Sally Baker, Aug. 27, 1815.
Ann and Israel Taft, Dec. 22, 1808.
Anna and Charles Colwell of Gloucester, R. I., int. Aug. 26, 1762.
Anna of Mendon, and Stephen Taft, in Mendon, Jan. 3, 1766.

* Intention not recorded.

TAFT, Anne C. and Origen Smith, Dec. 20, 1829.
Arnold (of Douglas, int.) and Nancy Thayer, Sept. 4, 1814.
Asa and Elizabeth Bucknam, Mar. 5, 1767.
Asa and Marcy Taft, int. Dec. 10, 1789.
Asenath A. and Asa Newell of Providence, R. I., Sept. 10, 1826. C.R.1.
Augustine C. and Deborah M. Taylor of Boston, int. Sept. 29, 1839.
Aurilla of Mendon, and Wilcome Ballou of Smithfield, Jan. 10, 1802.*
Azuba and Amos White, May 17, 1770.
Azuba and John Allen (Jr., int.) of Sutton, Oct. 28, 1828.
Bailey and Marinda Taft, Nov. 26, 1812.
Barshaba and James M. Shove of Burrillville, R. I., int. July 15, 1832.
Barzillai and Abigail Taft, in Mendon, Dec. 17, 1772.
Bathiah of Mendon, and Caleb Hill of New Sherborn, int. Nov. 24, 1739.
Benj[ami]n and Naomi Holbrook, Jan. 4, 1753.
Benj[ami]n and Barshaba Dicke, Jan. 14, 1762.
Benjamin and Martha (Abasha, int.) White, May 23, 1822.
Benjamin C. and Hopestill Taft, June 26, 1816.
Betsey and Moses Chapin, Dec. 15, 1796.
Betsy and Keith White, Aug. 16, 1809.
Beulah of Mendon, and Samuel Chapin, in Mendon, Feb. 26, 1761.
Bezaleel and Sarah Richardson, Jan. 2, 1777.
Bezaleel Jr. and Margaret S. Spring of Newburyport, int. June 13, 1807.
Bezaleel Jr., Esq., and Hannah Spring of Northbridge, int. Nov. 30, 1817.
Calista and Ezra Kidder of Alsted, N. H., Sept. 9, 1806.
Calvin and Molley Murdock, June 1, 1786.
Calvin (of Hawkinsville, Ga., int.) and Eliza Maria Taft, June 6, 1839.
Caroline J. and Philip Walden, int. July 11, 1847.
Catharine and John Hall, int. May 2, 1795.
Chandler and Abigail Taft, int. May 9, 1815.
Charles and Rachel P. Aldrich of Northbridge, int. Nov. 7, 1847.
Charles A. and Sarah E. Bowen of Worcester, int. Aug. 29, 1847.
Charlotte and Elbridge G. Daniels of Mendon, int. Dec. 3, 1815.
Charlotte and Moses Daniels (Jr. int.) of Mendon, Sept. 20, 1818.
Charlotte and Capt. George Carpenter, Nov. 5, 1818.

* Intention not recorded.

TAFT, Charlotte E., d. of Orsmus and Margaret, a. 18 y., and Samuel Taft 3d, s. of Warner and Mary, a. 22 y., Apr. 10, 1844.
Chloa and Robart Taft, Feb. 3, 1771.
Chloe and Easman Taft, Dec. 5, 1782.
Chloe and Ezra Southwick, int. May 1, 1803.
Chloe of Mendon, and Oliver Taft, int. Nov. 12, 1805.
Chloe and John Benson (Jr., int.) of Mendon, Dec. 19, 1805.
Chloe and Eaton Walker of New Haven, Conn., May 22, 1832.
Chloe A., d. of Samuel and Dorcas, a. 18 y., and Welcome Hall of Cumberland, R. I., s. of Andrew and Maranda, a. 23 y., Nov. 27, 1845.
Chloe Ann of Mendon, and Gardner Mowry, Jan. 7, 1836.
Chloe M., d. of Luke and Nancy, a. 26 y., and Luke S. Farnum of Northbridge, s. of Daniel and Mary, a. 32 y., Mar. 7, 1849.
Clarinda and Caleb Mowry of Mendon, Sept. 30, 1813.
Clarissa W. and Caleb T. Chapin, Nov. 1, 1830.
Cloe and Edward Lesuer, July 1, 1762.
Cloe and Joseph Thayer, Sept. 3, 1818.
Comfort of Mendon, and Benjamin Read, May 27, 1762.
Cummings and Marcy Green, June 2, 1796.
Daniel and Mary Sibley, Nov. 22, 1770.
Darias and Anna Murdock, int. Sept. 20, 1784.
Darius and Lois Cummings, in Mendon, Dec. 23, 1790.
David and Rachel Mowry of Smithfield, R. I., int. Feb. 18, 1791.
David and Seena Cummings, Nov. 20, 1793.
David and Henrietta Jepherson, in Mendon [no date] (int. Apr. 7, 1833).
Deborah of Mendon, and Noah Keith, int. Aug. 3, 1745.
Deborah and Samuel Penniman of Mendon, Oct. 25, 1770.
Deborah of Killingly, Conn., and David Hoopper, int. May 31, 1778.
Diana and Silvanus Thayer, in Mendon, Feb. 4, 1793.
Duty and Judy Rounds, int. May 1, 1825.
Easman and Chloe Taft, Dec. 5, 1782.
Easman Jr. and Sarah Carpenter, Apr. 11, 1805.
Eastman and Hannah Taft, int. Apr. 19, 1784.
Eber and Uranah Pickering of Mendon, int. Mar. 28, 1819.
Elenor and James O'Neil, Feb. 13, 1831.
Elijah of Mendon, and Phila Chapin, int. Oct. 8, 1789.
Elisabeth and Jonathan Penneman, Sept. 19, 1743.
Elisabeth and Elijah Alexander of Mendon, Oct. 31, 1765.
Elisabeth and Chapin Keith, June 26, 1790 (June 24 dup.).

TAFT, Elisha of Upton, and Expearence Taft, int. July 1, 1754.
Eliza Ann of Sutton, and Dutee Aldrich, in Douglas, May 8, 1837.
Eliza Maria and Calvin Taft (of Hawkinsville, Ga., int.), June 6, 1839.
Elizabeth and Peter Marvell of Providence, in Boston, Dec. 6, 1727.*
Elizabeth and Silas Rice of Lancaster, int. Dec. 31, 1775.
Elizabeth and Ephraim Taft of Boylston, Aug. 23, 1804.
Elkanah and Charlotte P. Hooton, int. Feb. 12, 1843.
Elkanah, widr., s. of Nathaniel and Abigail of Mendon, a. 63 y., and Catharine Aldrich, d. of Nathaniel and Rachel, a. 51 y., Mar. 24, 1847.
Elmira D. R. and George W. Rhodes of Northbridge, Nov. 30, 1843.
Emeline N. and Albert F. Wing, Oct. 15, 1839.
Enos of Mendon, and Phila Albee, in Mendon, Nov. 7, 1799.
Ephraim and Mary Taft, Jan. 3, 1739-40.
Ephraim and Anna Read of Smithfield, County of Providence, int. June 13, 1747.
Ephraim and Abigail Brown, int. Jan. 21, 1771.
Ephraim of Boylston, and Elizabeth Taft, Aug. 23, 1804.
Ephraim and Ann Haskell [no date] (int. Mar. 17, 1833).
Esther and James Taft, Nov. 19, 1767.
Esther and Fuller Murdock, Nov. 22, 1805.
Eunas and Levi Carpenter of Mendon, Nov. 25, 1804.
Eunice and Benjamin White, Jan. 23, 1734-5.
Eunice and Joseph Read, Nov. 22, 1753.
Eunice and Ephraim Spring of Northbridge, Aug. 25, 1774.
Eunice and Phineas Chapin, Sept. 3, 1795.
Expearence and Elisha Taft of Upton, int. July 1, 1754.
Experience and Elijah Holman of Millbury, Oct. 25, 1820.
Ezekiel and Olive Thayer, Nov. 29, 1804.
Ezra and Mercy G. (Mary C., int. and c.r.1) White, Apr. 18, 1821.
Ezra and Susan Keith, Mar. 20, 1823.
Frederick and Abigail Wood of Upton, int. June 4, 1782.
Garshom and Abigail Read, Mar. 22, 1764.
Genery Jr. of Upton, and Laura Hoit, int. Mar. 31, 1833.
George Washington and Nancy Hill of Grafton, int. July 17, 1803.
Hanna[h] and Elisha Benjamin, Sept. 9, 1747.*
Hannah and Peter Keith, Aug. 11, 1748.
Hannah and John Read, June 23, 1763.

* Intention not recorded.

TAFT, Hannah and Jesse Taft, Sept. 10, 1767.
Hannah and Benja[mi]n Murdock, int. Apr. 8, 1782.
Hannah and Eastman Taft, int. Apr. 19, 1784.
Hannah and Stephen Carpenter, Jan. 30, 1801.
Hannah and Benjamin Buffum, May 5, 1822.
Hannah T. and Angel Sweet of Upton, Nov. 27, 1817.
Harriet and (Dr., int.) Daniel Thurber of Mendon, Oct. 25, 1824. (Oct. 28, 1824. C.R.1.)
Harriet E. and Abraham Fletcher of Mendon, Aug. 21, 1839.
Henry and Hannah Rawson, int. Sept. 7, 1845.
Hopestill of Mendon, and David Farnum Jr., in Mendon, Jan. 21, 1796.
Hopestill and Benjamin C. Taft, June 26, 1816.
Huldah and Parker Tyler, Dec. 9, 1810.
Irene and Silas (Silas M., int.) Wheelock, May 5, 1841.
Irene and Girdon R. Spaulding (of Thompson, Conn., int.), May 24, 1843.
Isaac of Mendon, and Deborah White, int. Feb. 25, 1741-2.
Israel and Submit Read, Nov. 26, 1782.
Israel and Ann Taft, Dec. 22, 1808.
Jacob and Esther Marsh, Feb. 13, 1745-6.
Jacob Jr. and Mary Taft, int. Feb. 21, 1777.
Jacob, s. of John and Lucretia, a. 25 y., and Abby A. Wheelock, d. of Elias and Sarah, a. 22 y., Jan. 10, 1849.
James and Esther Taft, Nov. 19, 1767.
James M. and wid. Sally Law, int. June 21, 1829.
Jane T. and Silas B. Crawford (Elias B. of Grafton, int.) [no date] (int. Mar. 9, 1834).
Jason and Jerusha Newell, Dec. 24, 1818.
Jemima and Peter White, May 20, 1736.
Jesse and Lydia Sibley, May 12, 1763.
Jesse and Hannah Taft, Sept. 10, 1767.
Joanna B., d. of Zadock and Abigail, a. 39 y., and Russell Wilson of Mendon, s. of Jedediah and Polly of Mendon, a. 32 y., Dec. 11, 1844.
John and Hannah Cheney (of Medfield, int.), in Boston, Apr. 11, 1734.
John, Capt., and Deborah White, Feb. 22, 1759.
John and Sarah Wiley, int. Sept. 27, 1760.
John and Mary Harwood, Nov. 25, 1762.
John and Lucretia Newell, Sept. 9, 1818.
Joseph and Elizabeth Thayer, int. Jan. 23, 1740-1.
Joseph 3d (minor, int.) and Elisabeth Cumings, Feb. 12, 1752-3.
Joseph and Abigail Marsh, int. Oct. 19, 1772.

TAFT, Joseph 3d and Hannah Keath, Feb. —, 1773.
Joseph 3d and Sophia Boyd of Burrillville, R. I., in Burrillville, R. I., Aug. 19, 1821.
Joseph Warren and Susan Thayer of Smithfield, R. I., int. Mar. 8, 1824.
Joshua of Mendon, and Mary Johnson, in Mendon, Apr. 24, 1757.
Josiah and Lydia Taft of Mendon, in Mendon, June 11, 1755.
Josiah and Margree Green, int. Mar. 2, 1777.
Josiah Jr. and Anna Rist, int. June 10, 1791.
Judith, wid., and Samuel H. Green [no date] (int. Jan. 19, 1834).
Judson and Sally (Sarah B., int.) Keyes, Nov. 12, 1816.
Julia E. and Stephen Chapin of Milford, Mar. 19, 1826. C.R.1.
Katharin and Elisha Thompson of Douglas, Apr. 4, 1802.
Keith and Phebe Holbrook of Douglas, int. June 18, 1790.
Kesiah and William Hayward of Mendon, in Mendon, Nov. 11, 1741.
Lenard and Asenah Thayer of Douglas, int. July 30, 1790.
Levi, s. of Silas, and Mary Cook, d. of Ebenezer of Mendon, 2d day, 6th mo. 1775. C.R.3.*
Levina and Abraham Aldrich of Mendon, in Mendon, Mar. 31, 1768.*
Lewis and Silvia Green, Aug. 25, 1822.
Lois and Silas Taft 3d, int. Oct. 31, 1773.
Lois and Josiah Seagraves, Dec. 25, 1798.
Lois, Mrs., of Sutton, and Benjamin French, int. Dec. 14, 1834.
Lorin B., s. of Benjamin and Bathsheba, a. 24 y., and Paulina Wheelock, d. of Thomas and Paulina, Nov. 3, 1847.
Louisa M. and Frederick W. Patterson of Rochester, N. Y., Sept. 16, 1834.
Louisa M. and William Lee, int. May 15, 1836.
Lucretia (wid., int.) and (Lieut. int.) John Benson, Mar. 13, 1831.
Lucy and Samuel Cummings, Dec. 9, 1762.
Lucy and Webb Taft, Nov. 29, 1792.
Lucy and Ebenezer Winslow, Oct. 7, 1795.
Lucy and Bezaleel Seagraves (Jr., int.), Jan. 4, 1811.
Luke and Nancy Wood, Mar. 7, 1809.
Luther and Deborah Keith, Oct. 16, 1803.*
Lydia of Mendon, and Josiah Taft, in Mendon, June 11, 1755.
Lydia and John Cass of Richmond, int. Sept. 21, 1767.
Lydia and Royal Wheelock, in Mendon, Jan. 11, 1790.
Lydia and Alpheus White, Feb. 13, 1798. (Feb. 24, 1798. C.R.1.)

* Intention not recorded.

TAFT, Lydia and Jonathan Wood of Upton (Mendon, int. and c.r.1), Apr. 5, 1801.
Lyman and Deborah Wood, Apr. 11, 1786.
Marcy and Sweetin Taft, Jan. 19, 1785.
Marcy and Asa Taft, int. Dec. 10, 1789.
Marcy and Lieut. Joseph Torry of Mendon, Oct. 6, 1793.
Margaret and Levi White, Dec. 5, 1765.
Margaret and Mason Matthewson of Killingly, Conn., Aug. 28, 1808.
Margaret and Calvin Guild of Hookset, N. H., May 19, 1836.
Margaret L., d. of Bezaleel and Hannah, a. 30 y., and Dr. Alonzo W. Bennett, s. of James and Parna of Rindge, N. H., a. 29 y., Nov. 30, 1848.
Margarett and Ely Chapin of Worcester, int. Mar. 29, 1778.
Margery of Upton, and Simeon Wood, int. May 17, 1760.
Maria and Mellen Taft, Apr. 17, 1822.
Marinda and Bailey Taft, Nov. 26, 1812.
Martha of Burrillville, R. I., and Simon Richardson, int. Mar. 5, 1820.
Marvel of Northbridge, and Ruth Murdock, Apr. 29, 1784.
Marvel of Northbridge, and Molly Taft, Apr. 21, 1817.
Mary and Ephraim Taft, Jan. 3, 1739–40.
Mary and Rufus Smith of Smithfield, R. I., int. July 9, 1763.
Mary and Jacob Taft Jr., int. Feb. 21, 1777.
Mary and James Hewes of Gloucester, R. I., int. Aug. 6, 1785.
Mary (Marcy, int.) and Ezra Sibley of Sutton, June 1, 1815.
Mary and Joseph H. Perry, Feb. 16, 1820.
Mary and Reuben Green, int. Oct. 25, 1829.
Mary and James McNamara, int. May 9, 1830.
Mary A. of Mendon, and Stephen C. Jillson, int. Jan. 24, 1847.
Mary Ann and Hosea Aldrich, May 25, 1834.
Mary G. (Hannah G., int.) and Newell Taft, Oct. 26, 1822. (Oct. 24, 1822. c.r.1.)
Mehittabelle and Washington Hunt of Burrillville, R. I., Aug. 17, 1809.
Mellen and Maria Taft, Apr. 17, 1822.
Mercy and Rufus Smith of Gloucester, County of Providence, int. Sept. 28, 1751.
Michajah and Phebe Cummings, int. July 30, 1790.
Mijamin and Sarah Sweeting of Providence, R. I., int. Mar. 6, 1733–4.
Mijamin and Susanna Robins of Douglas, int. Dec. 12, 1779.
Mijamin and Mary Clark of Gloucester, R. I., int. May 5, 1787.

TAFT, Mijamin and Hannah Thayer, Mar. 15, 1798.
Milley and Ezekiel Clark, Mar. 26, 1792.
Molle and Simon Pain of Gloucester, R. I., int. Dec. 5, 1774.
Molly and Marvel Taft of Northbridge, Apr. 21, 1817.
Moses and Perscilla Thayer of Mendon, Sept. 3, 1735.
Moses Jr. and Nancy Taft, int. July 23, 1780.
Moses Jr. and Judith Cumming (Juda Cummings, int.), May 26, 1785.
Moses and Molly Wood, Apr. 25, 1817.
Moses 2d and Sylvia A. Wheelock, Apr. 27, 1834.
Mowry of Burrillville, R. I., and Sarah Rawson, Nov. 28, 1816. (Mowry Taft of Burrillville, R. I., and Sarah Richardson, int. Oct. 26, 1816.)
Murdock and Sally Capron, June 9, 1808.
Na[h]um and Rachel Allbee, Feb. 19, 1767.
Nancy and Moses Taft Jr., int. July 23, 1780.
Nancy and Josiah Southworth, Nov. 30, 1806.
Nancy, wid., of Gloucester, R. I., and Ezra Southwick, int. Nov. 26, 1837.
Nancy and Thomas A. Manchester of Millbury, int. Apr. 9, 1843.
Nathan and Mary Coopper of Gloucester, R. I., int. Nov. 22, 1758.
Nathan Jr. and Sarah Kimpton of Gloucester, R. I., int. Aug. 25, 1798.
Nathaniel, s. of Mijamin and Hannah Cass, d. of Daniel of Richmond, N. H., 4th day, 2d mo., called February, 1768. C.R.3.*
Nathaniel of Mendon, and Abagail Holbrook, in Mendon, May 31, 1768.*
Newell and Mary G. (Hannah G., int.) Taft, Oct. 26, 1822. (Oct. 24, 1822. C.R.1.)
Newell and Hannah Seagrave, Dec. 31, 1843.
Noah and Margret Keith, Nov. 23, 1752.
Noah Jr. and Charlotta Arnold of Gloucester, R. I., int. Jan. 30, 1790.
Olive and Ameriah Chapin, Jan. 4, 1787.
Olive and Othnial Tyler of Hopkinton, Mar. 8, 1789.
Olive of Sutton (wid., a. 40 y., int.), and Nicholas Baylies (a. 83 y., int.), July 3, 1823.
Oliver and Moley White, Nov. 21, 1772.
Oliver and Chloe Taft of Mendon, int. Nov. 12, 1805.
Oliver Jr. and Sarah Richardson, Nov. 8, 1843.
Orsamus and Margaret Smith of Mendon, int. Oct. 14, 1821.

* Intention not recorded.

TAFT, Otis, Capt. and Mary Ann Holroyd of Pawtuxet, R. I., int. Oct. 15, 1818.
Paris (Paris T., int.) and Julia Ann Burgess, Mar. 5, 1833.
Parla and Cornelius Wells of Montague, July 16, 1799. (July 8, 1799. C.R.1.)
Parly (Parla P., int.) and Amory Warren of Alstead, N. H., May 17, 1821.
Patience and Robart Gibbs Tillinghast, int. Oct. 21, 1781.
Patience and Abner Cooper of Northbridge, int. Sept. 18, 1803.
Paul and Mehitable Cook, May 10, 1750.*
Peter and Elizabeth Cheney of Medfield, in Medfield, Apr. 20, 1736.
Peter and Mary Arnold of Gloucester, R. I., June 4, 1767.
Phebe and Aaron Balkam of Douglas, in Douglas, Jan. 18, 1781.*
Phebe and William Salbury of Gloucester, R. I., int. Nov. 27, 1784.
Philena and Timothy Craggin of Douglas, June 6, 1799.
Phinehas and Jemime Thomson (of Douglas, int.), Sept. 22, 1774.
Phinehas and Relief Kimball of Milford, int. Mar. —, 1808.
Phinehas Smith and Laura Lesure, int. Feb. 16, 1834.
Polly of Mendon, and Bezaleel White, in Mendon, Apr. 25, 1793.
Polly (Dolley, int.), and Hezekiah Murdock, Feb. 7, 1798. (Feb. 13, 1798. C.R.1.)
Polly and Seth Seagraves, Feb. 21, 1810. (Feb. 11, 1810. C.R.1.)
Polly and Ebenezer H. Davis, May 11, 1836.
Priscilla and Timothy Taft, Dec. 6, 1770.
Reuben and Mercy Thayer of Mendon, int. Apr. 11, 1761.
Reuben and Faithful Thayer, int. July 19, 1761.
Reuben and Nancy Foster of Dudley, int. Jan. 13, 1805.
Rhoda and Robart Smith Jr. of Bellingham, int. June 19, 1774.
Rhoda and John Grant, int. Sept. 21, 1776.
Rhoda G. and Curtis Forbush of Grafton, int. Sept. 1, 1839.
Robart and Chloa Taft, Feb. 3, 1771.
Robert and Mary Balcom of Douglas, int. May 23, 1841.
Royal and Molly (or Polly, int.), Aldrich, Dec. 19, 1805.
Rozannah and Josiah Wood Jr. of Northbridge, May 25, 1791.
Ruth and Joseph Chapen, Mar. 9, 1758.
Ruth and William Smith Jr. of Dudley, Sept. 22, 1797.
Ruth S. of Mendon, and Jonas Nutting, int. Apr. 12, 1840.
Sally, Mrs., and James Lawler, Dec. 4, 1830.
Samuel and Hannah Jeperson of New Sherborn, Apr. 12, 1739.

* Intention not recorded.

TAFT, Samuel and Mary Murdocks, int. Dec. 16, 1758.
Samuel Jr. and Rachel Cumstock of Smithfield, R. I., int. Jan. 20, 1777.
Samuel and Experiance Humes, Jan. 9, 1786.
Samuel 2d and Sarah Mowry of Mendon, Aug. 25, 1803.
Samuel 2d and Dorcas Keith of Ward, int. Nov. 21, 1824.
Samuel and Maria Mowry, Apr. 27, 1828.
Samuel 3d, s. of Warner and Mary, a. 22 y., and Charlotte E. Taft, d. of Orsmus and Margaret, a. 18 y., Apr. 10, 1844.
Sarah and Daniel Read, Jan. 28, 1735-6.
Sarah and Jededeiah Buffum of Smithfield, R. I., int. Aug. 18, 1757.
Sarah and Thomas Joslen of Smithfield, R. I., int. Jan. 26, 1767.
Sarah and Benjamin Albb of Gloucester, R. I., int. Aug. 1, 1768.
Sarah and Otis Hunt, Feb. 20, 1796.
Sarah and John B. Brown of Wilmington, June 29, 1807.
Sarah and Amariah A. Wood, Sept. 10, 1834.
Selina and Jesse Murdock, Mar. 12, 1793.
Seth and Jemima Angel of Smithfield, R. I., int. Feb. 21, 1761.
Seth, s. of Willis and Margery, a. 51 y., and Eliza S. Scott, d. of Ira and Sophronia, a. 30 y., July 6, 1848.
Sibbel and Edward Ruggels of Pomfret, Conn., Feb. 14, 1786.
Silas and Mary Farnum, int. Dec. 30, 1748.
Silas, s. of Stephen and Elisabeth Cruff, d. of Samuel of Smithfield, Dec. 4, 1768.
Silas and Kezia Twitchel, Apr. 26, 1771.
Silas 3d and Lois Taft, int. Oct. 31, 1773.
Silvanus and Mrs. Margery Chillson of Smithfield, R. I., int. Dec. 29, 1822.
Simon P. and Lucretia M. Bemis of Spencer, int. Sept. 14, 1834.
Squire and Mary Pickering of Mendon, int. Sept. 2, 1827.
Stephen and Mary Lewis of New Sherborn, int. Feb. 15, 1733-4.
Stephen and Marcy Hazletine, Apr. 14, 1763.
Stephen and Anna Taft of Mendon, in Mendon, Jan. 3, 1766.
Stephen and Almira (Elmira, int.) Legg, Dec. 2, 1819.
Susan S. and Abner Aldrich of Smithfield, R. I., Feb. 29, 1844.
Susanna and Joel Thompson, int. Dec. 27, 1778.
Susanna and Isaac Dresser of Charlton, int. Dec. 4, 1780.
Susannah of Douglas, and Amory Thayer, int. June 12, 1816.
Suse and Ezra Southwick, int. Oct. 17, 1814.
Sweetin and Marcy Taft, Jan. 19, 1785.
Sweeting and Sarah Inman, Nov. 25, 1829.
Tabbrah (Tabatha, int.) and James Yates of Providence, Jan. 6, 1733-4.

TAFT, Tabitha and Simeon Fish of Mendon, Nov. 10, 1768.
Thadeous and Silence Holbrook, int. Apr. 8, 1777.
Thankfull and Stephen Sibley, May 30, 1765.
Thomas (Jr., int.) of Mendon, and Lidia Thompson, Mar. 8, 1732–3. C.R.1.
Thomas Jr. of Mendon, and Mary Spring, in Mendon, Jan. 30, 1777.
Timothy and Priscilla Taft, Dec. 6, 1770.
Timothy Jr. and Abigail Rite of Upton, int. Oct. 10, 1779.
Timothy and Polly Marsh of Douglas, int. May 31, 1818.
Trial and Joseph Tyler, June 23, 1809.
Unice and David Read, int. Sept. 5, 1732.
Warner and Mary Legg of Upton, int. Jan. 21, 1821.
Webb and Lucy Taft, Nov. 29, 1792.
Willard and Meritea (Maritta Boyd, int.) Bards of Burrillville, R. I., Mar. 3, 1816.
Willard and Ann H. Aldrich, int. Dec. 30, 1832. Banns forbid by Ann H. Aldrich, Dec. 31, 1832.
Willard and Mary Aldrich, Aug. 10, 1841.
William and Anna Harris of Gloucester, R. I., int. Feb. 8, 1777.
William and Winositt Preston, int. Feb. 21, 1779.
William H. and Arrina Loge of Burrillville, R. I., int. Oct. 7, 1832.
Willis and Margare Craggin of Mendon, in Mendon, Dec. 14, 1786.
Zadok and Abigail Bennet of Northbridge, int. Oct. 2, 1800.
Zadok A., s. of Zadock and Abigail, a. 27 y., and Mary M. Brown, d. of George and Sarah of Burrillville, R. I., a. 29 y., Jan. 17, 1845.
Zilpah and Nathan Fisher of Mendon, Dec. 20, 1795.

TALER (see Taylor), Joseph of Concord, and Hannah Wheat, int. Aug. 18, 1758.

TAMPLEN (see Tamplin), Dorithy and Thomas Ellison, Dec. 6, 1768.
William and Sarah Derumple, Nov. 27, 1739.

TAMPLIN (see Tamplen), Mary of Dighton, and John Ellison, int. Mar. 17, 1764.

TANCRED, James and Sarah Ledwick, int. Nov. 10, 1847.

TANNER, Mary B. and Levi M. Stoddard of Douglas, int. Jan. 27, 1833.

TAYLOR (see Taler), Abraham of Concord, and Jemima Wheat, int. Nov. 18, 1758.
Deborah M. of Boston, and Augustine C. Taft, int. Sept. 29, 1839.
Elizabeth of Douglas, and Josiah Reed, A.M., in Douglas, Apr. 21, 1782.
Emeline W. of Ludlow, and Ezbon Rist, int. Apr. 10, 1836.
Hannah of Grafton, and (Lieut., int.) Thaddeus Reed, in Grafton, May 24, 1780.
Humphry and Hannah Farnum, int. Oct. 19, 1828.
James of Sutton, and Mary Rice (Rist, int.), in Sutton, Nov. 21, 1781.
Lucina of Sutton, and Dutee S. White, int. Mar. 1, 1846.
Percival and Hannah Holbrook of Smithfield, R. I., in West Boylston, June 13, 1838.

TEFFT, Jemima of Smithfield, R. I., and Ebenezer Handy, int. Feb. 4, 1764.

TEMPLE, Lucinda of Marlborough, and Samuel S. Mowry, int. Sept. 4, 1831.

TENNEY (see Tenny, Tinney), John and Lillis Walling, both of Burrillville, R. I., May 15, 1843.*
Mary and Hiram H. Hervey, Aug. 20, 1833.
Sarah and Alfred Arnold, Nov. 13, 1833.

TENNY (see Tenney, Tinney), Nancy J. and Edwin C. Sayles of Burrillville, R. I., Feb. 23, 1843.

TERRY, Martha (Torry, int.) and John Hull, Oct. 25, 1773.

TEWKSBURY, Ezekiel F. and Olive Perry of Milford, int. Mar. 23, 1835.

THACHER, John and Dulcina Brigham of Grafton, int. Dec. 22, 1816.

THAYER, Abiel of Mendon, and Abigail S. Seagrave, June 5, 1836.
Abigail and Dan Alexander, int. Oct. 28, 1838.
Amory and Susannah Taft of Douglas, int. June 12, 1816.
Amos and Louis White, Sept. 15, 1785.
Arrilla of Douglas, and Mowry Richardson, int. Nov. 23, 1834.
Asa and Mary Murdock, int. Apr. 19, 1782.
Asa Jr. and Chloe (Chloe T., int.) Chapin, Sept. 24, 1827.
Asenah of Douglas, and Lenard Taft, int. July 30, 1790.

* Intention not recorded.

THAYER, Augustus and Maria (Sylvia M., int.) Ellison, Oct. 5, 1837.
Barbara of Mendon, and Henry Holbrook, in Mendon, Sept. 22, 1791.
Bathsheba of Mendon (of Uxbridge, int.), and Joseph Jackson (of Mendon, int.), May 8, 1760.
Beala and Deborah Keith, both of Mendon, Oct. 4, 1838.*
Bulah and Abner Belew, Sept. 5, 1750.*
Charles and Fanny Hall, June 25, 1837.
Charlotte of Sutton, and Warren Murdock, int. May 25, 1823.
Charlotte M., d. of Sullivan and Ruth, a. 23 y., and Samuel W. Wiggin of Ashland, a. 30 y., Nov. 2, 1846.
Collins and Almira Taft of Douglas, int. Aug. 9, 1819.
Comfort and James Keith, May 17, 1722.*
Deborah of Mendon, and Simeon Wheelock, in Mendon, Nov. 28, 1763.
Elisabeth of New Sherborn, and Benjamin Archer, Nov. 28, 1739.
Elisha of Douglas, and Molly Keith, int. May 16, 1812.
Elizabeth and Joseph Taft, int. Jan. 23, 1740–1.
Elizabeth and Israel Keith, both living at New Sherborn, int. May 13, 1741.
Enoch, Dr., of Gloucester, R. I., and Rhoda Aldrich, int. May 3, 1801.
Faithful and Reuben Taft, int. July 19, 1761.
Fisher E., s. of Jonathan W. and Polly, a. 24 y., and Achsah Lana Seagrave, d. of Dorrington and Jerusha, a. 26 y., Oct. 5, 1848.
Frances and Allen Packard, Jan. 1, 1839.
Grindal and Amy Mitchel, int. Oct. 6, 1787.
H. Adaline and Edwin Armsby of Northbridge, Nov. 30, 1842.
Hannah of Mendon, and Jonathan Cook (Jr., int.), in Mendon, Mar. 21, 1754.
Hannah and Mijamin Taft, int. Mar. 15, 1798.
Hannah of Blackstone, and Lyman Legg, int. June 15, 1845.
Henrietta and Gideon Frost of Wells, int. Mar. 11, 1781.
Henrietta and Manly Scott of Mendon, int. Mar. —, 1810.
Jared and Mary Rawson, both of Mendon, Jan. 16, 1803.*
Jemima of Mendon, and Joseph Baxter, in Mendon, Aug. 14, 1734.
Jeremiah and Allice Holbrook, Apr. 21, 1748.
Jerusha of Mendon, and Benjamin Corary (Crary, int.), Mar. 30, 1741.
Joel of Boston, and Abagail Brastow, Nov. 17, 1808.

* Intention not recorded.

THAYER, John of Mendon, and Ruth Ellis, int. July 8, 1749.
Joseph of Mendon or Bellingham, and Sarah Balcom, int. Feb. 27, 1740–1.
Joseph and Rachel Jepherson, Oct. 11, 1764.*
Joseph and Cloe Taft, Sept. 3, 1818.
Lois and Elias Philps (Philips, int.) of Milford, July 1, 1790.
Lucy J. of Douglas, d. of Turner and Lydia of Douglas, a. 21 y., and John C. Hammond of Douglas, s. of John and Nancy of Douglas, a. 20 y., Feb. 9, 1846.*
Luvina of Mendon, and Daniel Southwick, int. Oct. 4, 1801.
Lyman W. of Bellingham, and Chloe Ann Mowry, int. Mar. 19, 1848.
Margaret of Mendon, and Jonathan (Joshua, int.) Farnum, in Mendon, Nov. 16, 1752.
Marthay of New Sherborn, and Samuel Humes, Dec. 7, 1743.*
Marvel of Douglas, and Lucinda Aldrich, Apr. 27, 1820.
Mary and Jerimiah Cheson Jr., int. Oct. 19, 1750.
Mary and Ebenezer Coffin (of Boston, int.), May 28, 1786.
Mary of Amherst, and Frost Draper, int. Sept. 13, 1812.
Mary Jane, d. of Wiles and Polly, a. 19 y., and Isaac Alexander, s. of Samuel and Polly, a. 21 y., May 28, 1846.
Mary M. and Maj. Clark Sumner of Milford, Sept. 3, 1833.
Mehetible of Mendon, and Silas Aldrich, Aug. 9, 1774.
Mercy of Mendon, and Reuben Taft, int. Apr. 11, 1761.
Micah and Sarah Emerson, Mar. 2, 1757.
Molley and Silvenes Holbrook, int. Jan. 20, 1772.
Nancy and Arnold Taft (of Douglas, int.), Sept. 4, 1814.
Naomi of Mendon, and S[t]ephen Corray, int. Jan. 23, 1769.
Obed P. of Mendon, s. of Otis and Mercy of Mendon, a. 21 y., and Eliza Albee, d. of Ellis and Lavinia, a. 17 y., Nov. 14, 1844.
Olive and Ezekiel Taft, Nov. 29, 1804.
Oliver of Mendon, and Hannah Cook, Sept. 25, 1753.
Peletiah (Lieut., int.) of Mendon, and Hannah Blake, Mar. 21, 1793.
Perscilla of Mendon, and Moses Taft, Sept. 3, 1735.
Peter of Mendon, and Sarah Holbrook, in Mendon, June 12, 1740.
Phebe and Joseph Emerson, Dec. 3, 1767.*
Polly of Mendon, and Wheeler Aldrich, int. Sept. 12, 1841.
Reuben and Experience White, Mar. 21, 1765.
Reuben and Abagal Wood of Northbridge, int. Mar. 28, 1777.
Rhoda (of Douglas, int.) and Micah Holbrook, Nov. 27, 1766.
Rhoda of Mendon, and John Holbrook, in Mendon, Dec. 6, 1770.

* Intention not recorded.

THAYER, Royal and Hannah Seagraves, June 21, 1812.
Sally of Douglas, and Ezekiel Wood Jr., int. Nov. 9, 1798.
Samuel 3d of Mendon, and Sarah Farnum, May 9, 1754.
Samuel and Judah Walker of Ashford, int. Jan. 6, 1782.
Samuel of Douglas, and Amelia Blackman, Apr. 28, 1816.
Sarah and William Jepsson, both of New Sherborn, int. Aug. 1, 1740.
Sarah Ann and Henry Riedell, Sept. 26, 1837.
Sarah R. and Henry Chapin Esq., Oct. 7, 1839.
Sarah S. of Douglas, and Ananias Gifford, int. Mar. 24, 1822.
Sibel, d. of Uriah and Peter Darling, s. of Samuel, June 24, 1776.
Silvanus and Diana Taft, in Mendon, Feb. 4, 1793.
Sullivan and Charlotte Mowry, Sept. 6, 1814.
Susan of Smithfield, R. I., and Joseph Warren Taft, int. Mar. 8, 1824.
Susannah of Mendon, and Aaron White, in Mendon, Dec. 25, 1739.*
Tarzah of Douglas, and Aaron Aldrich, Jan. 23, 1769.
Thaddeus of Douglas, and Margarett Holbrook, int. May 24, 1778.
Thankful of Mendon, and Silvanus Holbrook, in Mendon, Oct. 25, 1748.
Turner and Lydia Batcheler of Douglas, int. Jan. 11, 1824.
Uriah of Mendon, and Abigal White, June 2, 1768.
Zilpah of Mendon, and John Holbrook, in Mendon, Mar. 11, 1732 (int. Jan. 13, 1742-3).

THOMAS, Thomas of Upton, and Sabra Thwing, Aug. 5, 1802.

THOMPSON (see Thomson), Abigail and Richard Aldrich, int. Nov. 22, 1801.
Alexander, s. of Elisha, a. 23 y., and Watee Ann Gifford, d. of Ananias, a. 17 y., Apr. 10, 1845.
Benja[min] and Eunice Morse, int. Mar. 2, 1791.
Elbridge G. and Julia Ann Whitaker, both of Mendon, Dec. 8, 1836.*
Elisha Jr. and Sarah Chace, int. Oct. 21, 1781.
Elisha of Douglas, and Katharin Taft, Apr. 4, 1802.
Elisha Jr. of Douglas, and Seviah Darling, int. May 30, 1813.
Ellis and Marcy Morse, int. Feb. 6, 1820.
Emily R., d. of Adams and Charity, a. 27 y., and Nahum W. Fay of Berlin, s. of Dexter and Zilpha, a. 23 y., Sept. 12, 1844.
Everett and Eliza Ann Chilson of Smithfield, R. I., Sept. 1, 1834.
Joel and Susanna Taft, int. Dec. 27, 1778.

* Intention not recorded.

THOMPSON, Joel, s. of Stephen of Smithfield, County of Providence, and Hannah Mitchel of Burrillville, in said county, d. of John Esten Esq., Oct. 24, 1819.*
John W. and Laura Marsh of Oxford, int. Jan. 19, 1823.
John W. and Phebe Howland of Douglas, int. July 24, 1825.
Lidia and Thomas Taft (Jr., int.) of Mendon, Mar. 8, 1732-3. c.r.1.
Marcy and Samuel Humes Jr., both of Douglas, Apr. 5, 1769.*
Mary and Nathan[ie]ll Potter (of Leicester, int.), Dec. 2, 1755.
Mary of Smithfield, R. I., and Micah Holbrook, int. May 30, 1779.
Peter of Douglas, and Elizabeth Baker of Oxford, Feb. 26, 1807.*
Polley and Nathaniel Emerson Jr., Jan. 27, 1797.
Sam[ue]ll and Mary Hill of Holliston, int. Jan. 28, 1745-6.
Stephen and Cynthia Williams, Sept. 13, 1798.
Stephen and Prudence Marcey, Feb. 6, 1834.
William and Lydia Dyer (of Hopkinton, int.), in Hopkinton, Jan. 10, 1769.
Willis and Armelia Aldrich, Dec. 1, 1803.

THOMSON (see Thompson), Benjamin and Mary Bly of Leicester, int. Aug. 10, 1732.
Elisabeth and John Rooks, int. Feb. 1, 1768.
Elisha and Abigail Cook, Feb. 20, 1745-6.
Jemime (of Douglas, int.) and Phinehas Taft, Sept. 22, 1774.
Jimima and William Stephens, int. Dec. 23, 1752.
Joseph and Marthay Thurston, Sept. 9, 1731.*
Keziah and Levi Walker of Pomfret, Conn., June 12, 1760.
Martha and John Connedy, Aug. 11, 1730.*
Mehetabel and John Hylord (Hillyard, int.), Feb. 14, 1765.
Moses and Mary Eliot, Nov. 12, 1741.
Nathaniel and Abigail Winter, int. Oct. 8, 1743.
Roger of Smithfield, R. I., and Elisabeth Fish, Jan. 12, 1769.
William and Mehitable Hillard of Hadley, Oct. 25, 1740.*
Woodlan and Sarah Danils of Mendon, Jan. 16, 1734-5.

THORNTON, William (Dr., int.) of Grafton, and Ruth A. Chapin, May 17, 1830.

THURBAR (see Thurber), Edward of Providence, R. I., and Mary Spring, Nov. 21, 1765.

THURBER (see Thurbar), Daniel (Dr., int.) of Mendon, and Harriet Taft, Oct. 25, 1824. (Oct. 28, 1824. c.r.1.)
Harriet, Mrs., and Adolphus Spring Esq., int. Aug. 4, 1839.

* Intention not recorded.

THURSTON (see Thurstun), Benjamin and Elizabeth Hayward of Mendon, in Mendon, Oct. 26, 1739.
Martha and Samuel Gary (of Pomfret, County of Windham, int.), Nov. 10, 1752.
Marthay and Joseph Thomson, Sept. 9, 1731.*

THURSTUN (see Thurston), David and Abigail Burks (Burke, int.), June 5, 1744.

THWING (see Twing), Albert and Laura Ann Fisher of Holliston, int. May 16, 1824.
Almon and Sarah Ann Darling, int. Aug. 19, 1832.
Anna and Ebenezer D. Draper, Sept. 11, 1834.
Asenath and Asa F. Onion of Bellingham, int. Oct. 23, 1819.
Asenath, wid., and John Persons, Feb. 20, 1827. C.R.1.
Benjamin and Molley Fisk of Mendon, int. Nov. 20, 1770.
Benjamin Jr. and Anna Mowry of Mendon, May 10, 1798.
Charles A. and Uraniah Keith, Oct. 5, 1828.
Hannah and Isaiah Burman (Buckman, int.) of Bethel, Vt., Jan. 7, 1794.
Hannah B. and George Draper of Palmer, Wednesday, Mar. 6, 1839.
John of District of Conway, and Ruth Holbrook, Oct. 6, 1771.
Luther and Olive Stockwell of Sutton, int. Sept. 26, 1802.
Mary M. and Freeman Nickerson, Oct. 21, 1830.
Mary Scott and Nathan Wheeler of Southborough, Jan. 16, 1827. C.R.1.
Mercy and Elihu Brown, in Mendon, Dec. 30, 1789.
Minerva and William Knight, Oct. 22, 1839.*
Molley and Samuel Rawson, June 23, 1785.
Paulina and Leonard (Leonard M., int.) Parker, Jan. 10, 1829.
Sabra and Thomas Thomas of Upton, Aug. 5, 1802.
Sarah and Aaron Batcheller of Northbridge, in Northbridge, Dec. 10, 1789.
Sarah M. and James A. Whipple, int. Sept. 23, 1832.
Susan A. and Manning W. Anson, Apr. 1, 1827. C.R.1.
Sylvia W., d. of Benjamin and Anna, a. 20 y., and Joseph B. Bancroft, s. of Samuel and Mary, a. 23 y., Sept. 11, 1844.

TIFFANY, George of Douglas, and Ann (Mary Ann, int.) Seagrave, Sept. 6, 1820.
Louisa T., b. in Attleboro, d. of Joseph, a. 38 y., and George W. Seagrave, 2d m., s. of Bezaleel, a. 41 y., Nov. 8, 1849.

* Intention not recorded.

TIFT (see Taf, Taft), Ann Elizabet[h] Niles and August Remick, int. Dec. 27, 1840.
Mary Ann (Taft, int.) and Farnum Gifford, Oct. —, 1834.

TILLEY, Betsey and W[illia]m Haskell, Oct. 5, 1805.*

TILLINGHAST, Anna and Levi Willard of Mendon, int. Mar. 26, 1780.
John (Capt. int.) and Hannah Russell, Aug. 7, 1803.
Patience and W[illia]m Holroyd of Providence, R. I., Nov. 28, 1805.
Robart Gibbs and Patience Taft, int. Oct. 21, 1781.
Sarah S. and Griffin Clark of Douglas, Apr. 1, 1832.

TILT, Rawson and Lucy A. Beckwith, both of Mendon, Apr. 30, 1837.*

TINNEY (see Tenney, Tenny), Mary, Mrs., and Independence Whipple, int. Apr. 7, 1833.
Moses of Mendon, and Hannah Whitney, Mar. 16, 1737-8.

TITUS, Elisabeth (of Douglas, int.) and James Yates, Dec. 26, 1753.
Elisabeth and John Sprage of Smithfield, R. I., Nov. 29, 1764.
Henry of Sutton, and Sarah Williams, May 22, 1822.

TOBY, Merchant (of Northbridge, int.) and Maria Spring, Mar. 26, 1818. (Mar. 25, 1818. C.R.1.)
Sarah A. of Worcester, and P. W. Dudley, int. Sept. 11, 1842.

TORREY (see Torry), Ebenezer Esq. of Fitchburg, and Sarah Arnold, Dec. 25, 1832.
Hannah of Mendon, and Eben[eze]r Read, int. Dec. 23, 1738.

TORRY (see Torrey), Caleb of Douglas, and Mary Tyler, Jan. 30, 1831.
Deborah and Seth Rawson, int. Nov. 20, 1780.
Joseph of Mendon, and Nabbe Wheelock, int. Sept. 25, 1788.
Joseph, Lieut., of Mendon, and Marcy Taft, Oct. 6, 1793.

TOURTELOTT, Betsy of Mendon, and James Albee, int. Feb. 11, 1821.

TRASK, Abir and William Southwick of Mendon, int. Sept. 29, 1822.
Anna and Samuel Lee, int. Dec. 3, 1820.
Esther and William Hunt, in Douglas, Dec. 13, 1787.
Marcy of Mendon, and Joseph Buxton, int. Mar. 3, 1805.

* Intention not recorded.

TRASK, Mary and Royal Aldrich, int. Mar. 16, 1828.
Rebecah, d. of Nicholas of Mendon, and Noah White, s. of John, 2d day, 6th mo., called August, 1750. C.R.3.*
Stephen and Juda Hunt of Northbridge, in Northbridge, Aug. 2, 1785.

TRAY, William of Worcester, and Azuba Stearns, in Worcester, Apr. 6, 1783.*

TREADWAY, Harriet of Salem, Conn., and William E. Keith, int. July 26, 1846.

TRIFLE (see Triphel), Jane and Mathew Colins, Oct. 31, 1765.

TRIPHEL (see Trifle), Mary and Ebenezer Chace, June 30, 1768.

TRIPP, Susan A., d. of David and Nancy, a. 19 y., and Richard B. Gibson, s. of Richard and Ann of Ware, a. 20 y., Feb. 26, 1846.

TRUSDEL, Sarah of Leicester, and Job Rutter of Northbridge, Apr. 15, 1774.*

TUCKER, Benjamin Jr. and Mary White, Apr. 30, 1826.
Chilion and Meribah Mowry of Douglas, int. July 20, 1816.
Jonathan and Esther Martin of Douglas, int. Oct. 26, 1817.
Laban of Winchendon, and Elvira S. Edmonds, Oct. 7, 1831.
Lydia and Theophilus S. Brown of Douglas, int. Aug. 4, 1833.
Mary and George Wall, int. Apr. 28, 1811.
Permila and Adolphus Jepherson, Mar. 26, 1826.
Phebe and Salmon (Solomon, C.R.1) Rhodes of Mendon (of Thompson, Conn., int.), Feb. 27, 1831.
Royal and Susan M. Bullock, Mar. 8, 1831.
Sarah M., d. of Benjamin and Mary, a. 18 y., and Welcome Ballou Jr. of Burrillville, R. I., s. of Welcome and Lavinia, a. 26 y., July 23, 1848.
Uranah Farnum and Henry Marshal of Saco, Me., int. June 2, 1833.

TURNER, Andrew E. and Mary W. Baker of Grafton, int. Sept. 9, 1832.
Rebecca of Medfield, and (Ens., int.) Edmund Rawson, in Medfield, Mar. 21, 1782.

TWICHEL (see Twitchel), Nathan and Hannah Kimpton, Dec. 18, 1766.

* Intention not recorded.

TWING (see Thwing), Annah· and Josiah Bucknam Jr. of Bethel, Vt., Jan. 9, 1794. c.r.1.*

TWIST, Lydia, d. of Lydia of Salem, and Benjamin Aldrich, s. of Abel, 6th day, 9th mo., called September, 1759. c.r.3.*

TWITCHEL (see Twichel), Daniel and Keziah Holbrook, July 12, 1742.
Jonas and Joana Aldrich, int. Feb. 1, 1768.
Kezia and Silas Taft, Apr. 26, 1771.

TYLER (see Tylor), Charlotte and Eber Arnold, Mar. 13, 1831.
Joseph and Mary Draper of Roxbury, int. Aug. 30, 1756.
Joseph and Ruth Read, Apr. 2, 1761.
Joseph and Trial Taft, June 23, 1809.
Kilita and Eleazer Keith of Thompson, Conn., Oct. 8, 1801.
Lawson and Sabina W. Smith of Mendon, int. Mar. 8, 1835.
Malinda and John Welds of Charlton, Oct. 26, 1806.
Mary and Ezekiel Morse of Sutton, Feb. 18, 1785.
Mary and Caleb Torry of Douglas, Jan. 30, 1831.
Mary A. and Saul S. Seagrave [no date] (int. Mar. 3, 1833).
Mehetable and Ezra Holbrook of Townsend, Nov. 18, 1771.
Nancy and Capt. Moses Whitney, Apr. 3, 1796.
Nathan and Nancy Man of Wrentham, int. Dec. 12, 1788.
Othnial of Hopkinton, and Olive Taft, Mar. 8, 1789.
Parker and Huldah Taft, Dec. 9, 1810.
Patty and Dr. James Mann of Wrentham, int. Dec. 12, 1788.
Phineas and Phila Benson of Mendon, in Mendon, Jan. 29, 1788.
Royal and Polley Weels of Canterbury, int. June 26, 1791.
Solomon and Mary Archer, int. Dec. 4, 1780.
Solomon and Jerusha Newell of Dudley, int. May —, 1809.
Timothy and Susanna Fish of Mendon, Dec. 10, 1774.

TYLOR (see Tyler), Elijah of Upton, and Ruth Owen of Mendon, Sept. 14, 1749.*

UNDERWOOD, Hannah C., Mrs., of Charlestown, and Jacob Aldrich, Nov. 29, 1838.

UPHAM, Danford of Dudley, and Waity G. Seagrave, Dec. 2, 1830.
Elizabeth, d. of Danforth and Watee, a. 19 y., and James W. Day, s. of Joseph and Abby, a. 29 y., Nov. 25, 1846.

* Intention not recorded.

USHER, Daniel Jr., s. of Daniel and Freelove, a. 22 y., and Hannah F. Hall, d. of Isaac and Polly, a. 19 y., Dec. 16, 1847.
James and Luc[e]na Sumner, Oct. 19, 1837.
John and Susan R. Lawrence, int. Jan. 25, 1846.
Joseph, b. in Smithfield, R. I., s. of Daniel and Freelove, a. 25 y., and Susan Hall, b. in Temple, Me., d. of John P. and Ann, a. 23 y., Dec. 25, 1845.

VARNEY (see Verney), Andrew J. and Amy G. Lewis, Nov. 29, 1836.
Lydia and Thomas J. Aldrich, Mar. 29, 1836.

VEAUX, Louisa (Voax, int.) and Joseph Chapin, Aug. 12, 1824.

VERNEY (see Varney), Susan H. of Spencer, and William Stanly, int. Sept. 12, 1841.

VERRY, Foster of Mendon, and Rachel Holbrook, int. Apr. 25, 1810.

VIAL, Jemima of Upton, and Henry Corban, July 27, 1826.

VOSS, Maria E. and Edwin M. Black, Mar. 31, 1828.

WADKINS, Miriam of Hopkinton, and Ezekiel Aldrich, in Hopkinton, Feb. 20, 1794.

WAICKFIELD, Silas and Ann Marsh, Feb. 17, 1767.*

WAIT (see Waite), Caroline G. and John D. Parker, int. Oct. 13, 1839.
Mary of Boston, and Dr. Josiah F. Flagg, int. Sept. 20, 1818.

WAITE (see Wait), Hipzebah of Sutton, and Isaac Bolster, June 4, 1735. (May 4, 1735. C.R.1.)*

WALDEN, Philip and Caroline J. Taft, int. July 11, 1847.

WALKER, Benjamin and Margaret Rawson of Mendon, Nov. 15, 1773.
David of New Salem, and Martha Jacobs, May 28, 1812.
Eaton of New Haven, Conn., and Chloe Taft, May 22, 1832.
Esther and Whitney Wood, Feb. 7, 1808.
Hipsibah and Henery Chace, int. Feb. 8, 1766.
Jemima of Union, Conn., and Haman Savery, int. Feb. 27, 1803.
Judah of Ashford, and Samuel Thayer, int. Jan. 6, 1782.

* Intention not recorded.

WALKER, Lemuel and Nabby D. Blanchard (of Sutton, int.), Apr. 3, 1835.
Levi of Pomfret, Conn., and Keziah Thomson, June 12, 1760.
Levi and Elisabeth Wallice, May 11, 1769.
Obediah of Sutton, and Eunice White, Oct. 28, 1745.
Reuben and Mary Read, Nov. 28, 1764.
Sylvia A. and Cyprian Whitney (Whiting, int.) of Douglas, Aug. 1, 1838.
Thomas and Lucy Rice of Upton, int. Feb. 8, 1766.
Timothy and Olive Arnold, in Mendon, Nov. 5, 1793.
William C. and Eliza H. Quint of Sanford, Me., int. Nov. 11, 1832.

WALKUP, Mary and Robert Follet, May 14, 1820.

WALL, George and Mary Tucker, int. Apr. 28, 1811.

WALLACE (see Wallice, Wallis), Rufus of Douglas (Sutton, int.) and Molly Paine, Jan. 18, 1827. C.R.1.

WALLCUTT, Elizabeth (of Attleborough, County of Bristol, alias Smithfield, County of Providence, int.) and Ebenezer Emerson, in Smithfield, R. I., last of March or beginning of April, 1733.

WALLICE (see Wallace, Wallis), Elisabeth and Levi Walker, May 11, 1769.

WALLING, Lillis and John Tenney, both of Burrillville, R. I., May 15, 1843.*
Whipple of Providence, R. I., and Calista Keech of Burrillville, R. I., May 15, 1843.*
Willard W. of Providence, R. I., and Adeline Morse, int. Sept. 25, 1848.

WALLIS (see Wallace, Wallice), Benjamin and Lydia Dudley, both of Douglas, Nov. 9, 1747.*
David of Douglas, and Abial Albee, int. Oct. 25, 1778.
Elisabeth of New Sherborn, and Benjamin Eliot, Sept. 29, 1737.
Joshua of Plainfield, County of Windham, and Hannah Winter, Nov. 6, 1739.
Lydia and Josiah Humes, Dec. 7, 1767.*
Mary and Francis Boon of Upton, June 10, 1786.
Nathaniel (of Douglas, int.) and Elisabeth Bardens, Dec. 9, 1758.

* Intention not recorded.

WARD, Bethiah of Pelham, and Horatio Seagrave, int. Apr. 6, 1834.
Daniel of Sutton, and Mary Rawson, in Mendon, Sept. 20, 1792.
Elijah and Alice Holebrook, Sept. 16, 1762.
Garshom of Grafton, and Prudance Powers, Sept. 1, 1768.
Polly of Sutton, and Isaac Rawson, int. Mar. 29, 1794.

WARE, Albert O. and Mehetabel Haws of Cumberland, R. I., int. Apr. 26, 1835.

WARFIELD, Experance and Jonathan Hibbard, Apr. 1, 1742.

WARMSLY, Elizabeth and William Anthony, int. July 15, 1832.
Samuel Judson and Dolly E. Smith of Providence, R. I., int. Nov. 20, 1842.

WARNER, Daniel and Mary Jane Horn, Mar. 17, 1833.
Harriet (Harriet B., int.) and Loring C. Guild, Sept. 28, 1836.

WARREN, Amory of Alstead, N. H., and Parly (Parla P., int.) Taft, May 17, 1821.
Elisabeth and Amariah Preston, int. Aug. 26, 1757.
John of Grafton, and Polly Chapin, May 20, 1797. (Aug. 20, 1797. C.R.I.) (July 30, 1797, int.)

WASHBURN, Susannah of Mendon, and John Kimpton, in Mendon, Dec. 1, 1768.

WATERMAN, Richard of Warwick, R. I., and Dianna Maria Chapin, Feb. 15, 1831.

WATERS, Joshua of Leverett, and Olive Packard, Apr. 26, 1819. (Joshua Waters of Leverett, and Ellis Packard, int. Nov. 30, 1818.)
Mary M. and John A. Bowen, Apr. 18, 1844.

WEBB, Elizabeth and Isaac Coit Esq. of Plainfield, Nov. 15, 1773.
Esther of Braintree, and Ebenezer Reed (Jr., int.), in Braintree, Jan. 26, 1736-7.
Mary and Peter Harwood, Apr. 22, 1756.
Nathan, Rev., and Ruth Adams of Braintree, in Braintree, Nov. 23, 1751 (int., Oct. 30, 1731).
Nathan, Rev., and Elisabeth Pratt of Medfield, int. Nov. 12, 1763.

WEELS, Polley of Canterbury, and Royal Tyler, int. June 26, 1791.

WEIGHTMAN, Ann (Mary Ann, int.) of Springfield, Vt., and Charles Murdock, Oct. 18, 1842.

WELCH, Hannah and John W. Chadwick, Sept. 4, 1836.
Lucy and Jeremiah Murphy, Aug. 3, 1834.
Palmer and Emely C. Willson of Mendon, int. Apr. 24, 1836.

WELD (see Welds), Mary of Charlton, and Daniel Seagrave, int. Jan. 31, 1830.

WELDS (see Weld), John of Charlton, and Malinda Tyler, Oct. 26, 1806.

WELLINGTON, Eliza W. of Waltham, and John A. Whitney, int. Mar. 19, 1837.

WELLS, Cornelius of Montague, and Parla Taft, July 16, 1799. (July 8, 1799. c.r.1.)

WESCOT, Damaris and Ezekiel Wood, int. Jan. 20, 1799.

WHEALER (see Wheeler, Wheler), Rachel of Grafton, and Timothy Winter, int. June 2, 1764.

WHEAT, Anna and John Burnap of Hopkinton, May 1, 1755.
Hannah and Joseph Taler of Concord, int. Aug. 18, 1758.
Jemima and Abraham Taylor of Concord, int. Nov. 18, 1758.

WHEATON, George of Taunton, and Frances (Fanny, int.) Willard, June 17, 1820. (June 7, 1820. c.r.1.)
Laban M. of Norton, and Eliza B. Chapin, June 25, 1829.

WHEELER (see Whealer, Wheler), Ambrose C. of Northbridge, s. of Ephraim and Charlotte, a. 21 y., and Gratia A. Lockwood of Northbridge, d. of Amasa and Henrietta, a. 19 y., Oct. 11, 1848.*
Nathan of Southborough, and Mary Scott Thwing, Jan. 16, 1827. c.r.1.
Sarah of Sutton, and Thomas Fuller, in Sutton, Feb. 6, 1749–50.

WHEELOCK, Abby A., d. of Elias and Sarah, a. 22 y., and Jacob Taft, s. of John and Lucretia, a. 25 y., Jan. 10, 1849.
Alpheus and Rachal Armstron of Gloucester, R. I., int. Nov. 28, 1785.
Charles A. and Nancy Seagrave, Apr. 20, 1834.

* Intention not recorded.

WHEELOCK, Daniel and Deborah Darling of Mendon, in Mendon, Mar. 30, 1732.
Deborah of Gloucester, R. I., and Enoch Aldrich, int. Oct. 21, 1774.
Elias and Sarah Wood, Sept. 12, 1819.
Eunice and Jesse Chapen, Nov. 20, 1783.
Hannah of Gloucester, R. I., and Henery Keith, int. Sept. 27, 1760.
Jerry and Sukey Day, Jan. 24, 1811.
Lucretia E., d. of Elias and Sarah, a. 23 y., and William H. Seagrave, s. of John dec., and ———, a. 29 y., Apr. 3, 1844.
Nabbe and Joseph Torry of Mendon, int. Sept. 25, 1788.
Nancy and Caleb N. Allen of Mendon, Jan. 17, 1807. (Jan. 11, 1807. c.r.1.)
Obediah and Rachel Rice, int. June 17, 1765.
Olive and Benjamin Buffum Jr. of Douglas, int. May —, 1810.
Paul and Deborah Morse, Aug. 30, 1784.
Paulina, d. of Thomas and Paulina, and Lorin B. Taft, s. of Benjamin and Bathsheba, a. 24 y., Nov. 3, 1847.
Phebe of Mendon, and (Lieut., int.) Nathan Keith, in Mendon, Jan. 10, 1788.
Philetas and Avis Handy of Gloucester, R. I., int. Nov. 10, 1790.
Rachel and Nath[anie]l Branch, Mar. 8, 1799.
Roena and Nicholas Salbury of Gloucester, R. I., int. Oct. 1, 1786.
Royal and Lydia Taft, in Mendon, Jan. 11, 1790.
Seth of Gloucester, R. I., and Levina Hunt, Feb. 17, 1796.
Silas (Silas M., int.) and Irene Taft, May 5, 1841.
Simeon and Deborah Thayer of Mendon, in Mendon, Nov. 28, 1763.
Simeon of Northbridge, and Catharine Croney, int. Sept. 16, 1804.
Sophia and Benjamin Buffum of Douglas, int. Nov. 18, 1849.
Sylvia A. and Moses Taft 2d, Apr. 27, 1834.

WHELER (see Whealer, Wheeler), Sarah of Sutton, and Simeon Black (Blake, int.), in Sutton, Nov. 4, 1779.

WHIPPLE, Elenor and Noah Arnold of Gloucester, County of Providence, int. Dec. 1, 1743.
Elmira, wid., of Douglas, and Daniel Seagrave, int. Mar. 26, 1845.
Eunice of Dana, and Samuel Emerson, int. Jan. 23, 1803.
Independence and Sophia Manton of Providence, R. I., int. Jan. 4, 1824.

WHIPPLE, Independence and Mrs. Mary Tinney, int. Apr. 7, 1833.
James A. and Sarah M. Thwing, int. Sept. 23, 1832.
John and Hannah Comstock of Smithfield, R. I., int. June 26, 1742.
Joseph C. and Chloe White of Douglas, int. July 30, 1820.
Mary and Joseph Manton (Marston, int.) of Johnston, R. I., May 6, 1812.
Mary Ann of Pelham, and John M. Keith, int. Sept. 1, 1833.

WHISTON, Joseph of Medway, and Permelia Smith, int. Mar. 5, 1800.

WHIT (see White, Wight), Lucina and Ezra Stone Jr. of Gloucester, R. I., int. Jan. 6, 1793.

WHITAKER, Julia Ann and Elbridge G. Thompson, both of Mendon, Dec. 8, 1836.*

WHITE (see Whit, Wight), Aaron and Sarah Holbrook, int. Apr. 19, 1738.
Aaron and Susannah Thayer of Mendon, in Mendon, Dec. 25, 1739.*
Aaron and Sarah Howland, Nov. 29, 1838.
Abiel and Abraham Fairfield of Gloucester, R. I., int. Apr. 10, 1798.
Abigail W., d. of John and Cynthia, a. 23 y., and James K. Robinson of Smithfield, R. I. (Slaterville, R. I., int.), s. of Gurdon and Clarissa of Mansfield, Conn., a. 27 y., June 17, 1845.
Abigal and Uriah Thayer of Mendon, June 2, 1768.
Adam and Sarah Craton of Douglas, Feb. 10, 1771.
Alpheus and Lydia Taft, Feb. 13, 1798. (Feb. 24, 1798. c.r.1.)
Alpheus of Mendon, and Rhoda Rawson, Oct. 14, 1802.
Ameriah and Phebe Wood, int. Oct. 6, 1786.
Amos and Azuba Taft, May 17, 1770.
Asa and Sally Steadly (Studley, int.) of Sutton, in Sutton, May 28, 1793.
Avery and Ruth Hartwell Billings of Dedham, int. Feb. 14, 1813.
Bathsheba and Ezekiel Wood 3d, int. Nov. 29, 1802.
Benjamin and Eunice Taft, Jan. 23, 1734-5.
Benjamin and Naoma Cook, Apr. 28, 1743.*
Benjamin and Philena Morse of Warwick (Philenda of Norwich, int.), in Warwick, May 28, 1786.

* Intention not recorded.

WHITE, Benjamin J. and Joann Allen of Barrington, R. I., int. May 11, 1834.
Bethany and Samuel Allen of Milford, Apr. 26, 1785.
Bezaleel and Polly Taft of Mendon, in Mendon, Apr. 25, 1793.
Chloe of Douglas, and Joseph C. Whipple, int. July 30, 1820.
Comfort and David Legg of Mendon, int. June 18, 1791.
David P., Dr., and Caroline Mowry, Sept. 7, 1837.
Deborah and Isaac Taft of Mendon, int. Feb. 25, 1741-2.
Deborah and Capt. John Taft, Feb. 22, 1759.
Deborah and David Hall, Apr. 28, 1785.
Douglas and Ruth Albee of Gloucester, int. June 10, 1771.
Dutee S. and Lucina Taylor of Sutton, int. Mar. 1, 1846.
Ebenezer (of Mendon, int.) and Elisabeth Ellis, Apr. 21, 1748.
Elizabeth of Douglas, and Silas Coy, int. Mar. 15, 1801.
Esther and William Creaton, int. Mar. 11, 1730-1.
Eunice and Obediah Walker of Sutton, Oct. 28, 1745.
Experience and Reuben Thayer, Mar. 21, 1765.
Ezra and Chloe Wood, Feb. 19, 1795. c.r.1.
Hannah and Nehemiah Hall (Jr., int.), June 1, 1786.
Hannah D. and Samuel O. White, Sept. 27, 1838.
Hannah Gould and Ellis Aldrich, Mar. 3, 1803.
Jemima and Joseph Cleaveland, May 24, 1770. (Joseph Clenelan and Jemima White, int. Dec. 18, 1769.)
Jesse and Elisabeth Archer, int. Feb. 7, 1764.
Jesse of Northbridge, and Anna Mason, int. Mar. 28, 1777.
John and Elisabeth Pane of Gloucester, R. I., int. Dec. 24, 1777.
John Jr. and Mercy Yates of Douglas, int. Jan. 3, 1800.
Jonathan and Abigail Bowker of Hopkinton, in Hopkinton, Jan. 21, 1785.
Jonathan and Mary Albee, Oct. 12, 1823.
Joseph Jr. and Judith Clark, Dec. 4, 1734.
Joseph and Deborah Fish of Mendon, in Mendon, Mar. 15, 1759.
Joseph of Smithfield, R. I., and Susanna Orrel, int. July 2, 1780.
Joseph Jr. and Naomi Wilson of Mendon, Feb. 17, 1792.
Josiah and Hannah Gould of Sutton, in Sutton, Nov. 14, 1765.
Josiah and Mary Green of Mendon, in Mendon, Jan. 26, 1769.
Josiah (Isaiah, int.) and May Perks (Mercy Parkes, int.) of Hardwick, in Hardwick, Sept. 20, 1798.
Josiah Gould and Marcy Roson (Rawson, int.), in Sutton, June 5, 1793.
Keith and Betsy Taft, Aug. 16, 1809.
Keith W. and Caroline Farnum of Ashford, Conn., int. Oct. 25, 1829.

WHITE, Leonard of Bellingham, and Maria Darling, Jan. 31, 1836.
Levi and Margaret Taft, Dec. 5, 1765.
Lewis S. and Sarah G. Flagg of Needham, int. Mar. 6, 1825.
Louis and Edward Seagrave, Jan. 6, 1757.
Louis and Amos Thayer, Sept. 15, 1785.
Lydia and Abraham Staples of Mendon, Oct. 1, 1740.*
Marcy and Jesse Morse, Jr., int Apr. 8, 1782.
Martha and Simon (Simeon, int.) Alexander of Mendon, in Mendon, May 21, 1786.
Martha (Abasha, int.) and Benjamin Taft, May 23, 1822.
Mary and Nathan Shippee of Smithfield, County of Providence, int. Dec. 12, 1743.
Mary and Nathan Rawson, Feb. 18, 1762.
Mary and Benjamin Tucker Jr., Apr. 30, 1826.
Mason of Smithfield, R. I., and Rhoda Wood, Feb. 5, 1822.
Mercy G. (Mary C., int. and C.R.1) and Ezra Taft, Apr. 18, 1821.
Miranda and Zara Howe, Oct. 14, 1822.
Moley and Oliver Taft, Nov. 21, 1772.
Moses and Abigail Fish, int. Feb. 7, 1746–7.
Moses and Abigal Keith, int. Mar. 4, 1748–9.
Moses and Abigail Holbrook of Mendon, in Mendon, Dec. 12, 1749.
Moses and Mary Cragin of Mendon, int. Nov. 5, 1757.
Nathan of Douglas, and Martha Combs, Mar. 16, 1770.*
Nathan and Eunice Chapin of Worcester, in Worcester, Jan. 14, 1779.
Nathan and Abigail Anthony of Gloucester, R. I., in Mendon, Mar. 6, 1793.
Nathan and Rachel Rist, Jan. 21, 1801.
Nathan Jr. of Worcester, and Elizabeth (Elizabeth H., int.) Read, Oct. 31, 1822.
Noah, s. of John, and Rebecah Trask, d. of Nicholas of Mendon, 2d day, 6th mo., called August, 1750. C.R.3.*
Olive and Joseph Morse, Jan. 13, 1785.
Orpah and Silas Morse, Feb. 15, 1791.
Paul and Mary Bolcum of Douglas, int. Jan. 25, 1768.
Paul and Susanna Parkas (Parkes, int.), Dec. 5, 1771.
Paul and Chloe Leshure, int. Nov. 19, 1777.
Paul (Jr., int.) and Martha Evans, in Hopkinton, June 18, 1778.
Pellatiah and Ellener Aldrich of Douglas, int. June 3, 1804.
Peter and Jemima Taft, May 20, 1736.
Peter Jr. and Chloe Farnum, Dec. 4, 1766.

* Intention not recorded.

WHITE, Philander and Mary Eddy of Mendon, int. Oct. 17, 1824.
Prudence and Benoni Benson of Mendon, Sept. 3, 1739.
Prudence of Mendon, and James Albee, in Mendon, Jan. 21, 1745 (prob. 1745–6) (int. Aug. 23, 1745).
Prudence and Caleb Handy, int. May 12, 1796.
Rachel and William Darling of Mendon, int. May 14, 1757.
Ruth of Mendon, and James Albee Jr., in Mendon, Feb. 29, 1776.
Sally of Sullivan, N. H., and Silas Rawson, int. Feb. 6, 1826.
Samuel and Elisabeth Cozens (Cuzans, int.), Sept. 23, 1731.
Samuel Jr. and Mary Fairbanks of Sherborn, int. Apr. 1, 1748.
Samuel and Mary Murdock, Feb. 12, 1752–3.
Samuel and Lois Emerson (of Gloucester, R. I., int.), May 8, 1766.
Samuel and Hannah Baker of Douglas, int. Jan. 7, 1801.
Samuel O. and Hannah D. White, Sept. 27, 1838.
Sarah and John Jonson, both of Providence, R. I., Dec. 29, 1729.*
Sarah Ann H. of Sutton, and Hosea Pheteplace, int. Apr. 30, 1837.
Semantha, d. of John and Cynthia, a. 19 y., and Samuel S. Ray of Slatersville, R. I., s. of Samuel and Susan of Slatersville, R. I., a. 20 y., Aug. 4, 1846.
Seth and Abigail Farnum, Aug. 20, 1740–1.
Seth and Jemima Keith, int. May 23, 1779.
Simon and Amey Lapham of Gloucester, R. I., int. Mar. 17, 1805.
Smith and Eunice Albee, int. Oct. 14, 1781.
Sophia and Charles S. (Charles Scott, int.) Capron, June 27, 1816.
Thomas and Elenor Brown, Oct. 29, 1747.
Thomas and Susanna Putnam of Sutton, int. Aug. 2, 1778.
Tryal and Abner Taft, Nov. 25, 1756.
Tryphena and James Barden, May 5, 1763.
William and Deborah Comstock of Gloucester, R. I., int. Nov. 12, 1799.

WHITEHILL, Christina and Edwin Hixon, int. Nov. 16, 1845.

WHITIN (see Whiting), Paul Jr. of New York, and Sarah R. Chapin, Aug. 26, 1822.

* Intention not recorded.

WHITING (see Whitin), Jesse and Nancy Fuller, int. Nov. 19, 1826.
Joel and Phebe Aldrich, int. July 25, 1819.
John and Hannah F. Kenney, int. Jan. 9, 1831.
John M. of Douglas, and Sarah Wood, int. Feb. 20, 1831.

WHITMAN, Charles S. and Lovina Lesure of Douglas, int. Nov. 21, 1830.
Saberry of North Providence, R. I., and Israel Green, int. Nov. 1, 1807.

WHITMORE, Paulina and Capt. Pemberton Brown, Sept. 25, 1838.
Sarah of Douglas and Samuel T. Willard, int. Dec. 16, 1832.

WHITNEY, Cyprian (Whiting, int.) of Douglas, and Sylvia A. Walker, Aug. 1, 1838.
Ebenezer of Montague, and Rachel Paine Rawson, Dec. 28, 1776.
Ezekiel and Jenet Patterson of Mendon, int. Mar. 31, 1743.
Ezra Esq. and Ruth Knop of Douglas, int. Nov. 8, 1795.
Hannah and Abraham Daniels of Mendon, int. Aug. 30, 1735.
Hannah and Moses Tinney of Mendon, Mar. 16, 1737-8.
Henrietta and Ephraim Baylies, Feb. 19, 1823.
John A. and Eliza W. Wellington of Waltham, int. Mar. 19, 1837.
Marcy of Douglas, and Samuel Read Jr., int. June 10, 1792.
Martha of Sherborn, and Ezekiel Wood, in Sherborn, Oct. 30, 1765.
Mason and Dolly (Polley, int.) Rawson, in Mendon, Mar. 29, 1792.
Moses, Capt., and Nancy Tyler, Apr. 3, 1796.
Patience, wid., of Sherborn, and Dea. Joseph Damon, May 13, 1759.
Persis and Joseph Lesuer of Upton, int. Aug. 15, 1768.
Ruth K. and Alanson Howard of New York City, Apr. 24, 1838.
Sally of Worcester, and Rev. David A. Grovesnor, int. Apr. 5, 1835.
Thankfull of Upton, and Jonathan Bachelder, int. Dec. 26, 1768.
William G. of Woodstock, Conn., s. of James and Mary, a. 32 y., and Martha Williams, d. of Chester, a. 42 y., Apr. 15, 1844.

WIGGIN, Samuel W. of Ashland, a. 30 y., and Charlotte M. Thayer, d. of Sullivan and Ruth, a. 23 y., Nov. 2, 1846.

WIGGLESWORTH, Charlotte, Mrs., and Samuel Read Esq., Nov. 2, 1836.

WIGHT (see Whit, White), Elnathan and Abigail Blood, both of Bellingham, Aug. 13, 1754.*

WILBER, Mary Ann and Benjamin F. Southwick (of Cumberland, R. I., int.), July 27, 1825.

WILCOX, Cornelia and Samuel M. Crocker (Jr., int.), Mar. 9, 1834.
David, s. of Willard and Hannah of Mendon, a. 23 y., and Mary J. Dodge, d. of Olney and Dorcas, a. 19 y., Dec. 12, 1844.
David R. and Mary Gorton, Oct. 10, 1839.
Otis and Mary Jepherson, Apr. 29, 1828.
Willard and Evelina Miller of Mendon, int. Nov. 21, 1830.

WILDE, Emily M. of Wrentham, and John D. Bullard, int. Nov. 10, 1844.

WILES, Sarah and Job Prince of Gloucester, County of Providence, int. Feb. 20, 1743-4.

WILEY, Sarah and John Taft, int. Sept. 27, 1760.
Susanna and Garshom Keith, int. Aug. 17, 1765.

WILLARD (see Willards), Agnes E. H., d. of George and Sylvia, a. 22 y., and William O. Bartlett of Worcester, s. of Otis of Smithfield, R. I., a. 25 y., Oct. 23, 1845.
Bezaleel and Rebecca Jaha, int. Mar. 21, 1841.
Cato and Lydia Braton of Smithfield, R. I., int. Jan. 3, 1802.
Emma C., d. of George and Sylvia, a. 28 y., and John C. Wyman of Worcester, s. of Abraham and Sarah, a. 25 y., Jan. 7, 1847.
Frances (Fanny, int.) and George Wheaton of Taunton, June 17, 1820. (June 7, 1820. c.r.1.)
George (Dr., int.) and Sylvia Chapin, Dec. 21, 1809.
George E. and Mary Lathrop of Canterbury in Westminster, Conn., Apr. 16, 1837.
Levi of Mendon, and Anna Tillinghast, int. Mar. 26, 1780.
Lydia and James Curles of Burrillville, R. I., Thursday, Apr. 28, 1842.
Samuel, Dr., and Olive Frost of Mendon, in Mendon, Nov. 3, 1774.
Samuel T. and Sarah Whitmore of Douglas, int. Dec. 16, 1832.

* Intention not recorded.

WILLARDS (see Willard), Abijah, Dr., and Fanny Hodges of Norton, int. Oct. 25, 1807.

WILLIAMS, Abigail, d. of Stephen and Nancy, a. 21 y., and Valentine M. Aldrich, s. of Jacob and Mary B., a. 29 y., July 2, 1844.
Andrew A. and Maria Green, Sept. 23, 1824.
Charles W. and Frances E. Messinger, Apr. 30, 1840.
Chester of Northbridge, and Sally Draper, June 13, 1797.
Cynthia and Stephen Thompson, Sept. 13, 1798.
Daniel W. and Chloe T. Baker, July 13, 1835.
Dorcas of New Sherborn, and Nicholas Humes, Mar. 28, 1744.
Elizabeth B. and Lewis Seagrave, Oct. 15, 1840.
George and Delilah Morse, Mar. 27, 1831. (Mar. 29, 1831. c.r.1.)
James M. of Burrillville, R. I., s. of George W. and Ruth of Burrillville, R. I., a. 22 y., and Eliza E. Aldrich, d. of Ahaz and Mary, a. 22 y., Mar. 2, 1846.
John D., widr., s. of Chester and Sarah, a. 46 y., and wid. Charity Chase, d. of James and Sally Tilly, a. 56 y., Mar. 6, 1848.
Louisa A., d. of Levi and Mahitable of Newton, a. 22 y., and Charles Hayward of Millbury, s. of Samuel and Sally of Hopkinton, a. 22 y., Feb. 10, 1846.
Louisa E. (Louisa Elizabeth, int.) and Elijah Hall, Sept. 5, 1838.
Mark of Batemans Precinct, N. Y., and Anna Ellison, int. Nov. 3, 1764.
Martha, d. of Chester, a. 42 y., and William G. Whitney of Woodstock, Conn., s. of James and Mary, a. 32 y., Apr. 15, 1844.
Mary of Taunton, and Rev. Josiah Spalding, int. Dec. 28, 1783.
Nelson, s. of Stephen and Nancy, a. 39 y., and Mary D. Paine, d. of David D. and Jemima, a. 20 y., Jan. 21, 1846.
Sarah and Richard Humes, Mar. 14, 1750–1.
Sarah and Manasseth Baker, in Northbridge, May 31, 1792.
Sarah and Henry Titus of Sutton, May 22, 1822.
Stephen and Lydia Hicks of Sutton, Oct. 16, 1766.
Stephen and Sarah Nelson of Upton, int. June 14, 1778.
Stephen (Jr., int.) and Nancy Baylies, June 21, 1803. (June 24, 1803. c.r.1.)

WILLISON, Samuel and Lydia Mitchel, int. Apr. 4, 1790.

WILLISTON, Sally and Norman M. Cheney, both of Newton, Nov. 9, 1841.*

* Intention not recorded.

WILLSON (see Wilson), Emely C. of Mendon, and Palmer Welch, int. Apr. 24, 1836.
Leah of Mendon, and Otis Holbrook, int. May 20, 1810.
Margaret of Killingly, Conn., and Ebenezer Harwood, int. Oct. 2, 1769.
Samuel and Alpha Fletcher of Mendon, int. Feb. 17, 1805.
Samuel and Nancy Swift, Nov. 27, 1806.

WILLY, John of Oxford, and Sussan[n]a Aldrich, int. Nov. 25, 1732.

WILMARTH, Hiram of Smithfield, R. I., and Joanna Darling, Sept. 23, 1829.
Welcome of Brooklyn, Conn., and Sarah Baylies, int. Apr. 24, 1831.

WILSON (see Willson), George and Hannah Green, July 25, 1833.
Naomi of Mendon, and Joseph White Jr., Feb. 17, 1792.
Russell of Mendon, s. of Jedediah and Polly of Mendon, a. 32 y., and Joanna B. Taft, d. of Zadock and Abigail, a. 39 y., Dec. 11, 1844.
Sylvia W., d. of Samuel and Celia, a. 18 y., and James H. Smith of Grafton, s. of Henry and Louisa, a. 23 y., Mar. 28, 1848.
Thomas and Lydia Buttler of Upton, Sept. 27, 1769.

WING, Albert F. and Emeline N. Taft, Oct. 15, 1839.
Charles and Mary G. Carpenter, Dec. 5, 1839.
Philip and Betsey Smith of Grafton, int. Apr. 1, 1821.

WINSLOW, Ebenezer and Lucy Taft, Oct. 7, 1795.

WINTER, Abigail and Joseph Provender, int. Aug. 19, 1737.
Abigail and Nathaniel Thomson, int. Oct. 8, 1743.
Abigail and Timothy Aldrich, Jan. 30, 1760.
Christopher and Ruth Aldrich, Jan. 28, 1737–8. (Jan. 18, 1737–8. c.r.1.)
Hannah and Joshua Wallis of Plainfield, County of Windham, Nov. 6, 1739.
Penellope and John Cooper, int. Nov. 21, 1771.
Rachel and Stephen Powers, Apr. 2, 1762.
Ruth and Ezra Cooper, Nov. 7, 1765.
Sarah and John Martin of Richmond, Nov. 7, 1765.*
Timothy and Rachel Whealer of Grafton, int. June 2, 1764.
Timothy and Hepsibah Cooper, both of Northbridge, Oct. 19, 1773.*

* Intention not recorded.

WITHERELL, Horace R. of Taunton, and Sarah Aldrich, Nov. 3, 1840.

WOOD (see Woods), Abagal of Northbridge, and Reuben Thayer, int. Mar. 28, 1777.
Abby and Luther Spring, Oct. 23, 1838.
Abigail and Nicolas Baylies, Apr. 24, 1760.
Abigail of Upton, and Frederick Taft, int. June 4, 1782.
Abigail and (Lieut., int.) Esek Pitts, Apr. 5, 1803.
(Abigail, c.r.1) and (Simon, c.r.1) Rawson, Mar. (28, c.r.1) 1804 (both of Mendon, c.r.1).*
Amariah A. and Sarah Taft, Sept. 10, 1834.
Amory of Northbridge, and Patience Wood, May 4, 1794.
Barshba (wid., int.) and James Burlingame of Burrillville, R. I., May 31, 1808.
Betsey E. of Northbridge, and Seymore Smith, int. Feb. 4, 1838.
Betsy and Nathan Wood of Milford, Dec. 5, 1822.
Chloe and Ebenezer Sterns, int. Oct. 16, 1769.
Chloe and Ezra White, Feb. 19, 1795. c.r.1.
Chloe and George Severy, int. Apr. 21, 1811.
Clarissa and Artemas Aldrich, Mar. 7, 1824.
Cynthia and Levi Woodward of Ashford, Conn., June 8, 1814.
Cynthia and Lyman Callum of Smithfield, R. I., Nov. 15, 1829.
Daniel and Rachel Aldrich, int. Mar. 20, 1755.
David and Molla Farnum, June 23, 1768.
David and Harriet Murdock, Mar. 18, 1841.
Deborah and Lyman Taft, Apr. 11, 1786.
Dexter and Deborah Chapen, Mar. 3, 1757.
Dorinda and Thomas Penniman of Plainfield, N. H., Jan. 4, 1814. (Jan. 30, 1814. c.r.1.)
Ester and Dr. John Anson of Dudley, Nov. 11, 1798.
Esther and Dependence Hayward of Mendon, Nov. 27, 1760.
Esther and George Persons, Apr. 5, 1818.
Eunace and Caleb Seagrave, June 20, 1802.
Eunice of Northbridge, and Daniel Carpenter, in Northbridge, Feb. 12, 1797.
Eunice S., d. of Reuben and Sally, a. 22 y., and Amasa B. Benson of Northbridge, s. of Amasa and Sarah, a. 29 y., May 28, 1845.
Ezekiel and Mary Brown, Mar. 25, 1732.*
Ezekiel and Martha Whitney of Sherborn, in Sherborn, Oct. 30, 1765.
Ezekiel and Sarah Albee of Mendon, int. Mar. 18, 1782.
Ezekiel Jr. and Sally Thayer of Douglas, int. Nov. 9, 1798.

* Intention not recorded.

WOOD, Ezekiel and Damaris Wescot, int. Jan. 20, 1799.
Ezekiel 3d and Bathsheba White, int. Nov. 29, 1802.
Ezekiel and Eunice Spring, Nov. 22, 1827.
Hannah C. and Sylvester Pickering of Mendon, Sept. 3, 1835.
Henry and Sarah Allen of Medway, in Medway, Aug. 1, 1759.
Howard and Waity Emerson, Apr. 22, 1804.
Jemima and George Jesseman, Dec. 5, 1765.
Jonah and Rachel Wood of Upton, int. Oct. 27, 1764.
Jonathan Jr. and Sarah Crosby, both of Upton, Feb. 20, 1750.*
Jonathan of Lunenburg, and Rachel Wood, Oct. 10, 1754.
Jonathan of Gloucester, R. I., and Molley Philips, int. Mar. 28, 1779.
Jonathan of Upton (Mendon, int. and c.r.1) and Lydia Taft, Apr. 5, 1801.
Josiah Jr. of Northbridge, and Rozannah Taft, May 25, 1791.
Lewis of Mendon, and Sophia Rawson, Oct. 20, 1833.
Lois and Jesse Penyman of Mendon, Dec. 8, 1763.
Lois and Joel Sibley, int. May 22, 1790.
Lucinda and Joseph Ellison of Northbridge, Nov. 27, 1798.
Lucinda and Comfort Rice of Millbury, int. Jan. 4, 1824.
Lyman and Sarah Eddy, Feb. 4, 1836.
Manning and Sarah H. Harvey, int. July 1, 1832.
Marcy and John Emerson, Feb. 27, 1745–6.*
Mark and Rachel Baker of Medfield, resident in Douglas, in Douglas, Sept. 1, 1796.
Martha and Jonathan Bacon, Jan. 1, 1750–1.
Martha and William Hall, int. June 6, 1789.
Mary and Timothy Sibley of Sutton, May 27, 1752.
Mary and Caleb Murdock, Apr. 11, 1786.
Mary and William Lee of Douglas, int. Sept. 3, 1791.
Mary and Adolphus Baylies, Mar. 9, 1825. c.r.1.
Molley and Hezekiah Bowin of Gloucester, R. I., int. May 29, 1791.
Molly and Moses Taft, Apr. 25, 1817.
Nancy and Luke Taft, Mar. 7, 1809.
Nathan and Rhoda Holbrook, int. July 22, 1771.
Nathan of Milford, and Betsy Wood, Dec. 5, 1822.
Obadiah and Esther Hayward of Mendon, int. Jan. 27, 1732–3.
Obadiah and Experience Hayward of Mendon, in Mendon, Nov. 22, 1759.
Olive and Cyrus Adams of Northbridge, Oct. 4, 1798.
Patience and Amory Wood of Northbridge, May 4, 1794.
Phebe and Ameriah White, int. Oct. 6, 1786.
Phineas and Harriet Murdock of Townsend, Vt., int. Oct. 3, 1830.

* Intention not recorded.

UXBRIDGE MARRIAGES.

WOOD, Phineas and Clarrissa Farnum, July 31, 1839.
Phineas and Sylvia Aldrich of Douglas, int. July 28, 1849.
Polly and Rufus Bennet of Northbridge, June 10, 1802.
Rachel and Jonathan Wood of Lunenburg, Oct. 10, 1754.
Rachel of Upton, and Jonah Wood, int. Oct. 27, 1764.
Reuben and Sally Grout, Feb. 2, 1817.*
Rhoda and Silas W. Stow of Boston, Apr. 7, 1807.
Rhoda and Mason White of Smithfield, R. I., Feb. 5, 1822.
Ruth and Samuel Ammidown of Douglas, Mar. 3, 1768.
Sally of Gloucester, R. I., and Joseph Emerson, int. Apr. 12, 1798.
Sally and Cyrus Grout, July 15, 1810.
Samuel and Rachel Albee of Mendon, in Mendon, June 22, 1794.
Sarah and Benjamin Lee, Oct. 17, 1759.
Sarah and Benjamin Fish, Feb. 16, 1764.
Sarah and Oliver Haden of Grafton, int. May 1, 1808.
Sarah and Elias Wheelock, Sept. 12, 1819.
Sarah and John M. Whiting of Douglas, int. Feb. 20, 1831.
Sarah Arnold of Burrillville, R. I., and Anan Richardson, int. Dec. 13, 1840.
Simeon and Margery Taft of Upton, int. May 17, 1760.
Solomon and Hannah Fish of Mendon, in Mendon, Oct. 1, 1765.
Sophia and Benjamin Jacobs, Oct. 8, 1820.
Submit and Joseph Pelton, Nov. 1, 1828.
Susanna and Ameriah Preston, Sept. 21, 1760.
Susanna of Mendon, and Samuel Bills, Mar. 6, 1803.
Timothy, Dr., and Molly Greene, int. Mar. 30, 1806.
Waity, wid., of Northbridge, and Capt. Jesse Aldrich, int. Nov. 15, 1840.
Wheelock and Hannah Comstock, int. Nov. 26, 1820.
Whitney and Esther Walker, Feb. 7, 1808.
William and Amy Legg of Mendon, int. May 5, 1839.
William W. of Northbridge, and Mary D. Smith, int. Sept. 18, 1842.

WOODING, Peter and Ruth Curtis of Gloucester, R. I., int. Aug. 29, 1785.

WOODS (see Wood), Lucy of Southboro, and Nathaniel Adames, int. Dec. 8, 1768.

WOODWARD, Bethiah and Isaac Richardson of Gloucester, R. I., Mar. 30, 1758.
Levi of Ashford, Conn., and Cynthia Wood, June 8, 1814.

* Intention not recorded.

WOODWELL, Mary and Jesse Corbet, in Hopkinton, May 28, 1755.

WORDEN, Mary M. and Andrew Cheeney, July 25, 1839.

WRIGHT (see Rite), John and Sarah Rist, Jan. 2, 1783.
Thomas B. (Thomas D. of Pawtucket, int.) and Charlotte Nicholls [no date] (int. Apr. 7, 1833).

WYMAN, John C. of Worcester, s. of Abraham and Sarah, a. 25 y., and Emma C. Willard, d. of George and Sylvia, a. 28 y., Jan. 7, 1847.

YATES, Abner and Ruth Emerson of Douglas, int. Apr. 30, 1770.
Elisabeth and Benjamin Read of Smithfield, R. I., int. Nov. 4, 1755.
James of Providence, R. I., and Tabbrah (Tabatha, int.) Taft, Jan. 6, 1733–4.
James and Elisabeth Titus (of Douglas, int.), Dec. 26, 1753.
Mercy of Douglas, and John White Jr., int. Jan. 3, 1800.

YORK, Mary B., d. of Hannah of Farmington, Me., a. 27 y., and Chauncey Aldrich, s. of Willard and Azubah, a. 34 y., May 21, 1848.

YOUNG, Charles and Roxana Batcheller, int. Apr. 8, 1832.
Susannay and Joseph Mosely of Sutton, Apr. 19, 1784.

NEGROES AND UNIDENTIFIED.

Cuff and Dinah, servants of Lieut. Draper, Mar. 6, 1760.
Dinah and Cuff, servants of Lieut. Draper, Mar. 6, 1760.
———, Ruth and Andrew Phillips of Gloucester, R. I., int. Jan. —, 1783.

UXBRIDGE DEATHS.

To the year 1850.

ABAN, Samuel, s. of Samuel and Hannah of Providence, Feb. 14, 1798, a. 9 m. 9 d. G.R.1.

ADAM (see Adames, Adams), Josiah, Mar. 15, 1828 (Mar. 14, G.R.1), a. 32 y. 2 m.

ADAMES (see Adam, Adams), James, s. of James and Elisabeth, June 20, 1755.
Ruth, d. of Joseph and Elisabeth, Sept. 12, 1761.

ADAMS (see Adam, Adames), Benjamin, Mar. 28, 1837, a. 72 y.
Betsey, w. of Benjamin Esq., Oct. 17, 1807, in her 38th y.
Betsey, d. of Benjamin Esq., Oct. 28, 1824, in her 21st y.
Charles G., s. of John and Fanny A., in Savannah, Ga., June 25, 1837, a. 14 y. G.R.1.
Christiania E., d. of Fleming (and Rebecca, G.R.1), Nov. 1, 1846, a. 2 y. Dysentery. (Oct. 31, 1846, a. 2 y. 4 m. 22 d. G.R.1.)
Elisabeth, w. of Joseph, Mar. 1, 1773, in her 38th y.
Elizabeth, d. of Joseph and Elizabeth, July 9, 1773.
Fanny, d. of Benjamin (and Betty, G.R.1), Mar. 9, 1797, a. 2 y. 4 m.
George, s. of Benjamin Esq., Sept. 2, 1832, in his 31st y.
John, ———, 1842. G.R.1.
Joseph, June 1, 1833, in his 70th y.
Joseph, Dr., Dec. 15, 1835, a. 81 y.
Martha B., d. of John and Charlotte, Aug. 28, 1844, a. 17 y. 2 m. 13 d. G.R.1.
Moses, s. of Joseph and Elisabeth. "Was killed by falling and going under the water wheel of a Grissmill on the Eleventh day of October, 1788." (In his 19th y. dup.)
Sally, d. of Benjamin Esq., June 8, 1824, in her 19th y.

ADAMS, Sally, w. of Dr. Joseph (formerly of Mendon, G.R.1), May 13, 1830. (a. 74 y. 4½ m. G.R.1.)
Samuel (Samuel G., G.R.1), s. of (Hon., G.R.1) Benjamin, Mar. 21, 1828, in his 29th y.
Susannah, wid. of Benjamin, Oct. 13, 1840, a. 73 y.

ALBEE, Elizabeth, w. of Ellis, May 22, 1827.
James, Aug. 18, 1814.
Laura (Laura S., G.R.24), d. of Ellis and Lavinia, Jan. 26, 1847, a. 15 y. Consumption. (Jan. 25, 1847, a. 17 y. 8 m. 21 d. G.R.24.)

ALDRICH, ———, s. of William and Dinah, Feb. 19, 1798. Twin.
———, s. of Laman, July 30, 1831, a. 4 d.
Abby E. (Abby Elizabeth, G.R.1), d. of Valentine M. and Abigail (Abigail W., G.R.1), Dec. 28, 1848, a. 9 m. 20 d. Dropsy in the head. (Dec. 29, 1848, a. 9 m. 11 d. G.R.1.)
Abel Jr., s. of Seth Jr., Aug. 14, 1810. Death caused by a fall from a tree.
Abel, Apr. 7, 1841, a. 91 y., in November, 1840. (Revolutionary soldier. G.R.1.)
Abel, Nov. 25, 1841, in his 53d y. G.R.1.
Abigail W., w. of Valentine M. and d. of Stephen Williams, Dec. 13, 1849. G.R.1.
Abraham, Sept. 22, 1811, a. 28 y.
Adaline, d. of Capt. Jesse, Aug. 28, 1834, a. 22 y. 9 m.
Almy, w. of Paul Jr., 6th day, 10th mo. 1829. C.R.4.
Alvina H., w. of Chauncey, Sept. 9, 1845, a. 30 y. Fits.
Amy, wid. of Seth, July 6, 1837, a. 93 y.
Anna, w. of Nehemiah, Sept. 22, 1813, a. 64 y.
Anna, 2d w. of John, 17th day, 2d mo. 1834. C.R.4.
Artemas, May 27, 1825, a. abt. 25 y.
Asahel, s. of Jesse, June 12, 1844, a. 47 y. Md. Consumption. (a. 47 y. 9 m. G.R.10.)
Austin, s. of Joseph, Aug. 23, 1825, a. 10 m.
Benjamin, s. of Seth Jr. and Audary, 3d day, 2d mo. 1812. C.R.4.
Brown, s. of David and Mary, 27th day, 4th mo. 1808. C.R.4.
Brown W., s. of John and Anna, 10th day, 7th mo. 1811. C.R.4.
Daniel, 6th day, 6th mo. 1812. C.R.4.
David, s. of David and Mary, 11th day, 11th mo. 1819. C.R.4.
David, 13th day, 7th mo. 182–. C.R.4.
Deborah, d. of Jacob and Joanna, Nov. 16, 1746.

ALDRICH, Dinah, wid. of William, Feb. 8, 1839, a. 77 y.
Dorcas, w. of Ephraim, Aug. 30, 1811, a. 39 y.
Dorcas, d. of Peleg and Huldah, 12th day, 11th mo. 1835.
    c.r.4.
Elisabeth, w. of John, 7th day, 1st mo. 1806. c.r.4.
Elisabeth, d. of John and Elisabeth, 23d day, 12th mo. 1820.
    c.r.4.
Elizabeth, w. of Abel, Nov. 19, 1837, a. 72 y.
Ellis, Oct. 2, 1838, a. 57 y. 2 m. 7 d. g.r.1.
Elvira H., w. of Chauncey, Sept. 9, 1845, a. 29 y. 11 m. 16 d.
    g.r.1.
Emeline (Emily E., g.r.1), d. of Chauncey (and Elvira H.,
    g.r.1), Oct. 18, 1842, a. abt. 3 m. (a. 3 m. 16 d. g.r.1.)
Emily (Emily M., g.r.21), w. of Robert (Robert H., g.r.21),
    July 28, 1840, a. 28 y. (a. 27 y. g.r.21.)
Enoch, Feb. 24, 1834, a. 82 y.
Ephraim, Aug. 24, 1826, a. 56 y. (25th day, 8th mo. 1826.
    c.r.4.)
Esther, d. of Jacob and Joanna, Feb. 19, 1754.
Esther, w. of Joel, June 12, 1808, a. 25 y.
George, s. of Abel, Nov. 30, 1802.
George Ellis, s. of Ellis and Sarah, Oct. 15, 1833, a. 14 m.
    g.r.1.
Gilbert Fay, s. of Lamond and Cynthia F., July 30, 1834, a.
    4 d. g.r.1.
Hannah, w. of Ellis, Apr. 4, 1828, in her 37th y. g.r.1.
Hellen, d. of Joseph, Nov. 8, 1839, a. abt. 3 y.
Hetty D., w. of Jacob, Feb. 4, 1833, a. 35 y. g.r.16.
Issabel, 2d w. of Peter, 3d day, 4th mo. 1790. c.r.4.
Jacob, s. of Jacob and Joanna, Nov. 9, 1740.
James, s. of Otis, Aug. 4, 1835, a. 2 y.
Jesse, Capt., Oct. 5, 1845, a. 73 y. Md. Typhus fever.
Joel, Dec. 26, 1838, a. 66 y. (25th day, 12th mo. 1838. c.r.4.)
John, Mar. 25, 1750.
John, 11th day, 3d mo. 1838. c.r.4.
John Seagrave, s. of Joseph, Aug. 22, 1825, in his 11th y.
Jonathan R. (Jonathan Richard, c.r.4), s. of Daniel H. (and
    Phebe M., g.r.16), Sept. 12, 1841, a. abt. 3 y. (a. 2 y.
    10 m. 12 d. g.r.16.)
Joseph, s. of Seth and Mary, Mar. 2, 1766, a. 1 y. 7 m.
Joseph, s. of Seth and Mary, July 23, 1785, a. 1 y. 2 m.
Joseph, 30th day, 12th mo. 1787. c.r.4.
Joseph, s. of Abel, Oct. 25, 1846, a. 57 y. Md. Consumption.
    (a. 58 y. g.r.1.)

ALDRICH, Joshua, s. of Joseph, 23d day, 5th mo. 1790. C.R.4.
Joshua, s. of John and Elisabeth, 13th day, 3d mo. 1808. C.R.4.
Josiah, s. of Daniel, Mar. 21, 1834, a. 3 y. (Josiah W. (Josiah Wilcox, C.R.4), s. of Daniel H. and Phebe M., Mar. 21, 1834, a. 3 y. 1 m. 8 d. G.R.16.)
Judith S., w. of Otis, Apr. 11, 1835, a. 44 y. G.R.23.
Lydia, d. of Benjamin and Lydia, July 26, 1788, a. nearly 5 y.
Lydia, wid. of Benjamin, May 20, 1824. (21st day, 5th mo. 1824. C.R.4.)
Maria, w. of Nathan, Aug. 16, 1844, a. 47 y. G.R.21.
Martha, d. of Samuel Jr. and Sarah, 6th day, 7th mo. 1791. C.R.4.
Martha, w. of Nathan, May 3, 1842, a. 54 y.
Martha, w. of Nathan, Aug. 13, 1845, a. 28 y. Consumption.
Mary, w. of Seth, 31st day, 12th mo. 1820. C.R.4.
Mary, w. of David, 10th day, 5th mo. 1842. C.R.4.
Mary B., w. of Jacob, June 16, 1816, a. 20 y. G.R.16.
Mary B., w. of Chauncey, June 19, 1849, a. 29 y. G.R.1.
Mary H., w. of Otis, Jan. 30, 1842, a. 31 y. 8 m. 17 d. G.R.23.
Mary R., d. of J[acob] and M[ary] B., Aug. 3, 1817, a. 14 m. G.R.16.
Mehitabel, w. of Jacob, Feb. 4, 1833.
Merrit, s. of Joseph, Aug. 17, 1833, a. abt. 6 y. Drowned.
Nathaniel, Mar. 31, 1840, a. 87 y.
Nehemiah, Feb. 20, 1803, a. 53 y. 9 m.
Nelly, d. of Nathaniel, Jan. 31, 1785, a. 9 m.
Noah, s. of Noah and Sarah, Jan. 31, 1745.
Noah, 13th day, 5th mo. 1812. C.R.4.
Noah, Nov. 14, 1835, a. 76 y.
Paul, 28th day, 7th mo. 1834. C.R.4.
Penellepy, Dec. 5, 1752.
Peter, 17th day, 3d mo. 1799. C.R.4.
Phebe Saben, d. of Paul Jr. and Almy, 24th day, 11th mo. 1818. C.R.4.
Phila, d. of Obed, Dec. 11, 1826.
Polly, w. of Arnold, Dec. 7, 1845. Cramp in the stomach.
Rachal, w. of Nathaniel, Mar. 12, 1836, a. 82 y. (8th day, 10th mo. 1836. C.R.4.)
Rachel, d. of Paul and Mary, 16th day, 8th mo. 1820. C.R.4.
Robert Bruce, s. of Peleg and Huldah, 2d day, 2d mo. 1826. C.R.4.
Robert Hall, s. of Ephraim, Sept. 9, 1805, a. 4 y.
Roby, d. of George, Sept. 7, 1822.
Rufus, s. of Benjamin and Lydia, Feb. 6, 1787, a. 13 y.

ALDRICH, Rufus (Rufus T., G.R.21), s. of Seth, Oct. 24, 1835, a. 22 y. (Oct. 29, 1835, a. 22 y. 4 m. G.R.21.) (22d day, 10th mo. 1835. C.R.4.)
Sally W., d. of Ellies and Hannah, Apr. 26, 1808, in her 4th y. G.R.1.
Samuel, s. of Samuel Jr. and Sarah, 30th day, 3d mo. 1794. C.R.4.
Samuel, 5th day, 7th mo. 1814. C.R.4.
Samuel, s. of George, Apr. 30, 1820, a. 26 y.
Samuel Jr., 5th day, 6th mo. 1820. C.R.4.
Samuel Cleark, s. of Samuel and Melissa, Jan. 24, 1846, a. 9 m. 12 d. G.R.21.
Sarah, w. of Noah, June 20, 1751.
Sarah, w. of Samuel Jr., 17th day, 12th mo. 1819. C.R.4.
Sarah, w. of Enoch, July 22, 1844, a. 63 y. G.R.10.
Sarah Jane, d. of Ellis and Sarah, Feb. 10, 1838, a. 4 y. G.R.1.
Seth, Oct. 15, 1737.
Seth, Dec. 26, 1817, a. 79 y.
Seth, June 5, 1824, a. 80 y.
Silas, June 15, 1798, a. 24 y.
Silvia, d. of Joseph, Dec. 24, 1826, a. 4 y. 9 m.
Susanna, w. of Paul, 3d day, 4th mo. 1804. C.R.4.
Susannah, w. of Capt. Jesse, May 20, 1837, a. 62 y.
Thankful, d. of William and Dinah, 19th day, 11th mo. 1802. C.R.4.
Waity, w. of Saval, June 13, 1841, a. abt. 60 y. (13th day, 7th mo. 1841. C.R.4.)
Willard, Nov. 6, 1839, a. 66 y.
William, s. of Remington, Sept. 21, 1832, a. abt. 14 m.
William, Feb. 1, 1837, a. 78 y. (2d day, 2d mo. 1837. C.R.4.)

ALEXANDER, Alanson, May 3, 1839, a. 26 y.
Polly, w. of Samuel, Aug. 11, 1840, a. 42 y.

ALLEN, ———, s. of John, Feb. 8, 1838, a. 5 w.
Azubah, w. of John and d. of Willis and Margery Taft, July 15, 1834, a. 31 y. G.R.1.

ALMEY, Robert, Dr., Dec. 23, 1845, a. 56 y. Consumption.

ANTHONY, ———, d. of John Jr., Aug. 31, 1839, a. 11 m.
———, w. of John Jr., Oct. 9, 1844.
Eliza, d. of John, Aug. 28, 1844, a. 16 y. Consumption.
Emeline, d. of William, Apr. 19, 1836, a. 2 y.

ARNOLD, Alise, d. of Elisha and Theodate, 24th day, 3d mo. 1793. c.r.4.
Benedict, 9th day, 2d mo. 1802. c.r.4.
Elisha, June 23, 1826, a. 70 y. (6th day, 7th mo. 1826. c.r.4.)
Hannah, w. of William, Oct. 21, 1844. g.r.21.
Lucy, d. of William (and Hannah, g.r.21), Oct. 1, 1826, in her 20th y.
Prudence S., d. of Eber and Charlotte, Jan. 31, 1849, a. 11 y. 10 m.
Rachel, w. of Eber, Jan. 25, 1801 (in her 36th y. g.r.1).
Sarah, wid. of Benedict, Feb. 14, 1836, a. 83 y.
Theodate, w. of Elisha, Jan. 25, 1817.

BACON, Asa of Natick, Oct. 13, 1810. Drowned.
Francis Loring, s. of (William and Eliza, g.r.1), Aug. 27, 1839, a. abt. 18 m. (a. 18 m. 20 d. g.r.1.)
Jonathan, s. of Jonathan and Martha, July 19, 1758.
Louis, Nov. 25, 1847, a. 82 y. g.r.16.
Miles, Mar. 17, 1830.
Solomon, s. of Jonathan and Martha, July 3, 1763.
William, Nov. 1, 1826. Apoplexy.

BAILEY, Louisa M., d. of Reuel, Aug. 5, 1847, a. 19 y. 6 m. 11 d. Typhus fever.
Polly, wid., Sept. 15, 1839, a. 69 y. (Mary, wid. of Dea. Stephen. g.r.1.)

BAKER, ———, ch. of John, Feb. 11, 1841, a. 3 w.
Caleb Strong, s. of Manasseh, Dec. 29, 1834, a. 18 y.
Ellen (Eleanor, g.r.1), Aug. 5, 1840, a. 18 y. (a. 18 y. 1 m. 5 d. g.r.1.)
Esther, wid. of ———, 24th day, 7th mo. 1793. c.r.4.
Hannah D., d. of Manasseh, July 3, 1836, in her 23d y.
Lois, wid. of Capt. Manassah, July 10, 1840, a. 66 y.
Manasseh, Capt., June 30, 1831, a. 66 y.
Sarah, w. of Manasseh, Jan. 19, 1793, a. 21 y.
Sawyer, s. of Manasseh, Oct. 14, 1802, a. 4 y. 11 m.

BALCKOM (see Balcom, Baulcom), Hannah, d. of Aaron and Phebe, Nov. 20, 1801.

BALCOM (see Balckom, Baulcom), Alanson, Col., Nov. 11, 1833, a. 26 y. g.r.1.
Mary Maria, d. of Col. Alanson and Maria, Aug. 27, 1835, a. 1 y. g.r.1.

BALLOU, Willard, s. of Martha Taft, Aug. 15, 1824, a. 34 y.

BARBER, Betsey Ann, w. of James, Dec. 25, 1847, a. 37 y.
G.R.1.

BARDEEN, Ferdinand, s. of Ferdinand and Amy, Aug. —, 1846. G.R.18.

BARDENS, Jerusha, d. of James, Jan. 10, 1750 (1751, a. 37 y. dup.).
Maribah, w. of James, Mar. 3, 1753.

BARRINGAN, Thomas, s. of John, Feb. 20, 1846, a. 9 y. Killed by accident in a machine shop.

BARTLET (see Bartlett), Elizabeth, wid. of (Walter Price of Salem, G.R.1) and mother of wife of Rev. Samuel Judson, May 28, 1824. (a. 77 y. G.R.1.)
John, May 19, 1837, a. abt. 14 y.

BARTLETT (see Bartlet), ———, w. of Jehu of Sutton, Apr. 23, 1815.
Betsey, Nov. 1, 1846, a. 64 y. Unm. Consumption. (Elizabeth Bartlett, youngest d. of Walter Price and Elizabeth of Salem, Oct. 31, 1846. G.R.1.)

BASSET (see Bassett), Hannah, d. of Joseph and Rachal, 20th day, 6th mo. 1815. C.R.4.
James C. (James Cumstock dup.), s. of Ephraim and Mercy, Sept. 22, 1815, a. 2 m: (a. 3 m. dup.).
Margery, w. of William, 18th day, 8th mo. 1791. C.R.4.
Mercy, w. of Ephraim, Dec. 27, 1825.
William, s. of William and Margery, 14th day, 3d mo. 1792. C.R.4.

BASSETT (see Basset), Joseph, July 26, 1836, a. 84 y.
Rachal, w. of Joseph, Sept. 29, 1832, in her 72d y. (28th day, 9th mo. 1828. C.R.4.)

BATCHELLER (see Batchellor), ———, ch. of William, July 30, 1839, a. 3 m.
Naomi, d. of Aaron, Aug. 19, 1838, a. abt. 8 or 9 y.
Perdiscus, Feb. 28, 1835, a. 30 y.

BATCHELLOR (see Batcheller), ———, wid. of David, June 29, 1837.

BATES, Daniel H., July 2, 1846, a. 1 y.

BATTEY (see Batty), Mary, d. of Nicholas and ———, 24th day, 1st mo. 1800. C.R.4.
Ruth S., d. of Richard and Rachel A., 8th day, 8th mo. 1836. C.R.4.

BATTY (see Battey), Anna, d. of Richard, Aug. 19, 1838, a. 8 y.

BAULCOM (see Balckom, Balcom), Mary, Apr. 4, 1740. Burned to death about 9 o'clock in the evening.

BAXTER, Frances, ———, 1833. C.R.1.

BAYLIES, Abigail, w. of (Dea., G.R.1) Nicholas, Jan. 16, 1788, at 5 minutes after 2 o'clock in the afternoon (in her 46th y. G.R.1).
(Abigail, G.R.1), 3d w. of Dea. Nicholas, May 24, 1822 (in her 63d y. G.R.1).
Adolpheus, s. of Nicholas and Abigail, Oct. 7, 1784, in his 5th y. G.R.1.
Alpheus, Oct. 25, 1826, a. 56 y.
Alpheus Wood, s. of Adolphus, Apr. 25, 1833, a. abt. 13 m.
Ephraim, s. of Alpheus, Sept. 21, 1848, a. 58 y. Md. Killed by a fall.
George (s. of Dea. Nicholas and Hannah, G.R.1), June 12, 1795, in his 5th y.
Hannah, w. of Dea. Nicholas, Jan. 9, 1800. (Jan. 4, 1800, in her 56th y. G.R.1.)
Nicholas, Dea., Jan. 19, 1831, in his 92d y.

BENSON, Charles Augustus, s. of Ezra (Ezra T. and Pamelia A., G.R.1), Oct. 13, 1833, a. abt. 13 m. (Oct. 14, 1833, a. 1 y. 18 d. G.R.1.)
Chloe, w. of Lieut. John, Apr. 25, 1826, in her 41st y. (Apr. 27, 1826, in her 42d y. G.R.1.)
John, s. of Lieut. John, Aug. 12, 1829, a. 10 y. (John M., s. of Capt. John and Chloe. G.R.1.)
John, Jan. 21, 1842, a. 60 y.

BIGELOW, Charles, s. of Charles, June 23, 1836, a. 3 y.

BIXBY, Crawford (Crawford A., G.R.1), s. of Uzeal (and Naomi, G.R.1), Nov. 10, 1837, a. abt. 1 y. (a. 13 m. G.R.1.)

BLAKE, Mary, w. of Joseph, Aug. 1, 1800, in her 86th y.

BLANCHARD, ———, d. of Joseph and Nancy, Apr. 15, 1849, a. 5 w. G.R.1.
Herbert J., s. of Joseph and Nancy, Mar. 17, 1848, a. 2 y. 1 m. G.R.1.
Isaac, Apr. 15, 1830, a. 40 y.
Phebe Ann, d. of Joseph and Nancy, Apr. 17, 1848, a. 4 y. G.R.1.
Victoria, d. of Joseph (and Nancy, G.R.1), Apr. 29, 1840, a. abt. 5 m. (Apr. 28, 1840. G.R.1.)

BOLSTER, ———, w. of Isaac, Feb. 6, 1846, a. 87 y. Md. Burned to death.
Betty, d. of Isaac and Hepzibah, June 5, 1741.
Hepzibah, w. of Isaac, July 20, 1741.
Isaac, Apr. 28, 1753.
Isaac, Feb. 7, 1846, a. 92 y. Md.

BOWDISH, Asa, Oct. 26, 1846, a. 74 y. 9 m. 22 d. Typhus fever.

BOWEN, Eliza Ann, d. of Thomas and Elisabeth, 3d day, 6th mo. 1811. C.R.4.
Ephraim, s. of Lemuel and Huldah, 7th day, 1st mo. 1791. C.R.4.
Isaac, s. of Thomas and Elisabeth, 24th day, 11th mo. 1798. C.R.4.
Smith, s. of Thomas and Elisabeth, 21st day, 11th mo. 1820. C.R.4.
Thomas, 3d day, 9th mo. 1842. C.R.4.

BRAMAN, William S., Aug. 5, 1846, a. 35 y. Md. Consumption.

BRANCH, Hamlet, s. of Nathaniel and Rachel, Sept. 17, 1814, a. 15 m. G.R.1.
Rachal, w. of Nathaniel, Feb. 23, 1825, in her 51st y. (Feb. 22, 1825. G.R.1.)
Silas W. (Silas Wheelock, G.R.1), s. of Nath[anie]ll and (Rachel, G.R.1), July 14, 1804, a. 2 y. 3 m. 5 d.

BRASTOW, Betsey (d. of David and Sabra, G.R.1), Oct. 16, 1802, a. 22 y.

BRAYTON, Hannah, wid. of ———, 28th day, 4th mo. 1816, C.R.4.

BREWER, George, Apr. 11, 1848, a. 14 y.

BRIDGE, Samuel H., Oct. 12, 1827.

BROOKS, Lavinia, d. of George and Betsey of Farmington, Me., Aug. 25, 1847, a. 19 y. Typhus fever.

BROWN, ———, ch. of Pemberton, Sept. 20, 1839, a. abt. 3 w.
———, ch. of Salmon, May 19, 1840.
———, d. of Chauncey, Nov. —, 1845, a. 1 m.
Abba Eliza, w. of Capt. Pemberton, Apr. 4, 1834, a. 25 y.
Andrus, Nov. 13, 1794. G.R.1.
Elihu, Oct. 25, 1840, a. 79 y. (Revolutionary soldier. G.R.1.)
Elizabeth, d. of Eleazer, Nov. 14, 1827, in her 18th y.
Francis, s. of Alpheus, Nov. 25, 1848, a. 23 y. Md. Consumption. (Nov. 26, 1848, a. 27 y. G.R.1.)
Frederic (Frederick Whitfield, G.R.1), s. of Henry A. (and Ann, G.R.1), Aug. 19, 1845, a. 7 y. 9 m. 16 d. Born in Maine. Typhus fever. (Aug. 18, 1845, a. 6 y. 9 m. 27 d. G.R.1.)
George, Oct. 3, 1831, a. 48 y. G.R.1.
Harriet F. E., d. of Henry and Harriet, July 30, 1844. (d. of H. A. and Ann, July 24, 1844, a. 6 w. 5 d. G.R.1.)
Jonathan of Seekonk, Feb. 14, 1823, a. 30 y.
Marcy, d. of Elihu, Dec. 30, 1796, a. 13 d.
Mercy, w. of Elihu, Sept. 9, 1839, a. 77 y. (a. 76 y. 23 d. G.R.1.)
Merrick D. F., s. of Martin S. and Clarissa (Clara L., G.R.1), Apr. 25, 1848, a. 4 m. 13 d. Dysentery.
Sarah, w. of (Dr., G.R.1), John B. and d. of Bezaleel Taft Esq., Nov. 12, 1808, a. abt. 25 y.
Sarah (Sarah A., G.R.1), d. of Alpheus (and Martha, G.R.1), Oct. 20, 1843, a. 19 y.
Thankful H., w. of Willis, Jan. 15, 1834, a. abt. 17 y. (Jan. 17, 1834. G.R.1.)
Walter, Capt., Mar. 18, 1845, a. 56 y. G.R.21.

BROWNING, William H., s. of Lewis, Aug. 1, 1838, a. 22 m.

BRUCE, Phinehas Esq., Oct. 5, 1809, in his 48th y. (Formerly of Machias, Oct. 3, 1809, a. 47 y. G.R.1.)

BUFFUM, Benjamin, 2d day, 5th mo. 1798. C.R.4.
Farnum, s. of Benjamin and Olive, Apr. 8, 1820, a. 10 m. G.R.25.
Susan, d. of Benjamin and Ellen H., 23d day, 10th mo. 1848. C.R.4.

BULLARD, Baruch, Apr. 12, 1837, a. 78 y. (Apr. 10, 1837. Revolutionary soldier. G.R.1.)
Elias (Elias D., G.R.1), s. of Luther and Hannah, Sept. 22 (Sept. 23, G.R.1), 1845, a. 18 y. (a. 16 y. 10 m. 5 d. G.R.1.) Typhus fever.
Hannah, w. of Luther, June 7, 1845, a. 50 y. Born in Oxford. Consumption. (a. 50 y. 6 m. 18 d. G.R.1.)
Julitta, wid. of Baruch, May 15, 1846, a. 84 y. G.R.1.
Luther, s. of Baruch and Julietta, Feb. 24, 1848, a. 59 y. 2 m. 21 d. G.R.1.
Samuel W. (s. of Baruch and Julitta, G.R.1), Aug. 10, 1820, a. 21 y.

BURLINGAME, Basheby, w. of James, Feb. 20, 1810, in her 28th y. G.R.1.

BURRILL, Henry R. (Henry Rothman, G.R.1), s. of Marcious E. (and Harriet N., G.R.1), Sept. 16, 1838, a. 1 y. (Sept. 15, 1838, a. 11 m. 24 d. G.R.1.)
Lucius, s. of Amor C. and Elethear, June 30, 1849, a. 7 y. 17 d. Born in Woonsocket, R. I. Killed by kick of a horse.

BUTLER, James, s. of wid. ———, Sept. 24, 1848, a. 13 y.

BUXTON, Frances, d. of Jonathan, Mar. 17, 1833, a. 8 m.

CALLUM, Henry Clay, s. of Lyman, Oct. 20, 1830, a. 4 m. 26 d.

CAMBEL, Wentworth, Mar. 23, 1831, a. 28 y. Scotchman.

CAPRON, Abigail, wid. of John, July 26, 1841, a. 83 y. (a. 82 y. G.R.1.)
Abigail M., w. of John W., May 22, 1828, in her 32d y. (May 21, 1828. G.R.1.)
Asenath, w. of John, Nov. 1, 1810 (Nov. 11, G.R.1), at 4 o'clock in the morning, a. 46 y. wanting 28 d.
Catherine M., d. of John W. and Catherine, Dec. 29, 1844, a. 6 m. Lung fever. (Dec. 30, 1844, a. 6 m. G.R.1.)
Charles, Nov. 9, 1812, a. 63 y.
Charles, s. of Charles S., Sept. 6, 1837, a. 20 y. (a. 19 y. G.R.1.)
Charles S. (Charles Scott, G.R.1), Sept. 20, 1836, a. 47 y. (a. 53 y. G.R.1.)
Hellen Maria, d. of Dea. William (William C. and Chloe D., G.R.1), July 26, 1838, a. 12 y. 6 m.
Henry Clay, s. of Charles Scott, Dec. 21, 1829, a. abt. 6 m.

CAPRON, Jehosabell, wid. of Charles, Mar. 15, 1821. (Mar. 15, 1820, a. 62 y. G.R.1.)
John, July 11, 1836, a. 78 y. (a. 79 y. Revolutionary soldier. G.R.1.)
John, s. of John W. (and Catherine B., G.R.1), Aug. 1, 1839, a. 1 y. (a. 14 m. G.R.1.)
Laura Southwick, d. of John, Oct. 27, 1823, a. 29 y.
Lucy Waldo, d. of John, Oct. 10, 1802, a. 3 y. 2 m. (Oct. 11, 1802. G.R.1.)
Mariah, d. of Charles (and Jehosheba, G.R.1), Jan. 7, 1826, a. 24 y. (Jan. 7, 1826, a. 23 y. G.R.1.)
Phebe (Phebe C., G.R.1), w. of Effingham L., Mar. 17, 1828.
Sarah W., d. of Charles S., Oct. 12, 1840, a. 17 y.
W[illia]m Banfield, s. of John and Asenath. Drowned at Pomfret, Conn., July 10, 1789.

CARPENTER, ———, inf. s. of Daniel and Eunice, June 25, 1812. G.R.1.
———, ch. of Olny, Sept. 3, 1827, a. 2 y. 4 m.
———, d. of Daniel G., June 19, 1829, a. 2 d.
———, d. of Daniel G., May 9, 1831, a. 30 h.
———, s. of Daniel G., Oct. 8, 1834, a. abt. 20 h.
Ann, w. of Col. John, July 31, 1833. (a. 43 y. G.R.1.)
Henry, Capt., July 2, 1841, a. 50 y. G.R.1.
Joseph, July 26, 1813, a. 63 y. (Revolutionary soldier. G.R.1.)
Joseph L., s. of Joseph and Sabra, Oct. 5, 1839, a. 10 m. G.R.1.
Maria Theresa, d. of Daniel and Eunice, Sept. 30, 1798.
Mark, s. of Joseph (and Sabra, G.R.1), July 6, 1848, a. 5 y., 9 m. Killed by a cart body falling on him.
Martha W., d. of William, May 6, 1819, a. 5 y.
Persis, wid. of Joseph, July 3, 1831, a. 80 y.
Sally Bartlett, d. of W[illia]m (and Abial, G.R.1), June 22, 1800. a. 14 m.
Sarah Ann, d. of Col. John (and Ann, G.R.1), Dec. 13, 1823, a. 1 y. 3 m.

CARTER, Nancy, w. of Alvan, July 23, 1808, a. 25 y. G.R.1.

CASS, Seth Augustus, s. of Edward, Dec. 13, 1839, a. 8 m.

CHADWICK, Sarah E., d. of John and Hannah, Oct. 4, 1845, a. 2 y. 5 m. Born in Douglas. Croup.

CHAPEN (see Chapin), Marcy, d. of Joseph and Ruth, Nov. 22, 1760.

CHAPIN (see Chapen), ———, s. of Royal, July 20, 1827, a. 30 min.
Abigail, wid. of Henry, May 25, 1847, a. 74 y. Consumption. (May 25, 1847, a. 75 y. G.R.1.)
Amariah, Sept. 18, 1840 (Aug. 7, 1840, G.R.1), a. 78 y. (Revolutionary soldier. G.R.1.)
Amos, Apr. 26, 1772, in his 72d y.
Anna, wid. of ———, Apr. 26, 1772.
Bartlet Judson, s. of Royal, Oct. 7, 1825, a. 10 d.
Deborah, w. of Gershom, Sept. 18, 1776, in her 42d y. G.R.1.
Edwin Fisk, s. of Caleb, Sept. 24, 1836, a. abt. 4 m.
Elizabeth, w. of Gershom, Sept. 11, 1761, in her 26th y. G.R.1.
Gershom, Aug. — (Aug. 23, 1801, in his 68th y., G.R.1).
Henry, Capt., in White Pigeon, Mich., Oct. 6, 1844, a. 79 y. 6 m. G.R.1.
John S., Dec. 19, 1849, a. 70 y. 4 m. 17 d. Md. Dropsy.
Joseph, Col., Aug. 18, 1809, in his 79th y. (Revolutionary soldier. G.R.1.)
Josiah Godard, s. of John S. and Polly, Feb. 27, 1811, a. 3 m.
Mary, wid. of (Gershom, G.R.1), Dec. 16, 1819, a. 76 y. (Dec. 15, 1819. G.R.1.)
Mary J. (Mary Judson, G.R.1), d. of Samuel A. and Maria, July 30, 1844, a. 7 m. (July 31, 1844. G.R.1.)
Moses S. (Moses Smedley, G.R.1), s. of Moses and Betsey (Nov. 14, G.R.1), 1819, a. 3 y. 4 m. (a. 3 y. 3 m. G.R.1.)
Nancy, d. of John S., Nov. 30, 1843, a. 31 y. 11 m.
Olive, w. of Amariah, May 3, 1839, a. 69 y.
Phineas, Dea., May 2, 1839, a. 69 y.
Reuben, Apr. 17, 1836, a. 66 y.
Royal Sibley, s. of Josiah, Aug. 12, 1824, a. abt. 2 y.
Ruth, w. of Col. Joseph, June 27, 1797, in her 58th y. G.R.1.
Samuel, Dea., Apr. 27, 1753, in his 51st year.
Sarah, d. of Amariah and Olive, Sept. 1, 1803, a. 7 y. G.R.1.
Sarah Maria, d. of Royal, Sept. 6, 1824, a. 2 y. 6 m.
Stephen, Mar. 9, 1843, a. 42 y.
Thomas Hoit, s. of Bezaleel T. (and Martha O., G.R.1), Aug. 14, 1840, a. 2 y. 6 m. (a. 2 y. 6 m. 3 d. G.R.1.)
W. P. B. Judson, s. of Royal and Maria T., Oct. 6, 1825. G.R.1.

CHAPMAN, Abigail, w. of Searle, May 31, 1831, in her 53d y.
Cyril, Dec. 23, 1831. Killed in the woods while at work felling a tree for Josiah Spring.
Thomas, ———, 1848. G.R.2.

CHASE, Elisabeth, d. of Jonathan Jr. and Elisabeth, 4th day, 5th mo. 1822. C.R.4.
Emeline B., d. of Josiah, Sept. 5, 1824, a. 3 y. 4 m. 23 d.
Israel, 2d day, 3d mo. 1797. C.R.4.
Jonathan, 10th day, 8th mo. 1800. C.R.4.
Joseph, 13th day, 12th mo. 1818. C.R.4.
Joseph, s. of Jonathan Jr. and Elisabeth, 13th day, 11th mo. 1829. C.R.4.
Keziah, d. of Joseph and Isabel, 24th day, 5th mo. 1809. C.R.4.
Silas, s. of Israel and Matilda, 1st day, 1st mo. 1797. C.R.4.

CHATMAN, Lucy, May 29, 1839, a. 21 y.

CHILLSON (see Chilson), David, Mar. 16, 1817, a. 59 y.
Jeremiah, Jan. 24, 1805.
Leah, Nov. 10, 1834, a. 77 y. (Nov. 12, 1834. G.R.1.)
Margaret or Peggy, Feb. 7, 1839, a. 73 y.
Rachal, wid. of Jeremiah, Feb. 23, 1824, a. 89 y.

CHILSON (see Chillson), Alvina, w. of Henry, Feb. 17, 1844, a. 33 y.

CISSCO, Marietta, w. of Ned, b. in Smithfield, R. I., Sept. 3, 1844, a. 28 y. Typhus fever.

CLAP (see Clapp), Eleazer, Oct. 23, 1805, in his 75th y. G.R.1.

CLAPP (see Clap), Daniel, 8th day, 8th mo. 1849. C.R.4.
Isabella, w. of Daniel, 13th day, 3d mo. 1818. C.R.4.
Sarah, w. of Daniel, 4th day, 7th mo. 1848. C.R.4.

CLARK, Susan (Susan Mariah, G.R.1), d. of Hiram (and Susan H., G.R.1), July 27, 1833, a. 6 y. Cholera. (a. 6 y. 4 m. 4d. G.R.1.)

COBURN (see Colburn), Ann Maria, d. of Josiah (and Betsey, G.R.1), July 12, 1833, a. 6 m. (a. 6 m. 2 d. G.R.1.)
Betsey, w. of Josiah, Oct. 3, 1847, a. 35 y. G.R.1.
Josiah Aldrich, s. of Josiah and Betsey, Sept. 24, 1835, a. 6 m. 22 d. G.R.1.
Julieis Anagustus, s. of Josiah and Betsey, Aug. 25, 1841, a. 3 w. G.R.1.

COFFIN (Mary, G.R.1), wid. of (Ebenezer, G.R.1), Apr. 3, 1818. (Apr. 2, 1818, a. 52 y. G.R.1.)

COLBURN (see Coburn), Delia E., d. of Charles O., Oct. 7, 1845, a. 10 m. Bowel complaint.
Salley, 22d day, 6th mo. 1811. c.r.4.

COLE, Mary, w. of Ariel, Oct. 27, 1848, a. 47 y. Consumption.

COLLINS, Abby C., d. of John S. and Sarah, July 11, 1845, a. 5 y. 6 m. Scarlet fever.
Daniel W., s. of John S., Jan. 11, 1837, a. 1 y. 10 m.
Mercy, Dec. 25, 1825, a. abt. 70 y.
Oscar Smith, s. of John S. and Sarah, Mar. 7, 1848, a. 3 y. 5 m. 24 d. Consumption.

COLTON, Anna K. Earle, w. of Samuel H., 28th day, 3d mo. 1842. c.r.4.

COMINGS (see Cumings, Cummins, Cummings), Ebenezer, s. of Samuel and Sarah, Aug. 15, 1758.
Thomas, s. of Samuel and Sarah, Aug. 27, 1765.

COMSTOCK (see Cumstock), Joseph, 2d day, 3d mo. 1800. c.r.4.
Susan, w. of Col. Silas A. and d. of Ezra and Chloe Southwick, July 22, 1843. g.r.18.

CONGDON, Albert, s. of Joshua and Sarah, 21st day, 10th mo. 1812. c.r.4.
Charles A., s. of Jennings B., Jan. 22, 1835, a. abt. 3½ m.
Charles M., s. of William and Lydia H., 25th day, 8th mo. 1824. c.r.4.
Eliza Ann, d. of William and Lydia H., 2d day, 10th mo. 1818. c.r.4.
Joseph, 2d day, 6th mo. 1834, a. 2 y. c.r.4.
Louisa, 23d day, 9th mo. 1836. c.r.4.
Susan M., d. of William and Lydia, 18th day, 8th mo. 1825. c.r.4.

COOK, Aaron, Apr. 11, 1814, a. 35 y. g.r.16.
Asenath, wid. of Aaron, June 29, 1838. (a. 56 y. g.r.16.)
Barton, s. of Amos, July 18, 1849, a. 38 y. 11 m. Md. Born in Cumberland.
Edwin Francis, s. of William and Abigail, June 8, 1846, a. 2 y. Scarlet fever.
Ellen A., d. of Joseph B. and Thankful, June 10, 1846, a. 3 y. Scarlet fever.
Emily A., w. of George W., Oct. 15, 1846, a. 27 y. 11 m. g.r.24.

Cook, Gertrude Irene, d. of Joseph B. and Thankful, June 24, 1846, a. 2 y. 2 m. Scarlet fever.
Hannah, w. of Jonathan, Feb. 11, 1763.
Helen A., d. of Joseph and Thankful, June 10, 1846, a. 3 y. G.R.7.
John, Lieut. (s. of Jonathan and Mehitable dup.), Apr. 13, 1753, in his 69th y.
Louis, d. of Jonathan, Mar. 13, 1827, a. 61 y.
Mehitable, d. of Jonathan and Hannah, Feb. 26, 1744.
Mehitable, w. of Jonathan, Apr. 7, 1753.
Miriam A., d. of Alvin (and Maria R., G.R.16), Mar. 20, 1835, a. 5 m. (Mar. 24, 1835, a. 4 m. 29 d. G.R.16.)
Paskco, 30th day, 7th mo. 1821. C.R.4.
Philadelphia (w. of Paskco, C.R.4), Sept. 8, 1845, a. 70 y. Md. Old age. (9th day, 9th mo. 1845. C.R.4.)

COOLIGE, Patience, 11th day, 3d mo. 1844. C.R.4.

COPELAND, ———, d. of Lyman, Mar. 30, 1840, a. abt. 1 y.
Danforth, s. of Lyman and Phebe, Sept. 8, 1844, a. 5 m. 6 d. Typhus fever.
Phebe, d. of Lyman and Phebe, Mar. 29, 1840. G.R.1.

CORARY, Esther, d. of Benjamin and Deborah, Jan. 18, 1773.

CRAGGIN, John, July 22, 1831, a. 84 y.
Keziah, w. of John, Jan. 19, 1831.
Mercy, wid. of Col. Samuel, Nov. 3, 1833, a. abt. 92 y.
Samuel, s. of Samuel and Marcy, Aug. 10, 1791, in his 2d y. G.R.1.
Samuel, Col., June 22, 1825, a. 87 y. (Revolutionary soldier. G.R.1.)

CRAGIN, Olive, w. of Ebenezer, May 7, 1848, a. 66 y. Consumption.

CROCKER, Mary, w. of ———, Jan. 24, 1843, a. 80 y. English woman.

CROSSMAN, Daniel, May 2, 1849, a. 37 y. 11 m. 24 d. G.R.1.
Sarah Josephine, d. of Daniel and Delphia B., Aug. 26, 1848, a. 7 y. 11 m. 9 d. G.R.1.

CUMINGS (see Comings, Cummins, Cummings), ———, s. of Charles and Sarah, Apr. 27, 1845, a. 1 m. 12 d. Whooping cough.

CUMINGS, Charles (Charles H., G.R.1), s. of Reuben and Lois, Nov. 1, 1846, a. 38 y. 9 m. 7 d. Md. Colic. (Nov. 1, 1847, in his 40th y. G.R.1.)
Isabella Frances, d. of Josiah (and Celia, G.R.1), Sept. 14, 1836, a. 2½ y. (a. 2 y. 5 m. G.R.1.)
John F., s. of Charles (and Sarah, G.R.1), Apr. 25, 1843, a. 4 y. 9 m. (Apr. 24, 1843, a. 4 y. 10 m. G.R.1.)
John Norris (John F., G.R.1), s. of Charles, May 20, 1838, a. 2 y. (a. 1 y. 9 m. 4 d. G.R.1.)
Lenord, s. of Samuel and Hannah, Dec. 4, 1740.
Maria, d. of Mary, ———, 1848. G.R.1.
Mary S., d. of Charles and Sarah, Aug. 15, 1842, a. 1 y. 4 m. 18 d. G.R.1.
Samuel, Lieut., May 13, 1758.
Samuel, s. of Samuel and Lucy, Sept. 14, 1778.
Samuel, s. of Reuben and Lois, Apr. 6, 1813, a. 18 y.

CUMMINS (see Comings, Cumings, Cummings), ———, ch. of Reuben, Oct. 9, 1802, a. a few hours.

CUMMINGS (see Comings, Cumings, Cummins), Reuben, Oct. 3, 1812. (a. 44 y. G.R.1.)

CUMSTOCK (see Comstock), Content, wid. of Laban, Jan. 22, 1843, a. 76 y. (a. 77 y. G.R.21.)
Laban, Sept. 24, 1829, a. 73 y.
Lucy, w. of Samuel, 3d day, 7th mo. 1825. C.R.4.
Samuel, 6th day, 6th mo. 1815. C.R.4.

CURLIS, Lydia (Lydia A., G.R.1), w. of James, Oct. 1, 1842, a. 23 y. (a. 24 y. G.R.1.)

DABORD, Magloria Jr., s. of Magloria and Catharine, Aug. 29, 1847, a. 1 y. 1 m. Fits.

DALEY, James, s. of Judah, Nov. 9, 1807, in his 68th y. G.R.14.
Judah, mother of James, ———, 1784, in her 64th y. G.R.14.

DALRIMPLE, Andrew, July 13, 1762, in his 87th y.

DALRUMPLE, Dorothy, ———, 1752.

DAMMON (see Damon), Ebenezer, s. of Joseph and Mary, July 1, 1749.
Eunice, d. of Joseph and Mary, Dec. 3, 1747.
Joseph, s. of Joseph and Mary, Dec. 2, 1747.
Mary, d. of Joseph and Mary, Dec. 2, 1747.
Thomas, s. of Joseph and Mary, Dec. 2, 1747.

DAMON (see Dammon), Joseph, Dea., Sept. 30, 1761.
Mary, w. of Dea. Joseph, May 18, 1758, in her 40th y.

DANIELS, ———, ch. of Nathan, Sept. 12, 1839, a. 36 h.
Abraham, Dr., Dec. 16, 1752.
Alsy Fowler, w. of Adolphus, ———, 1832. G.R.3. (26th day, 2d mo. 1832. C.R.4.)
Diame, d. of David and Ruth, 15th day, 2d mo. 1842. C.R.4.
Hetta, d. of Nathan and Sarah, 4th day, 2d mo. 1833. C.R.4.
Huldah, d. of David and Ruth, 15th day, 12th mo. 1842. C.R.4.
John Milton, s. of Adolphus and Alice, June 25, 1810, a. 4 y.
Joseph, s. of Dr. Abraham, Aug. 8, 1753.
Josiah, s. of Joseph and Mary, Aug. 15, 1783 (in his 2d y. dup.).
Mary, wid. of Darius, Apr. 11, 1842, a. 93 y. (Apr. 10, 1842, a. 94 y. G.R.1.)
Nathan, s. of Ruth and David, 10th day, 5th mo. 1839. C.R.4.
Ruth, w. of David, 15th day, 7th mo. 1801. C.R.4.
Sarah, w. of Nathan, 5th day, 1st mo. 1814. C.R.4.
Sarah, d. of Nathan and Sarah, 18th day, 1st mo. 1827. C.R.4.
Sarah F., ———, 1838. G.R.3.
Sarah Fowler, d. of Adolphus and Alice, June 24, 1810, a. 2 y.
Silence, d. of Nathan and Sarah, 26th day, 11th mo. 1804. C.R.4

DARLING, Abba Frances, d. of Benjamin, July 29, 1842, a. 5 m.
Atalatha, w. of Joshua, Dec. 20, 1833, a. 73 y. G.R.6.
Betsey, w. of Newton, Aug. 17, 1833, in her 39th y. G.R.5.
Caroline, d. of Newton and Betsey, Oct. 30, 1832, a. 5 y. G.R.5.
Charles, s. of Charles, Aug. 2, 1833, a. 3 y.
Charles, s. of Lyman, Aug. 26, 1836, a. abt. 2½ y.
Ebenezer, Sept. 3, 1835.
Hannah, w. of Jesse, 10th day, 4th mo. 1792. C.R.4.
Hannah A. Staples, w. of Cortes, Feb. 10, 1839, a. 29 y. 9 m. 28 d. G.R.1.
Josephine, d. of Newton and Malyna, Dec. 26, 1837, a. 8 y. 6 m. G.R.5.
Joshua, Apr. 21, 1834, a. 72 y. G.R.6.
Labiro, ch. of Joshua, July 3, 1799.
Leonard, Sept. 5, 1848, a. 26 y. G.R.5.
Malyna, w. of Newton, May 7, 1847, a. 49 y. G.R.5.
Margaret, w. of Stephen, July 14, 1832, a. 22 y.
Polly, w. of Nathan, May 26, 1846, a. 71 y. Born in Smithfield, R. I. Pleurisy. (May 25, 1846, a. 73 y. G.R.1.)

DAVIS, ———, w. of Samuel, Mar. 4, 1837.
———, Aug. 2, 1846. Dysentery.
Mary Jane, d. of Alonzo, Apr. 30, 1847, a. 6 m. 6 d.
Victoria A., d. of Dow, Oct. 29, 1846, a. 1 y. 4 m. 4 d. Dysentery.

DAY, ———, s. of James W. and Elizabeth, Sept. 26, 1847, a. 1 m.
Daniel, widr., Oct. 26, 1848, a. 81 y. Consumption. (Oct. 23, 1848. G.R.1.)
Peter, s. of Daniel, Nov. 29, 1815. (In his 23d y. G.R.1.)
Silvia, w. of Daniel, Jan. 28, 1842, a. 77 y.

DEAN (see Deane), Calvin, at Savannah, Ga., Oct. ——, 1812, a. 39 y.
James, s. of Calvin, Nov. ——, 1811. (James Pitcher, s. of Calvin and Fanny, Nov. 15, 1811, a. 7 y. 3 m. 3 d. G.R.1.)

DEANE (see Dean), Francis Brown, s. of Francis Jr., Esq. (and Mary Jane, G.R.1), Sept. 19, 1838, a. 17 m. 18 d.
James H., s. of James and Louisa, July 13, 1845, a. 6 m. Born in Taunton. Croup.

DENNIS, Elisabeth, w. of Obed, 12th day, 10th mo. 1840. C.R.4.
Hannah, d. of Obed and Elisabeth, 13th day, 9th mo. 1839. C.R.4.
Joseph, 24th day, 3d mo. 1822. C.R.4.
Sarah, w. of Joseph, 2d day, 12th mo. 1838. C.R.4.
Sarah C., d. of Asa and Sarah, 16th day, 8th mo. 1831. C.R.4.
Thomas C., s. of Obed and Elisabeth, 27th day, 9th mo. 1840. C.R.4.

DIX, George, s. of George, Nov. 3, 1833, a. abt. 7 m.

DODGE, Mary Frances, d. of Henry and Hannah T., Aug. 1, 1844, a. 9 m. 3 d. G.R.1.

DOOLITTLE, ———, ch. of ———, Sept. 7, 1843, a. 2 y.

DRAPER, Adolphus, s. of David and Martha, Dec. 5, 1787. Burned to death when their house was burned (a. 6 y. dup.).
Anna, w. of Lieut. David, Dec. 5, 1787.
Darius, s. of David and Martha, Sept. 11, 1807, a. 15 y. G.R.1.
David, Lieut., Dec. 5, 1787 (a. 81 y. dup.). He and his wife, Anna, and his granddaughter and grandson burned to death when their house was burned.

DRAPER, David, Oct. 23, 1823, a. 81 y. (In his 83d y. Revolutionary soldier. G.R.1.)
Elisabeth, d. of David and Martha, Nov. 2, 1776.
Elisabeth, d. of David and Martha, Dec. 5, 1787, a. 10 y. Burned to death when her grandfather's house was burned.
Elizabeth, w. of David, Dec. 8, 1787, a. 8– y.
Martha, w. of David, Jan. 25, 1803 (in her 51st y. G.R.1).
Mary Thayer, w. of Frost, Aug. 16, 1832, a. 47 y. G.R.1.
Milo, s. of Danford and Roxanna, Aug. 20, 1825, in his 2d year. G.R.1.
Rebekah, d. of Adolpheus and Belinda, Aug. 26, 1826, in her 9th y. G.R.1.
Samuel Judson, s. of Frost and Mary T., Aug. 22, 1835, a. 3 y. G.R.1.

DUDLEY, Amasa, Oct. 20, 1846, a. 54 y. Md. Consumption.
Mary (Miss, G.R.1), Aug. 1, 1837 (in her 33d y. G.R.1).

EARLE, Deborah, 26th day, 12th mo. 1804. C.R.4.
Hannah, d. of Robert Jr. and Sarah, 3d day, 11th mo. 1795. C.R.4.
Homer, s. of Marmaduke and Elisabeth, 30th day, 8th mo. 1804. C.R.4.
John Fry, s. of Henry and Miriam, 31st day, 8th mo. 1814. C.R.4.
Jonah, s. of Robert Jr. and Sarah, 20th day, 1st mo. 1846. C.R.4.
Lydia, d. of Henry and Ruth, his 3d w., 28th day, 2d mo. 1848. C.R.4.
Mary Folger, d. of John Milton and Sarah Hussey, 25th day, 8th mo. 1826. C.R.4.
Melissa, d. of Henry and Miriam, 30th day, 4th mo. 1846. C.R.4.
Miriam, w. of Henry, 14th day, 10th mo. 1814. C.R.4.
Patience, w. of Pliny, —— day, 11th mo. 1849. C.R.4.
Pliny, 29th day, 11th mo. 1832. C.R.4.
Richard, s. of Timothy and Ruth, 16th day, 10th mo. 1828. C.R.4.
Robert, 23d day, 1st mo. 1819. C.R.4.
Samuel, s. of Marmaduke and Elisabeth, 21st day, 6th mo. 1787. C.R.4.
Sam[ue]l Hussey, s. of John Milton and Sarah Hussey, 22d day, 9th mo. 1837. C.R.4.
Sarah, d. of Timothy and Ruth, 15th day, 3d mo. 1831. C.R.4.

EARLE, Silas, s. of Silas and Rachel, 8th day, 4th mo. 1833. c.r.4.
Silas, 26th day, 11th mo. 1842. c.r.4.
Timothy, 23d day, 3d mo. 1819. c.r.4.

EASTMAN, Albertine C. (Albertine A. C., g.r.1), d. of Lyman T. (and Caroline J., g.r.1), Aug. 20, 1841, a. 2 y. 7 m. (a. 2 y. 7 m. 7 d. g.r.1.)

EDDY, Arnold, Oct. 8, 1834, a. 34 y.
Hannah, d. of Jesse and Sarah, 9th day, 10th mo. 1797. c.r.4.
Lyman, s. of Thomas and Sarah, 8th day, 6th mo. 1787. c.r.4.
Sarah, w. of Thomas, 20th day, 1st mo. 1787. c.r.4.
Sarah, w. of Jesse, 3d day, 8th mo. 1805. c.r.4.
Sarah, b. in Maine, Sept. 19, 1847, a. 20 y. Typhus fever.
Thomas, 5th day, 10th mo. 1786. c.r.4.

EDWARDS, Henrietta, d. of William (William H. and Nancy S., g.r.1), Mar. 29, 1844, a. 1 y.
Josephine, d. of William (William H. and Nancy S., g.r.1), Feb. 27, 1844, a. 2 y. 10 m.
Nancy S., w. of William, Nov. 20, 1847, a. 31 y. Consumption.

ELLIOT, Asahel, Jan. 17, 1821.

ELLIS, Charles, s. of Charles (and Ruth, g.r.1), Aug. 24, 1838, a. 4 m. (a. 4 m. 5 d. g.r.1.)
Ruth (Ruth Stearns, g.r.1), w. of Charles, Feb. 1, 1841, a. 32 y.

ELLISON, Emily (Emily Augusta, g.r.1), d. of Adolphus (Adolphus S. and Julia A. Hunt, g.r.1), Oct. 8, 1843, a. 3 y. (a. 2 y. 11 m. g.r.1.)
Ezekiel, s. of Joseph, Oct. 27, 1825, a. abt. 16 y.
Joseph, Dec. 7, 1838, a. 66 y.
Julia Maria, d. of Adolphus (Adolphus S. and Julia A. Hunt, g.r.1), Oct. 5, 1843, a. 5 m. (a. 3 m. 9 d. g.r.1.)
Lorena, d. of Joseph and Lucinda, Oct. 25, 1802, a. 2 y. 9 m. 7 d. g.r.1.
Louis, s. of Joseph and Lucinda, Oct. 25, 1802, a. 16 m. 25 d., g.r.1.
Lucinda, wid. of Joseph, Feb. 14, 1841, a. 63 y.
Mary L., d. of Willard (and Sylvia, g.r.1), Sept. 8, 1843, a. abt. 9 m. (a. 9 m. 20 d. g.r.1.)

EMERSON, David, s. of Luke and Ruth, Jan. 17, 1756.
Eunice, w. of Samuel, Apr. 17, 1849, a. 68 y. g.r.1.

EMERSON, Jonathan, Apr. 27, 1842, a. 89 y. (Revolutionary soldier. G.R.1.)
Mary, d. of John, June 20, 1772.
Mary, w. of Jonathan, Oct. 24, 1841, a. 90 y.
Nathaniel, Feb. 6, 1846, a. 78 y. Md. Burned to death.
Pheeby, Jan. 1, 1760.
Reuben, s. of Lyman, Nov. 26, 1790, a. 10 m.
Rhoda, d. of Luke and Ruth, Feb. 10, 1763. "She expired of a Thursday at 3 o'clock in the afternoon."
Ruben, s. of Luke and Ruth, Feb. 7, 1763. "Died on Monday at 6 o'clock at night."
Susannah Rebekah, d. of James (James D. and Rebeckah W., G.R.1), Apr. 4, 1836, a. abt. 5 w. (Apr. 5, 1836, a. 1 m. 5 d. G.R.1.)
Warren, s. of Samuel (and Eunice, G.R.21), Apr. 15, 1817. (a. 11 y. G.R.21.)

EMERY, Anna M., wid. of ———, Jan. 23, 1849, a. 48 y. Consumption.

ENGLEY, Abby, d. of Joseph and Abby, June 20, 1843, a. 4 y. 8 m. G.R.1.

EVERETT, Olney W., s. of Silas S. and Almira M., Aug. 25, 1845, a. 2 m. 19 d. Canker in the mouth.

FAIRBANKS, Jonathan, July 31, 1772.

FARNUM, Abigail, wid. of Cornet John, Feb. 21, 1759, a. 71 y. G.R.21.
Abigail, wid. of (Moses, C.R.3), Oct. 2, 1773.
Adeline, d. of Capt. Thomas, Mar. 15, 1830, a. abt. 5 m.
Almira, d. of Easman, Jan. 24, 1829.
Amanda E., w. of Charles A., May 13, 1846, a. 44 y. G.R.1.
Amanda M., d. of Charles A. and Amanda E., Mar. 28, 1827, a. 4 m. 6 d. G.R.1.
Amanda M., d. of Charles A. and Amanda E., May 22, 1832, a. 2 y. 4 m. G.R.1.
Asa N., s. of Thomas and Matilda, Aug. 1, 1842, a. 21 y. G.R.1.
Caleb, Lieut., Jan. 3, 1829, a. 75 y. (a. 76 y. Revolutionary soldier. G.R.1.)
Charles, s. of Capt. Thomas, Sept. 20, 1828, a. abt. 3 m.
Charles Augustus, s. of Thomas and Matilda, Feb. 17, 1816, a. 3 m. G.R.1.
Charles Valentine, s. of Thomas, Feb. 18, 1816, a. abt. 3 m.
Daniel, s. of Moses (Jr., C.R.3) and Sarah, Oct. 14, 1772.

FARNUM, Daniel, Sept. 17, 1833, a. 58 y. (a. 59 y. G.R.I.)
David, 6th day, 5th mo. 1788. C.R.4.
David, Dec. 19, 1843, a. 72 y. G.R.I.
Deborah, w. of George, Nov. 8, 1827.
Elisabeth, wid. of Moses, 29th day, 4th mo. 1826. C.R.4.
Elizabeth, d. of George and Sarah, May 13, 1789.
Frost, s. of Royal, Feb. 8, 1845, a. 46 y. Unm.
George, 31st day, 12th mo. 1816. C.R.4.
George, Apr. 19, 1834, a. 74 y.
George, Mar. 15, 1837, a. 76 y.
George Augustus, s. of Charles A. and Amanda E., Feb. 5, 1836, a. 1 y. 2 m. G.R.I.
George L., s. of Charles A. and Amanda E., July 26, 1843, a. 9 m. G.R.I.
Hopestill, w. of David, Apr. 23, 1821, a. 44 y. G.R.I.
Job Pitts, s. of George and Deborah, Aug. 14, 1813, a. 3 y.
John, Cornet, Sept. 9, 1749, in his 78th y. G.R.21.
Jonathan S., s. of Daniel and Mary, July 21, 1814, a. 9 m. G.R.21.
Lois, w. of Lieut. Caleb, Feb. 10, 1792, in her 35th y.
Lois, d. of Lieut. Caleb and Azubah, July 25, 1822, a. 23 y. G.R.I.
Mary A., d. of Daniel and Mary, Dec. 31, 1829, a. 17 m. G.R.21.
Mary A., d. of Moses and Rachel, 29th day, 11th mo. 1836, a. 28 y. 3 m. 15 d. G.R.21.
Matilda, w. of Capt. Thomas, Aug. 28, 1830, a. 37 y.
Minerva E. (Minerva Elizabeth, C.R.4), d. of Jona. and Minerva, 22d day, 11th mo. 1828. G.R.21.
Moses, Sept. 8, 1770.
Moses, May 10, 1780, in his 50th y. (a. 49 y. 8 m. 14 d. G.R.21.)
Peter, 5th day, 5th mo. 1832. C.R.4.
Prudence, w. of Whipple, Aug. 30, 1833.
Rachel, w. of Moses, 11th day, 8th mo. 1846, a. 78 y. 7 m. 17 d. G.R.21.
Rosella, w. of Royal, Apr. 8, 1843, a. 80 y.
Ruth Daniels, d. of Moses and Rachel, Aug. 6, 1818, a. nearly 18 y. (a. 17 y. 10 m. 7 d. G.R.21.)
Sarah, w. of Moses, 1st day, 3d mo. 1776, a. 40 y. G.R.21.
Sarah, w. of George, Jan. 17, 1789.
Sarah, d. of George, Oct. 10, 1799, a. 4 y. 10 m. 7 d.
Stephen, s. of Moses and Abigail, Apr. 27, 1761.
Thomas, Sergt., s. of Capt. John, Nov. 9, 1765 (in his 40th y. G.R.I).
Urania, w. of Daniel Esq., May 14, 1822, a. 44 y. G.R.I.

FARRAR, Charles M., s. of Granville P. and Jane R., Sept. 9, 1847, a. 1 y. 3 m. 3 d. g.r.1.

FISH, Abigail, wid. of ———, Oct. 18, 1790, in her 91st y.
Benjamin, Apr. 21, 1773, in his 40th y.
Hannah, d. of Nathaniel and Susannah, Mar. 26, 1763.
Nathan[ie]l, Dec. 6, 1778, in his 56th y.
Olive, d. of Benjamin and Deborah, Aug. 28, 1757.
Reuben, s. of Nathaniel and Susanna, Aug. 27, 1762.
Stephen, Jan. 13, 1766.
Stephen, Jan. —, 1767.
Susannah, d. of Nathaniel and Susannah, Aug. 30, 1762.
Susannah, w. of Nathaniel, June 22, 1767.
Susannah, d. of Capt. Nathaniel, Aug. 22, 1791, a. 11 d.
Zadock, s. of Nathaniel and Susannah, June 16, 1766.

FISHER, Abigail (Abby Eliza, g.r.1), d. of Josiah (Josiah S. and Alma M., g.r.1), Oct. 27, 1832, a. 4 y. (a. 4 y. 7 m. 23 d. g.r.1.)
Adaline, d. of Josiah, Apr. 16, 1847, a. 6 m.
Adaline W., d. of Capt. Josiah S. and Alma M., Oct. 28, 1846, a. 1 y. 20 d. g.r.1.
Alma, d. of Capt. Josiah S. and Alma M., Apr. 7, 1847, a. 3 m. g.r.1.
Josiah, s. of Nathan and Zilpah, Apr. 11, 1799. g.r.1.
Lavinia, d. of Josiah S. and Alma M., Feb. 27, 1848, a. 23 y. Unm. Consumption.
Mary Ann, d. of Alfred, Aug. 12, 1827, a. 13 w.
Nathan, Mar. 21, 1847, a. 76 y. Md. Fit. (Feb. 21, 1847, a. 77 y. g.r.1.)
Zilpha, w. of Nathan, Feb. 24, 1848, a. 76 y. Consumption.

FLETCHER, Abby Spring (Abba Elizabeth, g.r.1), d. of Ephraim, Aug. 12, 1840. (Adopted d. of Josiah and Abba Spring, a. 5 y. 5 m. 17 d. g.r.1.)
Abram, May 18, 1848, a. 38 y. g.r.1.
Hannah, w. of Col. James and formerly w. of John Spring, Feb. 12, 1823, in her 76th y. g.r.1.
Olive, d. of Stacy and Rachel, ———, 1816, a. 4 y. g.r.16.
Olive, d. of Stacy and Rachel, 4th day, 2d mo. 1821. c.r.4.
Rachal, wid. of Stacy, Jan. 19, 1843, a. 54 y. (17th day, 2d mo. 1843. c.r.1.)
Stacy, Oct. 25, 1831.

FOLLETT, Samuel W., Nov. 17, 1848, a. 42 y. Jaundice. (Nov. 8, 1848, a. 41 y. 10 m. g.r.1.)

FOSTER, ———, Mr., of Taunton, Mar. 16, 1816.
George Bonfield, s. of Edward and Maranda, Aug. 21, 1819, a. 11 m. 25 d. G.R.1.
Maranda (Maranda C., G.R.1), w. of Edward, Nov. 7, 1848, a. 53 y. Consumption. (Nov. 5, 1848, a. 59 y. G.R.1.)
Ruth, w. of Alpheus, Oct. 5, 1841.

FOWLER, Ann Smith, d. of Henrietta, Mar. 14, 1841, a. 10 m.
Barnerd, 4th day, 4th mo. 1843. C.R.4.
David, s. of Ezekiel and Sarah, 27th day, 11th mo. 1794. C.R.4.
Ezekiel, 10th day, 9th mo. 1841. C.R.4.
Hannah, w. of Samuel, 13th day, 4th mo. 1809. C.R.4.
Huldah, w. of John, 15th day, 12th mo. 1842. C.R.4.
Mary, d. of Ezekiel and Sarah, 6th day, 4th mo. 1795. C.R.4.
Rebecca, w. of Barnerd, 6th day, 2d mo. 1805. C.R.4.
Samuel, 12th day, 3d mo. 1819. C.R.4.
Sarah, d. of Ezekiel and Sarah, 21st day, 9th mo. 1797. C.R.4.
Sarah, w. of Ezekiel, 11th day, 9th mo. 1814. C.R.4.

FRAZIER, Phillis, Aug. 15, 1842, a. between 60 and 70 y. Colored. (a. 68 y. G.R.1.)

FREBORN, Esther, w. of Sharp, 20th day, 8th mo. 1807.

FROST, Gideon, Dr., Jan. 7, 1835, a. 79 y. G.R.1.
Henrietta, w. of Dr. Gideon, Oct. 7, 1803 (in her 49th y. G.R.1).

FRY, Mary, d. of John and Miriam, 10th day, 4th mo. 1787. C.R.4.
Miriam, w. of John, 17th day, 5th mo. 1785. C.R.4.

GARDNER, Claudius B., s. of Emerson, Dec. 3, 1835, a. abt. 1 y.

GARSIDE, Albert (Albert W., G.R.1), s. of Joshua, Sept. 13, 1838, a. 10 m. (Feb. 15, 1838. G.R.1.)
Albert (Albert W., G.R.1), s. of Joshua and Helena, June 30, 1845, a. 2 y. 8 d. Cholera infantum.
Andrew Jackson, s. of Joshua, Feb. 11, 1837, a. abt. 5 m.
Henry A., s. of Joshua and Helena, June 6, 1848, a. 3 y. 1 d. Throat distemper.
James A., s. of Joshua and Helena, Sept. 14, 1837. G.R.1.
(Kaira M., G.R.1), ch. of Joshua (and Helena, G.R.1), Sept. 26, 1834, a. abt. 10 m.

GASKILL, Amy, w. of Benjamin, Jan. 16, 1817, a. 71 y.
Ann, d. of Joseph, Apr. 14, 1835, a. abt. 8 y. (Anne D., d. of Joseph and Isabella M., 14th day, 4th mo. 1835, a. 8 y. 1 m. 13 d. G.R.21.)
Benjamin, Apr. 22, 1818.
Elizabeth, w. of Ezekiel, 14th day, 2d mo. 1823. C.R.4.
Ezekiel, s. of Benja[min], Oct. 21, 1815.
Hosea, Aug. 10, 1840, a. 61 y.
Joanna, d. of Benjamin and Amy, 11th day, 7th mo. 1785. C.R.4.
Joseph, 14th day, 4th mo. 1785. C.R.4.
Joseph (Joseph G., C.R.4), s. of Joseph and Isabella M., 10th day, 9th mo. 1845, a. 1 m. G.R.21. (11th day, 9th mo. 1845. C.R.4.)
Lavinia, d. of Asa and Melissa M., 7th day, 2d mo. 1847. C.R.4.
Levina, d. of Benjamin and Amy, 10th day, 7th mo. 1785. C.R.4.
Lucy, July 25, 1785, in her 15th mo.
Nathan, s. of Benjamin and Amy, Apr. 16, 1779, a. 3 y.
Nathan, s. of Ezekiel and Elizabeth, Oct. 30, 1808, a. 5 y.
Susan Anne, d. of Joseph (and Isabella M., G.R.1), Apr. 26, 1839, a. 2½ y.
Verney, Apr. 19, 1795, in his 9th y. (25th day, 4th mo. 1795. C.R.4.)

GIFFORD, ———, ch. of Ananias, Mar. 23, 1827, a. 6 w.
———, s. of Ananias, July 26, 1839, a. abt. 1 y.
Ann, wid. of ———, June 15, 1833, in her 70th y.
Collins, s. of Seth, Mar. 31, 1827, a. 3 y.
Francis Henry, s. of Hastings and Maria, June 4, 1849, a. 1 y. 4 d. G.R.21.
Joanna, 30th day, 3d mo. 1798. C.R.4.
Mary Ann, d. of Farnum, Mar. 4, 1818, a. 1 y. 11 m.
Moses, Jan. 28, 1788, a. 18 m.
Sarah, d. of Seth, Sept. 6, 1783, a. 3 y.
Seth, June 1, 1824, a. 70 y.
Seth, Mar. 12, 1837, a. 42 y. (Mar. 19, 1837, a. 43 y. G.R.22.)
Thankful, wid. of Seth, May 24, 1841. (a. 49 y. G.R.22.)

GOLDTHWAIT, Eunice, w. of Benoni, Nov. 27, 1833, a. abt. 30 y.
Eunice M., d. of Abraham W. and Agnes, Jan. 30, 1847, a. 2 y. 5 m. G.R.16.
James, Apr. 7, 1846, a. 59 y. Consumption.
Milton, s. of Stephen, May 4, 1838, a. 5 y.

GRANT, Rebekah, d. of Calvin, July 30, 1838, a. 14 m.

GREEN (see Greene), Benjamin, Lieut., Aug. 16, 1797, in his 63d y. G.R.1.
Benjamin, Lieut., Feb. 24, 1825. (a. 71 y. G.R.1.)
Benjamin (Capt., G.R.1), July 26, 1837, a. 51 y. (Revolutionary soldier. G.R.1.)
Benjamin F., s. of Merrill and Mariah, Oct. 6, 1845, a. 4 y. 4 m. Croup. (Oct. 7, 1845. G.R.1.)
Hannah, d. of Benjamin, Aug. 12, 1821, a. 58 y.
John C., Aug. 21, 1813, a. 25 y. G.R.1.
Lucy, w. of David, Dec. 17, 1805, a. 38 y.
Martha C., d. of Benjamin, Sept. —, 1830, a. 49 y.
Mary, w. of Lieut. Benjamin, Aug. 14, 1824, in her 66th y.
Mercy, wid. of (Lieut., G.R.1), Benja[min], Mar. 27, 1801 (in her 68th y. G.R.1).
William Merrill, s. of Merrill, June 20, 1842, a. 7 y.

GREENE (see Green), Sabra, w. of Israel, Dec. 10, 1838, a. 53 y. 10 m. 26 d. G.R.1.
Sarah Jane, d. of Merrill and Maria, Feb. 13, 1848, a. 8 m. 5 d. Scarlet fever.
William M., s. of Merrill and Mariah, Dec. 31, 1846, a. 2 y. 6 m. Cholera infantum.

GREGORY, Samuel (s. of Daniel and Elizabeth, G.R.1), Nov. 8, 1844, a. 22 y. (Nov. 9, 1844, a. 21 y. 8 m. G.R.1.) Typhus fever.
Teresa, w. of Jonathan Esq., Dec. 27, 1834, a. 40 y.

GROSVENER, Ellen Louisa, inf. d. of Rev. D. P. and S., July —, 1842. G.R.1.

GROUT, Cyrus, Mar. 23, 1813. (Mar. 22, 1813, a. 27 y. G.R.1.)
John, Feb. 28, 1797, a. 50 y. G.R.1.
John, Capt., May 23, 1822. (a. 32 y. G.R.1.)
Nabby, w. of Capt. John, Oct. 14, 1821, a. 26 y.
Rhoda, wid. of John, Apr. 4, 1837, a. 84 y. (May 4, 1837. G.R.1.)

GUNN, Eugene A., s. of George and Mary, Sept. 24, 1848, a. 1 y. 8 m. Dysentery.

HALL, ———, s. of Parris and Bershebe, Feb. —, 1822, a. 15 d. G.R.1.

HALL, Andrew, s. of Nehemiah, June 27, 1848, a. 58 y. (June 28, 1848, a. 56 y. G.R.I.) Md. Consumption.
Andrew F., s. of Chandler and Ann M., June 3, 1848, a. 11 d. G.R.I.
Baxter, Capt., July 4, 1842, a. 84 y. (a. 85 y. 9 m. Revolutionary soldier. G.R.I.)
Charles, s. of Andrew (and Miranda, G.R.I), Nov. 22, 1840, a. abt. 3 m. (a. 3 m. 6 d. G.R.I.)
Charlotte, w. of Alvah, Sept. 5, 1845, a. 37 y. Typhus fever.
Clark, s. of David and Deborah, Mar. 4, 1797, a. 12 d.
David, July 25, 1798, in his 36th y. (Revolutionary soldier. G.R.I.)
Emely, d. of Alva (and Charlotte T., G.R.I), Sept. 9, 1838, a. 16 m.
Fanny, d. of Capt. Baxter (and Lydia, G.R.I), July 23, 1799. (a. 15 d. G.R.I.)
Frances E., d. of Welcome and Chloe A., Mar. 5, 1848, a. 4 m. 29 d. G.R.I.
George Franklin, s. of Elijah (and Louisa, G.R.I), June 8, 1840, a. abt. 7 m. (a. 7 m. 14 d. G.R.I.) Colored.
Hannah, d. of Nehemiah and Hannah, Feb. 12, 1800, in her 3d y. G.R.I.
Hope, d. of Nehemiah and Hannah, June 7, 1802, in her 15th y. G.R.I.
John, s. of Nehemiah and Sarah, May 30, 1755. a. 3 y. 7 m.
Nancy, d. of Isaac and Nancy, Feb. 7, 1848, a. 16 d. Consumption.
Nehemiah, Lieut., Dec. 21, 1797. (Dec. 22, in his 73d y. G.R.I.)
Nehemiah, Dec. 29, 1842, a. 78 y.
Perley Alvah, s. of Alvah and Charlotte T., Dec. 21, 1847, a. 2 y. 8 m. G.R.I.
Perry, s. of Nehemiah and Hannah, Nov. 14, 1810, in his 16th y. G.R.I.
Perry, s. of Parris and Bershebe, Mar. 2, 1819, in his 1st y. G.R.I.
Samuel, s. of David, Jan. 5, 1794, a. 4 m. 11 d.
Samuel, s. of David and Deborah, Dec. 19, 1794.
Stephen C., s. of Alvah and Charlotte, Dec. 23, 1847, a. 4 y. 4 m. 12 d.

HAMMOND, Mary, wid. of Col. Joseph, May 10, 1807, a. 78 y. G.R.I.

HANDY, Benjamin, Aug. 18, 1817, a. 70 y.
Caroline, d. of Benedict and Caroline, Sept. 1, 1838, a. 1 y. 1 m. G.R.18.
Charles, s. of Benedict A. and Caroline, Feb. 1, 1848. G.R.18.
Ebenezer, Dec. 21, 1846, in his 73d y. G.R.18.
George M., s. of Benedict A. and Caroline, Oct. 14, 1845, a. 14 y. G.R.18.
Mary, wid. of Benjamin, Mar. 2, 1837, a. 87 y.
Mary W., d. of Ebenezer and Patience, July 26, 1840, a. 18 y. G.R.18.
Samuel, s. of Ebenezer, in Pawtucket, Sept. 8, 1822.

HARDING, Augusta, d. of Judson, Oct. 29, 1826, a. 2 y.

HARKNESS, Elisha, 14th day, 5th mo. 1845. C.R.4.

HARRIS, ———, s. of Almon, Sept. — [entered among deaths in 1843], a. 10 m.
———, twin ch. of Almond, Sept. 3, 1845, a. 1 m. 2 d.
———, twin ch. of Almond, Sept. 5, 1845, a. 1 m. 4 d.
Anne, mother of Richard Mowry, abt. 1806. G.R.15.
Israel, July 5, 1811. Fell from his horse and was found dead in the road.

HARVEY, Margaret L., d. of John P. and Martha Ann, Aug. 12, 1849, a. 6 y. 9 m. 10 d. Measles.

HARWOOD, Ebenezer, s. of John and Hannah, Jan. 27, 1740.
Elizabeth, d. of John and Margaret, Feb. 4, 1762, in her 3d y. (Feb. 3 dup.).
Ezra, s. of John and Margaret, Jan. 1, 1760, in his 9th y.
Hannah, d. of John and Hannah, Mar. 26, 1735.
John Esq., Sept. 18, 1788, in his 89th y.
Mary, d. of John and Hannah, Dec. 9, 1736.
Mary, d. of John and Hannah, Mar. 10, 1738.

HASKELL, Elizabeth, w. of William, Apr. 7, 1827, a. 44 y.

HATCH, Mary M., w. of Charles, Dec. 20, 1849, a. 20 y. 3 m. 13 d. Born in Upton. Consumption.

HATHAWAY, Barker, Apr. 28, 1797.
Wesson, 21st day, 8th mo. 1825. C.R.4.

HAUGHTON, Eliza A., d. of Edward S., Aug. 13, 1846, a. 2 y. 3 m. Dysentery.

HAYDEN, Emily A., d. of Oliver and Sarah, Jan. 31, 1826, a. 17 y. G.R.1.
Rufus M., s. of Oliver and Sarah, Aug. 29, 1822, a. 17 m. G.R.1.

HAYWARD, Deborah A., d. of Elisha, Dec. 27, 1845, a. 19 y. Consumption.
Josiah Vose, s. of Ebenezer W. and Susan B., Mar. 21, 1838, a. 17 m. G.R.1.
Sarah, d. of Elisha, Feb. 20, 1846, a. 20 y. 11 m. 9 d. Consumption.

HEATH, George (George W., G.R.1), s. of Wilbur (Wilber W. and Caroline, G.R.1), Mar. 24, 1841, a. abt. 5 y. (a. 4 y. 9 m. 23 d. G.R.1.) Drowned.
Henry J., s. of Jesse C. and Sally, Sept. 17, 1848, a. 1 y. 1 m. Dysentery.

HEMENWAY, William K., Nov. 16, 1842, a. 21 y. Killed by being caught in a belt and carried round shafting.

HENDRAKE, Hannah Foster, adopted d. of Edward Foster, May 16, 1838, a. 30 y.

HEWETT, Surmilla, d. of Alanson, Oct. —, 1840, a. abt. 4 y.

HILL, Amos, s. of Thurber, Sept. 4, 1839, a. 1 y.
Caleb, Mar. —, 1796, in his 50th y.
Elizabeth, wid. of Caleb, June 13, 1808, in her 54th y.
Samuel, Sept. 20, 1836, a. 82 y.

HILLERD, Gideon, 29th day, 1st mo. 1815. C.R.4.

HIXON, Martha M., w. of Edwin, Jan. 22, 1845, a. 23 y. 7 m. 22 d. Consumption.

HODGES, Almira R., w. of William, Nov. 28, 1841, a. 24 y.
William, s. of William, Aug. 3, 1842, a. abt. 3 y.

HOLADAY, Phebe, Aug. —, 1844.

HOLBROOK, Amariah, Jan. 20, 1817.
Anna, w. of Moses, Feb. 18, 1848, a. 78 y. Liver complaint.
Annah, d. of William and Hopestil, July 15, 1737.
Bethiah, w. of Josiah, Nov. 11, 1744 (Nov. 10, 1744, in her 19th y. dup.).
Ellery, s. of Stephen, July 10, 1847, a. 37 y. 14 d. Md. Consumption.

HOLBROOK, Hopestil, w. of William, Mar. 16, 1762.
Jonathan, s. of Samuel, Oct. 28, 1740.
Lydia, d. of Samuel and Lydia, Jan. 5, 1757.
Nathan, s. of Samuel, Nov. 3, 1740.
Otis, July 15, 1838.
Stephen, Aug. 16, 1830, a. 66 y.
Thankful, wid. of ———, Dec. 10, 1798, a. 73 y.
Thomas, s. of William, Sept. 25, 1761.
William E. (William Ellery, G.R.1), s. of Ellery, Sept. 7, 1836, a. 6 m. (a. 6 m. 1 w. G.R.1.)

HOLDER, Daniel, s. of Thomas and Sarah, 19th day, 9th mo. 1787. C.R.4.

HOLROYD, Mary Ann Tillinghast, d. of Samuel T. (and Mary A., G.R.1), Oct. 18, 1822, in her 5th y. (a. 4 y. 6 m. 13 d. G.R.1.)
Samuel T., Oct. 26, 1817, on passage from Wilmington, N. C., to Providence, R. I. G.R.1.

HOLT, ———, ch. of William, Feb. 24, 1844, a. 1 y.
Elizabeth, d. of William and Jane, Oct. 25, 1847, a. 14 y. 9 m. 21 d. (a. 14 y. 10 m. 21 d. G.R.1.) Inflammation on the brain.
Hellen, d. of William and Jane, Oct. 13, 1847, a. 1 m. 3 d. Consumption.

HOWARD, Ira, s. of Amasa, Oct. 29, 1824, a. abt. 23 y.
Mary, evening of Nov. 8, 1842, a. 18 y. Drowned at Rogerson's village.

HOWE, Sarah of Providence, R. I., Jan. 23, 1807, a. 61 y. G.R.1.

HULL, ———, w. of James W., May 9, 1816.
Elias, s. of Will[ia]m (and Martha, G.R.1), Oct. 14, 1803, in his 7th y. (a. 6 y. 7 d. G.R.1.)
Joel, s. of Will[ia]m (and Martha, G.R.1), Oct. 16, 1803, a. 17 m.
Nancy, d. of William and Martha, Apr. 4, 1795, a. 4 y. G.R.1.
Nancy, d. of William and Martha, Sept. 24, 1795.
Paris, s. of Will[ia]m (and Martha, G.R.1), Oct. 6, 1803, in his 9th y. (a. 8 y. 2 m. 8 d., G.R.1.)
William Jr., s. of Will[ia]m (and Martha, G.R.1), Oct. 22, 1803, in his 4th y. (a. 3 y. 8 m. 11 d. G.R.1.)

HUMES, Ann, w. of John, July 10, 1756.
Daniel of Gloucester, 27th day, 10th mo. 1810. c.r.4.
Elisabeth, d. of Nicholas and Margaret, Sept. 6, 1740.
Margeret, w. of Nicholas, July 26, 1743.

HUSE, Alfred, widr., Aug. 19, 1844, a. 74 y.

INGERSOL, Sally, wid. of Capt. James P. (of Boston, g.r.1), June 26, 1848, a. 66 y.

INGLEY, Philena (Ingells, c.r.1), wid. of ———, Feb. 27, 1843, a. 89 y.

INMAN, Almira, d. of George and Ruth, 9th day, 3d mo. 1824. c.r.4.
Betsey, d. of James and Nancy, 28th day, 7th mo. 1825. c.r.4.
Buffum, s. of Samuel and Ann, 14th day, 4th mo. 1790. c.r.4.
Buffum, s. of George and Ruth, 5th day, 4th mo. 1830. c.r.4.
Eliza Ann, d. of George and Ruth, 20th day, 9th mo. 1829. c.r.4.
George, 9th day, 8th mo. 1842. c.r.4.
Hyrena Paine, d. of James and Nancy, 21st day, 3d mo. 1828. c.r.4.
Mary, d. of James and Nancy, 9th day, 5th mo. 1844. c.r.4.
Mary G., d. of George and Ruth, 1st day, 11th mo. 1837. c.r.4.
Matilda, Sept. 3, 1827.
Miranda, d. of Matilda, Sept. 23, 1827, a. 13 m.
Nathaniel, s. of George and Ruth, —— day, 2d mo. 1836. c.r.4.
Nelly, d. of George and Ruth, 9th day, 3d mo. 1822. c.r.4.
Samuel, 9th day, 8th mo. 1822. c.r.4.
Samuel, s. of George and Ruth, 20th day, 9th mo. 1829. c.r.4.
William Albert, s. of James and Nancy, 19th day, 3d mo. 1841. c.r.4.
Witham Henry, s. of James and Nancy, 29th day, 9th mo. 1811. c.r.4.

JACKSON, Sarah, Dec. 13, 1846, a. 51 y.

JACOBS, Benjamin, Mar. 22, 1830, in his 49th y.
Betsey (d. of Will[ia]m and Comfort, g.r.1), Oct. 7, 1798, in her 14th y.
Comfort, wid. of William, Mar. 14, 1819, in her 60th y. (a. 58 y. 11 m. g.r.1.)

JACOBS, John (s. of Will[ia]m and Comfort, G.R.1), Oct. 15, 1798, in his 12th y.
Sally, Oct. 25, 1798, a. 7 m. 7 d.
Susannah (d. of Will[ia]m and Comfort, G.R.1), Oct. 8, 1798, in her 7th y. (in her 8th y. G.R.1).
William, Aug. 19, 1805. (a. 55 y. G.R.1.)

JEFFERSON (see Jeperson, Jepherson), Mary Elizabeth, d. of Alpheus and Mary Ann, Oct. 6, 1846, a. 4 y. 7 m. G.R.1.
Orrin Fowler, s. of Alpheus and Mary Ann, Oct. 2, 1846, a. 1 y. 7 m. G.R.1.
Orrin Woodbury, s. of Alpheus and Mary Ann, Aug. 30, 1840, a. 5 y. 10 m. 27 d. G.R.1.

JENCKS, Mary, June 26, 1837, a. 20 y. Colored.
S. A. (Savalla, G.R.16), d. of Albert, Feb. 26, 1835, a. 3 y.

JEPERSON (see Jefferson, Jepherson), Elisabeth, d. of Thomas and Susannah, Oct. 10, 1730.

JEPHERSON (see Jefferson, Jeperson), ———, d. of Dutee, Aug. 27, 1839, a. abt. 2 y.
Adolphus, Oct. 10, 1841, a. 50 y.
Emily (Emily Adlaid, G.R.1), d. of Royal and Harriet, Oct. 28, 1844, a. 13 y. Dropsy on the heart. (Oct. 29, 1844, a. 12 y. 9 m. G.R.1.)
George Leonard, s. of Duty, May 14, 1835, a. 8 y.
Hellen Marantha, d. of Royal, Jan. 15, 1831, a. abt. 1 y. (Hellen M., d. of Royal and Harriet, Oct. 2, 1830, a. 9 m. G.R.1.)
Henry, s. of Duty, Jan. 6, 1834, a. abt. 14 m.
John, Nov. 24, 1844, a. 85 y. Md. Death caused by a fall. (Nov. 23, 1844. G.R.1.)
Mary, rep. d. of Reuben and real d. of Amy Gaskill, Apr. 24, 1817, a. 6 y.
Pamela, wid. of Adolphus, Nov. 1, 1842, a. 40 y. (a. 41 y. G.R.1.)
Polly (d. of Ruben and Mary, G.R.16), Mar. 15, 1847, a. 64 y. Unm. Consumption.

JESSEMAN, Jemima, d. of George, Sept. 5, 1785.

JOHNSON, Hannah, 31st day, 1st mo. 1791. C.R.4.
Horatio A., s. of Benjamin H. and Jane R., b. in Burrillville, R. I., May 16, 1849, a. 16 y. 1 m. 12 d.

JONES, Lucinda, w. of Thomas, Oct. 28, 1843, a. 44 y.
Simeon, s. of Benjamin and ———, Mar. 30, 1752. C.R.1.

JUDSON, Elizabeth Ann (eldest, G.R.1), d. of Rev. Samuel (and Sarah, G.R.1), Nov. 28, 1827, a. 24 y. 22 d. (Nov. 27, 1827. G.R.1.)
Samuel, Rev., Nov. 11, 1832, a. 65 y. Minister in the town for almost forty years.
Sarah, wid. of Rev. Samuel, Feb. 5, 1834, a. 64 y.
Walter Bartlet, s. of Rev. Sam[ue]l (and Sarah, G.R.1), Mar. 11 (Mar. 17, G.R.1), 1799, a. 11 m.
Walter Price Bartlet, Dr. (2d, G.R.1), s. of Rev. Sam[ue]l (and Sarah, G.R.1), in New Orleans, Nov. 1, 1825, a. 26 y. (a. 25 y. G.R.1.)

KEGAN, Patrick, Jan. 28, 1849, a. 24 y. Unm.

KEITH, Abigail, w. of Ichabod, Apr. 24, 1784, in her 23d y.
Anna, w. of Aaron, Sept. 10, 1844, a. 63 y. Death caused by taking opium.
Artemas Jr., s. of Artemas, Nov. 18, 1805, in his 3d y.
Asaal, Mar. 14, 1825, a. 28 y.
Chloa, d. of Garshom and Mary, Sept. 13, 1740.
Comfort, w. of James, Aug. 22, 1775, a. 75 y.
Cyrus A., Dec. 24, 1841. G.R.1.
David, June 23, 1819, a. 11 y.
Deborah, w. of Comfort, Dec. 7, 1774, a. 32 y.
Deborah, w. of Noah, Apr. 11, 1806, a. 78 y. G.R.1.
Deborah, May 8, 1822, a. 17 y.
Esther, d. of Peter and Hannah, Oct. 4, 1761, a. 3 y. 8 m. 12 d.
Gershom, Capt., Mar. 13, 1770, in his 70th y. Cancer on his face.
Gershom, Nov. 10, 1813, a. 72 y.
Hannah, w. of Henry, Oct. 12, 1761.
Hopestill, d. of James, Feb. 28, 1801.
James, s. of James and Comfort, Oct. —, 1735.
James, Nov. 16, 1770, a. 74 y.
John, s. of Garshom and Mary, Oct. 10, 1738.
Jonathan, s. of Garshom and Mary, June 2, 1732.
Kezia, d. of James and Comfort, Apr. 16, 1740.
Lois, d. of Comfort, Oct. 25, 1783, a. 18 m.
Lois, d. of Abijah, Sept. 12, 1791, a. 36 d.
Lois, d. of Comfort, June 10, 1793, a. 4 d.
Lucinda, d. of Artemas, Mar. 11, 1826, a. 12 y.
Lyman, Mar. 9, 1839, a. 51 y.
Mary, wid. of Capt. Gershom, June 24, 1787, in her 83d y.
Moses, July 21, 1775, in his 28th y.

KEITH, Noah, Oct. 9, 1800, in his 78th y. (Revolutionary soldier. G.R.1.)
Patience, d. of Comfort, Apr. 20, 1775, a. 4 m.
Pheebe, d. of Garshom and Mary, Sept. 12, 1740.
Rachel, d. of James and Comfort, Apr. 24, 1740.
Rhoda, d. of Artemas, June 30, 1829, a. 20 y.
Silance, d. of James and Comfort, May 9, 1740.
Susanna, w. of Garshom, Oct. 15, 1773.
Urania, w. of Maj. Artemas, Sept. 16, 1826.
Warren, s. of Comfort, Dec. 10, 1778, a. 9 m.

KELLEY (see Kelly), Thomas, June 2, 1817, a. 62 y. (a. 63 y. G.R.1.)

KELLY (see Kelley), Abbie, d. of Albert and Deborah Inman, 9th day, 9th mo. 1848. C.R.4.
(Abigail, G.R.1), wid. of Thomas, Sept. 7, 1818. (Sept. 8, 1818, a. 68 y. G.R.1.)
Benedict Arnold, s. of Daniel and Dorcas, 10th day, 7th mo. 1802. C.R.4.
Diame, w. of Wing, 15th day, 2d mo. 1842. C.R.4.

KEMPTON (see Kympton), Amanda M., d. of Daniel and Mary, Apr. 1, 1845, a. 18 y. 6 m. G.R.5.
Deliverance, w. of George, Jan. 4, 1827, a. 71 y.
Eliza, d. of Daniel and Mary, Feb. 2, 1846, a. 30 y. 4 m. G.R.5.
George, Sept. 1, 1841, a. 90 y.
Samuel, May 7, 1832.
Susannah, wid. of Samuel, Oct. 19, 1840.

KENDALL, Abijah, June 15, 1840, a. 63 y. G.R.1.
Mary Ann H., d. of Abijah and Waity Arnold, Nov. 10, 1818.

KENNEDY, Alonzo David, s. of William, May 2, 1836, a. 4 y. 3 m.
Robert Ira, s. of William, Aug. 8, 1831.

KEYES, Lois, w. of Oren, Mar. 8, 1819, a. 60 y.
Oran, Sept. 17, 1827, a. 70 y. G.R.1.

KIBBEY, Jacob, s. of Abigail, now w. of Timothy Maden, Nov. 24, 1769. Death caused by fall of a horse.

KING, Rhoda, 10th day, 2d mo. 1813. C.R.4.

KNOP, Susannah, d. of Joshua and Hannah, Mar. "about ye 30, 1738."

KYMPTON (see Kempton), Ephraim, s. of Ephraim and Abigail, Oct. 20, 1749.

LAIGHTON, Georgiana Augusta, d. of George (George E. and Sarah J., G.R.1), Aug. 13, 1843, a. 16 m. (a. 1 y. 4 m. 9 d. G.R.1.)

LAMEY, John, s. of Patrick and Mary, May 29, 1849, a. 3 y. 10 m. 21 d. Dysentery.

LAMPSON, Joseph C., Nov. 18, 1844, a. 21 y. 6 m. 23 d. Consumption.

LAPHAM, Abigail, d. of Jethro and Sarah, 5th day, 11th mo. 1826. C.R.4.
Elizabeth, wid. of ———, 25th day, 5th mo. 1790. C.R.4.
Jethro, 12th day, 5th mo. 1805. C.R.4.
Levi, s. of Jethro and Sarah, 24th day, 8th mo. 1847. C.R.4. (24th day, 5th mo. 1847 dup.)
Sarah, wid. of Jethro, 31st day, 7th mo. 1812. C.R.4.

LARMEY, John, s. of ———, wid. of ———, Aug. 10, 1849, a. 7 y. Born in New York. Fit.

LASURE (see Lesure), Thomas, Sept. 21, 1812.

LAWRENCE, ———, s. of Ethan, July 1, 1833, a. abt. 6 y.
Comfort, Feb. 17, 1847, a. 23 y. Unm. Typhus fever.
Mary, w. of Thomas G., Sept. 15, 1838, a. 45 y. 4 m. G.R.1.

LEACH, Eliza, Apr. 24, 1847, a. 14 y. Consumption. (Mary E., d. of Benjamin N. and Hannah S., Apr. 25, 1847, a. 13½ y. G.R.1.)

LEAR, George A. R., Aug. 3, 1828, a. 16 m.

LEE, Clara Caroline, w. of Newell and d. of Daniel Carpenter, Aug. 3, 1833, in her 30th y.
Fuller, ———, 1824.
George, Sept. 3, 1823. Cancer on his face.
Lydia, w. of John, Dec. 4, 1830 (in her 32d y. G.R.20).
Mary, w. of William and d. of Henry and Sarah Wood, Jan. 16, 1792 (in her 22d y. dup.).
Moses, Aug. 18, 1840, a. 56 y.
Polly, d. of Wil[lia]m, June 22, 1795, in her 4th y.
Ruth, w. of Briggs, Dec. 22, 1835.
Sarah Ann, d. of Samuel, Apr. 19, 1830, a. 3 y.
William, Dec. 1, 1800, in his 34th y.

LEGG, Aaron, Sept. 7, 1801, a. 70 y. (Revolutionary soldier. G.R.1.)
Abigail, w. of Asa, Nov. 10, 1821, a. abt. 28 y.
Angelana M., d. of Peter and Sarah W., Jan. 20, 1849, a. 5 m. Consumption.
Comfort, w. of David, July 31, 1800, a. 42 y.
David, Apr. 25, 1844, a. 87 y. 11 m. 14 d. Revolutionary soldier. G.R.1.
Judson, s. of Joel (and Sarah, G.R.1), Oct. 7 (Oct. 1, G.R.1), 1828, a. 22 y.
Margery Ann, d. of Joel (and Sarah, G.R.1), Dec. 2, 1828, a. abt. 19 y.
Samuel Adams, s. of Peter, Sept. 13, 1843, a. abt. 2 w.
Thankful Holbrook, w. of David, May 25, 1831, a. 74 y. G.R.1.

LEONARD, Nancy, Sept. 19, 1833, a. abt. 30 y. Colored.

LESURE (see Lasure), Edward, May 21, 1772.
Rhoda, d. of Gideon and Rhoda, Feb. 5, 1813, a. 27 y. G.R.1.
Sally, w. of Amos, May 26, 1823, in her 56th y.

LEWIS, ———, w. of Ebenezer of Lynn, Sept. 5, 1814.
James, Aug. 11, 1829. Colored.
Mary, d. of Enoch, Oct. 11, 1837, a. 25 y.
William, s. of William, Nov. 16, 1836, a. 3 y.

LOWELL, ———, twin d. of John, Feb. 25, 1840, a. 1 d.
———, ch. of John, Aug. 9, 1840, a. abt. 6 m.

MacNOMARA, (see McNamarra), Martha, w. of Timothy, Apr. 7, 1746.

MARSH, Betsey, w. of Joel, 10th day, 9th mo. 1837. C.R.4.
Douglass, 20th day, 5th mo. 1817. C.R.4.
Isabella, d. of Aaron, June 30, 1836, a. 18 m.
Maurice Lee, s. of Aaron and Sylvia, May 5, 1846, a. 3 y. 2 m. 11 d. Drowned.
Rachel, d. of Joel and Betsey, 30th day, 1st mo. 1818. C.R.4.
Ruth, 19th day, 6th mo. 1820. C.R.4.

MARTIN, John, 8th day, 8th mo. 1786. C.R.4.

MASON, Charles Rawson, s. of Charles and Sally, Sept. 18, 1806.

McCORNEY, Thomas, July 25, 1849, a. 27 y. Born in Ireland.

McCRILLIS, Abigail, w. of Joseph E. and d. of Caleb Rist, Aug. 26, 1835, a. 29 y. G.R.1.

McINTIER, Jedediah, s. of ———, Aug. 27, 1740.

McNAMARRA (see MacNomara), John, Aug. 14, 1801, in his 83d y.

MEHAM, Patrick, s. of Patrick, Nov. 17, 1845, a. 2 y.

MELLENDY, John, s. of John, Apr. 6, 1753.
John, Apr. 6, 1767.
William, s. of John, Aug. 6, 1760.

MERRIAM, Philena, w. of Samuel (Samuel F. and d. of Fuller Murdock, G.R.1), Jan. 31, 1835, a. 27 y.

MILLER, Hannah, wid. of ———, Jan. 7, 1827, a. 86 y.

MINOT, ———, ch. of Buckley, Sept. 29, 1827, a. abt. 3 h.
Clarissa Maria, d. of Buckley, Feb. 17, 1834, a. 1 y. 8 m.
George, s. of William (and Olive W., G.R.1), Sept. 2, 1841, a. abt. 3 m.
Louis, w. of (George, G.R.1), Mar. 29, 1832, a. 35 y. (Mar. 28, 1832. G.R.1.)
Lydia S., d. of William and Olive W., July 23, 1828, a. 9 m. G.R.1.
Maria, d. of Buckley, Feb. 10, 1833, a. 6 m.
Mary M., d. of William and Olive W., Sept. 11, 1828. G.R.1.

MOLONY, John, s. of Daniel and Catherine, July 15, 1844, a. 1 m. G.R.2.

MOOR (see Moore), Jonathan, 10th day, 12th mo. 1795. C.R.4.
Mary, w. of Jonathan, 20th day, 7th mo. 1795. C.R.4.

MOORE (see Moor), Louisa, w. of Nathan, a man of color, Mar. 23, 1835, a. 31 y.
Silvia, wid. of Jack, Mar. 17, 1842, a. abt. 90 y. Colored.

MORSE (see Morss), ———, s. of Nahum Jr., Oct. 2, 1833, a. abt. 6 m. (Nelson J., s. of Nahum and Mary T., Oct. 11, 1833, a. 5 m. 10 d. G.R.17.)
Charles, s. of Nahum Jr., Feb. 3, 1840, a. abt. 10 m. (Charles G., s. of Nahum and Mary T., Feb. 3, 1840, a. 8 m. 3 d. G.R.17.)
Cyrus, Mar. 28, 1836, a. 19 y.
Daniel, s. of James, Aug. 8, 1825, a. 1 y. 2 m.

MORSE, Jesse, Aug. 6, 1805, a. 76 y. Revolutionary soldier. G.R.1.
Jesse Jr., Apr. 7, 1834, a. 75 y. Revolutionary soldier. G.R.1.
Louisa, d. of Nahum Jr., Feb. 7, 1840, a. 4 y. (Louisa M., d. of Nahum and Mary T., Feb. 7, 1840, a. 4 y. 6 m. 3 d. G.R.17.)
Mercy W., d. of Marvel, Nov. 7, 1834, a. 16 y.
Nahum, Dec. 7, 1840, a. 75 y.
Rachel, w. of Jesse, Jan. 26, 1810, a. 78 y. G.R.1.
Samuel Read, s. of Timothy H., Feb. 8, 1834, a. 2 m.
Sarah, Miss, Jan. 31, 1804, in her 60th y.

MORSS (see Morse), Eunice, d. of Samuel and Jane, Apr. 17, 1763.
Samuel, May 8, 1770.

MOSHER, Meribah, 1st w. of Joseph, 3d day, 7th mo. 1778. C.R.4.

MOWRY, Amy, w. of Alanson, Sept. 28, 1837.
Caleb, May 16, 1845, a. 62 y. G.R.1.
Caleb Ellis, inf. s. of A. and H., Oct. —, 1849. G.R.1.
Duty, s. of Wanton and Mary, July 30, 1790.
Elizabeth, w. of David, 16th day, 4th mo. 1797. C.R.4.
Gardner, Nov. 9, 1843, a. 37 y.
Huldah, w. of Richard, Sept. 1, 1795, a. 50 y.
Isabel, w. of Richard (27th day, C.R.4), 10th mo. 1820, a. 60 y. G.R.15.
Jonathan, s. of Gideon, Nov. 21, 1832, in his 32d y. (a. 31 y. 9 m. 19 d. G.R.15.)
Mary, w. of Wanton, May 25, 1849, a. 81 y. Born in Smithfield, R. I. Consumption.
Richard, Jan. 24, 1835, a. 86 y. (23d day, 1st mo. 1835. C.R.4.)
Ruth, w. of Gideon, Mar. 1, 1816. (a. 35 y. 4 m. 27 d. G.R.15.)
Seth, s. of David and Elizabeth, 23d day, 3d mo. 1797. C.R.4.
Stephen, s. of Wanton, Sept. 14, 1826, a. abt. 23 y.
Wesley, s. of Caleb and Clarinda, May —, 1833, a. 3 y. 3 m. G.R.1.

MURDOCK, Abigail, Oct. 9, 1761, in her 78th y.
Bethiah, w. of John, Mar. 3, 1804 (in her 70th y. G.R.1).
Charlotte, w. of Warren, Mar. 7, 1829.
Elisha, Dec. 7, 1843, a. 88 y. (Revolutionary soldier. G.R.1.)
Gilbert Deblois, s. of Warren, Oct. 27, 1827, a. 3 y. 5 m.

MURDOCK, Hannah, w. of (Lieut., G.R.1) Elisha, Nov. 22, 1832, in her 74th y.
John Jr. (s. of John and Bethia, G.R.1), Mar. 20, 1799 (in his 46th y. G.R.1).
John, July 2, 1806, a. 79 y. G.R.1.
John, s. of Fuller (and Esther, G.R.1), Sept. 13, 1837, a. 25 y.
Mary Ann, d. of Fuller (and Ester, G.R.1), Aug. 27, 1834, a. 9 y. (a. 9 y. 2 m. G.R.1.)
Robbin, Mar. 26, 1812. Colored. (a. 72 y. G.R.1.)
Sarah A., d. of Moses (Moses T. and Dorinda W., G.R.1), Sept. 1, 1838, a. 14 m. (Aug. 13, 1838. G.R.1.)
Warren, Mar. 11, 1846, a. 51 y. G.R.1.
Zipporah, wid. of (Samuel, G.R.1), Jan. 21, 1804, a. 52 y.

MURPHY, Almira, w. of Isaac, Feb. 21, 1837.
Catharine A. (Catharine Amanda, G.R.1), d. of Isaac R. and Fanny, Aug. 6, 1848, a. 1 y. 10 m. 20 d. Dysentery. (Aug. 7, 1848, a. 1 y. 10 m. 21 d. G.R.1.)
Henry Clinton, s. of Isaac (Isaac R. and Fanny, G.R.1), Feb. 25, 1840, a. abt. 2 y. (a. 1 y. 2 m. 13 d. G.R.1.)

MURRAY, Mary, d. of Patrick and Mary, Dec. 24, 1845, a. 1 y. 6 m.

NEWELL, Ezbon C., Mar. 8, 1831, a. 40 y. (Mar. 10, 1832. G.R.1.)
John Taft, s. of Ezbon C., Jan. 17, 1831, a. abt. 6 m.
Patience, wid. of Esbon, Sept. 18, 1849, a. 54 y. Dysentery.

NEWTON, George, s. of Guy S. and Dorothy, 11th day, 9th mo. 1819. C.R.4.
Zelotes, d. of Guy S. and Dorothy, ——, 1839. C.R.4.

NICHOLS, ——, inf. ch. of Reuben and Mary, Feb. 16, 1845.
Samuel, Feb. 21, 1829.

NICHOLSON, Sarah A., May 7, 1847, a. 14 y. 8 m. Consumption.

NICKERSON, Benjamin, s. of Freeman and Mary, Aug. 1, 1835, a. 1 y. 10 d. G.R.1.
Mary, w. of Freeman and d. of Benjamin and Anna Thwing, Jan. 1, 1835, in her 25th y. G.R.1.
Sarah Ann, d. of Freeman and Mary, May 6, 1847, a. 11 y. 8 m. 15 d. G.R.1.

NOLEN, Thomas, b. in Ireland, Aug. 9, 1847, a. 53 y. Consumption.

O'BRIEN, ———, Aug. 4, 1827, a. 24 y. Drowned. Irishman.
James E., s. of Thomas and Bridget, July 25, 1849, a. 4 y. 9 m. 8 d. Dysentery.

PACKARD, Frances, w. of James A., Apr. 20, 1841, a. 22 y.

PAINE, Elbridge (Elbridge G., G.R.1), s. of Stephen (and Tirzah, G.R.1), Mar. 21, 1837, a. 27 y.
Leicester, July 6, 1821. (July 7, a. 79 y. G.R.1.)
Molly, wid. of Leicester, Nov. 6, 1830, a. 79 y. 11 m.
Polly, d. of Leicester, Oct. 20, 1833, in her 51st y. (Miss Mary G. G.R.1.)

PARKER, Augusta, d. of Prince, Feb. 6, 1843, a. abt. 15 m.
Charles, s. of W[illia]m. [No date, entered among deaths of 1803.]
George G., July 29, 1841, a. 43 y.
Joseph, 21st day, 1st mo. 1810. C.R.4.
Joseph A., 20th day, 6th mo. 1847. C.R.4.
Permala, d. of W[illia]m. [No date, entered among deaths of 1803.]
Samuel, Oct. 20, 1846, a. 20 y. 5 m. Consumption.

PARMENTER, Dorcas D. (Dorcas D. Farmer, w. of Joseph W. Parmenter, G.R.1), May 22, 1847, a. 17 y. Md. Brain fever. (a. 17 y. 3 m. G.R.1.)

PARSONS (see Persons), William, Jan. 25, 1819, a. abt. 87 y.

PATTERSON, Louisa (Louisa M., G.R.1), w. of Frederic W. (of Rochester, N. Y., G.R.1) and d. of Bezaleel Taft (Jr., G.R.1) Esq., Nov. 16, 1839, a. 28 y.

PEARCE (see Pierce), Cuff, May 28, 1815.
Patty, Miss, Jan. 21, 1833, a. abt. 85 y.

PEAVEY, Caroline, d. of John, Mar. 15, 1837, a. 1 m.

PEAVY, Henry, Jan. 25, 1845, a. 20 y.

PECK, Sarah, d. of Simon and Sarah, Feb. 5, 1732.

PENNIMAN, Adnah, s. of Jonathan and Elisabeth, Sept. 23, 1754.
Jonathan, s. of Jonathan and Elisabeth, Sept. 2, 1761 (in his 18th y. dup.).
Mary, d. of Jonathan and Elisabeth, July 5, 1749.

PERKINS, Jane Elizabeth, d. of Elijah C., Sept. 22, 1839, a. 4 m.
Mariamne, w. of John K. and d. of Daniel G. (and Wate, G.R.1) Carpenter, Sept. 9, 1843, a. 22 y.

PERRY, Chloe, w. of Josiah, June 30, 1830, a. 25 y. G.R.1.
Chloe F., d. of Josiah and Chloe, Aug. 30, 1830, a. 4 m. G.R.1.
Jemima, w. of (Dr., G.R.1) Adams, Aug. 10, 1847, a. 37 y. Childbirth.
William J., s. of Josiah and Chloe, June 5, 1829, a. 1 y. G.R.1.

PERSONS (see Parsons), ———, wid. of William, Aug. 12, 1821, a. 86 y.
———, inf. ch. of Paul Jr., Nov. 28, 1828.
Allen W. (Allen Wright, G.R.1), s. of Nathaniel and Sophia, Aug. 5, 1848, a. 11 m. 21 d. Dysentery.
Anne, d. of William, Sept. 4, 1822, a. 61 y.
Asenath, 2d w. of John, Feb. 14, 1834. (a. 69 y. G.R.1.)
Elias F., s. of Paul (and Nancy, G.R.1), July 27, 1826, a. 21 y. (July 26, 1826. G.R.1.)
John, Sept. 27, 1836, a. 76 y. G.R.1.
Lydia, w. of John, Nov. 10, 1825 (in her 68th y. G.R.1).
Rachel, June 26, 1794, a. 30 y.

PHELPS, Luke W., Sept. 9, 1839, a. 65 y.

PHETTEPLACE, Sarah, d. of Otis, June 12, 1843, a. 13 m.

PIERCE (see Pearce), Margaret B., wid. of William, May 11, 1831, in her 74th y. G.R.1.

PIKE, Caleb S., Dec. 27, 1845, a. 37 y. Md.
Polly, Nov. 5, 1831.

PITTS, Job, Aug. 10, 1831, a. 96 y., in April. Oldest person in town.
Lydia, w. of Job, June 5, 1830.

POLLOCK, Richard, Dec. 21, 1843, a. 24 y.

POTTER, Eunice, w. of Asa, 13th day, 1st mo. 1805. C.R.4.
John, 15th day, 11th mo. 1797. C.R.4.

PRESTON, Daniel, s. of Wilson and Susannah, Apr. 27, 1769. Death caused by fence falling on him.

RAWSON, Abner, Nov. 14, 1794, in his 74th y.
Betsey S., d. of Jones and Thankful, Mar. 22, 1826, a. 4 m. G.R.1.
Charles, Dec. 11, 1808 (in his 41st y. G.R.1).
Charles Mason, s. of Charles and Jarib, Sept. 18, 1806, in his 4th y. G.R.1.
Charles Newton, s. of Charles (Charles B. and Mary A., G.R.1), Feb. 4, 1840, a. 3 y. 3 m. (a. 3 y. 3 m. 6 d. G.R.1.)
Edmond, s. of Edmund and Martha, Feb. 27, 1745.
Edmund, Dea., Nov. 20, 1768, a. 81 y. Deacon for 38 years and Town Clerk 26 years.
Edward, ———, 1833, a. 63 y. G.R.1.
Elizabeth, w. of Dea. Edmund, June 15, 1759, in her 77th y.
Grindal, s. of John and Marcy, June 20, 1740.
Hooker, s. of John and Mary, June 5, 1741.
John Aldrich, s. of Simon Jr. (and Roxallana, G.R.1), Feb. 4, 1840, a. 2 y. 6 m. (Feb. 5, 1840, a. 2 y. 7 m. 4 d. G.R.1.)
Jonah, s. of John and Mary, June 12, 1741.
Lavina, d. of Capt. Simon (and Nabby, G.R.1), Oct. 10, 1828, in her 22d y.
Levina, w. of Lieut. Simon, Oct. 12, 1803 (in her 29th y. G.R.1).
Martha, w. of Edmund, Mar. 1, 1781 (in her 62d y. dup.).
Mary, d. of John and Mary, Mar. 8, 1740.
Mary, w. of John, June 7, 1741.
Mary, w. of Abner, Aug. 19, 1790 (in her 69th y. dup.).
Mary, wid. of ———, Nov. 26, 1802.
Mary, w. of Capt. Simon, Nov. 30, 1847, in her 73d y. G.R.1.
Merit, s. of Capt. James, Sept. 9, 1827, in his 23d y.
Molly, d. of John and Mary, June 12, 1741.
Nabby, w. of Capt. Simon, Nov. 30, 1847, a. 72 y. Consumption.
Nathan, Oct. 15, 1809, a. abt. 85 y.
Nathan, s. of Edward (and Lucy, G.R.1), May 27, 1824, in his 24th y.
Nathan Edward, s. of Abner and Martha, Aug. 30, 1832, a. 7 y. 1 m. 20 d. Drowned. G.R.1.
Otis, Mar. 17, 1822, a. 41 y.
Rhoda, d. of John and Mary, Jan. 21, 1746.
Sarah, wid. of Silas, Nov. 20, 1832, in her 88th y.
Seth, s. of Edmund and Martha, Dec. 13, 1754.
Seth, May 4, 1829, in his 70th y.
Silas, Mar. 6, 1825, in his 79th y.
William, s. of William and Desiar, July 28, 1766.

READ (see Reed), Abigail, wid. of Capt. Samuel, Feb. 4, 1806 (in her 73d y. G.R.1).
Daniel, Feb. 10, 1744, in his 33d y.
David, Jan. 6, 1805, a. abt. 97 y.
Ebenezer, Dec. 7, 1744.
Ebenezer, Apr. 22, 1824, a. 69 y.
Elizabeth, wid. of Josiah (and d. of Dr. John Taylor, dec., b. at Harvard, G.R.1), Feb. 16, 1819 (in her 62d y. G.R.1).
Elizebeth, 2d w. of Dea. Samuel, June 22, 1771 (in her 61st y. dup.).
Ezra, s. of Daniel and Sarah, Nov. —, 1737.
James, s. of Dea. Samuel, Dec. 19, 1752, in his 3d y.
Lydia, d. of David and Thankfull, Nov. 20, 1740.
Lydia, d. of Samuel and Ruth, Oct. 27, 1745.
Marcy, w. of Samuel Esq., Mar. 26, 1835, a. 67 y.
Mary, d. of Dea. Ebenezer and Sarah, Nov. 21, 1740 (in her 20th y. dup.).
Mary Green, d. of (Capt., G.R.1) Samuel (and Mercy, G.R.1), Sept. 13, 1806.
Ruth, w. of Dea. Samuel, Apr. 30, 1747.
Ruth, d. of Capt. Samuel and Abigail, Oct. 27, 1781, in her 17th y.
Samuel, Dea., in Townsend, Mar. 21, 1788, in his 81st y.
Samuel, Capt., Aug. 24, 1798, in his 69th y. (Revolutionary soldier. G.R.1.)
Samuel Esq., Apr. 19, 1839, a. 69 y.
Sarah, wid. of ———, May 16, 1773, in her 95th y.
Thomas, Jan. 12, 1789, in his 48th y.

REED (see Read), Jehiel H., s. of Jehiel H., Feb. 21, 1840, a. abt. 2 y.
John, Lieut., Jan. 18, 1771, in his 63d y. (64th y. dup.).

RHODES, ———, twin d. of George and Almira D. R., July 22, 1844, a. 1 d.
———, twin s. of George and Almira D. R., July 22, 1844, a. 1 d.
Abigail, w. of Zebulon (d. of James and Esther Taft, G.R.1), May 15, 1837, a. 46 y. (May 14, 1837. G.R.1.)
Patience Thayer, d. of Zebulon (and Abigail, G.R.1), Sept. 16, 1824, in her 7th y. (a. 6 y. 7 m. 15 d. G.R.1.)
Zebulon, Aug. 24, 1840, a. 50 y.

RICE, ———, Mr., July 22, 1847, a. 42 y.
Hannah, w. of Matthias, Nov. 28, 1834, a. 34 y.

RICHARDSON, ———, ch. of Simon, Sept. 13, 1827, a. abt. 1 y.
Charles, formerly of Concord, Aug. 18, 1814, a. abt. 23 y.
George G., s. of William and Nancy, Apr. 30, 1848, a. 22 y. 9 m. 2 d. Unm. Consumption.
(Henry, G.R.14), s. of Anan (and Sarah A., G.R.14), Sept. 1, 1843, a. 1 y. (a. 11 m. 24 d. G.R.14.)
Joseph, Capt., Jr., Feb. 6, 1825, in his 40th y. Smallpox.
Joseph, Jan. 13, 1835, a. 80 y. (a. 80 y. 8 m. 8 d. G.R.14.)
Mary, w. of Joseph, Mar. 20, 1820, a. 62 y. on monument, 63 y. on gravestone. G.R.14. (Mar. 11, 1820, T.R.)
Rosamond, w. of Joseph, June 30, 1848, a. 75 y. G.R.14.
Sarah, d. of Simon (and Martha, G.R.19), Oct. 3, 1837. (Oct. 2, 1837, a. 17 y. 5 m. G.R.19.)
Simon, Aug. 9, 1841, a. 41 y. (41 y. 6 m. G.R.19.)
Susan, d. of Joseph and Molly, Nov. 20, 1814, a. 18 y. 5 m. G.R.14.
Susan, d. of Sarah, May 15, 1815, a. 6 m. 9 d. G.R.14.

RICHMOND, Ann M., d. of Edward, Feb. 26, 1847, a. 18 y. Consumption.
James, s. of Edward, Aug. 23, 1845, a. 19 y. Born in Northbridge. Chronic disease of bowels.
Mercy, w. of Edward, Apr. 14, 1847 a. 48 y. Consumption.

RIEDEL (see Riedell), George, s. of George and Susan, Mar. 29, 1845, a. 2 y. Scarlet fever.

RIEDELL (see Riedel), Catharine E., d. of Henry and Sarah A., July 4, 1844, a. 5 m. G.R.1.
Edwin H., s. of Henry and Sarah, July 16, 1844, a. 4 y. G.R.1.
William Henry, s. of Henry and Sarah, Mar. 8, 1839, a. 12 w. G.R.1.

RIST, Alice, wid. of Joseph, May 16, 1826, a. more than 80 y.
Betsey, wid. of Caleb, Mar. 20, 1847, a. 67 y. Dropsy.
Caleb, Oct. 13, 1842, a. 73 y.
Charles T., d. of Luther and Betsey, Nov. 5, 1849, a. 17 y. G.R.1.
Charles Thomas, s. of Thaddeus, Mar. 5, 1831, in her 26th y.
Daniel Waldo, s. of Thaddeus, Nov. 28, 1831, in his 21st y.
Jerusha, w. of Joseph, Feb. 19, 1788.
Joseph, Apr. 19, 1740.
Joseph, Oct. 30, 1815, a. 75 y.
Luther Wayland, s. of Luther, Sept. 2, 1839, a. 3 y.
Mary, w. of Thomas, Dec. 23, 1736.

RIST, Nathaniel, June 8, 1825, a. 82 y.
Pheeby, w. of Joseph, Feb. 6, 1739.
Polly, wid. of Thaddeus, May 3, 1838, a. 56 y.
Rachel, w. of Joseph, Aug. 9, 1777.
Smith Capron, June 4, 1835, a. 26 y.
Thaddeus, Aug. 9, 1830, a. 55 y.
Thomas, Sept. 29, 1783.

ROBBINS, David H., Mar. 19, 1827, a. 19 y.
Edward, 30th day, 9th mo. 1820. C.R.4.
Patience, w. of Abel, Mar. 7, 1827, a. 50 y.

ROBINSON, Mary, Nov. 24, 1848, a. 20 y. Consumption.

ROGERSON, Elizabeth S. (Elizabeth Slater, G.R.1), d. of Robert, Jan. 19, 1842, a. 18 y.

ROOK, Deliverance, w. of John, Dec. 30, 1765.

RUSSELL, Jane, d. of Patrick, Oct. 20, 1846, a. 1 m. 5 d. Dropsy on the heart.

SABEN (see Sabin, Sabins), Richard M. (Richard Mowry, C.R.4), s. of Israel and Sarah, Oct. 10, 1829, a. 18 y. 3 d. G.R.1.
Sarah Ann, d. of Israel and Sarah, July 23, 1829, a. 10 m. 16 d. G.R.1.

SABIN (see Saben, Sabins), Huldah, d. of Israel (and Sarah, G.R.1), Sept. 18, 1842, a. abt. 12 y. (a. 11 y. 9 m. 25 d. G.R.1.)

SABINS (see Saben, Sabin), Gideon M., s. of Israel and Sarah, Aug. 17, 1849, a. 30 y. 6 m. 9 d. Born in Winchester, N. H. Md. Consumption.

SADLER, Lydia, d. of Joseph and Sarah, Nov. 12, 1748.
Mary, d. of Joseph and Sarah, Sept. 8, 1748.

SAINT CLAIR, Elizabeth, b. in Scotland, May 12, 1845, a. 47 y.

SALSBURY, ———, wid. of ———, Dec. 18, 1837, a. 89 y.

SAYLES, ———, d. of Albert and Maria, May 28, 1844. G.R.1.
———, s. of Albert and Maria, Mar. 16, 1845. G.R.1.
———, d. of Albert and Maria, Dec. 22, 1848. G.R.1.
Louisa J., d. of Horatio and Caroline M., Jan. 6, 1839. G.R.1.
Mary E., d. of Horatio and Caroline M., Dec. 20, 1838. G.R.1.
William, s. of Amasa and Mary, Jan. 6, 1818. G.R.1.

SCOTT, Anne Gray, d. of Manly and Henrietta, Mar. 31, 1815, in her 3d y. G.R.1.
Prevost St. Clair, s. of Manly and Henrietta, May 19, 1839, a. 25 y. 2 m. 20 d. G.R.1.

SCRIBNER, Sarah, w. of Cinkler, Sept. 27, 1848, a. 27 y. Consumption.

SEAGRAVE (see Seagraves), ———, ch. of Edward, Dec. 4, 1840, a. abt. 4 w.
———, d. of Edward 3d, Jan. 16, 1842, a. abt. 2½ w.
Betsey, w. of Samuel, Oct. 18, 1847, a. 62 y. 6 m. Liver complaint. (Oct. 19, 1847. G.R.1.)
Bezaleel, twin s. of Bezaleel and Mary, Nov. 18, 1805.
Bezaleel, Aug. 1, 1830, in his 64th y.
Caleb, s. of Josiah (and Lois, G.R.1), Nov. 13, 1823, a. 9 y. (Nov. 14, 1823. G.R.1.)
Caroline E., d. of Edward E. and Sarah F., Mar. 22, 1843, a. 1 y. 9 m. 27 d. G.R.1.
Clinton, s. of Bezaleel, Nov. 29, 1830, a. 18 y. 2 m.
Daniel, s. of Dorrington (and Jerusha, G.R.1), Feb. 25, 1828, a. abt. 18 m. (Feb. 20, a. 1 y. 3 m. G.R.1.)
Daniel, s. of John, Aug. 23, 1848, a. 53 y. Md. Consumption.
Dorrington, s. of John and Sarah D., Aug. 8, 1849, a. 67 y. 10 m. 16 d. Md. Dysentery.
Edwin C., s. of Charles E. and Abigail, Dec. 9, 1849, a. 9 m. 21 d. Dropsy on the brain.
Eliza Ann, d. of Edward (and Mary Ann, G.R.1), Sept. 29, 1841, a. 7 y. (a. 9 y. G.R.1.)
George W., s. of Dorrington and Jerusha, May 30, 1834, a. 22 y. G.R.1.
Henrietta (Henrietta F., G.R.1), d. of Josiah (and Louis, G.R.1), Sunday, June 1, 1823, a. 19 y.
Henry Martin, s. of John 2d, Dec. 1, 1839, a. 3 y. 6 m.
Henry W., s. of Edward E. and Sarah F., Aug. 10, 1841, a. 1 y. 6 m. 24 d. G.R.1.
James, s. of Edward, Feb. 6, 1839, a. 18 y. (James L., s. of Edward and Mary Ann. G.R.1.)
Jerusha, d. of Joseph D. and Rachel, July —, 1849, a. 9 m. Born in Milford. Dysentery.
Jerusha, wid. of Dorrington, Sept. 21, 1849, a. 63 y. 5 m. 11 d. Born in Bellingham. Dysentery.
John Jr., Oct. 14, 1836, a. 52 y. (53 y. G.R.1.)
John, Feb. 3, 1842, a. 84 y. (a. 85 y. Revolutionary soldier. G.R.1.)

SEAGRAVE, Laura Elizabeth, d. of Samuel, July 28, 1828, a. 2 y. (a. 1 y. 10 m. G.R.1.)
Lucy, w. of Bezaleel, June 21, 1847, a. 52 y. 2 m. Erysipelas.
Malvina, d. of Josiah (and Lois, G.R.1), Dec. 16, 1823, in her 11th y.
Mary, w. of Bezaleel, Nov. 5, 1805. (a. 36 y. G.R.1.)
Mary, twin d. of Bezaleel and Mary, Nov. 18, 1805.
Mary, w. of Capt. George W., Jan. 23, 1848, a. 39 y.
Mary E., d. of John and Almira, Aug. 25, 1849, a. 3 y. 5 m. 6 d. Dysentery.
Mary Lucinda, d. of Saul, Mar. 30, 1840, a. 4 y.
Mary W., w. of Daniel, Sept. 30, 1844, a. 38 y. (Sept. 28, 1844, a. 37 y. G.R.1.) Born in Charlton. Typhus fever.
Matilda, d. of Horatio (and Bethiah, G.R.1), Aug. 26, 1836, a. abt. 15 m.
Nancy Ann, d. of John, Feb. 27, 1842, a. abt. 3 y.
Sally, d. of John (and Sally, G.R.1), Dec. 17, 1806, a. 16 y.
Sally (Sarah D., G.R.1), w. of John, Sept. 19, 1831, in her 77th y.
Saloma (only, G.R.1), d. of Seth (and Mary, G.R.1), May 16, 1832, in her 20th y.
Sarah, d. of Bezaleel (and Lucy, G.R.1), Nov. 1, 1840, a. 15 y.
Sarah, d. of Bezaleel, Jan. 2, 1841, a. 42 y.
Silas Bamfield, s. of Capt. Scott (and Eliza, G.R.1), May 9, 1832, a. abt. 10 m. (May 10, a. 9 m. 25 d. G.R.1.)
Susan, d. of Bezaleel, Oct. 24, 1823, a. abt. 2 y.

SEAGRAVES (see Seagrave), Mary, d. of Samuel (and Betsey, G.R.1), Jan. 7, 1835, a. 29 y.
Melinda, d. of Daniel, Dec. 23, 1834, a. abt. 6 m. (Melinda Weld, d. of Daniel and Mary, Dec. 23, 1834, a. 9 m. 10 d. G.R.1.)

SEARLE, ———, s. of George, Sept. 2, 1843, a. abt. 3 m.

SERVEY, William, Feb. 21, 1836, a. 25 y.

SHEPHARD, John, Feb. 20, 1846, a. 50 y. Born in Manchester, Eng. Md. Consumption.

SHOVE, Alva, s. of James M., Nov. 6, 1835, a. abt. 3 y.
Avis, 2d w. of Josiah, 10th day, 12th mo. 1816. C.R.4.
Baxter, s. of Thomas B. and Hannah, Nov. 19, 1789.
Dexter, Jan. 30, 1839, a. 48 y.
Hannah, w. of Thomas (Thomas B., G.R.11), Nov. 6, 1847, a. 81 y. Old age. (a. 81 y. 7 d. G.R.11.)

SHOVE, Joanna, d. of Josiah and Joanna, 11th day, 12th mo. 1791. C.R.4.
Joanna, w. of Josiah, 10th day, 5th mo. 1796. C.R.4.
Josiah, s. of Josiah and Joanna, 23d day, 11th mo. 1811. C.R.4.
Josiah, 21st day, 2d mo. 1844. C.R.4.
Laura Ann, d. of Luther, July 18, 1842, a. 12 y.
Mary, w. of Jonathan Marble, 10th day, 7th mo. 1814. C.R.4.
Mary Spring, d. of Jonathan Marble and Mary, 23d day, 7th mo. 1814. C.R.4.
Sarah, 3d w. of Josiah, 23d day, 7th mo. 1838. C.R.4.
Simon, s. of Dexter, Aug. 1, 1838.
Squire, s. of Thomas and Hannah, Aug. 3, 1847, a. 47 y. Md. Dropsy. (a. 46 y. G.R.11.)
William Wilbur, only s. of Calvin and Sarah G., Dec. 4, 1848, a. 24 y. G.R.11.

SIBLEE (see Sibley), Mary, w. of Timothy and d. of Ezekiel and Mary Wood, Sept. 25, 1753, in her 18th y.

SIBLEY (see Siblee), ———, ch. of David, Sept. 14, 1843, a. 1 y.
Abigail, w. of John, Sept. 27, 1783.
Abigail, d. of Stephen and Thankful, Aug. 18, 1789.
Aldrich, June 4, 1818, a. 14 y. Drowned in Blackstone river.
Chloa, d. of Stephen and Thankful, Aug. 31, 1783.
Hannah, d. of Stephen, Mar. 22, 1825, in her 41st y. (Mar. 21, 1825. G.R.1.)
John, Mar. 4, 1790.
Keith, s. of Peter and Mary, May 7, 1788.
Molley, d. of Stephen and Thankfull, Feb. 10, 1786.
Nancy, d. of Lieut. Joel (and Louis, G.R.1), Mar. 31, 1800, a. 8 m. 2 d. (Mar. 29, 1800, a. 8 m. 1 d. G.R.1.)
Royal, Sept. 28, 1822, a. 27 y. (a. 28 y. G.R.1.)

SLADE, Dorcas, w. of Stephen, 28th day, 1st mo. 1808. C.R.4.
Stephen, s. of Howland and Mary, 31st day, 9th mo. 1807. C.R.4.
Stephen, 10th day, 12th mo. 1808. C.R.4.

SLEAD, Naomy, w. of Henry, 9th day, 7th mo. 1827. C.R.4.

SMITH, Amy, d. of Benja[min] of Smithfield, R. I., Feb. —, 1802.
Bethiah, w. of Lewis, Nov. 6, 1832, a. 66 y. G.R.1.
Katharine, w. of Asa, 19th day, 5th mo. 1784. C.R.4.
Lois, Apr. 18, 1832, a. 58 y.

SMITH, Lydia, d. of Lewis (and Bethiah, G.R.1), Sept. 19, 1829, in her 41st y.
Samuel, Oct. 12, 1842, a. 83 y.
Susannah, w. of Lewis, May 10, 1832, a. 67 y. G.R.1.
Thomas, s. of Asa and Katharine, 2d day, 5th mo. 1788. C.R.4.

SOUL, Nancy, d. of Asa and Nancy, July 28, 1847, a. 2 y. 6 m. Dysentery.

SOUTHWICK, Ailse, w. of Joseph, 11th day, 11th mo. 1844, a. 88 y. 9 m. G.R.21.
Amey, d. of Enoch and Mary, 8th day, 12th mo. 1793. C.R.4.
Bettey, wid. of ———, 3d day, 3d mo. 1800. C.R.4.
Chloe, w. of Ezra, Nov. 4, 1812, a. 28 y. 6 m. G.R.18.
Chloe, w. of John, 25th day, 4th mo. 1817. C.R.4.
Chloe Susan, d. of Joseph, Dec. 29, 1833, a. abt. 2 m.
David, 9th day, 8th mo. 1843. C.R.4.
Duty, s. of Joseph and Ailse, ——— day, 1st mo. 1803, a. 9 y. G.R.21. (2d day, 2d mo. C.R.4.)
Elizabeth A., d. of Arnold and Patience, Mar. 11, 1834. G.R.21.
Ellen Herbert, d. of Thomas, Feb. 8, 1843, a. between 2 and 3 y.
Ezra, Apr. 17, 1847, a. 67 y. Md. (Apr. 19, 1847, a. 67 y. 1 m. G.R.18.)
Farnum, s. of Royal, Sept. 14, 1801, a. 2 y.
Farnum, s. of Royal, Nov. 9, 1812, a. 13 y.
Farnum, 27th day, 1st mo. 1814. C.R.4.
George, ——— day, 3d mo. 1807. C.R.4.
George, Oct. 15, 1841, a. 52 y.
Hannah, d. of Jacob and Sarah, 4th day, 7th mo. 1810. C.R.4.
Hannah, d. of David and Lucretia, 18th day, 11th mo. 1813. C.R.4.
Jacob, 19th day, 8th mo. 1833. C.R.4.
James, s. of George, June 19, 1789, a. 5 m. 8 d.
James, s. of George and Judith, Aug. 22, 1842, in his 47th y. Drowned at Northbridge. G.R.23.
John, 23d day, 1st mo. 1821. C.R.4.
Jonathan, s. of Jacob and Sarah, 8th day, 11th mo. 1788. C.R.4.
Jonathan, s. of Jonathan F., July 21, 1840, a. abt. 8 m. (Jonathan F., s. of Jonathan F. and Chloe H., July 15, 1840, a. 7 m. G.R.21.)
Joseph, 19th day, 3d mo. 1814, a. 68 y. G.R.21.
Judith, wid. of (George, C.R.4), Feb. 11, 1836, a. 80 y. (2d mo. 1837. C.R.4.)
Laura W., w. of Willet H. of Poughkeepsie, N. Y., and d. of John Capron, Oct. 23, 1823, a. 29 y. G.R.1.

SOUTHWICK, Lucy, d. of John and Chloe, 17th day, 12th mo. 1805. C.R.4.
Luke, s. of Joseph and Ailse, 23d day, 3d mo. 1814, a. 24 y. G.R.21. (24th day, 3d mo. 1814. C.R.4.)
Lydia, d. of Enoch and Waity, Nov. 7, 1822. G.R.1. (27th day, 11th mo. 1822. C.R.4.)
Lydia, d. of Thomas and Harriet, July 24, 1844, a. 1 y. 7 m. 13 d. Consumption.
Lydia Capron, d. of Royal, Oct. 22, 1834, a. 27 y.
Mary, d. of David and Elisabeth, 30th day, 8th mo. 1797. C.R.4.
Nancy, d. of David and Lucretia, 24th day, 10th mo. 1816. C.R.4.
Phebe, wid. of Royal, June 2, 1843, a. 74 y.
Royal, Nov. 30, 1840 (1841, C.R.4), a. 80 y.
Royal A., s. of Israel (Israel M., G.R.1) and Lucy H., Apr. 5, 1846, a. 4 y. 10 m. 14 d. Scarlet fever.
Sarah, w. of Jacob, 28th day, 7th mo. 1829. C.R.4.
Suse (Susanna, G.R.18), w. of Ezra, Sept. 29, 1833, a. 56 y. (a. 56 y. 3 d. G.R.18.)
Urana, d. of Royal and Phebe, Apr. 14, 1811, a. 19 y.

SOUTHWORTH, Nancy, w. of Josiah, July 27, 1816, a. 29 y.

SPAULDING, James H., s. of Girdon R. and Irene, Mar. 25, 1846, a. 1 d.

SPINK, Ann S. (Miss Ann C., G.R.1), Dec. 28, 1847. (Dec. 29, a. 37 y. G.R.1.) Consumption.

SPRAGUE, Mercy, 5th day, 11th mo. 1835. C.R.4.
Silama, w. of Zebulon, 8th day, 12th mo. 1838. C.R.4.

SPRING, ———, s. of ——— Jr., Mar. 1, 1777, a. 10 y.
Abba C., w. of Josiah, Sept. 30, 1844, a. 48 y. 8 m. G.R.1.
Abigail, d. of John Jr. and Hannah, Feb. 13, 1777, in her 3d y.
Abigail 2d, d. of John (Jr. dup.) and Hannah, Sept. 8, 1778 (in her 1st y. dup.).
Abigail White, d. of John and Sarah, Sept. 25, 1739.
Adolphus Esq., Oct. 20, 1847, a. 75 y. Md. Old age. (a. 75 y. 5 m. G.R.1.)
Avary, s. of John Jr. and Hannah, Feb. 17, 1777, in his 1st y.
Calvin, Feb. 20, 1842, a. 50 y. (Dec. 10, 1841. G.R.1.)
Elias, s. of Lieut. Adolphus and Lydia, Mar. 14, 1804, a. 15 d. G.R.1.
Elkana, s. of John and Hannah, Mar. 1, 1777.

SPRING, Ephraim, cousin of John, Apr. 4, 1740. Burned to death about 9 o'clock in the evening.
Ephraim Jr., Jan. 30, 1821, a. 24 y.
Ephraim, Sept. 23, 1834, a. 84 y. (Revolutionary soldier. G.R.I.)
Eunice, w. of Ephraim, Oct. 11, 1827, a. 71 y.
Frances E., d. of George and Sabrina G., July 18, 1844, a. 5 m. 16 d. G.R.I.
Hannah, w. of Calvin, May 5, 1839, a. 45 y.
John, s. of John and Sarah, Apr. 4, 1740. Burned to death about 9 o'clock in the evening.
John, Jan. 2, 1797, in his 57th y. G.R.I.
Josiah, s. of Ephraim and Eunice, Dec. 29, 1780 (a. 2 y. 8 m. dup.).
Lewis, s. of Lieut. Adolphus and Lydia, Mar. 6, 1806, a. 3 m. G.R.I.
Lucy (Lucy E , G.R.I), d. of Elkanah (and Phebe C. of Brimfield, G.R.I), June 10, 1835. (a. 29 y. G.R.I.)
Lydia, w. of Adolphus, Mar. 15, 1838, a. 65 y. (a. 66 y. 3 m. G.R.I.)
Maria T., d. of Calvin and Hannah, July 11, 1847, a. 22 y. 10 m. 12 d. G.R.I.
Nabby, w. of Josiah, Oct. 1, 1844, a. 51 y.
Nancy Jane, d. of Luther, Dec. 28, 1838, a. abt. 3 y. and 6 m.
Sabrina, d. of George and Sabrina, July 19, 1844, a. 7 m. Dysentery.
Sarah, wid. of Dea. John, Sept. 13, 1800, in her 84th y.
Thomas Read, s. of John and Sarah, Mar. 1, 1739-40.

STANDLEY (see Stanly), Benoni, Nov. 23, 1846, a. 76 y. Old age.

STANLY (see Standley), Sarah, Dec. 30, 1843, a. 26 y.
Wells (Standley, G.R.I), Jan. 24, 1842, a. 77 y. (a. 76 y. G.R.I.)

STAPLES, Daniel Webster, s. of Charles, Sept. 2, 1835, a. abt. 6 m.
Ezra, Aug. 29, 1843, a. 60 y.
Seth, s. of Ezra, in Ashford, Conn., Apr. 22, 1848, a. 33 y. 4 m. 5 d. G.R.I.

STARBUCK, ———, s. of Uriah, 13th day, 12th mo. 1800. C.R.4.

STEARNS, ———, ch. of Edwin, Sept. 16, 1827, a. abt. 18 m.
Martha, w. of Nathan, June 17, 1808, in her 40th y. G.R.I.

STEPHENS, Nicholas, Dec. 3, 1830, a. abt. 35 y.

STONE, Cyrus, Aug. 27, 1833, a. abt. 22 y. Killed by kick of a horse.
Cyrus M., s. of Lorenzo D., Oct. 9, 1841, a. abt. 14 m.
Ezra, 20th day, 4th mo. 1816. c.r.4.
Freelove, w. of Ezra, 29th day, 6th mo. 1805. c.r.4.

STOWE, Charles Augustus, s. of Silas W., Mar. 14, 1836, a. 25 y.
Silas W., in Grafton, Nov. 27, 1828, in his 44th y. g.r.1.

SULLIVAN, Patrick T., s. of Timothy, Sept. 23, 1849, a. 1 y. 9 m. Born in Blackstone. Dysentery.

SWETT, Huldah, w. of Stephen, 28th day, 7th mo. 1797. c.r.4.
Stephen, 7th day, 6th mo. 1785. c.r.4.
Stephen, 12th day, 8th mo. 1787. c.r.4.

SYLVESTER, Joseph, 31st day, 4th mo. 1792. c.r.4.

TAFT, ———, s. of John (and Lucretia, g.r.1), Nov. 9, 1825, a. 3 m. (a. 8 w., g.r.1).
———, ch. of Willard dec. and ———, June 23, 1832, a. abt. 10 m.
———, s. of Oliver and Laura A. M., July 21, 1844, a. 14 d. Fits.
———, s. of David and Henrietta, Nov. 2, 1848, a. 6 h.
Aaron, Nov. 5, 1805, a. 78 y. (Revolutionary soldier. g.r.1.)
Abba L., d. of Warner and Mary, Aug. 19, 1827, a. 3 y. 3 m. g.r.1.
Abigail, d. of (Capt. g.r.1), Bezaleel and Sarah, Sept. 24, 1778 (in her 10th mo. g.r.1).
Abigail, w. of Joseph, Oct. 11, 1795, in her 64th y.
Abigail, w. of Dea. Gershom, Feb. 24, 1816, in her 80th y. g.r.1.
Abigail Caroline, d. of Zadock, Dec. 14, 1830, in her 24th y.
Abigal, w. of Bezaleel, Aug. 12, 1775 (in her 21st y. g.r.1).
Abner, May 30, 1809. (Lieut. Abner, May 30, 1809, in his 73d y. Revolutionary soldier.)
Adolphus Baylies, s. of Orsmus (and Margaret Smith, g.r.1), Oct. 22, 1832, a. abt. 4 m.
Albert F., s. of Artemas and Jane, Dec. 20, 1839, a. 3 y. g.r.1.
Amadison, s. of Sylvanus and Margary, Feb. 8, 1846, a. 19 y. g.r.1.

TAFT, Amanda M., d. of Eber and Uranah, Feb. 2, 1845. Scarlet fever.
Amos (Amos C., G.R.1), July 27, 1826, a. 39 y.
Andrew Jackson, s. of Eber, Mar. 13, 1833, a. 1 m. 14 d.
Anna, w. of Darias, May 4, 1790.
Arba, s. of Warner, Aug. 19, 1827, in his 4th y.
Asenath, w. of Leonard, July 22, 1824. (a. 54 y. G.R.1.)
Asenath Cummings, d. of Timothy (and Polly, G.R.1), Dec. 12, 1823, a. 4 y. 5 m. (a. 4 y. 4 m. 13 d. G.R.1.)
Augustus C., s. of Robert G. and Julia A., Oct. 6, 1845, a. 5 m. 17 d. G.R.1.
Austin, s. of Ezra (and Mary, G.R.1), Sept. 4, 1844 (Sept. 3, 1844, G.R.1), a. 22 y. 6 m. 6 d. Fits.
Azuba C., d. of Adna (and Emma C., G.R.1), Sept. 27, 1839, a. 2 y. 5 m. (Sept. 23, 1839. G.R.1.)
Bainbridge R., s. of Capt. Royal and Molly, Mar. 11, 1815, a. 1 y. 22 d. G.R.12.
Benjamin, s. of Cummins (and Mercy, G.R.1), May 29, 1799, a. 10 m. (May 30, a. 9 m. 20 d. G.R.1.)
Benjamin, Oct. 17, 1828, a. 30 y.
Bezaleel, June 21, 1839, a. 88 y. 7 m. (Revolutionary soldier. G.R.1.)
Bezaleel Esq., s. of Bezaleel Esq., July 16, 1846, a. 65 y. 9 m. 8 d. Md. Consumption.
Brainbridge, s. of Capt. Royal, Apr. 25, 1837, a. 15 y. (a. 15 y. 6 m. 6 d. G.R.12.)
Caleb, Sept. 19, 1756.
Caleb, s. of Bezaleel Esq., Nov. 3, 1805, a. abt. 19 y. (a. 18 y. 11 m. G.R.1.)
Calista Clirana, d. of Samuel 2d and Sarah, Oct. 7, 1815, in her 3d y. G.R.1.
Calvin (Capt., G.R.1), Feb. 12, 1816, a. 50 y.
Charles M., s. of Newell (and Hannah, G.R.1), Apr. 7, 1843, a. 3 m. (Apr. 6, a. 3 m. 5 d. G.R.1.)
Charlotte, d. of Noah and Margret, Jan. 21, 1777, in her 3d y.
Charlotte P., w. of Elkanah, Feb. 6, 1843, a. 45 y.
Cheny, Feb. 13, 1840, a. 52 y.
Chloe, w. of Easmon, May 4, 1783.
Chloe, w. of Amos C., Dec. 21, 1839, a. 48 y. G.R.1.
Chloe, w. of Oliver, Nov. 24, 1841, a. 59 y.
Clirana, d. of Sam[ue]l and Sarah, July 22, 1822, a. 3 m. 10 d. G.R.1.
Cummings, June 22, 1841, a. 70 y.
Dandridge, Aug. 10, 1832, a. 45 y. G.R.1.

TAFT, Darius, Feb. 18, 1838, a. 74 y.
David 3d, s. of Dutee, Mar. 26, 1826, a. 6 m.
David, May 5, 1832, in his 62d y. (a. 61 y. 9 m. G.R.1.)
Deborah, d. of Joseph and Hannah, Dec. 10, 1738.
Duty, Oct. 22, 1830, a. 34 y.
Easman, Apr. 29, 1829, a. 65 y. 10 m. Died suddenly while burning brush.
Ebenezer, s. of Joseph and Elisabeth, Aug. 28, 1732.
Ebenezer, s. of Josiah and Lydia, Oct. 16, 1735.
Edward G., s. of Henry, Oct. 3, 1841, a. abt. 14 w.
Elisabeth, d. of Gid[e]on, Dec. 5, 1741.
Elisabeth, w. of Capt. Peter, Sept. 21, 1783, in her 76th y.
Eliza, d. of Otis, July 10, 1833.
Elizabeth, wid. of Capt. Joseph, Mar. —, 1760 (Mar. 10, dup.), in her 73d y.
Elizabeth, w. of Joseph (Jr. dup.), Aug. 27, 1770, in her 41st y. (Aug. 27, 1771, in her 40th y. dup.).
Ephraim, May 6, 1748.
Ephraim, s. of Ephraim and Mary, June 29, 1748.
Esther, w. of Jacob, Mar. 14, 1802, in her 75th y.
Esther, wid. of James, Feb. 3, 1834, a. 86 y. 25 d.
Experience, wid. of Samuel, Jan. 15, 1837, a. 86 y. (Jan. 14, 1837, a. 87 y. G.R.1.)
Ezekiel, Apr. 24, 1821, in his 44th y. G.R.1.
Ezra, s. of Easman and Hannah, Feb. 19, 1808, in his 15th y. G.R.1.
Faithful, wid. of ———, May 29, 1831, a. abt. 85 y.
Francis Amariah, s. of Amariah and Mary, July 28, 1848, a. 10 m. 10 d. Bronchitis.
Frederic Esq., Feb. 10, 1846, a. 87 y. Md. Cancer. (Revolutionary soldier. G.R.1.)
George S., s. of Bezaleel and Hannah, Sept. 17, 1823, a. 1 y. 3 d. G.R.1.
Gershom, Dea., Apr. 29, 1813, a. 73 y. (Revolutionary soldier. G.R.1.)
Hannah, d. of John and Hannah, Feb. 2, 1740–1.
Hannah, w. of Sergt. Joseph, Aug. 2, 1771, in her 76th y. (70th y. dup.).
Hannah, wid. of Easman, July 3, 1832, in her 69th y.
Hannah, wid. of Joseph, Apr. 2, 1842, a. 88 y. 9 m.
Hannah, w. of Newell, Jan. 8, 1843, a. 40 y.
Hannah Jane, d. of Ezra and Urania (Susan, G.R.1), Apr. 7, 1848, a. 8 y. 4 m. 20 d. (a. 8 y. 7 m. 10 d. G.R.1.) Consumption.

TAFT, Harriet Jerusha, d. of Jason, May 13, 1836, a. 8 y., abt. 8 y. and 10 m.
Horace, s. of William, Jan. 27, 1840, a. abt. 5 y.
Irene, d. of James and Esther, May 29, 1790, a. 16 y. G.R.1.
Jacob, Mar. 15, 1802, in his 77th y.
Jacob, May 30, 1823, in his 72d y. (May 29, 1823. Revolutionary soldier. G.R.1.)
James, Jan. 14, 1826 (Jan. 16, 1826, G.R.1), in his 88th y.
James, s. of Luke and Mercy, May 15, 1829, a. 1 y. G.R.1.
James W., s. of Capt. Calvin, Aug. 8, 1834, a. 25 y.
Jemima, d. of Gidean and Elisabeth, Aug. 1, 1742.
Jesse, s. of Robart and Chloe, June 10, 1783.
Joanna, d. of Moses and Priscilla, Sept. 30, 1761.
Joanna, d. of Phineas and Relief, Aug. 11, 1813, a. 6 m. 1 d. G.R.1.
Joel, s. of Josiah and Lydia, Dec. 23, 1745, in his 4th y.
Joel, s. of Josiah and Lydia, Aug. 30, 1749.
Joel, s. of Peter and Elisabeth, Sept. 27, 1758, in his 12th y.
Joel, s. of Paris P. (and Julia Ann, G.R.1), Mar. (27, G.R.1), 1837, a. 8 m.
John, Capt., in Boston, Apr. 19, 1769, a. 58 y. Cancer on his leg.
John, May 29, 1826 (a. 33 y. 5 m. 26 d. G.R.11).
Joseph, Capt., July 18, 1747.
Joseph, Oct. 20, 1761, in his 69th y.
Joseph, Feb. 1, 1803, a. 78 y. (Revolutionary soldier. G.R.1.)
Joseph (Lieut., G.R.1), July 2, 1828, a. 77 y. (Revolutionary soldier. G.R.1.)
Joseph, s. of Noah, Aug. 23, 1830, a. 58 y. 5 m.
Joseph, s. of Willard, Oct. 7, 1831, in his 3d y.
Josiah, Capt., Sept. 30, 1756.
Josiah, Aug. 18, 1761.
Josiah, s. of Moses and Priscilla, Sept. 29, 1761.
Josiah Jr., s. of Maj. Josiah, Dec. 30, 1799 (in his 22d y. G.R.1).
Judith, w. of Moses, Nov. 26, 1816. (a. 50 y. G.R.1.)
Laura, d. of Jason, Feb. 24, 1835, a. 5 y.
Laura A. M., d. of Oliver and Laura A., Apr. 12, 1846, a. 1 y. 9 m. 5 d. Scarlet fever.
Leonard, widr., Feb. —, 1846, a. 77 y. Burned to death.
Lucinda, d. of Web (and Lucy, G.R.1), Nov. 10, 1841, a. 48 y.
Lucy, wid. of Webb, Mar. 14, 1846, a. 72 y. Palpitation of the heart.
Lurana Jane, d. of Eber, Sept. 7, 1842, a. 7 m. 28 d.
Lydia, w. of Jesse, Dec. 11, 1765.

TAFT, Lydia, d. of Jesse and Lydia, Jan. 22, 1766.
Lydia, d. of Siles and Mary, Oct. 1, 1768.
Lydia, w. of Capt. Josiah, Nov. 9, 1778, in her 67th y.
Lydia Arnold, d. of Timothy, Dec. 17, 1826, a. 3 y.
Marcy, w. of Stephen, Jan. 15, 1765.
Marcy, d. of Samuel and Mary, Apr. 25, 1768.
Marcy, wid. of Aaron, Jan. 22, 1806, a. abt. 72 y. (a. 77 y. G.R.1.)
Marcy, w. of Cummings, June 8, 1815. (June 9, 1815, in her 55th y. G.R.1.)
Marcy, d. of Newell and Hannah G., Apr. 12, 1830, a. 1 y. 10 m. G.R.1.
Margaret, w. of Noah, Apr. 15, 1803, in her 70th y.
Margaret, w. of Bezaleel Jr., Esq., July 25, 1816, a. 33 y. (Margaret S., only d. of Rev. Sam[ue]l Spring, D.D., of Newburyport, and Hannah, his wife, G.R.1.)
Margaret Spring (Margaret Stoddard, G.R.1), d. of Bezaleel Jr., Esq. (and Margaret, G.R.1), Dec. 13, 1816, a. 7 m. (a. 6 m. 22 d. G.R.1.)
Margery, wid. of Willis, Mar. 24, 1848, a. 82 y. Consumption. (a. 72 y. 8 m. G.R.1.)
Maria, d. of Royall and Molly, Oct. 13, 1810, a. 1 y. 11 m. 3 d. G.R.12.
Martha, Feb. 12, 1847, a. 78 y. Unm. Old age.
Mary, w. of Ephraim, June 15, 1746.
Mary, d. of Moses and Priscilla, Oct. 3, 1761.
Mary, w. of Siles, Aug. 25, 1770.
Mary, d. of Abner and Ryal, Aug. 18, 1775.
Mary, w. of John of Windsor, Mar. 12, 1782.
Mary, w. of Samuel, Mar. 26, 1785, in her 43d y.
Mary, d. of Calvin (and Molley, G.R.1), Feb. 20, 1816, a. 12 y.
Mary, wid. of Jacob, July 19, 1832, a. 74 y.
Mary, w. of Calvin, Feb. 12, 1847, in her 81st y. G.R.1.
Mary Ann, d. of Henry, Aug. 11, 1840, a. abt. 6 w.
Mary C., w. of Ezra, Mar. 14, 1822, a. 26 y. G.R.1.
Mary E. (Mary Elizabeth, G.R.1), d. of Amariah and Mary, Apr. 8, 1845, a. 1 y. 10 m. 15 d. Croup.
Mehetabel, w. of Paul, Feb. 1, 1800, in her 56th y. (a. 77 y. dup.).
Mellen, June 3, 1839, a. 39 y.
Mercy, d. of Col. Josiah (and Margery, G.R.1), June 12, 1803, in her 17th y.
Mercy, w. of Sweetin, July 10, 1827, a. 64 y. (a. 65 y. G.R.1.)
Mercy, d. of Newell, Apr. 12, 1830, a. abt. 2 y.

TAFT, Merinda, d. of Ephraim and w. of Bailey, Dec. 25, 1812, a. 20 y.
Micajah, s. of Noah, Sept. 9, 1849, a. 83 y. Md. Palsy. (a. 83½ y. G.R.1.)
Mijamin, June 23, 1817, a. 77 y.
Minerva, d. of Orsmus (and Margaret Smith, G.R.1), Feb. 1, 1837, a. 18 m.
Molly, w. of Moses, Apr. 13, 1836, in her 64th y.
Molly, wid. of Marvel, Feb. 12, 1847, a. 81 y. Old age.
Moses, Lieut., July 13, 1788, in his 76th y.
Moses, s. of James (and Esther, G.R.1), June 26, 1810, a. abt. 22 y. (June 27, 1810. G.R.1.)
Moses, widr., s. of Abner, Dec. 4, 1848, a. 88 y. Old age. (Revolutionary soldier. G.R.1.)
Mowry, July 25, 1822, in his 30th y. G.R.14.
Nathan, s. of Gid[e]on, Dec. 1, 1741.
Nathan, Mar. 14, 1817, a. 78 y.
Noah, Sept. 2, 1814 (in his 86th y. Revolutionary soldier. G.R.1).
Oliver, s. of Abner and Ryal at Roxbury camp, July 16, 1775. Revolutionary soldier.
Parney, May 3, 1814. (a. 45 y. G.R.1.)
Paul, Jan. 23, 1804, a. 75 y.
Perly, d. of Samuel and Mary, Apr. 13, 1768.
Peter, Capt., Dec. 12, 1783, in his 69th y.
Peter, Capt., Sept. 13, 1802, a. 61 y. (62 y. G.R.1.)
Phila, d. of Dea. Gershom and Abigail, Sept. 29, 1776, in her 2d y.
Phila, d. of Capt. Calvin (and Molley, G.R.1), Mar. 26, 1813, a. 17 y.
Phila, d. of Eber, Oct. 4, 1822, a. 2 y. 9 m. 2 d.
Phineas, s. of Silas and Mary, Mar. 12, 1768.
Phinehas, July 14, 1813 (in his 33d y. G.R.1).
Polly, d. of Samuel and Sally, Oct. 15, 1809, a. 3 m. 24 d. G.R.1.
Polly, w. of Ezra, Mar. 15, 1822.
Rawson, s. of Aaron and Rhoda, Oct. 26, 1776.
Reed, s. of Dea. Gershom and Abigail, Sept. 27, 1783 (in his 4th y. dup.).
Robert, Apr. 28, 1748.
Ruth, d. of Gershom and Abigail, Oct. 7, 1776.
Ruth, wid. of Nathan, Feb. 4, 1824, a. abt. 77 y.
S. A., ch. of Dexter, Apr. 12, 1837, a. 3 m.
Sally Ann, d. of Sylvanus and Margery, May 9, 1842, a. 18 y. 3 m. 14 d. G.R.1.

UXBRIDGE DEATHS.

TAFT, Samuel, Aug. 2, 1816, a. 80 y. (a. 80 y. 10 m. Revolutionary soldier. G.R.1.)
Samuel Judson, s. of Aaron and Rhoda, Mar. 20, 1794, in his 3d y.
Sarah, w. of Mijamin, July 2, 1785.
Sarah, w. of Bezaleel Esq., Apr. 27, 1809, a. 52 y. 7 m. 1 d.
Sarah, w. of Morey, and d. of Joseph and Molly Richardson, Mar. 22, 1818, a. 26 y. 9 m. G.R.14.
Sarah, wid. of John, Mar. 21, 1837, a. 99 y. 4 m.
Sarah Congdon, d. of Samuel (and Sarah, G.R.1), Nov. 16, 1826, a. 3 y.
Sarah M., d. of Timothy (and Polly, G.R.1), Nov. 5, 1843, a. 22 y.
Silence, wid. of Thaddeus, Aug. 16, 1849, a. 92 y. Dysentery.
Silvia Cordelia, d. of Samuel 2d (and Dorcas, G.R.1), July 27, 1828, in her 3d y. (a. 2 y. 2 m. G.R.1.)
Squire, Dec. 14, 1841, a. 44½ y. G.R.1.
Stephen, Lieut., Feb. 3, 1803 (in his 63d y. Revolutionary soldier. G.R.1).
Susanna, d. of Samuel and Sarah, Apr. 13, 1806, a. 7 m. G.R.1.
Sweeting, Sept. 26, 1833, in his 80th y. (Sept. 25, 1833. G.R.1.)
Sylvanus, s. of Sweeting, Dec. 16, 1844, a. 57 y. Md.
Sylvia, d. of Moses and Judith, Aug. 3, 1816, a. 6 y.
Tabirah, d. of Ephraim and Mary, Apr. 20, 1748, a. 2 y. 6 m.
Thaddeus, Sept. 5, 1831, a. 73 y. (Revolutionary soldier. G.R.1.)
Thomas, s. of Joseph and Elisabeth, June 5, 1751.
Timothy, s. of Gid[e]on, Nov. 23, 1741.
Timothy, s. of Sophia, Sept. 9, 1821, a. 6 y. G.R.1.
Tryal, wid. of Abner, June 14, 1814. (a. 77 y. G.R.1.)
Warner, Apr. 3, 1837, a. 47 y. (47 y. 7 m. G.R.1.)
Webb, Apr. 21, 1842, a. 70 y.
Willard, Feb. 25, 1832, a. 41 y.
William Adolphus, s. of Calvin (and Eliza M., G.R.1), Nov. 6, 1840, a. abt. 8 m. (Nov. 7, 1840. G.R.1.)
Willis, Dec. 6, 1841, a. 76 y.
Zadock, Nov. 15, 1843, a. 80 y. (Revolutionary soldier. G.R.1.)

TANKARD, Patrick, b. in Ireland, May 2, 1849, a. 64 y. Gravel.

TAYLOR, Caroline, d. of William, June 1, 1828, a. 13 m.
Charles W., Dec. —, 1848, a. 27 y. 10 m. 17 d. G.R.1.
Elvira A., d. of Charles and Susan, May 20, 1836, a. 16 y. 10 m. 10 d. G.R.1.

TAYLOR, Frost, s. of Rev. Hezekiah (and Sally, G.R.1) of Newfane, Sept. 23, 1802, a. 20 y. (gr. s. of Amariah Frost of Milford. G.R.1.)
Mary, w. of William, Sept. 8, 1844, a. 39 y. Colic.

THAYER, Alonzo, s. of Sullivan and Charlotte. Feb. 27, 1816, a. 5 m. 15 d. G.R.16.
Amos, s. of Grindal, ——, 1790, a. 1 y.
Amos, July 11, 1838, in his 82d y. G.R.1.
Asa, Apr. 9, 1828, a. 67 y. (Revolutionary soldier. G.R.1.)
Catharine, d. of Royal and Hannah, Aug. 13, 1844, a. 28 y. (Aug. 15, 1844, a. 31 y. G.R.1.)
Charlotte, w. of Sullivan, Dec. 30, 1815, a. 21 y. G.R.16.
Eliza A., w. of Obed P., July 5, 1848, a. 21 y. G.R.24.
(George E., G.R.1), s. of Sullivan (and Ruth, G.R.1), Feb. 20, 1835, a. 11 m. (a. 11 m. 11 d. G.R.1.)
Harriet T., d. of Seth, Oct. 15, 1839, a. 32 y.
Herbert Morton, s. of Sullivan, Jan. 10, 1844, a. abt. 11 m.
Hiram E. A., s. of Obed P. and Eliza A., ——, 184-, a. 15 m. G.R.24.
Levi Lincoln, ——, 1823. G.R.1.
Levi Lincoln, s. of Joseph Esq., Nov. 8, 1828, a. 4 y.
Lois, w. of Amos, Apr. 10, 1822, a. 74 y. G.R.1.
Lovisa, d. of Asa, Nov. 30, 1828, in her 23d y.
Mary, d. of Sullivan, June 1, 1837, a. 9 m. 9 d.
Mary, w. of ——, July 26, 1844, a. 80 y. G.R.1.
Mary J., d. of Sullivan and Ruth, June 2, 1835, a. 5 m. 9 d. G.R.1.
Mercy L. A., d. of Obed P. and Eliza A., June 3, 1847, a. 1 y. 6 m. 13 d. G.R.24.
Nancy, d. of Grindal, Feb. 24, 1797, in her 3d y.
Royal, s. of Royal (and Hannah, G.R.1), Mar. 21, 1829, a. 2 m.
Sarah, 29th day, 11th mo. 1797. C.R.4.
Seth, May 23, 1839, a. 74 y.
Susan S., ——, 1836. G.R.1.
Uriah, Lieut., Mar. 30, 1795, in his 89th y.
William B. (William Bainbridge, G.R.1), s. of Royal and Hannah, Nov. —, 1820. (Nov. 1, 1820, a. 1 y. 3 m. G.R.1.)
William W., s. of Augustus and Sylvia M., July 11, 1849, a. 11 y. 11 m. 11 d. G.R.1.

THOMPSON, ——, s. of Levi and Elizabeth, Jan. 17, 1831, a. 2 m. G.R.1.
Abigail, w. of Elisha, July 9, 1800.

UXBRIDGE DEATHS.

THOMPSON, Amy, w. of Eber, Oct. 5, 1827, a. 28 y. 6 m.
Benjamin, May 29, 1816, a. 56 y. G.R.16.
Catharine, Nov. 17, 1836, a. 84 y. (w. of Elisha, Dec. 17, 1836, a. 84 y. G.R.1.)
Ebenezer, Feb. 8, 1843, a. 74 y.
Elijah, s. of Benjamin dec., Feb. 1, 1821, a. 12 y. 3 m.
Emery, s. of Benjamin and Eunice, Apr. 15, 1795.
Emily Marie, d. of Levi and Elizabeth, Sept. 25, 1832, a. 6 m. 24 d. G.R.1.
Hannah, d. of Benjamin and Eunice, Apr. 22, 1795.
Joel, Jan. 9, 1833, a. 86 y.
Laura Ann, d. of Levi and Elizabeth, May 11, 1835, a. 1 y. 10 m. 16 d. G.R.1.
Lucy Ann, d. of Eber, Aug. 5, 1840, a. abt. 18 m.
Mary Ann, d. of Levi and Elizabeth, Sept. 25, 1837, a. 1 y. 4 m. 10 d. G.R.1.
Patty, d. of Benjamin and Eunice, Mar. 13, 1797.
Susan C. (Susan Charity, G.R.1), d. of Adams and Charity, Mar. 8, 1845, a. 13 y. 10 m. 28 d. Born in Wrentham. Consumption.
Susanna, w. of Joel, Feb. 12, 1846, a. 83 y. Heart disease.

THURSTON, Daniel, July 3, 1745.
Elisabeth, d. of Benjamin and Elisabeth, Feb. 24, 1744-5.
Mary, May 18, 1772.
Sarah, d. of Daniel and Martha, Apr. 9, 1742.

THWING, Benjamin (3d, G.R.1), s. of Benjamin Jr. (and Anna, G.R.1), Oct. 19, 1802.
Benjamin, only ch. of Almon and Sarah A., June 16, 1810, a. 3 y. 2 m. 13 d. G.R.1.
Benjamin, Sept. 19, 1813, a. 81 y.
Benjamin, June 26, 1830, a. 53 y.
Else Rawson, d. of Benjamin (and Anna, G.R.1), Sept. 24, 1827, a. 6 y. 11 m. (Sept. 23, 1827. G.R.1.)
Hellen, d. of Almond and Sarah A., Dec. 10, 1845, a. 9 m. Convulsions.
Molly, wid. of Benjamin, Aug. 20, 1815 (in her 72d y. G.R.1).
Samuel, s. of Benjamin and Mary, Nov. 29, 1762.

TIFFANY, Mary Ann, w. of George and d. of Josiah and Lois Seagrave, Feb. 11, 1825, in her 25th y. G.R.9.

TILLEY, Sarah, w. of James, Oct. 16, 1840, a. 83 y.

TILLINGHAST, Daniel Esq., formerly of Providence, R. I., Sept. 18, 1806, in his 75th y. G.R.1.
Hannah, d. of Robert G. (and Paticence, G.R.1), Jan. 24, 1800, in her 18th y. (Jan. 25, 1800. G.R.1.)
Hannah, w. of Capt. John, July 9, 1833, a. 64 y. (July 12, 1833, a. 63 y. G.R.1.)
Robert Gibbs, Ens., in Providence, June 24, 1799 (in his 39th y. G.R.1). Killed by falling into a cistern in a still.

TRASK, Lydia, 29th day, 7th mo. 1836. C.R.4.

TRIPP, Robert, Oct. 4, 1846, a. 76 y. Consumption.

TUCKER, Arnold, s. of Benjamin, Apr. 14, 1825, in his 16th y. (a. 15 y. 5 m. 19 d. G.R.8.)
Benjamin, July 29, 1845, a. 83 y. Md. Old age.
Caroline (Caroline C., G.R.1), d. of Benjamin Jr. and Mary W., June 28, 1845, a. 10 y. (June 26, 1845, a. 9 y. 2 m. G.R.1.) Scarlet fever.
Mary W., w. of Benjamin Jr., June 30, 1845, a. 43 y. (a. 42 y. 8 m. G.R.1.)
Newel, s. of Jonathan, Dec. 13, 1834, a. 15 y.

TUFTS, Cotton, Feb. 12, 1835, a. 63 y. Insane for 40 years.

TURNER, Alice, w. of James, July 29, 1848, in her 70th y. G.R.1.
John, Capt., of Salem, s. of John of Salem, Apr. 5, 1785, a. 40 y.
Theodosia L. (d. of James and Else, G.R.1), Sept. 16, 1844, a. 13 y. 3 m. 15 d. Typhus fever.

TWICHEL, Joanna, 28th day, 4th mo. 1820. C.R.4.

TYLER, Amary, Dec. 3, 1813, a. 21 y.
Doliver, s. of Newell and Watee H., Sept. 5, 1843, a. 6 y. G.R.1.
Hannah, d. of Parker and Huldah, Oct. 18, 1811, a. 7 d. G.R.1.
Huldah, w. of Parker, Oct. 11, 1811, a. 31 y. G.R.1.
Jerusha, wid. of Solomon, Sept. 26, 1834, a. 69 y. (Aug. 7, 1834. G.R.1.)
Mary, d. of Solomon and Mary, Apr. 23, 1798, a. 6 m. G.R.1.
Mary, w. of Solomon, July 17, 1808, a. 47 y. G.R.1.
Nahum Esq., Feb. 25, 1787, in his 55th y.
Nathan, Nov. 4, 1792, a. 35 y.
Solomon, Nov. 1, 1810. (a. 53 y. G.R.1.)
Taft, s. of Joseph (and Trial, G.R.1), May 26, 1830. (1826. G.R.1.)

TYLER, Trial, w. of Joseph, Aug. 18, 1815. (August 17, in her 39th y. G.R.1.)
Watee H., w. of Newell, Sept. 7, 1839, a. 31 y., G.R.1.

VIBBERT, Ferdinand M., Feb. 15, 1848, a. 13 m. G.R.1.

WALKER, Almira A., Sept. 2, 1845, a. 23 y. Unm. Typhus fever.
Isaac, Apr. 24, 1825, a. abt. 46 y. (a. 47 y. G.R.1.)
Mary, wid. of James, Jan. 17, 1849, a. 34 y. Consumption.

WALL, Caleb, 29th day, 1st mo. 1846. C.R.4.
Sarah, 23d day, 12th mo. 1835. C.R.4.

WALLIS, Byron, Jan. 30, 1848, a. 25 y. Inflammation of the lungs.

WARE, Polly Maria, d. of Albert O. (and Mehetable, G.R.1), Mar. 12, 1844, a. 7 y.

WARFIELD, Elizabeth, July 29, 1849, a. 66 y. G.R.5.

WARNER, Albert, s. of Daniel, Mar. 24, 1834, a. 2 m.
Mary Jane, w. of Daniel, Feb. 15, 1834.

WARREN, Hannah, wid. of Seth, Dec. 5, 1844, a. 79 y. Old age.

WATERS, Bethiah, wid. of ———, and sister of Benjamin Adams Esq., June 8, 1827.

WATSON, Elisabeth, d. of Thomas and Mary, 5th day, 11th mo. 1789. C.R.4.

WEBB, Nathan, Rev., Mar. 14, 1772, in his 67th y., and 42d year of his ministry.
Ruth, w. of Rev. Nathan, Aug. 26, 1761, in her 61st y.

WHEELER, ———, s. of Asa, Jan. 23, 1828, a. abt. 24 h.
Amanda, w. of Asa, Feb. 2, 1828, in her 24th y.
Buffum, s. of Jonathan Jr. and Mary, 25th day, 1st mo. 1792. C.R.4.
Charles, s. of Obediah Jr. and Phila, 8th day, 4th mo. 1836. C.R.4.
Content, d. of Jonathan Jr. and Mary, 30th day, 7th mo. 1793. C.R.4.
George W., s. of Asa, Aug. 31, 1829, a. 3 y.
Hannah, w. of Obadiah, 23d day, 3d mo. 1790. C.R.4.

WHEELER, Hannah, d. of Obadiah Jr. and Ann, 13th day, 2d mo. 1837. c.r.4.
Jonathan, 10th day, 8th mo. 1791. c.r.4.
Jonathan Jr., 14th day, 7th mo. 1797. c.r.4.
Joseph, s. of Obadiah Jr. and Ann, 16th day, 9th mo. 1798. c.r.4.
Lucy E., d. of Amasa and Roxcellana, Apr. 22, 1846, a. 3 y. 11 m. 15 d. Dropsy on the heart.
Lydia, d. of Abraham and Naomi, 18th day, 11th mo. 1785. c.r.4.
Miriam, w. of Stephen, 28th day, 12th mo. 1796. c.r.4.
Miriam, d. of Obadiah Jr. and Ann, — day, 7th mo. 1809. c.r.4.
Naomi, w. of Abraham, 5th day, 3d mo. 1791. c.r.4.
Obadiah Jr., 22d day, 12th mo. 1827. c.r.4.
Obediah, s. of Obadiah and Ann, 3d day, 10th mo. 1843. c.r.4.
Rhoda, w. of Benjamin, 16th day, 2d mo. 1846. c.r.4.
Samuel Aldrich, s. of Benjamin and Rhoda, 6th day, 11th mo. 1830. c.r.4.
Stephen, 3d day, 10th mo. 1845. c.r.4.
Stephen Sweat, s. of Benjamin and Rhoda, 6th day, — mo. 1845. c.r.4.
Thankful, d. of Jonathan Jr. and Mary, 1st day, 10th mo. 1789. c.r.4.
Thankful, d. of Jonathan Jr. and Mary, 24th day, 12th mo. 1790. c.r.4.

WHEELOCK, Alice A., d. of Charles A. and Nancy (Seagrave, g.r.1), July —, 1846, a. 10 m. Dysentery.
Deborah, w. of Paul, Jan. 24, 1800.
Deborah, wid. of (Simeon, g.r.1), Nov. 5, 1815. (Nov. 15, a. 74 y. g.r.1.)
Maria Isabella, d. of Jerry (and Sukey, g.r.1), Oct. 18, 1822, a. 1 y. 3 m.

WHIPPLE, Emma, d. of Virgil, Jan. 8, 1833, a. abt. 5 y.
Horace, s. of Jona[than] and Mary, Nov. 2, 1798, a. 1 y. 14 d. g.r.1.
Jonathan, Dec. 17, 1839, a. 87 y.
Mary, w. of Jonathan, Sept. 3, 1812, between 1 and 2 o'clock in the afternoon. (a. 57 y. g.r.1.)
Sophia, w. of Independence, July 14, 1830, in her 27th y.

WHITE, Abigail, d. of Moses (and Mary, g.r.1), Mar. 15, 1803, a. 42 y.

WHITE, Abner, s. of Benjamin and Mary, Nov. 2, 1743.
Abner, s. of Joseph and Judith, Apr. 5, 1758.
Amey B., d. of Sam[ue]l O. and Hannah D., July 31, 1839, a. 15 d. G.R.1.
Asa at No. 4, ———, 1759.
Bezaleel, Aug. 21, 1798, in his 31st y.
Chloe, wid. of Lieut. Peter, Dec. 27, 1830, in her 81st y.
Comfor[t], d. of Seth and Abigal, Apr. 9, 1758.
Deborah, w. of ———, Mar. 24, 1837, a. 72 y. G.R.1.
Easther, d. of Samuel and Louies, Apr. 22, 1769.
Edward, s. of Joseph and Judith, June 14, 1756.
Elisabeth, w. of John, 7th day, 6th mo. 1819. C.R.4.
Eliza Ann, 2d w. of Sam[ue]l O., Dec. 5, 1844, a. 18 y. G.R.1.
George, s. of Jonathan, Dec. 5, 1838, a. 4 m.
George, s. of Jonathan, Dec. 7, 1840, a. abt. 10 m.
Hannah D., w. of Sam[ue]l O., Aug. 8, 1841, a. 28 y. G.R.1.
Hannah D., w. of Samuel O., Dec. 5, 1844, a. 19 y. Typhus fever.
Henry, s. of Joseph and Deborah, Mar. 3, 1773, in his 8th y. (Mar. 4 dup.).
Jemima, w. of Seth, Sept. 3, 1818, a. 62 y. G.R.1.
Jennie, w. of Capt. Peter, Oct. 14, 1787, in her 76th y.
John, May 6, 1824, in his 82d y.
Jonathan, s. of Samuel and Mary, Oct. 18, 1761.
Joseph, Capt., June 15, 1737 (in his 54th y. dup.).
Joseph, s. of Joseph, Sept. 8, 1747.
Joseph, Mar. 22, 1829.
Josiah, Feb. 16, 1808, in his 87th y.
Judath, d. of Joseph, Sept. —, 1747.
Keith, in Savannah, Ga., Apr. 16, 1810.
Keith W., Oct. 16, 1836, a. 35 y.
Lydia, d. of Samuel and Mary, Oct. 9, 1761.
Mary, w. of Samuel, Dec. 19, 1765.
Mason, Apr. 15, 1839, a. 49 y. 11 m. 19 d. G.R.1.
Moses, s. of Joseph and Judith, Aug. 8, 1759.
Naomi, wid. of ———, Jan. 5, 1803, a. 81 y.
Nathan, s. of Thomas and Deborah, Aug. 12, 1736.
Noah, 3d day, 3d mo. 1791. C.R.4.
Obediah, s. of Joseph, Sept. —, 1747.
Oscar P., s. of Samuel O. and Judith L., Mar. 4, 1848, a. 6 m. 15 d. G.R.1.
Peter, Capt., May 8, 1782, in his 68th y.
Peter, Lieut., Dec. 2, 1821, a. 75 y. (Revolutionary soldier. G.R.1.)

WHITE, Polly, d. of Seth (and Jemima, G.R.1), Jan. 4, 1803, a. 16 y.
Rebecca, w. of Noah, 4th day, 1st mo. 1816. C.R.4.
Sally, d. of Amariah, Apr. 20, 1788. Twin.
Sally, d. of Seth, Mar. 14, 1822, a. 28 y. (Mar. 13, 1822. G.R.1.)
Sarah, d. of Joseph, Sept. —, 1747.
Seth, at Lake George, Aug. 20, 1758.
Suky, d. of Amariah, Apr. 20, 1788. Twin.
Willard, s. of Rachel Chillson and rep. s. of Seth White, July 9, 1833, a. abt. 28 y.

WHITING, ———, ch. of Jesse, Aug. 31, 1817, a. abt. 18 m.
(Emma G., G.R.1), d. of Prentice (and Harriet W., G.R.1), Aug. 7, 1848, a. 3 m. (Aug. 8, 1848. G.R.1.)
George N., s. of Nelson and Rhoda, Sept. 6, 1847, a. 10 m. 26 d. G.R.1.
Rebecca, wid. of ———, Aug. (20, G.R.1), 1848, a. 86 y. Old age.

WHITMAN, Valentine, Mar. 13, 1825, a. 74 y.

WHITNEY, Hannah, w. of Capt. Moses, May 30, 1793, in her 37th y.
Israel, Nov. 21, 1805.
Mercy, w. of Ezra, Sept. 23, 1794, in her 59th y.
Micah, s. of Ezra Esq., Feb. 12, 1795.

WILCOX, David, 13th day, 7th mo. 1819. C.R.4.
Emma S., d. of Otis and Polly, Mar. 30, 1848, a. 1 y. 3 m. 27 d. Inflammation of the lungs.
Lewis G. (Lewis Gilbert, G.R.1), s. of Otis, Feb. 12, 1838, a. abt. 2 y. (a. 1 y. 11 m. G.R.1).
Walter A., s. of Capt. Otis, Apr. 25, 1844, a. 2 y. 7 m. 23 d.

WILLARD, Abijah, Dr., Apr. 12, 1816, a. 34 y.
Cato, Aug. 14, 1834, a. abt. 65 y. Colored. (Aug. 15, 1834, a. 62 y. G.R.1.)
Elizabeth, w. of Dr. Nahum, Apr. 4, 1789, in her 65th y.
Emeline, d. of Dr. George and Sylvia, July 16, 1817, a. 20 m. (a. 1 y. 9 m. G.R.1.)
George, Dr., widr., s. of Samuel, Oct. 20, 1846, a. 57 y. Consumption.
Levi, s. of Col. Levi of Lancaster, Apr. 7, 1790, a. 34 y.
Nahum, Dr., Apr. 22, 1792, in his 72d y.
Nahum Ward, Dr., May 21, 1787, a. 27 y.

WILLARD, Olive, wid. of (Dr. Samuel, G.R.1), Apr. 30, 1831, a. 78 y.
Paris, s. of Cato, Dec. 7, 1839, a. 25 y. Colored. (Dec. 6, 1839, a. 24 y. G.R.1.)
Samuel, Dr., Sept. 9, 1811, a. 63 y. 5 m. 6 d.
Sarah Jane, d. of Samuel T., May 31, 1836, a. abt. 13 m.
Sylvia (Sylvia C., G.R.1), w. of Dr. George, Aug. 20, 1842, a. 52 y.

WILLIAMS, ———, Mr., Sept. 15, 1844, a. 63 y. Consumption.
Catharine (Catharine Larnard, G.R.1), d. of Charles (Charles W. and Frances E., G.R.1), Feb. 18, 1842, a. abt. 15 m. (a. 15 m. 13 d. G.R.1.)
Chester, Dec. 7, 1843, a. 76 y.
Eleanor, d. of Stephen (and Nancy, G.R.1), Dec. 12, 1841, a. 26 y.
Horace Waterman, s. of George and Delilah, Aug. 20, 1840, a. 5 w. 6 d. G.R.1.
James Henry, s. of George (and Delilah, G.R.1), May 6, 1839, a. 11 m. 23 d.
John, s. of Chester and Sarah, July 16, 1812, in his 3d y. G.R.1.
Lydia, w. of Stephen, July 5, 1773, in her 31st y.
Merilda, w. of John D., Oct. 1, 1847, a. 47 y. G.R.1.
Nancy, w. of Stephen (and d. of Dea. Nicholas Baylies dec., G.R.1), Aug. 6, 1843, a. 61 y.
Sarah, w. of Chester, Jan. 16, 1820, in her 49th y. G.R.1.
Sarah, wid. of Stephen, Sept. 23, 1825, a. 86 y. (Sept. 22, 1825. G.R.1.)
Stephen, Sept. 15, 1807. (a. 70 y. Revolutionary soldier. G.R.1.)

WILLMAN, John, July 12, 1845, a. 27 y. Scarlet fever.

WILLSON, Samuel, Sept. 8, 1822.

WILMARTH (see Wilmoth), George H., s. of Hiram and Joanna, Dec. 26, 1837, a. 4 y. 2 m. 23 d. G.R.1.

WILMOTH (see Wilmarth), Jason, s. of Ebenezer of Douglas, Apr. 9, 1801.

WILSON, Edwin, s. of Benjamin, Aug. 2, 1817, a. 4 m.
Nabby, w. of Henry, Feb. 23, 1836, a. 24 y.
Parley, s. of ——— of Upton, Sept. 15, 1815. Death caused by the upsetting of a cart.

WINDSOR, Mary, d. of James, Jan. 13, 1828, in her 4th y.

WING, Albert F., s. of Paul, Oct. 14, 1848, a. 30 y. Consumption.
Charles H., s. of Charles and Mary (Mary G., G.R.1), May 16, 1844, a. 10 m. 29 d. Whooping cough.
Edgar Taft, s. of Albert F. and Emeline N., Mar. 28, 1848, a. 3 m. 12 d. Consumption.
Emily H., d. of Albert and Emeline N., Oct. 27, 1844.
Francis C., s. of Charles and Mary, Feb. 4, 1848, a. 2 y. 10 m. Dropsy in the head.
Mehitebell, w. of Paul, Feb. 14, 1842, a. 57 y.
Nath[anie]l H., s. of Paul and Mercy Ann, 15th day, 6th mo. 1832. C.R.4.

WINSLOW (Oseanah M., G.R.1), d. of (Simeon A. and Mary, G.R.1), Sept. 22, 1844, a. 13 y. (Sept. 23, a. 13 y. 4 m. G.R.1.) Typhus fever.
Simon A., Saturday night, Dec. 26, 1835, about 12 o'clock, a. 32 y.

WOOD, ———, inf. s. of Samuel and Rachel, Sept. 11, 1811. G.R.1.
———, wid. of Capt. Josiah, Aug. 16, 1820, a. 86 y.
———, inf. ch. of Phineas (and Harriet M., G.R.1), Aug. 25, 1831. (Aug. 24, 1831. G.R.1.)
———, s. of Manning, Feb. 18, 1840, a. abt. 1 y.
Amaza, s. of Solomon and Susanna, Aug. 6, 1769.
Amory, Capt., in Worcester, Mar. 3, 1835, a. 67 y.
Amos, s. of David and Molley, Mar. 15, 1785.
Amos, s. of Ezekiel, Nov. 16, 1802, a. 4 y. 10 m.
Anna, d. of Dexter and Deborah, Aug. 29, 1797 (in her 23d y. G.R.1).
Anne, d. of Samuel (and Rachel, G.R.1), a. 27 y. this day, 19 Mar., 1824. (Mar. 29, 1824. G.R.1.)
Caleb, s. of Semeon and Margret, Dec. 24, 1769.
Charles P., s. of Phineas and Harriet, Aug. 30, 1849, a. 12 y. 27 d. Dysentery.
Clarissa (Clarissa F., G.R.1), w. of Phineas, May 26, 1848, a. 40 y. (41 y. G.R.1.)
David, s. of David and Molley, Nov. 15, 1794.
David, Sept. 26, 1835, a. 87 y. (Revolutionary soldier. G.R.1.)
Deborah, wid. of (Daniel, G.R.1), May 14, 1831, in her 94th y. (a. 91 y. G.R.1.)
Dexter, Mar. 4, 1811, a. 77 y. (Revolutionary soldier. G.R.1.)

WOOD, Esther, w. of James, Aug. 14, 1793, in her 87th y.
Esther, wid. of Obadiah (Mar. 29, G.R.1), 1799, in her 89th y. (a. 90 y. G.R.1.)
Ezekiel, Capt., May 16, 1772, in his 66th y.
Ezekiel 3d (s. of Henry and Sarah, G.R.1), Feb. 10, 1804, a. 26 y. Killed by fall of a tree.
Ezekiel, Dec. 15, 1811, a. 68 y. (a. 69 y. Revolutionary soldier. G.R.1.)
Ezekiel, Oct. 15, 1842, a. 70 y.
Harriet (Harriet M., G.R.1), w. of Phineas, May 5, 1838, a. 38 y. (39 y. G.R.1.)
Henry, Apr. 17, 1823, a. 86 y. 3 d.
James, Aug. 19, 1794, in his 90th y.
Jasius, Sept. 10, 1727, a. 29 y.
John, s. of Ezekiel and Mary, Jan. 6, 1738.
Joseph, Aug. 19, 1794, in his 90th y.
Josiah, s. of Ezekiel, Mar. 16, 1803, in his 10th y.
Josiah, Capt., Nov. 3, 1815.
Judah (Judeth dup.), d. of Henry, May 4, 1793, in her 18th y.
Keith, s. of David, Apr. 19, 1799, in his 27th y.
Lois, d. of Simeon and Margery, Apr. 20, 1773.
Maria, d. of Ezekiel 2d and Hannah, Apr. 30, 1811. G.R.1.
Marie, Apr. 30, 1814. G.R.1.
Mark, Apr. 17, 1831, a. 65 y.
Martha, w. of Ezekiel, Jan. 6, 1782.
Mary, d. of Dexter and Deborah [no date].
Mary, w. of Solomon, Feb. 21, 1749, in her 17th y.
Mary, d. of Henry and Sarah, Sept. 9, 1761.
Mary, w. of ———, Oct. 2, 1778, in her 73d y.
Mary B., d. of Amariah A. and Sarah (Sarah T., G.R.1), Sept. 9, 1847, a. 4 m. 11 d. (10 d. G.R.1.) Consumption.
Molly, w. of David, Jan. 12, 1832, in her 80th y.
Obediah, Aug. 16, 1792, a. 85 y. G.R.1.
Phinehas, s. of Henry and Sarah, Mar. 22, 1800, in his 32d y. (33d y. dup.).
Rachal, w. of Lieut. Mark, Oct. 28, 1825. (Oct. 27, 1825, a. 51 y. G.R.1.)
Rachal, w. of Samuel, June 21, 1834, a. 67 y.
Salley, d. of David and Molley, Mar. 22, 1787.
Sally, w. of Ezekiel, Aug. 25, 1819.
Samuel, Feb. 20, 1841, a. 76 y.
Sarah, w. of Ezekiel, Sept. 29, 1798.
Sarah, w. of Henry, Dec. 5, 1809, in her 68th y. G.R.1.
Sarah, w. of Ezekiel, Aug. 25, 1819, a. 41 y. G.R.1.

WOOD, Sarah A., d. of Amariah A. (and Sarah T., G.R.1), Sept. 26, 1837, a. 4 m. (a. 3 m. 23 d. G.R.1.)
Sibil, d. of Henry, July 23, 1779, in her 19th y.
Silvia, Jan. 14, 1816. G.R.1.
Solomon, s. of Solomon and Faithful, Nov. 9, 1727.
Solomon, Jan. 13, 1752, in his 83d y.
Susan (Susan A., G.R.1), d. of Ezekiel 2d, May 12, 1824, a. abt. 1 y. 10 m. (May 13, 1824. G.R.1.)
Thomas, s. of Ezekiel and Mary, Feb. 3, 1737–8.
Timothy, Dr., Oct. 12, 1813. (a. 51 y. Revolutionary soldier. G.R.1.)
Warfield, s. of Obediah and Esther, Feb. 1, 1733–4.
Whitney, July 27, 1810.

YATES, James, Apr. 1, 1772. Death caused by fall from a horse.
Marcy, d. of James and Tabberah, May 4, 1753.
Tabberah, w. of James, May 4, 1753.

YOUNG, ———, w. of Daniel, Jan. 6, 1832.
Daniel, Mar. 17, 1832, a. abt. 85 y.

NEGROES.

Felix, May —, 1800.
Fortune, negro boy of John Spring, Apr. 4, 1740. Burned to death about 9 o'clock in the evening.